中国—新加坡
“一带一路”国际商事审判案例选
第一卷

A COMPENDIUM OF CHINA–SINGAPORE INTERNATIONAL COMMERCIAL CASES CURATED FOR THEIR RELEVANCE TO THE BELT AND ROAD INITIATIVE

Volume 1

声 明

ACKNOWLEDGMENT

中国—新加坡
“一带一路”国际商事审判案例选

第一卷

A Compendium of China–Singapore International Commercial Cases

Curated for Their Relevance to

the Belt and Road Initiative

Volume 1

中华人民共和国最高人民法院
新 加 坡 共 和 国 最 高 法 院 | 主　编

The Supreme People's Court of the People's Republic of China
The Supreme Court of the Republic of Singapore | Chief Editors

法律出版社
LAW PRESS · CHINA

图书在版编目(CIP)数据

中国—新加坡"一带一路"国际商事审判案例选. 第一卷 / 中华人民共和国最高人民法院,新加坡共和国最高法院主编. -- 北京:法律出版社,2020
ISBN 978-7-5197-4920-0

Ⅰ. ①中… Ⅱ. ①中… ②新… Ⅲ. ①"一带一路"-国际商事仲裁-案例-中国、新加坡 Ⅳ. ①D997.4

中国版本图书馆 CIP 数据核字(2020)第 173150 号

中国—新加坡"一带一路"国际商事审判案例选(第一卷)
ZHONGGUO—XINJIAPO "YIDAIYILU" GUOJI SHANGSHI SHENPAN ANLI XUAN (DI-YI JUAN)

中华人民共和国最高人民法院
新加坡共和国最高法院
主编

策划编辑 朱 峰
责任编辑 韩泓宇 马秋婧
装帧设计 鲁 娟

出版 法律出版社
总发行 中国法律图书有限公司
经销 新华书店
印刷 中煤(北京)印务有限公司
责任印制 张建伟

编辑统筹 法律翻译与出版研发中心
开本 710 毫米×1000 毫米 1/16
印张 37.5
字数 501 千
版本 2020 年 10 月第 1 版
印次 2020 年 10 月第 1 次印刷

法律出版社 / 北京市丰台区莲花池西里 7 号(100073)
网址 / www.lawpress.com.cn
投稿邮箱 / info@lawpress.com.cn
举报维权邮箱 / jbwq@lawpress.com.cn
销售热线 / 400-660-8393
咨询电话 / 010-63939796

中国法律图书有限公司 / 北京市丰台区莲花池西里 7 号(100073)
全国各地中法图分、子公司销售电话:
统一销售客服 / 400-660-8393/6393
第一法律书店 / 010-83938432/8433 西安分公司 / 029-85330678 重庆分公司 / 023-67453036
上海分公司 / 021-62071639/1636 深圳分公司 / 0755-83072995

书号:ISBN 978-7-5197-4920-0 **定价**:398.00 元
(如有缺页或倒装,中国法律图书有限公司负责退换)

中国—新加坡
“一带一路”国际商事审判案例选
第一卷

A Compendium of China–Singapore International Commercial Cases Curated for Their Relevance to the Belt and Road Initiative
Volume 1

Panel of Senior Editors

China

ZHOU Qiang	The Honourable Chief Justice of the People's Republic of China, President of the Supreme People's Court
HE Rong	The Honourable Justice of the People's Republic of China, Executive Vice-President of the Supreme People's Court
YANG Wanming	The Honourable Justice of the People's Republic of China, Vice-President of the Supreme People's Court

Singapore

Sundaresh Menon	The Honourable the Chief Justice of the Supreme Court of the Republic of Singapore
Andrew Phang	The Honourable Justice of the Supreme Court of the Republic of Singapore, Judge of Appeal
Steven Chong	The Honourable Justice of the Supreme Court of the Republic of Singapore, Judge of Appeal
Ang Cheng Hock	The Honourable Justice of the Supreme Court of the Republic of Singapore, High Court Judge

编辑委员会
Panel of Editors

编辑委员会

新加坡

Panel of Editors

Singapore

Judicial Liaison	**Justin Yeo**	District Judge, Republic of Singapore
Commentators	**Goh Yihan**	Dean, School of Law, Professor of Law, Singapore Management University
	Lee Pey Woan	Professor of Law, Singapore Management University
	Daniel Seng	Associate Professor, Faculty of Law, National University of Singapore
	Adeline Chong	Associate Professor of Law, Singapore Management University
	Yip Man	Associate Professor of Law, Singapore Management University
	Justin Yeo	District Judge, Republic of Singapore
	Rachel Tan	Justices' Law Clerk, Supreme Court of the Republic of Singapore

Supreme Court Interpreters Section

Lim Cher Yeow	(Head, Language Services)	**Soh Hui San**	(Head Interpreter)
Wong Yin Ling	(Deputy Head Interpreter)	**Leong Yuan Hong**	(Senior Interpreter)
Marina Wang	(Senior Interpreter)	**Seah Wei Chun**	(Senior Interpreter)
Ng Lian Hua	(Senior Interpreter)	**Leung Shun Yee Yvonne**	(Interpreter)
Lim Zhong Wei	(Interpreter)		

Singapore Judicial College

Foo Chee Hock	Dean, Senior Counsel
Paul Quan	Executive Director, District Judge, Republic of Singapore
Rebecca Thaver	Deputy Director, Secretariat

序　言

2013年9月,中国国家主席习近平首次提出共同建设“丝绸之路经济带”的倡议。2015年3月,博鳌亚洲论坛2015年年会期间,中国政府发布了《推动共建丝绸之路经济带和21世纪海上丝绸之路的愿景与行动》,倡议“一带一路”沿线国家共同打造政治互信、经济融合、文化包容的利益共同体、责任共同体和命运共同体。习近平主席提出的共建“一带一路”倡议,秉持共商共建共享原则,为世界经济增长开辟了新空间,为国际贸易和投资搭建了新平台,为完善全球治理拓展了新实践,为推动构建人类命运共同体贡献了中国智慧和中国方案。中国最高人民法院高度重视加强与“一带一路”沿线各国司法合作,希望在国际商事争端解决、司法改革、信息化建设、案例研究、法官培训以及共同打击跨国犯罪等方面加强交流,开展务实有效合作,为中国与世界各国共同繁荣发展提供有力司法服务和保障,为人类法治文明发展做出积极贡献。

随着跨国商事活动日益增多,国际商事争端的有效解决已成为优化法治化营商环境、推动全球治理体系变革的重要保障。2018年6月29日,中国最高人民法院在广东省深圳市和陕西省西安市分别设立第一、第二国际商事法庭。同年8月26日,成立国际商事专家委员会,来自14个国家和地区的31名中外专家被聘任为首批专家委员。坚持高标准选任国际商事法庭法官,创新管辖、诉讼证据和裁判文书公开制度,创建“一站式”国际商事纠纷多元化解决平台,提出了一系列具有鲜明特色的创新举措,为国际商事争端解决机制建设做出积极探索。

近年来,中国最高人民法院先后发布两部关于为"一带一路"建设提供司法服务和保障的指导意见,全面总结中国法院服务保障"一带一路"建设的有益经验,积极借鉴国际法发展最新成果及国际民商事审判先进理念,在涉外民商事案件管辖权、合同效力和合同责任认定、国际海运责任承担、知识产权保护、国际商事法庭机制完善、域外法查明平台建设等方面做出新的探索。中国法院始终坚持共商共建共享的全球治理观,坚持尊重当事人意思自治原则,坚持纠纷解决方式多元化,促进营造市场化、法治化、国际化营商环境,积极推动全球治理规则法治化。

中国与新加坡自1990年建交以来,建立了与时俱进的全方位合作伙伴关系,在平等互利基础上开展了广泛合作。两国司法机关长期保持友好交往,人员往来日益密切,交流合作取得积极成果。2017年8月,我与新加坡首席大法官梅达顺先生共同出席首届中新法律和司法圆桌会议,签署《中华人民共和国最高人民法院与新加坡共和国最高法院合作谅解备忘录》。此后,两国建立法律和司法圆桌会议机制,迄今已成功举办三届圆桌会议。中新法律和司法圆桌会议作为双边法律司法合作和"一带一路"合作的重要平台,以司法合作助推全方位合作,有力促进了双方各项务实合作的开展,在造福两国人民、推动区域和平稳定发展中发挥着重要作用。

中华人民共和国最高人民法院与新加坡共和国最高法院联合编写的《中国—新加坡(新加坡—中国)"一带一路"国际商事审判案例选》,精心挑选了两国在"一带一路"涉外商事审判中的案例,并邀请两国知名学者对案例进行点评,是推动共建"一带一路"高质量发展的重要研究成果。本书的顺利出版,得益于中国国家法官学院和新加坡司法学院的倾力付出,凝聚了全体编撰人员的心血和智慧,是中国和新加坡两国司法合作领域的首创之举。

中国法院始终以开放的姿态面向世界,始终把立足本国国情、坚持自身特色同吸收各国司法文明成果有机结合起来。衷心希望中新两国司法界秉持开放包容的合作精神，坚持平等务实的合作理念，深化在法官培训、人员交流、案例研究等方面的合作，充分发挥中新法律和司法圆桌会议机制作用，在服务高质量共建“一带一路”等领域携手共进，推动形成更多互利共赢的合作成果，为促进地区和平发展、构建人类命运共同体提供有力司法服务和保障。

是为序。

中华人民共和国首席大法官

最高人民法院院长

周　强

2020 年 7 月

Foreword

In September 2013, XI Jinping, President of the People's Republic of China, first proposed the initiative of the Silk Road Economic Belt. In March 2015, during the Boao Forum for Asia Annual Conference 2015, the Chinese government released *Building a Silk Road Economic Belt and a 21st Century Maritime Silk Road — Vision and Actions*, which proposed that countries along the routes of the Belt and Road Initiative (BRI) jointly build the community of shared interests, the community of shared responsibility and the community of shared future with mutual political trust, economic integration and cultural inclusiveness. Guided by the principles of extensive consultation, joint contribution and shared benefits, the BRI proposed by President XI Jinping has opened up a new space for the world' s economic growth, set up a new platform for international trade and investment, demonstrated new practices for global governance, and offered the Chinese Wisdom and the Chinese Approach in promoting the building of the community of shared future for humanity. As a result, the Supreme People's Court of the People' s Republic of China (SPC) attaches great importance to enhancing judicial cooperation with other countries along the routes of the BRI. Moreover, SPC is eager to promote practical and effective cooperation in areas such as international commercial dispute resolution, judicial reform, information technology application, study of legal cases, professional training for judges, and jointly combating cross-border crimes, making every effort to provide effective judicial services and safeguards for the common development and prosperity of China and other countries, as well as making contributions to the development of a rule-based civilisation for humanity.

With transnational business activities increasingly on the rise, effective resolution of international commercial disputes plays a pivotal role in guaranteeing the optimisation of a rule-based environment for doing business and promoting the reform of global governance system. On June 29, 2018, China International Commercial Court (CICC) was established by SPC, with the First CICC in Shenzhen, Guangdong Province and the Second CICC in Xi'an, Shaanxi Province. On August 26, 2018, International Commercial Expert Committee (ICEC) was established by SPC, and 31 domestic and foreign experts from 14 countries and regions were appointed as its first members. Established as a one-stop platform for diversified international commercial dispute resolution mechanism, CICC actively explored the establishment of an international commercial dispute resolution mechanism by introducing a series of distinctive innovations in relation to jurisdiction, evidence in litigation and a system of publicizing judgments while adhering to the high standards of selection and appointment of judges to CICC.

In recent years, SPC has issued two consecutive guiding opinions on providing judicial services and safeguards for the BRI. Building on the useful experiences of the Chinese courts in safeguarding the construction of the BRI and drawing reference from the latest achievements in the development of international law as well as the advanced concepts in international civil and commercial trials, SPC has developed new practices on jurisdiction over foreign-related civil and commercial cases, validity of contracts and determination of contract liability, international maritime liability, protection of intellectual property rights, improvement of international commercial courts mechanism, as well as the construction of a platform for the access to foreign laws. Adhering to the principles of global governance through extensive consultation, joint contribution and shared benefits, Chinese courts have adopted diverse commercial dispute resolution mechanisms under the principle of party autonomy, in order to foster a market-oriented, rule-based international business environment, which promotes the rule of law in global governance.

Since the inception of diplomatic relations in 1990, China and Singapore have established all-round cooperative partnership that keeps pace with the times, and collaborated extensively on the basis of equality and mutual benefit. The judiciaries of our two countries have always maintained a friendly relationship, which have produced abundant fruits through increasingly frequent interaction, exchange and cooperation of personnel. In August 2017, the Honourable the Chief Justice of Singapore Sundaresh Menon and I attended the inaugural China-Singapore Legal and Judicial Roundtable and concluded the *Memorandum of Understanding Between the Supreme People's Court of the People's Republic of China and the Supreme Court of the Republic of Singapore on Cooperation*. Since then, our judiciaries have maintained this annual tradition and we have successfully held three Roundtables so far. The China-Singapore Legal and Judicial Roundtable is an important forum for bilateral legal and judicial cooperation as well as the BRI cooperation. Driven by legal and judicial cooperation, it has boosted all-round and practical cooperation between our countries, playing a significant role not only in delivering benefits to the two nations but also contributing to promoting peace and stability in the region.

Jointly published by the Supreme People's Court of the People's Republic of China and the Supreme Court of the Republic of Singapore, *A Compendium of China - Singapore (Singapore - China) International Commercial Cases Curated for Their Relevance to the Belt and Road Initiative*, is a significant achievement in the legal and judicial study of China and Singapore international commercial cases relevant to the BRI that promotes the high-quality development of the BRI construction. Renowned scholars from our two countries were invited to expound their views on these cases. Thanks to the unstinting efforts of the China National Judges College and the Singapore Judicial College, this publication has come into fruition like a blossom watered by the wisdom and labour of all the organisers, writers, translators and editors. It serves as a strong testament to the judicial cooperation between our two countries.

Based on our own national conditions, Chinese courts always engage the world with an open mind, forging our own path for our judicial system with Chinese characteristics and utilizing the finer attributes of other judicial cultures. Therefore, I sincerely hope that, the judiciaries of China and Singapore will, keeping to the spirit of openness and inclusiveness in their cooperation on equal and practical footing, deepen cooperation in the fields of professional training for judges, personnel exchanges and study of legal cases. To give full play to the role of the China－Singapore Legal and Judicial Roundtable, we should work together to build and take the BRI to greater heights, break new ground and produce more win-win outcomes, deliver robust judicial services and safeguards to promote regional peace and stability, as well as build the community of shared future for humanity.

This is the foreword to the publication.

The Honourable Chief Justice
President of the Supreme People's Court of
the People's Republic of China

ZHOU Qiang

July 2020

Foreword

It is both a pleasure and privilege to introduce *A Compendium of China-Singapore (Singapore-China) International Commercial Cases Curated for Their Relevance to the Belt and Road Initiative*, a joint publication by the Supreme Court of Singapore and the Supreme People's Court of the People's Republic of China. The Compendium is not only a reflection of the abiding friendship between the judiciaries of Singapore and China, but also an important milestone in our joint efforts since the inaugural Singapore-China Legal and Judicial Roundtable in Beijing in August 2017.

At the inaugural Roundtable, which was a historic first between China and an Asian country, I noted that the global economy was becoming ever more interconnected, with the consequence that cross-border commercial disputes were increasingly common and complex. In order to effectively meet the evolving dispute resolution needs of businesses, I suggested that national judicial and legal systems must pursue not only the harmonisation of court processes and practices but also of commercial laws. In this challenging but critical endeavour, judicial cooperation would be indispensable. I was greatly heartened by the Honourable Chief Justice ZHOU Qiang's warm affirmation of this profoundly important mission, as well as our shared recognition of the vital roles that our judiciaries have to play in supporting cross-border commerce, especially as the focal point of the global economy shifts toward Asia.

This common vision informed and gave direction to much of the work done at the first and subsequent Roundtables. The Honourable Chief Justice ZHOU and I recognised that our judiciaries' search for opportunities for closer collaboration, including the pursuit of greater harmonisation, must begin with a clearer and sounder understanding of *each other's* laws and procedures. That was one of the key inspirations behind the historic Memorandum of Understanding ("MOU") on cooperation between the Supreme Court of Singapore and the Supreme People's Court of the People's Republic of China, which the Honourable Chief Justice ZHOU and I signed that year. In that MOU, we acknowledged the need to promote the further understanding of each other's legal and judicial systems. To that end, we committed to the regular exchange of information and materials on our work and judgments, as well as cooperative research on areas of common interest. Above all, we affirmed our intention to perpetuate and deepen our cooperation by convening an annual Roundtable chaired by the Chief Justices of Singapore and China.

We built upon those foundations at the second Roundtable held in Singapore in August the next year. I presented to the Honourable Chief Justice ZHOU a compendium containing 24 selected commercial law judgments of the Supreme Court of Singapore. These covered key tenets of our commercial law such as *pacta sunt servanda* (agreements must be honoured), the role of good faith in contractual performance, the doctrine of estoppel, and our approach to unjust enrichment. Beyond this, the Honourable Chief Justice ZHOU and I signed a landmark Memorandum of Guidance between our courts on the recognition and enforcement of money judgments in commercial cases, with the aim of promoting mutual understanding in this essential area of law and procedure.

These developments were followed by a second MOU that the Honourable Chief Justice ZHOU and I signed at the third Roundtable in Beijing in August last year. In recognition of the need to establish frameworks to enable the continual learning and sharing that we envisioned, the second MOU lays the foundations for closer cooperation between the Singapore Judicial College and the China National Judges College. The colleges will work hand in hand to offer exchanges, visits and training programmes for members of the Singapore and Chinese judiciaries, with a view to advancing continuing judicial education in areas ranging from court administration to substantive issues of mutual interest.

The Compendium that you now hold represents the latest effort in the common enterprise of our judiciaries to achieve an ever-deeper and ever-closer understanding of each other's laws and procedures. The cases within this Compendium are drawn from the rich and varied jurisprudence of both the Singapore and Chinese courts on commercial law. They are accompanied by clear and succinct commentaries on their significance to commercial dispute resolution, and as such will be useful to judges, practitioners and academics alike. The Compendium is organised in two volumes and together, they explore a spectrum of important and topical issues within commercial law and practice.

As I perused the Compendium, what left the deepest impression on me was the remarkable resonance between the core principles, values and objectives of the commercial laws of our jurisdictions. Despite our different legal traditions and individual preferences in matters of procedure and practice, there remains unity of purpose in our laws' pursuit of fairness, certainty and consistency—all of which are key elements of the rule of law and basic premises for business and investor confidence. Indeed, we share common approaches in key aspects of commercial law. To take an example, the case of *Luck Treat Limited v. Shenzhen Zhongyuan City Commercial Investment Holding Co, Ltd for Application of Confirmation on the Validity of an Arbitration Agreement* emphasises the principle of separability between the arbitration agreement and the underlying contract. That is also a foundational principle of the law of arbitration in Singapore, manifested most clearly in Article 16(1) of the UNCITRAL Model Law on International Commercial Arbitration which [by virtue of s 3(1) of Singapore's International Arbitration Act (Cap. 143A, 2002 Rev Ed)] has the force of law in Singapore.

The resonance between our commercial laws is demonstrated in a different fashion by the decisions of the Singapore High Court in *Giant Light Metal Technology (Kunshan) Co Ltd v. Aksa Far East Pte Ltd* [2014] 2 SLR 545 ("*Giant Light Metal Technology*") and the Jiangsu Nanjing Intermediate People's Court in *Application of Kolmar Group AG for Recognition and Enforcement of Civil Judgment of Singapore High Court* ("*Kolmar Group*"). In *Giant Light Metal Technology*, the Singapore court recognised and enforced a judgment of the Suzhou Intermediate People's Court, Jiangsu Province; and that formed the basis of the Chinese court's decision in *Kolmar Group* that there is *de facto* reciprocity between the Singapore and Chinese courts in the recognition and enforcement of judgments, such that the Singapore judgment at issue in *Kolmar Group* could likewise be recognised and enforced in China. Although the two courts naturally applied different rules on recognition and enforcement, their decisions illustrate the dialectic between the common and civil law processes which ultimately promoted the finality of court judgments in commercial disputes.

I believe the Compendium will be an invaluable introduction for those seeking to learn more about, and to explore the commonalities between, the commercial laws of Singapore and China. I therefore warmly commend the Compendium to all who may take even the slightest interest in this area. It was an achievement made possible only by the unstinting efforts of a group of judges, academics and experts from both countries. I am deeply grateful to the

Honourable Chief Justice ZHOU for his unwavering support for this project, and to his team consisting of the Panel of Senior Editors, the Panel of Editors, the China National Judges College, and academic commentators. My gratitude also goes to the Singapore team consisting of Judges of Appeal Andrew Phang and Steven Chong, Justice Ang Cheng Hock, our judicial liaison District Judge Justin Yeo, the Singapore Judicial College, the Singapore Academy of Law, our expert commentators and court interpreters. These efforts have helped to build mutual understanding of our countries' laws and legal systems, and thereby laid a stepping-stone toward greater harmonisation and closer cooperation.

Let me conclude with a final observation. The bilateral relationship between Singapore and China has always been characterised by the same spirit of learning and understanding that underpins this Compendium. This year marks the 30th anniversary of the establishment of diplomatic relations between Singapore and China, which took place on 3 October 1990. But more than a decade before that—impelled by the visit of Singapore's founding Prime Minister Mr Lee Kuan Yew to China in 1976, which was followed by the state visit of then Vice-Premier Mr DENG Xiaoping to Singapore two years later—the friendship between our nations had already begun to flourish. In the 1990s, our officials conducted hundreds of mutual visits to learn from and engage each other, working toward the betterment of our societies and the strengthening of our ties. Today, both China and Singapore stand tall in the world economy—China as a global economic power, and Singapore as a leading financial, shipping and legal hub.

I suggest that our judiciaries must perpetuate this same spirit of friendship and learning that has helped to take our countries so far, and that still holds such promise for the future. I believe that if the past three Roundtables and this

Compendium are anything to go by, that future is bright indeed.

The Honourable the Chief Justice

Supreme Court of the Republic of Singapore

Sundaresh Menon

July 2020

序　言

我很高兴和荣幸地在此介绍《中国—新加坡(新加坡—中国)“一带一路”国际商事审判案例选》。这套选集由中华人民共和国最高人民法院与新加坡共和国最高法院联合主编,不仅反映了新加坡和中国司法机关源远流长的友谊,更是两国自2017年在北京召开首届新中法律和司法圆桌会议后共同努力的重要里程碑。

2017年8月,中国与另一个亚洲国家举办了首届法律和司法圆桌会议,这在历史上实属首创。我当时在会议上指出,全球经济联系日益紧密,跨境商事纠纷因此愈加普遍和复杂。为了有效应对企业不断变化的纠纷解决需求,我建议各国司法及法律体系不仅应促进法院程序与实践的协调,也须促进商事法律的协调。在这充满挑战但至关重要的工作中,司法合作是必不可少的。令我深受鼓舞的是,这极其重要的使命获得了中国首席大法官周强先生的积极肯定,且我们都认识到司法机关在支持跨境商务方面扮演着重要的角色,特别是在全球经济焦点转向亚洲这一时刻。

这一共同愿景为首届及后续举办的圆桌会议铺垫了道路,指明了方向。中国首席大法官周强先生和我认识到,两国司法机关若要寻求机会开展更紧密的合作,包括促进更大程度的法律协调,首先必须更清楚、更全面地了*解彼此的*法律和程序。这种共识带来的重要启发是,中国首席大法官周强先生和我也在那年签署了历史性的《中华人民共和国最高人民法院与新加坡共和国最高法院合作谅解备忘录》(以下简称《谅解备忘录》)。在《谅解备忘录》中,我们确认两国需要增进对彼此法律和司法制度的了解。为此,我们致力于定期就工作和判决的信息与资料进行交流,在两国共同感兴趣的领域展开合作研究。而新加坡和中国每年举办由两国首席大法官主持的圆桌会议,更是申明了两国延续和深化合作的意愿。

2018 年 8 月在新加坡举行的第二届圆桌会议便是建立在此基础上。我赠送给中国首席大法官周强先生关于新加坡最高法院商法判决的精选汇编,当中的 24 份商法判决涵盖了我国商法的主要原则,例如有约必守(*pacta sunt servanda*),秉诚行事在履行合同中的作用,不容反悔原则以及我院对不当得利的处理方式。此外,中国首席大法官周强先生和我也就两国法院之间承认与执行商事案件金钱判决签署了一份具有标志性意义的谅解备忘录,旨在促进两国法院在这个重要领域中的法律及程序的相互理解。

继这些进展之后,2019 年 8 月中国首席大法官周强先生和我在北京举行的第三届圆桌会议上签署了第二份谅解备忘录。鉴于实现持续学习与分享的愿景需要设立框架,第二份谅解备忘录为新加坡司法学院和中国国家法官学院奠定了密切合作的基础。两所学院将携手为新中两国司法机关人员提供交流、访问及培训课程合作机会,以便在法院行政管理及双方共同感兴趣的实质性问题等方面推动持续司法教育。

您手中的这套汇编是两国司法机关为了更深入、更密切了解彼此法律和程序这一共同事业做出的最新努力。这套汇编收录了新中两国法院丰富而多样的商事案例,也附有明确简洁的评注以说明案件对商事纠纷解决的重要性,法官、法律从业者及学者必能从中受益。汇编分成两卷,探讨了一系列商法及其实践中的重要热点问题。

在详读这套汇编后,令我印象最深刻的是,我们两个司法管辖区的商法在核心原则、价值观及目标方面有很多不谋而合之处。尽管我们的法律传统不同,程序及实践上也有各自倾向的方式,但我们的法律追求的目标统一,即公正、确定性和一致性,这些都是法治的关键要素,也是给予企业及投资者信心的基本前提。事实上,我们在商法的主要方面采用了相同的做法。

例如,“申请人运裕有限公司与被申请人深圳市中苑城商业投资控股有限公司申请确认仲裁协议效力”一案强调了仲裁协议与主合同之间的独立性原则,这也是新加坡仲裁法的基础原则,这一原则明确体现在《联合国国际贸易法委员会国际商事仲裁示范法》第 16 条第 1 款中,而根据新加坡的《国际仲裁法》(第 143A 章,2002 年修订版)第 3 条第 1 款,该条文在新加坡具有法律效力。

新加坡高等法庭的“捷安特轻合金科技(昆山)有限公司 v. 雅柯斯(远东)私人有限公司”[*Giant Light Metal Technology* (*Kunshan*) *Co Ltd v. Aksa Far East Pte Ltd*,以下简称“捷安特轻合金科技”]的裁决,以及江苏省南京市中级人民法院的“高尔集团股份有限公司申请承认和执行新加坡高等法院民事判决”(以下简称“高尔集团”)的裁决,分别以不同形式展现了两国商法上的不谋而合之处。在捷安特轻合金科技一案中,新加坡法院承认和执行了江苏省苏州市中级人民法院的判决,基于此,中国法院在高尔集团一案中裁定新中法院在承认和执行判决方面存有事实互惠关系,因此高尔集团一案中的新加坡判决同样可在中国获得承认和执行。两国法院在承认和执行判决上自然是适用了不同的规则,但它们的裁决说明了普通法和大陆法程序之间的辩证关系,最终促进了法院商事纠纷判决的终局性。

我相信这套汇编能让想要进一步了解及探讨新中两国商法共同点的人受益匪浅。因此,我极力将这套汇编推荐给所有对这一领域感兴趣的读者。这是两国法官、学者及专家不懈努力的成果。我由衷感谢中国首席大法官周强先生对这一项目的鼎力支持,也十分感激中方团队——编审委员会、编辑委员会、国家法官学院及学术界评论员。我也要感谢新加坡的团队:上诉庭法官潘文龙、上诉庭法官庄泓翔、法官洪清福、司法联络员兼地方法庭法官杨镕玮、新加坡司法学院、新加坡法律学会、专家评论员以及法庭通译员。各方的努力帮助增进了两国对彼此法律和法律制度的了解,为更大程度上的趋同与更密切的合作奠定了基石。

最后,我想提出自己的一些看法。相互学习和了解的精神是这套汇编的基础,而新中两国的双边关系向来也都本着同样的精神。新中两国于1990年10月3日建交,今年是两国建交30周年。两国友谊的种子早在正式建交的十多年前就已开始萌芽生长。新加坡建国总理李光耀先生于1976年访华,两年后,中国时任副总理邓小平先生也出访新加坡。到了20世纪90年代,两国官员进行了数百次互访,相互学习与交流,为改善社会福祉和加强联系共同努力。如今,中国和新加坡在世界经济中占据重要地位——中国是全球经济强国,新加坡则是重要的金融、海事及法律枢纽。

我建议,两国司法机关务必延续我们两国的友谊和相互学习的精神,这种精神让两国发展出今日的成就,也会让两国在未来取得更大的发展。从过去三届圆桌会议及这套汇编看来,我相信未来必定会一片光明!

新加坡共和国最高法院首席大法官

梅达顺

2020年7月

目　录

中国案例

新加坡案例

中国案例

中华人民共和国最高人民法院|主编

交通运输部南海救助局
诉
阿昌格罗斯投资公司、香港安达欧森有限公司上海代表处海难救助合同纠纷案

——雇佣救助合同依据合同法的相关规定确定当事人的权利义务

【裁判要旨】

1.《1989年国际救助公约》（以下简称《救助公约》）和《中华人民共和国海商法》（以下简称《海商法》）规定救助合同“无效果无报酬”，但均允许当事人对救助报酬的确定可以另行约定。若当事人明确约定，无论救助是否成功，被救助方均应支付报酬，且以救助船舶每马力小时和人工投入等作为计算报酬的标准时，则该合同系雇佣救助合同，而非上述国际公约和中国《海商法》规定的救助合同。

2. 在《救助公约》和中国《海商法》对雇佣救助合同没有具体规定的情况下，可以适用中国合同法的相关规定确定当事人的权利义务。

【专家点评】*

本案是中华人民共和国最高人民法院（以下简称最高人民法院）审理的第一例雇佣救助合同争议案，是重要的指导性案例。

2011年8月12日“加百利”轮在琼州海峡搁浅，救助人交通运输部

---

* 撰写人：司玉琢，大连海事大学教授、博士研究生导师。

南海救助局（以下简称南海救助局）与被救人“加百利”轮所有人阿昌格罗斯投资公司（以下简称投资公司）签订固定费率的雇佣救助合同，共产生救助费用7240998.24元人民币。南海救助局请求法院判令投资公司支付上述救助费用，投资公司抗辩，根据《海商法》第183条的规定，救助报酬的金额应当由获救的船舶和其他财产的各所有人，按照船舶和其他各项财产各自的获救价值占全部获救价值的比例承担。

一、雇佣救助合同的性质

雇佣救助是中国的习惯称谓，指救助方依据被救助方的请求，无论救助成功与否，都按照约定的费率或者固定的费用收取报酬的救助行为。据此，雇佣救助合同有两个构成要件：一是救助报酬与救助效果无关，二是报酬费率或费用固定。这是中国救助市场普遍存在的救助方式，法律并没有雇佣救助的相关规定，完全遵循意思自治原则。最高人民法院在本案中查明的事实是，投资公司与南海救助局经过充分磋商，明确约定无论救助成功与否，投资公司均应支付报酬，且“加百利”轮脱浅作业过程中如发生任何意外，南海救助局无须负责。因此，最高人民法院认为，本案所涉救助合同不属于《救助公约》和中国《海商法》所规定的“无效果无报酬”救助合同，而属雇佣救助合同。这一判决清晰地将雇佣救助合同与“无效果无报酬”救助合同区别开来，这是两种不同性质的救助合同。“无效果无报酬”救助合同是海商法特有的古老的海难救助法律制度，而根据合同构成要件，雇佣救助合同应属于海上服务合同。①

二、雇佣救助报酬的法律适用

“加百利”轮为希腊籍油轮，其船东——投资公司为希腊公司，该案具有涉外因素。由于各方当事人在庭审中均选择适用中华人民共和国法律，根据《中华人民共和国涉外民事关系法律适用法》（以下简称《涉外民事关系法律适用法》）第3条的规定，应适用中华人民共和国法律作为

① 参见司玉琢、吴煦：《雇佣救助的法律属性及法律适用》，载《中国海商法研究》2016年第3期。

处理该案实体争议的准据法。如果雇佣救助合同属于《海商法》第9章海难救助范畴，那么，作为调整海上运输关系、船舶关系的特别法，《海商法》应优先适用，当《海商法》的规定与我国参加的《救助公约》的规定不一致时，依据《最高人民法院关于适用〈中华人民共和国涉外民事关系法律适用法〉若干问题的解释（一）》第4条的规定，人民法院应当根据《海商法》第268条第1款的规定予以适用，即“中华人民共和国缔结或者参加的国际条约同本法有不同规定的，适用国际条约的规定；但是，中华人民共和国声明保留的条款除外”。这就是说，本案如果适用中国《海商法》，那么，凡是《海商法》规定与《救助公约》规定不一致之处，《救助公约》应优先适用。由于最高人民法院再审合议庭就该案雇佣救助合同的属性已认定为“不属于《救助公约》和《海商法》所规定的‘无效果无报酬’救助合同”，而《海商法》和《救助公约》又没有就雇佣救助报酬作出具体规定，在此情况下，最高人民法院适用《中华人民共和国合同法》（以下简称《合同法》）[①] 的相关规定确定该案雇佣救助报酬支付问题，符合法律适用规则。广州海事法院（即一审法院）、广东省高级人民法院（即二审法院）依据《海商法》第180条规定的相关因素对当事人在雇佣救助合同中约定的固定费率予以调整，属适用法律错误。

三、雇佣救助报酬的承担

本案争议的核心最终落在雇佣救助报酬的承担上。“加百利”轮船东主张雇佣救助报酬也是救助报酬，应适用《海商法》第183条之规定，由船货双方按比例承担，而不是船东一方承担，故而这一争议又回到雇佣救助到底适用还是不适用《救助公约》《海商法》的问题上。如果按整体不适用《救助公约》《海商法》海难救助特殊法律制度的观点，根本无须考虑雇佣救助报酬适用《救助公约》《海商法》的问题，自然也就无须考虑《海商法》第183条的适用，而直接适用《合同法》[②] 相关规定，雇佣救助

① 现为《中华人民共和国民法典》（以下简称《民法典》）合同编的相关规定。
② 现为《民法典》合同编的相关规定。

报酬只对合同双方产生约束力，对合同之外的第三方——货方没有约束力，即被救方履行雇佣救助合同义务，承担全部雇佣救助报酬后，可依据其与货方的合同约定进行分摊或追偿。但是，如果认为雇佣救助合同整体适用或者部分适用《救助公约》《海商法》，这就需要具体分析《救助公约》或《海商法》的报酬比例分摊条款是否适用雇佣救助报酬。

《海商法》第180条是关于计算“无效果无报酬”海难救助报酬应考虑的10项因素，第183条是关于海难救助报酬应由船货双方按比例分摊的规定。这两条与《救助公约》第13条规定的内容是一致的。但是，《海商法》并没有明确第180条和第183条之间的关系，这是《海商法》的一个漏洞。[①] 《救助公约》第13条规定的报酬与报酬分摊是有密切关联性的，《救助公约》第13条第1款是关于计算“无效果无报酬”海难救助报酬的标准（与《海商法》第180条内容一致），第2款接着规定，按照第1款确定的报酬应由船舶和其他财产利益方按其获救船舶和其他财产的价值比例进行支付。该条款关于按比例支付报酬的规定，有一个明确限定——按照第1款确定的报酬，即依据“无效果无报酬”原则确定的报酬，而不是泛指任何报酬。如果割裂开来单单依据《海商法》第183条规定解释雇佣救助报酬也可以按比例分摊，显然与《救助公约》第13条的规定不一致，当发生《海商法》与中国参加的国际公约规定不一致时，国际公约应优先适用，适用《救助公约》第13条，雇佣救助报酬不是依据《救助公约》第13条第1款规定的标准确定的，而是救助方与被救方平等协商确定的固定费率，不存在被救方按比例分摊的抗辩权。对此，最高人民法院认为，《海商法》第183条应适用于“无效果无报酬”的救助合同，但案涉合同属于雇佣救助合同，南海救助局以其与投资公司订立的合同为依据，要求投资公司全额支付约定的救助报酬并无不当。

---

① 参见张文广：《“加百利”轮海难救助合同纠纷再审案判决评析》，载《法律适用》2016年第8期。

四、本案判决的法律意义

中国现有三大救捞局，[①] 实践中，雇佣救助合同的比例远大于“无效果无报酬”救助合同的比例。如何使救助市场健康、有序发展，救助人知晓雇佣救助合同的性质、法律适用以及雇佣救助报酬的承担，这直接关系着救助人的利益。该案例的实践意义和理论价值在于：第一，雇佣救助费用（报酬）不属于“无效果无报酬”原则下的救助报酬，船舶优先权担保的救助报酬是指“无效果无报酬”原则下的救助报酬，雇佣救助费用不属于船舶优先权担保的债权；[②] 第二，救助报酬应由被救船东与其他财产利益方按比例分摊，一定是基于“无效果无报酬”原则的救助报酬，而不是基于雇佣救助产生的固定费用（报酬）；第三，雇佣救助的救助人是否有权享受海事赔偿责任限制或者就雇佣救助费用主张共同海损，这已超出救助法律关系，应依据海事赔偿责任限制权利主体的规定[③]或者共同海损构成要件[④]判断。本案一经落槌，在国内外救助实务界和海商法理论界产生很大反响，受到各界的好评。英国的《中国海商法案例汇编》（Chinese Maritime and Commercial Law Reports）对此作了专期报道。最高人民法院各审判业务庭和各高级人民法院经过层层筛选，后经评审委员会民主投票评审，在全国法院 2016 年生效的 1670 多万件案件中，本案被评选为“2016 年推动法治进程十大案件”之一。中国虽不是判例法国家，但是该指导性案例不仅对司法实践有着重要的指导意义，对海事立法也有不可忽视的影响力。

---

① 中国三大救捞局，分别为：南海救捞局、上海救捞局和烟台救捞局。

② 参见《1993 年船舶优先权和抵押权国际公约》第 4 条第 1 款第 3 项之规定。

③ 参见《海商法》第 204 条之规定。

④ 参见《海商法》第 193 条之规定。

【裁判文书】*

中华人民共和国最高人民法院
民事判决书

（2016）最高法民再61号

再审申请人（一审原告、二审被上诉人）：交通运输部南海救助局。住所地：中华人民共和国广东省广州市海珠区**路**号。

法定代表人：林某某，该局局长。

委托代理人：万某某，上海**律师事务所律师。

被申请人（一审被告、二审上诉人）：阿昌格罗斯投资公司（Archangelos Investments E. N. E.）。住所地：希腊共和国雅典****街**号（**** Street，**** Athens，Greece）。

代表人：巴拉巴诺斯（Balabanos），该公司董事长。

委托代理人：黄某，广东**律师事务所律师。

委托代理人：张某，广东**律师事务所律师。

一审被告：香港安达欧森有限公司上海代表处。住所地：中华人民共和国上海市徐汇区***路***号**大厦*号楼***室。

代表人：何某某（He X），该代表处首席代表。

委托代理人：黄某，广东**律师事务所律师。

再审申请人交通运输部南海救助局（以下简称南海救助局）因与被申请人阿昌格罗斯投资公司（以下简称投资公司）、一审被告香港安达欧森有限公司上海代表处（以下简称上海代表处）海难救助合同纠纷一案，不服广东省高级人民法院（以下简称二审法院）作出的（2014）粤高法民四终字第117号民事判决，向本院提出再审申请。本院于2015年12月24日

* 编者注：为保护案件当事人的个人信息，本书对案件当事人的名称、住所地等信息作了隐名处理，其他内容与原裁判文书相同。

作出（2015）民申字第3182号民事裁定提审本案，并依法由副院长、审判员贺荣，审判员张勇健、王淑梅、余晓汉，代理审判员郭载宇组成合议庭，于2016年7月7日公开开庭对本案进行了审理。南海救助局法定代表人林某某、委托代理人万某某，投资公司委托代理人黄某、张某，上海代表处委托代理人黄某到庭参加诉讼。本案现已审理终结。

南海救助局向广州海事法院（以下简称一审法院）诉称：投资公司是“加百利”（Archangelos Gabriel）轮的所有人，上海代表处是该公司的船舶代理人。2011年8月12日“加百利”轮在琼州海峡搁浅。南海救助局受投资公司委托派出“南海救116”轮、“南海救101”轮、“南海救201”轮以及一组潜水队员前往事故现场提供救助、交通、守护等服务，依双方约定，共产生救助费用人民币（以下若无特别说明，均为人民币）7240998.24元，但投资公司一直未付。请求法院判令：投资公司和上海代表处连带向南海救助局支付救助费用7240998.24元；投资公司和上海代表处连带向南海救助局支付自2011年8月20日起至实际支付之日的迟延付款利息（按中国人民银行同期贷款利率暂计至2012年8月19日的利息数额为476449.64元）；投资公司和上海代表处连带承担本案诉讼费用。

一审法院查明：

投资公司所属“加百利”轮系油轮，船籍国为希腊，登记港为比雷埃夫斯，总吨为40682。“加百利”轮载有卡宾达原油54580吨，自香港开往广西钦州，船上船员26人。2011年8月12日5时左右，该轮在琼州海峡北水道6#灯浮附近（北纬22°21′7.2″、东经110°48′7.8″）搁浅，左侧上有3度倾斜，船首尖舱在水位线下已出现裂痕且已有海水进舱，船舶及船载货物处于危险状态，严重威胁海域环境安全。

事故发生后，投资公司立即授权上海代表处就“加百利”轮搁浅事宜向南海救助局发出紧急邮件，请南海救助局根据经验安排两艘拖轮进行救助，并表示同意南海救助局的报价。

8月12日20时40分，上海代表处通过电子邮件向南海救助局提交委托书，委托南海救助局派出“南海救116”轮和“南海救101”轮到现场协助“加百利”轮出浅，承诺无论能否成功协助出浅，均同意按每马力小时3.2元的费率付费，计费周期为拖轮自其各自的值班待命点备车开始起算至上海代表处通知任务结束、拖轮回到原值班待命点为止。“南海救116”轮和“南海救101”轮只负责拖带作业，“加百利”轮脱浅作业过程中如发生任何意外南海救助局无需负责。另，请南海救助局派遣一组潜水队员前往“加百利”轮探摸，费用为：陆地调遣费10000元；水上交通费55000元；作业费每8小时40000元，计费周期为潜水员登上交通船开始起算，到作业完毕离开交通船上岸为止。

与此同时，为预防危险局面进一步恶化造成海上污染，中华人民共和国湛江海事局（以下简称湛江海事局）决定对“加百利”轮采取强制过驳减载脱浅措施。经湛江海事局组织安排，8月17日，中海发展股份有限公司油轮公司所属“丹池”轮对“加百利”轮上的原油进行了驳卸。18日，“加百利”轮利用高潮乘潮成功脱浅，之后安全到达目的港广西钦州港，驳卸的原油由“丹池”轮运抵目的港。

（一）“南海救116”轮的工作情况

南海救助局所属“南海救116”轮为救助船，总吨为3681，总功率为9000千瓦（12240马力）。“南海救116”轮到达事故现场后，因湛江海事局决定采取过驳减载脱浅方案，“南海救116”轮并未对“加百利”轮实施拖带救助，自8月12日7时45分至18日19时20分，该轮根据投资公司的指示，一直在事故现场对“加百利”轮进行守护，共工作155.58小时。南海救助局主张依约定的费率每马力小时3.2元计算，投资公司应向其支付救助费6093757.44元。投资公司与上海代表处则认为，其雇用“南海救116”轮及约定每马力小时3.2元费率的目的是由该轮进行拖带作业，但事实上该轮仅在现场待命、守候，未参与具体救助工作，不能按原约定费率计算救助费用。

（二）“南海救 101”轮的工作情况

南海救助局所属“南海救 101”轮为救助船，总吨为 4091，总功率为 13860 千瓦（18850 马力）。8 月 12 日 9 时 38 分，南海救助局发邮件要求上海代表处对第二艘拖轮“南海救 101”轮予以确认。9 时 57 分，上海代表处回复南海救助局，要求南海救助局安排前述两艘拖轮进行救助。

8 月 12 日 9 时 30 分，“南海救 101”轮前往事发海域救助“加百利”轮。该轮驶往事发海域途中，南海救助局于 15 时 19 分发邮件至上海代表处，称鉴于“加百利”轮船长坚持根据湛江海事局的意见，选择通过减载方式进行脱浅，建议只留“南海救 116”轮在现场作业，“南海救 101”轮返航回锚地。15 时 44 分，上海代表处回复邮件称，继之前确认，只留“南海救 116”轮在现场，取消“南海救 101”轮。15 时 50 分，该轮开始返航，未到达事发现场；23 时 05 分，该轮回到锚地。南海救助局主张该轮工作时间共计 13.58 小时，依约定的费率每马力小时 3.2 元，投资公司应向其支付救助费 819145.60 元。投资公司与上海代表处认为，“南海救 101”轮在驶往事故现场途中即已根据南海救助局的指示返回，更未实际进行任何拖带作业或其他作业，按原约定费率计算显失公平且极不合理。

（三）“南海救 201”轮的工作情况

南海救助局所属“南海救 201”轮为救助船，总吨为 552，总功率为 4480 千瓦（6093 马力）。8 月 13 日，投资公司提出租用“南海救 201”轮将其两名代表从海口运送至“加百利”轮。南海救助局向上海代表处发邮件称，“南海救 201”轮费率为每马力小时 1.5 元，根据租用时间计算总费用。上海代表处回复确认同意，称两名代表登上“加百利”轮后，“南海救 201”轮即可返回锚地。

8 月 13 日，该轮运送 2 名船东代表登上搁浅船，随后返航回海军码头完车。本次工作时间为 7.83 小时。

8 月 15 日 14 时 52 分，上海代表处向南海救助局发邮件，提出租用“南海救 201”轮，于 8 月 16 日 8 时运送相关人员及设备至“加百利”

轮，并询问该轮能否在现场等待数小时，费率能否定为每马力小时1.3元。16时，南海救助局回复称，费率仍为每马力小时1.5元，计费周期自该轮备车离开其值班锚地时起，至任务结束回到原值班锚地完车时止。且该轮本次仅作为交通船使用，不负责协助提供潜水探摸相关作业。20时02分，上海代表处回复称，通过艰难的谈判，同意南海救助局的方案，请立即安排。

8月16日，该轮运送相关人员及设备至搁浅船，随后缆带妥，完车。本次工作时间为7.75小时。

8月17日16时33分，上海代表处向南海救助局发出邮件，提出最终租用“南海救201”轮于8月18日作业一次，开航时间为18日2时，送船长、检验师等人登“加百利”轮。确认费率为每马力小时1.5元。

8月18日，该轮将相关人员及行李运送上过驳船，随后头尾缆带妥，完车。本次工作时间为8.83小时。

南海救助局主张依约定的费率每马力小时1.5元，按24.41小时工作时间计算，投资公司应向其支付救助费用223095.20元。投资公司与上海代表处则认为该轮总功率为6093马力，派出如此大马力的船舶作为交通船，属乘人之危而多收取费用。投资公司与上海代表处还认为，南海救助局对“南海救201”轮的航海日志进行了随意增删，不确认其真实性，但投资公司与上海代表处对此未举证加以证明。

（四）潜水队员的工作情况

8月12日9时57分，上海代表处向南海救助局发出邮件，要求南海救助局安排潜水队员探摸，以确认“加百利”轮受损情况及搁浅状况。15时54分，上海代表处向“加百利”轮的船代湛江外轮代理有限公司发出邮件称：南海救助局的人员和潜水员于15时左右离开基地，将于当日17时30分左右抵达现场进行水下探摸作业；委托湛江外轮代理有限公司作为船东代理人，配合湛江海事局进行救助并安排“加百利”轮继续驶往钦州。

8月13日18时08分，南海救助局向上海代表处发出邮件称，潜水队员登上交通船的时间为12日15时，离开交通船的时间为12日23时，潜水队员作业时间为8小时，请求上海代表处予以确认。该邮件同时还列出了“南海救101”轮12日的工作时间和“南海救201”轮13日的工作时间。19时35分，上海代表处回复对南海救助局的努力表示感谢，同时提出能否稍微减低费用，并建议取消“南海救101”轮12日9时30分至15时30分的作业费用，取消潜水作业费用100000元，取消“南海救201”轮13日的费用55000元。20时33分，南海救助局回复称，不能接受邮件中的请求。

南海救助局主张投资公司与上海代表处应依约定向其支付陆地调遣费10000元、水上交通费55000元、作业费40000元，共计105000元。投资公司与上海代表处则认为，陆地调遣费和水上交通费已涵盖了潜水员及设备的准备和出动费用，作业费每8小时40000元应仅指实际进行潜水探摸作业的费用，潜水队员未实际进行潜水探摸作业，南海救助局无权收取该项费用。

（五）与“南海救116”轮和“南海救101”轮的救助费率有关的其他事实

8月15日14时52分，上海代表处向南海救助局发出邮件协商相关费用问题，请求：1. 将“南海救116”轮的救助费率降低为每马力小时2.9元。2. 取消租用“南海救101”轮，稍微降低收费并报最低价。3. 潜水作业费用降低为100000元。4. 13日租用“南海救201”轮的费用为55000元。5. 欲租用“南海救201”轮于16日运送潜水员、港口船长及检验师登轮，能否把费率定为每马力小时1.3元。16时，南海救助局回复称：“南海救201”轮费率仍为每马力小时1.5元，其他因救助“加百利”轮所产生的费用，稍后再作讨论。

一审诉讼过程中，南海救助局确认无需上海代表处承担责任。

一审法院认为：

本案系海难救助合同纠纷。根据《最高人民法院关于海事法院受理案件范围的若干规定》第二十六条的规定，本案应由海事法院专门管辖。涉案事故船舶的被救助地属一审法院管辖范围，依照《中华人民共和国民事诉讼法》第三十一条的规定，一审法院对本案有管辖权。

因投资公司为希腊公司，“加百利”轮为希腊籍油轮，本案具有涉外因素。由于各方当事人在庭审中均选择适用中华人民共和国法律，根据《中华人民共和国涉外民事关系法律适用法》第三条的规定，应适用中华人民共和国法律作为处理本案实体争议的准据法。

（一）救助合同的成立及效力

搁浅事故发生后，投资公司的代理人上海代表处向南海救助局发出邮件，要求南海救助局安排两艘拖轮进行救助并称同意南海救助局的报价。此外，上海代表处通过邮件向南海救助局提交委托书，约定了救助所使用的船舶、人力（潜水员）及报酬计付标准等。从往来邮件来看，投资公司与上海代表处对“加百利”轮当时的危险状况是清楚的，上海代表处与南海救助局对相关费率等问题经过了充分的讨论，本案不存在重大误解及乘人之危情形。依照《中华人民共和国海商法》（以下简称《海商法》）第一百七十五条第一款关于“救助方与被救助方就海难救助达成协议，救助合同成立”之规定，南海救助局与投资公司之间救助合同成立，该合同并未违反现行法律、法规的强制性规定，合法有效，当事人双方应依约履行。

（二）是否应当追加货主中国联合石油有限公司作为第三人参加诉讼

投资公司申请中国联合石油有限公司参加诉讼的理由是本案系船货遭遇共同危险，依据《海商法》第一百八十三条的规定，救助报酬的金额应由获救的船舶和其他财产的各所有人按照船舶和其他财产各自的获救价值占全部获救价值的比例承担。一审法院认为，南海救助局系以救助合同为依据诉请投资公司依约定的费率支付救助费用，本案所涉法律关系与投资公司主张的共同海损费用分摊属不同的法律关系，投资公司追加货主作为第三人参加诉讼的主张不能成立。

（三）南海救助局实施的救助是否符合海难救助的构成要件

“加百利”轮是《海商法》第三条所称的船舶，是《海商法》所承认的救助标的；“加百利”轮搁浅后，船舶及船载货物处于危险状态，可能发生海洋污染事故，严重威胁海域环境安全，情况紧急，投资公司与上海代表处知悉“加百利”轮处于海上危险的事实；南海救助局派出了“南海救116”轮、“南海救101”轮、“南海救201”轮以及一组潜水队员前往事故现场提供交通、守护等，上述作业是成功救助“加百利”轮的重要组成部分。虽然“南海救116”轮并没有按原约定从事拖带作业，但其根据船东的安排一直在现场守护至“加百利”轮成功脱险，且《海商法》并未明确规定救助行为的具体形式。因此，南海救助局实施的上述行为属于救助行为。在救助过程中，南海救助局与投资公司的作为或不作为完全出于自愿，不存在《海商法》第一百八十六条规定的无权获得救助款项的情形。从整个救助过程来看，“加百利”轮成功脱浅，船上全部船员及货物最终安全抵达钦州港，成功获救。据此，南海救助局实施的救助符合海难救助的构成要件，其有权依据《海商法》第一百七十九条的规定获得相应救助报酬。

（四）救助报酬的数额及利息的确定

1. “南海救201”轮的救助费用

对于“南海救201”轮的作业时间，投资公司称南海救助局对该轮的航海日志进行了增删，但并未就此举证加以证明，该轮三次作业时间共24.41小时；该轮每马力小时1.5元的费率系南海救助局、投资公司充分协商而达成，一审法院予以确认；因该轮总功率为6093马力，依此计算，投资公司就该轮应支付的费用为223095.20元。

2. 潜水队员的费用

依投资公司发给南海救助局的委托书，潜水队员作业费的计费周期为潜水员登上交通船开始起算，到作业完毕离开交通船上岸为止。依据该约定，即便潜水员未下水作业，只要其登上交通船，投资公司即应向南海救助局支付潜水队员作业费用 40000 元，加上约定应付的陆地调遣费 10000 元、水上交通费 55000 元，三项费用共计 105000 元。

3. “南海救 116”轮及“南海救 101”轮的救助费用

投资公司对“南海救 116”轮和“南海救 101”轮的总功率及工作时间未提出异议，但认为因两轮未实施实际拖带作业，故原约定的费率应予以调低，可参照《中华人民共和国交通部国际航线海上救助打捞收费办法》《中华人民共和国交通部港口收费规则》《广东省港口收费规则》三个费率标准予以确定。一审法院认为，投资公司所提出的上述标准，第一个标准已废止，第二个、第三个标准仅适用于港口拖航，故上述标准均不适用于本案。

根据《海商法》第一百八十条的规定，确定报酬时应综合考虑救助方所用的时间、支出的费用和遭受的损失，救助方或者救助设备所冒的责任风险和其他风险等。在实际救助工作中，救助方守护作业的成本消耗、技术要求及责任风险等与拖带作业相比均有一定的差距。根据《海商法》第一百七十六条第二项规定，按照合同支付的救助款项明显过高或者过低于实际提供的救助服务的，诉讼或仲裁过程中法院或仲裁机构可以判决或者裁决变更救助合同。由于“南海救 116”轮和“南海救 101”轮均未按原约定实施拖带作业，南海救助局主张两轮的救助费率仍按约定的每马力小时 3.2 元计算，投资公司认为过高，提出异议，一审法院认为应予以调整。一方面，在往来邮件中，投资公司一直要求南海救助局调低该费率，南海救助局邮件回复称：其他因救助“加百利”轮所产生的费用，稍后再作讨论。可见当时南海救助局就该救助费率仍留有可调整的余地。另一方面，投资公司将救助方案变更为过驳减载脱浅并将这一变更告知南海救助局后，仍于 15 日的邮件中询问南海救助局可否将该轮的救助费率调整为每马力小时 2.9 元。可见投资公司在变更救助方案后仍愿意以每马力小时 2.9 元的费率付费，该费率的确定符合《海商法》鼓励救助的原则。据此，一审法院将“南海救116”轮和“南海救101”轮的救助费率调整至每马力小时2.9元。“南海救116”轮、“南海救101”轮的救助费用相应确定为5522467.68元和742350.70元。

上述“南海救116”轮、“南海救101”轮、“南海救201”轮及潜水队员的救助费用合计6592913.58元。

关于南海救助局请求的救助报酬的利息。南海救助局与投资公司未约定救助报酬的支付期限，事后未达成补充协议，也无法按照合同有关条款和交易习惯确定，依照《中华人民共和国合同法》（以下简称《合同法》）第六十二条关于“履行期限不明确的，债务人可以随时履行，债权人也可以随时要求履行，但应当给对方必要的准备时间”的规定，一审法院酌情认定完成救助作业后的两个月为准备时间，确定本案救助报酬的利息应从2011年10月19日起，按中国人民银行同期流动资金贷款利率计至判决确定应当支付之日止。

综上，一审法院经审判委员会讨论决定，依照《海商法》第一百七十五条第一款、第一百七十六条第二项、第一百七十九条、第一百八十条的规定，作出（2012）广海法初字第898号民事判决：投资公司向南海救助局支付救助报酬6592913.58元，及自2011年10月19日起至判决确定支付之日止按中国人民银行同期流动资金贷款利率计算的利息；驳回南海救助局的其他诉讼请求。一审案件受理费65822元，由南海救助局负担9591元，投资公司负担56231元。

投资公司不服一审判决提起上诉，请求二审法院撤销一审判决，依调整后的费率，按38.85%的比例改判投资公司承担相应的责任；判令南海救助局承担本案一、二审诉讼费用。

二审期间，除涉案救助报酬的认定之外，各方当事人对一审法院查明的其他事实无异议，二审法院予以确认。

二审法院另查明：

“加百利”轮搁浅后，该轮船长即向湛江海事局进行了汇报，湛江海事局责令该轮船长、船东尽快制定并实施脱浅方案。经研究，该轮船东/船长于事故当日决定选择过驳减载脱浅方案。为此，“加百利”轮船东先后从新加坡、荷兰、中国等地派遣了多名造船师、救助专家、检验师等登轮进行协助和指导。虽然湛江海事局的《“加百利”轮应急过驳脱浅综合保障预案》系于2011年8月17日发布，但过驳减载脱浅方案却是由“加百利”轮船方在8月12日14时25分之前即已明确并被湛江海事局认可。

涉案船舶的获救价值为30531856美元，货物的获救价值为48053870美元，船舶的获救价值占全部获救价值的比例为38.85%。

二审法院认为：

（一）关于涉案海难救助合同的效力

南海救助局与投资公司通过电子邮件磋商签订救助合同的过程中，“加百利”轮处于危险境地，“加百利”轮船东即委托相关领域专业人士参与研究确定救助方案，船东互保协会以及船方亦共同委托了专业律师及航海专业人士参与救助方案的确定及涉案合同的订立。上海代表处作为船东代表具体参与了涉案救助合同的谈判与订立。上海代表处与南海救助局的多次邮件往来可证明，投资公司对涉案事故的现场情况充分知悉，对涉案救助作业具有足够的专业认知，其在已选择过驳减载脱浅方案的情形下，与南海救助局经充分协商，最终订立了本案合同，同意南海救助局的合同报价，投资公司所称的对涉案合同的订立存在重大误解，二审法院不予支持。

投资公司确认，在涉案救助的同时期，南海救助局与案外人签订的拖轮作业合同显示，“南海救116”轮及同类拖轮的作业费用均不低于每马力小时3.0元，本案中不存在南海救助局乘人之危的情形。投资公司关于涉案救助合同应依《合同法》第五十四条的规定予以变更或撤销的理由，亦不能成立。

投资公司委托南海救助局派遣“南海救116”轮和“南海救101”轮到现场协助“加百利”轮出浅，并约定无论能否成功协助该轮出浅，投资公司均同意按照每马力小时3.2元的费率付费；“南海救116”轮和“南海救101”轮只负责拖带作业，“加百利”轮脱浅作业过程中如发生任何意外无需南海救助局负责。本案救助过程也显示，南海救助局在参与救助的过程中，实际服从于船方指示。故本案救助系合同救助，救助方按照被救助方的指挥进行救助，不论救助是否有效果，被救助方都应该按照《海商法》第一百七十九条的规定，根据救助方使用的人力和设备，按约定支付报酬。一审判决以“加百利”轮成功脱浅、救助效果良好作为本案救助报酬的取得依据之一，属适用法律不当。

（二）关于南海救助局请求的救助报酬是否合理

涉案委托书记载投资公司委托南海救助局派遣拖轮到现场协助“加百利”轮出浅，同时记载“南海救116”轮和“南海救101”轮只负责拖带作业。拖带出浅和过驳脱浅是两种不同的、独立的救助方式，过驳脱浅救助并不必然需要拖轮的守护。此外，投资公司请求南海救助局派遣“南海救116”轮和“南海救101”轮进行救助时尚未确定使用过驳减载脱浅方案，结合委托书的文义，应认定投资公司请求派遣拖轮到现场的目的是以拖轮合适的作业方式救助“加百利”轮脱浅，而非待命协助出浅。因拖轮抵达现场之后，投资公司救助方案发生变化，导致拖轮及潜水人员都未实际从事合同约定的救助作业，投资公司以南海救助局未实际实施合同约定的救助事项为由请求变更救助合同，于法有据。鉴于一审已根据投资公司的诉请，综合考虑《海商法》第一百八十条规定的因素对涉案救助报酬进行了调整，二审法院不再另行调整。各方当事人对依据一审判决认定的救助报酬基数6592913.58元无异议，予以确认。

（三）投资公司是否可以仅按船舶获救价值占全部获救价值的比例承担涉案救助报酬

《海商法》第一百七十五条规定：“遇险船舶的船长有权代表船舶所有人订立救助合同。遇险船舶的船长或者船舶所有人有权代表船上财产所有人订立救助合同。”《海商法》第一百八十三条规定：“救助报酬的金额，应当由获救的船舶和其他财产的各所有人，按照船舶和其他各项财产各自的获救价值占全部获救价值的比例承担。”在上述规定的适用上，《海商法》并未对不同类型的救助作出区分，故本案合同救助亦应适用。船舶在海上遇险，要求船舶所有人或船长亲自签订救助合同，不利于及时展开救助，也不符合海运实践。《海商法》第一百七十五条规定的两个法定代表权，与代理制度并不相悖，故南海救助局关于本案救助合同并非由“加百利”轮船长或船东签订、上海代表处从未向南海救助局披露其代表货主、本案不适用《海商法》第一百七十五条的理由均不能成立。

根据《海商法》第一百七十二条、第一百七十九条的规定，救助报酬是救助款项的一种形式，在合同救助中，救助方与被救助方可以对包括救助报酬形式在内的救助款项作出约定，南海救助局关于救助报酬仅适用于“无效果无报酬”救助合同的主张缺乏依据。双方约定的是被救助方对救助方的履约行为给予的经济回报，该约定费用应属于救助报酬，依法应适用《海商法》第一百八十三条的规定。故投资公司可仅按照船舶获救价值占全部获救价值的比例 38.85%向南海救助局承担救助报酬，投资公司应负担的救助报酬为 2561346.93 元。投资公司未向南海救助局支付救助报酬，构成违约，南海救助局请求其支付迟延付款利息于法有据，应予支持。一审法院酌情认定投资公司应在收到通知后两个月内支付涉案报酬合理，故本案利息应自 2011 年 10 月 19 日起算，按中国人民银行同期流动资金贷款利率计算至判决确定支付之日止。

综上，二审法院依照《海商法》第一百七十五条、第一百八十三条，《合同法》第一百零七条，《中华人民共和国民事诉讼法》第六十四条、第一百七十条第一款第二项的规定，作出（2014）粤高法民四终字第 117 号民事判决，撤销一审判决；投资公司向南海救助局支付救助报酬 2561346.93 元及其自 2011 年 10 月 19 日起至判决确定的支付之日止按中国人民银行同期流动资金贷款利率计算的利息；驳回南海救助局的其他诉讼请求。二审案件受理费 65822 元，由投资公司负担 23283.11 元，南海救助局负担42538.89元。

南海救助局不服二审判决，申请再审称：（一）投资公司委托书载明：无论是否能成功协助“加百利”轮出浅，投资公司同意按每马力小时3.2元的费率付费，表明双方已提前就费率计算等作出了约定，而南海救助局亦依约提供了救助、守护、交通等服务，双方合同已依法成立并履行。二审法院仅判令投资公司支付38.85%的救助费用，违反了合同的相对性，也与合同义务应全面履行之基本原则不符。（二）南海救助局申请再审时提交的《海损担保函》可以证明，货物的保险人已于2011年8月18日就承担货物所有人应分担的救助费用作出保证，但二审判决未查明这一事实，仅判令投资公司支付部分合同费用，使得船方和货方最终应承担的救助费用减少，也不利于实现《1989年国际救助公约》（以下简称《救助公约》）鼓励海上救助作业的宗旨。该证据足以推翻二审判决。（三）作为国家专业海上救助机构的南海救助局，既然参与了“加百利”轮的救助，就有权依据约定获得合同项下全部救助报酬。二审判决剥夺了南海救助局依约应得的合法权益，与鼓励海上救助之社会公共利益不符。（四）本案所涉合同以约定的费率和费用为救助报酬的计算依据，属雇佣救助合同。即使认为本案合同下的费用构成海难救助报酬，投资公司也有义务按照《海商法》第一百八十八条的规定，要求货方向救助人即南海救助局提供担保，而非如本案中投资公司所为，要求货物的保险人向投资公司提交担保。综上，南海救助局请求撤销二审判决，判令投资公司向其支付救助合同项下费用6592913.58元并支付相应利息，一、二审诉讼费用由投资公司承担。

投资公司答辩称：（一）二审法院判决投资公司按船舶获救价值占全部获救价值的比例承担救助报酬，恪守了合同相对性原则，适用法律正确。首先，《救助公约》第六条和《海商法》第一百七十五条赋予了船长和船舶所有人两个法定代表权。涉案救助合同是由投资公司代表货方一并与南海救助局订立，投资公司和货方均为合同甲方；其次，《海商法》第一百八十三条并未明确规定其所规范的报酬只适用于“无效果无报酬”救助合同而不适用于雇佣救助合同，南海救助局应获取的救助报酬属于《海商法》第一百八十三条调整范围。《海商法》第一百七十九条关于“或者合同另有约定外”之但书部分的规定，已对雇佣救助进行了制度设计和规范，救助人和被救助人可以通过约定使救助报酬的获得与否不与救助效果挂钩，无论救助成功与否，救助人均可按约定的固定费率主张救助款项（包括救助报酬、酬金或补偿）。本案救助为财产救助，南海救助局获得的应是、也只能是《海商法》所规定的救助报酬。（二）救助伊始或本案诉讼提起之前，至迟于本案二审庭审结束前，南海救助局应发现《海损担保函》的存在，但南海救助局直至二审结束后才发现该证据，系其主观过失而非客观原因所致，该证据不属于新证据。即使《海损担保函》属于新证据，南海救助局基于该证据要求投资公司全额支付救助报酬毫无依据。因为二审判决是基于船舶获救价值的比例判令投资公司支付其自身应分摊的部分，不涉及《海损担保函》所担保的应由货方分摊的部分。《海损担保函》和二审判决并未要求船方代货方垫付救助报酬，也没有剥夺南海救助局要求货方按比例支付救助报酬的权利，亦未免除货方的此项义务。（三）共同海损与海难救助是两项独立的制度，不能依共同海损理算规则剥夺投资公司仅需按比例支付救助报酬的法定权利。（四）因湛江海事局指示将救助方案从拖带脱浅变更为过驳减载脱浅，若继续依原先约定的针对拖带作业的费率（每马力小时 3.2 元）计费，将显失公平。根据情势变更原则，该费率应予以变更或调整。另外，南海救助局作为事业单位，为保障社会公共利益，其应仅收取足以弥补实际费用的报酬，而不应超额获利，进行人命救助更是其最主要的行政职责，不应收取任何报酬。即便对于调整后的救助报酬，人命救助所占比例（至少 50%）应予再次扣减。综上，投资公司请求驳回南海救助局的再审申请，维持二审判决。

上海代表处的陈述意见同投资公司答辩意见。

本院经审理，对一、二审判决认定的事实予以确认。

本院认为：

本案系海难救助合同纠纷。中华人民共和国加入了《救助公约》，《救助公约》所确立的宗旨，即鼓励对处于危险中的船舶和其他财产，以及对环境安全构成威胁的事件进行及时有效的救助，同时确保对实施救助作业的人员给予足够的鼓励，在本案中应予遵循。涉案事故发生后，投资公司及时寻求救助，南海救助局按照约定积极参与救助，对避免海洋污染事故的发生均发挥了作用，值得倡导。

因投资公司是希腊公司，“加百利”轮为希腊籍油轮，本案具有涉外因素。各方当事人在诉讼中一致选择适用中华人民共和国法律，根据《中华人民共和国涉外民事关系法律适用法》第三条的规定，本院适用中华人民共和国法律对本案进行审理。《海商法》作为调整海上运输关系、船舶关系的特别法，应优先适用。《海商法》没有规定的，适用《合同法》等相关法律的规定。

根据南海救助局的再审申请理由及投资公司、上海代表处的答辩意见，本案的争议焦点涉及事实和法律适用两个方面。具体包括：（一）南海救助局再审阶段提交的证据材料是否为法律规定的新的证据，如是，是否足以推翻二审判决；（二）如何理解《救助公约》和《海商法》所规定的救助合同；（三）本案所涉合同的性质及法律适用；（四）南海救助局诉请的救助报酬数额如何确定。

（一）关于南海救助局提交的证据材料是否为法律规定的新的证据及是否足以推翻二审判决

南海救助局申请再审期间，向本院提交了中国人民财产保险股份有限公司北京市分公司（以下简称人保财险北京公司）出具的《海损担保函》，目的在于证明投资公司在向南海救助局支付报酬后，可以从人保财险北京公司处获得补偿，认为该证据足以推翻二审判决。投资公司和上海代表处庭审质证称，对该证据材料的真实性、合法性无异议，但认为该证据材料不是新的证据，对其证明效力不予认可。

本院认为，该证据材料系人保财险北京公司针对“加百利”轮船东和其他可能的航程利益相关方而出具，该证据材料虽对本院了解案涉救助款项承担的相关情况有所帮助，但与本案当事人争议的救助报酬问题并无直接关联，本院不予采纳。

（二）关于如何理解《救助公约》和《海商法》所规定的救助合同

海难救助是一项传统的国际海事法律制度，《救助公约》和《海商法》对此作了专门规定。《海商法》第九章关于海难救助的规定，借鉴吸收了《救助公约》的主要内容。《救助公约》第十二条、《海商法》第一百七十九条规定了“无效果无报酬”的救助报酬支付原则，《救助公约》第十三条、《海商法》第一百八十条及第一百八十三条在该原则基础上进一步规定了报酬的评定标准与具体承担。上述条款是对当事人基于“无效果无报酬”原则确定救助报酬的海难救助合同的具体规定。与此同时，《救助公约》和《海商法》均允许当事人对救助报酬的确定另行约定。因此，在《救助公约》和《海商法》规定的“无效果无报酬”救助合同之外，还可以依当事人的约定形成雇佣救助合同。

（三）关于本案所涉合同的性质及法律适用

根据本案查明的事实，投资公司与南海救助局经过充分磋商，明确约定无论救助是否成功，投资公司均应支付报酬，且“加百利”轮脱浅作业过程中如发生任何意外，南海救助局无需负责。依据该约定，南海救助局救助报酬的获得与否和救助是否有实际效果并无直接联系，而救助报酬的计算，是以救助船舶每马力小时，以及人工投入等事先约定的固定费率和费用作为依据，与获救财产的价值并无关联。因此，本案所涉救助合同不属于《救助公约》和《海商法》所规定的“无效果无报酬”救助合同，而属雇佣救助合同。

关于雇佣救助合同下的报酬支付条件及标准，《救助公约》和《海商法》并未作具体规定。一、二审法院依据《海商法》第一百八十条规定的相关因素对当事人在雇佣救助合同中约定的固定费率予以调整，属适用法律错误。本案应依据《合同法》的相关规定，对当事人的权利义务予以规范和确定。

（四）关于南海救助局诉请的救助报酬数额如何确定

对于南海救助局诉请的救助报酬数额，投资公司主张，其应依照《海商法》第一百八十三条的规定，按照船舶获救价值占全部获救价值的比例承担救助报酬。本院认为，《海商法》第一百八十三条应适用于“无效果无报酬”的救助合同，而案涉合同属雇佣救助合同，南海救助局以其与投资公司订立的合同为依据，要求投资公司全额支付约定的救助报酬并无不当。

投资公司还提出，本案救助方案由此前的拖带作业、探摸作业变更为过驳减载，符合情势变更的有关情形，此前约定的救助报酬费率应予调整。本院认为，《最高人民法院关于适用〈中华人民共和国合同法〉若干问题的解释（二）》第二十六条规定：“合同成立以后客观情况发生了当事人在订立合同时无法预见的、非不可抗力造成的不属于商业风险的重大变化，继续履行合同对于一方当事人明显不公平或者不能实现合同目的，当事人请求人民法院变更或者解除合同的，人民法院应当根据公平原则，并结合案件的实际情况确定是否变更或者解除。”本案救助方案的调整并非基于客观情况的重大变化，而是包括当事人在内的相关方协商讨论的结果，且合同的继续履行对于投资公司并非明显不公平或者不能实现合同目的，救助方案的调整并不属于法律意义上的情势变更。投资公司以此主张降低约定的费率和费用，缺乏事实和法律依据，本院不予支持。

南海救助局根据其与投资公司的约定，投入了相应的船舶和人员用于涉案救助服务，投资公司应根据约定的费率，以及南海救助局投入的船舶和人员、耗费的时间等支付报酬。一审判决按照当事人的约定，确定投资公司应当向南海救助局支付“南海救 201”轮以及潜水队员的费用正确；同时，一审判决根据实际施救情况，将“南海救 116”轮和“南海救 101”轮的救助费率由每马力小时 3.2 元酌予调整至每马力小时 2.9 元，南海救助局对此未提起上诉，亦未就此问题提出再审请求，本院予以认可。

综上，二审法院以一审判决确定的救助报酬数额为基数，依照《海商法》的规定，判令投资公司按照船舶获救价值占全部获救财产价值的比例支付救助报酬，适用法律和处理结果错误，应予纠正。一审判决适用法律错误，但鉴于一审判决对相关费率的调整是以当事人的合同约定为基础，南海救助局对此并未行使相关诉讼权利提出异议，一审判决结果可予维持。本院依照《中华人民共和国合同法》第八条、第一百零七条，《中华人民共和国民事诉讼法》第一百七十条第一款第二项以及《最高人民法院关于适用〈中华人民共和国民事诉讼法〉的解释》第四百零七条第一款之规定，判决如下：

一、撤销广东省高级人民法院（2014）粤高法民四终字第117号民事判决；

二、维持广州海事法院（2012）广海法初字第898号民事判决。

本案一审案件受理费65822元，由交通运输部南海救助局负担9591元，阿昌格罗斯投资公司负担56231元；二审案件受理费65822元，由阿昌格罗斯投资公司负担。

本判决为终审判决。

审 判 长 贺 荣
审 判 员 张勇健
审 判 员 王淑梅
审 判 员 余晓汉
代理审判员 郭载宇
二〇一六年七月七日
法官助理 马 玲
书 记 员 李 娜

Nanhai Rescue Bureau of the Ministry of Transport

v.

Archangelos Investments E. N. E. and Shanghai Representative Office of Hong Kong Andaousen Co, Ltd for the Dispute over a Contract for Salvage at Sea

—To Determine the Rights and Obligations of the Parties to an Employment Contract for Salvage in Accordance with Relevant Provisions of the *Contract Law*

Holding

1. The *International Convention on Salvage of* 1989 (hereinafter referred to as *Convention*) and the *Maritime Law of the People's Republic of China* (hereinafter referred to as *Maritime Law*) provide that unless otherwise unanimously agreed upon by the Parties to salvage contracts, the principle of "No Cure, No Pay" shall apply. If and when a contract has explicit agreements that regardless of the results of the effort, the salved Party shall pay the remunerations based on the input of horsepower-hours of salvage ships and labours, the said contract is an employment contract for salvage rather than the salvage contract as defined in the above-mentioned *Convention* and the *Maritime Law*.

2. In the absence of definitive provisions on the employment contract for salvage in the *Convention* and the *Maritime Law*, relevant provisions of the *Contract Law of the People's Republic of China* (hereinafter referred to as *Contract Law*) can apply for determining the rights and obligations of the

Parties hereto.

Commentary*

This case is the first one for the dispute over an employment contract for salvage tried by the Supreme People's Court of the People's Republic of China (hereinafter referred to as SPC) and is an important guiding one.

On August 12, 2011, Gabriel tanker ran aground at Qiongzhou Strait. The salvor, Nanhai Rescue Bureau of the Ministry of Transport of the People's Republic of China (hereinafter referred to as NRB), entered into a fixed rate-based employment contract for salvage with the salvee, Archangelos Investments E. N. E. that is the owner of Gabriel tanker (hereinafter referred to as Archangelos) and incurred the salvage expenses of RMB 7, 240, 998. 24 in total during its salvage efforts. NRB lodged a lawsuit with the people's court, claiming that Archangelos should pay the aforesaid salvage expenses, whereas Archangelos rebutted that according to Article 183 of the *Maritime Law*, the salvage remunerations should be jointly borne by the owners of the salvaged ship and goods on board according to the proportion of their respective salvaged value to the total salvaged value.

1. Nature of Employment Contract for Salvage

The phrase, Employed Salvage Service, an idiomatic expression in China, means the salving Party makes the salvage efforts upon the request of and according to the requirements of the salved Party and, regardless of the results of such efforts, receives corresponding remunerations based on an agreed pay rate or a fixed pay. Therefore, for an employment contract for salvage, there are two constitutive elements including no relation of the salvage remunerations

* Author: SI Yuzhuo, Professor and Doctoral Supervisor, Dalian Maritime University.

to the salvage efforts and a pay rate or a fixed pay. This is a popular practice in the salvage service market in China, and there are no definitive legal provisions on the employed salvage services, so the principle of autonomy of will is widely followed. The facts in this case that SPC found were upon full consultation, Archangelos and NRB clearly agreed that whether or not the rescue was successful, Archangelos should pay the corresponding remunerations, and NRB should not be held liable for any accident in the course of the refloating operation to Gabriel tanker. Hence, SPC determined that the contract for salvage in this case was an employment contract for salvage rather than "No Cure, No Pay" contract for salvage defined in the *Convention* and the *Maritime Law*. This judgment clearly distinguished an employment contract for salvage from "No Cure, No Pay" contract for salvage, clarifying that it is a contract for salvage of completely different nature. A "No Cure, No Pay" contract for salvage is an ancient legal system of maritime salvage peculiar to the *Maritime Law*, whereas an employment contract for salvage is classified as a contract of maritime services by constitutive elements of a contract.①

2. Application of Laws Concerning the Remunerations for the Employed Salvage Services

Gabriel tanker is a Greek tanker and its shipowner, Archangelos, is a Greek company. Therefore this case was one involving foreign elements. Now that during the hearing stage of the court, both Parties to the dispute expressly agreed upon the application of the laws of the People's Republic of China, according to Article 3 of the *Law of the People's Republic of China on the Application of Laws Concerning Foreign-related Civil Relations* (hereinafter referred to as *Law on the Application of Laws*), the laws of the People's Republic of China shall be the governing law for handling the substantial dispute

① 参见司玉琢、吴煦:《雇佣救助的法律属性及法律适用》,载《中国海商法研究》2016 年第 3 期。

in this case. If and when an employment contract for salvage falls within the scope of Chapter 9: Maritime Salvage of the *Maritime Law*, it as a special law governing the relations arising from and/or pertaining to maritime transport and ocean vessels shall prevail. Where provisions of the *Maritime Law* are inconsistent with those of the *Convention* to which China is a party, according to Article 4 of the *Explanations (Ⅰ) of the Supreme People's Court on Several Issues Concerning the Application of the Law of the People's Republic of China on the Application of Laws Concerning Foreign-related Civil Relations*, the provisions of the *Convention* shall be applied by a people's court according to Article 268 (1) of the *Maritime Law*. Namely, "where provisions in an international treaty that the People's Republic of China has concluded or acceded to differ from those in this Law, the former shall prevail except for ones thereon the People's Republic of China has made reservations". That is to say, if and when China's *Maritime Law* applied to this case, wherever related provisions in the *Maritime Law* differed from those in the *Convention*, the latter should prevail. Given the employment contract for salvage in this case had been characterized by the case-reopening collegial panel of SPC as not being a "No Cure, No Pay" contract for salvage as defined in the *Convention* and the *Maritime Law*, and there exist no definitive provisions on the remunerations for the employed salvage services either in the *Maritime Law* and the *Convention*, therefore, SPC applied related provisions in the *Contract Law*① to determining the issues concerning the remunerations for the employed salvage services in this case, complying with rules of application of laws, and the adjustment to the fixed rate agreed upon by the Parties in the employment contract for salvage made by Guangzhou Maritime Court (namely CFI) and Guangdong Higher

① See related provisions in Part Ⅲ: Contracts of the *Civil Code of the People's Republic of China* (hereinafter referred to as *Civil Code*).

People's Court (namely CSI) according to related factors as prescribed in Article 180 of the *Maritime Law* was error in the application of laws.

3. Apportionment of the Remunerations for the Employed Salvage Services

The core issue at dispute in this case was, in essence, the apportionment of the remunerations for the employed salvage services among all Parties concerned. The shipowner of Gabriel tanker claimed that the remunerations for the employed salvage services was the salvage remunerations, and should be apportioned *pro rata* among the owners of the ship and the goods on board according to Article 183 of the *Maritime Law* rather than being exclusively borne by the shipowner. Hence, this dispute reverted to the issue that whether or not the *Convention* and the *Maritime Law* should apply to the employed salvage services. If and when the legal system of maritime salvage peculiar to the *Convention* and the *Maritime Law* in whole did not apply, there was no need to debate on the application of the *Convention* and the *Maritime Law* concerning the remunerations for the employed salvage services, and further, of course, the application of Article 183 of the *Maritime Law*, whereas relevant provisions of the *Contract Law*① directly applied. The remunerations for the employed salvage services were only binding on both Parties of the contract rather than a third party (the shippers) not involving in the contract. In short, having fulfilled its obligations under the employment contract for salvage and completed its payment of all the remunerations for the employed salvage services, the salved Party might as well request to share or reimburse corresponding costs with the shippers based on its own contractual stipulations with the shippers concerned. Yet, if and when the *Convention* and the *Maritime Law* applied in whole or in part to the employment contract for salvage, there was the need to make an idiographic analysis of the application of the

① See related provisions in Part Ⅲ: Contracts of the *Civil Code*.

proportional remuneration clause in the *Convention* or the *Maritime Law* to the remunerations for the employed salvage services in this case.

Article 180 of the *Maritime Law* deals with ten major considerations in calculating the maritime salvage remunerations under a “No Cure, No Pay” contract for salvage, while Article 183 thereof the provision on the proportional apportionment of maritime salvage remunerations among the shipowner and all the shippers. Despite being consistent in contents with Article 13 of the *Convention*, there are no clear relations between the two aforesaid Articles of the *Maritime Law*, leaving the *Maritime Law* with a loophole.① In contrast, there are close relations between the provisions on remunerations and the remuneration apportionment in Article 13 of the *Convention*, in which Article 13 (1) deals with the standards for calculating maritime salvage remunerations under a “No Cure, No Pay” contract for salvage (consistent in contents with Article 180 of the *Maritime Law*), and Article 13 (2) provides that the remunerations determined in Article 13 (1) shall be apportioned among the owner of the ship and the stakeholders of other properties on board according to the salvaged vessel and the values of other properties. There is a definitive restriction to the scope of the remunerations in this provision of the proportional remuneration payment, that is to say, the remunerations mean the one determined in Article 13 (1), namely, the remunerations determined based on the principle of “No Cure, No Pay” rather than any and all remunerations in a general sense. Although the remunerations for the employed salvage services defined only according to Article 183 of the *Maritime Law* can also be apportioned *pro rata*, it is obviously inconsistent with the provisions in Article 13 of the *Convention*. When provisions of the *Maritime Law* are inconsistent with related ones of international conventions to which China is a party, the

① 参见张文广:《“加百利”轮海难救助合同纠纷再审案判决评析》,载《法律适用》2016 年第 8 期。

latter shall prevail. Hence, Article 13 of the *Convention* shall apply. The remunerations for the employed salvage services are not determined according to Article 13 (1) of the *Convention*, but according to the fixed rate agreed upon by the salving Party and the salved Party consultation on the basis of equality, and thus the salved Party has no right of defense for proportional apportionment. In the view of SPC, Article 183 of the *Maritime Law* applies to "No Cure, No Pay" contract for salvage, and the contract in this case was an employment contract for salvage. Therefore, it was not inappropriate for NRB to request Archangelos to make full payment of the agreed salvage remunerations on the grounds of its contract with Archangelos.

4. The Legal Significance of the Judgment in This Case

In practice, an employment contract for salvage has been much more used by three major marine rescue bureaus[①] in China than "No Cure, No Pay" contract for salvage. In a healthy and orderly salvage market, full awareness of the nature of employment contract for salvage, its application of laws and its pattern of liability for the remunerations for the employed salvage services has direct bearing on their benefits of salvors. This case carries practical significance and theoretical value. (1) Expenses on employed salvage services (remunerations) are not the salvage remunerations under the principle of "No Cure, No Pay". The salvage remunerations secured by the maritime lien of ships are the salvage remunerations under the principle of "No Cure, No Pay", while the expenses on employed salvage services are not the claims secured by the maritime lien of ships;[②] (2) the salvage remunerations to be apportioned *pro rata* among the owner of the ship and the stakeholders of other properties on

① Three major rescue bureaus in China are Nanhai Rescue Bureau, Shanghai Rescue Bureau and Yantai Rescue Bureau.

② See Article 4 (1) (3) of the *International Convention on Maritime Liens and Mortgages of* 1993.

board must be the salvage remunerations under the principle of “No Cure, No Pay” rather than fixed expenses from employed salvage services (remunerations); and (3) the entitlement of salvors using employed salvage services to the limitation of liability for maritime claims or claims for general average on employed salvage service expenses are beyond the scope of salvage legal relations, and shall be judged according to relevant provisions on subjects of right to the limitation of liability for maritime claims① or the constitutive elements of general average.② The conclusion of this case raised strong repercussions both in the maritime salvage sector worldwide and the theoretical cycle of the *Maritime Law*, and won extensive praise in all circles. A special issue focusing on this case was added to the U. K. 's Chinese Maritime and Commercial Law Reports. Out of more than 1,670 cases tried by people's courts across the country in 2016, this one was cited among the “Top 10 Cases of 2016 Contributing to the Development of Rule of Law” based on strict screening by adjudication divisions under SPC and higher people's courts across the country and the democratic vote and evaluation from the Dispute Review Board. Although China is not a case-law country, this case not only carries important guiding value for its judicial practice but also delivers significant effects on its maritime legislation.

① See Article 204 of the *Maritime Law*.

② See Article 193 of the *Maritime Law*.

Grounds of Decision *

The Supreme People's Court of the People's Republic of China

Civil Judgment

No. 61 [2016], Case-reopening, Civ. Division, SPC

Petitioner for Case-reopening (Plaintiff of First Instance, Appellee of Second Instance): Nanhai Rescue Bureau of the Ministry of Transport.

Domicile: No. **, ** Avenue, Haizhu District, Guangzhou City, Guangdong Province, the People's Republic of China.

Legal Representative: Lin XX, Director-General.

Attorney: Wan XX, at Shanghai ** Law Firm.

Respondent (Defendant of First Instance, Appellant of Second Instance): Archangelos Investments E. N. E.

Domicile: **** Street, **** Athens, Greece.

Representative: Balabanos, Chairman.

Attorney: Huang X, at Guangdong ** Law Firm.

Attorney: Zhang X, at Guangdong ** Law Firm.

Defendant of First Instance: Shanghai Representative Office of Hong Kong Andaousen Co, Ltd.

Domicile: Room ***, Suite *, ** Mansion, No. ***, *** Avenue, Xuhui District, Shanghai, the People's Republic of China.

Representative: He X, Chief Representative.

Attorney: Huang X, at Guangdong ** Law Firm.

---

* Editor's note: all the contents herein are the same as in the original judgment documents except for personally identifiable information, including names and addresses, for the personal information security of the Parties involved.

The petitioner for case-reopening, Nanhai Rescue Bureau of the Ministry of Transport (hereinafter referred to as NRB), refused to accept the Civil Judgment of No. 117 [2014], Final, Fourth Civ. Division, Guangdong Higher People's Court made by Guangdong Higher People's Court (hereinafter referred to as CSI) on the dispute over the contract for salvage at sea between itself and the respondent, Archangelos Investments E. N. E., (hereinafter referred to as Archangelos), and the defendant of the first instance, Shanghai Representative Office of Hong Kong Andaousen Co, Ltd (hereinafter referred to as SHRO), and filed a petition for case-reopening with the Supreme People's Court of the People's Republic of China (hereinafter referred to as SPC). On December 24, 2015, SPC made the Civil Ruling of No. 3182 [2015], Civ. Appealing, SPC to reopen this case, and formed by law a collegial panel consisting of Vice-President and Justice HE Rong, Judges ZHANG Yongjian, WANG Shumei and YU Xiaohan, and Acting Judge GUO Zaiyu. On July 7, 2016, SPC heard this case *in curia*, where Lin XX, the legal representative of NRB; Wan XX, the attorney representing NRB; Huang X and Zhang X, attorneys representing Archangelos; and Huang X, the attorney representing SHRO, appeared and attended the proceedings in court. Now, the case-reopening procedure of this case has been concluded.

In its filings submitted with Guangzhou Maritime Court (hereinafter referred to as CFI), NRB alleged that Archangelos is the owner of Gabriel tanker (Archangelos Gabriel) and SHRO is its shipping agent. On August 12, 2011, Gabriel tanker ran aground in Qiongzhou Strait. At the request of Archangelos, NRB dispatched NRB No. 116 ship, NRB No. 101 ship and NRB No. 201 ship, together with a team of divers, to provide services, including salvage, transportation and safety protection, at the accident site, and incurred the salvage expenses of RMB 7,240,998.24 (denominated in RMB, the same below unless otherwise expressly specified) calculated based on prior agreement between the Parties, but Archangelos had failed to pay such expenses until now. NRB requested SPC to decide that Archangelos and SHRO jointly and severally paid to NRB the salvage expenses of RMB 7, 240, 998. 24 and the corresponding interest of RMB 476, 449. 64 accrued thereon during the period of deferred payment from August 20, 2011 to the date of actual payment (tentatively scheduled until August 19, 2012 at the benchmark interest rate of loans over the same period issued by the People's Bank of China); and Archangelos and SHRO jointly and severally bore all the legal costs of this case.

CFI found that:

Archangelos's Gabriel tanker is a oil tanker and is of Greek nationality, with its port of registration being Piraeus and the total tonnage 40, 682 tons. At around 05 : 00 on August 12, 2011 during its journey from Hong Kong to Qinzhou, Guangxi Province, the tanker, with 54, 580 tons of Cabinda crude oil and a 26-member crew on board, ran aground near No. 6 buoy light on the northern watercourse within Qiongzhou Strait (22°21'7. 2"N, 110°48'7. 8"E). With its hull tilted at an angle of 3 degrees to the left, cracks developing on the forepeak below the waterline, and water seeping into cabins, the ship and the goods on board were in danger, posing a serious threat to the environmental safety of the sea waters.

With the authorization from Archangelos, SHRO promptly sent an e-mail to NRB, briefing on the ship grounding of Gabriel tanker, requesting NRB to dispatch two tugboats to salvage the stranded tanker, and expressly agreeing to NRB's price offer for such operations.

At 20 : 40 on August 12, SHRO sent a Letter of Entrustment via e-mail, entrusting NRB to deploy NRB No. 116 ship and NRB No. 101 ship to assist with getting Gabriel tanker refloated at the accident site, and promising that, regardless of the results of the effort, the payment at the rate of RMB 3. 2/HP hour for the tugboats during the period from their preparation for the mission at their standby stations to their arrival back at their standby stations following the cessation of the salvage operations as required by SHRO would be made, and that two ships would only do the towing, and NRB should not be held liable for any possible accidents in the course. Moreover, NRB was also required to dispatch a team of divers to do the underwater inspection in and around Gabriel tanker, and besides a fixed sum of land deployment expenses of RMB 10, 000 and water transportation expenses of RMB 55, 000, the payment would be made for such mission at the rate of RMB 40, 000/8 hours during the period from the divers' getting on a traffic ship bound for Gabriel tanker to their getting off the traffic boat ashore following the completion of their underwater inspection operations.

Meanwhile, to prevent further deterioration of the dangerous situation and possible marine pollution, Zhanjiang Maritime Safety Administration of the People's Republic of China (hereinafter referred to as ZMSA) decided to take compulsory discharge measures with Gabriel tanker, helping get the ship refloated with the lighterage and load reduction. Under the arrangement of ZMSA, China Shipping Development Co, Ltd-affiliated Tanker Company deployed its Danchi ship on August 17 to unload the crude oil on Gabriel tanker. On August 18, Gabriel tanker managed to get refloated on rising tides, and then safely arrived at the port of destination, Qinzhou port in Guangxi Province. The unloaded crude oil was also sent to the port of destination by Danchi ship.

1. Facts about NRB No. 116 Ship

NRB No. 116 ship is a 3681-ton salvage ship with the total power of 9, 000 kilowatts (12, 240 horsepower). After arriving at the scene of the accident, due to ZMSA's decision to adopt the refloating arrangement with the lighterage and load reduction, NRB No. 116 ship did not perform the towing operations on Gabriel tanker. Throughout the 155. 58-hour period from 07 : 45 on August 12 to 19 : 20 on August 18, the ship had protected Gabriel tanker at the accident site as instructed by Archangelos. Therefore, NRB requested Archangelos to pay the salvage expenses of RMB 6, 093, 757. 44 in total according to the agreed pay rate of RMB 3. 2/HP hour. However, Archangelos and SHRO contended that the pay rate of RMB 3. 2/HP hour had been agreed upon for the towing operations. But in fact, the ship had been on standby at the site and protected the stranded tanker. Now that it did not take part in any specific salvage operations, the salvage expenses should not be calculated based on the original agreed pay rate of RMB 3. 2/HP hour.

2. Facts about NRB No. 101 Ship

NRB No. 101 ship is a 4091-ton salvage ship with the total power of 13, 860 kilowatts (18, 850 horsepower). At 09 : 38 on August 12, NRB requested SHRO via an e-mail to confirm that the second tugboat, NRB No. 101 ship, would be dispatched, and SHRO replied at 09 : 57 the same day, requesting NRB to arrange for aforesaid two tugboats to participate in the rescue effort.

At 09 : 30 on August 12, NRB No. 101 ship started off to rescue Gabriel tanker and during its race to the accident site, NRB sent an e-mail to SHRO at 15 : 19, saying that given the shipmaster of Gabriel tanker had insisted on adopting ZMSA's salvage scheme, refloating the tanker through load reduction, it was recommended that NRB No. 116 ship would continue to work at the site, while NRB No. 101 ship should return to its anchor station. At 15 : 44, SHRO replied, confirming that only NRB No. 116 ship would remain at the scene, and the engagement of NRB No. 101 ship was canceled. At 15 : 50, the ship began to return, that is to say, it did not arrive at the accident site. At 23 : 05, the ship was back at its anchor station. NRB claimed that the total working time for the ship was 13. 58 hours, and Archangelos should pay to NRB the salvage expenses of RMB 819, 145. 60 according to the agreed pay rate of RMB 3. 2/ HP hour. Yet, Archangelos and SHRO argued that given NRB No. 101 ship had been ordered back by NRB on the way to the accident site, having not done any towing or other operations, it was obviously unfair and extremely unreasonable for calculating the expenses at the agreed pay rate.

3. Facts about NRB No. 201 Ship

NRB No. 201 ship is a 552-ton salvage ship with the total power of 4, 480 kilowatts (6, 093 horsepower). On August 13, Archangelos offered to hire NRB No. 201 ship for sending two representatives from Haikou to the accident site of Gabriel tanker, and NRB replied through an e-mail to SHRO that the ship would be charged based on the rental time at the rate of RMB 1. 5/HP hour. SHRO replied to confirm that NRB No. 201 ship would be sent back upon arrival of its representatives at Gabriel tanker.

On August 13, the ship carried two representatives of the shipowner to the stranded Gabriel tanker and then returned to its naval terminal. The working time for the task was 7. 83 hours.

At 14 : 52 on August 15, SHRO e-mailed NRB, offering to hire NRB No. 201 ship for transporting related persons and devices to Gabriel tanker at 08 : 00 on August 16 and inquiring that whether or not the ship could wait for hours on the spot and whether or not the rental rate could be RMB 1. 3/HP hour, and received the reply from NRB at 16 : 00 the same day that the rental cost would remain calculated at the rate of RMB 1. 5/HP based on the rental time from its departure from the anchor station to its arrival back at the anchor station following the completion of the task, and that the ship would only work for the purpose of transportation, and did not take part in any underwater inspections. Following difficult negotiations, SHRO agreed to NRB's plan and replied at 20 : 02 the same day, requiring NRB to promptly make the arrangement for the task.

On August 16, the ship transported related persons and equipments to the stranded ship, and then returned to its anchor station. The working time for the task was 7. 75 hours.

At 16 : 33 on August 17, SHRO e-mailed NRB, offering to hire NRB No. 201 ship for transporting the shipmaster, inspectors and others to the stranded tanker on August 18, with the scheduled time of departure being 02 : 00 the same day and the confirmed rental rate being RMB 1. 5/HP hour.

On August 18, the ship transported related persons and luggages to a barge as scheduled, and then returned to its anchor station. The working time for the task was 8. 83 hours.

NRB claimed that based on the agreed pay rate of RMB 1. 5/HP hour and the working time of 24. 41 hours, Archangelos should pay for the salvage expenses of RMB 223, 095. 20. Yet, Archangelos and SHRO contended that the ship is a 6, 093 horsepower vessel, using such a powerful ship by NRB as a traffic ship was to profit from others' dilemma. Besides, Archangelos and SHRO also alleged that NRB tampered with the logbook of NRB No. 201 ship in its favor and thus did not recognize its authenticity, but failed to present the evidence supporting such allegation.

4. Facts about the Divers

At 09 : 57 on August 12, SHRO e-mailed NRB, requesting NRB to arrange divers to do underwater inspections for confirming the damage and grounding details of Gabriel tanker. In an e-mail at 15 : 54 the same day, SHRO notified Zhanjiang Foreign Shipping Agency Co, Ltd, the shipping agent of Gabriel tanker, that NRB's persons and divers had departed from their base at around 15：00, and would conduct underwater inspections at the accident site at around 17：30, and meanwhile entrusted Zhanjiang Foreign Shipping Agency Co, Ltd to be the shipowner's agent for assisting ZMSA with the salvage and making the arrangements for Gabriel tanker to sail to Qinzhou Port.

At 18：08 on August 13, NRB sent an e-mail to SHRO, notifying it that the divers got on the traffic ship at 15：00 on August 12, got off it at 23：00 on August 12, their working time was 8 hours, and requested SHRO to make a confirmation on these facts. Besides, in the same e-mail, NRB also listed the working hours of NRB No. 101 ship on August 12 and of NRB No. 201 ship on August 13. At 19：35, SHRO responded, thanking NRB's efforts and at the same time requesting NRB to reduce its charges including writing off the operation expenses of NRB No. 101 ship from 09：30 to 15：30 on August 12, the underwater operation expenses of RMB 100, 000 and the operation expenses of NRB No. 201 ship on August 13 of RMB 55, 000. At 20：33 the same day, NRB replied that it could not accept the request in the e-mail.

NRB claimed that Archangelos and SHRO should pay as agreed between the Parties the land deployment expenses of RMB 10, 000, the water transportation expenses of RMB 55, 000 and the operation expenses of RMB 40, 000, totaling RMB 105, 000, while Archangelos and SHRO rebutted that the land deployment expenses and the water transportation expenses had covered the expenses for preparations and movements of divers and equipment, and the operation expenses at the rate of RMB 40, 000/8 hours should be charged only based on the actual diving operations. Now that no actual diving operations took place for the divers, NRB was not entitled to such charges.

5. Other Facts about the Pay Rates of NRB No. 116 Ship and NRB No. 101 Ship

At 14 : 52 on August 15, SHRO e-mailed NRB to negotiate the costs, requesting (1) to reduce the pay rate of NRB No. 116 ship to RMB 2. 9/HP hour; (2) to cancel the hire of NRB No. 101 ship and to reduce the other expenses related with it to the lowest price level; (3) to reduce the expenses of underwater inspection operations to RMB 100, 000; (4) that the rent of NRB No. 201 ship on August 13 was RMB 55, 000; and (5) to reduce the pay rate of NRB No. 201 ship for transporting divers, shipmaster and inspectors to the stranded Gabriel tanker on August 16 to RMB 1. 3/HP hour. NRB replied at 16 : 00 the same day that the pay rate of NRB No. 201 ship remained RMB 1. 5/HP hour and other expenses related to the salvage of Gabriel tanker would be renegotiated later.

NRB confirmed in the proceedings of the first instance that SHRO did not have to assume its liability.

CFI held that:

This case was a dispute over a contract for salvage at sea. According to Article 26 of the *Provisions of the Supreme People's Court on Several Issues Concerning the Scope of Accepting Cases by Maritime Courts*, this case was subjected to the special jurisdiction of a maritime court and the site where the salvage of the distressed ship in this case took place fell within the jurisdiction of CFI. According to Article 31 of the *Civil Procedure Law of the People's Republic of China* (hereinafter referred to as *Civil Procedure Law*), CFI had jurisdiction over this case.

Now that Archangelos is a Greek company and Gabriel tanker is a Greek oil tanker, this case involved foreign factors. Given in the course of the court hearing, the Parties unanimously chose the laws of the People's Republic of

China for settling their dispute, according to Article 3 of the *Law on the Application of Laws*, the laws of the People's Republic of China should apply as the proper law for handling the substantive dispute in this case.

1. Establishment and Legal Validity of the Contract for Salvage

After the stranding accident took place, SHRO, the shipping agent of Archangelos, sent an e-mail to NRB, requesting NRB to dispatch two tugboats to salvage, and expressly agreeing to NRB's price offer for such operations. Furthermore, SHRO also issued via e-mail a Letter of Entrustment to NRB, and agreed on the pay rates and terms of payment on the salving ships, labors (divers) and remunerations. These e-mails between the Parties demonstrated that both Archangelos and SHRO were aware of the precarious situation Gabriel tanker was in, sufficient discussion and bargaining on the pay rates and related matters were made between SHRO and NRB, and thus there were no circumstances of significant misunderstanding or profiting from others' dilemma in this case. Given that Article 175 (1) of the *Maritime Law* provides that "where the salving Party and the salved Party reach an agreement on maritime salvage, the contract for salvage at sea is formed", the contract for salvage between NRB and Archangelos was established. Not violating any mandatory provisions in the effective laws and regulations, the contract was legal and valid and should be performed as provided therein by both Parties.

2. The Participation of the Additional Shipper, China National United Oil Corporation as the Third Party in the Legal Proceedings

The grounds on which Archangelos requested to add China National United Oil Corporation (ChinaOil) in the legal proceedings were that the tanker and the goods on board in this case suffered from common danger. According to Article 183 of the *Maritime Law*, the salvage remunerations shall be shared by the owners of the salvaged ship and the goods on board according to the proportions of their respective salvaged values to the total salvaged value. In the view of CFI, it was on the grounds of the contract for salvage that NRB litigated a lawsuit and requested Archangelos to pay the salvage expenses at the agreed pay rates, so the legal relation in this case was different from the one in the claim from Archangelos that the general average should be apportioned *pro rata*. Therefore, the request from Archangelos to add the shipper as the third party could not be established.

3. Conformity of Salvage Efforts by NRB with the Constitutive Elements of Maritime Salvage

Gabriel tanker is a ship as defined in Article 3 of the *Maritime Law*, and thus is the subject of salvage recognized by the *Maritime Law*. The grounding of Gabriel tanker landed the ship *per se* and the goods on board in danger, likely triggering marine pollution accidents and posing a serious threat to the environmental safety of the waters, and thus was an emergency. Both Archangelos and SHRO were aware of the dangerous fact that Gabriel tanker was stuck at sea. NRB dispatched NRB No. 116 ship, NRB No. 101 ship and NRB No. 201 ship, together with a team of divers, to provide various services at the accident site, including transportation and safety protection. The aforesaid efforts made by NRB were an important part of the success in rescuing Gabriel tanker. Despite having not performed the scheduled towing operations, NRB No. 116 ship had stood ready at the accident site as instructed by the shipowner and had protected Gabriel tanker until Gabriel tanker got out of danger. Furthermore, there are no definitive provisions on the specific forms and manners of salvage efforts in the *Maritime Law*. Hence, the aforesaid efforts made by NRB were salvage efforts. Now that performance and non-performance by NRB and Archangelos were entirely voluntary, there were no circumstances of not being entitled to salvage remunerations as provided in

Article 186 of the *Maritime Law*. By virtue of these salvage efforts, Gabriel tanker was successfully refloated, and all the crew and the goods on board finally arrived at Qinzhou Port safely and were rescued successfully. The result also demonstrated that the salvage efforts made by NRB conformed to constitutive elements of maritime salvage, and thus, NRB was entitled to the salvage remunerations according to Article 179 of the *Maritime Law*.

4. Determination of the Salvage Remunerations and the Corresponding Interest

(1) Salvage Expenses of NRB No. 201 Ship

As for the working time of NRB No. 201 ship, Archangelos alleged that NRB tampered with the logbook of NRB No. 201 ship in its favor but failed to present the evidence supporting its allegation. The total working time of 24.41 hours in three missions for the ship and the pay rate of RMB 1.5/HP hour for the ship, which was set based on sufficient consultation between NRB and Archangelos, were confirmed by CFI. With the total power of the ship being 6,093 horsepower, Archangelos should pay the operation expenses of RMB 223,095.20 to NRB.

(2) Labor Expenses of the Divers

According to the Letter of Entrustment issued by Archangelos to NRB, the charging time for divers' work lasted from the divers' getting on the traffic ship to their getting off the traffic ship ashore following the completion of their operations. According to the stipulation between the Parties, as long as that the divers got on a traffic ship, Archangelos should pay to NRB the underwater operation expenses of RMB 40,000, the agreed land deployment expenses of RMB 10,000 and the agreed water transportation expenses of RMB 55,000, totaling RMB 105,000, regardless of actual underwater operations for the divers.

(3) Salvage Expenses of NRB No. 116 Ship and NRB No. 101 Ship

Archangelos had no objection to the total power and the working time of NRB No. 116 ship and NRB No. 101 ship, but contended that given no actual towing operations for two ships, the agreed pay rates for them should be reduced and be determined in accordance with the charging standards of the Charging Measures of the Ministry of Transport of the People's Republic of China on Maritime Rescue & Salvage Operations on International Routes, the Charging Rules of the Ministry of Transport of the People's Republic of China on Port Services and the Charging Rules of Guangdong Province on Port Services. In the view of CFI, among the three charging standards invoked by Archangelos, the first one had been abolished and the other two only applied to the towing operations within a port. Hence, the aforesaid charging standards did not apply to the specific circumstance in this case.

According to Article 180 of the *Maritime Law*, in determining the remunerations, an overall consideration should be given to various factors, such as the time input, cost input and incurred loss of the salving Party, and the exposure of the salving Party and/or its equipment to liability and other risks. In contrast with towing operations, safety protection operations in an actual salvage effort entail significantly different requirements on the salving Party in cost input, technical requirements and liability risk. According to Article 176 (2) of the *Maritime Law*, where the salvage remunerations paid as provided in a contract are obviously higher or lower than the reasonable rewards for the actual salvage services, people's courts or arbitral institutions may rule or judge/reward on the change of the contracts for salvage in the course of litigations or arbitrations. NRB No. 116 ship and NRB No. 101 ship did not perform the scheduled towing operations, but NRB still requested to calculate the remunerations for two ships according to the agreed pay rate of RMB

3.2/HP hour. Archangelos challenged the calculation on the grounds that the agreed pay rate was excessively high. In the view of CFI, their pay rate should be adjusted. On the one hand, Archangelos had persistently requested NRB to reduce the agreed pay rate in its e-mails, and NRB had relied that other expenses related to the salvage of Gabriel tanker would be renegotiated later, which suggested that there was some adjustable leeway for the agreed pay rate. On the other hand, having replaced the original salvage scheme with the refloating the tanker through the lighterage and load reduction and notified NRB of the change, Archangelos still sent an e-mail on August 15 to NRB, inquiring about whether or not to reduce the pay rate of NRB No. 116 ship to RMB 2.9/HP hour, and suggesting that even after the change to the original salvage scheme, Archangelos remained ready to pay at the rate of RMB 2.9/HP hour, which was in compliance with the principle of encouraging salvage in the *Maritime Law*. Therefore, CFI readjusted the pay rates of NRB No. 116 ship and NRB No. 101 ship to RMB 2.9/HP hour, and accordingly the salvage expenses for NRB No. 116 ship and NRB No. 101 ship were determined at RMB 5,522,467.68 and RMB 742,350.70 respectively.

The total salvage remunerations involving the aforesaid NRB No. 116 ship, NRB No. 101 ship, NRB No. 201 ship and the divers were RMB 6,592,913.58.

As for the interest on the salvage remunerations that NRB claimed, there was no time limit of payment of the salvage remunerations stipulated between NRB and Archangelos or a supplementary agreement on the payment afterwards, and the time limit of payment could not be determined in the light of related contractual provisions or transaction practices. Article 62 of the *Contract Law* provides “if the time limit for performance is not clear, the obligor may perform and the obligee may require performance, at any time, provided that the other Party shall be given the time required for preparation". Therefore, based on discretionary circumstances, CFI determined that a two(2)-month period of time upon completion of the salvage operations should be deemed as the appropriate preparation time, and thus the interest on the salvage remunerations in this case should be calculated from October 19, 2011 to the date of payment as determined in this Judgment at the benchmark interest rate of working capital loans over the same period issued by the People's Bank of China.

To sum up, according to Articles 175 (1), 176 (2), 179 and 180 of the *Maritime Law*, CFI rendered through full discussion of the judicial committee the Civil Judgment of No. 898 [2012], FI, Guangzhou Maritime Court. Archangelos paid to NRB the salvage remunerations of RMB 6, 592, 913. 58, and the interest thereon during the period from October 19, 2011 to the date of payment as determined in this Judgment at the benchmark interest rate of working capital loans over the same period issued by the People's Bank of China; all the other claims from NRB were dismissed; the acceptance fee of the first instance was RMB 65, 822, RMB 9, 591 was borne by NRB and the remaining RMB 56, 231 was borne by Archangelos.

Archangelos appealed to CSI, requesting that the Judgment of CFI should be revoked, with Archangelos being only held liable for 38. 85% of the salvage remunerations calculated at the adjusted pay rate, and NRB should bear all the court costs of the first and second instances in this case.

During the trial of the second instance, both Parties raised no objection to the facts found by CFI except for the determined salvage remunerations. Therefore, CSI affirmed all the facts found by CFI.

CSI further found that:

After Gabriel tanker stranded, the shipmaster reported without delay to

ZMSA which instructed the shipmaster and shipowner to formulate and take schemes to refloat as soon as possible. Based on the study, the shipowner/shipmaster decided the same day on the refloating scheme by the lighterage and load reduction. So, the shipowner sent shipbuilders, salvage experts and inspectors from Singapore, the Netherlands, China and others to the accident site to provide assistance and guidance on the salvage operations. Although ZMSA's Comprehensive Safety Protection Scheme for Refloating Gabriel Tanker Through Emergency Load Reduction was publicly released on August 17, 2011, the refloating scheme through the lighterage and load reduction had, in fact, been decided upon by the shipowner of Gabriel tanker and approved by ZMSA before 14：25 on August 12.

The salvaged value of the ship *per se* was USD 30, 531, 856 and that of the salvaged goods on boardwas USD 48, 053, 870. Hence, the salvaged value of the ship *per se* accounted for 38. 85% of the total salvaged value.

CSI held that:

1. Legal Validity of the Contract for Salvage

While NRB and Archangelos negotiating and executing the contract for salvage via e-mails, Gabriel tanker was in danger. The owner of Gabriel tanker at once invited professionals to decide on a salvage scheme, and the Shipowners' Mutual Assurance Association and the shipowner also jointly engaged lawyers and maritime professionals to take part in working out a salvage scheme and concluding the contract for salvage in this case. As the representative of the shipowner, SHRO had taken part in the negotiation and conclusion of the contract for salvage involved in this case. The e-mails between SHRO and NRB proved that Archangelos was fully known of the ongoing actual situation at the accident site and also had sufficient professional knowledge of the salvage operations involved in this case. With the salvage scheme having been determined, it chose to conclude the contract with NRB based on full consultation and agreed to the price offer from NRB. Therefore, the claim from Archangelos that there was significant misunderstanding while executing the contract was not supported by CSI.

Archangelos confirmed that no pay rates for NRB No. 116 ship and the tugboats of similar capacities in other tugboat operation contracts between NRB and others not involved in this case executed during the salvage operations in this case were lower than 3. 0 RMB/HP hour, which proved that there were no circumstances of NRB's profiting from other' s dilemma in this case. Hence, Archangelos' request to rescind or change the contract for salvage according to Article 54 of the *Contract Law* could not be established.

Archangelos entrusted NRB to send NRB No. 116 ship and NRB No. 101 ship to help with Gabriel tank refloating at the accident site, and agreed that, regardless of the results of the effort, Archangelos would pay at the rate of RMB 3. 2/HP hour, NRB No. 116 ship and NRB No. 101 ship would only do the towing, and NRB should not be held liable for any possible accidents in the course. The salvage process in this case also showed that throughout the salvage period, NRB had in fact acted according to the instructions from the shipowner/shipmaster. Therefore, the salvage in this case was, in essence, a contractual salvage, namely the salving Party performed under the command of the salved Party to carry out the salvage operations, where, according to provisions of Article 179 of the *Maritime Law*, the salved Party should pay remunerations to the salving Party as agreed in advance between the Parties based on the actual inputs in labours and equipments, regardless of the results of the effort. Basing the salvage remunerations on the successful refloating of Gabriel tanker and the good salvage result, the Judgment made by CFI was improper in the application of laws.

2. Reasonability of the Salvage Remunerations that NRB Claimed

The Letter of Entrustment showed that Archangelos entrusted NRB to send tugboats to help get the stranded Gabriel tanker refloated at the site, and stipulated that NRB No. 116 ship and NRB No. 101 ship would only be responsible for towing operations. The towing and lighterage are different and independent salving approaches, and the lighterage does not necessarily entail safety protection operations by tugboats. Moreover, at the moment when Archangelos requested NRB to dispatch NRB No. 116 ship and NRB No. 101 ship to provide services, whether or not adopting the scheme of refloating the stranded tanker through the lighterage and load reduction had not been finally decided upon. In the light of the context of the Letter of Entrustment, it should be determined that the true purpose of Archangelos' request to send tugboats to the site was to get the stranded Gabriel tanker refloated through some appropriate operations of these tugboats, rather than to let these tugboats simply stand ready to provide assistance. It was the change of the salvage scheme on the side of Archangelos after the tugboats had arrived at the site that led to no actual salvage operations agreed in the contract for the tugboats and divers. Therefore, the request from Archangelos to change the contract for salvage on the grounds that NRB did not actually engage in the salvage operations agreed in the contract had a legal basis. CSI decided to make no further adjustment to the salvage remunerations in response to the request from Archangelos, as CFI had already adjusted the said salvage remunerations based on a comprehensive consideration of various factors set forth in Article 180 of the *Maritime Law*. Now that the Parties had no objection, the salvage remunerations of RMB 6, 592, 913. 58 determined by CFI was affirmed by CSI.

3. Proportional Apportionment of the Salvage Remunerations

Article 175 of the *Maritime Law* provides "the shipmaster of a distressed ship has the right to conclude a contract for salvage on behalf of the shipowner. The shipmaster or shipowner of a distressed ship has the right to conclude a contract for salvage on behalf of all the owners of the properties on board." Article 183 of the *Maritime Law* provides "the salvage remunerations shall be apportioned by the owners of the salvaged ship and the goods on board according to the proportions of their respective salvaged values to the total salvaged value." When it comes to the application of aforesaid provisions, the *Maritime Law* makes no distinction among various types of salvage, so, these provisions should also apply to the contractual salvage in this case. When a ship is in distress at sea, having the shipowner or shipmaster to conclude a contract for salvage in person is neither conducive to a timely salvage effort nor consistent with the shipping practice. Two legal rights as set forth in Article 175 of the *Maritime Law* are not in conflict with the agency system. Therefore, the claim by NRB that Article 175 of the *Maritime Law* should not apply to this case on the grounds that the contract for salvage in this case was not concluded by the shipmaster or shipowner of Gabriel tanker, and that SHRO had never divulged its capacity of representing the shippers to NRB was not established.

According to Articles 172 and 179 of the *Maritime Law*, salvage remunerations is one means of various salvage payments. In a contractual salvage, the salving Party and the salved Party may agree upon salvage payments including the means of salvage remunerations. NRB's claim that salvage remunerations exclusively apply to "No Cure, No Pay" contract for salvage had no basis. The matter agreed upon between the Parties was the economic reward the salved Party would give to the salving Party for the efforts the latter made in its contractual performance, so the expenses agreed upon between the Parties should be salvage remunerations, and the provision in Article 183 of the *Maritime Law* should apply to the contract for salvage. Thus, Archangelos was entitled to be only held liable for 38. 85% of the salvage remunerations to NRB according to the proportion of the salvaged value of the ship to the total salvaged value, that is to say, Archangelos should bear only a part of the salvage remunerations, namely RMB 2, 561, 346. 93. Given Archangels's failure to pay to NRB such part of the salvage remunerations constituted a breach of contract, NRB's request that Archangelos should pay the interest for the deferred payment thereon had legal basis and thus should be upheld. Based on discretionary circumstances, CFI determined that a two (2)-month period of time from Archangelos' receipt of a payment notification from NRB should be reasonable, and thus the interest in this case should be calculated from October 19, 2011 to the date of payment as determined in this judgment at the benchmark interest rate of working capital loans over the same period issued by the People's Bank of China.

To sum up, according to Articles 175 and 183 of the *Maritime Law*, Article 107 of the *Contract Law* and Articles 64 and 170 (1) (2) of the *Civil Procedure Law*, CSI made the Civil Judgment of No. 117 [2014], Final, Fourth Civ. Division, Guangdong Higher People's Court, deciding that the Civil Judgment made by CFI was rescinded, Archangelos paid to NRB for the salvage remunerations of RMB 2, 561, 346. 93 and the interest thereon over the period from October 19, 2011 to the date of payment as determined in this Judgment at the benchmark interest rate of working capital loans over the same period issued by the People's Bank of China; and all the other claims from NRB were dismissed. The acceptance fee of the second instance was RMB 65822, RMB 23283. 11 was borne by Archangelos and the remaining RMB 42, 538. 89 was borne by NRB.

NRB refused to accept the Judgment made by CSI, claiming in its petition for case-reopening that (1) Archangelos stated in its Letter of Entrustment that regardless of the results of the effort, Archangelos agreed to pay at the rate of RMB 3.2/HP hour, meaning that the Parties had agreed upon the calculated rate. NRB had offered its services, such as assistance, safety protection and transportation, and the Parties had established and performed the contract in accordance with the law. The decision by CSI that Archangelos should only be held liable for 38.85% of the salvage expenses not only violated the privity of contract, but also was inconsistent with the fundamental principle that the contractual obligations should be fully performed; (2) the Letter of Guarantee for Average that NRB submitted together with the case-reopening petition sufficed to prove that the insurer of the goods on board made the commitments on August 18, 2011 that it would cover the part of the salvage remunerations that should be shared *pro rata* by the owners of the goods, but CSI failed to find this fact, and ordered Archangelos to pay only a part of the salvage remunerations, thereby not only reducing the liability of the shipowner and shippers for the salvage remunerations but also frustrating the purpose of endorsing salvage operations at sea in the *Convention*. This evidence sufficed to overturn the Judgment made by CSI; (3) NRB, as a national professional maritime salvage agency, should be entitled to all the salvage remunerations as agreed in the contract for its efforts in salvaging Gabriel tanker. The deprivation of NRB of its legitimate rights and interests under the contract by the Judgment made by CSI was inconsistent with the social and public interests of encouraging maritime salvage; (4) with the agreed pay rate and expenses being the basis for calculating the salvage remunerations, the contract in this case is, in essence, an employment contract for salvage. Even if the expenses under the contract in this case constituted the maritime salvage remunerations, Archangelos should, as required by Article 188 of the *Maritime Law*, be obliged to request the shipper to provide guarantees to the salvor, namely NRB in this case, rather than request the insurer of the goods to provide guarantees to Archangelos as it was in this case. Based on the aforesaid analysis, NRB requested SPC to rescind the Judgment made by CSI, and to order Archangelos to pay the salvage remunerations of RMB 6, 592, 913. 58 under the contract for salvage and the corresponding interest; and required that Archangelos bore all the court costs of the first and second instances.

In its defense, Archangelos argued that (1) the Judgment by CSI that Archangelos should be held liable for a part of the salvage remunerations according to the proportion of the salvaged value of the ship to the total salvaged value complied with the doctrine of privity of contract and was a correct application of laws. First of all, Article 6 of the *Convention* and Article 175 of the *Maritime Law* granted two legal rights to the shipmaster and shipowner. The contract for salvage with NRB in this case was concluded by Archangelos on behalf of itself and its shipper, so Archangelos and the shipper acted both collectively or individually as the Party A to the said contract. Next, Article 183 of the *Maritime Law* does not definitely and specifically provide that the salvage remunerations as defined therein apply exclusively to “No Cure, No Pay” contract for salvage rather than an employment contract for salvage, and the salvage remunerations that NRB was entitled to should be subjected to Article 183 of the *Maritime Law*. The provision of “or unless otherwise agreed in the contract” in the Proviso under Article 179 of the *Maritime Law* provides systematical designs and regulations concerning employed salvage services, meaning that the salving Party and the salved Party may agree that the salvage remunerations are independent of the results of the salvage efforts. Under such circumstance, regardless of the result of the salvage efforts, the salvor has the right to claim the salvage payments from the salved Party at the agreed fixed pay rate (including salvage remunerations, rewards or compensations). In this case, the salvage was the salvage of the properties, so the acquisitions that NRB was entitled to should be, and should be limited to, the salvage remunerations as provided in the *Maritime Law*; (2) at the beginning of the salvage efforts or prior to the initiation of this lawsuit, or even at latest before the end of the second trial of this case, NRB should have known the existence of the Letter of Guarantee for Average, so the failure to discover this evidence by NRB until the conclusion of the second trial was NRB's subject fault rather than the consequences from some objective causes and thus this evidence should not be a new piece of evidence. Even if the Letter of Guarantee for Average was a new evidence, NRB's claim that Archangelos should fully pay the salvage remunerations on the grounds of this evidence had no basis as it was based on the proportion of the salvaged value of the ship to the total salvaged value that the Judgment was made by CSI that Archangelos paid the part of the salvage remunerations that should be apportioned *pro rata* by Archangelos, but the Judgment did not involve the part that the shipper should be held liable for, which was guaranteed under the Letter of Guarantee for Average. Neither did the Letter of Guarantee for Average or the Judgment made by CSI require the shipowner to pay the part of the salvage remunerations that the shipper should be held liable for, nor deprive NRB of its right to require the shipper to pay the part of the salvage remunerations that the shipper should be held liable for or to exempt the shipper from the obligation of payment; (3) general average and maritime salvage are two independent systems, and thus the rules for general average adjustment should not deprive Archangelos of its legal right to pay only the part of the salvage remunerations that it should apportion *pro rata*; and (4) now that the original towing-focused salvage scheme was replaced with the lighterage and load reduction-focused one under the instruction by ZMSA, the calculation of the salvage remunerations based on the agreed pay rate of RMB

3.2/HP hour specific to towing operations would obviously be unfair, so the agreed pay rate should be adjusted or changed following the principle of "the change of circumstances". Moreover, as a public institution with the mandate of protecting the public interests, NRB should limit its charges to the extent that its actual expenses could be reasonably covered rather than pursue excessive profits, and especially should not seek any remunerations from the fulfillment of its primary administrative duty of human life salvage. Even for the adjusted salvage remunerations, the remuneration share for human life salvage (at least accounting for 50%) should be further reduced. In conclusion, Archangelos requested SPC to reject the case-reopening petition from NRB and reaffirmed the Judgment made by CSI.

SHRO's statements were the same as the defense opinions of Archangelos.

Upon review, SPC reaffirmed the facts found by CFI and CSI.

SPC held that:

This case was a dispute over the contract for salvage at sea. The People's Republic of China has acceded to the *Convention*, the purpose therein of encouraging to provide timely and effective rescue to ships and other properties in danger or in the incidents endangering the environmental safety while ensuring adequate incentives for salving parties should be upheld in this case. After the accident happened, Archangelos promptly sought help, and NRB actively participated in the salvage operations as agreed upon between the Parties. The roles of both Parties in preventing marine pollution should be recognized and endorsed.

Now that Archangelos is a Greek company and Gabriel tanker is a Greek ship, this case involved foreign elements. Given in the course of the court hearing, the Parties unanimously chose the laws of the People's Republic of

China for settling their dispute, according to Article 3 of the *Law on the Application of Laws*, SPC should apply the laws of the People's Republic of China to hear this case. The *Maritime Law* as a special law governing the relations arising from and/or pertaining to maritime transport and ocean vessels shall prevail. In the absence of definitive provisions in the *Maritime Law*, relevant laws such as the *Contract Law* can apply.

In the light of the causes of NRB's petition for case-reopening and the defense opinions of Archangelos and SHRO, the dispute in this case focused on two aspects of issues including facts and application of laws. (1) Whether or not the evidential materials submitted by NRB during the case-reopening stage should be determined as a new piece of evidence defined by law, and further, if so, whether or not they sufficed to reverse the Judgment made by CSI; (2) how to understand the contract for salvage defined in the *Convention* and the *Maritime Law*; (3) the nature of the contract and its law application involved in this case; (4) how to determine the amount of salvage remunerations that NRB claimed.

1. Whether or Not the Evidential Materials Submitted by NRB during the Case-reopening Procedure Should be Determined as New Evidence Defined by Law, and Further, If So, Whether or Not They Sufficed to Reverse the Judgment Made by CSI

During the case-reopening procedure, NRB submitted to SPC the Letter of Guarantee for Average issued by Beijing Branch of PICC Property & Casualty Company Limited (hereinafter referred to as Beijing Property Insurance) to prove that Archangelos could be able to recover the salvage remunerations which paid to NRB from Beijing Property Insurance, asserting that this piece of evidence had the sufficient effect to reverse the Judgment made by CSI. Upon the cross-examination during the court hearing, Archangelos and SHRO raised no objection to its authenticity and legality, but contended that it was not a new piece of evidence and also did not recognize its evidentiary effect.

In the view of SPC, having been issued for purposes concerning the shipowner of Gabriel tanker and other stakeholders for this case and being helpful for SPC to get related information about the liability for the salvage expenses in this case, this piece of evidence from Beijing Property Insurance had no direct relevance to the salvage remunerations in dispute between the Parties in this case, and thus was not adopted by SPC.

2. How to Understand the Contract for Salvage Defined in the *Convention* and the *Maritime Law*

With maritime salvage being a traditionally international maritime legal system, there exist special provisions on it both in the *Convention* and the *Maritime Law*. The provisions on maritime salvage in Chapter 9 of the *Maritime Law* draw upon the main contents in the *Convention*. Article 12 of the *Convention* and Article 179 of the *Maritime Law* have established that "No Cure, No Pay" is the primary principle of the salvage remunerations payment, and both Article 13 of the *Convention* and Articles 180 and 183 of the *Maritime Law* proceed from such principle to provide the evaluation criteria and specific liabilities for such salvage remunerations. The aforesaid Articles are the specific provisions that govern how the Parties determine the remunerations for salvage services under a contract for salvage at sea based on the "No Cure, No Pay" principle. Meanwhile, both the *Convention* and the *Maritime Law* also allow the Parties to agree upon other approaches of determining their salvage remunerations. Therefore, besides the "No Cure, No Pay" contract for salvage as explicitly provided in the *Convention* and the *Maritime Law*, the Parties may choose to establish by the agreement an employment contract for salvage.

3. The Nature of the Contract and Its Law Application Involved in this Case

According to the facts found in this case, following full consultations and negotiations between the Parties, Archangelos and NRB expressly agreed that, irrespective of the success of the salvage, Archangelos should pay the agreed salvage remunerations to NRB, and NRB should not be held liable for any possible accidents in the course of the salvage operations to get Gabriel tanker refloated. In accordance with this agreement, the salvage remunerations for NRB had no direct relation to any actual consequences of salvage efforts, while the calculation of the salvage remunerations is based on the agreed fixed rates and fixed charges including the power capacity-HP hours of the rescue ships and labour inputs, which have no relation to the value of the salved properties. Therefore, the contract for salvage in this case was an employment contract for salvage rather than the "No Cure, No Pay" contract for salvage as defined in the *Convention* and the *Maritime Law*.

There exist no specific provisions on the terms and standards for salvage remunerations under an employment contract for salvage in the *Convention* and the *Maritime Law*, so the adjustment to the fixed rate agreed upon by the parties in the employment contract for salvage made by CFI and CSI according to related factors as prescribed in Article 180 of the *Maritime Law* was an error in the application of law. As far as this case was concerned, relevant provisions in the *Contract Law* should be applied to govern and determine the rights and obligations of the Parties.

4. How to Determine the Amount of Salvage Remunerations that NRB Claimed

In determining the amount of the salvage remunerations for NRB, Archangelos argued that, according to Article 183 of the *Maritime Law*, it should only be held liable for a part of the salvage remunerations according to the proportion of the salvaged value of the ship to the total salvaged value. In the view of SPC,

Article 183 of the *Maritime Law* applies to “No Cure, No Pay” contract for salvage, and the contract in this case was an employment contract for salvage. Therefore, it was not inappropriate for NRB to request Archangelos to make full payment of the agreed salvage remunerations on the grounds of its contract with Archangelos.

Archangelos further argued that the replacement of the salvage scheme of the previous towing operation and underwater inspection with the scheme of the lighterage and load reduction in this case satisfied the principle of “the change of circumstances”, so the agreed pay rate should be adjusted. In the view of SPC, Article 26 of the *Interpretations (Ⅱ) of the Supreme People's Court of the People's Republic of China on Several Issues Concerning the Application of the Contract Law of the People's Republic of China* provides “where significant changes, being unforeseeable by the Parties to a contract at the time of the execution thereof, not arising from *force majeure* events and not constituting business risks, take place to the objective circumstance under which such contract is concluded, and further performance thereof as is will be obviously unfair to one Party thereto or will remain impossible to realize the purpose thereof, a people's court may, upon the request from the Party thereto, determine the change or termination thereof following the principle of fairness and in the light of realities prevalent in a case.” Yet, the adjustment of the salvage scheme in this case was based on the consultations and discussions among stakeholders, including the Parties involved in this case, rather than significant changes to objective circumstances, and further performance the contract in this case as is will not be obviously unfair to Archangelos or render the purpose thereof impossible to achieve. Therefore, the adjustment of salvage scheme was not a change of circumstance in the legal sense. Therefore, Archangelos's claim that the agreed pay rates and charges on the grounds of such cause had no factual and legal basis and thus was not supported by SPC.

According to its agreement with Archangelos, NRB invested corresponding ships and persons in the salvage effort in the case. Thus, Archangelos should pay the salvage remunerations to NRB at the agreed pay rate based on NRB's input in ship equipments, labours and consumed time. The amount of remunerations determined by CFI based on the agreed pay rate between the Parties that Archangelos paid to NRB for NRB No. 201 ship and the divers was no error. Meanwhile, in the light of the actual salvage effort, CFI also adjusted the pay rate for NRB No. 116 ship and NRB No. 101 ship from RMB 3. 2/HP hour to RMB 2. 9/HP hour. Given NRB neither appealed against nor requested for case-reopening, such adjustment was affirmed by SPC.

To sum up, the Judgment made by CSI according to related provisions in the *Maritime Law* based on the salvage remunerations determined by CFI that Archangelos was held liable for a part of the salvage remunerations in accordance with the proportion of the salvaged value of the ship to the total salvaged value was error in the application of laws and the result of handling, and should be rectified. Despite the error in the application of laws in the Judgment made by CFI, the adjustment to related remunerations made by CFI was based on the agreement between the Parties, and NRB did not raise an objection to such adjustment by its litigation right, so the results of the Judgment made by CFI can be upheld. According to Articles 8 and 107 of the *Contract Law*, Article 170 (1) (2) of the *Civil Procedure Law* and Article 407 (1) of the *Interpretations of the Supreme People's Court of the People's Republic of China on the Application of the Civil Procedure Law of the People's Republic of China*, SPC makes the decisions as follows:

1. The Civil Judgment of No. 117 [2014], Final, Fourth Civ. Division, Guangdong Higher People's Court shall be revoked;

2. The Civil Judgment of No. 898 [2012], FI, Guangzhou Maritime Court shall be reaffirmed.

The acceptance fee of the first instance is RMB 65, 822, RMB 9, 591 shall be borne by Nanhai Rescue Bureau of the Ministry of Transport and the remaining, RMB 56, 231, shall be borne by Archangelos Investments E. N. E. The acceptance fee of the second instance, RMB 65, 822, shall be borne by Archangelos Investments E. N. E.

This Judgment shall be final and conclusive.

Presiding Justice: HE Rong
Judge: ZHANG Yongjian
Judge: WANG Shumei
Judge: YU Xiaohan
Acting Judge: GUO Zaiyu
July 7, 2006
Assistant Judge: MA Ling
Court Clerk: LI Na

申请人运裕有限公司
诉
被申请人深圳市中苑城商业投资控股有限公司
申请确认仲裁协议效力案

——仲裁条款可以独立于合同而成立

【裁判要旨】

1. 请求确认当事人之间不存在仲裁协议也属于广义的对仲裁协议效力的异议,人民法院应当立案审查。

2. 仲裁协议独立性是指仲裁协议与主合同可分,互相独立,它们的存在与效力以及适用于它们的准据法都是可分的。仲裁条款是仲裁协议的主要类型,赋予仲裁条款独立性,比强调独立的仲裁协议具有独立性更有实践意义。《中华人民共和国仲裁法》(以下简称《仲裁法》)第 19 条第 1 款"仲裁协议独立存在"的规定,涵盖仲裁协议是否存在,即是否成立的问题。《最高人民法院关于适用〈中华人民共和国仲裁法〉若干问题的解释》(以下简称《仲裁法解释》)第 10 条第 2 款进一步明确:"当事人在订立合同时就争议达成仲裁协议的,合同未成立不影响仲裁协议的效力。"在确定仲裁条款效力包括仲裁条款是否成立时,可先确定仲裁条款本身的效力;在确有必要时,才对整个合同的效力包括合同是否成立进行认定。在认定当事人已达成仲裁协议的情况下,对于合同是否成立的问题无须再行认定,该问题应在仲裁中解决。

【专家点评】*

本案涉及仲裁条款效力的认定问题。

申请人运裕有限公司(以下简称运裕公司)以合同未成立因而其中的仲裁条款亦未成立为由,请求确认其与被申请人深圳市中苑城商业投资控股有限公司(以下简称中苑城公司)之间的产权交易合同、债权清偿协议不存在有效的仲裁条款。中华人民共和国最高人民法院(以下简称最高人民法院)认为,本案属于广义的对仲裁协议效力的异议,应予立案审查。基于当事人的同意,案涉仲裁协议的效力认定适用中华人民共和国法律。依中国法律的规定,仲裁条款是否成立,主要指当事人双方是否有将争议提交仲裁的合意,即是否达成了仲裁协议。仲裁协议是一种合同,判断双方是否就仲裁达成合意,应适用《中华人民共和国合同法》(以下简称《合同法》)关于要约、承诺的规定。[①] 从案涉合同磋商情况看,当事人双方一致同意将争议提交仲裁。运裕公司等一方发出的合同草签版的仲裁条款,已将仲裁机构改为深圳国际仲裁院。就仲裁条款而言,这是运裕公司等发出的要约。中苑城公司在合同草签版上盖章,表示同意,并将盖章合同文本送交运裕公司,这是中苑城公司的承诺。根据《合同法》第 25 条、第 26 条的规定,[②]承诺通知到达要约人时生效,承诺生效时合同成立。据此,产权交易合同、债权清偿协议中的仲裁条款分别在两个合同的各方当事人之间成立,而案涉合同是否成立的问题应交由仲裁庭审理。本案并无阻却前述仲裁条款生效及导致其无效的法定情形,故最高人民法院驳回运裕公司的申请。

一、最高人民法院的裁判思路

在明晰案情的基础上,裁定书所显现的裁判思路环环相扣:

第一,权限问题。最高人民法院认定,仲裁协议是否存在,就是仲裁协议是否成立的问题,这是需要解决的先决问题,属于广义的对仲裁协议效力

---

* 撰写人:宋连斌,中国政法大学教授、博士研究生导师。

① 现为《民法典》合同编的相关规定。

② 现为《民法典》合同编的相关规定。

的异议,是申请确认仲裁协议效力的案件,应予立案审查。

第二,准据法的确定。最高人民法院基于当事人双方在案件审理过程中的共同选择,明确本案仲裁协议效力认定的准据法为中华人民共和国法律。

第三,厘清仲裁协议成立与效力的关系。囿于《仲裁法》第 20 条的规定,[①]实践中常有观点认为当事人仅可向法院申请确认仲裁协议的效力,仲裁协议的存在与否不属于法院审查范围。对此,最高人民法院国际商事法庭的法官运用文义解释的方法,分析了仲裁法、仲裁法解释中关于仲裁协议定义及仲裁协议独立性的规定,并指出认定仲裁条款的效力包括确定仲裁条款是否成立,为此可以先行确定仲裁条款本身的效力,确有必要时也考虑对整个合同的效力包括合同是否成立进行认定。

第四,仲裁协议的成立。最高人民法院认为,仲裁协议是否成立,主要指当事人是否有将争议提交仲裁的合意,即是否达成了仲裁协议。仲裁协议是一种合同,判断双方是否就仲裁达成合意,应适用合同法关于要约、承诺的规定。[②]

第五,仲裁协议的生效。鉴于双方在产权交易合同、债权清偿协议磋商过程中对仲裁条款达成一致,且不存在导致仲裁合同无效的法定情形,最高人民法院认定当事人之间存在有效的仲裁条款,相关合同争议应提交仲裁。

综上可知,这一认定过程逻辑性强,且恰当地运用了合同解释、法律选择等法律方法,裁定书也清晰展现了裁判者论理过程。通过本案的审理,与仲裁管辖权相关的一些长期存在争议的问题得到明确。归纳起来,有以下四点:(1)仲裁协议存在与否就是仲裁协议是否成立的认定问题。(2)当事人关于仲裁协议存在或不存在的异议,属于法院立案审查范围。(3)仲裁协议的成立,是指当事人有将争议提交仲裁的合意。(4)仲裁协议是一种合

① 《仲裁法》第 20 条规定:“当事人对仲裁协议的效力有异议的,可以请求仲裁委员会作出决定或者请求人民法院作出裁定。一方请求仲裁委员会作出决定,另一方请求人民法院作出裁定的,由人民法院裁定。当事人对仲裁协议的效力有异议,应当在仲裁庭首次开庭前提出。”

② 现为《民法典》合同编的相关规定。

同，判断双方是否达成仲裁合意，应适用合同法关于要约、承诺的规定。[①]

二、通过个案推进支持仲裁的政策

本案系最高人民法院第一国际商事法庭审结的首批案件之一。本案不仅有效地厘清了《仲裁法》第 20 条关于仲裁协议效力异议的外延以及仲裁协议效力认定案件的裁判思路，而且尝试了一个更妥帖、更灵活、更及时的支持仲裁的方法，即借鉴判例方法，通过裁判具体的个案争议，澄清已有规则、发展新规则，更好地连接理论法学与司法实践。本案中，第一国际商事法庭的法官对法条中“仲裁协议的效力”进行了解释。通过运用文义解释方法进而综合运用体系解释、类比解释的方法，对《仲裁法》第 19 条第 1 款“仲裁协议独立存在，合同的变更、解除、终止或者无效，不影响仲裁协议的效力”进行了解释，即从上下文关系看，该条是在该法第 16 条明确仲裁条款为仲裁协议的一种类型之后，规定了仲裁协议的独立性。因此，仲裁条款亦独立于合同，但仲裁条款是否完全独立于合同而成立，仲裁法缺乏明文规定，不如“已成立合同的变更、解除、终止或者无效不影响仲裁协议效力”的规定那么明确。在司法实践中，合同是否成立与其中的仲裁条款是否成立这两个问题时常纠缠不清。第一国际商事法庭的法官注意到，《仲裁法》第 19 条第 1 款中“仲裁协议独立存在”是概括性、总领性表述，应当涵盖仲裁协议是否存在即是否成立的问题。《仲裁法解释》第 10 条第 2 款进一步明确：“当事人在订立合同时就争议达成仲裁协议的，合同未成立不影响仲裁协议的效力。”由此推出，确定仲裁条款的效力包括认定仲裁条款是否成立。为此目的，可以先行确定仲裁条款本身的效力；在确有必要时，也可以考虑对整个合同的效力包括合同是否成立进行认定。通过以上解释，第一国际商事法庭也较好地界定了实践中仲裁协议效力认定的内涵与范围。

20 世纪以来，国际商事仲裁日益受到各国政府及经商者的重视，支持仲裁也成为越来越多的国家改进营商环境的选项。《仲裁法》实施以来，以最

① 现为《民法典》合同编的相关规定。

高人民法院为枢纽,我国法院对仲裁的支持愈来愈深化,以与最佳国际仲裁实践保持一致为目标,对维护开放的商业环境的作用也愈来愈显著。最高人民法院国际商事法庭的设立及通过个案推进支持仲裁,正是践行这一目标的得力举措。

【裁判文书】

中华人民共和国最高人民法院
民事裁定书

(2019)最高法民特1号

申请人:运裕有限公司(Luck Treat Limited)。住所地:英属维尔京群岛托尔托拉岛罗德城****号****楼(****,****,Road Town,Tortola,British Virgin Islands)。

代表人:陈某,该公司董事。

委托诉讼代理人:郭某,北京市**(郑州)律师事务所律师。

委托诉讼代理人:李某,北京市**(深圳)律师事务所律师。

被申请人:深圳市中苑城商业投资控股有限公司。住所地:中华人民共和国广东省深圳市福田区**路**楼。

法定代表人:周某某,该公司董事长。

委托诉讼代理人:朱某,北京市***(深圳)律师事务所律师。

委托诉讼代理人:伍某,北京市***(深圳)律师事务所律师。

申请人运裕有限公司(以下简称运裕公司)与被申请人深圳市中苑城商业投资控股有限公司(以下简称中苑城公司)申请确认仲裁协议效力一案,本院于2019年2月19日立案后进行了审查。现已审查终结。

运裕公司请求:确认运裕公司与中苑城公司之间就《产权交易合同》及《债权清偿协议》不存在有效的仲裁条款。事实和理由如下:合同本身未成立,因而其中的仲裁条款亦未成立。(一)合同未成立。运裕公司通过北京产权交易所(以下简称北交所)挂牌转让其持有的新劲企业公司(Newpower Enterprises Inc.,以下简称新劲公司)100%的股权,中苑城公司被确定为唯一合格意向受让方。之后,双方就《产权交易合同》及《债权清偿协议》通过电子邮件反复磋商,明确两份文件的草签版须经北交所及运裕公司等上级中国旅游集团公司(以下简称中旅公司)最终确认后方可签署。运裕公司还要求中苑城公司依据国家相关规定,办理境外投资手续并在境外以外汇方式支付交易价款。中苑城公司拒绝履行境外投资审批和外汇登记手续等法定义务。运裕公司在多次催告未果的情况下,通知中苑城公司取消交易。《中华人民共和国合同法》(以下简称《合同法》)第三十二条规定:“当事人采用合同书形式订立合同的,自双方当事人签字或者盖章时合同成立。”《产权交易合同》草签版本第十七条约定:“本合同经甲乙双方法定代表人或授权代表签字并盖章后,与《债权清偿协议》同时生效。”依据上述法律规定和约定,因中苑城公司拒绝履行法定义务与合规要求,合同文本未达成一致,更未能签署,故《产权交易合同》《债权清偿协议》均未成立。事实上,双方甚至未完成合同订立的要约和承诺过程。(二)合同中的仲裁条款亦未成立。两份文件草签版均包含如下仲裁条款:有关争议,提交深圳国际仲裁院仲裁。但仲裁条款不能脱离主合同而单独成立,双方当事人亦无脱离主合同成立而先行单独达成仲裁协议的明确意思表示。故仲裁条款也未成立,运裕公司与中苑城公司之间就《产权交易合同》文本所商讨事项不存在有效的仲裁条款。(三)运裕公司并非《债权清偿协议》的当事方,故该协议中的仲裁条款不能拘束运裕公司。

中苑城公司称,《产权交易合同》《债权清偿协议》已经成立并生效,双方在协商履行《产权交易合同》《债权清偿协议》中已就本案纠纷提交仲裁达成合意,双方之间存在有效的仲裁协议。(一)合同已成立并生效。本案产权转让是在北交所主持下、根据相关交易规则达成交易,交易合同依法成立并生效。运裕公司、新劲公司、深圳维景京华酒店有限公司(以下简称维景京华酒店公司)、北京港中旅维景国际酒店管理有限公司(以下简称维景酒店公司)(上述四公司以下合称运裕公司等)均应按照公告内容与中苑城公司签署《产权交易合同》《债权清偿协议》文本。1. 双方已就案涉产权的转让完成了要约和承诺。运裕公司委托北交所发布案涉交易公告,披露了交易的全部信息,并作出相关承诺。以上公告为运裕公司等发出的要约邀请。之后,中苑城公司向北交所提出受让申请。北交所向中苑城公司发出《受让资格确认通知书》,要求中苑城公司在 2017 年 5 月 4 日前支付保证金,"在上述时限内交纳保证金后获得资格确认",这是运裕公司等提出的要约。中苑城公司按照要求,当天即支付了人民币 2.7 亿元保证金,获得唯一受让资格,构成承诺。至此双方达成交易并按北交所交易规则开始履行。鉴于本案合同并非法律法规规定应办理批准生效手续的情形,本案交易合同依法已经成立和生效。2. 根据运裕公司挂牌公告的承诺和北交所交易规则,运裕公司等有义务在确定中苑城公司为最终受让人起五个工作日内,按照公告条件与中苑城公司在《产权交易合同》《债权清偿协议》文本上签字盖章。3. 运裕公司等在双方已按公告条件确认成交后,随意更改挂牌的交易条件,改变以人民币结算的交易规则,要求中苑城公司在境外以外汇方式向其支付本次交易价款,违反了自身承诺和北交所交易规则。4. 本案交易是在北交所进行,双方就交易的标的、价款、数量、履行方式、前置条件等实质性条款已经达成一致意见后摘牌成交的。书面交易合同并非双方之间关于本次交易的唯一法律文件,决定双方存在产权交易合同关系的文件还包括双方向北交所提出的申请书、承诺书、公告、通知、保证金支付凭证等,这些文件同样对双方具有约束力。本案产权交易不属于需经政府部门核准生效的境外投资事项,而属于政府部门备案事项,签署产权交易合同是办理本案交易合同备案手续的前提。(二)仲裁条款已成立。1. 2017 年 5 月 11 日,运裕公司等通过电子邮件向中苑城公司发来命名为"草签版"的交易合同文本,其中明确向中苑城公司提出了将争议提交深圳国际仲裁院仲裁的要约。中苑城公司于当天即在该交易合同文本上签字盖章,以电子签名、电子邮件和纸质签字盖章 EMS 邮递两种方式回复告知了运裕公司等。至此,双方之间已就仲裁协议达成合意,且仲裁合意之后保持不变。2. 仲裁条款独立性原则决定,即使双方还没有完成签署书面合同文本,仲裁条款的存在及生效也不受影响。《中华人民共和国仲裁法》(以下简称《仲裁法》)第十九条、《最高人民法院关于适用〈中华人民共和国仲裁法〉若干问题的解释》(以下简称《仲裁法解释》)第十条等规定确认了仲裁条款的独立性。根据上述规定,本案仲裁条款已经达成,独立存在且已生效。运裕公司等最终声称“取消交易”,但始终未要求取消仲裁协议。3. 运裕公司等以交易合同文本未经其集团内部最终审批同意,亦未签署为由,认为仲裁条款不存在,是将其内部审批的效力强加于中苑城公司,混淆了内部管理关系和外部法律关系。因此,本案“草签版”合同中的仲裁条款,应对双方有约束力。(三)运裕公司等尽管主体不同,但实质上权利全部归属于中旅公司,《产权交易合同》和《债权清偿协议》共同构成本案交易的完整内容,不可分割,应共同履行交易合同转让方的义务,接受仲裁条款约束。综上,本案双方之间的仲裁协议在形式上、内容上已经满足我国仲裁法规定的所有必要条件,请求依法认定双方之间存在有效的仲裁协议,驳回运裕公司的申请。

经审查查明:中国旅游集团有限公司,原名为中国旅游集团公司、中国港中旅集团公司,是国有独资公司。香港中旅(集团)有限公司(以下简称香港中旅公司)是中旅公司的全资子公司,注册于香港。运裕公司是香港中旅公司的全资子公司,注册于英属维尔京群岛。新劲公司是运裕公司的全资子公司,亦注册于英属维尔京群岛。

2016 年 3 月 24 日,中旅公司作出《关于同意挂牌转让 NEWPOWER ENTERPRISES INC. 100%股权的批复》,同意运裕公司依法合规转让其所持有的新劲公司 100%的股权。2017 年 3 月 29 日,运裕公司通过北交所公开挂牌转让其持有的新劲公司 100%的股权。挂牌转让公告中“与转让相关的其他条件”要求受让方“在签署《产权交易合同》的同时与转让方的关联方签署《债权清偿协议》,明确了解并同意《产权交易合同》约定的债权清偿是股权转让的重要前置条件”。4 月,中苑城公司与北京金羊泰和投资咨询有限公司签订《产权交易委托合同》,委托后者按照北交所的交易规则为中苑城公司收购新劲公司股权交易提供场内经纪服务。4 月 27 日,北交所向运裕公司出具《受让资格确认意见函》,载明案涉项目信息披露公告期满,征得意向受让方两个——中苑城公司和许某某。4 月 28 日,北交所向中苑城公司发出《受让资格确认通知书》,通知中苑城公司于 5 月 4 日前,将保证金人民币 2.7 亿元交付到北交所指定的结算账户,并明确中苑城公司在规定时限内交纳保证金后获得资格确认,如逾期未交,则视为放弃受让。同日,中苑城公司向北交所指定的结算账户转入人民币 2.7 亿元保证金。5 月 3 日,北交所向中苑城公司出具人民币 2.7 亿元保证金收据。由于许某某逾期未交纳保证金,故案涉项目仅剩中苑城公司一个意向受让人。

随后,中苑城公司与运裕公司等就签订案涉项目的产权交易合同等事宜开展磋商。5 月 9 日,深圳市泰隆金融控股集团有限公司(中苑城公司的上级集团公司)风控法务中心张某某代表中苑城公司向港中旅酒店有限公司(中旅公司的全资子公司)法务部法务经理刘某发送电子邮件,内容为:"请把合同及合同附件发送至本人这个邮箱(zha * * * * @ tljkjt.com)"。同日,刘某回复电子邮件称:"合同及附件文件会由我方指定对外联络人张某经理统一发给你们指定联系人李某总"。同日,港中旅酒店有限公司投资管理部经理张某发送电子邮件给张某某,内容为:"附件为此前提供给贵司的两份合同及附件,我司会尽快根据今天会议商议的条款对合同进行补充并提交北交所审核,同时也请贵司在我们此前提供的这版合同基础上将修改意见批注出来,尽快形成书面意见反馈给我们,下一步我们再综合北交所的反馈进行最终修订"。上述电子邮件的附件《产权交易合同》,系北交所提供的标准文本,载明甲方为运裕公司,乙方为中苑城公司,双方根据《合同法》和《企业国有产权转让管理暂行办法》等相关法律、法规、规章的规定,就运裕公司向中苑城公司转让其拥有的新劲公司 100%股权签订《产权交易合同》。合同主要内容为:1. 甲方拟转让其合法持有的标的企业的 100%股权;乙方拟收购上述股权。2. 乙方依本合同的约定受让甲方所拥有的转让标的事项,已依法律、行政法规和章程的规定,履行了相应的批准或授权、备案等程序。转让价格为人民币 9 亿元。3. 签订本合同所需的包括但不限于授权、审批、公司内部决策等在内的一切手续均已合法有效取得,本合同成立和产权转让的前提条件均已满足。4. 本合同经甲乙双方法定代表人或授权代表签字并盖章后，与《债权清偿协议》同时生效。5. 第十六条管辖及争议解决方式：16.1 本合同及产权交易中的行为均适用中华人民共和国法律；16.2 有关本合同的解释或履行，当事人之间发生争议的，应由双方协商解决；协商解决不成的，提交北京仲裁委员会仲裁。上述电子邮件的附件《债权清偿协议》，载明甲方一为香港中旅公司，甲方二为维景酒店公司，乙方为中苑城公司，丙方一为新劲公司，丙方二为维景京华酒店公司。该协议约定：1. 乙方同意自合同生效之日起五个工作日内代丙方一次性清偿甲方持有的人民币 107886893.15 元的债权及其资金占用费。2. 第十二条：本协议适用中华人民共和国法律。有关本协议的解释或履行，当事人之间发生争议的，应由各方协商解决；协商解决不成的，任何一方均有权提交北京仲裁委员会以仲裁方式解决。

5 月 10 日，张某某发送电子邮件给张某、刘某，内容为：“附件为我们公司对合同的一个修改意见，请贵公司在基于平等、公平的原则及合同签订后的有效原则慎重考虑加以确认”。在该邮件的附件中，《产权交易合同》文本第十六条“管辖及争议解决方式”修改为“16.1 本合同及产权交易中的行为均适用中华人民共和国法律。16.2 有关本合同的解释或履行，当事人之间发生争议的，应由双方协商解决；协商解决不成的，提交深圳国际仲裁院仲裁”；《债权清偿协议》文本第十二条修改为“本协议适用中华人民共和国法律。有关本协议的解释或履行，当事人之间发生争议的，应由各方协商解决；协商解决不成的，任何一方均有权提交【深圳国际仲裁院】以仲裁方式解决”。5 月 11 日 13 时 42 分，张某发送电子邮件给张某某和中苑城公司高级管理人员李某，针对中苑城公司对两个合同文本提出的修改意见进行了回应，并表示“现将修订后的合同草签版发送给贵司，请接到附件内容后尽快回复意见。贵方与我司确认后的合同将被提交至北交所及我司内部审批流程，经北交所及我司集团公司最终确认后方可签署（如有修改我司会再与贵司确认）”。该邮件附件《产权交易合同》（草签版）第十六条“管辖及争议解决方式”与《债权清偿协议》（草签版）第十二条和上述 5 月 10 日张某某发送给张某、刘某的电子邮件附件中的有关内容相同。同日 18 时 39 分，张某某发送电子邮件给张某，内容为“附件为我司签署完毕的产权交易合同(草签版)及债权清偿协议(草签版)、项目签约说明函等扫描件，请查收并回复”。该邮件附件《产权交易合同》(草签版)和《债权清偿协议》(草签版)的管辖及争议解决方式的内容与张某在同日发送电子邮件附件中的有关内容相同。中苑城公司在合同上盖章，并将该文本送达运裕公司。该电子邮件的另一附件为中苑城公司向运裕公司发出的《NEWPOWER ENTERPRISES INC. 100%股权签约说明函》，内容为：可于 2017 年 5 月 11 日与贵司签署《产权交易合同》(草签版)和《债权清偿协议》(草签版)；理解《产权交易合同》(草签版)和《债权清偿协议》(草签版)需经北交所进行合规性审核后报中旅公司批准签署，最终《产权交易合同》和《债权清偿协议》签署版本以正式版本内容为准；《产权交易合同》和《债权清偿协议》签署形式遵从贵司安排。

5 月 17 日，张某发送电子邮件给李某，载明：“深圳项目我司集团最终审批流程目前正进行中，如审批顺利计划可在本周五上午在北京维景国际大酒店举办签约仪式，具体情况待我司确认后通知贵司。现将《产权交易合同》及《债权清偿协议》拟签署版本提前发送给贵司以便核对。”该邮件附件 1 为《股权转让项目产权交易合同》(拟签署版)，附件 2 为《股权转让项目债权清偿协议》(拟签署版)。上述两个合同文本中的仲裁条款仍与草签版相同。

6 月 1 日，经法律合规性审核后，运裕公司向中苑城公司发出《复函》，主要内容为：1. 鉴于本次交易的转让方和转让的标的公司均系注册在境外英属维尔京群岛的公司，受让方贵司为注册在境内深圳的公司，本次交易属于境外投资，依据国家发改委 2014 年第 9 号令《境外投资项目核准和备案管理办法》、商务部 2014 年第 3 号令《境外投资管理办法》和国家外汇管理局《境内机构境外直接投资外汇管理规定》(汇发〔2009〕30 号)等有关规定，贵司依法应当为本项目办理境外投资所需的发改委、商务部备案或者核准等审批手续，并需要在外汇局办理境外直接投资外汇登记手续，在境外以外汇方式向转让方我司支付本次交易价款。2. 对于贵司来函所附《产权交易合同》

第15.3条款，我司法律顾问认为不符合3月29日本项目在北交所交易挂牌文件的要求。依据挂牌文件第四部分“与转让相关的其他条件”之3之(4)的规定，受让方未及时按照约定时限支付剩余价款的，意向受让方所缴纳的保证金将被全额扣除。因此，我司要求将该条款改为：乙方未按照合同约定期限付清全部转让价款，乙方所交纳的人民币2.7亿元保证金将被全额扣除，乙方无条件同意北交所将保证金人民币2.7亿元一次性划转至甲方指定账户。

中苑城公司分别于同年6月6日、8月29日及10月23日致函运裕公司，催促运裕公司尽快签署《产权交易合同》《债权清偿协议》。10月27日，运裕公司向中苑城公司发出《通知函》，称鉴于已多次告知并催促贵司依法办理法定手续，而贵司迟迟无法确认，故正式通知取消本次产权交易。11月12日，中苑城公司致函运裕公司，要求运裕公司尽快安排签约事宜，并请运裕公司配合出具向主管部门申办手续的相关文件。11月27日，运裕公司函复中苑城公司，表示已于10月27日向中苑城公司发出取消交易的通知，并提议双方立即向北交所办理保证金返还手续。

2018年4月4日，中苑城公司根据《产权交易合同》草签版本第16.2条及《债权清偿协议》草签版本第十二条的约定，向深圳国际仲裁院提出仲裁申请，将运裕公司等列为共同被申请人。在仲裁庭开庭前，运裕公司等分别向广东省深圳市中级人民法院提起诉讼，申请确认仲裁协议不存在。该院于2018年9月11日立案，形成了本案和另外两个关联案件。在该院审查期间，本院认为，本案及关联案件有重大法律意义，由国际商事法庭审查有利于统一适用法律，且有利于提高纠纷解决效率，故依照《中华人民共和国民事诉讼法》第三十八条第一款、《最高人民法院关于设立国际商事法庭若干问题的规定》第二条第五项之规定，裁定本案由本院第一国际商事法庭审查。本院在审查期间，询问了各方当事人，各方当事人同意就争议解决方式进行协商、调解。之后，当事人就争议解决方式及实体问题进行多次磋商，不能达成一致。本院恢复审查。

本院经审查认为,本案争议焦点是案涉仲裁条款是否成立。

运裕公司在中苑城公司申请仲裁后,以仲裁条款未成立为由,向人民法院申请确认双方之间不存在有效的仲裁条款。虽然这不同于要求确认仲裁协议无效,但是仲裁协议是否存在与是否有效同样直接影响到纠纷解决方式,同样属于需要解决的先决问题,因而要求确认当事人之间不存在仲裁协议也属于广义的对仲裁协议效力的异议。《仲裁法》第二十条第一款规定:当事人对仲裁协议的效力有异议的,可以请求仲裁委员会作出决定或者请求人民法院作出裁定。据此,当事人以仲裁条款未成立为由要求确认仲裁协议不存在的,属于申请确认仲裁协议效力案件,人民法院应予立案审查。

在确认仲裁协议效力时,首先要确定准据法。《中华人民共和国涉外民事关系法律适用法》第十八条规定:"当事人可以协议选择仲裁协议适用的法律。当事人没有选择的,适用仲裁机构所在地法律或者仲裁地法律。"在本院询问时,各方当事人均明确表示同意适用中华人民共和国法律确定案涉仲裁协议效力。因此,本案仲裁协议适用中华人民共和国法律。

《仲裁法》第十六条第一款规定:"仲裁协议包括合同中订立的仲裁条款和以其他书面方式在纠纷发生前或者纠纷发生后达成的请求仲裁的协议。"可见,合同中的仲裁条款和独立的仲裁协议这两种类型,都属于仲裁协议,仲裁条款的成立和效力的认定也适用关于仲裁协议的法律规定。

仲裁协议独立性是广泛认可的一项基本法律原则,是指仲裁协议与主合同是可分的,互相独立,它们的存在与效力,以及适用于它们的准据法都是可分的。由于仲裁条款是仲裁协议的主要类型,仲裁条款与合同其他条款出现在同一文件中,赋予仲裁条款独立性,比强调独立的仲裁协议具有独立性更有实践意义,甚至可以说仲裁协议独立性主要是指仲裁条款和主合同是可分的。对于仲裁协议的独立性,中华人民共和国法律和本院司法解释均有规定。《仲裁法》第十九条第一款规定:"仲裁协议独立存在,合同的变更、解除、终止或者无效,不影响仲裁协议的效力。"从上下文关系看,该条是在第十六条明确了仲裁条款属于仲裁协议之后,规定了仲裁协议的独立性。因此,仲裁条款独立于合同。对于仲裁条款能否完全独立于合同而成立,《仲裁法》的规定似乎不是特别清晰,不如已成立合同的变更、解除、终止或者无效不影响仲裁协议效力的规定那么明确。在司法实践中,合同是否成立与其中的仲裁条款是否成立这两个问题常常纠缠不清。但是,《仲裁法》第十九条第一款开头部分“仲裁协议独立存在”,是概括性、总领性的表述,应当涵盖仲裁协议是否存在即是否成立的问题,之后的表述则是进一步强调列举的几类情形也不能影响仲裁协议的效力。《仲裁法解释》第十条第二款进一步明确:“当事人在订立合同时就争议达成仲裁协议的,合同未成立不影响仲裁协议的效力。”因此,在确定仲裁条款效力包括仲裁条款是否成立时,可以先行确定仲裁条款本身的效力;在确有必要时,才考虑对整个合同的效力包括合同是否成立进行认定。本案亦依此规则,先根据本案具体情况来确定仲裁条款是否成立。

仲裁条款是否成立,主要是指当事人双方是否有将争议提交仲裁的合意,即是否达成了仲裁协议。仲裁协议是一种合同,判断双方是否就仲裁达成合意,应适用《合同法》关于要约、承诺的规定。从本案磋商情况看,当事人双方一直共同认可将争议提交仲裁解决。本案最早的《产权交易合同》,系北交所提供的标准文本,连同《债权清偿协议》由运裕公司等一方发给中苑城公司,两份合同均包含将争议提交北京仲裁委员会仲裁的条款。之后,当事人就仲裁机构进行了磋商。运裕公司等一方发出的合同草签版的仲裁条款,已将仲裁机构确定为深圳国际仲裁院。就仲裁条款而言,这是运裕公司等发出的要约。中苑城公司在合同草签版上盖章,表示同意,并于2017年5月11日将盖章合同文本送达运裕公司,这是中苑城公司的承诺。根据《合同法》第二十五条、第二十六条相关规定,承诺通知到达要约人时生效,承诺生效时合同成立。因此,《产权交易合同》《债权清偿协议》中的仲裁条款于2017年5月11日分别在两个合同的各方当事人之间成立。之后,当事人就合同某些其他事项进行交涉,但从未对仲裁条款有过争议。鉴于运裕公司等并未主张仲裁条款存在法定无效情形,故应当认定双方当事人之间存在有效的仲裁条款，双方争议应由深圳国际仲裁院进行仲裁。虽然运裕公司等没有在最后的合同文本上盖章，其法定代表人也未在文本上签字，不符合合同经双方法定代表人或授权代表签字并盖章后生效的要求，但根据《仲裁法解释》第十条第二款的规定，即使合同未成立，仲裁条款的效力也不受影响。在当事人已达成仲裁协议的情况下，对于本案合同是否成立的问题无需再行认定，该问题应在仲裁中解决。

运裕公司还提出其并非《债权清偿协议》当事人，其中的仲裁条款不能拘束运裕公司。鉴于《产权交易合同》中的仲裁条款已能约束运裕公司，其与中苑城公司之间的纠纷应通过仲裁解决，且运裕公司等为同一仲裁案件的共同被申请人，无需本院在本案中对《债权清偿协议》中的仲裁条款能否约束运裕公司进行判断。

综上，运裕公司的理由和请求不能成立。本院依照《中华人民共和国仲裁法》第十六条、第十九条、第二十条之规定，裁定如下：

驳回运裕有限公司的申请。

申请费人民币400元，由申请人运裕有限公司负担。

审判长　张勇健
审判员　高晓力
审判员　奚向阳
审判员　丁广宇
审判员　沈红雨
二〇一九年九月十八日
法官助理　李光琴
书记员　谢松珊

Luck Treat Limited

v.

Shenzhen Zhongyuan City Commercial Investment Holding Co, Ltd for Application of Confirmation on the Validity of an Arbitration Agreement

—Arbitration Clauses Can Have Effect Independent of the Contract

Holding

1. The request to confirm that no arbitration agreement exists between the Parties is also an objection to the validity of an arbitration agreement in a broad sense, which a people' s court shall accept and hear.

2. The independence of an arbitration agreement means that an arbitration agreement and its principal contract are separable and independent of each other, and their respective existence, effectiveness and proper laws are also separable. Arbitration clauses constitute the main form of arbitration agreements. Endowing arbitration clauses with independence is of more practical significance than emphasizing the independence of arbitration agreements. The paragraph "an arbitration agreement exists independently" in Article 19 (1) of the *Arbitration Law of the People's Republic of China* (hereinafter referred to as *Arbitration Law*) contains the issue of the existence of an arbitration agreement, that is, whether it is established. Article 10 (2) of the *Interpretations of the Supreme People's Court to Several Issues Concerning*

the Application of the Arbitration Law of the People's Republic of China (hereinafter referred to as *Interpretations of Arbitration Law*) further clarifies "if an arbitration agreement on related disputes is concluded between the Parties while a contract is formulated, the failure to establish the said contract shall not affect the validity of the said arbitration agreement." For the purpose of determining the validity of an arbitration clause, including its effective establishment, the validity of the said arbitration agreement itself can be determined firstly; but the validity of the entire contract, including its effective establishment, does not need to be determined except for being warranted by sufficient necessity. Once the establishment of an arbitration agreement between the Parties is determined, there is no need to determine the establishment of the contract, which should be solved during the arbitration.

Commentary *

This case involved the determination of the validity of an arbitration clause.

The Applicant, Luck Treat Limited (hereinafter referred to as Luck Treat), requested to confirm that there existed no valid arbitration clause in Equity Transaction Contract and Agreement on Creditor's Rights Settlement between itself and the Respondent, Shenzhen Zhongyuan City Commercial Investment Holding Co, Ltd (hereinafter referred to as Zhongyuan City), on the grounds that given the contracts were not established, so the arbitration clauses therein were not established either. In the view of the Supreme People's Court of the People's Republic of China (hereinafter referred to as SPC), this case represented in a broad sense an objection to the validity of an arbitration agreement, and should be accepted and heard. Upon the unanimous consent

---

* Author: SONG Lianbin, Professor and Doctoral Supervisor, China University of Political Science and Law.

from the Parties, the laws of the People's Republic of China applied to determining the validity of the arbitration agreement. Under the Chinese legal framework, the establishment of an arbitration clause primarily depends upon the existence of a consensus on dispute settlement through arbitration between the Parties, namely, whether or not the Parties reach an arbitration agreement. Given an arbitration agreement is a contract of a kind, related provisions on offer and acceptance in the *Contract Law of the People's Republic of China*① (hereinafter referred to as *Contract Law*) shall be applied for judging whether or not the Parties reach a consensus on arbitration. In the light of the negotiations in this case, the Parties had unanimously agreed to submit their disputes for arbitration.

Luck Treat & Others sent out the draft text of the contract where the arbitration clause was included and replaced the agreed arbitral institution with Shenzhen Court of International Arbitration. As far as the arbitration clause was concerned, such clause constituted an offer from Luck Treat & Others. Zhongyuan City sealed the draft text of the contract to express its consent and sent back the sealed contract to Luck Treat, constituting an acceptance of Zhongyuan City. According to Articles 25 and 26 of the *Contract Law*, ② upon its arrival at the offeror, an acceptance takes effect, and a contract is established once the acceptance became effective. Therefore, the arbitration clause in Equity Transaction Contract and Agreement on Creditor's Rights Settlement was established between the Parties thereto, respectively. As for the establishment of the contracts between the Parties in this case, it would be better to be determined by an arbitration tribunal. Now that there existed no legal circumstances in this case hindering the said arbitration clause from

① See related provisions in Part Ⅲ: Contracts of the *Civil Code*.

② See related provisions in Part Ⅲ: Contracts of the *Civil Code*.

becoming valid or rendering it invalidated, SPC dismissed the claim by Luck Treat.

Ⅰ. The Legal Reasoning of SPC

On the basis of clarifying the facts in the case, the legal reasoning in the Civil Ruling is closely linked with each other:

1. Jurisdiction

SPC held that the existence of an arbitration agreement is the establishment of an arbitration agreement, which is a prerequisite problem to be solved. Therefore, in a broad sense, the request to confirm that no arbitration agreement exists between the Parties is also an objection to the validity of a preexisting arbitration agreement, which a people's court shall accept and hear.

2. Determination of Proper Law

Upon the unanimous choice from the Parties during the trial of the case, SPC determined and clarified that the law of the People's Republic of China was the proper law for determining the validity of the arbitration agreement in this case.

3. Clarification of the Relation Between the Establishment and Validity of an Arbitration Agreement

Constrained by Article 20 of the *Arbitration Law*, ① common sense prevails in judicial practice that Parties can only turn to a people's court for determining the validity of an arbitration agreement, and the determination of the existence of an arbitration agreement falls out of the jurisdiction of a people's court. In response to this misunderstanding, judges at the China International Commercial

① Article 20 of the *Arbitration Law* provides "an objecting Party to the validity of an arbitration agreement may apply to an arbitration commission for a decision or to a people's court for a ruling. Where one Party seeks a decision from an arbitration commission while the other Party for a ruling from a people's court, the said people's court shall make a ruling. Any challenge by either Party of the validity of an arbitration agreement shall be raised to the arbitration tribunal prior to the first hearing."

Court of SPC (CICC) analyzed through semantic interpretation the definition of an arbitration agreement and related provisions on the independence of an arbitration agreement in the *Arbitration Law* and the *Interpretations of the Arbitration Law*, and came to a conclusion that the determination of the validity of an arbitration clause contains the issue of determining its establishment, and thus the validity of the arbitration clause *per se* may be determined firstly, but the validity of the entire contract, including its effective establishment, does not need to be determined except for being warranted by sufficient necessity.

4. Establishment of an Arbitration Agreement

SPC held that the establishment of an arbitration agreement primarily depends upon the existence of a consensus on dispute settlement through arbitration between the Parties, namely, whether or not the Parties reach an arbitration agreement. Since an arbitration agreement is a contract of a kind, related provisions on offer and acceptance in the *Contract Law*① shall be applied for judging whether or not the Parties reach a consensus on arbitration.

5. Validation of an Arbitration Agreement

Given the Parties reached a consensus on the arbitration clause during their negotiations on Equity Transaction Contract and Agreement on Creditor's Rights Settlement, and there were no legal circumstances that would invalidate an arbitration contract, SPC determined that there existed a valid arbitration clause between the Parties, and related disputes from the contract should be settled through arbitration.

In conclusion, the process of determination was of strong logic, various legal means, including contract interpretation and choice of laws, were applied properly, and the Civil Ruling clearly showed the judges' reasoning process. The hearing of this case contributed to clearing up some of longstanding

① See related provisions in Part Ⅲ: Contracts of the *Civil Code*.

controversial issues about the arbitration jurisdiction, especially the four major ones as listed below: (1) the determination of the existence of an arbitration agreement falls within the category of the determination of the establishment of an arbitration agreement; (2) any objection by either Party to the existence of an arbitration agreement falls within the jurisdiction of a people's court; (3) the establishment of an arbitration agreement means a consensus between the Parties on dispute settlement through arbitration; and (4) an arbitration agreement is a contract of a kind, and related provisions on offer and acceptance in the *Contract Law*① shall be applied for judging whether or not the Parties reach a consensus.

Ⅱ. The Policy Promotion to Support Arbitration Through Individual Cases

Among one of the first cases concluded by the First International Commercial Court of SPC, this case not only clearly defined the extension of the objection to the validity of an arbitration agreement in Article 20 of the *Arbitration Law* and effectively sorted out the legal reasoning of the ruling in determining the validity of an arbitration agreement, but also pioneered a more appropriate, flexible and timely approach to support arbitration. In other words, this case clarified the established rules, developed new rules and better harmonized theoretical jurisprudence and judicial practice through the adjudication of specific disputes with reference to the case-law methodology. During the hearing of this case, judges at the First International Commercial Court of SPC fully elucidated the explanations of the term "validity of an arbitration agreement" in related legal provisions, and by applying various methods, including semantic interpretation, systematic interpretation and analogy explanation, provided a clear-cut explanation of the provision in Article 19 (1) of the *Arbitration Law* that "an arbitration agreement exists independently, and

① See related provisions in Part Ⅲ: Contracts of the *Civil Code*.

its validity shall not be subject to the change, rescission, termination or invalidity of the contract”. That is to say, to put it in the context, the provision provides the independence of an arbitration agreement after Article 16 thereof clarifies the arbitration clause is a type of the arbitration agreement. Therefore, arbitration clauses are also independent of their contracts. However, on the issue of whether or not arbitration clauses can be established completely independently from their contracts, there are no such distinct provisions in the *Arbitration Law* as the one that “an arbitration agreement exists independently, and its validity shall not be subject to the change, rescission, termination or invalidity of the contract”. In judicial practice, the establishment of a contract has usually been entangled with the establishment of the arbitration clause therein. However, judges at the First International Commercial Court of SPC noticed that “an arbitration agreement exists independently” in Article 19 (1) of the *Arbitration Law* represents an encompassing and general expression, which shall contain the issue of the existence of an arbitration agreement, that is, whether it is established. Article 10 (2) of the *Interpretations of the Arbitration Law* further clarifies “if and when an arbitration agreement on related disputes is concluded between the Parties while a contract is formulated, the failure to establish the said contract shall not affect the validity of the said arbitration agreement.” Thus it can be concluded that the determination of the validity of an arbitration clause includes the determination of its establishment. To this end, the validity of the arbitration clause *per se* may be determined firstly, but the validity of the entire contract, including its effective establishment, does not need to be determined except for being warranted by sufficient necessity. Through the above explanations, the First International Commercial Court of SPC better defined the connotation and scope of the validity determination of an arbitration agreement in practice.

Since the 20th century, more importance has been attached by both governments and traders to international commercial arbitration, and supporting arbitration has also become an important approach for more countries to optimise their business environments. Since the enforcement of the *Arbitration Law*, people' s courts in the People' s Republic of China, with SPC as the hub, have steadily increased their support to arbitration and the goal of keeping consistence with the best international arbitration practices has played an increasing role in fostering an open business environment in the country. The establishment of the CICC and its support to arbitration through individual cases are effective measures in striving to achieve their goals.

Grounds of Decision

The Supreme People's Court of the People's Republic of China

Civil Ruling

No. 01 [2019], Special Procedure, Civ. Division, SPC

Applicant: Luck Treat Limited. Domicile: No. ∗∗∗∗, Building ∗∗∗∗, Road Town, Tortola, British Virgin Islands.

Representative: Chen X, Director.

Attorney: Guo X, at Beijing ∗∗ (Zhengzhou) Law Firm.

Attorney: Li X, at Beijing ∗∗ (Shenzhen) Law Firm.

Respondent: Shenzhen Zhongyuan City Commercial Investment Holding Co, Ltd. Domicile: Building ∗∗, ∗∗ Road, Futian District, Shenzhen City, Guangdong Province, the People's Republic of China.

Legal Representative: Zhou XX, Chairman.

Attorney: Zhu X, at Beijing ∗∗∗ (Shenzhen) Law Firm.

Attorney: Wu X, at Beijing ∗∗∗ (Shenzhen) Law Firm.

On February 19, 2019, the Applicant, Luck Treat Limited (hereinafter referred to as Luck Treat), filed an application with the Supreme People's Court of the People's Republic of China (hereinafter referred to as SPC), requesting the court to confirm the validity of its Arbitration Agreement with the Respondent, Shenzhen Zhongyuan City Commercial Investment Holding Co, Ltd (hereinafter referred to as Zhongyuan City). Now, the trial of this case has been concluded.

Luck Treat claimed to determine that there existed no valid arbitration clause in Equity Transaction Contract and Agreement on Creditor's Rights Settlement between Luck Treat and Zhongyuan City. Facts and Reasons are as follows: the contract *per se* was not formulated, and thus the arbitration clause therein was not established either. 1. The contract was not formulated. Luck Treat offered to transfer its 100% stake in Newpower Enterprises Inc. (hereinafter referred to as Newpower) on China Beijing Equity Exchange (hereinafter referred to as CBEX), and Zhongyuan City was determined as the only qualified prospective transferee. Upon multiple negotiations via e-mail, the Parties reached the agreement that, subject to confirmation from CBEX and the superior unit of Luck Treat China National Travel Service Group Corporation Limited (hereinafter referred to as CTS), two draft documents which were Equity Transaction Contract and Agreement on Creditor's Rights Settlement would be duly executed. Moreover, Luck Treat also requested Zhongyuan City to go through overseas investment formalities as required by national related regulations and to make the payments for the transaction in a foreign currency from outside the territory of the People's Republic of China, but Zhongyuan City refused to fulfill its legal obligations of completing the overseas investment approval and registration procedures of foreign exchange. Without effective response to its repeated requests, Luck Treat notified Zhongyuan City of cancelling the transaction. Article 32 of the *Contract Law of the People's Republic of China* (hereinafter referred to as *Contract Law*) provides "where a contract is in the form of a written contractual agreement, it has been established upon being signed or sealed by the Parties." Article 17 of Equity Transaction Contract (draft text) stipulated that "upon being signed and sealed by legal representatives or duly authorized representatives of the Parties, this Contract, together with Agreement on Creditor's Rights Settlement, takes effect." According to the legal provision and contractual stipulation mentioned above, neither Equity Transaction Contract nor Agreement on Creditor's Rights Settlement was formulated for Zhongyuan City's refusal to satisfy its legal obligations and compliance requirements led to the Parties' failure to reach an agreement on the text of the contract and have the contract duly executed. In fact, the Parties had not yet completed the process of offer and acceptance for the purpose of entering into a contract; 2. the arbitration clause in the contract was not established either. Two documents of draft text contained the following arbitration clause, any dispute shall be referred to Shenzhen Court of International Arbitration for settlement. However, no arbitration clause can be established separately from and independently of its principal contract, and the Parties also had no explicit expression of intention in entering into in advance a separate arbitration agreement independent of the principal contract. Therefore, the arbitration clause in the contract was not established either, that is to say, there was no valid arbitration clause between Luck Treat and Zhongyuan City concerning the matters having been discussed in Equity Transaction Contract; and 3. as Luck Treat was not a Party to Agreement on Creditor's Rights Settlement, the arbitration clause therein was not binding on Luck Treat.

Zhongyuan City argued that both Equity Transaction Contract and

Agreement on Creditor's Rights Settlement were established and effective. The Parties had reached an agreement that any dispute in this case should be settled through arbitration during the negotiations on the performance of two documents, so there existed a valid arbitration agreement between the Parties. 1. The contract had been formulated and was effective. The equity transfer in this case was executed under the administration of CBEX pursuant to related trading rules. Thus the transaction contract was formulated and became effective in accordance with the law. Luck Treat, Newpower, Shenzhen Metropark Hotel Co, Ltd (hereinafter referred to as SZ-Metropark) and Beijing HK CTS Grand Metropark Hotels Management Co, Ltd (hereinafter referred to as BJ-Metropark) (the four entities collectively hereinafter referred to as Luck Treat & Others) should sign Equity Transaction Contract and Agreement on Creditor's Rights Settlement with Zhongyuan City as instructed in the transaction announcements. (1) The Parties had completed the offer-and-acceptance process of the equity transfer in this case. Luck Treat disclosed all particulars of the transaction and made related commitments in CBEX's transaction announcements, constituting the invitation to offer from Luck Treat & Others. Then, Zhongyuan City filed an application for bidding for the proposed equity with CBEX that sent Notice of Confirmation of Transferee Qualification, required the former to pay a security deposit prior to May 4, 2017, and instructed that "the qualification will be confirmed after the payment of the said security deposit within the prescribed period", constituting the offer from Luck Treat & Others. Zhongyuan City paid the security deposit of RMB 270, 000, 000 as instructed on the same day, obtaining the qualification of the only transferee and constituting the acceptance. The Parties thereby concluded and began to execute the transaction in accordance with CBEX's trading rules. Now that the completion of approval procedures was not required by laws and regulations for the effectiveness of a contract in this case, so the contract involved in this case was established and effective in accordance with the law; (2) according to the acceptance made by Luck Treat in its listing announcement and CBEX's trading rules, Luck Treat & Others were obliged to sign and seal Equity Transaction Contract and Agreement on Creditor's Rights Settlement with Zhongyuan City in accordance with the conditions set forth in the listing announcement within five (5) business days from the confirmation of Zhongyuan City as the finalized transferee; (3) with the transaction having been confirmed by the Parties according to the conditions set forth in the listing announcement, the unilateral revision of the trading terms from Luck Treat & Others by changing the trading rule of payment in RMB into a foreign currency from outside the territory of the People's Republic of China violated both their own acceptance and CBEX's trading rules; (4) it was with the agreement on all substantive terms, including subject matter, price, quantity, way of performance, preconditions and others, having being reached that the equity was delisted in this case and the Parties clinched the transaction at CBEX. Hence, a written contract was not the only legal instrument on the transaction between the Parties. The other documents that determine the existence of Equity Transaction Contract relations between two Parties also included the applications from the Parties to CBEX, the letters of commitment from the Parties, the announcements, the notices and the acknowledge of security deposit payment, which were all binding on the Parties. The transaction in this case was not within the category of overseas investments subject to approval from regulatory authorities, but was just subject to the record keeping with regulatory authorities, so the execution of the contract was just the prerequisite for its record keeping with regulatory authorities in this case. 2. The arbitration clause was established. (1) Luck Treat & Others e-mailed Equity Transaction Contract marked "draft text" to

Zhongyuan City on May 11, 2017, explicitly making an offer that any dispute should be filed with Shenzhen Court of International Arbitration for settlement. Zhongyuan City returned the signed and sealed contract and informed both in electronic and hardcopy version to Luck Treat & Others on the same day via electronic signature, e-mail and EMS courier. Thus, the Parties by this moment reached a consensus on arbitration and since then had no change; (2) the principle of the independence of an arbitration clause mandates that its existence and validity are not subject to the contract even if the written copies thereof are not executed by the Parties. Article 19 of the *Arbitration Law of the People's Republic of China* (hereinafter referred to as *Arbitration Law*) and Article 10 of the *Interpretations of the Supreme People's Court to Several Issues Concerning the Application of the Arbitration Law of the People's Republic of China* (hereinafter referred to as *Interpretations of the Arbitration Law*) affirm the independence of an arbitration clause. According to the aforesaid regulations, the arbitration clause in this case was established, existed independently and was valid. Luck Treat & Others thereafter asserted that "the transaction was cancelled", but had never requested the arbitration agreement to be rescinded; (3) the claim from Luck Treat & Others that the arbitration clause did not exist on the grounds that the contract was not approved within its own business group and was not signed was, in effect, the imposition of the requirement of its internal approval on Zhongyuan City, confusing its internal management relationships with external legal relationships. Therefore, the arbitration clause in the contract of draft text in this case should be binding upon the Parties. 3. Despite being different subjects, all the rights of Luck Treat & Others under this transaction were, in essence, vested with CTS. Equity Transaction Contract and Agreement on Creditor's Rights Settlement collectively constituted the transaction in its entirety in this case and were inseparable, so

Luck Treat & Others should collectively fulfill all the obligations as the transferor in this transaction, and should be bound by the arbitration clause. In conclusion, the arbitration agreement between the Parties in this case satisfied all the necessary conditions both in form and in content as laid down in the *Arbitration Law*. Thus Zhongyuan City hereby requested SPC to affirm in accordance with the law that the arbitration agreement between the Parties existed and was valid, and dismissed the request from Luck Treat.

Upon review, SPC found that China National Travel Service Group Corporation Limited, the former China Tourism Group or the former China Travel Service (Holdings) Hong Kong Limited, is a wholly state-owned company, while China Travel Service (Holdings) Hong Kong Limited (hereinafter referred to as CTS Hong Kong) is a wholly-owned subsidiary of CTS incorporated in Hong Kong, Luck Treat is a wholly-owned subsidiary of CTS Hong Kong incorporated in the British Virgin Islands, and Newpower is a wholly-owned subsidiary of Luck Treat incorporated in the British Virgin Islands.

On March 24, 2016, CTS handed down the Approval Concerning the Transfer of 100% Equity in Newpower Enterprises Inc., giving the green light to Luck Treat to transfer its 100% stake in Newpower as required by related laws and regulations. On March 29, 2017, Luck Treat put for sale its 100% stake in Newpower on CBEX, stating in "the other conditions for the transfer section" of the listing announcement that, besides "Equity Transaction Contract with the transferor, the transferee is also required to sign Agreement on Creditor's Rights Settlement with all the related Parties of the transferor and clearly understand and agree that the liquidation of creditor's rights as agreed in the Contract is a critical precondition for the equity transfer". In April 2017, Zhongyuan City and Beijing Jinyang Taihe Investment Consulting Co, Ltd signed an Entrustment Contract for the Equity Transaction, whereby the former entrusted the latter to provide floor brokerage services for the transaction in accordance with the trading rules of CBEX. On April 27, CBEX issued to Luck Treat a Letter of Opinions on Confirmation of Transferee Qualification, stating that the disclosure period for the transaction expired and there were two candidates, Zhongyuan City and Xu XX, and on April 28, issued a Notice of Confirmation of Transferee Qualification to Zhongyuan City, notifying Zhongyuan City that the security deposit of RMB 270, 000, 000 should be remitted into a settlement account designated by CBEX prior to May 4 and stating that upon payment of the security deposit within the said period of time, Zhongyuan City's transferee qualification would be confirmed. Otherwise, it would be deemed as a waiver of the transfer. Zhongyuan City remitted the security deposit of RMB 270, 000, 000 into the designated settlement account on the same day, and received the acknowledge of security deposit payment on May 3 from CBEX. As the other candidate, Xu XX, failed to pay the security deposit within the said period of time, Zhongyuan City was left to be the only prospective transferee.

Subsequently, Zhongyuan City and Luck Treat & Others began to negotiate on related matters of the transaction, including the signing of Equity Transaction Contract. On May 9, Zhang XX at the Center of Risk Control & Legal Affairs of Shenzhen Tailong Financial Holdings Group Limited (Zhongyuan City's superior group company) sent on behalf of Zhongyuan City an e-mail to Liu X, legal manager at the Legal Department of Hong Kong CTS Hotel Co Ltd (a wholly-owned subsidiary of CTS), stating that "kindly drop the Contracts, together with their appendixes, at my e-mail box (zha * * * * @ tljkjt.com)". Liu X replied via e-mail on the same day that "our designated external contact: Manager Zhang X, will send the Contracts and their appendixes to your designated contact: Manager Li X." On the same day, Zhang X, manager of Investment Management Department of Hong Kong CTS Hotel Co Ltd, sent an email to Zhang XX, reading that "please find attached the two Contracts and their appendixes previously provided to your company. We will revise these Contracts according to the terms agreed upon at today's meeting and then submit them for the review by CBEX at an earlier day. BTW, you are kindly required to mark any places to be revised, if any, on these Contracts and give us written feedback as soon as possible so as to be incorporated, together with CBEX's review opinions, into the finalized texts." The attached in the aforesaid e-mail was CBEX's model form of an equity transaction contract. It was an "Equity Transaction Contract on Luck Treat's Transfer of Its 100% Equity in Newpower to Zhongyuan City" to be signed by Luck Treat as Party A and Zhongyuan City as Party B in accordance with related laws, regulations and rules, including the *Contract Law* and the *Interim Measures for the Administration of the Transfer of State-owned Property Rights in Enterprises*, with its main contents containing firstly, Party A desired to transfer its 100% legal holdings in the target company while Party B desired to acquire the mentioned above holdings; secondly, as stipulated in this contract, Party B had completed all the related procedures including approval, authorization, or record, in accordance with laws, administrative regulations and the articles of incorporation for receiving the target matter to be transferred from Party A, and the transfer price was RMB 900, 000, 000; thirdly, all the formalities necessary for the signing of this contract, including but not limited to authorization, examination, approval and corporate internal decisions, had been lawfully and validly obtained, and all preconditions for the formation of this contract and the equity transfer satisfied; fourthly, upon being signed and sealed by legal representatives or duly authorized representatives of the Parties, this contract, together with Agreement on Creditor's Rights Settlement, took effect; fifthly, Article 16 was jurisdiction and dispute settlement. In Article 16. 1, any acts under the Contract and in the equity transaction should be governed by the law of the People's Republic of China; in Article 16. 2, any dispute between the Parties arising from or pertaining to the interpretation or performance of the Contract should be resolved by the Parties through negotiation, and if such negotiation fails to find a solution, the dispute could be submitted to Beijing Arbitration Commission for settlement. The appendix, Agreement on Creditor's Rights Settlement, attached in the aforesaid e-mail stated that Party A1 was CTS Hong Kong, Party A2 was Beijing Metropark, Party B was Zhongyuan City, Party C1 was Newpower and Party C2 was Shenzhen Metropark, and stipulated that firstly, Party B agreed to repay on behalf of Party C, within five (5) business days from the effective date of the contract, the creditor's rights and its capital occupation fee of RMB 107, 886, 893. 15 in a lump sum due to Party A; secondly, Article 12 stipulated the agreement should be governed by the law of the People's Republic of China, and any dispute among the Parties arising from or pertaining to the interpretation or performance of the agreement should be resolved through negotiation, and if and when such negotiation failed to find a solution, any Party had the right to submit the dispute to Beijing Arbitration Commission for settlement.

On May 10, Zhang XX sent an e-mail to Zhang X and Liu X, reading that "please find attached one recommended revision to the Contract, and your careful consideration of and confirmation on such revision based on the principles of equality and fairness as well as the validity of a signed contract will be highly appreciated." In the attachment of the e-mail, Article 16 of Equity Transaction Contract, "Jurisdiction and Dispute Settlement" was revised into "16. 1 Any acts under the Contract and in the equity transaction shall be governed by the law of the People's Republic of China. 16. 2 Any dispute between the Parties arising from or pertaining to the interpretation or performance of the Contract shall be resolved by the Parties through negotiation, and if such negotiation fails to find a solution, the dispute is submitted to Shenzhen Court of International Arbitration for settlement", and Article 12 of Agreement on Creditor's Rights Settlement was revised into "the Agreement shall be governed by the law of the People's Republic of China, and any dispute among the Parties arising from or pertaining to the interpretation or performance of the Agreement shall be resolved through negotiation, and if such negotiation fails to find a solution, any Party has the right to submit the dispute to Shenzhen Court of International Arbitration for settlement." In response to the revision proposed by Zhongyuan City to the two documents, Zhang X sent an e-mail to Zhang XX and Li X, a senior executive of Zhongyuan City, at 13 : 42 on May 11, stating that "we hereby send the revised Contract (draft text) to you, and your earlier feedback on the revised Contract will be highly appreciated. Upon being confirmed by you and us, the revised Contract will be submitted to CBEX and our Group for examination and approval, and the execution thereof will be subject to final confirmation by CBEX and our Group (we will notify you of any further revisions, if any)." In the attachment of this e-mail, Article 16 of Equity Transaction Contract (draft text), "Jurisdiction and Dispute Settlement" and Article 12 of Agreement on Creditor's Rights Settlement (draft text) were respectively the same as related contents of the attachment in the aforesaid e-mail on May 10, 2017 from Zhang XX to Zhang X and Liu X. At 18 : 39 the same day, Zhang XX e-mailed Zhang X, saying that "please find attached the scanned copies of Equity Transaction Contract (draft text) and Agreement on Creditor's Rights Settlement (draft text) duly signed by us, together with the Instruction on the Signing of the Contract on Transferring 100% Stake in Newpower Enterprises Inc. and so on, and your early reply will be highly appreciated." In the attachment of this e-mail, the contents concerning jurisdiction and dispute settlement in both Equity Transaction Contract (draft text) and Agreement on Creditor's Rights Settlement (draft text) were respectively the same as related contents of the attachment in the e-mail sent on the same day from Zhang X. Zhongyuan City had affixed its seal on two documents and delivered them to Luck Treat. The Instruction on the Signing of the Contract on Transferring 100% Stake in Newpower Enterprises Inc., the other attachment in the same e-mail from Zhongyuan City to Luck Treat, contained that Equity Transaction Contract (draft text) and Agreement on Creditor's Rights Settlement (draft text) were scheduled to be executed on May 11, 2017; it was understood that the execution of the two documents should be subject to compliance review by CBEX and approval by CTS; the final signed versions of Equity Transaction Contract and Agreement on Creditor's Rights Settlement should be subject to the contents of the formal version; and the signing form of Equity Transaction Contract and Agreement on Creditor's Rights Settlement should be subject to your arrangement.

In an e-mail dated May 17 to Li X, Zhang X said that "as for the Shenzhen Project, the final review and approval is underway at our Group. If everything goes smoothly, the signing ceremony is expected to be held in the Friday morning at BJ-Metropark Hotel. Upon confirmation, we will notify you of detailed information. Now, we send the proposed texts of Equity Transaction Contract and Agreement on Creditor's Rights Settlement to you for a check." The Attachment-1 in this e-mail was the Contract on Property Right Transactions of Equity Transfer Project (proposed text) and the Attachment-2 was the Agreement on Creditor's Rights Settlement of Equity Transfer Project (proposed text). The arbitration clause in these two documents remained respectively the same as that in the previous ones (draft text).

Having completed the compliance review, Luck Treat sent a Reply on June 1, 2017 to Zhongyuan City, saying that 1. with the transferor and the target firm to be transferred being companies incorporated in the British Virgin Islands outside the territory of the People's Republic of China, and the transferee (i. e. your company), a company incorporated in Shenzhen within the territory of the People's Republic of China, this transaction fell within the category of overseas investments, and thus, in accordance with related provisions in the Administrative Measures for Approval and Registration on Overseas Investments (NDRC Directive of No. 9 [2014], the National Development and Reform Commission), the Administrative Measures for Overseas Investments (MOC Directive of No. 3 [2014], the Ministry of Commence) and the Provisions on Foreign Exchange Administration for Overseas Direct Investments of Domestic Institutions (SAFE Directive of No. 30 [2009], the State Administration of Foreign Exchange), your company was required by law to complete the record or approval formalities on overseas investments with the NDRC and the MOC, respectively, and the foreign exchange registration formalities on overseas direct investments with the SAFE for the transaction, and made the payments for the transaction in a foreign currency from outside the territory of the People's Republic of China to the transferor (i. e. our company); 2. with respect to Article 15. 3 of Equity Transaction Contract attached in your letter, our legal counsel believed that it did not comply with the requirements as set out in the listing announcement on the equity transfer in CBEX on March 29. Article 3. 4 of Section Ⅳ "Other Conditions for the Transfer" provides that where a transferee fails to pay the remaining transaction amount within the prescribed period of time, the security deposit paid by the said transferee shall be deducted in full. Therefore, we requested to have this clause revised as follows: where Party B fails to make a full payment for the transaction within the period of time as provided in the Contract, the security deposit of RMB 270, 000, 000 paid by Party B shall be deducted in full and Party B unconditionally agrees that CBEX may transfer the said security deposit of RMB 270, 000, 000 in a lump sum to the account designated by Party A.

On June 6, August 29 and October 23, 2017, Zhongyuan City sent letters to Luck Treat, urging Luck Treat to sign Equity Transaction Contract and Agreement on Creditor's Rights Settlement as soon as possible. On October 27, Luck Treat sent a Notification to Zhongyuan City, stating that given no affirmative response from you to our notification and repeated demand to timely complete related legal formalities, we hereby formally notify you that the transaction has been cancelled. On November 12, Zhongyuan City sent a letter to Luck Treat, requesting Luck Treat to arrange for the signing of the contract as soon as possible and to provide related documents for completing the legal formalities with competent authorities. On November 27, Luck Treat replied in writing, reaffirming that the notification of the cancellation of the transaction had been sent to Zhongyuan City on October 27, and proposing that the Parties immediately completed the procedures of refunding the security deposit with CBEX.

According to Article 16. 2 of Equity Transaction Contract (draft text) and Article 12 of Agreement on Creditor's Rights Settlement (draft text), Zhongyuan City filed an arbitration application with Shenzhen Court of International Arbitration on April 4, 2018 against Luck Treat & Others as co-respondents. However, before the arbitration hearing, Luck Treat & Others filed lawsuits respectively, requesting Shenzhen Intermediate People's Court of Guangdong Province (SZIPC) to confirm that there existed no arbitration agreement between the Parties. On September 11, 2018, SZIPC accepted these lawsuits, forming this case and two other connected cases. In consideration of the crucial legal significance carried by this case and its connected ones as well as the efficiency improvement in dispute resolution by uniform application of laws in a combined trial by the China International Commercial Court, and according to Article 38 (1) of the *Civil Procedure Law of the People's Republic of China* (hereinafter referred to as *Civil Procedure Law*) and Article 2 (5) of the *Regulations on the Supreme People's Court on Several Issues Regarding the Establishment of the International Commercial Court*, SPC made a ruling that this case was heard by the First International Commercial Court. During the court hearing of this case, the Parties agreed to settle their dispute through negotiation and mediation, but failed to achieve a consensus on the dispute resolution methods and substantive issues following repeated consultations. Therefore, SPC proceeded to resume its trial.

Upon review, SPC found that the issue in this case was the establishment of the arbitration clause.

In response to the arbitration application from Zhongyuan City, Luck Treat initiated legal proceedings, requesting the people's court to confirm that no valid arbitration clause existed between the Parties on the grounds that such arbitration clause had never been established. Despite different requests, either the invalidity of a preexisting arbitration agreement or the existence of an arbitration agreement will likewise have a direct influence on dispute resolution methods. Either of them is a prerequisite to be determined for dispute settlement. Therefore, in a broad sense, the request to confirm that no arbitration agreement exists between the Parties is also an objection to the validity of a preexisting arbitration agreement. Article 20 (1) of the *Arbitration Law* provides that an objecting Party to the validity of an arbitration agreement may apply to an arbitration commission for a decision or to a people's court for a ruling.

Therefore, the request by a Party to determine the non-existence of an arbitration agreement on the grounds that the arbitration clause has not been established falls into the same category of cases as a request to confirm the validity of an arbitration agreement, which a people's court shall accept and hear.

For the purpose of determining the validity of an arbitration agreement, the proper law shall be firstly chosen. Article 18 of the *Law of the People's Republic of China on the Application of Laws Concerning Foreign-related Civil Relations* (hereinafter referred to as *Law on the Application of Laws*) provides "the Parties to an arbitration agreement may choose by agreement proper laws for such arbitration agreement. In the absence of such choice, the laws in the place where the arbitral institution is located or the law of the place of arbitration shall apply." During the court hearing, all Parties explicitly agreed that the laws of the People's Republic of China should apply to determining the validity of the arbitration agreement involved in this case. Therefore, the arbitration agreement in this case was governed by the law of the People's Republic of China.

Article 16 (1) of the *Arbitration Law* provides "an arbitration agreement includes arbitration clauses stipulated in a contract and/or agreements on dispute settlement through arbitration concluded in other written forms before or after disputes arise." Thus, both arbitration clauses stipulated in a contract and independent arbitration agreements are classified as arbitration agreement. It follows that the laws and regulations on an arbitration agreement all the same apply to determining the establishment and validity of arbitration clauses.

As a widely accepted fundamental principle of law, the independence of an arbitration agreement means that an arbitration agreement and its principal contract are separable and independent of each other, and their respective existence, effectiveness and proper laws are also separable. Since arbitration clauses constitute the main form of arbitration agreements, endowing arbitration clauses with independence from other contractual clauses in the same documents is of more practical significance than emphasizing the independence of separate arbitration agreements. It may even be said that the independence of an arbitration agreement mainly refers to the separability of arbitration clauses from their principal contracts, which is stipulated in both the laws of the People's Republic of China and related judicial interpretations from SPC. Article 19 (1) of the *Arbitration Law* provides "an arbitration agreement exists independently, and its validity shall not be subject to the change, rescission, termination or invalidity of the contract." To put it in the context, this Article provides the independence of an arbitration agreement after Article 16 thereof clarifies that arbitration clauses are also arbitration agreements. Therefore, arbitration clauses are also independent of their contracts. However, on the issue of whether or not arbitration clauses can be established completely independently from their contracts, the provisions of the *Arbitration Law* are not so clear as that the change, rescission, termination or invalidity of the established contract will not affect the validity of the arbitration agreement. In judicial practice, the establishment of a contract has usually been entangled with the establishment of the arbitration clause therein. However, in the preface of Article 19 (1) of the *Arbitration Law,* "an arbitration agreement exists independently" represents an encompassing and general expression, which shall contain the issue of the existence of an arbitration agreement, namely, whether it is established, and the subsequent statements further specify in an itemized manner some circumstances that shall not affect the validity of the arbitration agreement. Besides, Article 10 (2) of the *Interpretation of the Arbitration Law* further clarifies "if and when an arbitration agreement on related disputes is concluded between the Parties while a contract is formulated, the failure to establish the said contract shall not affect the validity of the said arbitration agreement." Therefore, for the purpose of determining the validity of arbitration clauses, including their effective establishment, the validity of the said arbitration clauses *per se* may be determined firstly, but the validity of the principal contract, including its effective establishment, does not need to be determined except for being warranted by sufficient necessity. The same rule applies to this case, that is to say, the establishment of the arbitration clause should be determined firstly in accordance with the specific circumstances of this case.

The establishment of an arbitration clause primarily depends upon the existence of a consensus on dispute settlement through arbitration between the Parties, namely, whether or not the Parties reached an arbitration agreement. Given an arbitration agreement is a contract of a kind, so related provisions on offer and acceptance in the *Contract Law* should be applied for judging whether or not the Parties reached a consensus on arbitration. In the light of the negotiations in this case, the Parties had always jointly agreed to submit their disputes for arbitration. The initial Equity Transaction Contract in this case is the model form provided by CBEX, and was sent, together with Agreement on Creditor's Rights Settlement, by Luck Treat & Others to Zhongyuan City. The aforesaid documents contained a clause stating that any dispute shall be submitted to Beijing Arbitration Commission for settlement through arbitration, and subsequently, the Parties negotiated on the choice of an arbitration institution. The arbitration clause in the contract of draft text from Luck Treat & Others selected Shenzhen Court of International Arbitration as the arbitration institution for possible disputes. As far as the arbitration clause is concerned, this constituted an offer from Luck Treat & Others, and Zhongyuan City returned the sealed contract on May 11, 2017, signifying its consent to it and constituting its acceptance. According to Articles 25 and 26 of the *Contract Law*, upon its arrival at the offeror, an acceptance takes effect, and a contract is established. Therefore, the arbitration clause in Equity Transaction Contract and Agreement on Creditor's Rights Settlement were established between the Parties thereto respectively on May 11, 2017. Despite negotiations on other particulars in the contract thereafter, the Parties had never had any dispute over the arbitration clause. As Luck Treat & Others did not challenge the existence of invalid legal circumstances for the arbitration clause, it should be determined that there existed a valid arbitration clause between the Parties, and thus any dispute between the Parties should be submitted to Shenzhen Court of International Arbitration for settlement through arbitration. Even though Luck Treat & Others did not affix its seal on the finalized contract, nor did the legal representatives of the Parties sign the finalized contract, it did not meet the requirements that the contract should take effect after being signed and sealed by the legal representatives or authorized representatives of both Parties. However, according to Article 10 (2) of the *Interpretation of the Arbitration Law*, the validity of the arbitration clause shall not be affected even if the contract is not established. Under the circumstance that the Parties had already reached the arbitration agreement, there was no need to go further to determine the establishment of the contract in this case, leaving it to be resolved in arbitration.

Luck Treat also contended that not being a Party to Agreement on Creditor's Rights Settlement, it should not be bound by the arbitration clause therein. As the arbitration clause in Equity Transaction Contract was binding on Luck Treat, the dispute between Luck Treat and Zhongyuan City should be resolved through arbitration. Besides, given Luck Treat & Others were co-respondents in the same arbitration case, SPC had no need to make its judgment here on the issue.

In summary, the reasons and claims from Luck Treat could not be established. According to Articles 16, 19 and 20 of the *Arbitration Law* , SPC makes the ruling as follows:

The request from Luck Treat Limited shall be dismissed.

The application fee of RMB 400 shall be borne by the Applicant Luck Treat Limited.

Presiding Judge: ZHANG Yongjian

Judge: GAO Xiaoli

Judge: XI Xiangyang

Judge: DING Guangyu

Judge: SHEN Hongyu

September 18, 2019

Assistant Judge : LI Guangqin

Court Clerk: XIE Songshan

高尔集团股份有限公司
申请承认和执行
新加坡高等法庭民事判决案

——互惠原则在外国法院判决审查案件中的适用

【裁判要旨】

1. 在相互承认和执行外国法院判决领域,对互惠关系的认定应摒弃孤立、苛刻思维,以更加开放包容的态度进行审查,积极促进两国互惠关系的形成,促进国际司法协作。互惠条约或国际条约并非是审查两国之间是否存在互惠关系的唯一标准。

2. 在两国之间未有互惠条约的情形下,是否承认和执行外国法院判决,还需要审查两国之间是否存在事实互惠。事实互惠标准可适度放宽。如果外国法院以内国判决为依据,启动重新审理程序,并作出承认和执行的裁决,亦可视为该国对中国先行给予了互惠待遇。

【专家点评】*

本案涉及外国法院判决在中国的承认和执行问题。

在2016年高尔集团股份有限公司申请承认和执行新加坡共和国高等法庭民事判决案(以下简称高尔案)中,南京市中级人民法院首次依据互惠原则承认和执行了新加坡高等法庭的判决。南京市中级人民法院的裁定不仅

---

* 撰写人:何其生,北京大学法学院教授、博士研究生导师。
王雅菡,河南大学法学院讲师。

对中国、新加坡两国之间判决的相互承认和执行起到了积极的推进作用，而且在中国法院适用互惠原则方面也具有引领性价值。

一、高尔案所涉互惠问题

根据高尔案裁定书，南京市中级人民法院基于中国民事诉讼法的规定进行了如下的审查和分析：首先，新加坡高等法庭对江苏省纺织工业（集团）进出口有限公司作出了合法传唤，江苏省纺织工业（集团）进出口有限公司未参加庭审，但收到了案涉判决书。新加坡高等法庭的判决符合正当程序的要求。其次，在判决的承认和执行领域，中国与新加坡之间没有缔结和共同参加的国际条约，但新加坡高等法庭曾于2014年承认和执行了中国江苏省苏州市中级人民法院的民事判决。① “根据互惠原则，我国法院可以对符合条件的新加坡法院的民事判决予以承认和执行。”最后，法院经过审查，认为新加坡法院的判决并不违反我国法律的基本原则或者国家主权、安全、社会公共利益。综上，南京市中级人民法院作出承认和执行新加坡高等法庭013号民事判决的裁定。本案的裁定明确了中国司法实践中互惠的认定标准，即以原审国法院是否存在承认和执行中国法院判决的先例为判断依据。

值得关注的是，2018年8月31日，以高尔案为契机，中华人民共和国最高人民法院（以下简称最高人民法院）和新加坡共和国最高法院共同签署了《中华人民共和国最高人民法院和新加坡共和国最高法院关于承认与执行商事案件金钱判决的指导备忘录》（以下称为《指导备忘录》），进一步明确了两国间判决相互承认和执行的范围和条件。《指导备忘录》第6条规定，目前两国尚无有关一方判决可在另一方法院承认与执行的条约。在此情况下，根据中国民事诉讼法的规定，中国法院可以在互惠基础上，根据申请人的申请，承认与执行新加坡法院的判决。

---

① 参见本书“捷安特轻合金科技（昆山）有限公司 v. 雅柯斯（远东）私人有限公司”案，第383-441页。

二、高尔案在互惠关系解释上的引领性价值

作为依据互惠原则承认和执行外国法院判决的第一案以及“一带一路”建设典型案例之一，高尔案既是我国承认和执行外国法院判决司法实践中的转折点，同时也是“一带一路”建设推进下承认和执行外国法院判决的推动力。该案展现了我国在判决承认和执行领域加强国际合作的积极态度，同时也反映出我国以互惠促合作的意向。

虽然南京市中级人民法院对于互惠的认定仍采用事实互惠标准，但该案在一定程度上体现了我国在涉外审判司法实践中的进步，推动了我国法院以事实互惠承认外国法院判决的趋势。

在2017年受理的申请人刘某与被申请人陶某、童某申请承认和执行外国法院民事判决案①中，武汉市中级人民法院基于事实互惠承认与执行美国加利福尼亚州法院的判决。2019年3月，山东省青岛市中级人民法院承认和执行了韩国水原地方法院作出的一项借贷纠纷的民事判决，该院认为韩国法院的判决符合中国互惠原则的要求。② 2019年8月，浙江省温州市中级人民法院遵循了高尔案的裁判思路，再次承认和执行了新加坡高等法庭的另一个判决。③ 据此，互惠原则在我国已经开始发挥其积极合作的一面，而不是仅作为拒绝外国法院判决的理由。

随着“一带一路”建设的推进，最高人民法院也开展了一系列工作积极推进外国法院判决的承认和执行。2015年最高人民法院发布了《最高人民法院关于人民法院为“一带一路”建设提供司法服务和保障的若干意见》，其中第6条明确了要加强国际司法协助，保护中外当事人的合法权益，并在今后的司法实践中能够使互惠发挥更加积极的作用。2017年第二届中国—东盟大法官论坛上，中国与东盟国家在《南宁声明》中又达成推定互惠的共识。与司法实践相比，《南宁声明》所确立的推定互惠又进一步放宽了标准，即只

---

① 参见湖北省武汉市中级人民法院(2015)鄂武汉中民商外初字第00026号民事裁定书。

② 参见山东省青岛市中级人民法院(2018)鲁02协外认6号民事裁定书。

③ 参见海湾发展集团有限公司、陈某甲、陈某乙申请承认与执行法院判决、仲裁裁决案，浙江省温州市中级人民法院(2017)浙03协外认7号民事裁定书。

要对方国家没有以不存在互惠关系为由拒绝承认和执行的情况，即可推定为有互惠。[①]

综上分析，高尔案的灵活解释在判决承认与执行领域开启了我国对外司法合作的新局面，也使我国的判决得到越来越多国家的承认与执行。

【裁判文书】

中华人民共和国江苏省南京市中级人民法院
民事裁定书

（2016）苏 01 协外认 3 号

申请人：高尔集团股份有限公司（Kolmar Group AG）。住所地：****，Baarerstrasse **，**** Zug，Switzerland。

代表人：Sandelowsky，该公司董事长。

委托代理人：陈某某，江苏**律师事务所律师。

委托代理人：曹某，江苏**律师事务所律师。

被申请人：江苏省纺织工业（集团）进出口有限公司。住所地：中华人民共和国江苏省南京市***路***号。

法定代表人：梁某某，该公司总经理。

委托代理人：李某，**律师（南京）事务所律师。

委托代理人：周某，江苏****律师事务所律师。

申请人高尔集团股份有限公司（以下简称高尔集团）申请承认和执行新加坡共和国高等法院于 2015 年 10 月 22 日作出的 013 号民事判决一案，本

① 2017 年 6 月 8 日，中国与东盟国家就区域内国际司法协助等问题在《南宁声明》中达成了八项共识，其中第七项规定：“……尚未缔结有关外国民商事判决承认和执行国际条约的国家，在承认与执行对方国家民商事判决的司法程序中，如对方国家的法院不存在以互惠为理由拒绝承认和执行本国民商事判决的先例，在本国国内法允许的范围内，即可推定与对方国家之间存在互惠关系。”

院于2016年6月7日立案。本院依法组成了合议庭进行了审查,组织当事人进行了询问,现已审查终结。

高尔集团申请称,高尔集团因与江苏省纺织工业(集团)进出口有限公司(以下简称省纺集团)买卖合同纠纷,双方达成和解协议,省纺集团承诺赔偿高尔集团35万美元,后因省纺集团未履行和解协议,高尔集团依据和解协议中的约定管辖条款向新加坡共和国高等法院提起诉讼。经合法传唤,省纺集团未到庭,新加坡共和国高等法院于2015年10月22日作出013号缺席判决,判令省纺集团偿付35万美元及自传讯令状签发之日起至判决之日止按年利率5.33%计算的利息、费用4137.9新元,高尔集团亦向省纺集团进行了送达,但省纺集团完全不予理会。因省纺集团及其财产均在中国境内,现依据《中华人民共和国民事诉讼法》及司法解释相关规定,请求法院对该判决予以承认和执行。

省纺集团陈述意见称,《中华人民共和国民事诉讼法》第二百八十二条规定,"人民法院对申请或者请求承认和执行的外国法院作出的发生法律效力的判决、裁定,依照中华人民共和国缔结或者参加的国际条约,或者按照互惠原则进行审查后,认为不违反中华人民共和国法律的基本原则或者国家主权、安全、社会公共利益的,裁定承认其效力"。根据我国和新加坡共和国签署的《关于民事和商事司法协助的条约》的规定,两国之间的司法协助范围并不包括承认和执行法院的判决和裁定,故根据《中华人民共和国民事诉讼法》的规定,应驳回高尔集团的申请。

经审查认定:新加坡共和国高等法院于2015年10月22日作出013号民事判决,判令省纺集团支付高尔集团35万美元及自传讯令状签发之日起至判决之日止按年利率5.33%计算的利息,并且支付费用4137.9新元。省纺集团在本案听证中承认其得到了新加坡共和国高等法院的合法传唤,但未参加庭审,其亦收到了案涉判决书。另查明,2014年1月,新加坡共和国高等法院作出[2014]SGHC 16号判决,内容为对我国江苏省苏州市中级人民法院作出的判决进行承认和执行。

本院认为，《中华人民共和国民事诉讼法》第二百八十二条规定，“人民法院对申请或者请求承认和执行的外国法院作出的发生法律效力的判决、裁定，依照中华人民共和国缔结或者参加的国际条约，或者按照互惠原则进行审查后，认为不违反中华人民共和国法律的基本原则或者国家主权、安全、社会公共利益的，裁定承认其效力，需要执行的，发出执行令，依照本法的有关规定执行。违反中华人民共和国法律的基本原则或者国家主权、安全、社会公共利益的，不予承认和执行”，案涉民事判决系新加坡共和国法院作出，我国与新加坡共和国之间并未缔结或者共同参加关于相互承认和执行生效裁判文书的国际条约，但由于新加坡共和国高等法院曾于2014年1月对我国江苏省苏州市中级人民法院的民事判决进行了执行，根据互惠原则，我国法院可以对符合条件的新加坡法院的民事判决予以承认和执行。经审查，案涉判决亦不违反我国法律的基本原则或者国家主权、安全、社会公共利益，故依照《中华人民共和国民事诉讼法》第二百八十二条之规定，裁定如下：

承认和执行新加坡共和国高等法院于2015年10月22日作出的013号民事判决。

案件申请费80元，由被申请人省纺集团负担。

审 判 长　王　胜
审 判 员　姜　欣
审 判 员　陆红霞
二〇一六年十二月九日
书 记 员　杨文艳

Application of Kolmar Group AG for Recognition and Enforcement of Civil Judgment of Singapore High Court

—Application of the Principle of Reciprocity to Reviewing Cases Decided by Foreign Courts

Holding

1. In mutual recognition and execution of judicial decisions made by foreign courts, an open and inclusive mindset instead of insular and captious thinking should be adopted to determine reciprocal relations and review the cases settled at courts in other countries so as to promote reciprocal relations among countries and broader international judicial cooperation. Reciprocal treaties or international treaties are not the only criteria for examining the existence of reciprocal relationships between countries.

2. In the absence of a reciprocal treaty between two countries, recognition and execution of decisions made by foreign courts should be justified by the existence of *de facto* reciprocity between two countries, and the criteria for *de facto* reciprocity may be reasonably relaxed. If in response to decisions made by a Chinese court, a foreign court initiates retrial procedures and makes a decision to recognize and enforce the Chinese decisions, such a move may also be deemed that the said country has already granted reciprocal treatments to China.

Commentary *

This case involved the issue of recognition and enforcement of a judgment made by a foreign court in China.

In 2016, in the case of Kolmar Group AG's application for recognition and enforcement of a Civil Judgment made by the High Court of the Republic of Singapore (hereinafter referred to as Kolmar case), Nanjing Intermediate People's Court recognized and enforced the Judgment of Singapore High Court for the first time based on the principle of reciprocity. The Ruling of Nanjing Intermediate People's Court not only promotes the mutual recognition and enforcement of the judgments between China and Singapore, but also has a leading value in the application of the principle of reciprocity in China's courts.

1. The Issue of Reciprocity Involved in Kolmar Case

According to the Ruling of Kolmar case, Nanjing Intermediate People's Court conducted the following examination and analysis based on the provisions of China's *Civil Procedure Law*: firstly, Singapore High Court summoned legitimately to Jiangsu Textile Industry (Group) Import and Export Co, Ltd, who did not participate in the court trial, but received the relevant judgment. The Judgment made by Singapore High Court met the requirements of due process. Secondly, in the field of recognition and enforcement of the judgments, there are no international treaties concluded and jointly participated in between China and Singapore, but Singapore High Court recognized and enforced the Civil Judgment of Suzhou Intermediate People's Court of Jiangsu Province in 2014.① "In accordance with the principle of reciprocity, China's

---

* Authors: HE Qisheng, Professor and Doctoral Supervisor, Law School, Peking University.
WANG Yahan, Lecturer, Law School, Henan University.

① See the case of "*Giant Light Metal Technology (Kunshan) Co Ltd v. Aksa Far East Pte Ltd*" in this volume, pp. 383-441.

courts can recognize and enforce the civil judgments of Singapore courts that meet the requirements." Thirdly, Nanjing Intermediate People's Court through examination held that the judgment of Singapore court did not violate the basic principles of China's law(s) or national sovereignty, security, and social and public interests. In conclusion, Nanjing Intermediate People's Court made a ruling to recognize and enforce the Civil Judgment of No. 013 made by Singapore High Court. The Ruling of this case clarified the identified criterion of reciprocity in China's judicial practice which is based on whether there was a precedent in the original hearing country to recognize and enforce the judgments of China's courts.

It is remarkable to see that on August 31, 2018, taking the Kolmar case as an opportunity, the Supreme People's Court of the People's Republic of China (hereinafter referred to as SPC) and the Supreme Court of the Republic of Singapore jointly signed the Memorandum of Guidance Between the Supreme People's Court of the People's Republic of China and the Supreme Court of Singapore on Recognition and Enforcement of Money Judgments in Commercial Cases (hereinafter referred to as Guidance Memorandum), which further clarifies the scope and conditions of mutual recognition and enforcement of the judgments between two countries. Article 6 of Guidance Memorandum stipulates there is no treaty between two countries that the judgment of one party can be recognized and enforced in the court of the other party. Under such circumstances, according to the provisions of China's *Civil Procedure Law*, China's courts can recognize and enforce the judgments of Singapore courts on the basis of reciprocity in accordance with the application of applicants.

2. The Leading Value of Kolmar Case on the Interpretation of Reciprocal Relationship

As the first case of recognizing and enforcing the judgment of a foreign court based on the principle of reciprocity and one of typical cases under the construction of the Belt and Road Initiative, Kolmar case in China is not only a turning point concerning recognition and enforcement of the judgments of foreign courts in judicial practice, but also a driving force for recognition and enforcement of the judgments of foreign courts to push on the construction of the Belt and Road Initiative. This case shows China's positive attitude to strengthen international cooperation in the field of recognition and enforcement of the judgments, and also reflects China's intention to promote cooperation through reciprocity.

Although Nanjing Intermediate People's Court still adopts the standard of factual reciprocity for the determination of reciprocity, this case reflects the progress of China's foreign-related judicial practice to a certain degree, and pushes forward the trend of China's courts to recognize the judgments of foreign courts with factual reciprocity.

In 2017, having accepted the case of the Applicant Liu X and the Respondents Tao X and Tong X who applied for recognition and enforcement of the civil judgment of a foreign court, Wuhan Intermediate People's Court recognized and enforced the Judgment of California State Court, the United States, on the basis of factual reciprocity.① In March 2019, Qingdao Intermediate People's Court of Shandong Province recognized and enforced a Civil Judgment concerning a debit and credit dispute made by Suwon District Court of South Korea, and held that the judgment of South Korean court met the requirements of China's principle of reciprocity.② In August 2019, Wenzhou Intermediate People's Court of Zhejiang Province followed the ruling

① See the Civil Ruling of Wuhan Intermediate People's Court of Hubei Province, No. 00026 [2015], FI, Civil and Commercial Division, Wuhan Intermediate People's Court.

② See the Civil Ruling of Qingdao Intermediate People's Court of Shandong Province, No. 6 [2018], Shandong Province 02, Assistance, Foreign Judgment Recognition.

analysis of Kolmar case and once again recognized and enforced another Judgment made by Singapore High Court.① Therefore, the principle of reciprocity began to play the side of its positive cooperation in China, rather than just as a reason to refuse the judgments of foreign courts.

With the promotion of the construction of the Belt and Road Initiative, SPC has also launched a series of work to actively push forward recognition and enforcement of the judgments made by foreign courts. In 2015, SPC issued the *Opinions of the Supreme People's Court on Several Issues Concerning People's Court Providing for Judicial Services and Safeguards for the Construction of the Belt and Road Initiative*, among which Article 6 clarifies to strengthen international judicial assistance, to protect the legitimate rights and interests of Chinese and foreign parties, and to enable reciprocity to play a more active role in the future judicial practice. At the Second China-ASEAN Chief Justice Forum in 2017, China and ASEAN countries also reached a consensus on presumptive reciprocity in Nanning Declaration. Compared with judicial practice, the standard of presumptive reciprocity established in Nanning Declaration was further relaxed, which meant as long as the other country does not refuse to recognize and enforce it on the ground that there is no reciprocal relationship, it can be presumed that there is reciprocity.②

① See the case of Gulf Development Group Co, Ltd, Chen X(A) and Chen X(B)'s application for recognition and enforcement made by the judgment of the court and the arbitration award, a Civil Ruling made by Wenzhou Intermediate People's Court of Zhejiang Province, No. 7 [2017], Zhejiang Province 03, Assistance, Foreign Judgment Recognition.

② On June 8, 2017, China and ASEAN countries reached eight consensus in the Nanning Declaration on issues such as international judicial assistance in this region, among which Article 7 provides "... a country that has not yet concluded an international treaty on the recognition and enforcement of foreign civil and commercial judgments, in the judicial process of recognizing and enforcing the civil and commercial judgments of the other countries, if the courts of the other countries do not have the precedent of refusing to recognize and enforce the civil and commercial judgments in the home country on the ground that there is no reciprocity, it can be presumed that there exists a reciprocal relationship with the other country within the scope prescribed by its domestic laws".

In conclusion, the flexible interpretation of Kolmar case has opened a new situation of China's foreign judicial cooperation in the field of recognition and enforcement of the judgments, and has also enabled China's judgments to be recognized and enforced by more and more countries.

Grounds of Decision

The People's Republic of China

Intermediate People's Court of Nanjing, Jiangsu Province

Civil Ruling

No. 3 [2016], Jiangsu Province 01, Assistance, Foreign Judgment Recognition

Applicant: Kolmar Group AG.

Domicile: ****, Baarerstrasse **, **** Zug, Switzerland.

Representative: Sandelowsky, Chairman of the company.

Attorney: Chen XX, at Jiangsu ** Law Firm.

Attorney: Cao X, at Jiangsu ** Law Firm.

Respondent: Jiangsu Textile Industry (Group) Import and Export Co, Ltd.

Domicile: No. *** Road, Nanjing City, Jiangsu Province, the People's Republic of China.

Legal Representative: Liang XX, General Manager of the company.

Attorney: Li X, at Nanjing ** Law Firm.

Attorney: Zhou X, at Jiangsu **** Law Firm.

Applicant Kolmar Group AG (hereinafter referred to as Kolmar) applied for recognition and enforcement of the Civil Judgment No. 013 by the High Court of the Republic of Singapore on October 22, 2015, which was filed by Nanjing Intermediate People's Court on June 7, 2016. The Court formed a collegial bench to conduct examination according to law, and organized the related Parties for inquiry. Now the examination of this case has been concluded.

Kolmar claimed that it had reached a settlement agreement with Jiangsu Textile Industry (Group) Import and Export Co, Ltd (hereinafter referred to as SUTEX) concerning the dispute over a sale and purchase contract, whereby SUTEX agreed to pay USD 350, 000 to Kolmar for compensation. Since SUTEX failed to perform the settlement agreement, Kolmar filed a lawsuit in the High Court of the Republic of Singapore according to the jurisdiction clause agreed upon in the settlement agreement. After being summoned legitimately, SUTEX did not appear in court, and the High Court of the Republic of Singapore issued a default Judgment (No. 013) on October 22, 2015, ordering SUTEX to pay USD 350, 000, plus interest at an annual rate of 5.33% from the date of issuance of the writ of summons to the date of Judgment, and a legal fee of SGD 4, 137. 90. Kolmar also served SUTEX with the Judgment, but SUTEX did not make any response. Given that the domicile of SUTEX and its property are in China, Kolmar was now requesting Nanjing Intermediate People's Court to recognize and enforce the Judgment in accordance with the *Civil Procedure Law of the People's Republic of China* (hereinafter referred to as *Civil Procedure Law*) and the provisions of the relevant judicial interpretation.

SUTEX argued that Article 282 of the *Civil Procedure Law* provides "the people's court shall, for applications or requests for recognition and enforcement of legally effective judgments and rulings by foreign courts, rule to recognize its effectiveness after it reviews in accordance with international treaties concluded or acceded to by the People's Republic of China, or in accordance with the principle of reciprocity and decides that they do not violate the basic principles of the laws of the People's Republic of China, or national sovereignty, security, social and public interests." According to the Treaty

Between the People's Republic of China and the Republic of Singapore on Judicial Assistance in Civil and Commercial Matters, the scope of legal assistance between two countries does not include recognition and enforcement of the judgments and rulings by the courts, and thus the application of Kolmar should be rejected in line with the *Civil Procedure Law*.

Upon examination, Nanjing Intermediate People's Court finds that the High Court of the Republic of Singapore issued the Civil Judgment No. 013 on October 22, 2015, ordering SUTEX to pay Kolmar USD 350, 000, plus interest at an annual rate of 5.33% from the date of issuance of the writ of summons to the date of Judgment, and a legal fee of SGD 4, 137. 90. SUTEX admitted in the hearing of this case that it was legitimately summoned by the High Court of the Republic of Singapore, but did not participate in the court trial, and it also received the relevant judgment. Nanjing Intermediate People's Court also finds that in January 2014, the High Court of the Republic of Singapore issued the Judgment [2014] SGHC No. 16, which was to recognize and enforce the Judgment made by the Intermediate People's Court of Suzhou, Jiangsu Province, the People's Republie of China.

In the view of Nanjing Intermediate People's Court, in accordance with Article 282 of the *Civil Procedure Law*, which provides that "the people's court shall, for applications or requests for recognition or enforcement of legally effective judgments and rulings by foreign courts, rule to recognize their effectiveness after it reviews in accordance with international treaties concluded or acceded to by the People's Republic of China, or in accordance with the principle of reciprocity, hold that they do not violate the basic principles of the laws of the People's Republic of China, or national sovereignty, security, social and public interests, and if and when enforcement is needed, issue enforcement orders in accordance with relevant provisions of this Law. The court shall refuse to recognize or enforce the relevant judgments or rulings by foreign courts if and when it finds the judgments or rulings by foreign courts violate the basic principles of the law of the People's Republic of China, or national sovereignty, security, social and public interests." The Civil Judgment was made by the High Court of the Republic of Singapore, and there is no international treaty between the People's Republic of China and the Republic of Singapore in respect of mutual recognition and enforcement of legally effective judgments and rulings. However, in January 2014, the High Court of the Republic of Singapore enforced the Judgment by the Intermediate People's Court of Suzhou, Jiangsu Province, the People's Republie of China, and based upon the principle of reciprocity, courts in our country may recognize and enforce civil judgments by eligible Singapore courts. Upon the examination, Nanjing Intermediate People's Court found that the relevant civil judgment did not violate the basic principles of the law of the People's Republic of China, nor national sovereignty, security, social and public interests. In conclusion, in accordance with Article 282 of the *Civil Procedure Law*, Nanjing Intermediate People's Court rules as follows:

Nanjing Intermediate People's Court shall recognize and enforce the No. 013 Civil Judgment by the High Court of the Republic of Singapore on October 22, 2015.

The application fee of RMB 80 shall be borne by SUTEX.

Presiding Judge: WANG Sheng

Judge: JIANG Xin

Judge: LU Hongxia

December 9, 2016

Court Clerk: YANG Wenyan

浙江隆达不锈钢有限公司
诉
A. P. 穆勒-马士基有限公司
海上货物运输合同纠纷案

——托运人变更运输合同的权利及合理规制

【裁判要旨】

在海上货物运输合同中,依据《中华人民共和国合同法》(以下简称《合同法》)第 308 条①的规定,承运人将货物交付收货人之前,托运人享有要求变更运输合同的权利,但双方当事人仍要遵循《合同法》第 5 条②规定的公平原则确定各方的权利和义务。托运人行使此项权利时,承运人也可相应行使一定的抗辩权。如果变更海上货物运输合同难以实现或者将严重影响承运人正常营运,承运人可以拒绝托运人改港或者退运的请求,但应当及时通知托运人不能变更的原因。

【专家点评】*

该案是我国第一起海上货物运输合同中涉及控制权纠纷的案件,极具典型意义。

本案承运人 A. P. 穆勒-马士基有限公司(以下简称马士基公司)承运

---

① 现为《民法典》合同编的相关规定。

② 现为《民法典》总则编的相关规定。

* 撰写人:司玉琢,大连海事大学教授、博士研究生导师。

托运人浙江隆达不锈钢有限公司(以下简称隆达公司)一批不锈钢产品,从宁波运至科隆坡,船到目的地前两天左右,托运人要求改港或者退运,承运人回复称改港或者退运不具可操作性,托运人主张承运人未按其指示改港或退运,应承担违约责任。中华人民共和国最高人民法院组成合议庭再审此案,准确适用法律,对此案件作出了公正判决。

一、隆达公司作为托运人有权向承运人发出改港或者退运的指示

《中华人民共和国海商法》(以下简称《海商法》)尚未引入货物控制权制度,《合同法》第 308 条[①]虽未明确是控制权条款,但包含货物控制权的内容,在特别法《海商法》没有规定的情况下,托运人依据一般法《合同法》第 308 条[②]之规定,主张变更卸货港或者退运货物是有法律依据的。再审合议庭认为:“隆达公司在涉案货物海上运输途中请求承运人改港或者退运,因海商法未就航程中托运人请求变更运输合同的权利予以规定,故本案适用《合同法》的有关规定。依据《合同法》第三百零八条的规定,在承运人将货物交付收货人之前,托运人享有请求变更运输合同的权利。”这一判决表明,在承运人责任期间内,根据《合同法》第 308 条[③]规定,托运人享有变更运输合同的权利,可要求承运人变更交货港或者退运货物。

二、马士基公司作为承运人不应无条件地执行托运人变更合同的指示

中国《合同法》仅设一个条款尚不能形成运输合同变更的完整制度,其中设定限制合同变更权的条件是制约托运人滥用此项权利的重要规定。根据国际班轮海上货物运输的实际情况,托运人在依据《合同法》第 308 条[④]规定主张变更运输合同时,应不得致使海上货物运输的各利益方的利益显失公平,不得妨碍承运人履行对其他托运人应承担的合同义务,不得剥夺承运人对托运人主张合同变更权利的抗辩权。如果托运人发出的变更合同的指示不能合理执行,干扰了承运人的正常营运,承运人应有权拒绝执行。因为

① 现为《民法典》合同编的相关规定。
② 现为《民法典》合同编的相关规定。
③ 现为《民法典》合同编的相关规定。
④ 现为《民法典》合同编的相关规定。

《合同法》“运输合同”一章[①]没有规定合同变更权的限制性条件，再审合议庭适用《合同法》总则[②]的一般规定，即公平原则，弥补《合同法》第 308 条[③]规定的缺失。再审合议庭认为，托运人虽享有请求变更运输合同的权利，“但双方当事人仍要遵循《合同法》第五条规定的公平原则确定各方的权利和义务”。如果要求承运人无条件服从托运人变更运输合同的请求，则显失公平。为合理平衡海上货物运输合同中各方当事人的利益，托运人可以行使请求变更运输合同权利，承运人也应享有相应的抗辩权。如果变更运输合同难以实现或者将严重影响承运人正常营运，承运人可以拒绝托运人改港或者退运的请求，但应当及时通知托运人不能执行的原因。

三、马士基公司无须赔偿隆达公司的货损

马士基公司作为承运人拒绝执行隆达公司改港或返还货物的指示，于 2014 年 7 月 13 日将货物运抵目的港，这批货物在之后长达 8 个月的时间里，因隆达公司未曾提货而被海关拍卖。马士基公司拒绝执行隆达公司改港或返还货物的指示的抗辩已经得到合议庭的支持，也就是说，马士基公司拒绝执行隆达公司变更合同的指示并无过错，后来货物发生的损失与承运人拒绝执行托运人变更合同的指示没有关联性，已转变为货物到港后无人提货的法律关系，即承运人对货物的处置权问题，《海商法》第 86 条规定：“在卸货港无人提取货物或者收货人迟延、拒绝提取货物的，船长可以将货物卸在仓库或者其他适当场所，由此产生的费用和风险由收货人承担。”再审合议庭认为，马士基公司将涉案货物运至目的港后，因无人提货，将货物卸载至目的港码头符合前述法律规定。马士基公司卸货后所产生的费用和风险应由收货人承担，马士基公司作为承运人无须承担相应的风险。至此，这起运输合同纠纷案以托运人主张合同变更权开始，以承运人行使货物处置权告终。

---

① 现为《民法典》合同编的相关规定。
② 现为《民法典》总则编的相关规定。
③ 现为《民法典》合同编的相关规定。

四、本案的启示：准确适用法律是保证本案公正判决的基础

本案是一起具有涉外因素的海上货物运输合同纠纷案。双方当事人在诉讼中一致选择适用中华人民共和国法律，根据《中华人民共和国涉外民事关系法律适用法》第3条的规定，再审合议庭适用中华人民共和国法律审理了本案。中国《海商法》作为调整海上运输关系、船舶关系的特别法，应优先适用于本案。《海商法》没有规定的，适用《合同法》①等相关法律的规定。鉴于《海商法》对于运输合同的变更未作规定，合议庭适用《合同法》第308条②："在承运人将货物交付收货人之前，托运人可以要求承运人中止运输、返还货物、变更到达地或者将货物交给其他收货人，但是应当赔偿承运人因此受到的损失。"这是有关货物控制权的规定。

为了保持海上运输法与贸易法的衔接，保护买卖合同的卖方，同时也因应电子商务发展的需要，非海运的运输公约早已引入了有关货物控制权和控制方的专门规定，③涉及海运的《联合国全程或部分海上国际货物运输合同公约》（以下称《鹿特丹规则》）也开始规定控制权和控制方。④ 由此可见，无论是海运还是非海运的国际货物运输公约都有关于货物控制权的规定。

所谓控制权是指货物到达目的地之前请求变更收货人、货物交付地，以及其他不构成对运输合同变更的指示和修改此种指示的权利。《合同法》第308条⑤规定的"中止运输、返还货物"已超出了通常货物控制权的范围，如果机械地执行"返还货物"的规定，将对海上货物运输的承运人产生不公。再审合议庭并没有以返还货物会对承运人不利，违反公平原则，判决承运人胜诉，而是以《合同法》第308条⑥没有规定托运人行使控制权的限制条

---

① 现为《民法典》合同编的相关规定。

② 现为《民法典》合同编的相关规定。

③ 参见《统一国际航空运输某些规则的公约》（1999年《蒙特利尔公约》）第12条，《国际公路货物运输合同公约》（CMR）第12条、第14—16条，《国际铁路货物运输合同统一规则》（CIM－COTIF）第18—22条以及《内河水道货物运输合同布达佩斯公约》（CMNI）第14—15条之规定。

④ 参见《鹿特丹规则》第10章第50—56条之规定。

⑤ 现为《民法典》合同编的相关规定。

⑥ 现为《民法典》合同编的相关规定。

件,即没有规定承运人对控制权的抗辩权,判决需要《合同法》第 5 条①的公平原则作补充。这样判决既符合法律的规定,又合理地平衡了承托双方的利益。《鹿特丹规则》第 10 章就控制权的权利主体、控制权的范围、行使控制权的期间、行使控制权的限制条件、违反控制权规定的法律后果以及为行使控制权提供担保等作出全面完整的规定,这为未来中国海商法的完善提供了借鉴。

【裁判文书】

中华人民共和国最高人民法院
民事判决书

(2017)最高法民再 412 号

再审申请人(一审被告、二审被上诉人):A. P. 穆勒-马士基有限公司(A. P. Moller-Maersk A/S)。住所地:丹麦王国哥本哈根 * * * *,埃斯普兰那登 * * 号(Esplanaden * *, * * * * Copenhagen K, Denmark)。

代表人:汉尼伯格(Henneberg)、克加文科(Kjarvik),该公司授权代表。

委托代理人:曹某,上海市 * * * 律师事务所律师。

委托代理人:陈某某,上海市 * * * 律师事务所律师。

被申请人(一审原告、二审上诉人):浙江隆达不锈钢有限公司。住所地:中华人民共和国浙江省丽水市松阳县 * * 街道 * * 大道 * * * 号。

法定代表人:项某某,该公司总经理。

委托代理人:袁某,北京 * * (上海)律师事务所律师。

委托代理人:温某,北京 * * (宁波)律师事务所律师。

再审申请人 A. P. 穆勒-马士基有限公司(以下简称马士基公司)因与

① 现为《民法典》合同编的相关规定。

被申请人浙江隆达不锈钢有限公司(以下简称隆达公司)海上货物运输合同纠纷一案,不服浙江省高级人民法院(以下简称二审法院)作出的(2016)浙民终222号民事判决,向本院申请再审。本院于2017年10月31日作出(2017)最高法民申3552号民事裁定提审本案,并依法组成合议庭于2017年12月20日公开开庭审理了本案。马士基公司委托代理人曹某、陈某某,隆达公司委托代理人袁某到庭参加诉讼。本案现已审理终结。

隆达公司向宁波海事法院(以下简称一审法院)诉称:2014年6月,隆达公司出口一批价值366918.97美元的不锈钢无缝产品,从中国宁波港运至斯里兰卡民主社会主义共和国(以下简称斯里兰卡)科伦坡(COLOMBO)港。同年6月28日,涉案货物装至马士基公司所属的“GUNDE MAERSK”船上出运。货物到达目的港后,因收货人未支付货款,隆达公司向马士基公司提出退运要求,马士基公司也同意安排退运,但马士基公司至今未能安排退运,并声称涉案货物在目的港已被拍卖但未提供任何文件予以证明。马士基公司未尽到妥善保管货物的义务或已实施无单放货,导致隆达公司提单物权落空,应向隆达公司承担赔偿责任。请求判令马士基公司向隆达公司赔偿货物损失366918.97美元(按2015年5月29日美元兑人民币汇率1:6.2002折合人民币2274971元)及利息(按中国人民银行同期贷款利率自2015年5月29日起计算至实际履行之日止)。

一审法院查明:

2014年6月,隆达公司由中国宁波港出口一批不锈钢无缝产品至科伦坡,货物报关价值为366918.97美元。隆达公司通过货代向马士基公司订舱,涉案货物于同年6月28日装载于4个集装箱内装船出运,出运时隆达公司要求做电放处理。2014年7月9日,隆达公司通过货代向马士基公司发邮件称,发现货物运错目的地要求改港或者退运。马士基公司于同日回复,因货物距抵达目的港不足2天,无法安排改港,如需退运则需与目的港确认后回复。次日,隆达公司的货代询问货物退运是否可以原船带回,马士基公司于当日回复“原船退回不具有操作性,货物在目的港卸货后,需要由现在的收货人在目的港清关后,再向当地海关申请退运。海关批准后,才可以安排退运事宜”。涉案货物于 2014 年 7 月 12 日左右到达目的港。马士基公司应隆达公司的要求于 2015 年 1 月 29 日向其签发了编号 603386880 的全套正本提单。根据提单记载,托运人为隆达公司,收货人及通知方均为 VENUS STEEL PVT LTD,起运港中国宁波,卸货港科伦坡。2015 年 5 月 18 日,隆达公司向货代发邮件称决定向马士基公司申请退运。次日,隆达公司向马士基公司发邮件表示已按马士基公司要求申请退运。马士基公司随后告知隆达公司涉案货物已被拍卖。

一审法院另认定,涉案货物在 2015 年 3 月 13 日被目的港海关拍卖。

一审法院认为:

本案系具有涉外因素的海上货物运输合同纠纷。因双方当事人明确同意适用中国法,按照《中华人民共和国涉外民事关系法律适用法》(以下简称《涉外民事关系法律适用法》)第三条的规定,本案适用中华人民共和国法律。

隆达公司系涉案货物托运人且持有全套正本提单,马士基公司系承运人,双方当事人之间成立海上货物运输合同法律关系。货物到港前,隆达公司要求马士基公司改港或者退运,但马士基公司已明确告知货物距抵达目的港不足 2 天,无法安排改港或退运。货物抵港后,隆达公司作为涉案货物的托运人和正本提单持有人,理应及时关注货物状态并采取有效措施,但直至货物被海关拍卖长达半年时间内,隆达公司均未采取自行提货等有效措施,相应货损风险应由隆达公司承担。隆达公司主张马士基公司未按指示改港或者退运,违反法定义务,但证据与理由不足,不予采信。一审法院依据《涉外民事关系法律适用法》第三条,《最高人民法院关于审理无正本提单交付货物案件适用法律若干问题的规定》(以下简称《无单放货司法解释》)第八条,《中华人民共和国民事诉讼法》(以下简称《民事诉讼法》)第二十七条、第二百五十九条的规定,判决:驳回隆达公司的诉讼请求。一审案件受理费人民币 25000 元,由隆达公司负担。

隆达公司不服一审判决提起上诉，请求二审法院撤销一审判决，改判支持隆达公司一审诉讼请求。

二审法院对一审判决认定的事实予以确认。另查明：隆达公司在马士基公司告知需由原收货人在目的港办理清关才可以安排退运后，于2014年7月10日又提出“这个货要安排退运，就是因为清关清不了，所以才退回宁波的，有其他办法吗”。此后，马士基公司再未回复邮件。

二审法院认为：

双方当事人对隆达公司是涉案提单项下货物的托运人、马士基公司是承运人，双方之间成立海上货物运输合同法律关系均无异议。本案争议的焦点是隆达公司是否享有改港或者退运的权利以及马士基公司对隆达公司的涉案货损是否应当承担赔偿责任。

（一）隆达公司是否享有改港或者退运的权利。隆达公司系涉案货物托运人，持有全套正本提单，对涉案货物享有控制权。《中华人民共和国合同法》（以下简称《合同法》）第三百零八条规定：“在承运人将货物交付收货人之前，托运人可以要求承运人中止运输、返还货物、变更到达地或者将货物交给其他收货人，但应当赔偿承运人因此受到的损失。”《无单放货司法解释》第九条规定：“承运人按照记名提单托运人的要求中止运输、返还货物、变更到达地或者将货物交给其他收货人，持有记名提单的收货人要求承运人承担无正本提单交付货物民事责任的，人民法院不予支持。”根据双方当事人确认的事实，涉案货物于2014年7月12日到达目的港，在此之前的7月9日，隆达公司通过货代向马士基公司申请改港或者退运。依据以上法律规定，隆达公司作为涉案货物的托运人，在货物交付收货人之前，可以要求承运人马士基公司改港或者退运。若马士基公司采取措施配合隆达公司变更或解除合同，依法可向隆达公司主张相应损失。因此，隆达公司上诉提出其享有改港及退运的权利有相应法律依据，二审法院予以支持。

（二）马士基公司对隆达公司的涉案货损是否应当承担赔偿责任。马士基公司以其已尽到管货义务及货物被海关拍卖属于免责事项为由，认为其无需对隆达公司涉案货损承担赔偿责任。《中华人民共和国海商法》(以下简称《海商法》)第四十六条规定:“承运人对集装箱装运的货物的责任期间,是指从装货港接收货物时起至卸货港交付货物时止,货物处于承运人掌管之下的全部期间。”该法第四十八条规定了承运人妥善管理货物的义务。因此,从装货港接收货物时起至卸货港交付货物止,承运人应尽到谨慎管货的义务。马士基公司于 2014 年 7 月 9 日收到隆达公司改港或者退运的要求后,当即表示不能改港。次日,隆达公司提出“想要做原船带回的那种退运”,马士基公司回复称“原船带回不具有操作性”,退运需先清关再向海关申请才可安排。隆达公司立即重申“这个货要安排退运”,并询问“有其他办法吗”。从隆达公司的邮件内容看,应认定隆达公司于7 月 10 日已明确提出退运的要求。但是,马士基公司对隆达公司明确要求办理退运的邮件未予回复,卸货后也未通知隆达公司自行处理或安排退运事宜,致使涉案货物处于无人看管状态。对于涉案货物于 2015 年 3 月 13 日在目的港被拍卖的相关情况,马士基公司直到 2015 年 5 月都未能了解并通知到隆达公司。因此,不应认定马士基公司已尽到海商法规定的谨慎管货义务,对涉案货损应承担相应赔偿责任。隆达公司作为涉案货物的权利人,在阻止承运人向提单记载的收货人交货后,仍应积极关注货物到港后的状态,在合理时间内对货物进行处置。隆达公司在货物到港 10 个月后才再次联系马士基公司,对涉案货损也应承担责任。虽然《海商法》第五十一条规定货损是由于“政府或者主管部门的行为、检疫限制或者司法扣押”等原因造成的,承运人不负赔偿责任,但本案拍卖行为发生在货物到港八个月之后,马士基公司有足够时间通知隆达公司自行处置货物,隆达公司作为托运人亦有足够的时间了解货物状态并对货物进行处置。本案拍卖行为并非必然发生,故不属于《海商法》规定的免责事由。马士基公司主张免责的理由不能成立,不予支持。

综上,在隆达公司提出退运要求后,马士基公司既未明确拒绝安排退运,也未通知隆达公司自行处理,对涉案货损应承担相应的赔偿责任,酌定责任比例为 50%。隆达公司系涉案货物托运人,虽然依法可以在货物交付收货人之前要求马士基公司改港或者退运，但在马士基公司拒绝改港且对退运事宜未作出明确答复时，未积极采取有效措施防止损失发生，对本案货损也应承担责任。马士基公司未能举证拍卖款的金额且在诉讼中确认未能收回拍卖款，应推定涉案货物全损。隆达公司一审中提交了涉案货物报关单，证明货物价值为 366918.97 美元。故马士基公司应赔偿隆达公司 366918.97 美元×50%＝183459.49 美元。二审法院依照《合同法》第三百零八条、《民事诉讼法》第一百七十条第一款第二项之规定，判决：（一）撤销一审判决；（二）马士基公司于判决送达之日起十日内赔偿隆达公司货物损失 183459.49 美元及利息；（三）驳回隆达公司其他诉讼请求。本案一、二审案件受理费各人民币 25000 元，由隆达公司各负担 12500 元，由马士基公司各负担 12500 元。

马士基公司不服二审判决，申请再审称：（一）二审判决认定马士基公司应配合隆达公司退运或者改港系适用法律错误。第一，二审判决适用《合同法》《无单放货司法解释》不恰当。马士基公司是否有配合隆达公司改港或者退运的义务，应根据斯里兰卡当地的法律规定。依据斯里兰卡海关条例的相关规定，涉案货物客观不能转港和退运，只能先办理进口清关手续再退运，且办理进口清关手续系进口方的义务。马士基公司作为承运人，无法协助也没有能力办理进口清关手续。二审判决苛责马士基公司应进一步配合隆达公司办理进口清关手续，于法无据也违背航运实践和惯例。第二，马士基公司已将涉案货物运抵目的港，海上货物运输合同项下的义务已经履行完毕。如果托运人选择回运，应另行订舱并建立新的海上货物运输合同关系，否则，承运人不负有当然的回运义务。第三，即使隆达公司行使的是中途停运权，该权利系基于国际货物买卖合同的不安抗辩权，并不必然约束作为运输合同当事人的承运人。且在班轮运输的方式下，托运人行使中途停运权将侵害同船其他货主的权益，也不具有实际可操作性，承运人没有必须配合变更或解除原海上运输合同关系的义务。（二）二审判决认定马士基公司未尽谨慎管货义务缺乏事实及法律依据。涉案货物抵达目的港后，马士基公司已通知隆达公司，隆达公司即负有及时了解货物状态并提领货物的义务。隆达公司持有全套正本提单，有义务处置该货物。隆达公司应承担未尽以上义务而导致货物灭失的风险。二审判决加重了承运人的通知义务，显失公平。涉案货物卸载于目的港码头后堆存于港区内的堆场，由港区实际占有保管并收取堆存费。承运人此时的义务在于提供完好的集装箱装载货物，马士基公司已经履行了该项谨慎管货的义务。（三）二审判决认定马士基公司应承担赔偿责任错误。《无单放货司法解释》第八条规定，承运到港的货物超过法律规定期限无人向海关申报，被海关提取并依法变卖处理，或者法院依法裁定拍卖承运人留置的货物，承运人主张免除交付货物责任的，人民法院应予支持。马士基公司已告知隆达公司涉案货物须办理清关手续后方可退运，隆达公司完全可以委托其目的港代理完成清关手续并另行订舱退运，但隆达公司对滞港货物置之不理八个月之久，导致货物被目的港海关拍卖，隆达公司应该自行承担损失。《海商法》第五十一条第一款第五项规定，政府或者主管部门的行为、检疫限制或者司法扣押造成的货损，承运人可以免责。海关拍卖涉案货物的行为属于政府行为，马士基公司作为承运人可以免责。综上，请求撤销二审判决，驳回隆达公司的全部诉讼请求，本案诉讼费用由隆达公司承担。

隆达公司答辩称：（一）托运人在海上运输合同中可以行使要求改港或者退运的权利。二审判决适用《合同法》第三百零八条、《无单放货司法解释》第九条正确。《合同法》和《海商法》是一般法和特别法的关系。海商法未规定的，应当适用合同法。《无单放货司法解释》第九条赋予托运人中途停运权，源于《合同法》第三百零八条的规定。司法实践中也有大量支持托运人行使中途停运权的案例。马士基公司关于无法改港或者退运的抗辩缺乏依据。马士基公司至今仍未尽到目的港外国法的查明义务，该公司引用的斯里兰卡海关条例的规定无法核实。（二）马士基公司未尽到谨慎管货的义务。依据《海商法》第四十六条的规定，承运人在将货物交付于收货人之前都要尽到保管、照料货物的义务。既然目的港无人提货时托运人要支付滞箱费,承运人也应该承担对应的管货义务。马士基公司未完成货物交付,在其责任期间,涉案货物被拍卖灭失,马士基公司应当承担赔偿责任。马士基公司于2015年1月签发提单也表明,此时涉案货物还在马士基公司的控制之下。(三)本案不能适用《海商法》第五十一条免责条款。马士基公司至今未提交任何证据证明涉案货物系目的港海关依职权拍卖的,应承担举证不能的后果。拍卖行为发生在货物到港8个月之后,马士基公司有足够的时间通知隆达公司处置货物。拍卖行为并非必然发生,本案不构成《海商法》规定的免责事项。综上,请求维持二审判决。

本案再审期间,双方当事人均未提交新的证据材料。对于原审认定的事实,隆达公司无异议。马士基公司认为二审判决没有认定其员工在货物运抵目的港后继续与隆达公司进行联系的事实,认定涉案货物在卸货港处于无人看管的状态与事实不符。本院经审理,对二审判决认定的事实予以确认。

本院认为:

本案是具有涉外因素的海上货物运输合同纠纷。双方当事人在诉讼中一致选择适用中华人民共和国法律,根据《涉外民事关系法律适用法》第三条的规定,本院适用中华人民共和国法律审理本案。海商法作为调整海上运输关系、船舶关系的特别法,应优先适用。海商法没有规定的,适用合同法等相关法律的规定。根据马士基公司的再审申请和隆达公司的答辩意见,本案的争议焦点为:(一)马士基公司应否为涉案货物安排改港或者退运;(二)马士基公司是否应当赔偿隆达公司的货损。

(一)马士基公司应否为涉案货物安排改港或者退运

隆达公司在涉案货物海上运输途中请求承运人改港或者退运,因海商法未就航程中托运人请求变更运输合同的权利予以规定,故本案适用《合同法》的有关规定。依据《合同法》第三百零八条的规定,在承运人将货物交付收货人之前,托运人享有请求变更运输合同的权利,但双方当事人仍要遵循《合同法》第五条规定的公平原则确定各方的权利和义务。海上货物运输具有运输量大、航程预先拟定、航线相对固定等特殊性,托运人要求改港或者退运的请求有时不仅不易操作,还会妨碍承运人的正常营运或者给其他货物的托运人或收货人带来较大损害。在此情形下,如果要求承运人无条件服从托运人变更运输合同的请求,显失公平。因此,在海上货物运输合同下,托运人并非可以无限制地行使请求变更运输合同的权利,承运人也并非在任何情况下都应无条件服从托运人请求变更运输合同的指示。为合理平衡海上货物运输合同中各方当事人的利益,在托运人可以行使请求变更运输合同权利的同时,承运人也相应地享有一定的抗辩权。如果变更运输合同难以实现或者将严重影响承运人正常营运,承运人可以拒绝托运人改港或者退运的请求,但应当及时通知托运人不能执行的原因。涉案运输方式为国际班轮运输,载货船舶除运载隆达公司托运的 4 个集装箱外,还运载了其他货主托运的众多货物。涉案货物于 2014 年 6 月 28 日装船出运,7 月 12 日左右到达目的港,而隆达公司于 7 月 9 日才要求马士基公司改港或者退运。在承运船舶距离到达目的港只有两三天时间的情形下,马士基公司主张由于航程等原因无法安排改港、原船退回不具有操作性,客观合理。一审判决支持马士基公司的上述主张,符合公平原则,本院予以维持。

(二)马士基公司是否应当赔偿隆达公司的货损

《海商法》第八十六条规定:“在卸货港无人提取货物或者收货人迟延、拒绝提取货物的,船长可以将货物卸在仓库或者其他适当场所,由此产生的费用和风险由收货人承担。”马士基公司将涉案货物运至目的港后,因无人提货,将货物卸载至目的港码头符合前述法律规定。马士基公司于 2014 年 7 月 9 日通过邮件回复隆达公司距抵达目的港不足 2 日。隆达公司已了解货物到港的大体时间并明知涉案货物在目的港无人提货,但在长达 8 个月的时间里未采取措施处理涉案货物致其被海关拍卖。隆达公司虽主张马士基公司未尽到谨慎管货义务,但并未举证证明马士基公司存在管货不当的事实。隆达公司的该项主张缺乏依据,本院不予支持。依据《海商法》第八十六条的规定,马士基公司卸货后所产生的费用和风险应由收货人承担,马士基公司作为承运人无需承担相应的风险。二审判决判令马士基公司承担涉案货物一半的损失，缺乏事实依据，适用法律不当，应予纠正。一审判决适用《无单放货司法解释》的规定，与本案事实及争议的法律问题不符，应予纠正，但判决结果正确，可予维持。

综上，本院依照《中华人民共和国合同法》第五条、第三百零八条，《中华人民共和国海商法》第四十八条、第八十六条，《中华人民共和国民事诉讼法》第二百零七条第一款、第一百七十条第一款第二项的规定，判决如下：

一、撤销浙江省高级人民法院（2016）浙民终222号判决；

二、维持宁波海事法院（2015）甬海法商初字第534号判决。

一、二审案件受理费各人民币25000元，均由浙江隆达不锈钢有限公司承担。

本判决为终审判决。

审 判 长　王淑梅
审 判 员　余晓汉
审 判 员　黄西武
二〇一七年十二月二十九日
法官助理　赵　珂
书 记 员　陈　晖

Zhejiang Longda Stainless Steel Co, Ltd

v.

A. P. Moller-Maersk A/S

for the Dispute over a Contract for Carriage of Goods by Sea

—A Shipper's Right to Change or Modify Transport Contracts and Reasonable Institutions

Holding

For a contract for carriage of goods by sea, in accordance with the Article 308 of the *Contract Law of the People's Republic of China* [1] (hereinafter referred to as *Contract Law*), a shipper shall, before the delivery of the goods under a contract by the carrier to the consignee, have the right to request to modify the said contract, but both Parties hereto shall redefine the rights and obligations of the Parties following the principle of fairness as provided in Article 5 of the *Contract Law*. [2] If the shipper exercises this right, the carrier is entitled to exercise the right to defense accordingly. If such modification renders performance of the modified contract impossible or may have material impacts on the normal operation of the carrier, the carrier shall have the right to refuse the shipper's request to have the goods under the contract rerouted or shipped back, with a notification without delay to the shipper stating the reasons for such refusal.

---

① See related provisions in Part Ⅲ: Contracts of the *Civil Code*.

② See related provisions in Part Ⅲ: Contracts of the *Civil Code*.

Commentary*

This case is the first one involving the dispute over the right to control under a contract for carriage of goods by sea in China, which is of significance.

The carrier of this case, A. P. Moller-Maersk A/S (hereinafter referred to as Maersk), transported a batch of stainless steel products consigned by the shipper Zhejiang Longda Stainless Steel Co, Ltd (hereinafter referred to as Longda) from Ningbo to Colombo. Around two (2) days before the arrival of the said goods at the port of destination, the shipper requested to change the port or ship back, and the carrier replied it was impracticable. The shipper asserted that the carrier should be held liable for a breach of contract for its failure to follow the instruction to change the port or ship back. The Supreme People's Court of the People's Republic of China formed a collegial panel to reopen this case, accurately applied laws, and made an impartial judgment on the dispute.

1. Longda as the Shipper Had the Right to Instruct the Carrier to Change the Port or Ship back

There is no relevant regulation on the right to control of goods in the *Maritime Law of the People's Republic of China* (hereinafter referred to as *Maritime Law*). Despite not being expressed explicitly as the clause of the right to control, Article 308 of the *Contract Law* ① has contents on the right to control. In the absence of relevant provisions in a special law, namely the *Maritime Law* in this case, the shipper's request to change the port or ship back according to related provisions of a general law, namely Article 308 of the

* Authors: SI Yuzhuo, Professor and Doctoral Supervisor, Dalian Maritime University.

① See related provisions in Part Ⅲ: Contracts of the *Civil Code*.

Contract Law ① in this case, had a legal basis. In the view of the case-reopening collegial panel, "as far as Longda's request to the carrier to change the port or ship back the goods is concerned, given there are no provisions in the *Maritime Law* on the right of a shipper to request to change a contract for carriage of goods by sea during the voyage. Therefore, relevant provisions of the *Contract Law* apply to this case. Under Article 308 ② thereof, a shipper has the right to request to change a contract for carriage of goods by sea prior to the delivery by a carrier of the goods to a consignee". This Judgment demonstrated that, according to Article 308 of the *Contract Law*, ③ a shipper is entitled to change a contract for carriage of goods during the period of responsibility of a carrier, and may request the carrier to change the port of delivery or ship back goods.

2. Maersk as the Carrier Should Not Unconditionally Implement the Shipper's Request to Change the Contract

Only one provision relates to the right to change transport contracts in the *Contract Law*, and thus fails to establish a complete set of regulation in the change of transport contracts. The conditions for the change of transport contracts in the provision are the vital basis for constraining the possible abuse of such right by a shipper. In the light of the actual situation of the carriage of goods by international liners, a shipper, according to Article 308 of the *Contract Law*, ④ when claiming to change transport contracts shall not lead to obvious injustice among all the stakeholders of the carriage of goods by sea, hinder the carrier's from performing its contractual obligations to other shippers,

---

① See related provisions in Part Ⅲ: Contracts of the *Civil Code*.

② See related provisions in Part Ⅲ: Contracts of the *Civil Code*.

③ See related provisions in Part Ⅲ: Contracts of the *Civil Code*.

④ See related provisions in Part Ⅲ: Contracts of the *Civil Code*.

and deprive the carrier of the right to defense against the shipper's such right of claiming to change the contracts. If and when a shipper's instruction to change transport contracts may not be reasonably operable or may hinder the normal operation of the carrier, the carrier shall have the right to refuse to perform. Now that there are no restrictive conditions for the right to change transport contracts in the chapter of Transport Contract under the *Contract Law*,[①] the case-reopening collegial panel applied the general provisions, namely the principle of fairness, in the chapter of General Rules under the *Contract Law*,[②] making up the absence of provisions in Article 308 of the *Contract Law*.[③] In the view of the case-reopening collegial panel, notwithstanding a shipper had the right to request to change transport contracts, "... but both Parties to the said contract shall determine the rights and obligations of each Party following the principle of fairness as provided in Article 5 of the *Contract Law*". It would be obviously unfair to require a carrier to unconditionally obey the shipper's request to change a transport contract. To strike a reasonable balance between the interests of all Parties to a contract for carriage of goods by sea, whereas a shipper may exercise the right to request for change of a contract, the carrier shall also have the corresponding right to defense. If and when the change may render the corresponding performance of the changed contract impossible or may have serious impacts on the normal operation of the carrier, the carrier shall have the right to refuse the shipper's request to change the port or ship back with a written notification without delay to the shipper stating the reasons for such refusal.

---

① See related provisions in Part Ⅲ: Contracts of the *Civil Code*.

② See related provisions in Part Ⅲ: Contracts of the *Civil Code*.

③ See related provisions in Part Ⅲ: Contracts of the *Civil Code*.

3. Maersk Did Not Have to be Held Liable for the Damage of the Goods to Longda

Having refused to follow Longda's instruction to change the port of destination or ship back the goods, the carrier Maersk shipped goods at the port of destination on July 13, 2014, and this batch of goods were auctioned by the customs after eight (8) months since Longda did not take delivery of goods. Maersk's defense on its refusal to follow Longda's instruction was supported by the case-reopening collegial panel. That is to say, Maersk did nothing wrong in refusing to carry out Longda's instruction of changing the port or shipping back. The subsequent loss of goods had no relation with the carrier's refusal to carry out the shipper's instruction of changing the contract, and evolved into a new legal relationship that no one took delivery of goods after they arrived at the port of destination, namely the carrier's right to dispose of goods. Article 86 of the *Maritime Law* provides that if and when no one takes delivery of goods at the port of discharge or the consignee delays or refuses to take delivery of goods, the ship master may store the goods at a warehouse or other appropriate place, and all the costs and risks arising therefrom shall be borne by the consignee. In the view of the case-reopening collegial panel, Maersk, after transporting goods involved in the case to the port of destination, unloaded goods at the warehouse of the port of destination because no one took delivery of goods, which met the foregoing legal provision. All the costs and risks after the discharge of goods at the port of destination shall be borne by the consignee. So in this case, Maersk as the carrier shall not be held liable for any costs and risks incurred thereafter. Thus, this dispute over a transport contract started with the shipper claiming the right to change the contract and ended with the carrier exercising the right to dispose of goods.

4. Inspiration from this Case: Accurate Application of Laws is the Basis of Ensuring an Impartial Judgment in this Case

This case is a dispute over the contract for carriage of goods by sea with foreign factors. Now that both Parties to the dispute unanimously chose to apply the law of the People's Republic of China, according to the provisions of Article 3 of the *Law of the People's Republic of China on the Application of Laws Concerning Foreign-related Civil Relations*, and the case-reopening collegial panel applied the law of the People's Republic of China to hear this case. China's *Maritime Law* as a special law governing the relations arising from and/or pertaining to maritime transport and ocean vessels shall prevail, and where there are no provisions therein, provisions of relevant laws, including the *Contract Law*, ① shall apply. Given there are no provisions in the *Maritime Law* on the alteration of transport contracts, therefore, the case-reopening collegial panel applied Article 308 of the *Contract Law*. ② "Prior to delivery by a carrier of goods under a contract to the consignee, the shipper may require the carrier to suspend the shipment, ship back, change the place of arrival, or deliver to other consignees, but shall compensate the carrier for the loss he/she suffered". This is the relevant provision on the right to control of goods.

To maintain the connection between maritime transport laws and trade laws and protect sellers in sales and purchases contracts as well as to meet the needs of a booming e-commerce, non-maritime transport conventions had already introduced some special provisions on the right to control of goods and the

① See related provisions in Part Ⅲ: Contracts of the *Civil Code*.

② See related provisions in Part Ⅲ: Contracts of the *Civil Code*.

controlling parties, [1] and the *United Nations Convention on Contacts for the International Carriage of Goods Wholly or Partly by Sea* (hereinafter referred to as *Rotterdam Rules*) involving maritime transport also began to stipulate the right to control and the controlling party. [2] Thus, it can be seen that both maritime and non-maritime conventions on international carriage of goods have related provisions on the right to control of goods.

The right to control means the right to change consignees and/or places of delivery, and/or to give other instructions that do not constitute changes to the transport contract and the right to modify such instructions prior to the arrival of goods at the place of destination. The provision of "suspension of transportation and return of goods" in Article 308 of the *Contract Law* [3] goes beyond the scope of the right to control of goods in general. Rigid application of the provision of "return of goods" would have been unjust to the carrier of goods by sea. Rather than the judgment in favor of the carrier on the grounds that "return of goods" would lead to adverse consequences to the carrier and would violate the principle of fairness, the case-reopening collegial panel judged that the principle of fairness as provided in Article 5 of the *Contract Law* [4] should be followed as a supplementary provision on the grounds that there are no provisions in Article 308 of the *Contract Law* [5] on restrictive conditions for a shipper's exercise of its right to control, namely, no provisions on the carrier's right to defense

---

① See Article 12 of the *Convention for the Unification of Certain Rules for International Carriage by Air* (*Montreal Convention of* 1999), Articles 12 and 14-16 of the *Convention on the Contract for the International Carriage of Goods by Road* (CMR), Articles 18-22 of the *Uniform Rules Concerning the Contract of International Carriage of Goods by Rail* (CIM-COTIF) and Articles 14-15 of the *Budapest Convention on the Contract for the Carriage of Goods by Inland Waterways* (CMNI).

② See Articles 50-56 in Chapter 10 of the *Rotterdam Rules*.

③ See related provisions in Part Ⅲ: Contracts of the *Civil Code*.

④ See related provisions in Part Ⅲ: Contracts of the *Civil Code*.

⑤ See related provisions in Part Ⅲ: Contracts of the *Civil Code*.

against the right to control. Not only did such judgment conform to the provisions of law but also balanced the interests of both Parties. In Chapter 10 of the *Rotterdam Rules*, there are comprehensive and complete provisions on the right to control, including the subject, the scope, the period of its exercise, restrictive conditions, the legal consequences of its violation, and guarantee needed for its exercise, providing a reference for the improvement of China's *Maritime Law* in the future.

Grounds of Decision

The Supreme People's Court of the People's Republic of China Civil Judgment

No. 412 [2017], Case-reopening, Civ. Division, SPC

Petitioner for Case-reopening (Defendant of First Instance, Appellee of Second Instance): A. P. Moller-Maersk A/S.

Domicile: Esplanaden **, **** Copenhagen K, Denmark.

Representative: Henneberg and Kjarvik, authorized representatives of this company.

Attorney: Cao X, at Shanghai *** Law Firm.

Attorney: Chen XX, at Shanghai *** Law Firm.

Respondent (Plaintiff of First Instance, Appellant of Second Instance): Zhejiang Longda Stainless Steel Co, Ltd.

Domicile: No. XX, XXX Avenue, Songyang County, Lishui City, Zhejiang Province, the People's Republic of China.

Legal Representative: Xiang XX, General Manager of this company.

Attorney: Yuan X, at Beijing ** (Shanghai) Law Firm.

Attorney: Wen X, at Beijing ** (Ningbo) Law Firm.

Petitioner for Case-reopening: A. P. Moller-Maersk A/S (hereinafter referred to as Maersk) appealed against the Judgment of No. 222 [2016], FI, Civ. Division, Zhejiang Higher People's Court (hereinafter referred to as CSI) on the dispute over the Contract for Carriage of Goods by Sea between itself and the respondent of Zhejiang Longda Stainless Steel Co, Ltd (hereinafter referred to as Longda) and filed a petition for case-reopening with the Supreme People's Court of the People's Republic of China (hereinafter referred to as SPC). On October 31, 2017, SPC made a Civil Ruling of No. 3552 [2017], Appealing, Civ. Division, SPC to try this case via certiorari, and formed a collegial panel by law to review this case *in curia* on December 20, 2017, where both Cao X and Chen XX, the attorneys representing Maersk, and Yuan X, the attorney representing Longda, appeared and attended the proceedings in court. Now the retrial of this case was concluded.

In its filings submitted with Ningbo Maritime Court (hereinafterreferred to as CFI), Longda alleged that in June 2014, Longda exported a batch of stainless-steel seamless products with the value of USD 366, 918. 97 from port of Ningbo, China, to port of Colombo, the Democratic Socialist Republic of Sri Lanka (hereinafter referred to as Sri Lanka). On June 28, 2014, the goods were shipped on board of Maersk's "GUNDE MAERSK" vessel. Due to the failure by the consignee to pay for the goods arriving at the port of destination, Longda requested to, and Maersk agreed to, ship back the goods. Yet, Maersk had never done so and claimed with no documentation that the goods were auctioned at the port of destination. Maersk should be liable to Longda for its failure to fulfill the carrier's obligation of keeping the goods properly or for its delivery of the goods without the original B/L, which lead to the loss of Longda's property rights under the B/L, and requested CFI to order that

Maersk should compensate to Longda for the loss of the goods in the amount of USD 366, 918. 97 (or RMB 2, 274, 971 based on the prevailing exchange rate of 1 : 6. 2002 on May 29, 2015) and interest (based on the PBOC's lending interest rates during the same period from May 29, 2015 to the date of the actual performance).

Upon review, CFI found that:

In June 2014, Longda exported stainless-steel seamless products of USD 366, 918. 97 in customs value from Port of Ningbo, China, to Colombo, and booked the goods space with Maersk through a forwarder for the goods, which was loaded on aboard in four containers on June 28, 2014, and the B/L telex release was required to be completed by Longda at the time of shipment. On July 9, 2014, Longda sent via the forwarder an e-mail to Maersk stating that the port of destination was the wrong place of delivery, and the goods were requested to change the port or ship back. On the same day, Maersk replied that with less than two days left away from the arrival at the port of destination, the goods could not be changed the port, and the reply could only be made upon the confirmation with the port of destination should the goods be requested to be shipped back. The forwarder inquired the following day that whether the goods could be shipped back by the same vessel, and was replied the same day that "it is not operable to ship back the said goods by the same vessel since it is required that the consignee completes the customs clearance firstly after the said goods being unloaded at the port of destination and shipping back can only be arranged upon the approval by the local customs with the application by the said consignee". The goods in dispute arrived at the port of destination around July 12, 2014. At the request of Longda, Maersk issued a full set of the original B/L No. 603386880 on January 29, 2015 thereon stating that the shipper was Longda, the consignee and the Notifying Party both were Venus Steel Pvt Ltd, the port of departure was Port of Ningbo, China, and the port of discharge was port of Colombo. On May 18, 2015, Longda sent an e-mail to the forwarder stating that he/she decided to apply to Maersk for shipping back the goods. On the following day, Longda sent an e-mail to Maersk stating that as required by Maersk, Longda had applied for shipping back the goods, but was subsequently informed by Maersk that the goods had already been auctioned.

CFI further found that the goods in dispute were auctioned by the customs of the port of destination on March 13, 2015.

CFI concluded that:

This case is a contract dispute over the carriage of goods by sea with foreign factors. Now that both Parties to the dispute expressly agreed upon the application of China's laws, according to Article 3 of the *Law of the People's Republic of China on the Application of Laws Concerning Foreign-related Civil Relations* (hereinafter referred to as *Law on the Application of Laws Concerning Foreign-related Civil Relations*), laws of the People's Republic of China shall apply to this case.

Given that Longda was the shipper of the goods and the holder of a full set of the original B/L and Maersk was the carrier of the goods, the legal relationship for a contract for carriage of goods by sea was established between both Parties. Before the goods arrived at the port of destination, Longda required to change the port or shipped back, and was clearly informed by Maersk that with less than two days left away from the arrival at the port of destination, the goods couldn't be changed the port or shipped back. Longda had never paid due care to and taken any effective measures to the goods upon and from their arrival at the port of destination, such as taking delivery of the goods by itself, as it should have done as the shipper of the goods and the holder of the original B/L, until the goods were auctioned by the local customs nearly half a year after their arrival at the port of destination, and thus should assume all risks of the damage of the goods. Longda claimed that the failure by Maersk to have the goods changed the port or shipped back as required by Longda constituted a breach of the legal obligation. However, this claim was not supported by enough evidence and reasons, thus it was not accepted by SPC. According to Article 3 of the *Law on the Application of Laws Concerning Foreign-related Civil Relations,* Article 8 of the *Rules of the Supreme People's Court on Related Issues Concerning Proper Laws in Hearing Cases of Delivery of Goods Without the Original B/L* (hereinafter referred to as *Judicial Interpretations on Delivery Without the Original B/L*), and relevant provisions in Articles 27 and 259 of the *Civil Procedure Law of the People's Republic of China* (hereinafter referred to as *Civil Procedure Law*), CFI judged that the claims from Longda were dismissed and the fees for accepting the case of RMB 25, 000 were borne by Longda.

Longda appealed against the Judgment of CFI, requesting CSI to revoke the Judgment of CFI and made a judgment in favor of the claims of the first instance lodged by Longda.

CSI affirmd the facts found in the Judgment of CFI, and further found that having been informed by Maersk that the goods could not be shipped back unless and until the original consignee at the port of destination cleared the customs, Longda went on to inquire on July 10, 2014, saying that "the reason why to have them shipped back to Ningbo is just that the customs clearance cannot be completed" and asking "if there are any alternatives". But Longda had since then received no reply from Maersk.

The CSI concluded that:

Given the fact that neither Party had an objection to the legal relationship for a contract for carriage of goods by sea between Longda as the shipper and Maersk as the carrier of the goods under the B/L, the legal issues of this case were whether or not Longda had the right to change the port or ship back, and whether or not Maersk should be liable to Longda for the damage of the goods.

(1) Whether or not Longda had the right to change the port or ship back. Longda was the shipper of the goods and the holder of a full set of the original B/L, and thus had the control over the goods. Article 308 of the *Contract Law of the People's Republic of China* (hereinafter referred to as *Contract Law*) provides "prior to delivery by a carrier of goods under a contract to the consignee, the shipper may require the carrier to suspend the shipment, ship back, change the place of arrival, or deliver to a new consignee, subject to compensating for any loss or losses incurred by the said carrier as the result of such requirement by the said shipper." Article 9 of the *Judicial Interpretations on Delivery of Goods Without the Original B/L* provides "if the carrier suspends the shipment, ships back the goods, changed the place of arrival or delivers the goods to other consignees according to the requirements of the consignor with straight B/L, the people's court shall not support the request of the consignee holding a straight B/L to the carrier for civil liabilities for delivery of goods without original B/L." On the basis of the facts confirmed by both Parties, the goods arrived at the port of destination on July 12, 2014, and it was on July 9 that Longda applied via the forwarder to Maersk for having the goods changed the port or shipped back. According to the foregoing legal provisions, Longda as the shipper of the goods might, any time before delivery of the goods by the carrier to the consignee, require Maersk as the carrier to change the port or ship back the goods. Had some measures been taken to cooperate with Longda in changing or terminating the contract, Maersk might have claimed relevant loss

incurred to Longda according to law. Therefore, the claim that Longda had the right to change the port or ship back the goods had a legal basis, and was upheld by CSI.

(2) Whether or not Maersk should be held liable for damage of Longda's goods in dispute. On the grounds that it had fulfilled the obligation of prudently taking care of the goods and that the auction of the goods by the local customs was a legal exemption, Maersk insisted that it should not be held liable for the damage of the goods to Longda. Article 46 of the *Maritime Law of the People's Republic of China* (hereinafter referred to as *Maritime Law*) provides "the period of liability for the containerized goods of a carrier means the whole period of the goods being under the control of a carrier, namely starting at the moment of receiving the goods at the port of loading and ending at the moment of delivering the goods at the port of discharge", and Article 48 thereof provides the obligation of a carrier to prudently manage the goods. Therefore, throughout the period from the receipt of the goods at the port of loading to the delivery of the goods at the port of discharge, the carrier shall fulfill the obligation of prudent management of the goods. Upon receipt of the request from Longda on July 9, 2014 to change the port or ship back the goods, Maersk replied promptly that it could not be changed the port. The next day, Longda required "to have the goods shipped back on the same vessel", Maersk replied that "it (having the goods shipped back on the same vessel) is not operable", and the customs clearance must be completed before applying for the shipping back. Longda reaffirmed promptly that "the shipping back of the goods needs to be arranged" and inquired "if there are any alternatives". Based on the e-mail from Longda, it was established that the request to ship back the goods was expressly put forward by Longda on July 10, 2014. But Maersk

neither replied to the express requirement to ship back the goods from Longda nor notified Longda of any arrangement of handling by itself (Longda) or shipping back the goods, leaving the goods unloaded at the port of destination unattended. The auction of the goods at the port of destination on March 13, 2015 was neither known to Maersk nor notified to Longda until May 2015. Therefore, the fulfillment by Maersk of the obligation of prudent management of the goods under control of a carrier as set forth in the *Maritime Law* shall not be established, and thus Maersk shall be held liable for the damage of the goods. Having prevented the carrier from delivering the goods to the consignee designated on the B/L, Longda, as the holder of the goods in this case, should actively take care of the goods unloaded at the port of destination and dispose of it within a reasonable period. Longda did not contact Maersk until ten (10) months later following the arrival of the goods at the port of destination, and thus should also be held liable for the damage of the goods. Notwithstanding the provision in Article 51 of the *Maritime Law* provides that a carrier is not held liable for the damage of the goods under its control arising from "acts of governments or competent authorities, quarantine restrictions or judicial seizures", but the auction in this case did not occur until eight (8) months later following the arrival of the goods at the port of destination, so there was sufficient time for Maersk to notify Longda to dispose of the goods on its own, and Longda as the shipper of the goods to get knowledge of the whereabouts of, and dispose of, the goods. The auction in this case was not an inevitable event, and did not constitute any one of the exemption as provided in the *Maritime Law*. Maersk's claim for exemption could not be established and was not upheld by SPC.

In conclusion, to Longda's requirement to have the goods shipped back,

Maersk neither expressly refused to do so nor notified Longda to deal with the goods at the port of destination on its own, and thus should be partially held liable for the damage of the goods, which was 50% at the discretion of SPC. Although having the right to require Maersk as the carrier of the goods to change the port of destination or ship back the goods before the delivery of the goods to the consignee, Longda as the shipper of the goods failed to take effective measures to actively prevent the possible damage of the goods while Maersk refused to change the port of destination and had not received an explicit reply from Maersk to its requirement to ship back the goods, and thus should also be partially held liable for the damage of the goods in this case. Given that Maersk failed to prove the amount of the auction and confirmed its failure to take back money from the auction in the proceedings, the damage of the goods should be presumed to the total loss of the goods, and Longda submitted the customs declaration for the goods with CFI proving that the value of the goods was USD 366, 918. 97. Therefore, Maersk should compensate Longda for the damages of USD 366, 918. 97×50 percent = USD 183, 459. 49. According to the provisions of Article 308 of the *Contract Law* and Article 170 (1) (2) of the *Civil Procedure Law*, CSI judged as follows: (1) the Judgment made by CFI shall be revoked; (2) Maersk shall, within ten (10) days upon the date of service of this Judgment, compensate Longda for the damage to the goods of USD 183, 459. 49 and interest thereon; (3) all the other claims from Longda shall be rejected; the litigation fees for the trials of the first and second instance respectively were RMB 25, 000, with RMB 12, 500 for each trial borne by Longda and the remaining RMB 12, 500 for each trial borne by Maersk.

Unsatisfied with the Judgment made by CSI, Maersk filed a case-reopening petition with SPC, claiming that (1) the conclusion that Maersk should cooperate with Longda to change the port of destination or ship back the goods in the trial of the second instance was an error in the application of laws. Firstly, the application of the *Contract Law* and the *Judicial Interpretations on Delivery of Goods Without the Original B/L* invoked in the trial of the first instance and the second instance were inappropriate for this case. The local laws of Sri Lanka should apply to decide whether or not Maersk had the obligation to cooperate with Longda to change the port of destination or ship back the goods. According to relevant provisions of the *Sri Lanka Customs Regulations*, the goods cannot be changed the port or shipped back objectively before the completion of customs clearance, and the obligation of completing customs clearance rests with the importer of the goods. Maersk as the carrier of the goods should not be held liable to, and also did not have the ability to, complete the customs clearance. CSI held severely that Maersk should cooperate with Longda to complete the customs clearance, which had no legal basis and violated the shipping practices and customs. Secondly, Maersk had already shipped the goods at the port of destination, and thus had fully performed its obligations under the contract for carriage of goods by Sea. If the shipper chooses to ship back the goods, it shall make a reservation for the separate shipping space for the goods and establish a new contractual relationship for carriage of the goods by sea. Otherwise, the carrier shall not be obliged to ship back the goods. Thirdly, even if the requirement by Longda to ship back the goods was to exercise its right of stoppage in transit, yet, such right was based on the unsafe right to defense arising from or pertaining to contracts for the international sales of goods, and not necessarily binding on the carrier as a Party to a contract for carriage of goods by sea. Furthermore, under the mode of liner transportation, not only did the exercise by a shipper of the right of stoppage in transit infringe the rights and interests of other goods owners of the same vessel, but also was not practically operable, so a carrier was under no obligation to cooperate with a shipper to change or terminate the original contract for carriage of goods by sea; (2) the conclusion in the trial of the second instance that Maersk failed to conduct prudent management of the goods was unjustified by any factual or legal basis. After the goods arrived at the port of destination, Maersk had notified Longda who had the obligation to get knowledge of the whereabouts of, and take delivery of, the goods unloaded at the port of destination. Longda as the holder of a full set of the original B/L had the obligation of disposing of the goods, so Longda should assume all the risks of the damage of the goods arising from its failure to perform such obligation. The Judgment of CSI aggravated the carrier's duty of notice, which was obviously unfair. The unloaded goods left in the storage yard at port of destination was under actual possession and custody of the port and charged with the stockpiling fees. By now, the carrier's obligation was limited to providing the containerized goods in a good condition, so Maersk had fully performed its obligation of conducting prudent management of the goods; (3) the conclusion that Maersk should assume the liability for damage in the trial of the second instance was an error. Article 8 of the *Judicial Interpretations of Delivery of Goods Without the Original B/L* provides "a carrier's claim for exemption from the liability for taking delivery of goods shall be upheld by a people's court if the said goods shipped at the port is undeclared with the customs beyond a legal period and auctioned or disposed of by the customs prescribed by law or by a ruling of the court on basis of law." Maersk had notified Longda that the customs clearance for the goods must be completed before being shipped back, and Longda could have entrusted its forwarder at the port of destination to complete customs clearance, and could have made a reservation for a new goods space for shipping back the goods. But Longda made no action, and ignored the goods at the port for eight(8) months, leaving it to be auctioned by the customs at the port of destination, so Longda should be exclusively held liable for the damage of goods. Article 51 (1) (5) of the *Maritime Law* provides "a carrier may be exempted from liability for the damage of goods arising from the acts of the government or competent authorities, quarantine restrictions or judicial seizures." The auction of goods by the customs is the act of the government. Therefore, Maersk as the carrier might be exempted from the liability. In conclusion, Maersk requested that the Judgment of CSI shall be revoked, all the claims from Longda shall be rejected and the costs of litigation for this case shall be borne by Longda.

Longda argued that (1) a shipper in a contract for carriage of goods by sea might exercise the right to request to change the port or ship back, and Article 308 of the *Contract Law* and Article 9 of the *Judicial Interpretations on Delivery of Goods Without the Original B/L* applied in the trial of the second instance were no error. The relationship between the *Contract Law* and the *Maritime Law* is the one between a general law and a special law. In the absence of relevant provisions in the *Maritime Law*, the *Contract Law* shall apply. The right of a shipper to require stoppage in transit granted by Article 9 of the *Judicial Interpretations on Delivery of Goods Without the Original B/L*, derives from the provision of Article 308 of the *Contract Law*. In judicial practice, there exist many cases supporting the exercise by a shipper of the right to require stoppage in transit. Maersk's argument that the goods could not be changed the port or shipped back had no basis. Maersk had so far failed to meet its obligation of identifying the laws of the port of destination, and the provisions of the Sri Lanka Customs Regulations invoked by Maersk could not be verified; (2) Maersk failed to perform its obligation of prudent management of the goods. Under the provision of Article 46 of the *Maritime Law,* a carrier has the obligation to keep and take care of the goods properly until the goods is delivered to the consignee. Since a shipper shall pay the container demurrage until the goods are picked up at the port of destination, a carrier shall also assume the corresponding obligation to manage the goods. Maersk failed to complete the delivery of the goods and should be held liable for the damage of the goods arising from the customs auction exactly within its period of liability. The B/L issued by Maersk in January 2015 also indicated that the goods remained under the control of Maersk at least by this moment; (3) the exemption clause as set forth in Article 51 of the *Maritime Law* shall not apply to this case. Maersk had not presented any evidence that the auction of the goods was an *ex officio* action by the customs at the port of destination, and thus should bear the consequences of the failure of proof. Since the auction took place eight (8) months later after the arrival of the goods at the port of destination, Maersk had sufficient time to notify Longda to dispose of the goods. Therefore, the auction was not inevitable, and the basic elements underlying an exemption clause as set forth in the *Maritime Law* did not exist in this case. In summary, the Judgment of CSI was requested to be upheld.

During the case-reopening procedure, neither Party submitted new evidence. Longda had no objection to the facts found in the original trials. Maersk claimed that the fact that its employees continued communicating with Longda after the goods arrived at the port of destination failed to be established in the trial of the second instance, and the conclusion that the goods were left unattended at the port of discharge was inconsistent with the facts. Upon the case-reopening procedure, SPC reaffirmed the facts found in the trial of the second instance.

In the view of SPC:

This case is a contractual dispute over the carriage of goods by sea involving foreign-related relations. Both Parties to the dispute agreed upon the application of China's laws, according to Article 3 of the *Law on the Application of Laws*, laws of the People's Republic of China shall be applied in the reopening process of this case by SPC. The *Maritime Law* as a special law governing the relations arising from and/or pertaining to maritime transportation and ocean vessels shall apply in priority, and where there are no provisions therein, provisions of relevant laws, including the *Contract Law,* shall apply. According to Maersk's case-reopening petition and Longda's defense opinion, the issues of this case were (1) whether or not Maersk shall arrange the goods in dispute to change the port or ship back; and (2) whether or not Maersk shall be held liable for the damage of goods to Longda.

1. Whether or Not Maersk Shall Arrange the Goods in Dispute to Change the Port or Ship back

Longda requested the carrier to change the port or ship back the goods by sea in transit, and given that there are no provisions in the *Maritime Law* on the right of a shipper to request to change a contract for carriage of goods by sea during the voyage. Therefore, relevant provisions of the *Contract Law* shall apply in this case. Under Article 308 thereof, a shipper has the right to request to change a contract for carriage of goods by sea prior to the delivery of the goods by a carrier to a consignee, but both Parties to the said contract shall determine the rights and obligations of each Party following the principle of fairness as provided in Article 5 thereof. With unique characteristics for the carriage of goods by sea such as large volumes of transportation, prearranged voyages, relatively fixed routes and so on, not only may a shipper's request to change the port of destination or ship back of the goods, under some circumstances, be difficult to operate but also hinder the normal operation of the carrier or cause great damage to the shippers and/or consignees of other goods. In this case, it would be obviously unfair to require a carrier to unconditionally obey the shipper's request to modify or change a contract for carriage of goods. Therefore, under the contract for carriage of goods by sea, a shipper has no unrestricted right to require to exercise the right to change a contract, and a carrier shall not unconditionally obey the shipper's instruction to change such a transport contract under any circumstances. To strike a reasonable balance between the interests of the Parties to a contract for carriage of goods by sea, whereas a shipper may exercise the right to request to change a contract for carriage of goods by sea, the carrier shall also have the corresponding right to defense. If such change renders the performance of the changed contract impossible or may have serious impacts on the normal operation of the carrier, the carrier shall have the right to refuse the shipper's request to change the port or ship back with a notification without delay to the shipper stating the reasons for such refusal. The mode of transport in this case is the international liner transport. Besides four containers for Longda, there was a large quantity of goods for other shippers on the same vessel. The goods were loaded and shipped on June 28, 2014, arrived at the port of destination around July 12, and Longda had not required for changing the port or shipping back until July 9. With only two or three days left away from arrival at the port of destination, Maersk's claim that it was not operable to arrange to change the port or ship back on the same vessel due to the voyage was objective and reasonable. The

Judgment made by CFI that the above-mentioned claim by Maersk was upheld was consistent with the principle of fairness, which was affirmed by SPC.

2. Whether or Not Maersk Shall be Held Liable for the Damage of Goods to Longda

Article 86 of the *Maritime Law* provides "if and when no one takes delivery of the goods at the port of discharge or the consignee delays or refuses to take delivery of the goods, the ship master may store the goods at a warehouse or other appropriate place, and all the costs and risks arising therefrom shall be borne by the consignee." What Maersk had the goods shipped to the port of destination and stored at the port of destination after being unclaimed was in conformity with the foregoing legal provision. On July 9, 2014, Maersk replied via an e-mail to Longda that there were less than two days left away from the arrival at the port of destination. By then Longda had known the approximate date of arrival of the goods at the port of destination. Longda had perfectly known that no one would take delivery of goods at the port of destination, and took no measures for up to eight (8) months thereafter, leading to the goods being auctioned by the customs. Although it claimed that Maersk failed to perform the obligation of a carrier to prudently manage the goods, Longda did not present evidence of improper handling of the goods by Maersk. Therefore, this claim by Longda had no basis, and shall not be upheld by SPC. According to Article 86 of the *Maritime Law*, all the costs and risks incurred upon and from the discharge of the goods shall be borne by the consignee. Maersk as the carrier shall not be held liable for any costs and risks incurred thereafter. The Judgment of CSI that Maersk assumed one half of the loss of goods involved in this case was lack of factual basis and was improper in the application of laws, and shall be reversed. The application of related provisions of the *Judicial*

Interpretations on Delivery of Goods Without the Original B/L in the trial of the first instance was inconsistent with the facts and the issues in this case, and shall be rectified, but the result of the judgment is no error and shall be upheld.

In conclusion, according to Articles 5 and 308 of the *Contract Law*, Articles 48 and 86 of the *Maritime Law*, and Articles 207(1) and 170 (1) (2) of the *Civil Procedure Law*, the Judgment is made as follows:

1. The Judgment of No. 222 [2016], Final, Civ. Division, Zhejiang Higher People's Court shall be revoked;

2. The Judgment of No. 534 [2015], FI, Commercial Division, Ningbo Maritime Court shall be affirmed;

The court acceptance fees of RMB 25,000 respectively for the trial of the first and second instances shall be borne by Longda.

This Judgment shall be final and inclusive.

Presiding Judge: WANG Shumei

Judge: YU Xiaohan

Judge: HUANG Xiwu

December 29, 2017

Assistant Judge: ZHAO Ke

Court Clerk: CHEN Hui

中化国际(新加坡)有限公司
诉
蒂森克虏伯冶金产品有限责任公司
国际货物买卖合同纠纷案

——《联合国国际货物销售合同公约》的适用及根本违约的认定

【裁判要旨】

1. 国际货物买卖合同的当事各方所在国为《联合国国际货物销售合同公约》(以下简称《销售公约》)的缔约国,应优先适用公约的规定,公约没有规定的内容,适用合同中约定适用的法律。国际货物买卖合同中当事人明确排除适用《销售公约》的,则不应适用该公约。

2. 在国际货物买卖合同中,卖方交付的货物虽然存在缺陷,但只要买方经过合理努力就能使用货物或转售货物,不应视为构成《销售公约》规定的根本违约的情形。

【专家点评】*

本案主要涉及国际货物买卖合同履行过程中因货物缺陷而引起的合同解除和损害赔偿问题。

上诉人德国蒂森克虏伯冶金产品有限责任公司(以下简称德国克虏伯

---

* 撰写人:左海聪,对外经济贸易大学二级教授、博士研究生导师,中国法学会国际经济法学研究会副会长。

公司）与被上诉人中化国际（新加坡）有限公司（以下简称中化新加坡公司）国际货物买卖合同纠纷一案的基本案情是：卖方德国克虏伯公司与买方中化新加坡公司签订采购合同，销售一单石油焦。货物运到后，买方发现货物规格与合同约定不符，向卖方索赔。后买方找到下家将货物转卖，转卖价格低于合同价格。买方诉至江苏省高级人民法院，认为卖方的瑕疵履行构成根本违约，要求解除合同并由卖方承担所有损失。卖方认为货物虽有缺陷，但不严重，买方的损失是由货物价格下跌造成的，因而主张货物损失应该由买方自行承担，买方也无权解除合同。采购合同约定，案件由美国纽约州的法律管辖。江苏省高级人民法院（即一审法院）判决支持原告中化新加坡公司的诉讼请求，被告德国克虏伯公司不服一审判决，上诉至中华人民共和国最高人民法院（以下简称最高人民法院）。最高人民法院（即二审法院）于2014年6月作出判决：卖方交付货物存在缺陷但尚不构成根本违约，买方不能主张解除合同；买方的损失，部分归因于卖方货物的缺陷导致买方转售困难，部分归因于货物价格的下跌，卖方只承担可归因于货物缺陷的损害赔偿。

最高人民法院上述判决中的一些法律推理和适用具有创造性，其裁判理念和方法具有典型性和指导性。该案不但被列入最高人民法院的指导性案例和“一带一路”典型案例，也被联合国贸易法委员会秘书处编写的《〈联合国国际货物销售合同公约〉判例法摘要汇编》（2016年版，以下简称《贸法会判例法摘要汇编》）多次引用，作为《销售公约》第1条、第7条、第25条、第74条解释和适用的典型案例。

最高人民法院在本案中的创造性裁判理念和方法主要体现在法律适用、根本违约认定和损害赔偿额确定三个方面。

一、延续优良传统，正确适用国际公约和外国法

本案双方当事人在法律适用上存在争议。上诉人（即一审被告）认为，关于本案的准据法，根据采购合同约定以及我国的冲突规范，本案应适用美国纽约州法律。此外，《销售公约》也应适用于本案，《销售公约》的解释、美国《统一商法典》以及商业惯例等同样适用于本案,《贸法会判例法摘要汇编》也是审理本案的依据。一审法院认定只有《销售公约》适用于本案是错误的。

在应该适用《销售公约》而合同当事人选择缔约国法律为准据法时,对于如何适用《销售公约》,各国法院的做法有些差异。德国法院一般认为,如果合同选择德国法,则《销售公约》作为德国法的一部分应优先适用且排除国内法的适用。美国法院通常会将《销售公约》视为自执行条约而直接适用。中国法院一般依据《销售公约》第1条第1款第1项将《销售公约》作为准据法直接适用,同时对公约未作规定的事项适用该缔约国法律。例如,在上诉人美国联合企业有限公司诉被上诉人中国山东省对外贸易总公司烟台公司购销合同纠纷案[1998(经终字)第358号]中,最高人民法院认定,由于双方当事人的营业地位于中国和美国,而中国和美国均为公约的缔约国,该纠纷应适用《销售公约》,对上诉人关于应依据最密切联系原则确认美国法为准据法的主张不予支持。

本案双方当事人在合同中约定,合同应当根据美国纽约州当时有效的法律订立、管辖和解释。最高人民法院认可一审法院的解释和适用,认为这一法律选择条款有效。考虑到当事人双方营业地分别位于德国和新加坡,而德国和新加坡均为《销售公约》缔约国,且双方当事人并没有明确排除公约的适用,因此,依据《销售公约》第1条第1款第1项,本案的准据法应为《销售公约》,在涉及《销售公约》没有规定的问题上,应当选择适用当事人在采购合同中约定的美国纽约州法律。

在销售合同效力问题上,最高人民法院援引《销售公约》第4条,认定《销售公约》对于合同效力问题未作规定,进而认为应该适用合同约定的美国纽约州法律的规定。法院经查明和适用美国纽约州的法律,认定本案的采购合同有效。

这种将《销售公约》作为准据法、将当事人选择的缔约国法律作为补充适用的法律的做法,将法律适用中的不同事项分割开来,既尊重当事人的意思自治,又履行了我国加入《销售公约》所承担的义务,是一种先进的法律适用理念和方法,彰显了中国法官的司法智慧。

《销售公约》是目前世界范围内适用频次最高的国际公约,截至 2016 年 5 月,已经在不少于 4500 个诉讼或仲裁案件中得到适用。《销售公约》的广泛适用为国际货物买卖合同提供了统一的法律,为国际货物买卖交易提供了法律保障和可预见性。中国法院对《销售公约》的适用一直持积极态度。截至 2016 年,中国法院和仲裁机构已经在 400 余件涉外货物买卖合同案件中适用了《销售公约》进行案件审理。中国法院的一贯做法促进了《销售公约》的适用,扩大了《销售公约》的影响力,也降低了国际货物买卖当事人的交易成本,提高了交易的可预见性和法律保障。

二、参照外国判例,准确认定违约方行为不构成根本违约

本案中违约方的违约行为是否构成根本违约是双方当事人的争议焦点之一。一审法院支持被上诉人(即一审原告)的主张,认为根本违约成立,原告可以行使解约权。上诉人就此提起上诉。

《销售公约》第 25 条对根本违约的构成要件作了规定,即如果一方当事人的违约使另一方当事人蒙受损害以致实质上剥夺了他依据合同可以得到的东西,即构成根本违约。违约方可以其在订约时无法预见而且一个理性的人在相同情形下也无法预见该损失为由进行抗辩。由于《销售公约》采用了“实质剥夺”的表达,只表明了损害需要达到一定严重程度,但究竟何种情形、何种损害可以构成根本违约,需要法庭依据案件的具体情形作出判断。一审法院认为,一审被告(即上诉人)交付的货物规格低于合同所约定规格的下限,构成根本违约。

最高人民法院认为,上诉人关于将《贸法会判例法摘要汇编》作为判案依据的主张虽然不能成立,但判例摘要可以作为法院理解和适用相关规则的参考。关于交付货物存在缺陷是否构成根本违约,在本案之前《贸法会判例法摘要汇编》有两个判例可供借鉴。第一个判例是德国最高法院 1996 年审理的一个案件(判例 171)。该案中,荷兰卖方提供的硝酸钴不符合合同约定,不是英国产的而是南非产的,质量较差。德国买方宣布解除合同。德国最高法院认为,在卖方已经交付货物的情况下,买方仅以货物质量较差、原产地不符合合同约定为由解除合同理由不足,而且买方不能证明南非产的货物不能在德国或外国销售,因而根本违约不能成立,买方也无权解除合同。第二个判例是瑞士联邦高等上诉法院 1998 年审理的一个案件(判例 248)。该案中,德国卖方交付的冻肉太肥,含水率太高,结果其价值比合同规定的质量低了 25.5%,瑞士买方主张根本违约成立。法官认为:成立根本违约进而解除合同是买方可以主张的最严厉的救济方式,通常只在异常情形下使用。本案中的情形不能视为根本违约,因为买方仍能以较低的价格转售或以其他方式进行加工。

最高人民法院据此综合考量上述判例对《销售公约》中关于根本违约条款的理解,认为:买方在不存在不合理麻烦的情况下,能使用货物或转售货物,甚至打些折扣,质量不符并不构成根本违约。被上诉人将货物成功转售,而且没有低于当时的合理价格。最高人民法院由此确认,本案上诉人交付货物与合同不符,构成违约,但这种类型的违约不构成根本违约,因而被上诉人也没有解除合同的权利,从而令人信服地解决了本案的主要争议焦点问题。

《销售公约》第 7 条规定,解释公约时应考虑本公约的国际性质以及促进其适用的统一,这为各国缔约国法院和仲裁机构设定了统一解释《销售公约》的义务。由于各国法院均在本国司法体系下对《销售公约》进行解释和适用,没有共同的上诉法院,实践中要实现《销售公约》的统一解释和适用,只有依赖各国法院相互参照和借鉴对方的判决,《贸法会判例法摘要汇编》为各国法院相互参照判决提供了有益的参考资料。本案中,最高人民法院通过参照外国法院的判决,解释和适用《销售公约》的相关条款,既参照了其他国家法院的司法智慧,又履行了促进《销售公约》的统一解释的义务,具有十分重要的意义,为中国法院今后参照外国法院判例进行法律解释和促进《销售公约》的统一适用提供了范例。

三、核清事实，分清责任，准确决定违约的损害赔偿数额

本案中违约的损害赔偿计算问题也是一个争议焦点。上诉人主张被上诉人的损失是由货物价格下降造成的，与货物质量无关。被上诉人主张，货物损失是由于上诉人交付货物有严重瑕疵，使被上诉人难以找到下一买家造成的。一审法院支持了被上诉人的主张，判决上诉人承担赔付所有损害赔偿的责任。最高人民法院认真核实事实，确认被上诉人的损失部分是由上诉人的货物质量问题造成的，部分是由货物价格下降造成的，从而改判上诉人只承担由货物质量问题造成的部分的损害赔偿。

损害赔偿是《销售公约》规定的主要救济方式，损害赔偿额往往是诉讼当事人最为重视的诉讼结果。《销售公约》第 74 条规定，一方当事人违反合同应付的损害赔偿额，应与另一方当事人因其违约而遭受的包括利润在内的损失金额相等。这一规定从字面上看，似乎并没有对损失是由双因或多因造成时如何计算损失额作出规定。但事实上从第 74 条规定中可以推断，不是由一方当事人违约所造成的损失，该当事人对此不承担赔偿责任。最高人民法院查明双因造成损害的事实，判决违约方承担部分损失的法律推理，符合第 74 条的规定，是一种有效解释，也是裁判理念和方法上的一种创新。

综合而言，最高人民法院的上述判决在法律适用问题上运用新方法，在根本违约认定问题上开放借鉴外国判例，在损害赔偿问题上对关键词进行有效的演进性解释，是国际货物买卖领域适用《销售公约》的里程碑式的判决，不仅对中国法院和仲裁机构今后审理类似案件具有指导意义，对外国法院和仲裁机构审理类似案件也具有参考借鉴价值。

【裁判文书】

中华人民共和国最高人民法院
民事判决书

(2013)民四终字第35号

上诉人(一审被告):蒂森克虏伯冶金产品有限责任公司(ThyssenKrupp Metallurgical Products GmbH)。住所地:德国埃森市***大街**号(**** ** Essen,Germany)。

法定代表人:Knötsch,该公司执行董事。

Nelken,该公司执行董事。

委托代理人:徐某某,广东**(天津)律师事务所律师。

委托代理人:闫某某,广东**(天津)律师事务所律师。

被上诉人(一审原告):中化国际(新加坡)有限公司〔Sinochem International (Overseas) Pte Ltd〕。住所地:新加坡海滨景*号亚洲广场塔*****(** Marina view,**** Asia Square Tower *,Singapore)。

法定代表人:李某,该公司董事。

委托代理人:陈某某,上海虹桥**律师事务所律师。

委托代理人:郑某,北京市**律师事务所律师。

上诉人蒂森克虏伯冶金产品有限责任公司(以下简称德国克虏伯公司)因与被上诉人中化国际(新加坡)有限公司(以下简称中化新加坡公司)国际货物买卖合同纠纷一案,不服江苏省高级人民法院(以下简称江苏高院)于2012年12月19日作出的(2009)苏民三初字第0004号民事判决,向本院提起上诉。本院依法组成合议庭于2013年12月26日公开开庭审理了本案。德国克虏伯公司的委托代理人徐某某、闫某某,中化新加坡公司的委托代理人陈某某、郑某到庭参加诉讼。本案现已审理终结。

中化新加坡公司向一审法院江苏高院起诉称：2008年4月11日，中化新加坡公司与德国克虏伯公司签订《采购合同》，约定中化新加坡公司向德国克虏伯公司购买石油焦25000吨，石油焦的HGI指数应在36至46之间。中化新加坡公司按约支付了全部货款，但德国克虏伯公司交付的石油焦HGI指数仅为32，严重影响中化新加坡公司在中国市场销售，构成根本违约。中化新加坡公司有权解除合同，要求德国克虏伯公司返还全部货款，并赔偿中化新加坡公司由此遭受的全部损失。因此请求判令：1. 解除双方订立的《采购合同》；2. 德国克虏伯公司返还货款7756828.55美元（按2009年5月6日基准汇率6.8232计算为人民币52926392.56元）及自2008年9月24日至德国克虏伯公司实际返还货款之日的利息（按中国银行同期美元贷款利率计算）；3. 德国克虏伯公司赔偿中化新加坡公司港口包干费、堆存费人民币1523052元（暂计算至2009年5月6日）；4. 德国克虏伯公司承担本案诉讼费用。

德国克虏伯公司答辩称：1. 德国克虏伯公司交付的石油焦HGI值是32，表面看与合同约定不符，但该值不是强制性的，HGI值为32的石油焦并不影响其使用，德国克虏伯公司的行为不构成违约。2. 石油焦运抵南京港后，中化新加坡公司支付了货款，并未提出异议。中化新加坡公司之所以后来提出质量异议，是因为2009年9、10月份，石油焦市场价格大幅下跌。3. 即使德国克虏伯公司构成违约，中化新加坡公司因未在合同约定的石油焦抵达目的港之日起60日内向德国克虏伯公司索赔，中化新加坡公司丧失索赔权。4. 中化新加坡公司已将石油焦以与涉案《采购合同》基本相同的价格出售给其母公司中化国际（控股）股份有限公司（以下简称中化控股公司），中化新加坡公司没有损失。因此请求判令：1. 驳回中化新加坡公司的诉讼请求；2. 本案诉讼费用由中化新加坡公司负担。

江苏高院经审理查明：

一、双方当事人一致认可的事实

2008年4月11日,中化新加坡公司与德国克虏伯公司签订《采购合同》,约定:1. 中化新加坡公司向德国克虏伯公司采购燃料级石油焦25000吨,数量可有10%浮动,石油焦的HGI指数典型值在36至46之间。2. 石油焦的装货港为加利福尼亚匹兹堡,目的港为中国港口,具体港口由中化新加坡公司确定。3. 由双方确认的独立检验人在装货港船上采样检验并出具检验证书,该检测结果是终局的并对双方有约束力。中化新加坡公司有权在卸货港对石油焦的数量和品质进行检验,德国克虏伯公司有权委托独立检验人见证上述检验过程并自行承担相应费用。如果中化新加坡公司发现石油焦的品质或数量与在装货港确定的品质或数量不符,其应向德国克虏伯公司发出索赔通知,并有权在石油焦到达目的港之日起60日内向德国克虏伯公司提出索赔(采购合同第7.2.3条)。4. 本合同应当根据美国纽约州当时有效的法律订立、管辖和解释。双方还就合同履行作了其他约定。

2008年8月8日,双方认可的检验人A. J. EDMODN公司在装货港出具的检验证书载明,石油焦的HGI指数为32。同年8月11日的重量检验证书载明,德国克虏伯公司实际交付石油焦26079.63吨。

2008年7月31日,中化新加坡公司在中国交通银行新加坡分行(以下简称新加坡交行)开立信用证,信用证45A规定:石油焦HGI指数为CA. 36-46。2008年8月27日,德国克虏伯公司向新加坡交行提示包括A. J. EDMODN公司在装货港出具的检验证书在内的议付单据。该行于2008年9月2日支付了大部分货款。2008年9月11日,德国克虏伯公司开具最终商业发票,确定石油焦单价为301.56美元/吨。2008年9月25日,中化新加坡公司通过电汇方式支付了剩余小部分货款。中化新加坡公司向德国克虏伯公司总计支付货款7756828.55美元。

2008年9月8日,石油焦到达南京港。2008年11月10日,中国检验认证集团江苏有限公司出具的化验证书载明,石油焦的HGI指数为32。

2008年10月至12月,中国市场石油焦价格下跌,中硫焦出厂含税价10

月下跌为人民币2048元/吨，11月跌至人民币1357元/吨，12月下跌为人民币1305元/吨。

中化控股公司是中化新加坡公司的母公司。

德国克虏伯公司公司名称原为蒂森克虏伯矿业能源公司（ThyssenKrupp Minenergy GmbH），住所地德国埃森市****街***号（**** Strasse *** Essen），2011年6月24日变更为蒂森克虏伯冶金产品有限责任公司（ThyssenKrupp Metallurgical Products GmbH），住所地变更为德国埃森市****街**号（**** ** Essen, Germany）。

二、双方当事人关于涉案石油焦的HGI指数是否符合合同约定的观点

中化新加坡公司认为德国克虏伯公司交付的石油焦的HGI指数为32，不符合合同的约定，难以在中国市场销售，构成根本违约。为证明其主张，中化新加坡公司提供了上海大学材料科学与工程学院出具的关于石油焦特性的说明。该说明称：燃料级石油焦的硬度（HGI指数）是其核心指标，通常的大型企业对于所采购的燃料级石油焦的硬度指标要求不低于45，在磨机型号允许的情况下，也接受部分硬度在35以上的石油焦，而硬度指标低于35的燃料级石油焦用途非常有限，所以国内燃料级石油焦市场上并不多见此类需求。德国克虏伯公司认为，该证据属于证人证言，证人没有出庭作证，故对其真实性不予确认。

德国克虏伯公司认为，虽然其交付的石油焦的HGI指数为32，表面上看与合同约定不符，但实际上并不构成违约，合同约定的HGI指数是典型值。HGI指数为32的石油焦仍然可以在中国市场销售。为证明其主张，德国克虏伯公司申请从事石油焦行业三十余年的美国人Fisher先生、中铝公司郑州轻金属研究院原副院长王某某先生和华北电力大学教授李某某先生三位专家证人出庭作证。该三位专家证人一致认可：HGI指数表示石油焦的研磨指数，指数越低，石油焦的硬度越大，研磨难度越大，指数越高，则石油焦的硬度越低，研磨难度越低。HGI指数为32的石油焦具有使用价值，符合涉案采购合同的目的。此外，Fisher先生称，其见过的最低HGI指数为35，最高

HGI 指数为 85。石油焦的 HGI 指数难以准确测定,通常用一个典型值的范围表示。王某某先生称,对硬度大的石油焦,在使用前,需要对磨机的喂料速度、风压和流量、磨机转速等磨粉参数进行调整。李某某先生称,HGI 指数是燃料制粉系统的选型依据,不能作为其是否是燃料的判断依据。HGI 指数较低的石油焦需要更换研磨设备方可使用。

中化新加坡公司对德国克虏伯公司证人证言的真实性没有异议,但强调 Fisher 先生的证言表明其在三十年的专业生涯中,从未见过 HGI 指数为 32 的石油焦,其见过的石油焦 HGI 指数最低为 35。王某某先生本人未做过 HGI 指数的测定工作,也没有使用过不同 HGI 指数的石油焦,其证言的权威性值得商榷。李某某先生的证言表明,不同 HGI 指数的石油焦对研磨设备的要求不同,HGI 指数硬度大的石油焦需要更换设备方可使用。

江苏高院认为,德国克虏伯公司提供的三位专家证人的证言中关于石油焦 HGI 指数与硬度的关系以及涉案 HGI 指数为 32 的石油焦具有使用价值部分的内容能够互相印证,具有科学依据,可以采信;关于 HGI 指数为 32 的石油焦是否符合合同目的,属于裁判性事项,证人无权对此作出判断,故对该三位专家证言中关于涉案 HGI 指数为 32 的石油焦符合合同目的部分的内容,该院不予采信。关于涉案 HGI 指数为 32 的石油焦是否符合合同目,该院将在判决裁判理由部分予以详细论证。中化新加坡公司提供的关于石油焦特性的说明并非以个人名义出具,而是以上海大学材料科学与工程学院名义出具,且加盖了单位公章,其内容并不否认 HGI 指数为 32 的石油焦可以使用,只是认为其用途有限。该说明的内容在一定程度上与德国克虏伯公司提供的三位专家证人的证言也可以互相印证,具有科学依据,可以采信。

此外,德国克虏伯公司还提供了中国检验认证集团北京有限公司出具的品质检验证书,用于证明其交付石油焦的 HGI 指数为 36。中化新加坡公司对该证据的真实性、合法性及关联性不予认可,理由是:1. 涉案石油焦到达目的港之后,一直处于中化新加坡公司的控制之下,德国克虏伯公司并未向中化新加坡公司提取涉案石油焦作检验样品，因此德国克虏伯公司用于检验的石油焦样品并非涉案石油焦。2. 德国克虏伯公司未经中化新加坡公司同意单独委托中国检验认证集团北京有限公司进行检验，没有合同和法律依据。江苏高院认为，由于德国克虏伯公司用于检验的石油焦样品是否取自涉案石油焦不能确定，且其单方委托检验没有合同依据，故对该证据的关联性、合法性不予确认。

三、关于双方当事人就涉案石油焦的 HGI 指数进行交涉的事实

2008 年 10 月 15 日，中化控股公司发函给德国克虏伯公司，提出其交付的涉案石油焦的 HGI 指数与合同约定的范围严重不符，下家用户无法使用，拒绝接货，事态严重，请德国克虏伯公司尽快拿出处理意见。德国克虏伯公司在本案第一次庭审答辩时，认可中化控股公司的该行为代表中化新加坡公司。2008 年 11 月 4 日，中化新加坡公司再次发函给德国克虏伯公司，称德国克虏伯公司交付的石油焦的 HGI 指数严重偏离合同约定的范围，构成实质性违约，并要求德国克虏伯公司妥善处理。德国克虏伯公司于同年 11 月 12 日回函给中化新加坡公司，称其交付的石油焦的 HGI 指数只是略低于采购合同约定的范围，不构成实质性违约，并同意举行会晤，商讨解决办法。同年 11 月 27 日，中化新加坡公司发函给德国克虏伯公司要求双方尽快会晤。同年 12 月 8 日，德国克虏伯公司回函给中化新加坡公司称，2008 年年底之前会晤困难，建议在 2009 年 1 月会晤。

上述事实有中化新加坡公司提供的 2008 年 10 月 15 日中化新加坡公司发给德国克虏伯公司的传真、11 月 4 日及 11 月 27 日发给德国克虏伯公司的函件，德国克虏伯公司 2008 年 11 月 12 日、12 月 8 日的回函为证。德国克虏伯公司对上述证据的真实性没有异议，江苏高院对上述双方就涉案石油焦的 HGI 指数进行交涉的事实予以确认。

中化新加坡公司称，除了通过书面函件交涉之外，中化新加坡公司还与德国克虏伯公司进行多次口头交涉。德国克虏伯公司对此不予认可。中化新加坡公司亦未提供相关证据予以证明。

四、涉案石油焦的处置

在本案审理过程中,为了避免涉案石油焦长期存放南京港造成损失的进一步扩大,中化新加坡公司于2009年11月11日致函德国克虏伯公司,告知与潜在买受人初步商定的价格等信息,并征询德国克虏伯公司的意见。2009年11月18日,德国克虏伯公司回函认为其已完成交货义务,中化新加坡公司处理涉案石油焦无需与其商量,更无需其同意,对于中化新加坡公司所提出的价格,也无法给出任何评论意见。2009年11月26日,中化新加坡公司委托中化控股公司与威海金猴进出口贸易有限公司(以下简称金猴公司)签订销售合同,将系争石油焦以人民币1575.50元/吨的价格出售给该公司。中化新加坡公司处置涉案石油焦收回货款人民币34637187.25元(分别按汇率6.8284和6.8283计算,折合美元5072525.65元)。中化新加坡公司在出售系争石油焦过程中承担了以下额外费用:(1)税费人民币1600255.71元(按汇率6.8359计算折合美元234095.83元);(2)包干费人民币834549元(按汇率6.8309计算折合美元122172.63元);(3)堆存费人民币1120000元(按汇率6.8263计算折合美元164071.31元);(4)商检费人民币10000元(按汇率6.8317计算折合美元1463.76元);(5)报关费用人民币27029.36元(按汇率6.8261计算折合美元3959.71元);(6)财务费用美元2490元。中化新加坡公司在出售系争石油焦过程中承担的额外费用合计528253.24美元。

上述事实有2009年11月11日中化新加坡公司关于处理系争石油焦及时减少损失的函、2009年11月18日德国克虏伯公司律师回函、委托出售系争石油焦的函、2009年11月26日销售合同、2009年12月17-30日发票五张、原油价格及石油焦价格走势图、发票5张、海关保证金、风险担保金、抵押金专用收据、进口税率表、南京新生圩海关进口关税专用缴款书、检验费用付款单据及发票、报关费用支付单据及发票、港口存储及代理合同为证,德国克虏伯公司除认为委托出售涉案石油焦的函没有公证认证外,对其他证据的真实性没有异议。江苏高院认为,中化控股公司与中化新加坡公司是母子公司关系，委托出售系争石油焦的函系在中国国内取得，不需要办理公证认证手续，该证据的真实性可以确认。故江苏高院对上述事实予以确认。

五、关于中化新加坡公司的损失

德国克虏伯公司认为，中化新加坡公司已将涉案石油焦以原价卖给了其母公司中化控股公司，其没有任何损失。中化新加坡公司认可其与中化控股公司之间存在石油焦买卖合同，且价格与涉案采购合同价基本相同，但认为其与中化控股公司之间并不是真正的买卖关系，而是委托销售关系。中化新加坡公司向德国克虏伯公司采购涉案石油焦的目的是在中国境内销售，中化新加坡公司与中化控股公司签订的买卖合同系用于报关目的，是使涉案石油焦顺利进入中国境内，便于其委托中化控股公司代其在中国境内销售。为证明其主张，中化新加坡公司提交了其委托中化控股公司销售涉案石油焦的委托函。德国克虏伯公司对该委托函的形式真实性没有异议，但怀疑该委托函是中化新加坡公司为了本案的索赔事后补签的。江苏高院认为，中化新加坡公司提供的委托函是原件，在没有相反证据推翻的情况下，可以采信。

中化新加坡公司认为，其支付德国克虏伯公司的货款金额为7756828.55美元，扣除处置涉案石油焦后收回的货款5072525.65美元，德国克虏伯公司还应返还中化新加坡公司货款2684302.9美元，并向其支付自2008年9月25日至实际返还之日按中国银行同期美元贷款利率计算的利息。德国克虏伯公司认为，中化新加坡公司的差价损失，是石油焦市场下跌造成的，并非涉案石油焦的HGI指数与采购合同不符所致。该损失是正常的商业风险，应由中化新加坡公司承担。

除此之外，中化新加坡公司还要求德国克虏伯公司赔偿其在处置涉案石油焦过程中额外支出的税费234095.83美元、包干费122172.63美元、堆存费164071.31美元，合计520339.77美元；至于商检费、报关费和财务费等费用，中化新加坡公司明确表示不要求德国克虏伯公司赔偿。德国克虏伯公司则认为，其行为不构成违约，该费用系中化新加坡公司转卖涉案石油焦应当承担的成本,不应由德国克虏伯公司承担。

江苏高院认为:

一、关于本案的法律适用

中化新加坡公司系新加坡公司,德国克虏伯公司系德国公司,故本案系国际石油焦买卖合同纠纷。虽然双方当事人在合同中约定涉案合同应当根据美国纽约州当时有效的法律订立、管辖和解释,但在诉讼中双方当事人均选择《联合国国际货物销售合同公约》(以下简称《销售公约》)作为确定其权利义务关系的依据,而新加坡与德国均为《销售公约》的缔约国,故涉案合同应适用公约的有关规定。

二、德国克虏伯公司的行为构成根本违约

双方当事人在买卖合同中明确约定,涉案石油焦的 HGI 指数典型值在 36 至 46 之间。经双方认可的检验人在装货港检验,涉案石油焦的 HGI 指数为 32;中化新加坡公司依据《采购合同》的约定在目的港复检的结果亦表明涉案石油焦的 HGI 指数为 32。中化新加坡公司据此主张,涉案石油焦的 HGI 指数远远低于双方买卖合同所约定的标准,亦低于国内销售的一般石油焦的质量,导致涉案石油焦难以在国内市场销售,签订买卖合同时的预期目的无法实现,故德国克虏伯公司的行为构成根本违约。德国克虏伯公司则认为,双方在买卖合同中约定的 HGI 指数为典型值,并非强制性指标,仅仅是一个大约的范围,合同并未对涉案石油焦的 HGI 指数设定最低和最高的范围,超出该范围不仅不构成根本违约,亦不构成一般违约。对于德国克虏伯公司的这一主张,中化新加坡公司反驳认为,双方在合同中未约定石油焦的 HGI 指数的精确值,而是约定了一个典型值的范围,正是基于对石油焦的 HGI 指数不确定性的考虑。石油焦的 HGI 指数具有不确定性并不意味着双方约定的 HGI 指数典型值的可变范围不具有约束力。对此,江苏高院认为,既然双方在采购合同中约定涉案石油焦 HGI 指数典型值在 36 至 46 之间,那就意味着德国克虏伯公司交付的石油焦的 HGI 指数典型值最低不应低于 36,最高不应高于 46,超出这个范围即构成违约。德国克虏伯公司关于双方在《采购合同》中并未对涉案石油焦 HGI 指数的典型值设定最低和最高的范围，涉案《采购合同》约定的石油焦 HGI 指数的典型值范围并非强制性指标，不具有强制性的主张没有依据，该院不予支持。江苏高院认为，由于双方在涉案《采购合同》中约定石油焦的 HGI 指数为典型值，涉案检验检测的就应当是涉案石油焦 HGI 指数的典型值。经装货港和目的港两次检验，德国克虏伯公司实际交付的石油焦的 HGI 指数典型值均为 32，低于双方约定的 HGI 指数典型值的最低值。该院据此认定，德国克虏伯公司交付的石油焦的 HGI 指数与合同约定不符，构成违约。

中化新加坡公司认为，其作为贸易商购买涉案石油焦的目的是在中国境内销售，德国克虏伯公司交付的石油焦的 HGI 指数与合同约定不符，导致其在中国境内无法正常销售，最终剥夺了其期待的利益，构成根本违约。而德国克虏伯公司认为，德国克虏伯公司的三位专家证人的意见、中化新加坡公司将涉案石油焦转售给金猴公司的事实，均证明涉案 HGI 指数为 32 的石油焦可以在国内实际使用。江苏高院认为，双方当事人一致认可，HGI 指数表示石油焦的硬度，指数越高，硬度越低；指数越低，硬度越高。这表明，HGI 指数的高低对石油焦的硬度有着重要的影响。德国克虏伯公司专家证人 Fisher 先生是长期从事石油焦行业的专业人士，Fisher 先生出庭作证称其在从业经历中见到的 HGI 指数最低为 35。Fisher 先生的这一证言表明 HGI 指数为 32 的石油焦的确极为罕见，或者说涉案石油焦的 HGI 指数偏离双方在合同中约定的范围的程度相当严重。德国克虏伯公司专家证人李某某先生出庭作证称，HGI 指数是燃料制粉系统的选型依据，HGI 指数低、硬度大的石油焦需要更换设备方可使用。这表明，HGI 指数不同的石油焦，对研磨设备的要求也就不同。HGI 指数低达 32 的石油焦必然会对研磨设备有特殊的要求，这也就意味着此类石油焦的市场需求极为有限。因此，德国克虏伯公司交付 HGI 指数低达 32 的石油焦给中化新加坡公司，必然会给中化新加坡公司的销售造成极大困难，这等于实际上剥夺了中化新加坡公司签订涉案采购合同期望得到的利益。作为从事石油焦贸易的专业公司，德国克虏伯公司不可能不知道其违约行为可能给中化新加坡公司造成的损失。江苏高院据此认定,德国克虏伯公司的行为构成根本违约。

三、中化新加坡公司有权宣告合同无效

中化新加坡公司以德国克虏伯公司根本违约为由,请求法院判令解除合同,应理解为其请求法院依据《销售公约》的规定宣告合同无效。德国克虏伯公司认为,根据《销售公约》第四十九条(1)(a)和(2)(b)(一)的规定,在卖方已经交付货物的情况下,买方若要以卖方交货不符合合同约定构成根本违约为由宣告合同无效,必须在已知道或理应知道根本违约事由后一段合理时间内提出。中化新加坡公司没有在合理的时间内发出宣告合同无效的通知,丧失了宣告合同无效的权利。江苏高院认为,德国克虏伯公司的这一主张不能成立。理由如下:

《销售公约》第三十九条(1)规定,买方对货物不符合同,必须在发现或理应发现不符情形后一段合理时间内通知卖方,说明不符合同情形的性质,否则就丧失声称货物不符合同的权利。第四十条规定,如果货物不符合同规定指的是卖方知道或不可能不知道而又没有告知买方的一些事实,则卖方无权援引第三十九条规定的合理期限进行抗辩。虽然从文义上看,该规定适用于一般违约,但根据举轻以明重的原理,该规定同样适用于因交货与合同严重不符构成根本违约而宣告合同无效的情形。本案中,德国克虏伯公司在装货港就已知道其交付的石油焦的 HGI 指数为 32,严重偏离双方约定的指标。其既没有将这一事实在发货前告知中化新加坡公司,也没有询问中化新加坡公司是否愿意接受 HGI 指数为 32 的石油焦,而是直接将货物运交中化新加坡公司。在此种情形下,德国克虏伯公司无权以中化新加坡公司没有在合理的时间内发出宣告合同无效的通知为由,主张中化新加坡公司丧失了宣告合同无效的权利。

实际上,中化新加坡公司宣告合同无效并未超出合理期限。2008 年 9 月 8 日石油焦到达目的港,中化新加坡公司发现 HGI 指数为 32 后,依据采购合同第 7.2.3 条于同年 10 月 15 日即发函给德国克虏伯公司,提出其交付的涉案石油焦的HGI指数与合同约定的范围严重不符,下家用户无法使用,拒绝接货,事态严重,请德国克虏伯公司尽快拿出处理意见。为了进一步核实石油焦品质,中化新加坡公司对石油焦进行了复检。复检结果表明涉案石油焦的HGI指数为32,与合同约定不符。此后,中化新加坡公司多次发函给德国克虏伯公司,提出德国克虏伯公司交付的石油焦的HGI指数严重偏离合同约定的范围,构成实质性违约,要求妥善处理石油焦质量问题,但终因德国克虏伯公司不予配合,未能得到解决。江苏高院认为,中化新加坡公司在发现涉案石油焦的HGI指数与合同约定严重不符之后,毫不迟延地与德国克虏伯公司进行交涉,且在交涉无果之后,进而提起诉讼要求宣告合同无效,应当视为中化新加坡公司在知道或理应知道根本违约事由后一段合理时间内向德国克虏伯公司发出了符合公约第二十六条规定的宣告合同无效的通知。德国克虏伯公司关于中化新加坡公司未在合理时间内向其发出宣告合同无效的通知,因而丧失了宣告合同无效的权利的主张没有依据,江苏高院不予支持。

德国克虏伯公司还认为,中化新加坡公司已于2009年11月将涉案石油焦卖给金猴公司,已经不可能按实际收到货物的原状返还货物,根据公约第八十二条(1)的规定,中化新加坡公司已丧失宣告合同无效的权利。江苏高院认为,中化新加坡公司在发现德国克虏伯公司交货构成实质性违约后,即与德国克虏伯公司进行交涉,但德国克虏伯公司不予配合,致使中化新加坡公司不得不提起诉讼。在本案审理过程中,为避免损失进一步扩大,中化新加坡公司再次与德国克虏伯公司商谈涉案石油焦的妥善处置,德国克虏伯公司明确拒绝,中化新加坡公司不得已将涉案石油焦出售给金猴公司。因此,造成涉案石油焦不能按实际收到时的原状返还给德国克虏伯公司的责任在德国克虏伯公司而不在中化新加坡公司。根据公约第八十二条(2)(a)的规定,中化新加坡公司并未丧失宣告合同无效的权利。

此外,德国克虏伯公司认为,中化新加坡公司已经支付全额货款,中化新加坡公司的这一行为表明其对石油焦的质量是满意的,且已经接受了涉案石油焦,其无权再对石油焦的质量提出异议。江苏高院认为,根据涉案《采购合同》的约定,中化新加坡公司有权对石油焦质量提出异议并寻求救济的期限是货物到港后60日内,该权限与中化新加坡公司是否支付货款没有关系。这就意味着,即使中化新加坡公司已经支付了货款,只要不超过货物到港后60日,中化新加坡公司仍有权对石油焦的质量提出异议并寻求救济。德国克虏伯公司关于中化新加坡公司支付全额货款的行为应视为其对涉案石油焦的质量满意并接受货物,因而丧失对涉案石油焦的质量提出异议并寻求救济的权利的主张,没有依据,江苏高院不予支持。

四、德国克虏伯公司应承担的责任

根据《销售公约》第七十四条和七十七条、第八十一条和八十四条的规定,中化新加坡公司宣告合同无效后,有权要求德国克虏伯公司返还已经支付的货款并支付从收取货款之日起的利息,以及赔偿中化新加坡公司因德国克虏伯公司违约而遭受的经济损失。在本案中,中化新加坡公司支付德国克虏伯公司的货款金额为7756828.55美元,中化新加坡公司为了减轻由于德国克虏伯公司违约而引起的损失,设法将涉案石油焦处置收回货款5072525.65美元。扣除该款后,德国克虏伯公司还应返还中化新加坡公司货款2684302.9美元,并支付该部分货款自中化新加坡公司支付货款之日(2008年9月25日)至实际返还之日的利息。中化新加坡公司在处置涉案石油焦的过程中承担额外费用528253.24美元,该款属于中化新加坡公司因德国克虏伯公司违约而遭受的损失,中化新加坡公司只要求德国克虏伯公司赔偿520339.77美元,应予支持。

德国克虏伯公司认为,中化新加坡公司并无损失,中化新加坡公司已将涉案石油焦以原价卖给了其母公司中化控股公司。江苏高院认为,德国克虏伯公司的这一主张不能成立。中化新加坡公司称,其与中化控股公司签订买卖合同是为了报关需要,以使涉案石油焦顺利进入中国境内,便于其委托中化控股公司代其在中国境内销售,其与中化控股公司之间并不是真正的买卖关系,而是委托销售关系,并提交了其与中化控股公司之间的委托销售合同为证。2008 年 10 月 15 日代中化新加坡公司就涉案石油焦的 HGI 指数向德国克虏伯公司提出交涉就是中化控股公司，德国克虏伯公司并未提出异议。此后，中化新加坡公司还多次与德国克虏伯公司就涉案石油焦的 HGI 指数进行交涉，德国克虏伯公司亦未提出中化新加坡公司已将涉案石油焦转售给中化控股公司，无权再对涉案石油焦的 HGI 指数提出异议。由此可见，德国克虏伯公司对中化新加坡公司与中化控股公司之间的委托销售关系是明知的。在本案审理过程中，中化新加坡公司为减轻损失而处理涉案石油焦也是委托中化控股公司代为销售。这也进一步印证了中化新加坡公司关于其与中化控股公司之间是委托销售关系，而非买卖合同关系的主张。江苏高院据此认定，中化新加坡公司与中化控股公司之间并非买卖合同关系，而是委托销售关系。德国克虏伯公司关于中化新加坡公司已将涉案石油焦以原合同价格出售给中化控股公司因而不存在损失的主张，没有依据，江苏高院不予支持。

德国克虏伯公司还认为，中化新加坡公司的损失是由于石油焦价格下跌所致，其不应当承担赔偿责任。江苏高院认为，导致宣告涉案《采购合同》无效的原因是德国克虏伯公司构成根本违约，而不是市场价格下跌；如果德国克虏伯公司交付的石油焦的 HGI 指数符合合同约定，即使价格下跌，中化新加坡公司亦无权以此为由宣告合同无效，此时，价格下跌属中化新加坡公司应当承担的商业风险。在涉案采购合同系因德国克虏伯公司的根本违约而被宣告无效的情况下，价格下跌的风险则属于德国克虏伯公司应当承担的商业风险。因此，在本案中，即使存在因石油焦市场行情发生变化而导致的损失，亦应由德国克虏伯公司承担。

综上所述，德国克虏伯公司交付石油焦的 HGI 指数与涉案《采购合同》的约定严重不符，构成根本违约，其应承担宣告合同无效的后果。江苏高院依照《销售公约》第二十五条、二十六条、三十九条(1)、四十条、四十九条(1)(a)和(2)(b)(一)、七十四条、七十七条、八十一条、八十二条(1)和(2)(a)、八十四条，《中华人民共和国民事诉讼法》第一百二十八条的规定，判决如下:(一)宣告德国克虏伯公司与中化新加坡公司于2008年4月11日签订的《采购合同》无效。(二)德国克虏伯公司于本判决生效之日起30日内返还中化新加坡公司货款2684302.9美元并支付自2008年9月25日至本判决确定的给付之日的利息(按中国银行同期美元贷款利率计算)。(三)德国克虏伯公司于本判决生效之日起30日内赔偿中化新加坡公司损失520339.77美元。如果未按本判决指定的期间履行上述给付义务,应当依照《中华人民共和国民事诉讼法》第二百二十九条之规定,加倍支付迟延履行期间的债务利息。本案案件受理费人民币306432元,由德国克虏伯公司负担。

德国克虏伯公司不服江苏高院一审判决,向本院提起上诉称:一、一审判决对本案适用法律认定错误。根据合同约定以及我国的冲突规范,本案应适用美国纽约州法律。《销售公约》应适用于本案,《销售公约》的解释、美国《统一商法典》以及商业惯例等同样适用于本案,《〈联合国国际货物销售合同公约〉判例法摘要汇编》也是审理本案的依据。江苏高院认定只有《销售公约》才适用于本案是错误的。二、江苏高院错误认定中化新加坡公司与中化控股公司是委托代理关系。中化新加坡公司与中化控股公司是买卖合同关系,中化新加坡公司在已将货物顺利转卖的情况下,无权主张本案中的诉讼请求。三、一审判决错误认定德国克虏伯公司交付HGI指数为32的石油焦构成根本违约。1. 德国克虏伯公司交付HGI指数为32的石油焦不构成一般性违约。HGI指数不是强制性指标,仅仅是一个大约的范围。合同对于HGI值这样一个非重要指标,并未作出价格调整的安排。从合同当事人的行为考虑,一个理性的买方如果认为石油焦HGI值为32与合同不符构成根本违约,不会在收到检验证书2个月后,甚至已接收了货物并付清全额货款后才对货物品质提出异议。2. 德国克虏伯公司交付HGI指数为32的石油焦不构成根本违约。案涉石油焦尽管HGI值较低,但完全具备其应有的使用价值和商业价值。并且中化新加坡公司于2009年11月将涉案货物转卖,转卖价格高于同期市场价格。因此涉案HGI指数为32的石油焦并未从根本上剥夺中化新加坡公司在合同下有权得到的东西导致其合同目的不能实现。江苏高院认定德国克虏伯公司构成根本违约，与事实相悖，于法无据。四、中化新加坡公司未在合理时间内作出宣告合同无效的通知，已丧失宣告合同无效的权利。其在得知 HGI 指数为 32 的数月之后并且是在市场发生大跌的背景下作出合同无效的宣告，不能认为是在合理期限内作出。江苏高院在合理期限的认定上，严重违背了《销售公约》的相关规定和立法精神。五、即使德国克虏伯公司交付 HGI 值为 32 的石油焦构成一般性违约，由于中化新加坡公司未在合理期限内提出质量异议，其已丧失主张质量不符的权利。六、一审判决在损失数额的认定上存在严重错误。根据《销售公约》第七十六条的规定，本案中假设中化新加坡公司有权宣告合同无效，那么损害赔偿的计算应按合同约定价格与中化新加坡公司接收货物时的价格之差进行计算。然而一审判决错误地按合同价格减去 2009 年 11 月转卖给金猴公司的价格之差计算，明显与《销售公约》的规定相悖。七、中化新加坡公司在一审中的诉讼请求为请求法院解除双方订立的《采购合同》，从未向法院提出过宣告《采购合同》无效的诉讼请求。江苏高院径自判决宣告涉案合同无效，判非所请，违反法律规定。综上，请求：1. 依法改判驳回中化新加坡公司的全部诉讼请求；2. 依法判令中化新加坡公司承担一、二审全部诉讼费用。

中化新加坡公司答辩称：一、一审判决根据双方当事人的选择适用《销售公约》审理本案是正确的。依据双方在《采购合同》中的约定，应适用美国纽约州法律，德国克虏伯公司主张《销售公约》为纽约州法律的一部分。而《〈联合国国际货物销售合同公约〉判例法摘要汇编》不是《销售公约》的组成部分，也非公约的官方解释，不能作为本案的法律依据。二、中化新加坡公司委托中化控股公司代为销售案涉石油焦，两者之间是委托关系而非买卖关系，一审判决对此认定正确。中化新加坡公司委托中化控股公司代为销售涉案石油焦，已经得到德国克虏伯公司的认可。在涉案石油焦运抵南京港后，中化控股公司作为中化新加坡公司的代理人直接与德国克虏伯公司联系,德国克虏伯公司也认可其代理人身份,其在本案诉讼发生后再就中化控股公司受托人的身份问题提出异议,有违"允诺禁反言"原则。三、案涉石油焦的HGI指数为双方明确约定的重要质量指标。德国克虏伯公司交付石油焦的HGI值为32,严重低于双方的约定,造成中化新加坡公司在转售时的极大困难,合同目的无法实现,构成根本违约。中化新加坡公司向德国克虏伯公司付款,不能视为接受质量不合格货物。根据合同约定,对货物的质量异议在石油焦抵达目的港60日内提出即可。四、根据《销售公约》,德国克虏伯公司因未告知货物不符情况,而无权主张"合理时间"抗辩,且中化新加坡公司已在合理时间内启动了双方约定的纠纷解决机制,并向德国克虏伯公司主张货物不符的根本违约,一审判决认定中化新加坡公司宣告合同无效并未超出合理期限是正确的。五、一审判决对中化新加坡公司损失的认定是正确的。中化新加坡公司根据《销售公约》第七十四条主张损失,但德国克虏伯公司却错误地理解和援引《销售公约》第七十六条规定,没有任何依据。中化新加坡公司主张损失的总额,是中化新加坡公司实际遭受的损失,并不因时价计算时点的变化而变化。六、《销售公约》中规定的宣告合同无效与我国法律所述合同解除,其内涵是一致的,本案不存在判非所请的情况。综上,一审判决认定事实清楚,适用法律正确,请求依法驳回德国克虏伯公司的上诉。

江苏高院一审查明的事实,有相关证据予以佐证,各方当事人亦均无异议,本院予以确认。

本院另查明:中化新加坡公司于2009年11月11日至德国克虏伯公司关于处理系争货物及时减少损失的函件中载明:"鉴于贵司拒绝与我司签订处理货物止损之协议,为减少系争货物所产生的损失,维护贵司与我司的共同权利,我司已觅得系争货物买受人,并且通过我司的代理方即中化国际(控股)股份有限公司与潜在买受人就价格等事宜已初步商定,即结算数量为25722.339吨(BALTIC FRONTIER轮进口石油焦原堆原转),单价为1575.50元/吨,南京惠宁码头舱底交货价,该价格未低于市场合理价格。"

德国克虏伯公司在二审期间向本院提交了美国《统一商法典》和相关案例〔Lomaglio Assocs. v. LBK Mktg. Corp.，1999 美国州地方法院莱克西斯14185(S. D. N. Y. 1999)〕，认为根据美国法律，案涉合同成立并有效。

中化新加坡公司未对德国克虏伯公司提交的美国法律提出异议，但认为应由具备美国法律从业资格的专业人士对法律作出说明，不认可本案德国克虏伯公司委托代理人所作的说明。中化新加坡公司同时认为《销售公约》是认定案涉合同效力的依据，根据《销售公约》，案涉合同合法成立并有效，且即使适用我国法律，案涉合同也应认定合法有效。

本院认为：

一、本案法律适用以及合同效力问题

本案为国际货物买卖合同纠纷，双方当事人均为外国公司，案件具有涉外因素。最高人民法院《关于适用〈中华人民共和国涉外民事关系法律适用法〉若干问题的解释(一)》第二条规定："涉外民事关系法律适用法实施以前发生的涉外民事关系，人民法院应当根据该涉外民事关系发生时的有关法律规定确定应当适用的法律；当时法律没有规定的，可以参照涉外民事关系法律适用法的规定确定。"案涉《采购合同》签订于 2008 年 4 月 11 日，在《中华人民共和国涉外民事关系法律适用法》实施之前，当事人签订《采购合同》时的《中华人民共和国民法通则》第一百四十五条规定："涉外合同的当事人可以选择处理合同争议所适用的法律，法律另有规定的除外。涉外合同的当事人没有选择的，适用与合同有最密切联系的国家的法律。"本案双方当事人在合同中约定应当根据美国纽约州当时有效的法律订立、管辖和解释，该约定不违反法律规定，应认定有效。由于本案当事人营业地所在国新加坡和德国均为《销售公约》缔约国，美国亦为《销售公约》缔约国，且在一审审理期间双方当事人一致选择适用《销售公约》作为确定其权利义务的依据，并未排除《销售公约》的适用，江苏高院适用《销售公约》审理本案是正确的。而对于审理案件中涉及到的问题《销售公约》没有规定的，应当适用当事人选择的美国纽约州法律。《〈联合国国际货物销售合同公约〉判例法摘要汇编》并非公约的组成部分,其不能作为审理本案的法律依据。但在如何准确理解公约相关条款的含义方面,其可以作为适当的参考资料。

人民法院审理合同纠纷案件,无论当事人是否对合同效力存在异议,均应首先对该问题作出认定。《销售公约》第四条规定:“本公约只适用于销售合同的订立和卖方和买方因此种合同而产生的权利和义务。特别是,本公约除非另有明文规定,与以下事项无关:(a)合同的效力,或其任何条款的效力,或任何惯例的效力;(b)合同对所售货物所有权可能产生的影响。”由于公约并未对合同效力问题作出规定,故本案应适用当事人在合同中选择的美国纽约州法律对此问题作出认定。德国克虏伯公司在本院二审期间提交了美国《统一商法典》和相关判例,认为案涉合同应认定有效。中化新加坡公司虽对德国克虏伯公司代理人关于美国法律的说明不予认可,但对于德国克虏伯公司提交的相关美国法律并未提出异议,且亦认为案涉合同应认定有效。对德国克虏伯公司提交的美国法律,本院予以确认。根据双方当事人提交并确认的美国法律,案涉《采购合同》并不存在应认定无效的情形,《采购合同》有效。

二、江苏高院是否判非所请的问题

中化新加坡公司一审起诉的一项诉讼请求是其认为德国克虏伯公司根本违约,请求解除双方订立的《采购合同》。《销售公约》并未类似于我国相关法律规定,对合同解除和无效加以区别并作出规定,其规定一方当事人构成根本违约的情况下,另一方当事人有权宣告合同无效。此处规定的宣告无效实质等同于我国法律中的解除合同。江苏高院根据中化新加坡公司的诉请及其依据的事实和理由,结合《销售公约》的相关规定,认为其请求法院判令解除合同应理解为请求法院依据《销售公约》的规定宣告合同无效,符合中化新加坡公司的真实意思表示,对此中化新加坡公司亦表示认可,并无异议。江苏高院并不存在判非所请的情形。德国克虏伯公司关于江苏高院超过当事人诉讼请求,判非所请的上诉理由不能成立。

三、中化新加坡公司与中化控股公司是否委托代理关系的问题

中化新加坡公司主张其与中化控股公司之间系委托关系，其对与中化控股公司签订买卖合同是为办理报关需要进行了合理解释，并提交了委托销售合同，且中化控股公司2008年10月15日代中化新加坡公司就涉案石油焦的HGI指数向德国克虏伯公司提出交涉，此后中化新加坡公司还多次与德国克虏伯公司就涉案石油焦的HGI指数进行交涉，德国克虏伯公司并未提出中化新加坡公司已将案涉石油焦转售给中化控股公司，无权再对案涉石油焦的HGI指数提出异议。在本案一审过程中，中化新加坡公司为减轻损失而处理涉案石油焦也是委托中化控股公司代为销售。江苏高院据此认定中化新加坡公司与中化控股公司之间系委托销售关系，对于德国克虏伯公司关于中化新加坡公司与中化控股公司之间系买卖关系，中化新加坡公司已将涉案石油焦以原合同价格出售给中化控股公司因而不存在损失的主张不予支持并无不当。德国克虏伯公司关于江苏高院错误认定中化新加坡公司与中化控股公司是委托代理关系的上诉理由不能成立。

四、德国克虏伯公司是否构成根本违约的问题

双方当事人在《采购合同》中约定的石油焦HGI指数典型值在36至46之间，而德国克虏伯公司实际交付的石油焦HGI指数为32，低于双方约定的HGI指数典型值的最低值，不符合合同约定。江苏高院认定德国克虏伯公司构成违约是正确的。

本案争议的焦点问题在于德国克虏伯公司的上述违约行为是否构成根本违约。首先，从双方当事人在合同中对石油焦需符合的化学和物理特性规格约定的内容看，合同对石油焦的受潮率、硫含量、灰含量、挥发物含量、尺寸、热值、硬度(HGI值)等七个方面作出了约定。而从目前事实看，对于德国克虏伯公司交付的石油焦，中化新加坡公司仅认为HGI指数一项不符合同约定，而对于其他六项指标，中化新加坡公司并未提出异议。结合当事人提交的证人证言以及证人出庭的陈述，HGI指数表示石油焦的研磨指数，指数越低，石油焦的硬度越大，研磨难度越大。但正如江苏高院在一审

判决中指出的即使是中化新加坡公司一方提交的上海大学材料科学与工程学院出具的说明,亦不否认HGI指数为32的石油焦可以使用,只是认为其用途有限。故可以认定虽然案涉石油焦HGI指数与合同约定不符,但该批石油焦仍然具有使用价值。其次,本案一审审理期间,中化新加坡公司为减少损失,经过积极的努力将案涉石油焦予以转售,且其在就将相关问题至德国克虏伯公司的函件中明确表示该批石油焦转售的价格"未低于市场合理价格。"这一事实说明案涉石油焦是可以以合理价格予以销售的。第三、综合考量其他国家裁判对《销售公约》中关于根本违约条款的理解,买方在不存在不合理的麻烦的情况下,能使用货物或转售货物,甚至打些折扣,质量不符依然不过是非根本违约。故本院认为德国克虏伯公司交付HGI指数为32的石油焦的行为,并不构成根本违约。江苏高院认定德国克虏伯公司构成根本违约并判决宣告《采购合同》无效,适用法律错误,本院应予纠正。德国克虏伯公司对其是否构成根本违约这一问题的上诉理由成立,本院予以支持。

鉴于德国克虏伯公司的行为不构成根本违约,中化新加坡公司无权据此宣告合同无效,则德国克虏伯公司上诉提出的中化新加坡公司是否以根本违约为由在合理时间内作出宣告合同无效通知的问题,已无进一步审查的必要,本院对此问题不再评判。

五、当事人责任承担问题

虽然德国克虏伯公司交付与合同约定的HGI值不符的石油焦并不构成根本违约,但如前所述,由于所交货物与合同约定不符,江苏高院认定其违约是正确的。根据《采购合同》的约定,如果中化新加坡公司发现石油焦的品质或数量与在装货港确定的品质或数量不符,有权在石油焦到达目的港之日起60日内向德国克虏伯公司提出索赔。本案货物2008年9月8日到达南京港,2008年10月15日,中化控股公司发函给德国克虏伯公司,提出其交付的石油焦HGI指数与合同约定的范围严重不符,下家用户无法使用,拒绝接货,事态严重,请德国克虏伯公司尽快拿出处理意见。德国克虏伯公司在一审庭审答辩时，认可中化控股公司的该行为代表中化新加坡公司。2008年11月4日，中化新加坡公司再次发函给德国克虏伯公司，称德国克虏伯公司交付的石油焦HGI指数严重偏离合同约定的范围，构成实质性违约，并要求德国克虏伯公司妥善处理。上述事实说明中化新加坡公司在合同约定的期限内已就货物质量提出异议，主张相关权利。故德国克虏伯公司关于中化新加坡公司未在合理期限内提出质量异议，已丧失主张质量不符的权利的上诉理由不能成立，本院不予支持。

德国克虏伯公司交付的石油焦HGI指数不符合合同约定，客观上造成中化新加坡公司不能及时转售。虽然中化新加坡公司经过努力予以转售，但受市场价格变动影响，产生损失。故对于货款差价损失2684302.9美元及利息和堆存费164071.31美元，德国克虏伯公司应承担相应的赔偿责任。上述损失的产生，亦有市场风险的原因，故中化新加坡公司亦应自行承担相应的损失。税费、包干费均是合同履行中应由中化新加坡公司承担的费用，在其宣告合同无效的请求不能得到支持的情况下，税费和包干费均应由中化新加坡公司自行承担。

综上，江苏高院一审判决认定事实基本清楚，但部分法律适用错误，责任认定不当，本院予以纠正。根据《中华人民共和国民法通则》第一百四十五条，《联合国国际货物销售合同公约》第一条、第四条、第二十五条、第三十九条、第四十九条、第七十四条、第七十八条，《中华人民共和国民事诉讼法》第一百七十条第一款第（二）项，最高人民法院《关于适用〈中华人民共和国涉外民事关系法律适用法〉若干问题的解释（一）》第二条之规定，判决如下：

一、撤销江苏省高级人民法院（2009）苏民三初字第0004号民事判决第一项。

二、变更江苏省高级人民法院（2009）苏民三初字第0004号民事判决第二项为蒂森克虏伯冶金产品有限责任公司于本判决生效之日起30日内赔偿中化国际（新加坡）有限公司货款损失1610581.74美元并支付自2008年9月25日至本判决确定的给付之日的利息（按中国银行同期美元贷款利率计算）。

三、变更江苏省高级人民法院(2009)苏民三初字第0004号民事判决第三项为蒂森克虏伯冶金产品有限责任公司于本判决生效之日起30日内赔偿中化国际(新加坡)有限公司堆存费损失98442.79美元。

四、驳回中化国际(新加坡)有限公司的其他诉讼请求。

如果未按本判决指定的期间履行上述给付义务,应当依照《中华人民共和国民事诉讼法》第二百五十三条之规定,加倍支付迟延履行期间的债务利息。

一审案件受理费人民币306432元,由蒂森克虏伯冶金产品有限责任公司负担人民币183859.2元,中化国际(新加坡)有限公司负担人民币122572.8元。二审案件受理费人民币306432元,由蒂森克虏伯冶金产品有限责任公司负担人民币183859.2元,中化国际(新加坡)有限公司负担人民币122572.8元。

本判决为终审判决。

审 判 长 任雪峰

代理审判员 成明珠

代理审判员 朱 科

二〇一四年六月三十日

书 记 员 丁 一

Sinochem International (Singapore) Pte Ltd

v.

ThyssenKrupp Metallurgical Products GmbH for the Dispute over a Contract for the International Sale of Goods

—Application of the *United Nations Convention on Contracts for the International Sale of Goods* and Determination of Fundamental Breach of Contract

Holding

1. If and when the countries where the Parties to a contract for the international sale of goods are located are signatories to the *United Nations Convention on Contracts for the International Sale of Goods* (hereinafter referred to as CISG), the provisions thereof shall prevail, and further then, where there are no relevant provisions therein, the proper laws set forth in the said contract shall prevail. The CISG shall not apply provided that its application is explicitly excluded by the parties hereto.

2. For a contract for the international sale of goods, even if the goods delivered under the contract by the Seller are found to be defective, such case shall not be deemed as the fundamental breach of contract as defined in the CISG provided that the said goods can remain to be used or resold by the Buyer with reasonable efforts.

Commentary *

This case mainly relates to the rescission of contract and damages claims arising from the performance of a contract for the international sale of goods.

The essential facts in the dispute over the contract for the international sale of goods between the Appellant ThyssenKrupp Metallurgical Products GmbH (hereinafter referred to as ThyssenKrupp) and the Appellee Sinochem International (Overseas) Pte Ltd (hereinafter referred to as Sinochem-SG) go as follows: the Seller ThyssenKrupp and the Buyer Sinochem-SG signed a Purchase Contract on Petroleum Coke. Having found the goods delivered defective, the Buyer claimed for damages against the Seller on the grounds of the non-conformity of the goods with that stipulated in the Purchase Contract, and thereafter resold the goods to another buyer at a price lower than the original contract price. Having failed to find out a solution to the dispute through negotiations between the Parties, the Buyer filed a lawsuit with the Higher People's Court of Jiangsu Province (hereinafter referred to as CFI), claiming that the Seller's defective performance constituted a fundamental breach and requesting that the Purchase Contract is rescinded and all the losses are borne by the Seller. Yet, the Seller contended that, with the defect in the goods not being a material one, its performance didn't constitute a breach of contract, and all the losses incurred to the Buyer were the consequence of the declining prices of the goods, asserting that the Buyer is exclusively held liable for all the losses and has no right to rescind the Purchase Contract. In addition, it was also stipulated in the Purchase Contract that any possible disputes concerning the Purchase Contract shall be governed by the law of the State of

* Author: ZUO Haicong, Professor (T2) and Doctoral Supervisor, University of International Business and Economics; Vice-President, Research Institute of International Economic Laws of China Law Society.

New York, the United States. The Defendant ThyssenKrupp appealed against the Judgment made by CFI, which upheld the claims from the Plaintiff Sinochem-SG, to the Supreme People's Court of the People's Republic of China (hereinafter referred to as SPC or CSI), and SPC rendered the Judgment in June 2014 that: the defect in the goods delivered by the Seller didn't suffice in constituting a fundamental breach from the Seller, and thus the Buyer has no right to request to have the Purchase Contract rescinded on the grounds thereof; and all the losses incurred to the Buyer are attributable in part to the defect in the goods delivered by the Seller, which led to the Buyer's difficulty in reselling the goods, and in part to the declining prices of the goods, and thus the Seller is held liable only for the damages attributable to the defect in the goods.

The mentioned above Judgment made by SPC embodies some creativity in the legal reasoning and application of laws, and carries typical and guiding significance in its adjudication concept and approach. This case has not only been listed among SPC's guiding cases and the BRI-related typical cases but also cited repeatedly by the UNCITRAL Secretariat in its Digest of Case Law on the United Nations Convention on the International Sale of Goods (2016 Revision) (hereinafter referred to as Digest of Case Law) as a typical case in interpreting and applying Article 1, Article 7, Article 25 and Article 74 of the CISG.

The creativity in SPC's adjudication concept and approach in this case is mainly reflected in the application of laws, the definition of fundamental breach and the determination of damages.

1. Uphold the Good Tradition in Proper Application of International Conventions and Foreign Laws

The dispute on the application of laws arose between the Parties. The Appellant affirmed that as for the governing law, according to the contractual stipulation and the rule of the conflict of laws in China, laws in the State of New York, the United States, shall apply to this case. Besides, the CISG and its interpretations, the U. S. *Uniform Commercial Code*, commercial practices, etc. shall also apply hereto, and the Digest of Case Law shall also be the basis for the trial of this case. The determination that only the CISG was applicable in this case by CFI was an error.

The approach to applying the CISG adopted by courts varies with countries when the laws of signatory states are chosen as the governing law by the Parties while the CISG shall applies. In general, German courts hold that if German laws are chosen by the Parties, the CISG, as a part of German laws, prevails and excludes the application of domestic laws, whereas in U. S. courts, the CISG as a self-executing treaty directly applies. But in Chinese courts, the CISG directly applies as the governing law according to its Article 1 (1)(1), and then, when it comes to the matters on which there are no relevant provisions therein, the laws of signatory states shall apply. For example, in the case of the sales contract dispute between Appellant United Enterprise Co, Ltd of the United States and Appellee Shandong Foreign Trade (Yantai) Company in eastern China (No. 358[1998], Final, Eco. Division), given China and the United States where the principal places of business of the Parties to the dispute are located respectively are both signatory states to the CISG, SPC determined that the CISG shall apply to the dispute, and dismissed the claim by the Appellant that United States laws shall be the governing law based on the doctrine of the most significant relationship.

It was stipulated in the Purchase Contract that it is concluded in accordance with laws of the New York State, the United States, in force at the time of the execution thereof, and shall be governed and interpreted by the said laws. SPC accept the interpretation and application of the CFIG, and ruled that this choice of law clause is valid. Given that Germany and Singapore where the principal places of business of the Parties to the dispute are located respectively are both signatory states to the CISG, and the Parties didn't expressly exclude the application thereof, and now, therefore, the CISG shall apply as the governing law according to its Article 1 (1)(1), and when it comes to the issues on which there are no relevant provisions therein, laws of the New York State, the United States, which were stipulated by the Parties in the Contract, shall apply.

With regard to the validity of a sale contract, SPC found by reference to Article 4 of the CISG that there are no related provisions therein on this issue and determined that the legal provisions of the New York State, the United States, which were stipulated by the Parties in the Purchase Contract, shall apply. Having determined and applied laws of the United States State of New York, SPC concluded that the Purchase Contract in this case is valid.

The practice of the CISG prevailing as the governing law and the laws of signatory states chosen by parties applying as the supplementary laws distinguishes and separates different issues in the application of laws, not only respecting the principle of party autonomy but also performing the obligations of China as a signatory state to the CISG. So, it is an advanced concept and approach of law application, demonstrating the judicial wisdom of Chinese judges.

By May 2016, the CISG, the international convention applied most frequently worldwide, had been applied in at least 4, 500 litigation or arbitration cases. Extensive application of the CISG creates a uniform law governing contracts for the international sale of goods, providing legal guarantee and foreseeability for transactions for the international sale of goods. Chinese courts have been very acceptive of the application of the CISG. As of 2016, Chinese courts and arbitration institutions had applied the CISG to more than 400 cases of foreign-related purchase contracts for goods. The consistent practice of Chinese courts contributes to the application and influence of the CISG, reduces the transaction costs for Parties involved in the international sale of goods, and enhances the foreseeability and legal guarantee of transactions.

2. Accurately Determine the Nature of a Breach by Reference to Foreign Precedents

In this case, whether or not the breach of contract constitutes a fundamental breach is one of the issues between the Parties. CFI supported the claim of Appellee (the Plaintiff of First Instance) that a fundamental breach was established, and the Plaintiff was entitled to rescind the Purchase Contract. Appellant (the Defendant of First Instance) appealed against CFI's Judgment.

Article 25 of the CISG provides the constitutive elements of a fundamental breach, that is, when one Party's breach causes the other Party to suffer the loss or damage to the extent that it materially deprives the latter of what it otherwise can be able to obtain under a contract, such breach constitutes a fundamental breach. However, the breaching Party may lodge a defense if and when the said loss or damage is unforeseeable at the time of the execution thereof by itself or a reasonable person in a similar situation. Now that the expression "materially deprive" in the CISG only indicates the severity of the loss or damage, so that under what circumstances and at what levels of severity of the said loss or damage does a breach suffice in constituting a fundamental breach is up to a court to make a judgment based on specific circumstances in different cases. In this case, CFI found that with the specification of the goods delivered being lower than the floor of the range stipulated in the Purchase Contract, the Defendant's breach constituted a fundamental breach.

In the view of SPC, although the Appellant's claim that the Digest of Case Law served as the basis of judgment wasn't justified, the essentials of judicial precedents could be drawn upon to understand and apply relevant rules. Two judicial precedents in the Digest of Case Law have certain reference value in determining whether or not the defective goods delivered in this case constituted a fundamental breach. The first is the one (Case 171) handled by the Supreme Court of Germany in 1996, where with the place of origin not being the U. K. but South Africa and the quality poor, the cobaltnitrate delivered by the Dutch Seller did not conform to the contract, and the German Buyer declared the contract to be rescinded on the grounds of the non-conformity. But in the view of the Supreme Court of Germany, when the goods had been delivered by the Seller, the Buyer's request to rescind the contract only on the grounds of the poor quality of the goods and the non-conformity of the place of origin of the goods with the stipulation in the contract wasn't sufficiently justified. Furthermore, the Buyer failed to prove that the goods being originated in South Africa could not sell in Germany or other countries. Therefore, the Supreme Court of Germany ruled that the fundamental breach couldn't be established, and the Buyer also hadn't the right to rescind the contract. The second case is the one (Case 248) handled by the Swiss Federal High Court of Appeal in 1998, where with the fat and moisture contents being too high, the frozen meat delivered by the German Seller had a 25. 5% lower value than the quality stipulated in the contract, and the Swiss Buyer claimed that the Seller committed a fundamental breach. The judge asserted that the constitution of a fundamental breach and the resulting rescission of contract were the most severe remedies that the Buyer could claim, and thus were applied only under unusual circumstances. In the end, the judge ruled that the circumstance in this case couldn't be regarded as a fundamental breach as the Buyer could still be able to resell at a lower price, or otherwise process, the goods.

In the light of the understanding of the fundamental breach provisions in the CISG in the above-mentioned judicial precedents, SPC concluded that the non-conformity of the quality of the goods didn't suffice in constituting a fundamental breach providing that the Buyer can use or resell the said goods without unreasonable troubles or even at a discounted price. In this case, the Appellee not only successfully resold the goods but also did it at a price not lower than the reasonable price at that time. SPC thus determined that the Appellant's delivery of the goods not in conformity with the contract in this case constituted a breach of contract but did not suffice in constituting a fundamental breach, and therefore the Appellee did not have the right to rescind the Purchase Contract, convincingly resolving the main legal issue in dispute in this case.

Article 7 of the CISG provides that in interpreting the CISG, due regard shall be given to its international nature and better uniformity of its application, which is an obligation for courts and arbitration institutions of signatory states in uniformly interpreting the CISG. Given courts in various jurisdictions interpret and apply the CISG under their respective judicial systems and institutions, and there is no common court of appeal for harmonizing different interpretations, to achieve a unified interpretation and application of the CISG in practice can only rely on the cross-reference and mutual learning of judgments from courts in other countries. The Digest of Case Law provides a useful way for courts from different jurisdictions to learn from each other. By referring to the interpretation and application of related provisions of the CISG and judgments by foreign courts in this case, SPC not only drew upon the judicial wisdom of courts in other countries but also fulfilled its obligation of promoting a uniform interpretation of the CISG. Therefore, SPC's Judgment in this case is of great importance, providing an example for Chinese courts in legal interpretations by referring to judicial precedents in foreign courts and promotion of the uniform application of the CISG.

3. Clarify Facts, Define Liabilities for Parties and Determine Damages Accurately

The calculation of damages for breach of contract in this case was also a point of dispute. Appellant (Defendant of First Instance) claimed that the losses incurred to the Appellee (Plaintiff of First Instance) were caused by the declining prices of the goods, having no relation with the quality of the goods delivered, whereas the Appellee maintained that the losses should be attributable to the serious defect of the goods, which created the difficulty for Appellee to find a buyer. CFI supported Appellee's claim and ruled that the Appellant is exclusively held liable for compensating all the losses. Upon the close examination and verification of all the facts, SPC concluded that the losses incurred to the Appellee were caused partially by the poor quality of the goods in Appellant and partially by the declining price of the goods, and rendered the judgment that the Appellant is only held liable for the part of the losses attributable to the poor quality of the goods.

Compensation for damages is the main way of remedies provided in the CISG, and the amount of damages is often the point of focus for all Parties in a lawsuit. Article 74 of the CISG provides that the amount of damages payable by one Party for breach of contract shall be equal to the amount of losses, including the corresponding interest, suffered by the other Party arising from breach of contract. Literally, this Provision does not seem to provide methods for calculating the losses arising from more than one cause. But as a matter of fact, it can be inferred from Article 74 that either Party shall not be held liable for the losses not caused by its breach of contract. Based on the clarified fact that the losses in this case were caused by two causes, SPC determined that the breaching Party bears a corresponding part of the losses. The SPC's legal reasoning conforms to Article 74 of the CISG, which is an effective interpretation and also an innovation in the ruling concept and approach.

To sum up, in the above-mentioned judgment, SPC adopted an innovative approach in applying laws, drew on judicial precedents in foreign courts in defining a fundamental breach, and made effective evolutionary interpretation of critical terms in determining the amount of damages. This Judgment is a landmark achievement in the application of the CISG in the field of international sale of goods, not only having the guiding significance for Chinese courts and arbitration institutions in handling similar cases but also the reference value for foreign courts and arbitration institutions.

Judicial Opinion

The Supreme People's Court of the People's Republic of China

Civil Judgment

No. 35 [2013], Final, Fourth Civ. Division, SPC

Appellant(Defendant of First Instance): ThyssenKrupp Metallurgical Products GmbH.

Domicile: ****** Essen, Germany.

Legal Representative: Knötsch, Executive Director; Nelken, Executive Director.

Attorney: Xu XX, at Guangdong ** (Tianjin) Law Firm.

Attorney: Yan XX, at Guangdong ** (Tianjin) Law Firm.

Appellee (Plaintiff of First Instance): Sinochem International (Overseas) Pte Ltd.

Domicile: ** Marina View, **** Asia Square Tower *, Singapore.

Legal Representative: Li X, Director.

Attorney: Chen XX, at Shanghai Hongqiao ** Law Firm.

Attorney: Zheng X, at Beijing ** Law Firm.

Appellant ThyssenKrupp Metallurgical Products GmbH (hereinafter referred to as ThyssenKrupp) appealed against the Civil Judgment of No. 0004 [2009], FI, Third Civ. Division, the Higher People's Court of Jiangsu Province (hereinafter referred to as CFI) on December 19, 2012 on the dispute over the Contract for International Sale of Goods (hereinafter referred to as Purchase Contract) between itself and the Appellee Sinochem International (Overseas) Pte Ltd (hereinafter referred to as Sinochem-SG) and filed an appellate petition with SPC. On December 26, 2013, SPC formed a collegial panel by law this case in public, where Xu XX and Yan XX, the attorneys representing ThyssenKrupp, and Chen XX and Zheng X, the attorneys representing Sinochem-SG, appeared and attended the proceedings in court. Now, the trial of this case has been concluded.

In its pleadings submitted with CFI, Sinochem-SG alleged that on April 11, 2008, Sinochem-SG entered into the Purchase Contract with ThyssenKrupp on the purchase of 25,000 tons of petroleum coke from ThyssenKrupp, with its Hardgrove Grindability Index (HGI) in the range of 36-46, and made the full payment as stipulated in the Purchase Contract. Yet, the HGI of the petroleum coke delivered by ThyssenKrupp was just 32, which seriously affected its sale in the Chinese market and constituted a fundamental breach of contract. Therefore, Sinochem-SG held that it had the right to rescind the Purchase Contract, and required ThyssenKrupp to refund the full payment it had made and compensate it for all the losses it suffered therefrom. To this end, Sinochem-SG requested CFI to rule that: (1) the Parties rescinded the Purchase

Contract; (2) ThyssenKrupp refunded the full payment of USD 7, 756, 828. 55 (RMB 52, 926, 392. 56 based on the USD/RMB basic exchange rate of 1 : 6. 8232 on May 6, 2009) and paid the interest accrued thereon from September 24, 2008 to the date of the actual refund (based on the Bank of China's US dollar lending rate for the same period) to Sinochem-SG; (3) ThyssenKrupp compensated the local charges and the overtime storage charges totaling RMB 1, 523, 052 (calculated provisionally as of May 6, 2009) for the petroleum coke incurred on Sinochem-SG; and (4) ThyssenKrupp bore all the court costs of this case.

In its defense against the allegations and claims from Sinochem-SG, ThyssenKrupp argued that: (1) the HGI value of the petroleum coke delivered by ThyssenKrupp was, indeed, 32. Despite seemingly deviating from the stipulation in the said Contract, but the said stipulation on the HGI value was not mandatory, and the HGI value being 32 had no effect on the usability of the said petroleum coke. Therefore, ThyssenKrupp did not constitute a breach of contract; (2) when the petroleum coke arrived at the Port of Nanjing, Sinochem-SG paid for the goods without objection. The real reason why Sinochem-SG raised the quality objection thereafter was that the market prices of petroleum coke fell sharply in September and October 2009; (3) even if ThyssenKrupp actually constituted a breach of contract, Sinochem-SG should lose its right to claim due to its failure to raise such an objection and make a claim to ThyssenKrupp within sixty (60) days from the date of arrival (incl.) of the petroleum coke at the Port of destination as set forth in the Purchase Contract; and (4) Sinochem-SG sold the petroleum coke to its parent company, Sinochem International (Holding) Co, Ltd (hereinafter referred to as Sinochem Holdings), at a price substantially identical to that as set in the Purchase Contract, and Sinochem-SG did not suffer any loss. Based on the mentioned above, ThyssenKrupp requested CFI to rule that: (1) Sinochem-SG's claim was rejected; and (2) all the court costs of this case were borne by Sinochem-SG.

Upon the hearing, CFI found that:

1. Undisputed Facts Affirmed by Both Parties

On April 11, 2008, Sinochem-SG and ThyssenKrupp signed the Purchase Contract, which stipulated that: (1) Sinochem-SG purchased 25, 000 tons of fuel-grade petroleum coke from ThyssenKrupp, with a 10% more or less in the shipping quantity and a typical HGI value in the range of 36 - 46 being acceptable; (2) the Port of loading of the petroleum coke was a port at Pittsburgh, California, and the Port of destination was a Chinese port (subject to the determination by Sinochem-SG later); (3) an independent inspector appointed by both Parties made the sampling testing on the petroleum coke on board at the Port of loading and issued the certificate of inspection, with the testing results being final and binding upon both Parties. Sinochem-SG had the right to inspect the quantity and quality of the petroleum coke delivered at the Port of discharging, and ThyssenKrupp had the right to appoint, at its own expense, an independent inspector to witness on the site of the mentioned above inspection. If the quality or quantity of the petroleum coke found at the Port of discharge was not in conformity with stipulated at the Port of loading, Sinochem-SG should send a notice of claims to ThyssenKrupp and had the right to lodge a claim within sixty (60) days from the date of arrival of the petroleum coke at the Port of destination (Article 7. 2. 3 of the Purchase Contract); and (4) the Purchase Contract should be concluded in accordance with laws of the New York State, the United States, in force at the time of the execution thereof, and should be governed and interpreted by the said laws. In addition, the Parties also entered into other agreements on the performance of the said

Purchase Contract.

On August 8, 2008, the Inspection Certificate issued at the Port of loading by A. J. EDMODN Co appointed by both Parties showed that the HGI value of the petroleum coke was 32. The Inspection Certificate of Weight dated August 11, 2008 showed that the petroleum coke actually delivered by ThyssenKrupp was 26, 079. 63 tons.

On July 31, 2008, Sinochem-SG opened a Letter of Credit (L/C) through the Singaporean Branch of Bank of Communications of China (hereinafter referred to as BOCOM-SG), providing in the L/C A45 that the HGI value of the petroleum coke was CA. 36-46. On August 27, 2008, ThyssenKrupp presented to BOCOM-SG the negotiable instruments including the Inspection Certificate issued at the Port of loading by A. J. EDMODN Co, and BOCOM-SG paid the bulk of the payment for the goods on September 2, 2008. On September 11, 2008, ThyssenKrupp issued the final commercial invoice confirming the unit price of the petroleum coke was USD 301. 56/ton. On September 25, 2008, Sinochem-SG paid off the balance under the L/C by T/T. So, Sinochem-SG made the payment of USD 7, 756, 828. 55 in total to ThyssenKrupp.

On September 8, 2008, the petroleum coke arrived at the Port of Nanjing. On November 10, 2008, the Certificate of Material Quality Testing issued by China Certification & Inspection Group Jiangsu Co, Ltd stated that the HGI value of the petroleum coke was 32.

The price of the petroleum coke in China slid from October to December 2008, with the pretax ex-factory price for medium sulfur coke falling to RMB 2, 048 per ton in October, RMB 1, 357 per ton in November and RMB 1, 305 per ton in December.

Sinochem Holdings is the parent company of Sinochem-SG.

ThyssenKrupp (the former ThyssenKrupp Minenergy GmbH domiciled at **** Strasse *** Essen) was changed on June 24, 2011 into ThyssenKrupp Metallurgical Products GmbH domiciled at ****** Essen, Germany.

2. The Opinions from Both Parties over the Conformity of the HGI Value of the Petroleum Coke with the Said Contract

Sinochem-SG claimed that the HGI value of the petroleum coke delivered by ThyssenKrupp was 32, which was not in conformity with the stipulation in the Purchase Contract and led to the difficulty in selling it in China, as a result, constituted a fundamental breach of contract. To support its claim, Sinochem-SG provided the Property Description on the Petroleum Coke HGI Values issued by the School of Materials Science and Engineering of Shanghai University, which states that the hardness (HGI value) is a core indicator of fuel-grade petroleum coke. The required hardness at large enterprises is generally not lower than 45. The fuel-grade petroleum coke with the hardness higher than 35 may be acceptable for some grinding millers, but that with the hardness of being lower than 35 has very limited uses and a very thin demand on the domestic market in China. ThyssenKrupp contended that the above evidence presented by Sinochem-SG was the witness' testimony, and its authenticity couldn't be ascertained now that the witness did not testify in court.

ThyssenKrupp argued that while the HGI value of the petroleum coke delivered was 32, which seemingly wasn't in conformity with the stipulation in the Purchase Contract but did not constitute a breach of contract as the HGI value stipulated therein was a typical value, the petroleum coke with an HGI value at 32 could still be sold in China. To prove its argument, ThyssenKrupp requested to allow Mr. Fisher, a U. S. citizen working for more than 30 years in the petroleum coke sector, Mr. Wang XX, a former Vice-President at Zhengzhou Light Metals Research Institute of Chinalco, and Mr. Li XX, a professor at North China Electric Power University, to testify in court as expert witnesses, who all affirmed that the HGI value means the grinding index of petroleum coke: the lower the index, the harder the petroleum coke is and the more difficult to grind, whereas the higher the index, the softer the petroleum coke is and the easier to grind. The petroleum coke with an HGI value at 32 has use-value, and satisfies the purpose under the Purchase Contract. In addition, Mr. Fisher also testified that the lowest and highest HGI values he had ever experienced were 35 and 85, respectively, and given it is very difficult to measure the accurate HGI value of petroleum coke, so a range centered on a typical value is usually used as its proxy indicator. Mr. Wang XX testified that for the petroleum coke with higher hardness, various grinding parameters of a grinding mill, such as feeding speed, airflow pressure, airflow rate and rotation rate, have to be adjusted in advance. Mr. Li XX testified that the HGI value is the basis of model selection for a fuel pulverizing system, but not the criterion for whether or not a kind of petroleum coke falls within the fuel grade. To grind the petroleum coke with a lower HGI value, a different model has to be used.

Sinochem-SG had no objection to the truth and authenticity of the testimonies from ThyssenKrupp's witnesses, but emphasized that Mr. Fisher's testimony showed that in his professional life of thirty years, he had never experienced the petroleum coke with an HGI value at 32, and the petroleum coke with the lowest HGI value he experienced was that at 35. Mr. Wang XX did not do the HGI value measuring in person and did not use the petroleum coke with different HGI values, so the authority of his testimony was questionable. Mr. Li XX's testimony showed that the petroleum coke with different HGI values has different requirements on the grinding equipment, and to grind the petroleum coke with a higher hardness of the HGI value, the grinding equipment has to be changed.

CFI concluded that:

In the testimonies from the three expert witnesses provided by ThyssenKrupp, the relation between the HGI value and the hardness of the petroleum coke and the contents about the use-value of the petroleum coke with the HGI value of 32 in this case could be mutually corroborated, had the scientific basis, and thus were accepted; the issue of the petroleum coke with the HGI value of 32 in this case serving the purpose under the Purchase Contract was about a matter of judgment within the scope of determination and decision by SPC, which a witness had no right to make a judgment on it, so the contents in the mentioned above expert testimonies of the petroleum coke with the HGI value of 32 in this case serving the purpose under the Purchase Contract weren't accepted by SPC; and the issue of the petroleum coke with the HGI value of 32 herein serving the purpose under the Purchase Contract would be demonstrated by SPC in detail in the Section: Reasons for Decisions. The Property Description on the petroleum coke submitted as evidence with SPC by Sinochem-SG was provided in the capacity of School of Materials Science and Engineering of Shanghai University rather than in the capacity of a natural person, and affixed with its official seal, not denying the usability of the petroleum coke with the HGI value of 32 but just stating its limit use. The contents in the Property Description were also mutually corroborated with the testimonies from the three expert witnesses provided by ThyssenKrupp, had a scientific basis, and thus were accepted by SPC.

In addition, ThyssenKrupp also provided a Quality Inspection Certificate issued by China (Beijing) Inspection and Certification Group Co, Ltd to prove that the HGI value of the petroleum coke delivered was 36, but was challenged by Sinochem-SG in its authenticity, legality and relevance on the grounds as follows: (1) the petroleum coke had, since its arrival at the Port of destination, been in the control of Sinochem-SG, and ThyssenKrupp had never taken any inspection samples of the petroleum coke from Sinochem-SG. Therefore, the petroleum coke sampled and tested by ThyssenKrupp was not from the petroleum coke in this case; and (2) without the consent of Sinochem-SG, the inspection that ThyssenKrupp unilaterally entrusted China (Beijing) Inspection and Certification Group Co, Ltd to conduct had no contractual and/or legal basis. In the view of CFI, now that whether or not the petroleum coke samples tested by ThyssenKrupp were sourced from the petroleum coke in this case couldn't be ascertained, and there was no contractual basis for such inspection unilaterally commissioned by ThyssenKrupp, the relevance and legality of the evidence weren't affirmed.

3. Facts of Negotiations on the HGI Value of the Petroleum Coke

On October 15, 2008, Sinochem Holdings notified in writing ThyssenKrupp that due to the material non-conformity with the range of the HGI value stipulated in the Purchase Contract, the petroleum coke it delivered was unsuitable for use, and was rejected by customers, and at the same time required ThyssenKrupp to work out a solution to the serious problem as soon as possible. During the defense inthe first court hearing, ThyssenKrupp recognized that this action by Sinochem Holdings was taken on behalf of Sinochem-SG. On November 4, 2008, Sinochem-SG sent a letter once again to ThyssenKrupp, stated that the HGI value of the petroleum coke delivered by ThyssenKrupp seriously deviated from the range of the HGI value stipulated in the Purchase Contract, constituting a material breach of contract, and requiring ThyssenKrupp to handle the matter properly. In a written reply on November 12, 2008 to Sinochem-SG, ThyssenKrupp stated that the HGI value of the petroleum coke it had delivered was only slightly below the range of the HGI value stipulated in the Purchase Contract, not constituting a material breach, and agreed to meet to discuss a solution. On November 27, 2008, Sinochem-SG sent a letter to ThyssenKrupp, requesting the Parties to meet as soon as possible. On December 8, 2008, ThyssenKrupp replied to Sinochem-SG that it was difficult to meet before the end of 2008 and suggested that the meeting was to be held in January 2009.

These facts were evidenced by the faxed letter dated October 15, 2008 from Sinochem-SG to ThyssenKrupp, the letters dated November 4 and 27, 2008 from Sinochem-SG to ThyssenKrupp and the replies dated November 12 and December 8, 2008 from Thyssenkrupp. ThyssenKrupp raised no objection to the authenticity of the mentioned above evidence presented by Sinochem-SG, and CFI confirmed the facts that the Parties had engaged over the HGI value of the petroleum coke.

Sinochem-SG claimed that, in addition to the foregoing facts of written engagement between the Parties, Sinochem-SG raised the issue to ThyssenKrupp in oral communication on several occasions, which was not recognized by ThyssenKrupp, and was also not supported by any related evidence from Sinochem-SG.

4. Disposal of the Petroleum Coke Involving in this Case

To avoid additional loss from extended storage of the petroleum coke at the Port of Nanjing during the trial, Sinochem-SG notified in writing on November 11, 2009 ThyssenKrupp of the price terms initially agreed on with a potential buyer and related information and tried to seek views and advice from ThyssenKrupp. In its written reply on November 18, 2009, ThyssenKrupp stated that it had performed its delivery obligation, and was neither obliged to consult with Sinochem-SG on or to give its consent to the disposal of the petroleum coke nor to make any comments on the proposed price terms.

Sinochem-SG sold the petroleum coke to Weihai Golden Monkey Import & Export Trade Co, Ltd (hereinafter referred to as Golden Monkey) at the price rate of RMB 1,575.50/ton under a Sale Contract concluded on November 26, 2009 through Sinochem Holdings, receiving payment of RMB 34,637,187.25 (USD 5,072,525.65 based on the USD/RMB rates of 6.8284 and 6.8283) and incurring the following costs from the disposal of the petroleum coke: (1) the taxes & charges of RMB 1,600,255.71 (USD 234,095.83 based on the USD/RMB rate of 6.8359); (2) the local charges of RMB 834,549 (USD 122,172.63 based on the USD/RMB rate of 6.8309); (3) the overtime storage charges of RMB 1,120,000 (USD 164,071.31 based on the USD/RMB rate of 6.8263); (4) the inspection fees of RMB 10,000 (USD 1,463.76 based on the USD/RMB rate of 6.8317); (5) the customs clearance fee of RMB 27,029.36 (USD 3,959.71 based on the USD/RMB rate of 6.8261); and (6) financial expenses of USD 2,490. The costs incurred by Sinochem-SG in the disposal of the petroleum coke totaled USD 528,253.24.

The supporting evidence of the foregoing facts included: the letter dated November 11, 2009 from Sinochem-SG to ThyssenKrupp regarding the disposal of the petroleum coke and timely reduction of possible losses, the written reply dated November 18, 2009 from ThyssenKrupp's attorney, the Letter of Entrustment on the sale of the petroleum coke, the Sale Contract concluded on November 26, 2009, five invoices dated December 17-30, 2009, a price chart of the Crude Oil & Petroleum Coke, five invoices, Custom Deposit, Risk Guaranty Fund, Special Receipts for Mortgage, Import Tariff Schedules, the Special Form of Import Duty Payments issued by Xinshengyu Customs of Nanjing, receipts and invoices of inspection fees, receipts and invoices of customs clearance fees, and the Port Storage and Agency Contract. ThyssenKrupp had no objection to the authenticity of all the evidence except the

Letter of Entrustment on the grounds that it wasn't notarially certified. In the view of CFI, given the parent-subsidiary relation exists between Sinochem Holdings and Sinochem-SG, and the Letter of Entrustment was produced within the People's Republic of China, no notarial certification should be conducted and its authenticity could be confirmed. Therefore, CFI affirmed the above facts.

5. The Loss Incurred to Sinochem-SG

ThyssenKrupp contended that now that the petroleum coke had been sold to its parent company Sinochem Holdings at the original price, Sinochem-SG suffered no loss. While recognizing the petroleum coke sale contract existed between itself and Sinochem Holdings and the sale price to Sinochem Holdings was basically identical to the purchase price in the Purchase Contract, Sinochem-SG argued that its relation with Sinochem Holdings was not a real relation of a buyer and a seller but a relation of the commission sale. Its procurement of the petroleum coke from ThyssenKrupp was to sell it in China, and its conclusion of the sale contract with Sinochem Holdings was to streamline the customs clearance, enabling the petroleum coke to get into China smoothly, and facilitate its sale through Sinochem Holdings in China. To prove its argument, Sinochem-SG submitted the Letter of Entrustment whereby it entrusted Sinochem Holdings to sell the petroleum coke. ThyssenKrupp had no objection to the formal authenticity of the Letter of Entrustment but suspected that the Letter of Entrustment was signed ex-post for the claim in this case. CFI concluded that the Letter of Entrustment provided by Sinochem-SG was original and could be accepted in the absence of evidence to the contrary.

Sinochem-SG contended that the payment for the petroleum coke to ThyssenKrupp was USD 7, 756, 828. 55. ThyssenKrupp should refund the price difference of USD 2, 684, 302. 9 between the proceeds of USD 5, 072, 525. 65

from the disposal and the payment of USD 7, 756, 828. 55, and pay the corresponding interest accrued on the payment for the petroleum coke during the period from September 25, 2008 to the actual refund date based on Bank of China's USD lending rate for the same period. ThyssenKrupp argued that the price difference was attributed to the declining prices in the market of the petroleum coke in China rather than the non-conformity of the HGI value of the petroleum coke with which was stipulated in the Purchase Contract. The loss in price difference was from normal commercial risks, and thus should be borne by Sinochem-SG.

In addition, Sinochem-SG also requested ThyssenKrupp to make compensation for the additional costs of USD 520, 339. 77 in total from the disposal that wouldn't otherwise have been incurred by it, including the taxes & charges of USD 234, 095. 83, the local charges of USD 122, 172. 63 and the overtime storage charges of USD 164, 071. 31 from the disposal, and made it clear that it chose not to require ThyssenKrupp to make compensation for other expenses incurred to Sinochem-SG, including the inspection fees, customs clearance fees and financial fees. ThyssenKrupp refuted that its act didn't constitute a breach of contract, all these additional costs mentioned above were the costs that Sinochem-SG should bear from its resale of the petroleum coke, and thus should not be borne by ThyssenKrupp.

CFI concluded that:

1. The Application of Laws

With Sinochem-SG being a Singaporean company and ThyssenKrupp a German company, this case was about a dispute over an internationalsale contract on the petroleum coke. Despite the stipulation that the Purchase Contract was concluded in accordance with laws of the New York State, the United States, in force at the time of the execution thereof, and should be governed and interpreted by the said laws, the Parties agreed in the trial that the *United Nations Convention on Contracts for the International Sale of Goods* (hereinafter referred to as CISG) was the basis for determining their respective rights and obligations. Furthermore, both Singapore and Germany are signatory states to the CISG. Therefore, relevant provisions thereof apply to the Purchase Contract.

2. The Fundamental Breach of Contract from ThyssenKrupp

The Parties stipulated in the Purchase Contract that the typical HGI value of the petroleum coke was in the range of 36-46. The HGI value of the petroleum coke tested by the inspector appointed by both Parties at the Port of loading was 32, and the result from the retesting by Sinochem-SG according to the provisions of the Purchase Contract at the Port of destination also showed that the HGI value of the petroleum coke was 32. Based on these testing results, Sinochem-SG argued that the HGI value of the petroleum coke was not only far lower than the stipulated value in the Purchase Contract but also below the quality of general petroleum coke in the Chinese market, rendering it hard to sell in the Chinese market and the expected purpose of Sinochem-SG at the execution of the Purchase Contract unachievable, and therefore ThyssenKrupp committed a fundamental breach of contract. ThyssenKrupp maintained that the HGI value stipulated by the Parties in the Purchase Contract was only an approximate range rather than a mandatory indicator, and that the Purchase Contract didn't set a floor and a ceiling for the HGI value of the petroleum coke, so being beyond the approximate range constituted neither a fundamental breach nor a general breach. Sinochem-SG retorted that that the Parties didn't prescribe an exact HGI value but rather a range of a typical value was exactly to factor in its uncertainty. The uncertainty didn't mean the variable range of a typical HGI value stipulated by the Parties had no constraints. Therewith, CFI concluded that now that the typical HGI value stipulated by the Parties was between 36 and 46, which meant the floor was 36, the ceiling 46, and being beyond this range constituted a breach of contract. ThyssenKrupp's claimed that the Parties did not set a floor and a ceiling for the typical HGI value of the petroleum coke in the Purchase Contract and that the range of the typical HGI value stipulated by the Parties in the Purchase Contract was not a mandatory indicator and was not binding had no basis and weren't upheld by CFI. In the view of CFI, now that the Parties had stipulated in the Purchase Contract that the HGI value of the petroleum coke was a typical value, the tested value should be that typical value. However, the tested typical HGI values of the petroleum coke delivered by ThyssenKrupp both at the Port of loading and the Port of destination were 32 both of which were lower than the floor of the range of the typical HGI value stipulated by both Parties. Therefore, CFI determined that the HGI value of the petroleum coke delivered by ThyssenKrupp wasn't in conformity with that in the Purchase Contract, and thus constituted a breach of contract.

Sinochem-SG asserted that as a trader, its purpose of purchasing the petroleum coke is to sell it in China, and that the non-conformity of the HGI value of the petroleum coke delivered by ThyssenKrupp with the contractual stipulation rendered the subject matter difficult to sell normally in China and ultimately deprived it of its expected benefits. Therefore, the act of ThyssenKrupp constituted a fundamental breach of contract. ThyssenKrupp refuted that the testimonies of its three expert witnesses and the fact that Sinochem-SG resold the petroleum coke to Golden Monkey sufficed in proving that the petroleum coke with the HGI value of 32 could actually be used in China. In the view of CFI, the Parties agreed that the HGI value signifies the hardness of petroleum coke: the higher the HGI value, the lower the hardness, whereas the lower the HGI value, the higher the hardness. That means that the level of the HGI value has a significant effect on the hardness of petroleum coke. ThyssenKrupp's expert witness, Mr. Fisher who is a veteran professional in petroleum coke sector, testified in the court that the petroleum coke with the lowest HGI value he had experienced in his professional life was that at 35, signifying that the petroleum coke with an HGI value at 32 was, indeed, extremely rare, and in other words, the HGI value of the petroleum coke delivered by ThyssenKrupp deviated from the range stipulated by both Parties in the Purchase Contract by a very wide margin. ThyssenKrupp's expert witness, Mr. Li XX, testified that the HGI value is the basis of model selection for a fuel pulverizing system, and to grind the petroleum coke with a lower HGI value or a higher hardness, a different model has to be used. That means that the petroleum coke with a different HGI value has different requirements on the grinding equipment, and it follows that the petroleum coke with an HGI value at as low as 32 necessarily has some unusual requirements on the grinding equipment and thus has very limited demand in the market. Therefore, the petroleum coke with an HGI value at as low as 32 delivered by ThyssenKrupp was extremely hard to sell in the market inevitably, which *de facto* amounted to having Sinochem-SG be deprived of its expected benefits at the execution of the Purchase Contract. ThyssenKrupp as a professional company in the petroleum coke sector could not be unaware of the loss that its breach of contract may cause to Sinochem-SG. CFI, therefore, determined that ThyssenKrupp's act constituted a fundamental breach of contract.

3. Sinochem-SG's Right to Declare the Contract Avoided

Sinochem-SG's request on the grounds of ThyssenKrupp's fundamental breach of contract to CFI to rule that the Purchase Contract was canceled should be construed as a request to CFI to declare the Purchase Contract avoided according to relevant provisions of the CISG. ThyssenKrupp contended that, under Articles 49 (1) (1) and (2)(2)(1) of the CISG, where the goods have been delivered, the request to declare the contract avoided on the grounds that the Seller's non-compliance with the contract constitutes a fundamental breach of contract shall be given a notification to the Seller within a reasonable period of time after the Buyer has known or should have known such a fundamental breach of contract. Sinochem-SG did not give such notification to ThyssenKrupp within a reasonable period of time, and thus lost the right to declare the Purchase Contract avoided. In the view of CFI, ThyssenKrupp's argument was unjustified by virtue of the reasons as follows:

Article 39 (1) of the CISG provides that unless the Buyer notifies the Seller of the non-conformity of the goods with the contract, stating the nature of the said non-conformity, within a reasonable period of time after the Buyer has discovered or should have discovered the said non-conformity, the Buyer shall lose the right to declare the said non-conformity of the goods with the contract. Article 40 provides that in its defense, the Seller has no right to invoke "a reasonable period of time" as provided in Article 39 if the non-conformity of the goods refers to facts that the Seller knows or can not fail to know but fails to notify the Buyer. Notwithstanding, in its literal sense, the application of the foregoing Provision is limited to a general breaches of contract, yet, following the principle of *argumentum a maiore ad minus* (*argumentum a fortiori*), the same Provision shall also apply to the circumstance where a contract is declared avoided based on a fundamental breach of contract arising from the material non-conformity of the goods delivered with the contract. Since its delivery of the goods at the Port of loading, ThyssenKrupp had known the HGI value of the petroleum coke delivered was 32, which seriously deviated from the range stipulated by both Parties. Instead of notifying Sinochem-SG of the fact or inquiring of Sinochem-SG whether or not the latter would still accept the petroleum coke with an HGI value at 32, ThyssenKrupp continued to ship and deliver it to the latter. Under this circumstance, ThyssenKrupp had not the right to claim that Sinochem-SG lost its right to declare the Purchase Contract avoided on the grounds that no notification of avoidance of contract had been given by the latter within a reasonable period of time.

In fact, Sinochem-SG declared the contract avoidance without exceeding a reasonable period of time. It was on September 8, 2008 that the petroleum coke arrived at the Port of destination, and on October 15, 2008 that, having found the HGI value was 32, Sinochem-SG sent a letter to ThyssenKrupp according to Article 7 (2)(3) of the Purchase Contract, notifying the latter of the fact that due to the material non-conformity with the range of the HGI value stipulated in the Purchase Contract, the petroleum coke it delivered was unsuitable for use, and was rejected by customers, and at the same time requiring ThyssenKrupp to work out a solution to the serious problem as soon as possible. To further verify the quality of the petroleum coke, Sinochem-SG had it retested. The result from the retesting also showed that the HGI value of the petroleum coke was 32, which wasn't in conformity with the specified range. Sinochem-SG had since sent several letters to ThyssenKrupp, claiming that the HGI value of the petroleum coke was substantially out of the stipulated range and constituted a material breach of contract, and demanding it to properly handle the quality problem. It was ThyssenKrupp's failure to cooperate that led to no solution to the problem. In the view of CFI, having found the material non-conformity of the HGI value of the petroleum coke with the stipulated range, Sinochem-SG had negotiated without delay with ThyssenKrupp for a solution, and it was following the failure to have a solution through mentioned above negotiations that Sinochem-SG proceeded to initiate a lawsuit, requesting that the Purchase

Contract be declared avoided. Such an act from Sinochem-SG should be construed as that notification of declaring a contract avoided as provided in Article 26 of the CISG was issued to ThyssenKrupp within a reasonable period of time from "a fundamental breach has been known or should have been known". Therefore, ThyssenKrupp's claim that Sinochem-SG had lost its right to declare the Purchase Contract avoided due to its failure to give such notification within a reasonable period was no basis and was not upheld by CFI.

ThyssenKrupp also contented that now that Sinochem-SG had sold the petroleum coke to Golden Monkey in November 2009, it was no longer possible to return the goods in its original condition, therefore, under Article 82 (1) of the CISG, Sinochem-SG lost the right to declare the Purchase Contract avoided. In the view of CFI, having found ThyssenKrupp constituted a material breach of contract, Sinochem-SG had without delay negotiated with ThyssenKrupp. It was ThyssenKrupp's failure to cooperate that Sinochem-SG had to file a lawsuit. To avoid additional loss during the trial of this case, Sinochem-SG again tried to discuss with ThyssenKrupp on properly handling the petroleum coke. It was the explicit refusal from ThyssenKrupp that Sinochem-SG was forced to sell the petroleum coke to Golden Monkey. Therefore, the responsibility for rendering the petroleum coke unable to be returned to ThyssenKrupp in the original condition at the time of receipt rested with ThyssenKrupp rather than with Sinochem-SG. Under Article 82 (2) (1) of the CISG, Sinochem-SG did not lose the right to declare the Purchase Contract avoided.

Furthermore, ThyssenKrupp argued that Sinochem-SG had made the full payment, which showed it was satisfied with the quality of the petroleum coke and accepted the petroleum coke, and that it no longer had the right to raise an objection to the quality of the petroleum coke. In the view of CFI, according to the stipulation of the Purchase Contract, Sinochem-SG had the right to object to the quality of the petroleum coke and to seek remedies within sixty(60) days of the arrival of the goods at the Port of destination. Such right had nothing to do with whether or not Sinochem-SG had paid for the goods, meaning that even if the payment had been made, Sinochem-SG still had the right to object to the quality of the petroleum coke and to seek remedies provided that its objection was raised within sixty (60) days of the arrival of the goods at the Port of destination. ThyssenKrupp's claim that Sinochem-SG's full payment should be deemed that Sinochem-SG was satisfied with and accepted the quality of the petroleum coke and then lost the right to object to and seek remedies for the quality of the petroleum coke was no basis and was not upheld by CFI.

4. Liabilities that ThyssenKrupp Should Assume

Under relevant provisions in Article 74, Article 77, Article 81 and Article 84 of the CISG, after declaring the Purchase Contract avoided, Sinochem-SG had the right to request ThyssenKrupp to refund the payment of the goods already made, to pay the corresponding interest thereon as from the date of ThyssenKrupp's receipt of the payment, and to compensate for all the losses it suffered arising from ThyssenKrupp's breach of contract. In this case, the payment for the petroleum coke made by Sinochem-SG to ThyssenKrupp was USD 7, 756, 828. 55. To mitigate further losses from ThyssenKrupp's breach of contract, Sinochem-SG managed to reap the proceeds of USD 5, 072, 525. 65 from the disposal of the petroleum coke, so ThyssenKrupp should refund the price difference of USD 2, 684, 302. 9 between the proceeds of USD 5, 072, 525. 65 from the disposal and the payment of USD 7, 756, 828. 55, pay the corresponding interest accrued on the payment for the petroleum coke during the period as from the date of the said payment made (September 25, 2008) to the actual refund date, and compensate Sinochem-SG for the additional cost of USD 528, 253. 24 incurred to Sinochem-SG from its disposal of the petroleum coke. The additional cost was the loss suffered by Sinochem-SG as a result of ThyssenKrupp's breach of contract, and for which Sinochem-SG only requested the compensation of USD 520, 339. 77, which should be supported by CFI.

ThyssenKrupp contended that now that the petroleum coke had been sold to its parent company Sinochem Holdings at the original price, Sinochem-SG suffered no loss. CFI determined this claim by ThyssenKrupp was not found. Sinochem-SG refuted that its conclusion of the Sale Contract with Sinochem Holdings was to streamline the customs clearance, enabling the petroleum coke to get into China smoothly, and to facilitate its sale through Sinochem Holdings in China, so its relation with Sinochem Holdings was not a real contract relation of a buyer and a seller but the commission sale relation, and presented its commission sale contract with Sinochem Holdings as the evidence. Neither did ThyssenKrupp have any objection to the first negotiation with itself by Sinochem Holdings on behalf of Sinochem-SG concerning the HGI value of the petroleum coke on October 15, 2008, nor did raise the claim in the subsequent negotiations directly with Sinochem-SG that Sinochem-SG no longer had the right to have any objection to the HGI value of the petroleum coke on the grounds that the petroleum coke had been resold to Sinochem Holdings, it thus followed that ThyssenKrupp had clearly known that the relation between Sinochem-SG and Sinochem Holdings was the commission sale relation. To avoid additional loss during the trial, the petroleum coke was also sold by entrusting Sinochem Holdings, which further confirmed Sinochem-SG's claim that its relation with Sinochem Holdings was a commission sale relation rather than a sale contract relation between a buyer and a seller. On this basis, CFI determined that the relation between Sinochem-SG and Sinochem Holdings was not the sale contract relation of a buyer and a seller but the commission sale relation. Therefore, ThyssenKrupp's claim that Sinochem-SG had sold the petroleum coke to Sinochem Holdings at the original contract price and thus suffered no loss was no basis and was not upheld by CFI.

ThyssenKrupp argued that Sinochem-SG's loss was attributed to the declining price of petroleum coke in China, and thus ThyssenKrupp was not obliged to compensate Sinochem-SG for the loss. In the view of CFI, the cause behind Sinochem-SG's declaration of the Purchase Contract being avoided was ThyssenKrupp's fundamental default rather than the declining prices. Should the HGI value of the petroleum coke ThyssenKrupp delivered have conformed to the contractual stipulation, Sinochem-SG wouldn't have the right to declare the Purchase Contract avoided even if the price declined, as in that case, the declining price was the commercial risk that Sinochem-SG should bear. The declaration of the Purchase Contract being avoided in this case was a result of ThyssenKrupp's fundamental breach of contract, so the risk of the declining price was the commercial risk that ThyssenKrupp had to bear. Therefore, in this case, ThyssenKrupp should be liable for any loss resulting from a change in the petroleum coke market.

In conclusion, the HGI value of the petroleum coke ThyssenKrupp delivered was seriously in non-conformity with the stipulation in the Purchase Contract, which constituted a fundamental breach of contract, and ThyssenKrupp should bear the consequences of the Purchase Contract being declared avoided. According to Article 25, Article 26, Article 39 (1), Article 40, Articles 49 (1) (1) and (2) (2) (1), Article 74, Article 77, Article 81, Articles 82(1) and (2)(1) and Article 84 of the CISG and Article 128 of the *Civil Procedure Law of the People's Republic of China* (hereinafter referred to as *Civil Procedure*

Law), CFI made the Judgment as follows: (1) the Purchase Contract signed on April 11, 2008 between ThyssenKrupp and Sinochem-SG was declared avoided; (2) within thirty(30) days from the effective date of this Judgment, ThyssenKrupp refunded the payment of the goods of USD 2, 684, 302. 9 to Sinochem-SG, and pays the interest thereon during the period from September 25, 2008 to the date of payment as determined by this Judgment (based on the Bank of China's US dollar lending rate for the same period); and (3) within thirty (30) days from the effective date of this Judgment, ThyssenKrupp compensated Sinochem-SG for the loss of USD 520, 339. 77. If the aforesaid obligations of payment were not honored within the period as determined in this Judgment, the interest on the outstanding debt during the delayed period shall be doubled according to the provisions of Article 229 of the *Civil Procedure Law*. ThyssenKrupp bore the court fees of RMB 306, 432 for this case.
ThyssenKrupp appealed against CFI's Judgment to SPC, claiming that:

Firstly, there was an error in determining proper laws to this case in the trial of the first instance. According to contractual provisions and the rule of the conflict of laws in China, laws in the State of New York, the United States, shall apply to this case. The CISG, the interpretations of the CISG, the U. S. *Uniform Commercial Code*, commercial practices, etc. shall also apply to this case, and the UNCITRAL Digest of Case Law on the United Nations Convention on the International Sale of Goods (hereinafter referred to as Digest of Case Law) shall also be the basis for the trial of this case. The judgment that only the CISG was applicable in this case by CFI was an error; secondly, the judgment by CFI that the relation between Sinochem-SG and Sinochem Holdings was the principal-agent relation was an error. The relation between Sinochem-SG and Sinochem Holdings was the sale contract relation of a buyer and a seller, and Sinochem-SG had no right to raise the claims in this case after the goods had been sold; thirdly, the conclusion in CFI's Judgment that ThyssenKrupp's delivery of the petroleum coke with the HGI value of 32 constituted a fundamental breach of contract was an error. (1) ThyssenKrupp's delivery of the petroleum coke with the HGI value of 32 didn't constitute a general breach of contract. The HGI value wasn't a mandatory indicator but an approximate range. For an insignificant indicator such as the HGI value, there were no price adjustments specified in the Purchase Contract. In addition, putting in perspective the acts of the Parties to a contract, a reasonable buyer who asserts that the petroleum coke with the HGI value of 32 isn't in conformity with the contract and constitutes a fundamental breach of contract won't object to the quality of the goods until as late as two (2) months after the receipt of the inspection certificate, or even after the goods have been received and the full payment has been made. (2) ThyssenKrupp's delivery of the petroleum coke with the HGI value of 32 didn't constitute a fundamental breach of contract. Despite a lower HGI value, the petroleum coke had all its proper use-value and commercial value, and was sold in November 2009 by Sinochem-SG even at a price higher than the market price for the same period. Thus, the petroleum coke with the HGI value of 32 did not fundamentally deprive Sinochem-SG of what it would be entitled to under the Purchase Contract, thereby rendering its purpose of contract unachievable. The conclusion by CFI that ThyssenKrupp constituted a fundamental breach of contract was contrary to the facts, and also had no legal basis; fourthly, Sinochem-SG failed to give a notice of declaring the Purchase Contract avoided within a reasonable period of time, and thus lost the right to do so. Its avoidance of the Purchase Contract as late as until a few months after it had known that the HGI value was 32 and amid a market crash couldn't be deemed as a declaration within a reasonable period of time. The judgment of a reasonable period of time by CFI seriously violated relevant provisions of the CISG and the spirits of legislation; fifthly, even if ThyssenKrupp's delivery of the petroleum coke with the HGI value of 32, indeed, constituted a general breach of contract, Sinochem-SG lost the right to claim the non-conformity of the goods with the Purchase Contract given it failed to file a quality objection within a reasonable time; sixthly, the judgment of the amount of loss in the trial of the first instance was a serious error. Under the provisions in Article 76 of the CISG, assuming that Sinochem-SG had the right to declare the Purchase Contract avoided in this case, then the calculation of damages should have been based on the difference between the price stipulated in the Purchase Contract and the actual price at which Sinochem-SG took delivery of the goods. Yet, in the trial of the first instance, the damages were mistakenly calculated as the difference between the price stipulated in the Purchase Contract and the price at which the goods were resold in November 2009 to Golden Monkey. Such calculation was obviously inconsistent with related provisions in the CISG; and seventhly, throughout the trial of the first instance, Sinochem-SG only requested to CFI that the Purchase Contract between the Parties was rescinded rather than that the Purchase Contract was declared avoided. However, CFI on its own ruled that the Purchase Contract was declared avoided. CFI's Judgment on a matter other than the claim from the Plaintiff wasn't a claim-specific judgment, and thus was in violation of related legal provisions. To sum up the mentioned-above, ThyssenKrupp requested to SPC to rule that: (1) CFI should reject all the claims from Sinochem-SG in accordance with the law; and (2) Sinochem-SG should bear all the court costs for the trials of the first and second instances.

In its defense, Sinochem-SG argued that: firstly, CFI's Judgment was correct in applying the CISG to this case by respecting the choice of the Parties. The laws of the State of New York, the United States, shall apply as agreed by the Parties in the Purchase Contract. ThyssenKrupp contended that the CISG is the integral part of the laws in the State of New York, the United States, but the Digest of Case Law is neither a part nor the official explanations of the CISG, and thus couldn't serve as the legal basis for hearing this case; secondly, Sinochem-SG entrusted Sinochem Holdings on behalf of itself to sell the petroleum coke, and their relation was the principal-agent relation rather than the sale contract relation of a buyer and a seller. The judgment of their relation in CFI's Judgment was correct. The entrustment of Sinochem Holdings by Sinochem-SG to sell the petroleum coke had been approved by ThyssenKrupp, and Sinochem Holdings also had, in the capacity of the agent of Sinochem-SG, contacted directly and negotiated with ThyssenKrupp after the petroleum coke arrived at the Port of Nanjing. The act that ThyssenKrupp thereafter came to raise an objection to the status of Sinochem Holdings as the agent of Sinochem-SG which it had recognized before the proceedings was against the rule of promissory estoppel; thirdly, the HGI value of the petroleum coke in this case was an important quality indicator clearly stipulated by both Parties in the Purchase Contract. The HGI value of the petroleum coke delivered by ThyssenKrupp was 32, much lower than the range stipulated by both Parties, which led to great difficulties for Sinochem-SG to sell, and rendered the purpose of contract unachievable, thus constituting a fundamental breach of contract. The payment to ThyssenKrupp by Sinochem-SG didn't mean, and couldn't be construed as, its acceptance of the unqualified goods. Under the Purchase Contract, any objection to the quality of the goods could be raised anytime within sixty (60) days of the arrival of the petroleum coke at the Port of destination; fourthly, in accordance with the CISG, ThyssenKrupp had no right of defense on the grounds of "a reasonable period of time" due to its failure to notify Sinochem-SG the fact that the goods weren't in conformity with the contractual stipulations, while Sinochem-SG initiated the dispute settlement mechanism mutually agreed by both Parties within a reasonable period of time and also lodged a claim to ThyssenKrupp over the fundamental breach of contract on the grounds of the non-conformity of the goods with the contractual stipulations, therefore, the decision in CFI's Judgment that the time at which the Purchase Contract was declared avoided by Sinochem-SG did not exceed a reasonable period of time was correct; fifthly, the decision of Sinochem-SG's losses in CFI's Judgment was correct. The claim for the losses was made by Sinochem-SG based on Article 74 of the CISG, whereas the misunderstanding and quotation of Article 76 of the CISG by ThyssenKrupp had no basis. The total loss that Sinochem-SG claimed was the actual losses incurred to Sinochem-SG and didn't wary with the time point of calculation; and sixthly, the "Avoidance of Contract" defined in the CISG is consistent in the connotation with the "Rescission of Contract" defined in the Chinese laws, so it didn't exist such a case as "judgment on a matter other than the claim from the Plaintiff" as claimed by ThyssenKrupp. To sum up the mentioned-above, the facts were clearly determined, and right proper laws were correctly applied in the trial of the first instance. Hence, Sinochem-SG requested that ThyssenKrupp's appeal was rejected in accordance with law.

All the facts found by CFI in the trial of the first instance were supported by relevant evidence, to which both Parties had no objection, and thus was affirmed by SPC.

SPC further found that:

The letter that Sinochem-SG sent on November 11, 2009 to ThyssenKrupp on the disposal of the disputed goods for timely reducing losses stated: "given your firmly refused to enter into an agreement with us on the disposal of the goods in dispute to stop the rise of losses, and for the purpose of reducing the losses from the goods in dispute and protecting the common rights of your firm and us, we have managed to find a potential buyer of the goods in dispute, and have negotiated with the potential buyer on the transaction through our agent Sinochem Holdings, including the prices. Now, the price terms initially agreed on with the potential buyer are: settlement quantity: 25, 722. 339 tons (BALTIC FRONTIER ship, imported petroleum coke, original Container Yard and original Transfer Station); Unit Price: RMB 1, 575. 50/ton, Ex ship's hold Huining Nanjing, not lower than the reasonable market price".

During the trial of the second instance, ThyssenKrupp submitted to SPC the U. S. *Uniform Commercial Code* and a relevant U. S. precedent [*Lomaglio Assocs. v. LBK Mktg. Corp.*, 1999 U. S. District Court in Lexis 14185 (S. D. N. Y. 1999)], arguing that the Purchase Contract in question was established and valid under the U. S. law.

Sinochem-SG did not object to the United States law submitted by ThyssenKrupp, but maintained that the explanations of the law should be given by some professionals with the U. S. legal practice qualification rather than the descriptive statement from ThyssenKrupp's entrusted agents's corporate attorney in this case. In addition, Sinochem-SG also asserted that the CISG was the basis for determining the validity of the Purchase Contract in this case, and that in accordance with the CISG, the Purchase Contract was legally established and valid, and even if the Chinese laws apply, the Purchase Contract shall all the same be found to be legal and effective.

In the view of SPC:

1. Proper Laws and the Validity of the Purchase Contract

Given both Parties to the dispute were foreign entities, this case was a commercial dispute on a contract for the international sale of goods involving foreign factors. Article 2 of the *Explanations (I) of the Supreme People's*

Court on Several Issues Concerning the Application of the Law of the People's Republic of China on the Application of Laws Concerning foreign-related Civil Relations [hereinafter referred to as *Explanations (I)*] provides: "for the foreign-related civil relations having been established prior to the implementation of the *Law of the People's Republic of China on the Application of Laws Concerning foreign-related Civil Relations* (hereinafter referred to as *Law on the Application of Laws*), a people's court shall determine applicable laws for the said foreign-related civil relations according to related laws and regulations in effect at the time of the establishment of the said foreign-related civil relations, and in the absence of such provisions in related laws and regulations in effect at the time, such determination may be made by referring to related provisions of the *Law on the Application of Laws*." The Purchase Contract was signed on April 11, 2008 and prior to the implementation of the *Law on the Application of Laws*. When the Purchase Contract was established, the *General Principles of the Civil Law of the People's Republic of China* (hereinafter referred to as *General Principles*) has been effective and its Article 145 provides: "unless otherwise provided by law, the Parties to a foreign-related contract may choose proper laws for the settlement of their contract disputes. In the absence of such proper laws chosen, the laws of the country most closely related to the said contract shall apply". In this case, the Parties stipulated that the Purchase Contract was concluded in accordance with laws of the State of New York, the United States, in force at the time of the execution thereof, and shall be governed and interpreted by the said laws. This stipulation did not violate laws and shall be deemed valid. Singapore and Germany, where the Parties have their places of business respectively, and the United States are signatory states to the CISG, and the Parties unanimously chose the CISG as the basis for determining their respective rights and obligations in the trial of the first instance and didn't preclude the application of the CISG, therefore, the application of the CISG to this case in the trial of the first instance by CFI was correct. In case of no provisions related to the issues in this case in the CISG, laws of the State of New York, the United States, which were chosen by the Parties, shall apply. The Digest of Case Law is not an integral part of the CISG, and thus couldn't serve as the legal basis for hearing this case, though accurate comprehensions of the meanings of relevant provisions in the CISG could serve as an appropriate reference during the trial of this case.

While settling a contract dispute, a people's court shall, first of all, determine the validity of contract no matter whether or not the Parties have objections to it. Article 4 of the CISG provides: "the CISG applies only to the conclusion of a sales contract and the rights and obligations of the Seller and the Buyer under such contract, and in particular, shall, unless otherwise expressly provided, have nothing to do with one or more of the following issues: (a) the validity of such contract, or its provisions, and/or any practice; (b) the possible effects of such contract on the ownership of the said goods." Given no provisions on the validity of contract exist in the CISG, laws of the State of New York, the United States, which were chosen by the Parties, shall apply in determining this issue in this case. During the trial of the second instance, ThyssenKrupp submitted to SPC the U. S. *Uniform Commercial Code* and a relevant precedent, asserting that the validity of the Purchase Contract in question should be affirmed. While disapproving of the descriptive statement of the United States law submitted by ThyssenKrupp from the ThyssenKrupp's corporate attorney in this case, Sinochem-SG did not challenge the law *per se*, and also asserted that the validity of the Purchase Contract in question should be affirmed. Therefore, the United States laws submitted by ThyssenKrupp were affirmed by SPC. In accordance with the United States laws submitted by

ThyssenKrupp and approved by both Parties, there existed no causes found for invalidating the Purchase Contract, and therefore the Purchase Contract was valid.

2. The Issue of CFI's Judgment on a Matter Other Than the Claim from the Plaintiff

Throughout the trial of the first instance, one of the claims from Sinochem-SG was to request to rescind the Purchase Contract on the grounds of the fundamental breach of contract by ThyssenKrupp. Yet, unlike the Chinese laws, the CISG, without making a distinction between the terms: Avoidance of Contract and Rescission of Contract, has no separate provisions on them, but only provides that either Party has the right to declare a contract avoided providing that the other Party constitutes a fundamental breach of contract. The phrase "Declare a Contract Avoided" therein is, in essence, equivalent to the definition of the Rescission of Contract in the Chinese laws. On the basis of Sinochem-SG's claims and the facts and reasons on which such claims were based, and in the light of relevant provisions of the CISG, CFI affirmed that Sinochem-SG's request to CFI to rule that the Purchase Contract was rescinded shall be construed as a request to CFI to rule in accordance with the provisions of the CISG that the Purchase Contract was declared avoided. Such construction by CFI fitted in with the true meaning of the expression from, and was also approved without objection by, Sinochem-SG. It didn't exist such a case as "CFI's Judgment on a matter other than the claim from the Plaintiff" as claimed by ThyssenKrupp. Therefore, ThyssenKrupp's grounds of appeal against CFI's Judgment exceeding the scope of claim from the Plaintiff weren't established.

3. The Issue of Principal-Agent Relation Between Sinochem-SG and Sinochem Holdings

Sinochem-SG argued that its relation with Sinochem Holdings was a commission sale relation, gave a reasonable explanation that its conclusion of the sale contract with Sinochem Holdings was to streamline the customs clearance, and presented its commission sale contract with Sinochem Holdings. In addition, on October 15, 2008, Sinochem Holdings on behalf of Sinochem-SG negotiated with ThyssenKrupp concerning the HGI value of the petroleum coke, and thereafter Sinochem Holdings also negotiated with ThyssenKrupp on several occasions concerning the same issue. Given having never had an objection to the fact that Sinochem-SG had sold the petroleum coke to Sinochem Holdings throughout all these negotiations, ThyssenKrupp no longer had the right to have any objection to the HGI value of the petroleum coke. To avoid additional loss during the trial of the first instance, the petroleum coke was also sold by entrusting Sinochem Holdings. Based on the mentioned-above, CFI judged that the relation between Sinochem-SG and Sinochem Holdings was the commission sale relation, and it was no error that CFI judged that ThyssenKrupp's claims that the relation between Sinochem-SG and Sinochem Holdings was the sale contract relation of a buyer and a seller, and that Sinochem-SG had sold the petroleum coke to Sinochem Holdings at the original contract price, thus suffering no loss, were not upheld. Therefore, ThyssenKrupp's grounds of appeal against CFI's wrong determination of the relation between Sinochem-SG and Sinochem Holdings as the commission sale relation weren't established.

4. The Issue of ThyssenKrupp's Fundamental Breach of Contract

The Parties stipulated in the Purchase Contract that the typical HGI value of the petroleum coke was in the range of 36-46. The HGI value of the petroleum coke delivered by ThyssenKrupp was 32, lower than the floor of the range of the typical HGI value stipulated by both Parties and thus constituting the non-conformity with that in the Purchase Contract. Therefore, it was correct that CFI determined that ThyssenKrupp constituted a breach of contract.

The issue in this case was whether or not ThyssenKrupp's breach of contract constituted a fundamental breach of contract. First of all, in terms of the required chemical and physical feature specifications of the petroleum coke including seven indicators: moisture, sulfur content, ash content, volatile content, size, heat value and hardness (HGI value) were stipulated by the Parties in the Purchase Contract. Based on the facts so far, Sinochem-SG asserted that only one indicator of the petroleum coke delivered by ThyssenKrupp, namely the HGI value, wasn't compliant with the stipulation, and had no objection to the other six ones. According to the witness' testimonies submitted by the Parties and the statements by witnesses in court hearings, the HGI value means the grinding index of petroleum coke: the lower the index, the harder the petroleum coke is and the more difficult to grind. However, just as CFI in its Judgment put it, even the property description on petroleum coke submitted as evidence with CFI by Sinochem-SG, which was issued by School of Materials Science and Engineering of Shanghai University, didn't deny that the petroleum coke with the HGI value of 32 could be used except that its use was limited. Therefore, it could be concluded that despite the non-conformity of its HGI value with that stipulated in the Purchase Contract, the petroleum coke still had use-value; next, to reduce losses during the first trial of this case, Sinochem-SG made active efforts to resell the petroleum coke in this case. In its letter concerning related issues to ThyssenKrupp, Sinochem-SG clearly stated that the resale price of the petroleum coke was "not lower than the reasonable market price". This fact showed that the petroleum coke could be sold at a reasonable price; and finally, according to the understanding of the fundamental breach of contract clauses in the CISG in judicial judgments in other countries, the non-conformity of the quality of goods at worst constitutes only a non-fundamental breach of contract providing that the Buyer can use or resell the said goods without unreasonable troubles or even at a discounted price. SPC, therefore, determined that ThyssenKrupp's delivery of the petroleum coke with the HGI value of 32 didn't constitute a fundamental breach of contract. The judgment by CFI that ThyssenKrupp constituted a fundamental breach of contract and the resulting judgment that the Purchase Contract was declared avoided were errors in the application of laws, and were rectified by SPC. ThyssenKrupp's grounds of appeal against the fundamental breach of contract were established and upheld by SPC.

Now that ThyssenKrupp didn't constitute a fundamental breach of contract and Sinochem-SG had no right to declare the Purchase Contract avoided accordingly, there was no need for examining and making comments on the challenge raised by ThyssenKrupp in its appellate petition that the notification of avoidance of contract was issued by Sinochem-SG within a reasonable period of time on the grounds of a fundamental breach of contract.

5. Liabilities of the Parties

Despite not being a fundamental breach of contract as mentioned above, ThyssenKrupp's delivery of the petroleum coke in non-conformity with the contractual stipulation constituted a breach of contract. This conclusion made by CFI was correct. According to the stipulation in the Purchase Contract, Sinochem-SG had the right to lodge a claim to ThyssenKrupp within sixty (60) days from the date of the arrival of the petroleum coke at the Port of destination if the quality or quantity of the goods wasn't in conformity with that stipulated by the Parties at the Port of loading. On September 8, 2008, the goods involved in this case arrived at the Port of Nanjing, and on October 15, 2008, Sinochem Holdings sent a letter to ThyssenKrupp, stating that due to the material non-conformity with the range of the HGI value specified in the Purchase Contract, the petroleum coke it delivered was unsuitable for use, and was rejected by customers, and at the same time requiring ThyssenKrupp to work out a solution to the serious problem as soon as possible. In its defense in court hearings of the first instance, ThyssenKrupp recognized that this action by Sinochem Holdings was taken on behalf of Sinochem-SG. On November 4, 2008, Sinochem-SG sent a letter once again to ThyssenKrupp, stating that the HGI value of the petroleum coke delivered by ThyssenKrupp seriously deviated from the range of the HGI value specified in the Purchase Contract, constituting a material breach of contract, and requesting ThyssenKrupp to handle the matter properly. These facts indicated that Sinochem-SG lodged an objection to the quality of the goods and claimed the relevant rights within the period of time specified in the Purchase Contract. Therefore, ThyssenKrupp's grounds of appeal that Sinochem-SG failed to raise the quality objection within a reasonable period of time and thus lost the right to claim the non-conformity of quality couldn't be established and weren't upheld by SPC.

The non-conformity of the HGI value of the petroleum coke delivered by ThyssenKrupp with that stipulated in the Purchase Contract objectively rendered Sinochem-SG unable to sell it in time. Despite having sold it at last after hard efforts, Sinochem-SG suffered losses that otherwise would not have been incurred from the declining market prices. Therefore, ThyssenKrupp should compensate for the price difference of the goods of USD 2, 684, 302. 9, the corresponding interest thereon, and the overtime storage charges of USD 164, 071. 31. However, given the losses mentioned above were also partially attributable to market risks, Sinochem-SG should also bear a corresponding part of the losses. Taxes & charges, and local charges were the costs that should be borne by Sinochem-SG in its performance of the Purchase Contract. Now that its request to declare the Purchase Contract avoided shall not be supported, so all the taxes & charges and the local charges shall be exclusively borne by Sinochem-SG.

In conclusion, the facts were, in principle, clearly determined, some laws were incorrectly applied, and liabilities of the Parties were improperly defined in the trial of the first instance. All these errors in CFI's Judgment shall be rectified by SPC. According to Article 145 of the *General Principles*, Article 1, Article 4, Article 25, Article 39, Article 49, Article 74 and Article 78 of the CISG, Article 170 (1) (2) of the *Civil Procedure Law*, and Article 2 of the *Explanations (I)*, SPC rules as follows:

1. Paragraph 1 of the Civil Judgment of No. 0004 [2009], FI, Third Civ. Division, the Higher People's Court of Jiangsu Province shall be revoked;

2. Paragraph 2 of the Civil Judgment of No. 0004 [2009], FI, Third Civ. Division, the Higher People's Court of Jiangsu Province shall be amended as: "within thirty (30) days from the effective date of this Judgment, ThyssenKrupp compensates Sinochem-SG for the loss of USD 1, 610, 581. 74 in the payment of goods, and pays the interest thereon during the period from September 25, 2008 to the date of payment as determined by this Judgment (based on the Bank of China's US dollar lending rate for the same period)";

3. Paragraph 3 of the Civil Judgment of No. 0004 [2009], FI, Third Civ. Division, the Higher People's Court of Jiangsu Province shall be amended as: "within thirty (30) days from the effective date of this Judgment, ThyssenKrupp compensates Sinochem-SG for the loss of USD 98, 442. 79 in the overtime storage charges";

4. All the other claims from Sinochem-SG shall be dismissed;

If the aforesaid obligations of payment are not honored within the period of time as determined in this Judgment, the interest on the outstanding debt during the delayed period shall be doubled according to the provisions of Article 253 of the *Civil Procedure Law*;

A part of the court costs for the first instance of RMB 306, 432, namely

RMB 183, 859. 2, shall be borne by ThyssenKrupp, and the remaining RMB 122, 572. 8 by Sinochem-SG. A part of the court costs for the second instance of RMB 306, 432, namely RMB 183, 859. 2, shall be borne by ThyssenKrupp, and the remaining RMB 122, 572. 8 by Sinochem-SG.

This Judgment shall be final and conclusive.

Presiding Judge: REN Xuefeng
Acting Judge: CHENG Mingzhu
Acting Judge: ZHU Ke
June 30, 2014
Court Clerk: DING Yi

新加坡案例

新加坡共和国最高法院 | 主编

JIO Minerals FZC and others
v.
Mineral Enterprises Ltd

——用以确定哪个国家为申索的自然行诉地时所适用的普通法原则(与法院不方便审理有关)

上诉庭——2010 民事上诉第 72 号

上诉庭法官赵锡燊及上诉庭法官潘文龙

2010 年 9 月 9 日;2010 年 11 月 11 日

【简要案情】

答辩方 Mineral Enterprises Ltd(以下简称"答辩方")是一家专营采矿及铁矿石销售的印度公司。答辩方有兴趣在印度尼西亚开采铁矿石。第二上诉方 Jimmy Singh (以下简称"第二上诉方")和第三上诉方 Raman Srinivasan(以下简称"第三上诉方")管控一家名为 PT JIO Energi Resources(以下简称"PT JIO")的印度尼西亚公司,该公司持有在加里曼丹珀莱哈里开采铁矿石的特许权(以下简称"珀莱哈里特许权")。第二上诉方与第三上诉方居住于印度尼西亚。答辩方的代理人和第二上诉方、第三上诉方在印度尼西亚开会进行协商。

第一上诉方 JIO Minerals FZC(以下简称"第一上诉方")于 2006 年 8 月在阿拉伯联合酋长国(以下简称"阿联酋")成立。第二上诉方与第三上诉方是第一上诉方营业执照的持有人。第一上诉方之后与 PT JIO 签订了一份

“独家的、不可撤销的勘探、开发、采矿协议”(以下简称“独家采矿协议”),获得在印度尼西亚开采铁矿石的特许权,独家采矿协议受阿联酋阿治曼法律管辖。

第一上诉方随后发出一封要约书给答辩方。该要约书通过电子邮件的方式从印度尼西亚发往答辩方位于印度的办公室。第一上诉方在要约书中表述,自己拥有储备量高达100万吨的优质铁矿石。答辩方通过从第二上诉方与第三上诉方处购买第一上诉方的股份,接受了要约书中的要约,由此形成了合同,下称“投资协议”。答辩方将股份的买入价(以下简称“投资资金”)汇款至第二上诉方与第三上诉方的新加坡银行账户。

签订投资协议后,答辩方在珀莱哈里特许权区域内展开钻探工作,但后来停止了钻探活动。上诉方称,答辩方所进行的钻探活动不足以让答辩方对珀莱哈里特许权区的铁矿石产量作出定论。上诉方还称,有印度尼西亚籍证人目睹了答辩方的钻探活动。

上诉方过后将部分投资资金返还给答辩方。答辩方随后向新加坡高等法庭起诉上诉方,要求法庭宣判答辩方正当撤销投资协议,并要求上诉方返还投资资金的余额并作出损害赔偿,以及根据《不实陈述法》(第390章,1994年修订版)对欺诈性不实陈述或不实陈述作出进一步或替代性的损害赔偿。

上诉方以法院不方便审理(*forum non conveniens*)为由,申请中止诉讼程序。助理主簿批准了上诉方的申请。答辩方就此提出上诉。高等法庭法官(以下简称“法官”)以新加坡法院并非是不方便审理本案的法院为由,裁定答辩方上诉得直。

【裁判要旨】

裁定,上诉得直:

(1)新加坡法院适用 *Spiliada Maritime Corporation v. Cansulex Ltd* [1987] AC 460 案件的两阶段测试(以下简称“*Spiliada* 测试”)来确定是否应以法院不方便审理为由准予中止诉讼程序。*Spiliada* 测试的第一阶段会考虑连结因素,如与个人有关的连结、与事件和交易有关的连结,以及管辖法、其他诉讼程序以及诉讼形式等连结因素,以确定另一个诉讼地是否清楚明确地比新加坡更适合作为诉讼地。*Spiliada* 测试的第二阶段需要考虑的是,出于维护正义,是否存在促使法庭驳回中止诉讼申请的情况:见[38]和[42]。

(2) 法官可酌情准予或驳回中止诉讼程序的申请。除非法官本人在原则问题上有所误解,或考虑了不该考虑的事项,或没有考虑应该考虑的事项,或作出了明显错误的决定,否则上诉庭不会干涉法官行使酌情权。上诉方作出申辩,指出法官可能错误地适用了某些原则。因此,本上诉庭必须就本案案情重新适用 *Spiliada* 测试标准:见[40]和[60]。

(3) 各方之间与纠纷相关的连结点都在印度尼西亚:见[61]和[62]。

(4) 至于是否有非诉讼方证人作证,应分别分析两个因素:①以证人的经常居住地为诉讼地的便利性(以下称"便利证人因素");以及②证人是否被强制作证(以下称"强制证人作证因素"):见[63]。

(5) 在分析便利证人因素时,法庭不应预先确定当事人应传唤的证人。被告方只须证明外国证人的证词至少与其抗辩立场相关就足够了。上诉方已达到这一门槛。但由于印度尼西亚籍证人可能会通过视频连线作证,而且印度尼西亚与新加坡距离不远,所以便利证人因素在本案并不是一个重要的因素:见[66],[67],[69],[70]和[110]。

(6) 就强制证人作证因素而言,最好有证据证明印度尼西亚籍证人是否可以被强制在印度尼西亚法庭作证。但是,印度尼西亚籍证人在印度尼西亚法庭作证的可能性较大:见[74]和[110]。

(7) 投资协议并没有明确规定管辖法,但由于独家采矿协议中选择适用阿联酋法律,而该协议也与投资协议密切相关,因此可以合理推断各方有意适用阿联酋法律作为投资协议的管辖法:见[80]和[85]。

(8) 法官不应在没有要求各方就阿联酋法律的潜在适用性作出陈词的情况下,就假定阿联酋法律是投资协议的管辖法。但由于双方在上诉时都有机会就阿联酋法律的适用性作出陈词,因此上诉庭可初步认为阿联酋法律是投资协议的管辖法:见[86]和[87]。

(9) 在侵权案中,新加坡法院采用的选择法律规则是双重可起诉性规则。此规则规定,侵权行为必须根据法院地法和侵权行为地法都可以起诉。但双重可起诉性规则可能会被推翻。法庭要确认侵权行为地法,就必须先确定侵权行为的发生地。通常用以确定侵权行为发生地的测试是实质测试。根据实质测试,法庭需要审视构成侵权行为的事件,并查问诉因实质上在何地产生。对于在单一司法辖区内收到并据此行事的不实陈述,法庭建议用更为具体的规则来确定不实陈述的侵权行为地(见以下意见)。对于不在该规则范围内的案件,则可适用更为一般的实质测试及其可能的标准。然而,本庭无须对所建议的规则之地位作出确定裁决,因为根据本上诉案的案情无法适用该建议的规则,原因有二:第一,虽然实际的不实陈述是在印度收到的,但上诉方也辩称其他陈述是在印度尼西亚开会时作出的。第二,各方在印度和印度尼西亚两个司法辖区都有根据这些陈述行事。因此,法庭必须适用一般的实质测试。由此得出,印度尼西亚是侵权行为地,因为大多数的协商都在那里进行,而且答辩方也在该地依据这些陈述采取了措施:见[88],[90]和[93]—[95]。

(10) 没有必要严格证明印度尼西亚法律与新加坡法律的差异。法庭会注意到其他司法辖区的法律可能不同:见[96]。

(11) 对于根据《不实陈述法》提出的诉因,法庭有必要确定《不实陈述法》的适用范围,以确定该法是否有可能适用于本案。法庭应根据推定不具有域外效力的两个方面来确定《不实陈述法》的适用范围。一方面,只有在相关的连结因素指出诉讼地法为管辖法时,才可以推定适用某法律条文。另一方面,推定适用原则仅会影响诉讼地域内发生的活动,或是诉讼地国民在国外的活动:见[98]。

(12) 关于推定不具有域外效力的第一个方面,首先要做的是,对答辩方主张上诉方通过不实陈述诱使其签订合同这一系争点作出定性。无论该系争点被定性为侵权问题还是合同问题,其管辖法都不是新加坡法律。因

此,就推定的第一方面而言,《不实陈述法》并不适用于本案:见[101]。

(13) 关于推定不具有域外效力的第二个方面,则是推定《不实陈述法》只适用于在新加坡领域内作出的不实陈述。如果有清楚的迹象表明国会有让《不实陈述法》具有域外适用效力的意图,那么该推定就可能被推翻,但《不实陈述法》并没有明文的域外适用规定。然而,如果该法适用于域外,则相关合同的适用法律必须是新加坡法律,方能贯彻法律的意旨。由于不实陈述在新加坡域外发生,而且投资协议也不受新加坡法律管辖,因此就该推定的第二个方面而言,《不实陈述法》并不适用于本案:见[102]—[105]。

(14) 初步认定,侵权行为地是自然行诉地。如果侵权行为的发生地是偶然的,"初步认定"的立场可能会被推翻。本案的侵权行为地是印度尼西亚,而且侵权行为在那里发生也并非偶然:见[106]和[107]。

(15) 答辩方与新加坡之间的一般联系以及投资资金支付到新加坡银行账户的事实都与 *Spiliada* 测试的第一阶段无关,因为这些联系都与答辩方提出的诉求无关。法庭应只考虑与纠纷相关的联系:见[109]。

(16) 总的来说,本庭认为印度尼西亚明显比新加坡更适合作为诉讼地。投资协议虽受阿联酋法律管辖,但这并不是支持新加坡成为自然行诉地的因素。针对法院不方便审理原则的分析具有相对性。即便第三诉讼地能作出与印度尼西亚同等或比之更强有力的自然行诉地主张,新加坡也不会仅因此就成为自然行诉地:见[110]和[111]。

(17) 鉴于提交本庭的案情,当事人没有针对 *Spiliada* 测试的第二阶段提出任何论点,这并不奇怪:见[115]。

意见:新加坡法院拒绝采用澳大利亚高等法院在 *Oceanic Sun Line Special Shipping Co v. Fay* (1988) 165 CLR 197 和 *Voth v. Manildra Flour Mills Proprietary Limited* (1990) 171 CLR 538 案件中确立的方法。澳大利亚法院的方法涉及裁定本土诉讼地是否明显不适合作为诉讼地:见[45]和[46]。

英国法院将确定侵权行为发生地的实质测试具体化,针对不实陈述在一个司法辖区发生但在另一个司法辖区收到的情形确立了更切实的规则。这个方法是有可取之处的。实质测试的范围宽泛且没有限制,针对特殊侵权案件,更具体的规则以及恰当的例外情况是有帮助的。有人建议,如果是在单一司法辖区收到陈述并据以行事的情形,该地点就应是侵权行为地,除非事件只是偶然在那里发生,或者收到陈述和据此行事的地点在不同国家。尽管如此,一般的实质测试可能仍适用于不符合该规则的案件:见[91],[93]和[94]。

【专家点评】*

一、简介

随着亚洲经济的崛起以及中国推动实施宏伟的“一带一路”倡议,区域内跨国经济活动持续加速发展,国际商业纠纷也随之激增。国际商业纠纷往往涉及应在何地提起诉讼的司法管辖权争议,需要适用明确而复杂的国际私法规则来解决。本评注将归纳新加坡 *JIO Minerals FZC and others v. Mineral Enterprises Ltd*①这一标志性判决中所确定的法院不方便审理(*forum non conveniens*)的主要原则,并解释这些原则如何与国际社会相关联。

二、案情与裁决

原告是一家有兴趣在印度尼西亚开采铁矿石的印度公司,得知第二被告和第三被告管控的印度尼西亚公司 PT JIO 持有印度尼西亚铁矿石特许权。根据各方的协商,第一被告 JIO Minerals FZC 作为合资经营项目的公司,在阿联酋成立。

PT JIO 与 JIO Minerals FZC 签订了一份协议,指定后者为唯一和独家的国际代理商,就该铁矿石特许权拥有不可撤销的开采及营销权利(独家采矿协议)。PT JIO 在独家采矿协议中称自己拥有铁矿石特许权,且铁矿石的储

---

* 本评注撰写人:叶曼(Yip Man),新加坡管理大学法学院副教授、李光前研究计划研究员。

① [2011] 1 SLR 391.

量约有100万吨。独家采矿协议中的法律选择条款约定的是阿联酋法律。独家采矿协议的副本也给原告发送了一份。原告声称,在印度尼西亚进行协商时也曾作出类似陈述。

JIO Minerals FZC之后从印度尼西亚发出一份要约书,提议将其50%的股权卖给原告,原告在印度收到该要约书。JIO Minerals FZC在要约书中称其拥有100万吨的优质铁矿石,但要约书不含法律选择条款或诉讼地选择条款。原告接受了要约并支付了对价,双方因此缔结了合同(投资协议)。

各方就其中一个特许权区内的铁矿石储量发生纠纷。在投资协议下支付的对价部分退还给了原告,虽然退款的目的存有争议。随后,原告在新加坡对被告提起诉讼,要求法庭宣判撤销投资协议,并要求被告返还剩余的对价款及作出损害赔偿;或者根据《不实陈述法》,[1]原告就不实陈述侵权行为或不实陈述提出申索。被告申请中止新加坡的诉讼程序,并辩称印度尼西亚更适合作为诉讼地。新加坡高等法庭驳回被告的中止程序申请,但上诉庭推翻该裁决,并裁定印度尼西亚是该诉讼的自然行诉地。

1. 法院不方便审理:*Spiliada* 测试

上诉庭适用了 *Spiliada* 测试[2]来确定原告申索的自然行诉地是新加坡还是印度尼西亚。依据该测试,法院须确定"为了各方利益及司法公正,更适合审理"纠纷的诉讼地。[3] 倘若有其他诉讼地现成可用,且也更适合展开该诉讼,那么本地的诉讼程序将予以中止。

2. 两阶段审查

Spiliada 测试需要进行两个阶段的酌情审查。在第一阶段,法院会考虑一般的连结因素以确定哪个诉讼地与纠纷具有最真实和实质的连结。举证责任归于被告。连结因素包括:

---

① (Cap 390, 1994 Rev Ed).

② 取自英国法院在 *Spiliada Maritime Corp v. Cansulex Ltd* [1987] AC 460 的裁决中所制定的原则。

③ Ibid, at 476.

(1)与个人有关的连结;

(2)与事件和交易有关的连结;

(3)管辖法;

(4)其他诉讼程序;

(5)诉讼的形式。

在第二阶段,法庭主要考虑的是,实质正义能否在初步认定的自然行诉地获得。所有因素都得到审查。举证责任由原告承担:原告必须列出有力的证据证明自己无法在外国法院取得实体公正。上诉庭认为,须谨慎质疑外国法律体系的司法质量,仅指出原告在本地诉讼地拥有法律或司法优势是不够的。

3. 比较方法

重要的是,*Spiliada* 测试采用比较方法,其目的并不是抽象地确定最适合的诉讼地或证明新加坡显然不适合作为诉讼地。被告必须证明,显然有更适合的外国诉讼地,且其有意在该外国诉讼地进行诉讼。仅证明纠纷与新加坡之间没有任何实质的连结因素是不够的,因为这没有说明纠纷和所建议的外国诉讼地之间有什么连结点。

三、适用

上诉庭的分析着重于 *Spiliada* 测试的第一阶段,因为各方并没有就测试的第二阶段提出任何论点。上诉庭裁定,根据下面提到的连结点,可证明印度尼西亚显然是更适合审理申索的诉讼地,与申索无关的连结点则不予理会。例如,将对价款支付到新加坡银行账户,以及各方与新加坡之间的某些一般连结点。

1. 便利证人

便利证人因素关乎证人的实际所在位置。本案中,被告打算传唤居住在印度尼西亚的证人。但是,法官认为该因素并非特别重要,因为新加坡和印度尼西亚距离不远,而且可以通过视频连线取得证人的证词。

2. 强制证人作证

相反地，强制证人作证因素是更重要的连结点。被告辩称，可能需要强制在印度尼西亚的证人出席庭审。新加坡法院不能强制外国证人到新加坡法院作证。[①] 虽然被告没有援引专家证据来证明能否强制印度尼西亚证人在印度尼西亚法院作证，但上诉庭认为案件若在印度尼西亚进行审理，印度尼西亚证人作证的可能性较大。因此，该因素支持印度尼西亚为自然行诉地。

3. 申索的管辖法

申索的管辖法是 *Spiliada* 测试第一阶段的一个重要因素。在法律适用地的法院提起申索可以节省时间和费用，比起适用外国法律，法院更擅于适用本国的法律。

(1)合同申索及返还申索

与投资协议密切相关的独家采矿协议中有明示的法律选择条款，由此推断出投资协议有选择阿联酋法律的默示条款。因此，合同申索，即要求法庭宣判有效撤销投资协议以及就合同中的不实陈述提出损害赔偿，受阿联酋法律管辖。

对于要求返还对价款余额的申索，上诉庭裁定该申索也受投资协议的准据法(阿联酋法律)管辖，因为该申索是合同无效产生的后果。

(2)侵权申索——多地侵权

在侵权案中，新加坡的法律选择规则是双重可起诉性规则。此规则规定，侵权行为必须根据法院地法(*lex fori*，法院当地的法律)和侵权行为地法(*lex loci delicti*，侵权行为发生地的法律)都可以起诉。这一主要规则受制于一个可变通的例外情况，若援引该例外情况，适用的法律就是与侵权行为发生以及与各方之间有最重大连结关系的国家的法律，无论是法院地的法律、侵权行为发生地的法律，甚至是第三国的法律。

确定侵权行为地是适用双重可起诉性规则的关键。当构成侵权的事件

① Rules of Court (Cap 322, R 5, 2006 Rev Ed), Order 38, rule 18(2).

在多于一个司法管辖区内发生时(即多地侵权),确定侵权行为发生地就会变得复杂。根据新加坡法律,侵权行为发生地是依据侵权实质测试确定的——诉因实质上是在何地产生的。上诉庭指出,根据英国普通法,不实陈述申索的侵权行为地为收到陈述并据以行事之地。但是,英国法院的处理方式不适用于 *JIO Minerals FZC* 案的案情,因为原告在不同的司法管辖区收到陈述并据以行事。原告在印度收到陈述,但原告依据这些陈述在印度和印度尼西亚两地行事。

综合考虑各种情况,上诉庭裁定侵权行为地为印度尼西亚,因为那是(在当地进行协商时)作出陈述的地方,也是原告据以行事(进行钻探活动)的地方。收到陈述的地方反而不重要——陈述在印度收到是因为原告在那里。因此,就不实陈述提出的侵权申索受印度尼西亚法律管辖。

(3)法定申索——推定不具有域外效力

根据《不实陈述法》提出的申索引出了该法地域范围的问题,从而引发了推定不具有域外效力原则的应用。上诉庭认为,该推定有两个方面,两者皆与认清国会的立法意图有关。第一方面的操作属于法律选择的一部分:只有当法律选择规则将新加坡法律作为系争点的管辖法时,本地的成文法才适用。由于不实陈述的申索,无论是侵权的还是合同的,都不涉及适用新加坡法律,因此可推定国会并无意让《不实陈述法》适用于本案。

第二方面则是一般操作:一般推定国会有意让本地法律适用于在新加坡境内发生的活动,除非国会另有明确的相反意图。上诉庭确认,《不实陈述法》未就地域范围作出规定,所以推定只适用于在新加坡境内作出的不实陈述。如果该法适用于在新加坡境外作出的不实陈述,以及适用于与受外国法律管辖的合同有关的不实陈述,那就无法更好地实现立法目的。

4. 侵权行为地

侵权行为地本身是一个重要的连结因素。初步认定,侵权行为地就是侵权案件的自然行诉地,除非侵权行为在那里是偶然发生的。上诉庭在本案中裁定,在印度尼西亚,即重大活动进行的地方,发生侵权行为并不是偶然的。

由于新加坡法律乍看来并不适用于任何一项申索,所以这一因素也不支持新加坡为任何一项申索的自然行诉地。就其他侵权申索而言,印度尼西亚法律是管辖法,因此支持印度尼西亚为侵权的自然行诉地。虽然合同申索及返还申索可能受阿联酋法律管辖,上诉庭提醒,审查本案自然行诉地时须将印度尼西亚和新加坡作比较,而不是同阿联酋作比较。

四、结语

虽然 *JIO Minerals FZC* 案论及的是在新加坡法律下法院不方便审理的普通法原则,但是该裁决对其他司法管辖区有着重大的借鉴价值。

中国虽是大陆法系(民法法系)司法管辖区,但也将中国式的法院不方便审理原则正式纳入了《最高人民法院关于适用〈中华人民共和国民事诉讼法〉的解释》的第 532 条中。[①]事实上,中国法院自 20 世纪 90 年代起就开始适用一套受到较多约束的法院不方便审理原则。[②] 虽然"中国式"和"新加坡式"有所区别,[③]但中国法律接受这一原则使两个司法管辖区能够就该原则的未来发展开展建设性对话,同时在司法管辖规则协调问题上便利双方或多边协商。

① 第 532 条大体上反映了中国在早前一些官方文件里所重申的意见。See ZS Tang, Y Xiao and Z Huo, *Conflict of Laws in the People's Republic of China* (Edward Elgar, 2016), p 108.

② Ibid, pp 107-108; G Tu, "*Forum Non Conveniens* in the People's Republic of China" (2012) Chinese Journal of International Law 341.

③ Ibid, pp 108-117.

JIO Minerals FZC and others

v.

Mineral Enterprises Ltd

—Common Law Principles (Relating to *Forum Non Conveniens*) for Determining Which Country is the Natural Forum for the Claims in Question

Court of Appeal — Civil Appeal No 72 of 2010
Chao Hick Tin JA and Andrew Phang Boon Leong JA
9 September; 11 November 2010

Facts

The respondent ("the Respondent"), Mineral Enterprises Ltd, was an Indian company with expertise in mining and marketing iron ore. The Respondent was interested in mining iron ore in Indonesia. Jimmy Singh and Raman Srinivasan, the second and third appellants ("the Second and Third Appellants") respectively, controlled PT JIO Energi Resources ("PT JIO"), an Indonesian company with concessions to mine iron ore in Pelaihari, Kalimantan ("the Pelaihari Concession"). The Second and Third Appellants were resident in Indonesia. The Respondent's representatives and the Second and Third Appellants engaged in negotiations during meetings in Indonesia.

The First Appellant ("the First Appellant"), JIO Minerals FZC, was formed in the United Arab Emirates ("UAE") in August 2006. The Second and

Third Appellants were the First Appellant's commercial licensees. The First Appellant then acquired rights to iron ore mining concessions in Indonesia by entering into an "Exclusive Irrevocable Exploration, Exploitation, Mining Agreement" ("the Exclusive Mining Agreement") with PT JIO. The Exclusive Mining Agreement was governed by the laws of Ajman, UAE.

The First Appellant subsequently sent the Respondent a letter of offer ("Letter of Offer"). The Letter of Offer was sent from Indonesia via e-mail to the Respondent's office in India. The Letter of Offer contained a representation that the First Appellant had a high grade iron ore reserve amounting to one million tonnes. The Respondent accepted the offer contained in the Letter of Offer by purchasing shares in the First Appellant from the Second and Third Appellants. The resulting contract will be referred to as "the Investment Agreement". The Respondent paid the purchase price ("the Investment Funds") for the shares into the Singapore bank accounts of the Second and Third Appellants.

The Respondent commenced drilling at the Pelaihari Concession after entering into the Investment Agreement. The Respondent later stopped its drilling activities. The Appellants alleged that the Respondent's drilling activities were insufficient for it to have formed a firm view of the amount of iron ore deposits in the Pelaihari Concession. The Appellants also alleged that there were Indonesian witnesses who witnessed the Respondent's drilling activities.

The Appellants later returned the Respondent part of the Investment Funds. The Respondent subsequently commenced proceedings against the Appellants in the Singapore High Court for a declaration that the Respondent had validly rescinded the Investment Agreement, the return of the balance of the Investment Funds, damages and, further or alternatively, damages for fraudulent misrepresentation or misrepresentation under the Misrepresentation Act (Cap 390, 1994 Rev Ed).

The Appellants applied to stay the proceedings on the ground of *forum non conveniens*. An assistant registrar granted the Appellants' application. The Respondent appealed. The High Court judge ("the Judge") allowed the appeal on the ground that Singapore was not *forum non conveniens*.

Holding

Held allowing the appeal:

(1) Singapore courts applied the two stage test in *Spiliada Maritime Corporation v. Cansulex Ltd* [1987] AC 460 ("the *Spiliada* test") to determine whether a stay should be granted on the ground of *forum non conveniens*. In stage one of the *Spiliada* test, connecting factors such as personal connections, connections to events and transactions, the governing law, other proceedings and the shape of the litigation, were considered to determine whether another forum was clearly or distinctly more appropriate than Singapore. Stage two of the *Spiliada* test required a consideration of whether there were circumstances by reason of which justice required that a stay should be refused: at [38] and [42].

(2) The decision to grant or refuse a stay of proceedings was discretionary. An appellate court would not interfere with an exercise of discretion unless the Judge had misdirected himself on a matter of principle, or had taken into account matters which he ought not to have taken into account or had failed to take into account matters which he ought to have taken into account or his decision was plainly wrong. The Appellants' arguments suggested that the Judge might have misapplied certain principles. Hence, the court had to apply the *Spiliada* test afresh to the facts: at [40] and [60].

(3) Indonesia was the place where all the parties had some connection that was relevant to the dispute: at [61] and [62].

(4) As for the availability of non-party witnesses, two factors should be analysed separately: (a) the convenience in having the case decided in the forum where the witnesses were ordinarily resident ("the Witness Convenience Factor"); and (b) the compellability of those witnesses ("the Witness Compellability Factor"): at [63].

(5) In analysing the Witness Convenience Factor, the court should not predetermine the witnesses that the parties should call. It was sufficient for a defendant to show that evidence from foreign witnesses was at least arguably relevant to its defence. The Appellants had met this threshold. However, the Witness Convenience Factor was not a significant factor in the present case because of the possibility of the Indonesian witnesses giving evidence via video-link and the proximity of Indonesia to Singapore: at [66], [67], [69], [70] and [110].

(6) In relation to the Witness Compellability Factor, it would have been preferable to have had evidence on whether the Indonesian witnesses were compellable to testify in an Indonesian court. However, it was more likely that the Indonesian witnesses would testify in an Indonesian court: at [74] and [110].

(7) The Investment Agreement did not have an express governing law. However, it was reasonable to infer that the parties intended UAE law to govern the Investment Agreement because of a choice of UAE law in the Exclusive Mining Agreement, which was a closely related contract: at [80] and [85].

(8) The Judge should not have suggested that UAE law was the applicable law of the Investment Agreement without inviting the parties to submit on the

potential applicability of UAE law. However, it was open to the Court of Appeal to take the provisional view that the governing law of the Investment Agreement was UAE law because both parties had the opportunity to submit on the applicability of UAE law in the appeal: at [86] and [87].

(9) The choice of law rule that the Singapore courts applied for torts was the double actionability rule, which provided that the tort had to be actionable under both the *lex fori* and the *lex loci delicti*. The double actionability rule might, however, be displaced. In order to ascertain the *lex loci delicti*, the court had to determine the place of the tort. The test that was commonly applied for determining the place of the tort was the Substance Test. The Substance Test required the court to look at the events constituting the tort and ask where, in substance, the cause of action arose. The court suggested a more specific rule for determining the place of the tort for misrepresentations for which the representation was received and acted upon in a single jurisdiction (see the observations, below). The Substance Test, in its more general form and possible "incarnations", could be resorted to in cases not falling within the suggested rule. However, it was not necessary to rule definitively on the status of the suggested rule as the court was, on the facts of the present appeal, unable to apply the suggested rule for two reasons. First, although the actual misrepresentation was received in India, the Appellants also contended that other representations were made during meetings in Indonesia. Second, the representations were acted upon in two jurisdictions: India and Indonesia. Therefore, the court had to apply the *general* Substance Test. Applying the Substance Test, the place of the tort was Indonesia because that was the place where most of the negotiations took place and where the respondent took steps in reliance of the representations: at [88], [90] and [93] to [95].

(10) Strict proof of the differences between Indonesian law and Singapore

law was not necessary. The court could take notice that the laws of other jurisdictions were likely to be different: at [96].

(11) As for the cause of action based on the Misrepresentation Act, it was necessary for the court to determine whether the scope of the Misrepresentation Act was such that it potentially applied in the present case. Two aspects to the presumption against extraterritoriality should be applied to determine the scope of the Misrepresentation Act. The first aspect was that a statutory provision was presumed to apply only where the relevant connecting factor pointed to the law of the forum as the governing law. The second aspect was that statutes were presumed only to be intended to affect activities occurring within the territory of the forum or to activities abroad of nationals of the forum: at [98].

(12) On the first aspect of the presumption against extraterritoriality, the starting point was to characterise the issue that the respondent raised with its claim that the appellants induced it to enter into a contract through a misrepresentation. The Misrepresentation Act did not apply in the present case on the first aspect of the presumption because the governing law of the issue was not Singapore law, whether the issue was characterised as a tort issue or a contract issue: at [101].

(13) On the second aspect of the presumption against extraterritoriality, the Misrepresentation Act was presumed to only apply to misrepresentations within Singapore territory. This presumption might be displaced by a clear indication that Parliament intended for the Misrepresentation Act to apply extraterritorially. The Misrepresentation Act did not expressly provide that it was to apply extraterritorially. However, its purpose would be furthered if it were to apply extraterritorially, but only if the applicable law of the relevant contract were Singapore law. Hence, on the second aspect of the presumption, the Misrepresentation Act was not applicable because the misrepresentation occurred

outside Singapore territory and the Investment Agreement was not governed by Singapore law: at [102] to [105].

(14) The place of the tort was *prima facie* the natural forum. The *prima facie* position could be displaced if the place of the tort was fortuitous. The place of the tort in the present case was Indonesia and it was not fortuitous that the tort occurred there: at [106] and [107].

(15) The general connections of the Respondent to Singapore and the fact that the Investment Funds were paid into Singapore bank accounts were not relevant in stage one of the *Spiliada* test because those connections were not relevant to the claims that the Respondent had framed. Only connections that were relevant to the disputes should be considered: at [109].

(16) On the whole, the court was satisfied that Indonesia was clearly or distinctly a more appropriate forum than Singapore. Even though the Investment Agreement might be governed by UAE law, this was not a factor that favoured Singapore's candidacy as the natural forum. *Forum non conveniens* analysis was relative. Singapore would not become the natural forum simply because a third forum had a better or as strong a claim as Indonesia as the natural forum: at [110] and [111].

(17) As for the second stage of the *Spiliada* test, the parties did not proffer any arguments, which was not surprising because of the facts before the court: at [115].

Observation: Singapore courts rejected the approach taken by the Australian courts, as established by the High Court of Australia in *Oceanic Sun Line Special Shipping Co v. Fay* (1988) 165 CLR 197 and *Voth v. Manildra Flour Mills Proprietary Limited* (1990) 171 CLR 538. The Australian approach involved a determination of whether the local forum was a clearly inappropriate forum: at [45] and [46].

The English courts had crystallised the Substance Test for determining the place where a tort occurred into more certain rules for misrepresentations made in one jurisdiction and received in another jurisdiction. There was some merit in this approach. The Substance Test was broad and open-ended. It would help to have more concrete rules, with appropriate exceptions, for particular torts. It was suggested that if a representation was received and acted upon in a single jurisdiction, that place should be the place of the tort unless that place was fortuitous or the receipt and reliance occurred in different countries. The Substance Test, in its general form, might nevertheless be applied in cases not falling within the suggested rule: at [91], [93] and [94].

Commentary *

Introduction

The rise of Asian economies and the implementation of the ambitious Belt and Road Initiative by the People's Republic of China ("PRC") will continue to accelerate cross-border economic activities in the region and lead to a concomitant proliferation in international commercial disputes. International commercial disputes often involve jurisdictional battles over where to litigate, calling for the application of clear and sophisticated private international law rules. This commentary distils the key principles of *forum non conveniens* that have been laid down in the Singapore landmark judgment of *JIO Minerals FZC v. Mineral Enterprises Ltd*, ① and explain how they are of relevance to an international audience.

---

* Author: Yip Man, Associate Professor, Lee Kong Chian Fellow, Singapore Management University, School of Law.

① [2011] 1 SLR 391.

Facts and Decision

The plaintiff, an Indian company, was interested in mining iron ore in Indonesia and came to know of the iron ore concessions owned by an Indonesian company, PT JIO Energi Resources (“PT JIO”), controlled by the second and third defendants. Pursuant to the parties’ negotiations, the first defendant, JIO Minerals FZC (“JIO Minerals”) was incorporated in United Arab Emirates (“UAE”) as a vehicle for the joint venture.

PT JIO entered into an agreement with JIO Minerals, appointing the latter as its sole and exclusive international agent with irrevocable rights of mining and marketing of iron ore concessions (the “Exclusive Mining Agreement”). PT JIO represented in the Exclusive Mining Agreement that it owned iron ore concessions with an estimated reserve of 1 million tonnes of iron ore. The Exclusive Mining Agreement contained a UAE choice of law clause. A copy of the Exclusive Mining Agreement was sent to the plaintiff. The plaintiff also alleged that similar representations were made in negotiations conducted in Indonesia.

JIO Minerals then offered to sell 50% of its shareholding to the plaintiff under a Letter of Offer sent from Indonesia and received by the plaintiff in India. JIO Minerals represented therein that it owned 1 million tonnes of high grade iron ore. The Letter of Offer did not contain a choice of law clause or a choice of forum clause. The plaintiff accepted the offer by paying the consideration and a contract was thus concluded between the parties (“Investment Agreement”).

The Parties fell into dispute on the amount of iron ore deposits in one of the concessions. The plaintiff was repaid a portion of the consideration paid under the Investment Agreement, although the purpose of repayment was in dispute. Subsequently, the plaintiff commenced proceedings against the defendants in Singapore, seeking a declaration that the Investment Agreement was rescinded, the return of the balance of the consideration and damages. In the alternative, it claimed for the tort of misrepresentation or misrepresentation under the Misrepresentation Act.[①] The defendants applied for a stay of the Singapore proceedings, arguing that Indonesia was the more appropriate forum. The Singapore Court of Appeal overturned the High Court's rejection of the defendants' stay application and held that Indonesia was the natural forum for the action.

***Forum non conveniens*: the *Spiliada* test**

The Court of Appeal applied the *Spiliada* test[②] to determine whether Singapore or Indonesia was the natural forum for the plaintiff's claims. Under this test, the court is to identify the forum in which the dispute may be "tried more suitably for the interests of all the parties and for the ends of justice".[③] Local proceedings will be stayed if there is some other *available and more appropriate forum* for the trial of the action.

A two-stage inquiry

The *Spiliada* test entails a two-stage, discretionary inquiry. At the first stage, the court considers general connecting factors to identify the forum with the most real and substantial connection with the dispute. The burden of proof is on the defendant. The connecting factors include:

(1) Personal connections

(2) Connections to events and transactions

(3) Governing law

(4) Other proceedings

---

① (Cap 390, 1994 Rev Ed).

② Derived from the principles laid down in the English decision of *Spiliada Maritime Corp v. Cansulex Ltd* [1987] AC 460.

③ Ibid, at 476.

(5) Shape of the litigation

At the second stage, the court considers primarily if substantial justice may be obtained in the *prima facie* (foreign) natural forum. All factors will be examined. The plaintiff bears the burden of proof: he must demonstrate with cogent evidence that he would be denied substantial justice in the foreign court. The Court advised caution in questioning the quality of justice in the foreign legal system. The mere fact that a plaintiff has a legitimate or juridical advantage in the local forum will not suffice.

A comparative approach

Importantly, the *Spiliada* test involves a comparative approach. Its objective is not to identify the most appropriate forum in the abstract or to show that Singapore is a clearly inappropriate forum. The defendant must show that there is a clearly more appropriate and available foreign forum in which he intends to pursue litigation. Proving that the dispute has no substantive connecting factors with Singapore is insufficient, for it says nothing about the connection between the dispute and the suggested foreign forum.

Application

The Court of Appeal's analysis focused on stage one of the *Spiliada* test as no arguments were made in respect of stage two of the test. The Court held that Indonesia was shown to be a clearly more appropriate forum for the trial of the claims, based on the connections discussed below. Connections that were irrelevant to the claims were disregarded: for example, the fact that the consideration was paid into Singapore bank accounts and certain general connections that the parties had with Singapore.

Witness convenience

The witness convenience factor concerns the physical location of the witnesses. In this case, the defendants intended to call witnesses resident in

Indonesia. However, the Court considered that this factor is not particularly significant because of the proximity between Singapore and Indonesia, as well as the possibility of obtaining evidence through video-link.

Witness compellability

In contrast, the witness compellability factor was a more significant connection. The defendants had argued that the witnesses based in Indonesia may need to be compelled to attend court proceedings. A Singapore court is not able to compel a foreign witness to testify in a Singapore court. ① Although the defendants did not adduce expert evidence on whether the Indonesian witnesses are compellable to testify in an Indonesian court, the Court took the view that there was a greater chance that the Indonesian witnesses would testify if the case were tried in Indonesia. As such, this factor favours Indonesia as the natural forum.

The governing laws of the claims

The governing law of a claim is a significant factor under stage one of the *Spiliada* test. Time and expenses could be saved if the claim were brought in the forum of the applicable law, as a forum is more adept at applying its own than a foreign law.

Contractual and restitutionary claims

A choice of UAE law was implied into the Investment Agreement based on the express choice of law provision in the closely related contract, the Exclusive Mining Agreement. As such, the claim for a declaration that the Investment Agreement was validly rescinded and the claim for damages for misrepresentation in contract, characterised as contractual claims, were governed by UAE law.

The restitutionary claim for the balance of the consideration was held to be

① Rules of Court (Cap 322, R 5, 2006 Rev Ed), Order 38, rule 18(2).

also governed by the proper law of the Investment Agreement (ie UAE law) because it arose as a consequence of the failure of the contract.

Tort claim—multiple locality torts

The Singapore choice of law rule for torts is the double actionability rule, which provides that the tort must be actionable under both the *lex fori* (law of the forum) and *lex loci delicti* (law of the place of the tort). This main rule is subject to a flexible exception which may be invoked to apply the law of the country with the most significant connection to the occurrence of the tort and the parties, whether it is the law of the forum, the law of the place of the tort, or even the law of a third country.

The determination of the place of the tort is key to the double actionability rule. This exercise becomes complex where the events constituting the tort occurs in more than one jurisdiction ("multiple locality torts"). Under Singapore law, the place of the tort is determined based on the "substance of the tort test": where, in substance, did the cause of action arise? The Court noted that under English common law, the place of the tort for misrepresentation claims is the place where the representation was received and acted upon. However, the English approach was inapplicable to the facts of *JIO Minerals* because the representations were received and acted upon by the plaintiff in different jurisdictions. The representations were received by the plaintiff in India, but they were acted upon by the plaintiff in both India and Indonesia.

Considering all circumstances, the Court held that the place of the tort was Indonesia because it was the place where the representations were made (during the negotiations that were conducted there) and where the plaintiff had acted upon the representations (drilling activities). The place of receipt was, however, not significant: the representations were received in India because the plaintiff was based there. Thus, Indonesian law governed the tortious claim in misrepresentation.

Statutory claim—presumption against extraterritoriality

The claim under the Misrepresentation Act raised the question as to the geographical scope of the statute, thereby bringing the principle of presumption against extraterritoriality into play. The Court of Appeal explained that there are two aspects to the presumption, and both are related to the discernment of parliamentary intention. The first aspect operates as part of the choice of law exercise: the local statutory law would only be applicable if the choice of law rules point to Singapore law as the governing law of the issue. As the claim for misrepresentation, on either a tortious or contractual characterisation, would not engage the application of Singapore law, it may be presumed that Parliament did not intend for the Misrepresentation Act to apply to the present case.

The second aspect operates generally: save for clear intention to the contrary, it is generally presumed that Parliament intends for domestic laws to apply to activities that occur in Singapore. The Court affirmed that the Misrepresentation Act, which is silent as to its geographical scope, is presumed to only apply to misrepresentations made in Singapore. The statutory purposes underlining the legislation would not be better served if it were to apply to misrepresentations occurring outside Singapore and in relation to contracts governed by foreign law.

The place of the tort

The place of the tort is a significant connecting factor on its own. The place of the tort is *prima facie* the natural forum for the tort, unless the place of the tort was fortuitous. In the case, the Court held that Indonesia, where significant activities took place, was not fortuitous.

As Singapore law did not *prima facie* apply to any of the claims, this factor did not favour Singapore as a natural forum for any of the claims. In so far as the alternative tort claim was concerned, Indonesian law was the governing law and it thus favoured Indonesia as the natural forum for the tort. Although UAE law might govern the contractual and restitutionary claims, the Court reminded that the "natural forum" inquiry in the case required a comparison between Indonesia and Singapore, and not with UAE.

Conclusion

Although *JIO Minerals* addresses the common law principles of *forum non conveniens* under Singapore law, the decision is of great comparative value to other jurisdictions.

Although the PRC is a civil law jurisdiction, Article 532 of the Supreme People's Court's Interpretation on the Application of the Civil Procedural Law of the PRC formally incorporated the Chinese version of the doctrine of *forum non conveniens*.① Indeed, the Chinese courts have been applying a more constrained version of *forum non conveniens* since 1990s.② Although there are differences between the Chinese version and the Singapore version,③ the acceptance of the doctrine in Chinese law enables constructive dialogue on future developments of the doctrine in the two jurisdictions, as well as facilitates bilateral or multilateral negotiations on the harmonisation of jurisdictional rules.

---

① Article 532 substantially echoed the guidance given in earlier Chinese official documents. See ZS Tang, Y Xiao and Z Huo, *Conflict of Laws in the People's Republic of China* (Edward Elgar, 2016), p 108.

② Ibid, pp 107–108; G Tu, "*Forum Non Conveniens* in the People's Republic of China" (2012) Chinese Journal of International Law 341.

③ Ibid, pp 108–117.

Grounds of Decision

JIO Minerals FZC and others

v.

Mineral Enterprises Ltd

[2011] 1 SLR 391

11 November 2010

Andrew Phang Boon Leong JA (delivering the grounds of decision of the court):

Introduction and facts

1 This was an appeal against the decision of the High Court judge ("the Judge") who had refused to grant the defendants a stay of the action brought against them by the plaintiff (see *Mineral Enterprises Ltd v. JIO Minerals FZC* [2010] SGHC 109).

2 Dissatisfied with the decision of the Judge, the defendants appealed. After hearing counsel, we allowed the appeal. We now give the detailed grounds for our decision.

The parties

3 Mineral Enterprises Ltd ("the Respondent") is the plaintiff. It is an Indian company with expertise in mining and marketing iron ore in India and internationally. The Respondent has projects in Indonesia which are coordinated by its Mining and Operations Manager, Joseph Cyriac ("Cyriac").

4 JIO Minerals FZC ("the First Appellant") is a company incorporated in the United Arab Emirates ("UAE") and was set up by Jimmy Singh ("the Second Appellant") and Raman Srinivasan ("the Third Appellant"). The First, Second and Third Appellants are the defendants and we will refer to them collectively as

"the Appellants". The Second Appellant is the President and Director of an Indonesian company known as PT JIO Energi Resources ("PT JIO"). The Second Appellant is also a commercial licensee and manager of the First Appellant. PT JIO owns iron ore mining concessions in 12 hectares of land in Pelaihari, Kalimantan ("the Pelaihari Concession").

5 The Third Appellant is a commercial licensee of the First Appellant. Although it was suggested that the Third Appellant had control over PT JIO, together with the Second Appellant, the exact nature of the Third Appellant's association with PT JIO was not addressed by the parties.

Initial meetings in Indonesia

6 Cyriac met the Second and Third Appellants in Indonesia around August 2005. At this first meeting, Cyriac told the Second and Third Appellants that the Respondent was interested in mining iron ore in Indonesia. The Second and Third Appellants told Cyriac that a company that they controlled, PT JIO, had mining concessions in Pelaihari, Kalimantan.

7 Cyriac later visited the Pelaihari Concession. The outcome of this visit is disputed. The Appellants' version is that Cyriac assessed that the Pelaihari Concession contained approximately 300,000 to 500,000 tonnes of iron ore and that Cyriac communicated this assessment to the Respondent's directors. The Respondent's version was that Cyriac did not explore the Pelaihari Concession because the Appellants did not provide sufficient facilities and logistical arrangements for Cyriac to do so.

The Singapore joint venture

8 On 7 April 2006, the Respondent entered into a joint venture agreement ("the Singapore JVA") with JIO Corporation Pte Ltd ("JIO Singapore"), a Singapore company. The Second Appellant was the majority shareholder and a director of JIO Singapore.

9 The Singapore JVA provided for the incorporation of a joint venture company in Singapore. JIO Singapore was to procure marketing rights over at least one million tonnes of iron ore from Indonesia for the joint venture company. The Respondent and JIO Singapore were to have an equal number of shares in the joint venture company.

10 The Singapore JVA stipulated Singapore law as its governing law and included both a Singapore International Arbitration Centre arbitration clause and a forum selection clause for the Singapore courts.

11 After an amendment on 9 May 2006 to the Singapore JVA's payment provisions, the Singapore JVA was, however, not pursued further. The Respondent's director, H R Jain, deposed in his affidavit dated 18 January 2010 that the Singapore JVA was not pursued because of "the more advantageous income tax benefits" of forming the joint venture vehicle in the UAE instead.

12 JIO Singapore was struck off the register of companies in Singapore on 4 July 2008.

Visits to the Tanah Bumbu Concession

13 From February to August 2006, the Respondent's representatives visited a mining concession in Tanah Bumbu, Kalimantan ("the Tanah Bumbu Concession").

14 The Second Appellant deposed in his affidavit dated 23 November 2009 that two representatives of the local government in charge of the Tanah Bumbu Concession were aware of these visits by the Respondent's representatives.

The Exclusive Mining Agreement

15 On 2 August 2006, the UAE Government of Ajman issued a commercial license to the First Appellant. Shortly thereafter, on 7 August 2006, the First Appellant entered into an agreement with PT JIO. This agreement was termed an "Exclusive Irrevocable Exploration, Exploitation, Mining and Marketing

Agreement” (“the Exclusive Mining Agreement”). Under the Exclusive Mining Agreement, PT JIO appointed the First Appellant as “its sole and exclusive international agent with irrevocable rights of exploration, exploitation, mining and marketing of Iron Ore Concession [*sic*]”. The Exclusive Mining Agreement did not define the term “Iron Ore Concession”.

16 Under Article 5. 1 of the Exclusive Mining Agreement, however, PT JIO represented that it had iron ore concessions with an estimated reserve of one million tonnes of “+65 Fe iron ore”.

17 The Exclusive Mining Agreement selected the laws of Ajman, UAE, as its governing law. The Exclusive Mining Agreement provided for disputes in connection with it to be resolved “under the rules of the UAE International Arbitration [*sic*]”.

18 On 7 September 2006, PT JIO sent the Respondent a copy of the Exclusive Mining Agreement via e-mail. PT JIO sent the copy from Indonesia and the copy was received by the Respondent in India.

Meetings in Indonesia

19 The Respondent's representatives had meetings and negotiations with the Second and Third Appellants in Indonesia in or around August 2006. The outcome of the meetings is material to the dispute between the parties.

20 According to the Appellants, the Respondent and the Appellants had agreed that the Pelaihari Concession was to be used as a “pilot project”. The Appellants further allege that the parties agreed that the Appellants would procure mining concessions with iron ore deposits of one million tonnes. In procuring these iron ore deposits, the Appellants were *not* to be limited to the Pelaihari Concession.

21 According to the Respondent, the outcome of the meetings was that the Respondent was to be given a first right of refusal for all other concessions that

the Appellants held and that the Pelaihari Concession was to be the first project for the parties. The Respondent further alleged that the Appellants assured it at the meetings that they had control over the Tanah Bumbu Concession and could bring that concession within the scope of the joint venture that the parties intended to enter.

The Letter of Offer

22 On 7 September 2006, the First Appellant sent a letter of offer to the Respondent ("the Letter of Offer"). The Second Appellant signed the Letter of Offer.

23 The material terms of the Letter of Offer were as follows:

(a) The First Appellant offered the Respondent 50% shareholding in the First Appellant.

(b) The First Appellant represented that it "has a high grade iron ore reserve of 1 million tones [*sic*]".

24 The Letter of Offer was sent from Indonesia. The Respondent received the Letter of Offer in India.

Cyriac's Assessment of the Tanah Bumbu Concession

25 Cyriac visited the Tanah Bumbu Concession around the time when the First Appellant sent the Letter of Offer to the Respondent. After the visit, Cyriac made a written report ("the Cyriac Report") that stated that the Tanah Bumbu Concession had approximately five to six million tonnes of iron ore deposits. The Cyriac Report was dated 14 September 2006.

26 The Appellants argued that the Respondent only accepted the Letter of Offer after it received the Cyriac Report. In contrast, the Respondent argued that it was not aware of the contents of the Cyriac Report before it accepted the Letter of Offer.

Payment of consideration

27 The Respondent accepted the offer in the Letter of Offer by paying the requisite consideration ("the Investment Funds") to the bank accounts of the Second and Third Appellants in Singapore on 27 September 2006. We will refer to the resulting contract between the parties as the "Investment Agreement".

28 The Second and Third Appellants then transferred 30 and 20 shares, respectively, in the First Appellant to the Respondent.

The Respondent's drilling activities at the Pelaihari Concession

29 The Respondent started drilling at the Pelaihari Concession some time after the Investment Agreement was concluded. The exact date when the Respondent's drilling commenced and the extent of the Respondent's drilling activities are, however, disputed.

30 The Appellants alleged that the Respondent's drilling activities were insufficient for it to form a firm view on the amount of iron ore deposits in the Pelaihari Concession. The Appellants alleged that representatives of the local government in charge of the Pelaihari Concession witnessed the Respondent's drilling activities and would be able to give evidence on those activities.

Partial repayment of the Investment Funds

31 The Appellants returned the Respondent a sum of US $699, 000. The purpose of this repayment is disputed.

32 The Appellants argued that the sum was returned because they felt that they had no choice but to return the unutilised portion of the Investment Funds because the Respondent was not going to restart drilling. The Appellants further argued that they did not agree to return the balance of the Investment Funds.

33 The Respondent alleged that the Appellants returned that sum because they admitted that the Pelaihari Concession did not contain sufficient deposits. The Respondent also argued that the Appellants promised to return the balance of the

Investment Funds.

The claim

34 On 19 February 2009, the Respondent commenced proceedings against the Appellants in the Singapore High Court for, *inter alia*:

(a) a declaration that the Respondent had validly rescinded the Investment Agreement;

(b) the return of the balance of the Investment Funds (amounting to US $1,028,695);

(c) damages to be assessed; and

(d) further or alternatively, damages for fraudulent misrepresentation or misrepresentation under the Misrepresentation Act (Cap 390, 1994 Rev Ed).

The decision below

35 The Judge allowed the Respondent's appeal from the assistant registrar's decision to stay the action on the ground of *forum non conveniens*.

36 The Judge's reasons for holding that Singapore was not *forum non conveniens* were as follows:

(a) The only legally significant geographical connections that the dispute had with Indonesia were: (i) the location of the concessions in Indonesia; and (ii) the Indonesian residency of the Second Appellant, who, in the Judge's opinion, was the "directing mind behind the corporate structures and documentation".

(b) The Appellants did not raise a compelling argument that the Investment Agreement was governed by Indonesian law. Rather, reasonable persons in the position of the parties would not have concluded that Indonesian law should govern the Investment Agreement, given that: (i) the Exclusive Mining Agreement was governed by UAE law; and (ii) the Singapore JVA was governed by Singapore law.

(c) The Appellants' arguments on the law governing the alternative tort claims did not present "insurmountable obstacles".

(d) The Appellants were not able to show that the evidence of two Indonesian witnesses who allegedly witnessed the extent of the Respondent's drilling operations would be material. The Appellants also failed to show whether these witnesses would be available or whether other witnesses would be able to provide the same evidence.

(e) On the whole, the Appellants had failed to demonstrate the presence of another more appropriate forum for the dispute.

The issue

37 The sole issue on appeal was whether the Respondent's action should be stayed on the ground of *forum non conveniens*. In particular, we were concerned with whether or not Indonesia was a clearly or distinctly more appropriate forum than Singapore for the hearing of the dispute between the parties.

The applicable legal principles

***The approach in* Spiliada**

38 The general principles to be applied in the context of the present appeal are well-established and may be traced back to the seminal House of Lords decision of *Spiliada Maritime Corporation v. Cansulex Ltd* [1987] AC 460 ("*Spiliada*"). Indeed, the principles set out in *Spiliada* have been approved and applied a great many times by the Singapore courts. The applicable principles were recently summarised in the decision of this court in *CIMB Bank Bhd v. Dresdner Kleinwort Ltd* [2008] 4 SLR(R) 543 ("*CIMB Bank*"), as

follows (at [25]-[26]):

> 25 The *locus classicus* on the question of when a stay would be granted on the basis of *forum non conveniens* is *Spiliada Maritime Corporation v. Cansulex Ltd* [1987] AC 460 ('*Spiliada*'), a decision of the House of Lords where Lord Goff of Chieveley, in delivering the leading judgment, laid down certain guiding principles (at 476-478) for determining the question of *forum non conveniens* ('the *Spiliada* test'). Those principles have been adopted by this court in several cases such as *Brinkerhoff Maritime Drilling Corp v. PT Airfast Services Indonesia* [1992] 2 SLR(R) 345, *Eng Liat Kiang v. Eng Bak Hern* [1995] 2 SLR(R) 851, *PT Hutan Domas Raya v. Yue Xiu Enterprises (Holdings) Ltd* [2001] 1 SLR(R) 104 and *Rickshaw Investments Ltd v. Nicolai Baron von Uexkull* [2007] 1 SLR(R) 377 ('*Rickshaw Investments*').
>
> 26 The gist of these principles is that, under the doctrine of *forum non conveniens*, a stay will only be granted where the court is satisfied that there is some other available and more appropriate forum for the trial of the action. The burden of establishing this rests on the defendant and it is not enough just to show that Singapore is not the natural or appropriate forum. The defendant must also establish that there is another available forum which is clearly or distinctly more appropriate than Singapore. The natural forum is one with which the action has the most real and substantial connection. In this regard, the factors which the court will take into consideration include not only factors affecting convenience or expense (such as the availability of witnesses) but also other factors such as the law governing the

> transaction and the places where the parties respectively reside or carry on business. If the court concludes, at this stage of the inquiry ('stage one of the *Spiliada* test'), that there is no other available forum which is clearly more appropriate for the trial of the action, it will ordinarily refuse a stay. If, at this stage, it concludes that there is some other available forum which *prima facie* is clearly more appropriate for the trial of the action, it will ordinarily grant a stay, unless there are circumstances by reason of which justice requires that a stay should nevertheless be refused. In this connection, the court will consider all the circumstances of the case. For this second stage inquiry ('stage two of the *Spiliada* test'), the legal burden is on the plaintiff to establish the existence of those special circumstances.

39 We will, in fact, proceed to analyse the facts of the present appeal in accordance with the two stages enunciated in *Spiliada* and, consistent with the terminology adopted in *CIMB Bank*, will refer to each stage as "stage one of the *Spiliada* test" and "stage two of the *Spiliada* test", respectively.

40 It is worth noting that a decision on whether to grant a stay of proceedings is, ultimately, a discretionary one. The discretionary nature of the determination necessarily limits the role of an appellate court; as this court has observed in *CIMB Bank* (at [84]):

> It is clear that in determining whether or not to grant a stay of proceedings, the judge will be exercising a discretion. Such an exercise of discretion should not be interfered with by an appellate court unless the judge had misdirected himself on a matter of principle, or he had taken into account matters which he ought not to

have taken into account or had failed to take into account matters which he ought to have taken into account, or his decision is plainly wrong (see *The Abidin Daver* [1984] AC 398 at 420 *per* Lord Brandon of Oakbrook).

Factors to consider under stage one of the* Spiliada *test

41 The courts will generally consider the relevant connecting factors at *stage one* of the *Spiliada* test. Although the list of factors is obviously not closed and much will depend upon the precise factual matrix concerned, Prof Yeo Tiong Min has furnished some helpful guidance, as follows (see *Halsbury's Laws of Singapore* vol 6(2) (LexisNexis, 2009) ("*Halsbury's Laws of Singapore*") at para 75.090):

> General connecting factors are considered at this stage. These include the locations of the parties, relevant witnesses, facts, and evidence, and the applicable law to the issues in dispute. As the search is for the forum that is prima facie clearly more appropriate to try the case, it is important to see what the case is about, and connections which have no or little bearing on adjudication of the issues in dispute between the parties will carry little weight. While there is a natural emphasis on the minimisation of expense and inconvenience of trial at this stage, it should be borne in mind that the true test is appropriateness.
>
> At this stage, differences in legal systems are generally ignored. In general, five types of connections may conveniently be identified, but they are not exhaustive.

42 The learned author then proceeds to list the following "five types of

connections” which he states (and as also observed in the preceding paragraph) “are not exhaustive” (and see generally the very helpful and perceptive account of these factors in *Halsbury's Laws of Singapore* at paras 75.091–75.095):

(1) Personal Connections

(2) Connections to Events and Transactions

(3) Governing Law

(4) Other Proceedings

(5) Shape of the Litigation

Stage two of the* Spiliada *test

43 In so far as *stage two* of the *Spiliada* test is concerned, Prof Yeo observes as follows (see *Halsbury's Laws of Singapore* at para 75.096):

> In Stage Two, the court is primarily concerned with the question whether there are circumstances by reason of justice why it should exercise its jurisdiction even if it is not the prima facie natural forum. The ultimate question of where the case should be heard for the interests of the parties and the ends of justice must not be lost sight of. This part of the test requires all circumstances to be taken into consideration, including factors already taken into consideration in Stage One. The main consideration in Stage Two is whether substantial justice can be obtained in the foreign *prima facie* natural forum. The court of the forum needs to tread a fine balance between justice to the parties and international comity. In considering this question, the court will not pass judgment on the competence or independence of the judiciary of another country, all the more so of a friendly foreign country, and will assiduously avoid comparing the quality of justice obtainable under its own legal system and the foreign

legal system. It is not true that the quality of foreign judiciary will never be questioned, but the court of the forum will take a very cautious approach. The mere fact that the plaintiff has a legitimate or juridical advantage in proceedings in Singapore will not be decisive. The plaintiff must establish with cogent evidence that he will be denied substantial justice if the case is not heard in the forum.

44 The learned author then proceeds to consider a number of related issues under the following headings (and see generally (again) the very helpful and perceptive account in *Halsbury's Laws of Singapore* at paras 75.097–75.101):

(1) Denial of Substantial Justice

(2) Contractual Choice of Law

(3) Time Bar

(4) Negative Declarations

(5) Substantial Justice in the Forum

Australian approach not followed

45 Before proceeding to apply the principles just stated, it might be appropriate to emphasise, once again, that the approach adopted in the Singapore context may be *contrasted with* that adopted in the *Australian* context (consisting in what has been termed the "clearly inappropriate forum test", which is elaborated upon below). In so far as the present Australian approach is concerned, it may, in fact, be traced back to the seminal High Court of Australia decisions of *Oceanic Sun Line Special Shipping Co Inc v. Fay* (1988) 165 CLR 197 ("*Oceanic Sun*") and *Voth v. Manildra Flour Mills Proprietary Limited* (1990) 171 CLR 538 ("*Voth*"). However, it should be noted that the Singapore courts *rejected* the Australian approach (in favour of the approach in *Spiliada*) fairly early on. In the Singapore Court of Appeal decision of *Eng Liat*

Kiang v. Eng Bak Hern [1995] 2 SLR(R) 851, for example, L P Thean JA, delivering the judgment of the court, observed thus (at [24]-[25]):

> 24 Counsel for the appellant sought to set out the basis for the *Spiliada* test and submitted that it was formulated at the time to prevent 'forum shopping' when the parties had little or no connection with the forum in which the case was brought. On the strength of the Australian authorities counsel submitted that the test in *Oceanic Sun* and approved in *Voth* should apply and urged this court to depart from the principles enunciated in *Spiliada Maritime Corp v. Cansulex Ltd*.
>
> 25 On authority and on principle we cannot agree. *The Spiliada* has been considered and approved in *Brinkerhoff* and we can see no reason for departing from that authority. The underlying basis in this test is whether the local court is clearly an appropriate forum or not and whether there is another forum which is distinctly and clearly more appropriate. It has a more liberal approach which cut down local parochialism as regards judicial adjudication and attaches greater importance to consideration of international comity.

46 It is notable that, whilst it was decided first, *Oceanic Sun* was only a bare majority decision of 3 to 2 in so far as the general approach to be adopted was concerned (unlike the majority, both Wilson and Toohey JJ preferred the test in *Spiliada* and (not surprisingly) arrived at a different decision on the facts). However, the judgments of the majority also raised a number of uncertainties inasmuch as it could not be said that there was a clear majority (amongst the majority judges in *Oceanic Sun*) in favour of what is presently known as the

"clearly inappropriate forum test" in the Australian context. Indeed, this last-mentioned test was clearly set out in the judgment by Deane J (at 247 – 248). However, only Gaudron J (albeit not Brennan J) agreed with Deane J in this particular regard (at 266).

47 The "clearly inappropriate forum test" was, however, clearly endorsed in *Voth* (with only one judge (Toohey J (who was also in the minority in *Oceanic Sun*)) being in the minority, the learned judge stating (at 590) that he was "impenitent in adhering to the view which Wilson J. and [he] expressed in *Oceanic Sun*"). Significantly, Brennan J, who adopted a narrower approach than "the clearly inappropriate forum test" in *Oceanic Sun* (see above at [45]), endorsed this particular test in *Voth*; as the learned judge put it (at 572):

> As I think it is more important that a test be authoritatively settled than that I adhere to the test I prefer, and as any such test is judge-made law, I add my acceptance of the test proposed by the majority. It is unnecessary to consider whether the performance of the institutional duty of enunciating the law authoritatively should prevail when Justices' individual views diverge on questions of the true construction of the Constitution or perhaps on questions of the true construction of a statute, for that is not the present case. I therefore join in the decision that the 'clearly inappropriate' test be adopted for the determination of applications of the three classes mentioned.

However, although Brennan J agreed with the majority of the court in *Voth* as to the particular test to be applied, he did "respectfully dissent from the result of its application" (*id*). In contrast, Toohey J, who (as we have just seen) adopted the approach in *Spiliada* instead, nevertheless arrived at the *same* conclusion as the majority (who applied "the clearly inappropriate forum test" instead)—thus illustrating the following observation made by Mason CJ, Deane, Dawson and Gaudron JJ in their joint judgment in the same decision (at 558) (see also below at [54]):

> The 'clearly inappropriate forum' test is similar to and, for that reason, is likely to yield the same result as the 'more appropriate forum' test in the majority of cases. The difference between the two tests will be of critical significance only in those cases—probably rare—in which it is held that an available foreign tribunal is the natural or more appropriate forum but in which it cannot be said that the local tribunal is a clearly inappropriate one.

Reference may, in this regard, also be made to the following observations by Prof Yeo (see *Halsbury's Laws of Singapore* at para 75.083):

> A notable variation is found in Australian jurisprudence, where the courts have struck a different balance. The Australian court will refuse to exercise its jurisdiction only if it is demonstrated that it is a clearly inappropriate forum. In many cases, the result will be the same as the approach in *The Spiliada*, but there may be a marginal case where it may be demonstrated that there is a clearly more appropriate forum available elsewhere yet the forum is not a clearly inappropriate forum, in which case stay of proceedings would *prima facie* be granted under the *Spiliada* approach but denied under the Australian approach. The Singapore courts apply the *Spiliada* approach because it is thought to be more consistent with international comity.

48 *Voth* therefore marks the clear establishment of the "clearly inappropriate forum test" (see also Martin Davies, Andrew Bell and Paul Le Gay Bereton, *Nygh's Conflict of Laws in Australia* (LexisNexis, 8th ed, 2010) ("*Nygh's Conflict of Laws in Australia*") at paras 8.13-8.24).

49 And, in the decision of this court in *Murukami Takako v. Wiryadi Louise Maria* [2009] 1 SLR(R) 508, the current Australian position was summarised thus (at [32]-[35]):

> 32 In so far as those of the disputed foreign properties situated in Australia ('the Australian properties') are concerned, the appellant also previously brought claims in the Supreme Court of New South Wales. Gzell J, in *Murakami v. Wiryadi* [2006] NSWSC 1354 ('Murakami'), stayed those proceedings on the ground of *forum non conveniens*. The learned judge applied the Australian approach to *forum non conveniens* as set out in the Australian High Court decisions of *Oceanic Sun Line Special Shipping Co Inc v. Fay* (1988) 165 CLR 197 ('*Oceanic Sun Line*'), *Voth v. Manildra Flour Mills Proprietary Limited* (1990) 171 CLR 538 ('*Voth*'), *Henry v. Henry* (1996) 185 CLR 571 and *CSR Limited v. Cigna Insurance Australia Limited* (1997) 189 CLR 345 to the effect that the court may stay or dismiss proceedings if, having regard to the circumstances of the case and the availability of the foreign tribunal, the forum is clearly inappropriate for the determination of the dispute (reference may similarly be made to the (also) Australian High Court decision of *Regie Nationale des Usines Renault SA v. Zhang* (2002) 210 CLR 491).

33 Although the test applied in the Australian context to the issue of *forum non conveniens* is quite different from that set out in *Spiliada* ([26] *supra*), there would (on most occasions) be no difference in the actual result arrived at by the court (see, for example, *Oceanic Sun Line* at 251-252 (*per* Deane J) and 265-266 (*per* Gaudron J), *Voth* at 558 (*per* Mason CJ and Deane, Dawson and Gaudron JJ), *Eng Liat Kiang* ([9] *supra*) at [23] and Peter Brereton, '*Forum Non Conveniens* in Australia: A Case Note on *Voth v. Manildra Flour Mills*' (1991) 40 ICLQ 895 at 897 - 898; *cf*, however, *Civil Jurisdiction and Judgments* ([6] *supra*) at para 4. 20 (reference may also be made to Richard Garnett, 'Stay of Proceedings in Australia: A "Clearly Inappropriate" Test?' (1999) 23 Melb Univ L Rev 30)). That having been said, it is important to guard against simply equating the two tests because (if nothing else) their respective points of emphasis are quite different (see, for example, *Voth* at 558 *per* Mason CJ and Deane, Dawson and Gaudron JJ; the learned judges, however, also observed that, in applying the test under Australian law, 'the discussion by Lord Goff in *Spiliada* of relevant "connecting factors" and "a legitimate personal or juridical advantage" provide[d] valuable assistance' (*id* at 564-565)—observations which were also cited and applied by Gzell J in *Murakami* at [39]).

34 While we have previously rejected the Australian approach to *forum non conveniens* in favour of the test in *Spiliada*, which calls for a determination of whether there is another forum which is clearly or distinctly more appropriate than Singapore (see, for example, the decision of this court in *Eng Liat Kiang* at [26]), Gzell J's observations in *Murakami* ([32] supra) are nevertheless helpful. This

is because the factors which the learned judge considered would apply with equal force in the context of the doctrine of *forum non conveniens* as set out in *Spiliada*. In particular, Gzell J noted that (see *Murakami* at [45]):

> The connecting factors ... do not favour New South Wales against Indonesia. [The appellant] is not resident in New South Wales and [the first respondent] and [the fourth respondent] do not live in Australia. The events [which are] the subject of complaint are just as much centred in Indonesia where the non-disclosure of the New South Wales assets is alleged to have occurred as in New South Wales where the assets were acquired.

The learned judge also noted (*id* at [46]), just as we have (see [29] above), that the *lex causae* was Indonesian law. He further commented (at [47] of *Murakami*) that:

> If matters are to be determined in the New South Wales court expert evidence will be required. If the issues are to be determined in the Indonesian courts there is no need for experts.

Indeed, Gzell J was of the view (*id* at [52]) that 'it [was] in the interests of the parties that a proper resolution of the issues be made in proceedings to be commenced in Indonesia'.

35 The factors and the arguments considered by Gzell J in the preceding paragraph, although analysed in the context of the Australian approach to *forum non conveniens*, apply equally in the context of the approach of this court as embodied in *Spiliada* ([26] *supra*). Indeed, there is a considerable overlap between the factors

> and the arguments considered by Gzell J in *Murakami* and those discussed above in the context of the present proceedings. There is, in fact, good reason to believe that this is one instance where there would be no difference in result regardless of whether the Australian approach or the approach in *Spiliada* is adopted (see also above at [33]).

50 It should be noted that the decision of Gzell J in *Murakami v. Wiryadi* [2006] NSWSC 1354 was in fact reversed on appeal in the decision of the New South Wales Court of Appeal decision of *Murakami v. Wiryadi* [2010] NSWCA 7. However, the general principles as well as observations set out in the quotation in the preceding paragraph continue to represent the Australian approach towards the issue of *forum non conveniens*, notwithstanding the following observations by Kirby J in the High Court of Australia decision of *Regie Nationale des Usines Renault SA v. Zhang* (2002) 210 CLR 491 ("*Zhang*") (at 525):

> Like the Pilgrim I have not lost faith. One day *Voth* may be overruled and a principle of the common law may be established more appropriate to contemporary circumstances of global and regional disputes in which Australian courts, like those of every country, must now operate. But until overruled by this Court or replaced by valid legislation, *Voth* must be applied.

51 Indeed, a challenge mounted recently against the present Australian approach in the subsequent (also) High Court of Australia decision of *Puttick v. Tenon Ltd* (2008) 238 CLR 265 was rejected, in no uncertain, terms by the

majority. The challenge (which was mounted by the Respondent) was, in fact, framed by way of an invitation to the court to either overrule the "clearly inappropriate forum test" in *Voth* ([45] *supra*) *or* to *restate* the test in *Voth* in a *modified* form by also permitting a stay when there was a more appropriate forum for the resolution of the dispute. The latter was, in effect, an invitation to introduce the *Spiliada* test *in addition to* the "clearly inappropriate forum test". Not surprisingly, perhaps, French CJ, Gummow, Hayne and Kiefel JJ *rejected* this invitation and reaffirmed the "clearly inappropriate forum test" in *Voth*. Heydon and Crennan JJ, however, whilst clearly of the view that *Voth* could not be overruled in that particular case, did (perhaps somewhat curiously) add thus (at [38]):

> *Voth's* case should simply be followed until the time comes, if it ever comes, for full argument to be developed about its correctness, and for an argument that it is wrong to be accepted.

The learned judges proceeded to give reasons as to why the test in *Voth* could not be challenged in that particular case. These included, first, that there was no "satisfactory forensic background against which to explore the correctness of *Voth's* case" (at [39]); that it was not satisfactorily explained in detail how the considerations relevant to overruling prior authorities (here, *Voth*) had been satisfied (at [40]); that the written submissions advanced by the Respondent in relation to the correctness of *Voth* "were not developed in the detail which is desirable when a question of this important kind is presented" (at [41]); that "it was not demonstrated that even if the *Voth* test were overruled or modified, there would be any difference in the result of the appeal"; and that "[i]n the absence of that demonstration, any observations making a change to the *Voth* test would in one sense be dicta only”, which was “not in general a satisfactory method of developing the law” (at [42]).

52 The observations of both Heydon and Crennan JJ are, on one reading at least, ambiguous although it might, on another reading, be open to the interpretation that they were at least open to the “clearly inappropriate forum test” in *Voth* being revisted on an appropriate occasion in the foreseeable future. Looked at in this light, the following observations by the authors of a leading Australian textbook may appear a little too strong (see *Nygh's Conflict of Laws in Australia* ([48] *supra*) at para 8.24):

> [*Voth v. Manildra Flour Mills Proprietary Limited* (1990) 171 CLR 538] has been part of Australian law for twenty years. In [*Puttick v. Tenon Ltd* (2008) 250 ALR 482], a new generation of High Court justices, none of whom participated in *Voth*, showed no inclination to reconsider the ‘clearly inappropriate forum’ test. Despite all the academic lamentation and complaint, judicial reform of the *Voth* test appears to be past praying for. Without legislative change, the test is entrenched in Australian law and critics must just grin and bear it.

A final point—relativity of natural forum

53 A final point might be noted. Counsel for the Appellant, Mr Cavinder Bull, laid great emphasis upon the fact that there were, in effect, no substantive connecting factors in relation to *Singapore*. He argued that this was a relevant factor as stage one of the *Spiliada* test was *comparative* in nature. There is some force in this argument inasmuch as the defendant must, under the first limb of the test in the *Spiliada*, establish that there is *another* available forum which is clearly or distinctly more appropriate than

Singapore. To *that* end, the number as well as quality of connecting factors in the *Singapore* context *is* relevant from a comparative (or relational) perspective. And, to the extent that there are *no* substantive connecting factors in relation to Singapore, that must surely weigh in favour of the defendant. However, as this court pointed out in *CIMB Bank* ([38] *supra* at [26]; also reproduced above at [38]), "it is not enough just to show that Singapore is not the natural or appropriate forum"—which would, of course, be the situation if there were, in the case concerned, *no* substantive connecting factors in relation to *Singapore*. The defendant must, as we have already noted, go *further* and establish that there is *another* available forum which is *clearly or distinctly more appropriate than Singapore* (see also the decision of this court in *Siemens AG v. Holdrich Investment Ltd* [2010] 3 SLR 1007 at [4] ("*Siemens AG*")). Hence, notwithstanding the fact that there might be few—or even *no*—substantive connecting factors in relation to *Singapore*, this does *not necessarily* mean that the defendant would have discharged the burden that is placed upon it under the first limb of the test in the *Spiliada*. This is, in fact, an excellent example of the more *general* principle that *every* perspective in a given legal test *must* be considered. Indeed, in so far as this particular issue is concerned, the following summary by Prof Yeo is particularly helpful (see *Halsbury's Laws of Singapore* ([41] *supra* at para 75. 089), appropriately entitled "Relativity of Natural Forum"):

> The principle of the natural forum does not seek to identify *the* most clearly appropriate forum in the absolute sense. The search is for *a* natural forum, not *the* natural forum. Four implications follow.
>
> Firstly, there may be cases where no forum can be said to be comparatively more appropriate than any other. In such a case, stay

will not be granted because it cannot be shown that there is another forum that is clearly more appropriate. Similarly, in a service out of jurisdiction case, it cannot be rebutted that Singapore is the proper forum to hear the case. The Singapore court will exercise its jurisdiction in such cases, even if it means multiplicity of proceedings.

Secondly, although the formulation in *The Spiliada* is that the defendant seeking a stay of proceedings must not only show that Singapore is not an appropriate forum, but that there is clearly another more appropriate forum elsewhere, it should be borne in mind that the inappropriateness of Singapore as a forum is relative to the existence of a clearly more appropriate forum elsewhere. It is not necessary to show that Singapore is a clearly inappropriate forum.

Thirdly, the defendant may show that two (or more) fora are clearly more appropriate than Singapore, without having to identify one of them specifically as *the* most appropriate forum.

Fourthly, if the parties have chosen not to have their dispute decided in the foreign forum with the strongest connections with the case, and this alternative forum is not put forward to the court for consideration, the court is still obliged to consider whether any other forum put forward by the defendant is a clearly more appropriate forum than Singapore. A more difficult situation arises where the defendant applies to stay Singapore proceedings on the basis that forum X is clearly more appropriate than Singapore, while the plaintiff presents evidence that forum Y is clearly more appropriate than either X or Singapore (but neither the plaintiff nor the defendant is interested in litigating in Y). In principle, this does not affect the proposition that

> the court should *prima facie* stay the proceedings when the defendant has demonstrated that there is a clearly more appropriate and available forum elsewhere.
>
> [emphasis in original]

54 We should note—parenthetically—that, in *contrast* to the *Singapore* position, the *Australian* position (see above at [47]-[48]) tends, by its very nature, to be focused, instead, on (as Mason CJ, Deane, Dawson and Gaudron JJ put it in *Voth* (at 565)) "the inappropriateness of the local court and not the appropriateness or comparative appropriateness of the suggested foreign forum". And, in the same decision, the learned judges also observed, in a similar vein (at 558), that:

> ... the question which the ["clearly inappropriate forum"] test presents is slightly different [from the approach in *Spiliada*] in that it focuses on the advantages and disadvantages arising from a continuation of the proceedings in the selected forum rather than on the need to make a comparative judgment between the two forums.

Likewise, Gleeson CJ, Gaudron, McHugh, Gummow and Hayne JJ observed in *Zhang* (at 503) that "it should at once be noted that a court is not an inappropriate forum merely because another is more appropriate". However, we would think that, on a practical level at least, some comparative analysis is probably inevitable in most cases. Indeed, in *Voth*, Mason CJ, Deane, Dawson and Gaudron JJ observed (at 558) that:

> [The focus on the inappropriateness of the local forum] is not to deny

> that considerations relating to the suitability of the alternative forum are relevant to the examination of the appropriateness or inappropriateness of the selected forum.

(See also *Voth* at 564–565 and [47] above).

55 Let us turn now to apply both the first limb as well as the second limb of the test in the *Spiliada* to the facts of the present appeal. Before proceeding to do so, it would be appropriate to review—in summary form—the main arguments proffered on behalf of both parties.

The parties' arguments

The Appellants' arguments

56 The Appellants argued that, as between Singapore and Indonesia, Indonesia was the more appropriate forum for hearing the dispute between the parties. The Appellants emphasised that the following connecting factors pointed towards Indonesia as the natural forum:

(a) Events relevant to the dispute occurred in Indonesia. For example, Indonesia was the place where Cyriac first met the Second and Third Appellants. Indonesia is also the location of the mining concessions that are the subject of the dispute.

(b) The parties have connections with Indonesia. The First Appellant is a UAE company but it has a registered office in Indonesia. Both the Second and Third Appellants are resident in Indonesia. The Respondent carries out projects in Indonesia and its representative, Cyriac, spends a significant amount of time there.

(c) The Appellants will have to rely on non-party witnesses who are resident in Indonesia ("the Indonesian Witnesses"). Some of these witnesses may have to be compelled to testify. In this regard, the Judge erred in predetermining the witnesses that the Appellants wished to call for the trial on the merits.

(d) Documentary evidence relevant to the dispute is presently located in Indonesia.

(e) In so far, at least, as the Respondent's alternative claim for misrepresentation in tort is concerned, the natural forum is Indonesia because that is the place where the tort occurred.

(f) The Respondent's claims are governed by Indonesian law. The claim for misrepresentation is governed by Indonesian law because Indonesian law is the *lex loci delicti*. Indonesian law is also the law governing the Investment Agreement because that is the law which has the closest and most real connection with the Investment Agreement. In relation to the governing law of the Investment Agreement, the Judge erred in suggesting that UAE law might govern the Investment Agreement even though neither party raised the applicability of UAE law in the hearing below.

(g) The Appellants sought leave to raise a new argument on the Respondent's claim under the Misrepresentation Act. The Appellants argued that the Respondent has no claim under the Misrepresentation Act because the Misrepresentation Act does not have extraterritorial effect, *ie*, that this Act does not apply to misrepresentations occurring outside the territory of Singapore.

57 On the whole, the Appellants submitted that, as between Singapore and Indonesia, Indonesia is the more appropriate forum for hearing the dispute. The Appellants further argued that, even if the Investment Agreement was governed by UAE law, the connecting factors were still overwhelmingly in favour of Indonesia. In any case, the Appellants urged us to only consider whether Singapore was a more appropriate forum than Indonesia since neither party was

contending that the dispute should be heard in any forum apart from Singapore or Indonesia.

The Respondent's arguments

58 The Respondent submitted that the following connecting factors pointed towards Singapore as the more appropriate forum for hearing the dispute:

(a) The Appellants chose to receive the Investment Funds in Singapore.

(b) Both the Second and Third Appellants have connections with Singapore. The Second Appellant studied in Singapore. He also has a Singapore bank account and he previously owned an apartment in Singapore. The Second Appellant also previously held shares and directorships in Singapore companies. The Third Appellant also holds shares and directorships in Singapore companies. The Respondent also has connections with Singapore in the form of a wholly-owned subsidiary incorporated in Singapore.

(c) As for the location of witnesses, the dispute is in relation to the discussions between the Appellants and the Respondent. Therefore, the party witnesses (*ie*, the Second and Third Appellants and the Respondent's representatives) are the most relevant witnesses. In any case, the Appellants have not shown that adducing evidence via video-link would be unsuitable. Furthermore, the travel time between Indonesia and Singapore is not long and so the inconvenience occasioned by having the case heard in Singapore is not significant. As for the need to compel the witnesses, the Appellants have not adduced evidence on whether the witnesses are compellable in Indonesia.

(d) The location of documents should not be given any weight. The expense of transporting the documents to Singapore may be compensated with an appropriate costs order.

(e) Indonesian law is not the governing law of the Investment

Agreement. Rather, the Investment Agreement is governed by Singapore law because the Singapore JVA was abandoned only because of the more advantageous tax benefits of using a UAE entity. The parties always intended for Singapore law to govern the Investment Agreement. Alternatively, the governing law is UAE law. As for the misrepresentation claim, the Judge did not err in considering that the application of Indonesian law was not an insurmountable obstacle. The Judge was merely ascribing the weight that he was giving to the governing law as a connecting factor. In any event, the Indonesian law issues for the tort claim are not complex.

(f) The place of the tort is indeed the *prima facie* natural forum for the misrepresentation claim. However, this is just one of the factors that the court should consider. Furthermore, this factor should be given less weight because Indonesian tort law has not been shown to be different from Singapore law.

(g) As for the Respondent's claim under the Misrepresentation Act, the Respondent took issue with the Appellants' raising of a new point that was not canvassed before the Judge. On the merits, the Respondent argued that the applicability of the Misrepresentation Act has no bearing on the *forum non conveniens* analysis because it is not a connecting factor.

(h) On balance, the connecting factors do not point clearly and distinctly away from Singapore to Indonesia. The connecting factors in favour of Indonesia should be given little weight.

Our decision

Introduction

59 It is perhaps important to state an obvious point right at the outset. Notwithstanding the principles stated above, the *facts* of each case are of equal importance. Put simply, there is no mechanistic method that can be utilised in

this—indeed, any—legal context. To adopt such an approach would be a sure recipe for legal disaster, producing (in the majority of cases at least) great injustice. Hence, a close attention to the factual matrix of the present appeal is imperative.

The Judge's discretion

60 As we noted earlier (at [40]), a decision to grant, or to refuse to grant, a stay of proceedings is discretionary. We were of the view that the appeal could not be allowed merely because we disagreed with the Judge's exercise of his discretion inasmuch as we might have arrived at a different conclusion on the facts. To reiterate, the guiding principles in this regard were, as this court stated in *CIMB Bank* ([38] *supra* at [84] reproduced above at [40]), that:

> … an exercise of discretion should not be interfered with by an appellate court unless the judge had misdirected himself on a matter of principle, or he had taken into account matters which he ought not to have taken into account or had failed to take into account matters which he ought to have taken into account, or his decision is plainly wrong.

In this regard, the Appellants' arguments suggested that the Judge might have misapplied certain principles. For example, the Appellants submitted that the Judge failed to correctly apply the *Albaforth* principle, which, as will be seen below (at [106]), is a principle that, in a dispute involving a tort, the place where the tort occurred is *prima facie* the natural forum. It was, therefore, necessary for us to apply the *Spiliada* test afresh to the facts in order to ascertain whether or not the Judge had misapplied the principles just stated. We pause to observe—parenthetically—that the relevant factors in the context of the facts of the present appeal fall (as we shall see) principally within the purview of the first three categories of connections identified by Prof Yeo (above at [42]).

Stage one of the* Spiliada *test

The residence and place of business of the parties

61 The First Appellant is a UAE corporation. However, it has a representative office in Jakarta. The First Appellant appears to have conducted most of its business from that office, as evidenced by the following facts: (a) it sent the Letter of Offer to the Respondent from Indonesia; (b) it conducted its meeting of its board of directors to increase its share capital at the representative office; and (c) it sent the Respondent a copy of the Exclusive Mining Agreement from Indonesia.

62 As for the other parties, the Second and Third Appellants are resident in Indonesia. The Respondent is an Indian company with operations in Indonesia.

The availability of non-party witnesses

63 We were of the view that the parties were conflating two factors: (a) the *convenience* in having the case decided in the forum where the witnesses are ordinarily resident ("the Witness Convenience Factor"); and (b) the *compellability* of those witnesses ("the Witness Compellability Factor"). We should analyse these factors separately because each may suggest that different forums are the natural forum. In addition, the Witness Compellability Factor could also be a relevant factor under the second stage of the *Spiliada* test, as was the argument of counsel in *Rickshaw Investments Ltd v. Nicolai Baron von Uexkull* [2007] 1 SLR(R) 377 at [91]-[92] ("*Rickshaw Investments*"). In this regard, we agreed with the following observations of Prof Yeo (*Halsbury's Laws of Singapore* at para 75.091):

The connections of relevant witnesses can be important too. The physical locations of witnesses are generally of less significance today given the ease of travel and the possible use of information and communication technology. *A more important consideration is the compellability of the witnesses*. This has been considered as a Stage One factor although it involves a comparison of the procedures of different legal systems. *Arguably, it sits more naturally as a Stage Two factor*—a juridical advantage of trial in a particular forum. However, *the benefit of considering this as a Stage One factor is that compellability of the defendant's witnesses in the foreign court will be weighed in the equation as well*, whereas as a Stage Two factor, the defendant would have to prove that non-compellability in Singapore is a denial of substantial justice, a very difficult case to make out. This point, while illustrating the different objectives of the two stages, also demonstrates the need to take a holistic view. [emphasis added]

64 Given the differences between the two factors, we considered them separately.

(1) The Witness Convenience Factor

65 In so far as the Witness Convenience Factor was concerned, our view was that the Judge had, with respect, erred for two reasons in holding that the Appellants had not shown that the evidence of the Indonesian Witnesses is material.

66 First, as this court in *Good Earth Agricultural Co Ltd v. Novus International Pte Ltd* [2008] 2 SLR(R) 711 ("*Good Earth*") has held (at [21]), the court hearing an application for a stay should not predetermine the witnesses that the parties should call. In fairness to the Judge, he did not hold

that the evidence of the Indonesian Witnesses was not necessary for the Appellants' defence. Rather, the Judge indicated that *the Appellants had failed to demonstrate* that the evidence of the Indonesian Witnesses' would be material. However, we were of the view that the Judge had, in substance, predetermined that the Appellants did not need testimony from the Indonesian Witnesses to advance their defence.

67 Second, the Appellants have endeavoured to explain the reasons why they require the testimony of the Indonesian Witnesses. It would not be appropriate to require the Appellants to demonstrate *exactly* how they would use the testimony of the Indonesian Witnesses at this interlocutory stage. The Appellants have not yet prepared their Defence. We acknowledge, on the other hand, that a defendant applying for a stay should not be permitted to assert, without substantiation, that it requires foreign witnesses because that would make it easy for defendants to manufacture a connecting factor. Our view was that a defendant should at least show that evidence from foreign witnesses is at least arguably relevant to its defence. The Appellants have, in our view, met that threshold.

68 Since the Appellants require the testimony of the Indonesian Witnesses, it appears that this factor points to Indonesia as the natural forum. However, our analysis did not end there. It was necessary for us to consider whether (a) the possibility of obtaining evidence from the Indonesian Witnesses through video-link and (b) the fact that Indonesia is relatively close to Singapore suggest that this factor should not be given substantial weight. Our view was that both considerations were persuasive and hence operated against the Appellants on this particular sub-issue.

69 With regard to the first consideration, this court has endorsed the views of the High Court in *Peters Roger May v. Pinder Lillian Gek Lian* [2006] 2 SLR

(R) 381 (at [26]) on how the possibility of obtaining video-link evidence should impact the stage one analysis of the *Spiliada* test (see *Good Earth* at [21]). The Appellants have not explained why the evidence of the Indonesian Witnesses cannot be given via video-link.

70 As for the second consideration, we note that this court in *Chan Chin Cheung v. Chan Fatt Cheung* [2010] 1 SLR 1192 held (at [35]) that the availability of witnesses should not be a significant factor if the witnesses are from Malaysia because of the proximity of Singapore to Malaysia. This consideration applies with equal force to Indonesia, which (as the Respondent has argued) is also relatively near to Singapore.

(2) The Witness Compellability Factor

71 In so far as the Witness Compellability Factor is concerned, a Singapore court cannot compel a foreign witness to testify in a Singapore court (see O 38 r 18(2) of the Rules of Court (Cap 322, R 5, 2006 Rev Ed)). Therefore, the fact that the Indonesian Witnesses cannot be compelled by a Singapore court to either testify in person in Singapore or to give evidence via video-link is a factor that points to Indonesia as being the natural forum. The Appellants have argued that the Indonesian Witnesses may need to be compelled to testify.

72 A countervailing consideration is, as the Respondent has argued, that the Appellants have not shown that the Indonesian Witnesses would be compellable in an Indonesian court if this dispute were heard in Indonesia. The Respondent cited the recent Singapore High Court decision of *Sun Jin Engineering Pte Ltd v. Hwang Jae Woo* [2010] SGHC 111 ("*Sun Jin Engineering*") in support of the argument that the Appellants should have led evidence on the compellability of the Indonesian Witnesses in the Indonesian courts. In *Sun Jin Engineering*, the court had the benefit of expert evidence on whether foreign witnesses were compellable in the alternative forum (the Maldives).

73 With respect, the Respondent has misunderstood this particular aspect of the decision in *Sun Jin Engineering*. The Appellants have correctly explained that in *Sun Jin Engineering*, the court considered that the expert evidence on whether witnesses were compellable in the Maldives was unclear. Notwithstanding this, the court considered that it was *more likely* that the Maldivian witnesses would testify if the case were heard in the Maldives (see *Sun Jin Engineering* at [40]).

74 We took a similar view in this appeal. Although it would have been preferable to have had expert evidence on whether the Indonesian Witnesses are compellable to testify in an Indonesian court, it is more likely that the Indonesian Witnesses would testify if the dispute were heard in an Indonesian court.

The governing law of the claims

75 As this court has observed (in *Rickshaw Investments* ([63] *supra*) at [42]), the governing law of the claims raised by the parties is a significant factor in stage one of the *Spiliada* test.

(1) Characterising the issues

76 Before determining the governing law of the claims, it is necessary for us to characterise the issues raised by the claims. The first stage of any choice of law analysis is to characterise the issues that the parties have raised (see, for example, the English Court of Appeal decision of *Macmillan Inc v. Bishopsgate Investment Trust plc (No* 3*)* [1996] 1 WLR 387 at 407).

77 The Respondent has made claims (see also above at [34]) for the following: (a) a declaration that the contract was validly rescinded; (b) restitution of the remainder of the Investment Funds; (c) damages for misrepresentation in contract; (d) damages for misrepresentation in tort; and (e) damages for misrepresentation under the Misrepresentation Act.

78 The first and the third claims are claims in contract. The second claim is a claim in restitution. However, the choice of law analysis for the restitutionary claim is the same as the choice of law analysis for the contract claims because the restitutionary claim is consequential on the failure of the Investment Agreement (see *CIMB Bank* ([38] *supra*) at [41]). The fourth claim is a claim in tort and the fifth claim is a statutory claim.

(2) The governing law for the contractual and restitutionary claims

(A) THE CHOICE OF LAW RULE

79 It is well established that a three-stage approach is applied to determine the governing law of a contract (see, for example, the decision of this court in *Pacific Recreation Pte Ltd v. S Y Technology Inc* [2008] 2 SLR(R) 491 ("*Pacific Recreation*") at [36]). At the first stage, the court considers if the contract expressly states its governing law ("the Express Law"). If the contract is silent, the court proceeds to the second stage and considers whether it can infer the governing law from the intentions of the parties ("the Implied Law"). If the court is unable to infer the parties' intentions, it moves to the third stage and determines the law which has the closest and most real connection with the contract ("the Objective Law").

(B) ANALYSIS

80 It is clear that there was no Express Law. We were of the view, however, that it is possible to determine the Implied Law. It is reasonable to infer that the parties intended that UAE law govern the Investment Agreement given the choice of that law in a closely related contract, *viz*, the Exclusive Mining Agreement. The Exclusive Mining Agreement was, in fact, sent to the Respondent. The Letter of Offer also refers to the Exclusive Mining Agreement three times. Furthermore, the Exclusive Mining Agreement was essential to the Investment Agreement. Without it, the First Appellant would have had nothing

of value to offer the Respondent in exchange for its provision of expertise.

81 As the editors of the 11th Edition of *Dicey and Morris on the Conflict of Laws* (Stevens & Sons, 11th Ed, 1987) ("*Dicey and Morris (11th Ed)*") note, it is possible to infer that the parties intended that a contract be governed by the same law that governs a closely related contract (at p 1185):

> ... The legal or commercial connection between one contract and another may enable a court to say that the parties must be held implicitly to have submitted both contracts to the same law. ...

The editors of the 11th Edition of *Chesire and North's Private International Law* (Butterworths, 11th Ed, 1987) make a similar assertion (at pp 459–460).

82 The editors of *Dicey and Morris (11th Ed)* cite a number of cases for this proposition, including the English Court of Appeal decision in *In re United Railways of the Havana and Regla Warehouses Ltd* [1960] Ch 52 ("*Re United Railways of Havana*"). *Re United Railways of Havana* involved two related contracts that were part of a transaction for an English railway company to obtain finance to purchase rolling stock. The English railway company incorporated a subsidiary in Pennsylvania and sold the rolling stock to that subsidiary. The subsidiary then leased the rolling stock to the English railway company ("the First Contract"). Under the terms of the First Contract, the English railway company was to pay rentals to the subsidiary. The subsidiary entered into a contemporaneous contract with a trust company ("the Second Contract"). Under the terms of the Second Contract, the subsidiary assigned its rights under the First Contract to the trust company. In effect, this arrangement meant that the English railway company would pay the rentals to the trust

company which would in turn pay the rentals to holders of trust certificates.

83 One of the issues in *Re United Railways of Havana* was the governing law of the First Contract. Having held that the Second Contract was governed by *Pennsylvanian* law, the English Court of Appeal proceeded to hold that the First Contract was also governed by Pennsylvanian law because that was both the Implied Law and the Objective Law. The following portion of the court's judgment is instructive (*Re United Railways of Havana* at 94):

> It has been material to consider the agreement in this connection because it was held by the judge, and argued before us by counsel for the respondents, that *the proper law of the agreement and of the lease was intended to be the same. This is probably, though not, we think, inevitably, true*. In the words of the judge: 'The lease is expressly recited in the agreement, and in the lease there is a recital of the intention immediately to assign the benefit of the lease to the trustee. *The two documents are essential parts of the same transaction*, namely, the Philadelphia Plan. In those circumstances one would expect that they would each have the same proper law, and I hold that they have.' One certainly cannot ignore the fact that *each of the two documents constituted essential parts of one entire transaction and it would, we think, be unusual if the parties concerned in that transaction should desire one part to be governed by the law of Cuba (which is in many relevant respects totally different from American law) and the other part to be governed by the law of Pennsylvania*. [emphasis added]

It should be noted that *Re United Railways of Havana* proceeded on appeal to the House of Lords (see *Tomkinson v. First Pennsylvania Banking and Trust Co; Appeal in In re United Railways of Havana and Regla Warehouses Ltd* [1961] AC 1007 ("*Re United Railways of Havana (HL)*")). On this particular point, the House of Lords considered that the Objective Law was Pennsylvanian law (see *Re United Railways of Havana (HL)* at 1068 (*per* Lord Denning) and 1081 (*per* Lord Morris)). The judgment at the House of Lords did not consider whether the Implied Law was Pennsylvanian law (and was, incidentally, one of the rare decisions that was overruled (pursuant to the House of Lords Practice Statement (Judicial Precedent) [1966] 1 WLR 1234) by the House of Lords in *Miliangos v. George Frank (Textiles) Ltd* [1976] AC 443 (albeit with Lord Simon of Glaisdale dissenting (on the issue as to whether or not the "breach date conversion" rule in *Re United Railways of Havana (HL)* ought to be departed from and be substituted with the rule that an English court was entitled to give judgment for a sum of money expressed in a foreign currency in the case of obligations of a money character to pay foreign currency under a contract, the proper law of which was that of a foreign country and when the money of account was that of that country or possibly some country other than the United Kingdom))).

84 We also considered decisions such as the English High Court decisions in *The Njegos* [1936] P 90 ("*The Njegos*") and *The Adriatic* [1931] P 241 to be relevant because they consider that it is possible to infer that the parties concerned intended that a contract be governed by the same law as the governing law of a related contract. In *The Njegos*, for example, a bill of lading incorporated the terms of a charterparty. The charterparty contained an arbitration clause providing for arbitration in England. The parties agreed that the proper law of the charterparty was English law. The issue related to the governing law of the bills of lading. The court found that the bills of lading did

not incorporate the arbitration clause and hence the governing law could not be inferred from the arbitration clause. However, the court nevertheless held that English law governed the bills of lading because the parties should be presumed to have intended that the bills of lading be governed by the same law as the law governing the charterparty (*The Njegos* at 107). It might also be noted that the Singapore High Court in *Las Vegas Hilton Corp v. Khoo Teng Hock Sunny* [1996] 2 SLR(R) 589 referred (at [39]) to *The Njegos* when discussing the circumstances in which an inference may be drawn in relation to the governing law of a contract.

85 Returning to the relevant facts of the present appeal, we considered that it was possible to infer that the parties intended that the Investment Agreement be governed by the same law that governs the Exclusive Mining Agreement (UAE law) because of the close relation between the contracts. We did not consider it to be material that the Exclusive Mining Agreement and the Investment Agreement were not between the same parties. The related contracts in the decisions referred to above (at [83] and [84]) were also between different parties. The crucial point is that the two contracts in each of those decisions were so closely related that the parties could not reasonably be considered as having intended that different laws govern the related contracts.

86 This raises the issue as to whether the Judge was entitled to suggest that the applicable law was UAE law when the parties proceeded on the basis that the applicable law was either Singapore law or Indonesian law. The Appellants argued that the Judge should not have suggested that the applicable law was UAE law without inviting the parties to make submissions on the potential applicability of UAE law. The Appellants relied on the decision of this court in *Pacific Recreation* ([79] *supra*) as support for this argument.

87 It is indeed true that the Judge should have allowed the parties to submit on

the potential applicability of UAE law. However, it is open to us to reach a provisional view that the governing law of the Investment Agreement is UAE law because both parties had the opportunity to submit, in this appeal, on the potential applicability of UAE law—which opportunity they in fact availed themselves of.

(3) The governing law for the alternative tort claim

(A) THE CHOICE OF LAW RULE

88 The choice of law rule that Singapore courts apply for torts is the double actionability rule (see *Rickshaw Investments* ([63] *supra*) at [53]). The double actionability rule provides that the tort must be actionable under both the *lex fori* and the *lex loci delicti*. Exceptionally, the double actionability rule may be displaced such that the tort may be actionable in Singapore even though it is not actionable under either the *lex loci delicti* or the *lex fori*. The exception may even be applied to provide that the law of a third country is the applicable law for the tort (see *Rickshaw Investments* at [56]).

(B) ANALYSIS

89 We have to first determine the place of the tort in order to ascertain the *lex loci delicti*. This posed some difficulty in the present appeal because the elements constituting the tort of misrepresentation did not occur in a single jurisdiction. The alleged misrepresentations were made in Indonesia. But at least some of the misrepresentations were received in India.

90 The test that is commonly applied for determining the place of the tort is that which looks at the events constituting the tort and asks where, in substance, the cause of action arose ("the Substance Test") (see, for example, the House of Lords decision of *Distillers Co (Biochemicals) Ltd v. Laura Anne Thompson* [1971] AC 458 at 468 and the English Court of Appeal decision of *Metal und Rohstoff AG v. Donaldson Lufkin & Jenrette Inc* [1990] 1 QB 391 at

443). The Singapore courts have also applied the Substance Test (see, for example, the Singapore High Court decisions of *Wing Hak Man v. Bio-Treat Technology Ltd* [2009] 1 SLR(R) 446 at [26] and *Focus Energy Ltd v. Aye Aye Soe* [2009] 1 SLR(R) 1086 at [14]).

91 The English courts have crystallised the Substance Test into a more certain rule in cases of misrepresentations made in one jurisdiction and received in another jurisdiction. In the context of determining the place of tort for the purpose of leave to serve out of jurisdiction, the English Court of Appeal has held that the place of the tort is the place where the representation is "received and acted upon" (see the English Court of Appeal decisions of *Cordoba Shipping Co Ltd v. National State Bank, Elizabeth, New Jersey (The "Albaforth")* [1984] 2 Lloyd's Rep 91 at 92 ("*The Albaforth*") and *Diamond v. Bank of London and Montreal Ltd* [1979] QB 333 at 345-346). A different approach, however, was taken in a case where the misrepresentation occurred in one jurisdiction to an *unspecified class* of persons and was received and relied upon in a second jurisdiction. The court found that the tort occurred in the first jurisdiction (see the English Court of Appeal decision of *Cordova Land Co Ltd v. Victor Brothers Inc* [1966] 1 WLR 793 at 801). Prof Yeo, in *Halsbury's Laws of Singapore*, concisely states the approach taken in these misrepresentation cases thus (at para 75.378):

> The tort of misrepresentation is generally committed in the country where the representation is *received and acted upon*, at least where the representation is directed specifically at the plaintiff, *unless the place is fortuitous in the circumstances*, or if the receipt and reliance occur in different countries. If the representation is made *at large*, then the tort may have occurred in the *place where the representation*

is made. [emphasis added]

92 It should be noted, in passing, that the English courts *now* apply a *different* test for determining the place of the tort. For cases arising before the date when the Rome II Regulation came into force (11 January 2009), the test for the place of the tort is found in s 11(2) of the Private International Law (Miscellaneous Provisions) Act 1995 (c 42) (UK) ("the PILMPA") (which is, of course, not applicable in Singapore). That provision defines the place of the tort differently for personal injury cases (see s 11(2)(a) of the PILMPA), property damage cases (see s 11(2)(b) of the PILMPA) and all other cases (see s 11(2)(c) of the PILMPA). The present case would have come within the scope of s 11(2)(c) of the PILMPA, under which the place of the tort would be the place where "the most significant element or elements" of the events constituting the tort in question occurred (see *Dicey, Morris and Collins on the Conflict of Laws* (Sweet & Maxwell, 14th Ed, 2006) at paras 35-088–35-089 ("*Dicey, Morris and Collins*")). For cases coming within the purview of the Rome II Regulation, there is no longer a need to consider the place of the tort because other connecting factors, such as the place where the damage occurs and the place of habitual residence, are utilised instead (see generally *Dicey, Morris and Collins on the Conflict of Laws*, Third Cumulative Supplement to the Fourteenth Edition at paras S35-194–S35-200).

93 We were of the view that the approach adopted by the English courts (as discussed above at [91]) has some merit. The Substance Test is itself rather broad and open-ended. There is, for example, room for debate as to whether the place where the representation was made is more significant than the place where the representation was received—and *vice versa*. More importantly, both would, theoretically at least, satisfy the Substance Test. It would therefore help

to have more concrete rules, with appropriate exceptions, for particular torts. For misrepresentations, it is suggested that, if the representation was received and acted upon in a single jurisdiction, that place should be the place of the tort unless that place was fortuitous or if the receipt and reliance occur in different countries. The Substance Test (in its more general form and possible "incarnations") may nevertheless still be resorted to in cases not falling comfortably within this suggested (and more specific) rule. However, for reasons which we will elaborate upon in a moment, there is no need to rule definitively on this point in the present appeal. In particular, the circumstances are such that the suggested rule cannot (as we shall see) be applied.

94 As just mentioned, the present appeal is, in fact, a case that does not fit comfortably within the suggested rule. The actual misrepresentation was *received* in India because that was the place where the First Appellant sent the Letter of Offer and the Exclusive Mining Agreement. Both those documents contained a representation that the First Appellant had mining concessions with one million tonnes of iron ore. However, the Appellants contend that other representations were also made during meetings in Indonesia as to the mining concessions that the First Appellant could rely on to make up a total of one million tonnes of iron ore. The representations were also *acted upon* in *two* jurisdictions. The Respondent acted on the representation by remitting funds from India. The Respondent also acted on the representation in Indonesia by conducting drilling works at the Pelaihari Concession. Accordingly, it is not possible to apply the suggested rule. Instead, we applied the general Substance Test.

95 Applying the general Substance Test, we were of the view that the place of the tort was Indonesia. Indonesia was the place where most of the negotiations took place. The Respondent also took steps in reliance of the representations in

Indonesia. The only reason why the representations in the Letter of Offer and the Exclusive Mining Agreement were received in India was because the Respondent was based in India. Accordingly, we were of the view that the *lex loci delicti* is Indonesian law.

96 It remained for us to consider the Respondent's contention that Indonesian law has not been shown to be different from Singapore law. In this regard, we noted that strict proof of the differences between Indonesian and Singapore law was not necessary. As this court observed in *Rickshaw Investments*, we may take notice that the laws of other jurisdictions are likely to be different (at [43]):

> Choice of law questions raise a related issue regarding a party's evidential burden to plead foreign law. In *Goh Chok Tong v. Tang Liang Hong* [1997] 1 SLR(R) 811, Lai Kew Chai J pointed pertinently to *the need for foreign law to be pleaded*, and held that if foreign law was not in fact pleaded, it would be presumed to be the same as the relevant position under Singapore law (see generally at [77]-[84], and especially at [79]): see also *Ertel Bieber and Company v. Rio Tinto Company, Limited* [1918] AC 260 at 294-295. Where this evidentiary presumption can be invoked, the applicability of a foreign *lex causae* under choice of law rules may therefore be reduced in significance since the forum is unlikely to have difficulty applying a foreign law which is (assumed to be) identical to the *lex fori*. In this regard, however, a number of cases suggest that a court may, despite a party's failure to adduce proof of foreign law, have regard to the fact that the principles in the foreign jurisdiction concerned will, in all likelihood, differ from the *lex fori* in some

respects (see, for example, the Singapore High Court decision of *PT Jaya Putra Kundur Indah v. Guthrie Overseas Investments Pte Ltd* [1996] SGHC 285 at [44] ('*PT Jaya*')). Hence, in the present case, the mere factum of a foreign *lex causae*, *ie*, German law, may be accorded due weight *despite* the respondent's failure to adduce evidence regarding the content of this law. [emphasis in original]

(4) The statutory claim

97 Contrary to the Respondent's submissions (see above at [58 (g)]), whether the Misrepresentation Act potentially applies is a relevant consideration under stage one of the *Spiliada* test because it is relevant for this court to consider the law governing the claims raised by the Respondent. For example, if the scope of the Misrepresentation Act is such that it potentially applies to the present case, then that would be a factor against Indonesia being the natural forum because greater expense and inconvenience would result in having the application of a Singapore statute heard in an Indonesian court. This is *not* to state that we are determining the *substantive* issue as to whether the Respondent's claim under the Misrepresentation Act is sustainable on the facts, as we cannot, *ex hypothesi*, make this determination in the context of the present proceedings. Rather, we are determining whether the *scope* of the Misrepresentation Act is such that it *potentially* applies in the present case.

98 Before considering the scope of the Misrepresentation Act, we should elucidate the approach that we took in our analysis. The Appellants approached the issue of the scope of the Misrepresentation Act from the perspective of the presumption against extraterritoriality. It is useful to clarify that there are in fact two aspects to this presumption in the conflict of laws context. Prof Yeo notes as follows (see *Halsbury's Laws of Singapore* ([41] *supra*) at para 75.292):

> Where the conflictual scope of legislation is not spelt out, it has often been said that there is a presumption that legislation of the forum is intended only to have territorial effect. There are two overlapping aspects to this presumption. *Firstly*, as a matter of *private international law*, the presumption is that the statutory provision *only applies if the relevant connecting factor points to the law of the forum as the law governing the issue*. *Secondly*, *whatever the basis that the statute applies* (whether as forum mandatory law, or as the substantive law governing the issue by reason of the forum's choice of law rule, or as forum procedural law), it is presumably *only intended to affect activities occurring within the territory of the forum*, or to *activities abroad of nationals of the forum*. [emphasis added]

99 *Dicey, Morris and Collins* ([92] *supra*) note that there are two approaches to determining the scope of a statute in the conflict of laws context. However, the editors do not consider the two approaches to be part of a common exercise of deriving parliamentary intention. The following remarks by the editors, in the context of a discussion on the scope of s 2 of the Marriage Act 1949 (c 76) (UK), are instructive (at para 1-040):

> A court, when confronted by a statute of its own law or of foreign law which is expressed in general terms like this, could use one of the two methods to determine its scope. The *first* is to *interpret the statute in the light of its purpose and background* so as to read into it the limitations which the legislature would have expressed if it had given thought to the matter. This is an artificial method, and perhaps a

> dangerous one, because *ex hypothesi* the legislature gave no thought to the matter—if it had done so it would have expressed the limitations. The *second method* is to *apply general principles derived from the conflict of laws*—i. e. *first characterise the question* as relating to capacity to marry [as noted above, this quotation is from a discussion on the scope of s 2 of the Marriage Act 1949 (c 76) (UK), which provides that "[a] marriage between persons either of whom is under the age of sixteen shall be void"], and then apply the relevant conflict rule to the question so characterised. [emphasis added]

100 Our view was that, conceptually, it is better to consider the two approaches as part of a common exercise of discerning parliamentary intention. If Parliament clearly intended for a statute to apply even where the choice of law rules suggest that Singapore law does not apply, the courts must not disregard Parliamentary intention and refuse to apply the statute. Parliament has the power to legislate extraterritorially (see the decision of this court in *PP v. Taw Cheng Kong* [1998] 2 SLR(R) 489 at [37]). The choice of law rules are simply useful tools in ascertaining Parliamentary intention on the geographical scope of our laws.

101 On the first aspect of the presumption, the starting point is to characterise the issue that the Respondent has raised with its claim that the Appellants have induced it to enter into a contract through a misrepresentation. The competing characterisations are a tort and a contract characterisation. It is not necessary to reach a firm conclusion on the proper characterisation because, on either characterisation, the applicable law is not Singapore law. As considered above, the applicable law on a contract characterisation is UAE law (see above at

[85]) and the applicable law based on a tort characterisation is Indonesian law (see above at [95]). Therefore, on the first aspect of the presumption, we may presume that Parliament did not intend that the Misrepresentation Act apply to the present case because Singapore law does not govern the issue that the Respondent has raised.

102 The second aspect of the presumption does not rely on choice of law rules. Parliament is *generally* presumed to have intended for its laws to only apply to activity in Singapore (see the decision of this court in *Parno v. SC Marine Pte Ltd* [1999] 3 SLR(R) 377 at [38]-[39] ("*Parno*")). This presumption may be displaced by clear indication of Parliamentary intention that the statute concerned is intended to apply extraterritorially (see *Parno* at [39]). This intention need not be stated expressly (see *Parno* at [38]). As an illustration, the Singapore High Court recently held that the presumption against extraterritoriality was rebutted in the Traditional Chinese Medicine Practitioners Act (Cap 333A, 2001 Rev Ed) on the basis that extraterritorial application of that statute would serve Parliamentary intention and would not cause any difficulty with international comity and enforcement of the statute (see *Huang Danmin v. Traditional Chinese Medicine Practitioners Board* [2010] 3 SLR 1108 at [36]-[38]).

103 Applying this general presumption, the Misrepresentation Act is presumed to apply only to misrepresentations within Singapore territory. Unlike, for example, s 37 of the Prevention of Corruption Act (Cap 241, 1993 Rev Ed), the Misrepresentation Act is silent as to its geographical scope. It is clear, therefore, that the Singapore Parliament has not *expressly* stipulated that it intended that the Misrepresentation Act apply extraterritorially. However, it seems that the intention underlying the Misrepresentation Act would be furthered if the Misrepresentation Act were applied to misrepresentations occurring outside

Singapore territory but *only if* the applicable law of the relevant contract were Singapore law. The purpose of the Misrepresentation Act, which is based on the Misrepresentation Act 1967 (c 7) (UK), is well known and is concisely stated by the editors of *Chitty on Contracts* (Sweet & Maxwell, 30th Ed, 2008) in the following manner (at para 6-001):

> … Prior to the enactment of the Misrepresentation Act 1967, the position broadly speaking was that a misrepresentation which induced a person to enter into a contract gave the representee the right to rescind the contract, subject to certain conditions, but *generally gave him no right to damages unless the misrepresentation had contractual force*. Since the coming into force of the Misrepresentation Act the representee *will always be able to claim damages for negligent misrepresentation* in circumstances in which he could have recovered damages had the misrepresentation been fraudulent. In addition the Act *gives the court a discretion to refuse to permit a representee to rescind a contract, but to award him damages in lieu of rescission*, if the misrepresentation is negligent or wholly innocent; but it leaves the representee with an absolute right to rescind where the misrepresentation is fraudulent. The Act of 1967 *does not, however, alter the rules as to what constitutes an effective misrepresentation* …
> [emphasis added]

104 It appears, therefore, that the purposes underlying the Misrepresentation Act are two-fold: (a) to supplement the remedies available to a representee under common law (more accurately, under the then common law as the seminal House of Lords decision in *Hedley Byrne & Co Ltd v. Heller & Partners*

Ltd [1964] AC 465 had been decided by the time the Misrepresentation Act had been enacted and had filled the then existing gap, albeit in different manner than that provided for pursuant to s 2(1) of the Misrepresentation Act (see, for example, *Cheshire, Fifoot and Furmston's Law of Contract—Second Singapore and Malaysian Edition* (Butterworths Asia, 1998) ("*Cheshire, Fifoot and Furmston*") at pp 468–471)); and (b) to confer the courts with flexibility in remedial matters by allowing courts to award damages in lieu of rescission, which flexibility was not available under the common law (pursuant to s 2(2) of the Misrepresentation Act (see also *Cheshire, Fifoot and Furmston* at pp 482–484)). These purposes would not appear to be enhanced if the Misrepresentation Act were applicable to misrepresentations occurring outside Singapore territory in relation to contracts governed by foreign law. Unlike, for example, the Prevention of Corruption Act or the Traditional Chinese Medicine Practitioners Act, the Misrepresentation Act is not intended to regulate conduct or protect classes of persons. The purposes of such conduct regulating and protective statutes would, perhaps, be advanced if they are applied without strict regard to territorial links. A statute that merely supplements existing common law remedies with respect to the *Singapore* common law of contract, without serving a conduct regulating or protective function, on the other hand, does not appear to require *general* extraterritorial application to have its purposes advanced. If, however, the relevant contract were governed by Singapore law (whether by express choice or otherwise), it would appear to be consistent with the purposes of the Misrepresentation Act to say that it applies even to misrepresentations occurring outside Singapore territory. In fact, we would suggest that it would be highly artificial if a choice of Singapore law in a contract only brings into operation Singapore *common law* for misrepresentations occurring outside Singapore territory without the supplementary or facilitative provisions of the Misrepresentation Act.

105 As we have held, the Investment Agreement might be governed by UAE law (see above at [85]). It follows, therefore, that the Misrepresentation Act does not apply because the misrepresentation occurred outside the territory of Singapore and the Investment Agreement was not governed by Singapore law. Therefore, the fact that the Respondent has raised a claim based on the Misrepresentation Act should not be a relevant factor in stage one of the *Spiliada* test.

Other connecting factors

(1) The place of the tort

106 As this court accepted in *Rickshaw Investments* ([63] *supra* at [39]), for tort claims, the place of the tort is *prima facie* the natural forum. This principle is derived from *The Albaforth* ([91] *supra* at 96) and was accepted by the House of Lords in *Berezovsky v. Michaels* [2000] 1 WLR 1004 (at 1014). However, as was observed in *Rickshaw Investments* (at [40]), *The Albaforth* principle is only a *prima facie* position. As the Hong Kong Court of Appeal recently noted, the place of the tort may, in some cases, be fortuitous (see *The Peng Yan* [2009] 1 HKLRD 144 at [28] *per* Ma CJHC (with whom Cheung J agreed)):

> It is therefore important when applying *The Albaforth* principle in the context of *forum non conveniens* applications, to examine just how close a connection there really exists with any given *forum*. In some cases, the place of the commission of the tort may be decisive; in others, perhaps not weighty at all. The underlying principle to be firmly borne in mind is the basic test in *The Spiliada* and *The Adhiguna Meranti*. The place of the

> commission of the tort may in some cases be quite fortuitous and may provide no more than a convenient starting point or *prima facie* position. The court is required to look into more substantial factors in the application of the basic test. The present case involved a collision where, quite often, there is no obvious or natural forum: see *The Spiliada* at p. 477C–D.

107 As we held earlier (see above at [95]), the place of the tort was Indonesia. Applying the *Albaforth* principle, Indonesia would, *prima facie*, be the natural forum, at least for the alternative tort claim. We were of the view that there was nothing on the facts of this case to displace the *prima facie* position. The place of the tort was not fortuitous. Indonesia was the place from which the misrepresentations were made. Indonesia was also the place where substantial acts in reliance of the misrepresentation took place: the Respondent conducted drilling at the Pelaihari Concession because of the Appellants' alleged misrepresentations. This is not to say that the *Albaforth* principle, whilst applicable in the context of the present proceedings, is decisive in the present appeal. We were aware that the Respondent's claim in tort was framed as an *alternative* cause of action.

(2) General connections with Singapore and the payment of the Investment Funds in Singapore

108 The Respondent placed considerable emphasis on certain general connections that the parties have or have had with Singapore. The Respondent also relied on the fact that the Investment Funds were paid into Singapore bank accounts.

109 We did not consider these connections to be relevant in stage one of the *Spiliada* test. The general connections to Singapore and the payment of the

Investment Funds into Singapore bank accounts have no relevance to the claims that the Respondent has framed. Only connections that are relevant to the disputes should be considered in the *forum non conveniens* analysis (see, for example, the decision of this court in *The Rainbow Joy* [2005] 3 SLR(R) 719 at [52] and the English High Court decision of *Vetco Gray UK Ltd v. FMC Technologies Inc* [2007] EWHC 540 (Pat) at [26]). The underlying purpose of the *forum non conveniens* analysis is to determine whether there is a more appropriate forum, *viz*, one "in which the case may be tried more suitably for the interests of all the parties and the ends of justice" (see *Spiliada* ([38] *supra*) at 476), and the core inquiry is to determine the place which has the "most real and substantial connection" with the case (see *Spiliada* at 478). This purpose and core inquiry will not be advanced by considering connecting factors that are not relevant to the dispute because those factors are not really and substantially connected with the case at hand.

Conclusion on stage one of the Spiliada *test*

110 On the whole, we were satisfied that Indonesia was clearly or distinctly a more appropriate forum than Singapore for the trial of the claims concerned. Indonesia is the place where all the parties have some connection that is relevant to the dispute. Although not a significant factor in so far as the proximity of Indonesia to Singapore and the possibility of obtaining evidence via video-link are concerned, we gave some weight to the fact that the Appellants intend to call witnesses based in Indonesia. The Appellants have also argued that they need to rely on Indonesian Witnesses who may have to be compelled, and the Appellants will more likely be able to compel these witnesses if the case was heard in Indonesia. In relation to the alternative claim in tort, it was relevant that Indonesian law was the *lex loci delicti* and that the place of the tort was Indonesia.

111 Although (as noted above) we considered that UAE law might govern the Investment Agreement, this was not a factor in favour of Singapore's candidacy as the natural forum. It should be recalled that the *forum non conveniens* analysis is a relative one (see above at [53]). The choice in the present proceedings was between Indonesia and Singapore. Between Indonesia and Singapore, it would not be logical for us to consider that Singapore was the natural forum simply because a third forum, the UAE, had a better or as strong a claim as Indonesia as the natural forum. In this regard, we found the English Court of Appeal decision of *Macsteel Commercial Holdings (Pty) Ltd v. Thermasteel V (Canada) Inc* [1996] CLC 1403 ("*Macsteel*"), which the Appellants discussed at length in their Appellants' Case, to be a useful illustration (incidentally, *Macsteel* was recently considered by this court in *Siemens AG* ([53] *supra* at [15])). *Macsteel* was a case where the dispute had links to Ontario and South Africa. The only link with England was that English law was expressed to be the governing law of the contract. On those facts, the court held that the action should be stayed even though both South Africa and Ontario had *equally* strong links with the dispute. The court considered it relevant that the parties were not arguing that the case should be heard in South Africa. The only comparison was between England and Ontario. As between England and Ontario, Ontario was the clearly more appropriate forum.

112 In fact, the Singapore High Court case adopted a similar approach to the English Court of Appeal in *Macsteel*. In *Lehman Brothers Special Financing Inc v. Hartadi Angkosubroto* [1998] 3 SLR(R) 664, the court considered that the natural forum was either New York or Indonesia and not Singapore (at [35]). The High Court accordingly granted the stay.

113 Reference in this regard may also be made to the following views of Prof Yeo, which were also reproduced above (see above at [53]) (see *Halsbury's*

Laws of Singapore ([41] *supra*) at para 75.089):

> Fourthly, if the parties have chosen not to have their dispute decided in the foreign forum with the strongest connections with the case, and this alternative forum is not put forward to the court for consideration, the court is still obliged to consider whether any other forum put forward by the defendant is a clearly more appropriate forum than Singapore. A more difficult situation arises where the defendant applies to stay Singapore proceedings on the basis that forum X is clearly more appropriate than Singapore, while the plaintiff presents evidence that forum Y is clearly more appropriate than either X or Singapore (but neither the plaintiff nor the defendant is interested in litigating in Y). In principle, this does not affect the proposition that the court should *prima facie* stay the proceedings when the defendant has demonstrated that there is a clearly more appropriate and available forum elsewhere.

114 We were satisfied that, on a relative analysis, Indonesia was clearly a more appropriate forum than Singapore. Accordingly, stage one of the *Spiliada* analysis pointed firmly in favour of granting a stay of proceedings.

Stage two of the* Spiliada *test

115 It should be noted that no arguments were proffered with respect to this particular limb of the test in the *Spiliada*. This was not surprising, in our view, having regard to the relevant facts before us, and we therefore need say no more about this particular limb.

Conclusion

116 For the reasons set out above, it was clear that Indonesia was clearly and more distinctly the appropriate forum for the trial of the claims concerned. We therefore allowed the appeal with costs, and with the usual consequential orders.

117 We would also like to take this opportunity to commend both Mr Bull and Ms Gan for their clear arguments. In particular, neither sought to either exaggerate or even embellish their respective client's cases but simply presented their arguments to this court in as cogent and as persuasive a fashion as possible.

Reported by Rajaram Vikram Raja.

BNA v. BNB and another

——仲裁协议准据法的确定以及在确定是否执行各方的仲裁意图时应对仲裁协议作出适当解释

上诉庭——2018 民事上诉第 159 号

大法官梅达顺、上诉庭法官朱迪柏拉卡斯及上诉庭法官庄泓翔

2019 年 10 月 15 日;2019 年 12 月 27 日

【简要案情】

该争议由上诉方与答辩方签订的一份协议(以下称《返销协议》)所引起。根据《返销协议》,上诉方为某种产品的买方,答辩方则为卖方。上诉方未能依据《返销协议》的条款作出必要付款,因而引发了争议。

《返销协议》第 14 条对解决争议的约定如下:

> 第 14 条　争议
>
> 14.1　本协议适用中华人民共和国法律。
>
> 14.2　对于由本协议引起或与本协议有关的任何及所有争议,双方应首先本着诚意友好解决。如果协商不成,双方同意最终将争议提交至新加坡国际仲裁中心(新仲)在上海仲裁,并根据新仲的仲裁规则进行仲裁。仲裁具有终局性,对双方都具有约束力。

答辩方就争议向新加坡国际仲裁中心(以下简称“新仲”)提起仲裁,新仲正式委任三人组成仲裁庭。上诉方对仲裁庭的管辖权提出异议,理由是仲裁协议的准据法为中华人民共和国法律,而根据中国法,此仲裁协议无效,争议应当在中国法院进行诉讼。这一论点的依据是,双方明确选择了中国法为实体合同即《返销协议》的适用法,且实体合同中约定上海为仲裁地,故仲裁地法也是中国法。但适用中国法会使仲裁协议变得无效,因为中国法不允许外国仲裁机构,如新仲,裁决以中国为仲裁地的仲裁或由此类纯属中国国内争议所引起的仲裁。

针对是否有管辖权审理争议仲裁庭未能达成一致决定,最终多数仲裁员裁定仲裁庭有管辖权。多数仲裁员认为,若双方特意选择的适用法最终会使仲裁协议变得无效,这根本就不符合商业价值或逻辑。多数仲裁员因此认定上海不是仲裁地,而仅仅是开庭地。相反地,新加坡才是仲裁地,仲裁庭依据新加坡法律具有管辖权。持异议的仲裁员则认为,上海是仲裁地,中国法是仲裁地法。既然中国法也是实体合同的适用法,中国法应当是仲裁协议的准据法。中国法不允许将此争议提交仲裁,仲裁庭也因此不具有审理争议的管辖权。

上诉方向高等法庭提出申请,请求裁定仲裁庭不具有审理争议的管辖权。主审法官驳回了管辖权异议的诉求。法官裁定,双方并没有就仲裁协议的准据法作出明确选择;仅仅在第 14.1 条中规定中国法为《返销协议》的准据法,并不足以认定中国法同样是第 14.2 条仲裁协议的准据法的明示选择。相反地,法官认为双方作出了以新加坡法为仲裁协议准据法的默示选择。法官裁定,仲裁协议的仲裁地为新加坡。双方将《新加坡国际仲裁中心仲裁规则》(第 5 版,2013 年,以下简称《新仲规则》)作为相关仲裁规则,而《新仲规则》第 18.1 条规定,双方没有明确约定的,默认仲裁地应当是新加坡。第 14.2 条提及了两个地理位置——新加坡及上海。鉴于第 18.1 条明确规定当双方没有明确选择时,仲裁地应为新加坡,法官因此认为“在上海仲裁”的表述是指以上海为仲裁开庭地。新加坡是法域而上海不是,这一事实也支持了这样的解读。所以,提及新加坡时,更好的理解是新加坡为仲裁地。

法官认为,中国法作为实体合同的适用法,且实体合同载有仲裁协议,因此可视为双方对准据法默示选择的一个起点。但法官也考虑到,以新加坡法为仲裁地法会使该默示选择被取代,因为如果中国法是准据法,双方之间的仲裁协议很可能无效。因此,新加坡法才是仲裁协议的准据法。上诉方就此提出上诉。

【裁判要旨】

裁定,上诉得直:

(1) 双方在《返销协议》第14.2条没有对仲裁协议的适用法作出明示选择。单凭第14.2条出现在第14.1条后,并不能表示第14.1条所载明的《返销协议》的适用法应同样被认定是第14.2条仲裁协议的明示适用法:见[56]及[59]—[61]。

(2) 作为起点,双方接受《返销协议》的适用法同样也是仲裁协议的适用法。但如果仲裁地法与该起点大不相同,该起点将被取代:见[62]及[63]。

(3) 第14.2条"在上海仲裁"的表述是指上海为仲裁地,而并不只是开庭地。"在上海仲裁"这一表述的正常含义为上海是仲裁地。仲裁地的选择对仲裁协议有重要的法律意义,开庭地的选择在法律意义上的重要性则小得多。若双方在仲裁协议中仅载明一个地理位置,特别是双方明确选择"在[那个地点]仲裁",就如本案的情况,那么"那个地点"自然而然就会被理解为双方选择的仲裁地。这一解释有一系列典据支持,这些典据表明对于相似的用语均理解为仲裁地的选择而不仅仅是开庭地的选择:见[65]—[69]。

(4) 对于"在上海仲裁"这一表述的正常含义指的就是仲裁地,不存在可以取代这样理解的相反征象。答辩方不能依赖双方在签订合同前洽商时,据称曾属意的中立仲裁地并非上海这一证据。该证据仅在高等法庭审理管辖权异议时被诉请采纳,但仲裁庭并没有采纳。不同于仲裁庭,高等法庭及上诉庭要遵守口头证据规则及《证据法》(第97章,1997年修订版)第94—99节例外情况,因此这类证据不能按照当然权利被采纳。虽然这类证据没有被全面禁止采纳,但由于它们并非所有缔约方可合理取得,也不关乎任何明确清晰的背景,因此在这起案件中无法被采纳。无论如何,答辩方证人的证词削弱了答辩方称“双方有意在中立的地方就他们的争议进行仲裁”这一说法,因为证人在供证时说自己不理解仲裁地的概念:见[76]—[78]及[81]—[88]。

(5) 答辩方赖以为据的根据中国法仲裁协议属无效以及双方签订《返销协议》时现行中国法的情况,同样不能构成用以理解第14.2条的背景内容。没有证据显示双方察觉到中国法及选择新仲为管理机构之间的相互影响,更不用说这两个选择的结合会带来无效的结果:见[90]。

(6) 答辩方辩称“新加坡是法域而上海不是”,这一论点对他们没有帮助。双方均没有在提交下级法院的书面陈词中提到或处理这一点,仲裁庭也没有依据这一点。无论如何,商业当事人在仲裁协议中仅注明城市或国家是常见的做法。因此,单单提及上海就足以明确表示是仲裁地而非开庭地:见[92]及[93]。

(7) 最终的结果是,上海是仲裁地。“在上海仲裁”这一表述的正常含义就是以上海为仲裁地,且没有相反的征象表明存在另一种理解。反过来说,仲裁地法以及双方对仲裁协议准据法的默示选择,是相同的,即中国法。因此,中国法是仲裁协议的准据法。也就是说,中国法作为准据法的默示选择是否应被仲裁地法取代,以便双方的仲裁意愿不会失效,这一问题根本不存在:见[94]。

(8) 裁定上诉得直,但仅针对新加坡不是仲裁地这一部分。上诉庭对于仲裁庭是否有管辖权没有定论。如果新加坡不是仲裁地,新加坡法院对管辖权的任何决定无论如何都不会对仲裁庭具有约束力。再者,《国际仲裁法》(第143A章,2002年修订版)也没有规定法院必须对管辖权作出明确的裁决:见[95][97][98]。

(9) 虽然上诉庭对于仲裁庭是否有管辖权没有明确的定论,但这并不表示在高等法庭提出管辖权异议是不当的。上诉方在高等法庭提出的申请是妥当的,因为多数仲裁员认定新加坡是仲裁地。更何况,基于双方对仲裁地的选择地点有分歧,高等法庭和中国法院一样,具有审理管辖权异议的资格。在这种情况下,要求审理管辖权异议的法院同时也是仲裁地法院,将会产生一个无法调和的矛盾:审理管辖权异议的法院应是双方选择的仲裁地的法院,但审理管辖权异议的法院必须决定哪里是仲裁地,以及须决定本身是否是仲裁地法院:见[100]及[101]。

意见:仲裁协议的准据法如果不是仲裁地法,往往也不会是仲裁地法院在撤销仲裁裁决阶段适用的法律。相反地,仲裁地法院在审理任何撤销申请时所适用的法律最终取决于申请人在程序中提出的异议理由。这是《国际仲裁法》第24节以及《联合国国际贸易法委员会国际商事仲裁示范法》(以下简称《示范法》)第34条第2款所规定的,这两条规定载明了可撤销仲裁裁决的理由。这些规定清楚载明,仲裁地法院有权针对某些异议理由适用自身法律,最明显的就是以可仲裁性以及与仲裁地公共政策有冲突为理由的异议:见《示范法》第34条第2款第2项。另外,有些异议理由是仲裁地法院在审理撤销申请时有权适用自身法律以外的其他法律,最明显的就是"协议依据缔约方选择适用法属无效"的情况:见《示范法》第34条第2款第1项第1目。一般而言,仲裁地的法院会适用仲裁地法,如果仲裁地法指引法院适用另一套法律体系(通常是仲裁协议的准据法),则法院会适用该法。一般来说,仲裁协议的准据法与仲裁协议的构成、有效性、效力及履行等密切关联:见[51]—[55]。

【专家点评】*

在没有明示条款的情况下,法院应该如何裁定仲裁协议的准据法?这个问题曾提交新加坡和其他司法管辖区的法院,也是上诉庭的 *BNA v. BNB*

---

* 本评注是作者以个人身份撰写的,所表达的意见纯属作者个人的看法,不反映新加坡最高法院的观点。本评注的所有失误,纯属作者个人的失误。本评注撰写人:杨镕玮(Justin Yeo),上诉庭事务处副主簿,最高法院助理主簿,新加坡地方法庭法官。陈佳琪(Rachel Tan),最高法院法律秘书。

and another [2020] 1 SLR 456 (以下简称“*BNA*”)[①]裁决中的主要系争点。

在 *BNA* 案中,上诉庭的审理依据是双方同意以高等法庭在 *BCY v. BCZ* [2017] 3 SLR 357 (以下简称“*BCY*”)[②]裁决中载明的框架作为裁定仲裁协议准据法的适用分析框架。在 *BCY* 案中,高等法庭采用了与英国上诉法院在 *Sulamérica Cia Nacional de Seguros SA and others v. Enesa Engelharia SA and others* [2013] 1 WLR 102 案中的分析法类似的一项三阶段分析法。简而言之,这三个阶段分为:

第一,如果双方已作出明确选择,那将是仲裁协议的准据法。

第二,如果没有作出明确选择,法院将考虑双方是否作出了默示选择,如果是,那将是仲裁协议的准据法。

第三,如果没有明示或默示选择准据法,与仲裁协议有最密切且最真实联系的法律体系将是仲裁协议的准据法。[③]

上诉庭在 *BNA* 案中作出的裁决意义重大,原因有三:

第一,上诉庭表示,如果仲裁协议仅注明一个地理位置,在没有明确的相反表示的情况下,自然而然就会理解为仲裁地的选择。[④] 在下级法院,法官裁定“在上海仲裁”只是指仲裁的开庭地,原因是:(1)仲裁协议提及两个地理位置是因为双方明确纳入了仲裁规则,[⑤]该规则规定除非另有明确约定,否则默认仲裁地为新加坡;以及(2)“上海”指的是一个城市而不是一个法域(有别于,例如,中华人民共和国即中国)[⑥]。上诉庭不认同,并裁定“在上海仲裁”的正常含义应解读为选择了上海为仲裁地,尽管这一正常含义可能会被相反的征象所取代。[⑦] 这种理解地理位置的方法也获得了一系列国

---

① *BNA* 是针对 *BNA v. BNB and another* 的高等法庭判决[2019]SGHC 142 的上诉裁决。

② *BNA* at [44].

③ *BCY* at [40].

④ *BNA* at [65].

⑤ 该仲裁规则是指《新仲规则》。

⑥ *BNA* at [30].

⑦ BNA at [65] and [69].

际权威典据和学术评论的支持。[1] 事实上,我们注意到英国上诉法院最近在 *Enka Insaat ve Sanayi AS v. OOO Insurance Company Chubb and other companies* [2020] EWCA Civ 754[2] 案中也发表了类似的观点。

第二,*BNA* 案裁决强调 *BCY* 案框架第二阶段的重点在于,双方就仲裁协议选择准据法的意图。上诉人辩称,上海不可能是选定的仲裁地,因为(1)背景资料(有关合同签订前的洽商)显示,双方有意以一个"中立"的地方为仲裁地;(2)中国法可能使仲裁协议无效,而这与双方明确的仲裁意图相悖。[3] 前一项论点遭驳回,因为上诉人所依据的合同签订前的洽商这一证据不被采纳。[4] 上诉庭也驳回了后一项论点,因为上诉人未能证明双方至少意识到仲裁协议准据法的选择可能对仲裁协议的有效性造成影响。[5] 在我们看来,这样的处理方式有助于避免事后因结论与合同订立时的意图不符而产生人为的和理论上的争议。另外,该处理方式强调,尽管有仲裁的意图但不一定会被赋予效力(例如,当双方选择的仲裁地使仲裁协议无效时)。[6] 综上所述,这几点说明了在当事人选择仲裁协议准据法时,确保他们获得充分法律咨询是重要的,可能还有必要就拟适用的法律对仲裁协议的潜在影响征求外国的法律意见。

第三,上诉庭裁定,尽管上诉人的立场为上海是仲裁地,但上诉人在新加坡提出管辖权异议却是妥当的。这是因为仲裁庭多数成员已裁定新加坡是仲裁地,尽管就这一点双方有所争议。上诉庭指出,在这种情况下,新加

---

① BNA at [66], citing English decisions such as *Naviera Amazonica Peruana SA v. Compania Internacional de Seguros del Peru* [1988] 1 Lloyd' s Rep 116 ("arbitration in London"), *Shagang South-Asia (Hong Kong) Trading Co Ltd v. Daewoo Logistics* [2015] 1 Lloyd' s Rep 504 ("[a]rbitration to be held in Hong Kong"), as well as academic commentaries such as David Joseph, *Jurisdiction and Arbitration Agreements and Their Enforcement* (Sweet & Maxwell, 3rd Ed, 2015) and Gary Born, *International Commercial Arbitration* (Kluwer Law International, 2nd Ed, 2014).

② See *Enka Insaat ve Sanayi AS v. OOO Insurance Company Chubb and other companies* [2020] EWCA Civ 754 at [46].

③ *BNA* at [70].

④ *BNA* at [71]-[88].

⑤ *BNA* at [89]-[90].

⑥ 这与 *BNA*[2]的意见一致。

坡法院与上海法院一样具有审理管辖权异议的资格。[①] 这对于未来与上诉人处在相同情况的争议方而言,具有指导意义。

上诉庭在*BNA*案中的裁定被认为"具有商业合理性",[②]并因"对仲裁协议的适用法作出让人欣见的澄清"而获得赞许。[③] 此外,该裁决有一个重要提示:双方的仲裁意图是否应获得执行取决于仲裁协议的措辞和恰当解释,从而也强调了必须确保仲裁协议是审慎拟定的。

① *BNA* at [101].

② See Thio Shen Yi SC & Thara Rubini Gopalan, "BNA v. BNB: Cappuccino Without The Foam" [2020] SAL Prac 6 at para 39, which observed that "The Court of Appeal reached the most commercially sound decision possible in its decision on *BNA v. BNB.*"

③ See Mahesh Rai, Case Note on *BNA v. BNB* (2020) 1 Singapore Arbitration Journal 72.

BNA v. BNB and another

—The Determination of the Proper Law of an Arbitration Agreement, and the Proper Construction to be Given to an Arbitration Agreement in Determining Whether the Parties' Intention to Arbitrate Should be Enforced

Court of Appeal—Civil Appeal No 159 of 2018

Sundaresh Menon CJ, Judith Prakash JA and Steven Chong JA

15 October 2019; 27 December 2019

Facts

The dispute arose in relation to an agreement (the "Takeout Agreement") that had been entered into by the appellant and the respondents. The appellant was the buyer, and the respondents were the sellers, of certain products under the Takeout Agreement. The dispute arose when the appellant failed to make the necessary payments under the Takeout Agreement.

The Takeout Agreement contained a dispute resolution provision in Art 14:

ARTICLE 14: DISPUTES

14.1 This Agreement shall be governed by the laws of the People's Republic of China.

14.2 With respect to any and all disputes arising out of or relating to this Agreement, the [p]arties shall initially attempt in good faith to

> resolve all disputes amicably between themselves. If such negotiations fail, it is agreed by both parties that such disputes shall be finally submitted to the Singapore International Arbitration Centre (SIAC) for arbitration in Shanghai, which will be conducted in accordance with its Arbitration Rules. The arbitration award shall be final and binding on both [p]arties.

The respondents initiated arbitration proceedings administered by the Singapore International Arbitration Centre ("SIAC"), which duly appointed a three-person arbitral tribunal. The appellant challenged the jurisdiction of the arbitral tribunal, on the grounds that the proper law of the arbitration agreement was the law of the People's Republic of China ("PRC"), which law rendered the arbitration agreement invalid, and entailed that the dispute had to be litigated in the PRC courts instead. This argument was mounted on the basis that the law of the substantive contract, the Takeout Agreement, was expressly chosen to be PRC law, and that the law of the seat, too, was PRC law, given that it was provided that Shanghai was to be the seat of the arbitration. PRC law, however, would have invalidated the arbitration agreement because PRC law did not allow a foreign arbitral institution such as the SIAC to administer an arbitration with the PRC as its seat or which arose from a purely domestic dispute such as this.

The arbitral tribunal arrived at a split decision on the question of its jurisdiction to hear the dispute, with the majority holding that the tribunal had jurisdiction. The majority considered that it would have made no commercial or logical sense for parties to have intentionally selected a law to govern the arbitration agreement which would then invalidate it. It therefore took the view that Shanghai was not the seat, but merely the venue of the arbitration. Instead,

Singapore was the seat, and the tribunal had jurisdiction under Singapore law. The dissenting arbitrator took the view that Shanghai was the seat of the arbitration, and thus PRC law was the law of the seat. Given that PRC law was also the law of the substantive contract, PRC law was the proper law of the arbitration agreement. PRC law did not allow this dispute to be referred to arbitration, thus the tribunal lacked jurisdiction to hear the dispute.

The appellant applied to the High Court for a declaration that the tribunal lacked jurisdiction to hear the dispute. The judge ("Judge") dismissed the jurisdictional challenge. The Judge ruled that the parties had not made an express choice of proper law of the arbitration agreement; simply providing in Art 14. 1 that the proper law of the Takeout Agreement was PRC law was insufficient to similarly render it an express choice of proper law for the arbitration agreement in Art 14. 2. The Judge found, however, that the parties had made an implied choice of Singapore law as the proper law of the arbitration agreement. The Judge found that Singapore was the seat of the arbitration agreement. The parties had incorporated the Arbitration Rules of the Singapore International Arbitration Centre (5th Ed, 2013) ("the SIAC Rules") as the relevant arbitral rules, and r 18. 1 of the SIAC Rules provided that in the absence of the parties' express provision, the default seat would be Singapore. This meant that Art 14. 2 made reference to two geographical locations: Singapore and Shanghai. Given that r 18. 1 explicitly provided that the seat of an arbitration would, absent the parties' express selection, be Singapore, the Judge considered that the phrase "arbitration in Shanghai" referred to Shanghai as the venue of the arbitration instead. This reading was buttressed by the fact that Singapore, but not Shanghai, was a law district, and thus the reference to Singapore was better understood as a reference to Singapore being the seat of the arbitration.

The Judge accepted that PRC law, as the law of the substantive contract into which the arbitration agreement was integrated, would serve as the starting point of the parties' implied choice of proper law. But he considered that Singapore law, as the law of the seat, would displace that implied choice, because it was likely that the parties' arbitration agreement would be invalid if PRC law was its proper law. Thus, Singapore law was the proper law of the arbitration agreement. The appellant appealed.

Holding

Held, allowing the appeal:

(1) The parties had not made an express choice of law for the arbitration agreement in Art 14. 2 of the Takeout Agreement. The mere fact that Art 14. 2 followed Art 14. 1 did not mean that the governing law specified in Art 14. 1 to govern the Takeout Agreement should also be taken as the express governing law of the arbitration agreement in Art 14. 2: at [56] and [59] to [61].

(2) The parties accepted that the starting point was that the governing law of the Takeout Agreement would similarly be the governing law of the arbitration agreement. However, this starting point could be displaced if the law of the seat materially differed from that starting point: at [62] and [63].

(3) The phrase "arbitration in Shanghai" in Art 14. 2 was a reference to Shanghai as the seat of the arbitration, and not merely its venue. The natural meaning of the phrase "arbitration in Shanghai" was that Shanghai was the seat of the arbitration. The selection of a seat had immense legal significance to an arbitration agreement, whereas the choice of venue was far less legally important. Where parties had specified only one geographical location in an arbitration agreement, and particularly where, as here, the parties had expressed a choice for "arbitration in [that location]", that location was most

naturally construed as a reference to the parties' choice of seat. This was buttressed by a line of authorities that had interpreted similar phraseology as indicating a choice of seat, and not merely of venue: at [65] to [69].

(4) There were no contrary indicia to displace the natural reading of the phrase "arbitration in Shanghai" as referring to the seat of the arbitration. The respondent was precluded from relying on evidence of the parties' pre-contractual negotiations that allegedly pointed to the parties desiring a neutral seat that was not Shanghai. The evidence had only been sought to be admitted in the jurisdictional challenge in the High Court, and had not been admitted by the arbitral tribunal itself. The High Court and the Court of Appeal, unlike the arbitral tribunal, were both bound by the parol evidence rule and its exceptions in ss 94 to 99 of the Evidence Act (Cap 97, 1997 Rev Ed), thus the evidence was not admissible as of right. Although there was no blanket prohibition on the admissibility of such evidence, the evidence could not be admitted in this case as it was neither reasonably available to all the contracting parties, nor did it relate to a clear and obvious context. In any event, the respondents' witness's own evidence undermined the respondents' argument that the parties intended to have a neutral forum in which to arbitrate their disputes, because the witness himself attested that he did not understand the concept of the seat of an arbitration: at [76] to [78] and [81] to [88].

(5) The respondents' reliance on the invalidating effect of PRC law on the arbitration agreement, on the state of PRC law as existed at the time the parties entered into the Takeout Agreement, similarly could not form part of the context in construing Art 14.2. There was nothing in the evidence to show that the parties were sensitive to the interplay between PRC law and the choice of the SIAC as the administering institution, much less to the invalidating effect of this particular combination of choices: at [90].

(6) The respondents' arguments that Singapore, but not Shanghai, was a law district, did not assist them. This was not an argument raised or addressed by either party in their written submissions below, nor was it relied upon by the tribunal. In any event, it was common for commercial parties to only specify either a city or country in their arbitration agreements, and thus the reference to Shanghai alone was sufficient as a clear reference to a seat, and not a venue: at [92] and [93].

(7) The sum result was that Shanghai was the seat of the arbitration. The natural reading of the phrase "arbitration in Shanghai" pointed to Shanghai as the seat, and there were no contrary indicia to point away from this natural reading. This in turn meant that the law of the seat, and the parties' implied choice of proper law of the arbitration agreement, was one and the same: PRC law. It followed that PRC law was the proper law of the arbitration agreement. Hence the question whether the implied choice of PRC law as the proper law should be displaced by the law of the seat in order not to nullify the parties' intention to arbitrate simply did not arise: at [94].

(8) The appeal was allowed, but only to the extent that Singapore was not the seat of the arbitration. The Court of Appeal took no concluded view as to whether the tribunal did or did not have jurisdiction. If Singapore was not the seat, any decision of the Singapore courts on jurisdiction would not be binding upon the tribunal anyway. Further, s 10 of the International Arbitration Act (Cap 143A, 2002 Rev Ed) ("IAA") did not require the court to make a positive finding as to jurisdiction either way: at [95], [97] and [98].

(9) Although the Court of Appeal did not express a concluded view as to the tribunal's jurisdiction, this did not mean that the jurisdictional challenge was not properly brought in the High Court. The appellant's application was properly filed in the High Court because the majority of the tribunal had determined that

Singapore was the seat. Moreover, given that the parties had disagreed about the location of the seat, the High Court had as good a claim as the PRC courts to hear the jurisdictional challenge. In this case, requiring that the court hearing the jurisdictional challenge be the court of the seat would create an unsolvable contradiction: the court which should hear the challenge ought to be the court of the seat chosen by the parties, but the court hearing the challenge would have to decide what was the seat and, by extension, whether it was the seat court: at [100] and [101].

Observation: The proper law of the arbitration agreement, if it was not the law of the seat, was not invariably the law that the seat court would apply at the stage of setting aside an arbitral award. Instead, the law that the seat court would apply in any setting-aside application would ultimately depend on the grounds of challenge raised by the applicant in those proceedings. This was what s 24 of the IAA and Art 34(2) of the UNCITRAL Model Law on International Commercial Arbitration ("Model Law"), which together set out the grounds upon which an arbitral award might be set aside, provided. These provisions made it clear that there were some grounds of challenge for which the seat court was mandated to apply its own law, most obviously, where the challenge was made on the grounds of arbitrability and of alleged conflict with the public policy of the seat: see Art 34(2)(b) of the Model Law. On the other hand, there were grounds of challenge where the seat court in hearing the setting-aside application was mandated to apply some law *other* than its own, most obviously, when the "said agreement [was] not valid under the law to which the parties [had] subjected it": see Art 34(2)(a)(i). In general, the seat court would apply the law of the seat and where that law directed it to some other system of law, usually the proper law of the arbitration agreement, then it would apply that law. The proper law of the arbitration agreement would generally be most relevant to questions as to formation, validity, effect and discharge of the arbitration agreement: at [51] to [55].

Commentary *

How should a court determine the proper law of the arbitration agreement in the absence of an express provision? This issue has been brought before courts in Singapore and other jurisdictions. It was the central issue in the Court of Appeal's decision of *BNA v. BNB and another* [2020] 1 SLR 456 ("*BNA*"). ①

In *BNA*, the Court of Appeal proceeded on the basis of the parties' agreement that the applicable analytical framework for determining the proper law of the arbitration agreement was that set out in the High Court decision of *BCY v. BCZ* [2017] 3 SLR 357 ("*BCY*"). ② In *BCY*, the High Court adopted a three-stage analysis similar to that applied by the English Court of Appeal in *Sulamérica Cia Nacional de Seguros SA and others v. Enesa Engelharia SA and others* [2013] 1 WLR 102. In gist, the three stages are as follows:

First, if the parties had made an *express* choice, that would be the proper law of the arbitration agreement.

Second, if no express choice had been made, the court would consider whether the parties had made an *implied* choice and, if so, that would be the proper law of the arbitration agreement.

---

* This commentary is written in the authors' personal capacity. The opinions expressed in this commentary are entirely the authors' own views and are not to be understood as reflecting the views of the Supreme Court of Singapore. All errors in this commentary remain solely the authors' own. Author: Justin YEO, Deputy Divisional Registrar, Court of Appeal; Assistant Registrar, Supreme Court; District Judge, Singapore. TAN Jia Qi, Rachel, Justices' Law Clerk, Supreme Court.

① *BNA* is a decision on appeal from a decision of the High Court in *BNA v. BNB and another* [2019] SGHC 142.

② *BNA* at [44].

Third, if the proper law had neither been expressly nor impliedly chosen, the system of law with which the arbitration agreement has the closest and most real connection would be the proper law of the arbitration agreement. ①

The Court of Appeal's decision in *BNA* is significant for three reasons.

First, the Court of Appeal made clear that where an arbitration agreement specifies only one geographical location, this is most naturally construed as a reference to a choice of seat in the absence of clear contrary indication. ② In the court below, the Judge had found that the reference to "arbitration in Shanghai" was merely a reference to the "venue" of the arbitration, given that (i) the arbitration agreement referred to two geographical locations because the parties had expressly incorporated arbitration rules③ which provided that the default seat would be Singapore unless expressly provided otherwise; and (ii) "Shanghai" is a reference to a city and not a law district (unlike, for instance, a reference to the People's Republic of China (the "PRC")). ④ The Court of Appeal disagreed, and held that the natural reading of "arbitration in Shanghai" should be construed to mean that Shanghai had been chosen as the seat of the arbitration, although this natural reading could be displaced by contrary indicia. ⑤ This approach towards construing geographical references finds support in a line of international authorities and academic commentaries. ⑥

① *BCY* at [40].

② *BNA* at [65].

③ This is a reference to the Arbitration Rules of the Singapore International Arbitration Centre (5th Ed, 2013) ("SIAC Rules").

④ *BNA* at [30].

⑤ *BNA* at [65] and [69].

⑥ *BNA* at [66], citing English decisions such as *Naviera Amazonica Peruana SA v. Compania Internacional de Seguros del Peru* [1988] 1 Lloyd's Rep 116 ("arbitration in London"), *Shagang South-Asia (Hong Kong) Trading Co Ltd v. Daewoo Logistics* [2015] EWHC 194 (Comm) ("[a]rbitration to be held in Hong Kong"), as well as academic commentaries such as David Joseph, *Jurisdiction and Arbitration Agreements and Their Enforcement* (Sweet & Maxwell, 3rd Ed, 2015) and Gary Born, *International Commercial Arbitration* (Kluwer Law International, 2nd Ed, 2014).

Indeed, we note that the English Court of Appeal recently made a similar observation in *Enka Insaat ve Sanayi AS v. "OOO Insurance Company Chubb" and other companies* [2020] EWCA Civ 574. ①

Second, the *BNA* decision emphasises that the focus at the second stage of the *BCY* framework is on the parties' intentions relating to the choice of proper law of the arbitration agreement. The appellant had argued that Shanghai could not have been the chosen seat, because (i) the background contextual material (relating to pre-contractual negotiations) showed that the parties intended that the arbitration be seated in a "neutral" forum; and (ii) PRC law might invalidate the arbitration agreement, which would be contrary to the parties' express intention to arbitrate. ② The former argument was rejected as the evidence of pre-contractual negotiations relied upon by the appellant was inadmissible. ③ The Court of Appeal also rejected the latter argument as the appellant failed to show that the parties were, at the very least, aware of the impact that the choice of proper law of the arbitration agreement could have on its validity. ④ In our view, this approach helps to avoid artificial and theoretical arguments that may be raised after the fact to justify conclusions that do not accord with the reality of the parties' intentions at the time of contracting. In addition, the approach emphasises that an intention to arbitrate may not invariably be given effect to (if, for instance, the parties' choice of law invalidates the arbitration agreement). ⑤ Taken together, these points demonstrate the importance of ensuring that one is adequately advised on the

---

① See *Enka Insaat ve Sanayi AS v. "OOO Insurance Company Chubb" and other companies* [2020] EWCA Civ 574 at [46].

② *BNA* at [70].

③ *BNA* at [71]-[88].

④ *BNA* at [89]-[90].

⑤ This is in line with the observation made in *BNA* at [2].

choice of the proper law of the arbitration agreement. It may well be necessary to obtain foreign legal advice on potential effects that the intended law may have on the arbitration agreement.

Third, the Court of Appeal found that notwithstanding the appellant's position that Shanghai was the seat of the arbitration, the jurisdictional challenge had been properly brought by the appellant in Singapore. This was because the majority of the arbitral tribunal had found that Singapore was the seat, a point which had in any event been disputed between the parties. The Court of Appeal observed that in such a situation, the Singapore courts had as good a claim as the Shanghai courts to hear the jurisdictional challenge. ① This is instructive for future disputants who find themselves in a position similar to the appellant's.

The Court of Appeal's decision in *BNA* has been described as "commercially sound", ② and praised for providing "welcome clarification on the law applicable to arbitration agreements". ③ Amongst other things, the decision serves as an important reminder that whether the parties' intention to arbitrate should be enforced depends on the wording and proper construction of the arbitration agreement, and—in so doing—underscores the need to ensure that arbitration agreements are carefully drafted.

---

① *BNA* at [101].

② See Thio Shen Yi SC & Thara Rubini Gopalan, "BNA v. BNB: Cappuccino Without The Foam" [2020] SAL Prac 6 at para 39, which observed that "The Court of Appeal reached the most commercially sound decision possible in its decision on *BNA v. BNB*".

③ See Mahesh Rai, Case Note on *BNA v. BNB* (2020) 1 Singapore Arbitration Journal 72.

Grounds of Decision

BNA v. BNB and another

[2020] 1 SLR 456

27 December 2019

Steven Chong JA (delivering the grounds of decision of the court):

Introduction

1 An arbitration agreement by definition is the product of negotiations between the parties. By incorporating an arbitration agreement into an underlying contract, the parties contemplate that should a dispute arise, it should be referred to arbitration strictly in accordance with the terms of the arbitration agreement and no more.

2 However, it does not follow that the parties' manifest intention to arbitrate must always be given effect to come what may. Ultimately, whether the parties' intention to arbitrate should be enforced invariably depends on the wording and proper construction of the arbitration agreement. What must not be overlooked is that arbitration agreements, despite the best of intentions of the parties, can at times be invalid for any one of a variety of reasons. After all, the Convention on the Recognition and Enforcement of Foreign Arbitral Awards (10 June 1958) 330 UNTS 38 (entered into force 7 June 1959, accession by Singapore 21 August 1986) ("the New York Convention") expressly contemplates in Art Ⅱ(3) that arbitration agreements can be "*null and void, inoperative or incapable of being performed*" [emphasis added].

3 Within the text of any arbitration agreement, parties may expressly provide for, *inter alia*, a seat for the arbitration, the arbitral institution, the arbitral

rules and the governing law of the arbitration agreement. These choices would be informed by what each party perceives to be most advantageous or favourable to it. It is therefore not uncommon that the eventual text of an arbitration agreement involves some *compromise* between the parties' preferred positions.

4 This appeal arose from a dispute over the proper interpretation of an arbitration agreement that was indeed the product of negotiations and compromise between the parties. It came before the Singapore courts because the majority of the tribunal in its jurisdictional decision found Singapore to be the seat of the arbitration. This finding was affirmed by the High Court. We heard the appeal on 15 October 2019 and allowed it to the extent that we found that Shanghai was the seat of the arbitration instead. The impact of our decision made it inappropriate for us to decide whether the arbitration agreement was invalid under what we determined to be the governing law of the arbitration agreement, *ie*, the law of the People's Republic of China (the "PRC"). In our view, any such determination should rightly be decided by the relevant PRC court as the seat court applying PRC law.

5 At the time of giving our decision we stated that we would explain our decision with full grounds. This we do now.

Background

The parties

6 The appellant ("BNA") is a corporation organised and existing under the laws of the PRC, with its principal place of business in the PRC. It is the buyer under the "Takeout Agreement".

7 The first respondent ("BNB") is a company organised and existing under the laws of the Republic of Korea, with its principal place of business in the

Republic of Korea. It was the original seller under the Takeout Agreement.

8 The second respondent (“BNC”) is a company organised and existing under the laws of the PRC, with its principal place of business in the PRC. It took on BNB’s rights and obligations under the Takeout Agreement by way of an addendum to the Takeout Agreement.

The Takeout Agreement and addendum

9 The Takeout Agreement was a contract for the sale of industrial gases (“the products”) by the first respondent, BNB, to the appellant, BNA. BNA and BNB entered into the Takeout Agreement on 7 August 2012.

10 On 1 February 2013, BNA, BNB and BNC entered into an addendum to the Takeout Agreement (the “Addendum”). Clause 2 of the Addendum relevantly provided that “[BNA, BNB and BNC] agree that the rights and obligations of [BNB] under the [Takeout Agreement] [would] be fully assigned to [BNC] effective from February 1, 2013”. The Addendum was also specifically provided to be “an indivisible part of the [Takeout Agreement]”, with the Addendum to prevail in the event of any conflict or discrepancy between it and the Takeout Agreement. Like the judge below (“Judge”), we use the term “Takeout Agreement” hereafter in this judgment to refer to the single indivisible agreement comprising both the original Takeout Agreement and the Addendum.

11 The primary obligation of BNA as the buyer under the Takeout Agreement was to buy specified quantities of the products from, at first, BNB, and later, BNC. The Takeout Agreement required BNA to pay the respondents on a monthly basis for the products purchased and delivered. The products which are the subject of the Takeout Agreement were manufactured in the PRC by the respondents. The products were to be sold and transported from the respondents’ facilities to the appellant’s facilities. The relevant facilities were all

located in the PRC.

12 The critical provision in the Takeout Agreement is Art 14:

> ARTICLE 14: DISPUTES
>
> 14. 1 This Agreement shall be governed by the laws of the People's Republic of China.
>
> 14. 2 With respect to any and all disputes arising out of or relating to this Agreement, the [p]arties shall initially attempt in good faith to resolve all disputes amicably between themselves. If such negotiations fail, it is agreed by both parties that such disputes shall be finally submitted to the Singapore International Arbitration Centre (SIAC) for arbitration in Shanghai, which will be conducted in accordance with its Arbitration Rules. The arbitration award shall be final and binding on both [p]arties.

As the Judge below noted, Art 14 serves two purposes. It records the parties' express choice of PRC law to govern the Takeout Agreement and it contains the parties' arbitration agreement.

The arbitral proceedings

13 BNA failed to make the necessary payments under the Takeout Agreement, and the respondents filed a notice of arbitration dated 2 March 2016. BNA responded by challenging the tribunal's jurisdiction.

14 The Singapore International Arbitration Centre ("SIAC") appointed a tribunal comprising three arbitrators. The tribunal first dealt with the appellant's challenge to its jurisdiction.

15 The crux of the jurisdictional dispute before the tribunal was whether the

proper law of the arbitration agreement was Singapore law, or PRC law. The appellant took the position that PRC law was the proper law, but the respondents contended that it was Singapore law instead. The appellant argued that if PRC law was the proper law of the arbitration agreement, the arbitration agreement would be invalid. This was so for two reasons. First, because Shanghai was the seat of the arbitration, and PRC law did not permit a foreign arbitral institution such as the SIAC to administer a PRC-seated arbitration. Second, because the dispute was a purely domestic dispute, and PRC law did not permit a foreign arbitral institution such as the SIAC to administer such a dispute. It followed that the tribunal therefore could not have jurisdiction if PRC law was the proper law. We foreshadow that the potentially invalidating effect of PRC law on the arbitration agreement remained at the heart of the jurisdictional challenge in the High Court, and before us in the appeal as well.

16 The tribunal gave its decision on jurisdiction on 18 July 2017. The majority ruled that the tribunal *did* have jurisdiction. The dissenting arbitrator took the view that the tribunal did not.

17 It will suffice for us to make some brief observations of the reasons provided by the majority and the minority.

18 The majority's decision reveals a deep concern that it should find as the proper law of the arbitration agreement a law that would not invalidate the arbitration. After examining some authorities dealing with the "validation principle" and the principle of "effective interpretation", the majority summarised those authorities as standing for an overarching principle: "it makes no commercial or logical sense for parties to intentionally select a law to govern an arbitration agreement which would then invalidate it". This drove the majority to find Singapore to be the seat of the arbitration. The reference to

Shanghai in Art 14. 2 was insufficient to make it the seat of arbitration, because if Shanghai were the seat, PRC law would apply, and if PRC law applied, the arbitration agreement would be exposed to the risk of being held invalid and illegal. To avoid the possibility of the parties' manifest intention to arbitrate their dispute being nullified, the majority took the view that the reference to Shanghai was intended to be a reference to the venue of the arbitration. Singapore, instead, was the seat.

19 The majority accepted that the governing law of the Takeout Agreement, PRC law, would presumptively be the proper law of the arbitration agreement as well. But it considered that this presumptive choice of PRC law was displaced by Singapore law, because the application of PRC law might invalidate the arbitration agreement. On the other hand, the arbitration agreement would be valid if Singapore law, as the law of the seat, governed the arbitration agreement instead. The majority thus concluded that Singapore law was the proper law of the arbitration agreement.

20 The dissenting arbitrator issued a separate opinion. Her view was that Shanghai was the seat of the arbitration, and there was nothing to displace PRC law as the proper law of the arbitration agreement. It was significant to her that this dispute bore multiple connections to the PRC, in that the Takeout Agreement was concluded in the PRC; the products were manufactured, supplied and delivered in the PRC; and the place of performance was the PRC. Further, the parties had expressly chosen PRC law as the applicable law governing the Takeout Agreement in Art 14. 1. This choice naturally extended to the arbitration agreement as well, because the parties had specifically chosen arbitration "in Shanghai" in Art 14. 2. The reference to the SIAC did not change the analysis; the domicile or nationality of an arbitral institution was irrelevant in the proper law analysis.

The decision below

21 The appellant applied to the High Court of Singapore for a declaration that the tribunal lacked jurisdiction to hear the dispute. This application was brought under s 10(3) of the International Arbitration Act (Cap 143A, 2002 Rev Ed) ("IAA"), which permits any party to apply to the High Court to challenge a tribunal's decision on jurisdiction.

22 The application was duly heard by a single judge in the High Court in June and August 2018. The Judge dismissed the jurisdictional challenge in August 2018, giving brief oral grounds, and later supplemented those grounds with full written grounds on 1 July 2019 in *BNA v. BNB and another* [2019] SGHC 142 ("the GD").

23 It was common ground before the Judge that the appropriate legal framework for determining the proper law of an arbitration agreement was the three-stage framework set out by the High Court in *BCY v. BCZ* [2017] 3 SLR 357 ("*BCY*") ("*BCY* framework"). The Judge agreed and applied the *BCY* framework in his decision. Before he did so, however, he disposed of four preliminary points. We will revisit some of these in our judgment, so we briefly set them out here for context.

24 The Judge considered the respondents' invitation to him to rely on pre-contractual negotiations as evidence that the parties had intended for arbitration at a "neutral" seat, which the respondents contended meant Singapore, and not Shanghai. The respondents had not put forward the documents containing the parties' pre-contractual negotiations in the jurisdictional challenge before the tribunal, but sought to rely on them to buttress their case before the Judge. The Judge refused this invitation. In his view, the entire agreement clause at Art 16. 3 of the Takeout Agreement precluded reliance on any pre-contractual

negotiations: GD at [41].

25 The Judge rejected the respondents' submissions that there existed a specialised or unique principle of effective interpretation applicable only to arbitration agreements that required him to give the arbitration agreement in Art 14.2 an interpretation which, at the least, kept it alive. In his view, such a principle required two competing interpretations before it could apply; further, it had the nakedly instrumental objective of ensuring an arbitration agreement was effective: GD at [47] and [48].

26 The Judge also rejected the applicability of the validation principle in Singapore law. The validation principle provides that "if an international arbitration agreement is substantively valid under any of the laws that may potentially be applicable to it, then its validity will be upheld, even if it is not valid under any of the other potentially applicable choices of law": GD at [51]. The Judge considered that adopting the validation principle was impermissibly instrumental (at [53]); could be inconsistent with the parties' intentions (at [55]); was unnecessary because Singapore law already endorsed the *ut res magis* principle (at [62]); and could create problems at the enforcement stage (at [65]).

27 Finally, the Judge considered that the doctrine of separability applied even in this case, where the validity of the main contract (the Takeout Agreement) had not been challenged, to allow the arbitration agreement to stand apart from the Takeout Agreement and for each to have different governing laws. The Judge considered that separability also applied because the governing law clause of the Takeout Agreement, into which the arbitration agreement was integrated, operated to render the arbitration agreement invalid: GD at [73]-[74]. Thus, a broader reading of the doctrine of separability was necessary to save the arbitration agreement from being made invalid, and, correspondingly, to give

effect to the parties' manifest intention to arbitrate their disputes: GD at [76].

28 The Judge then turned to apply the three-stage *BCY* framework. The first stage of the approach required the Judge to examine if the parties had expressly chosen a law to govern the arbitration agreement. The Judge considered that the parties had not made any such express provision. They had only expressly provided in Art 14. 1 that PRC law was the proper law of the Takeout Agreement, but this did not by itself mean that PRC law was also the law of the arbitration agreement: GD at [80].

29 The Judge therefore had to turn to the second stage of the *BCY* framework, which required him to consider whether the parties had instead made an *implied* choice of proper law for the arbitration agreement. As is apparent from the GD itself, the Judge devoted the bulk of his analysis to this stage of the framework, but for convenience we consider that the Judge's decision can essentially be reduced to two steps.

30 The Judge found that Singapore was the seat of the arbitration. He considered that the phrase "arbitration in Shanghai" in Art 14. 2 did not mean that Shanghai was the seat of arbitration. Although the mere reference to a geographical location might have been sufficient in previous cases to make that location the seat of the arbitration, this was not a question to be resolved by resort to the precedents: GD at [98]. The parties had expressly incorporated the Arbitration Rules of the Singapore International Arbitration Centre (5th Ed, 2013) ("the SIAC Rules") as the relevant arbitral rules for their arbitration, and r 18. 1 of the SIAC Rules provided that in the absence of parties' express provision, the default seat would be Singapore. This meant that the arbitration agreement in fact referred to two geographical locations, Shanghai and Singapore. Given that r 18. 1 explicitly provided that the *seat* of an arbitration would, in the absence of express selection by the parties, be Singapore, the

Judge interpreted "arbitration in Shanghai" to mean the selection of Shanghai as the *venue* of the arbitration: GD at [109]. The Judge found further support for this conclusion from the fact that the arbitration agreement in Art 14. 2 did not refer to arbitration in the PRC, but instead only referred to "arbitration in Shanghai". The PRC was a law district, but Shanghai was only a city and not a law district. Because Singapore *was* a law district, and Shanghai was not, the Judge considered that the reference to Shanghai was more naturally construed as a reference to a venue rather than a seat: GD at [110].

31 As he found Singapore was the seat, the Judge held that Singapore law as the law of the seat could displace the implied choice of PRC law as the governing law of the arbitration agreement. The Judge recognised that it was not the mere fact that the law of the seat (Singapore law) was different from the governing law of the Takeout Agreement (PRC law), that the latter would be displaced. This followed from the statement of principle in *BCY* that the starting point is that the governing law of the substantive contract—in this case, PRC law—was the parties' implied choice as the proper law of their arbitration agreement. He considered that this was an appropriate case, however, for PRC law to be displaced in favour of Singapore law because it was likely that the parties' arbitration agreement would be invalid if PRC law was its proper law: GD at [116]. On the other hand, the tribunal would have jurisdiction to hear the dispute under Singapore law. The Judge thus held that Singapore law was the proper law of the arbitration agreement, dismissed the appellant's jurisdictional challenge, and affirmed the majority's decision that the tribunal did have jurisdiction.

32 Under s 10(4) of the IAA, no appeal shall lie from a decision of the High Court on a s 10(3) IAA jurisdictional challenge except with leave of the High Court. The Judge did, however, grant the appellant leave to appeal to us. He

explained that it was somewhat arbitrary that the mere choice of the SIAC's arbitral rules was decisive in this dispute, when the default provision making Singapore the seat was almost certainly an unintended effect of the selection of the SIAC Rules: GD at [122]. He also considered that the three-stage inquiry might operate to give effect to the parties' intentions not at the time they entered into the arbitration agreement, but at the time the arbitration was commenced. The Judge observed that if PRC law had changed from the time the parties concluded the Takeout Agreement, such that the arbitration agreement would not have been invalid under PRC law, then it was "virtually certain" that no jurisdictional challenge would have been mounted, and the parties would have arbitrated in the PRC, with PRC law as the proper law of the arbitration agreement. It might therefore be said that in such a case, the three-stage inquiry, by following the shifting state of the law and transforming what would have been invalid at the time the parties contracted to instead be valid, was simply the validation principle in disguise: GD at [123].

The parties' cases

33 The parties agreed in the appeal, as they had before the Judge, that the *BCY* three-stage framework was the proper framework for determining the proper law of the arbitration agreement. Their arguments were therefore chiefly directed at addressing each of the three stages of the framework.

34 The appellant's case was that the dispute could be resolved at the first stage of the *BCY* framework. Its position was that an express choice of PRC law to govern the arbitration agreement had been made by the parties, because Art 14.1 expressly provided that the Takeout Agreement "shall be governed by the laws of the [PRC]", and Art 14 was a provision entitled "Disputes", thus extending that choice of law not only to the substantive contract, *ie*, the

Takeout Agreement, but also to the arbitration agreement in Art 14. 2. The appellant also disagreed with the Judge that separability had any role to play when neither party challenged the validity of the Takeout Agreement.

35 Alternatively, the appellant contended that the parties had made an implied choice of PRC law as the proper law at the second stage of the *BCY* inquiry. The starting point was that the law of the Takeout Agreement, PRC law, applied to the arbitration agreement, and there was nothing to displace it. The seat of the arbitration was Shanghai, and the mere reference to the SIAC Rules did not make Singapore the seat. The appellant also agreed with the Judge's refusal to admit evidence of the parties' pre-contractual negotiations because these were excluded by the entire agreement clause and the evidence was, in any event, unreliable.

36 If it was necessary to go to the third stage of the *BCY* inquiry, the appellant also contended that the law with the closest and most real connection to the dispute was PRC law.

37 In addition, the appellant affirmed the position it had consistently taken throughout the proceedings that PRC law would operate to invalidate the arbitration agreement, for the same two reasons we have already set out above at [15].

38 The respondents, on the other hand, mounted a defence of the Judge's decision. They argued that the Judge was correct in finding at the first stage of the *BCY* inquiry that no express choice of the proper law of the arbitration agreement had been made.

39 At the second stage of the *BCY* framework, the respondents also aligned themselves with the Judge's analysis that the selection of the SIAC Rules had also incorporated the default choice of Singapore as the seat of the arbitration. The respondents went further, however, in also arguing that the

Judge should have admitted the evidence of the parties' pre-contractual negotiations, which would have strengthened this finding. Citing *BQP v. BQQ* [2018] 4 SLR 1364 ("*BQP*"), the respondents contended that there was, in fact, no prohibition against such material being admitted, because the exclusionary rule did not apply at all in a case arising out of arbitration such as this. The pre-contractual negotiations would show that the parties had always intended to have their disputes arbitrated in a neutral forum, which in this case meant Singapore.

40 Although the starting point was that PRC law, as the law of the Takeout Agreement, also extended to the arbitration agreement in Art 14. 2, the respondents contended that there were strong factors to displace that starting point. They relied on the parties' emphasis on having a neutral forum and the fact that, at the time the parties entered into the Takeout Agreement, there was a "serious risk" that a choice of PRC law would completely undermine the parties' agreement. As such, the parties could not have made an implied choice of PRC law as that would simply have invalidated their agreement to arbitrate.

41 In addition, the respondents took the position that the arbitration agreement would not be invalid under PRC law as it currently stands. The respondents contended that PRC law had changed from the time the parties entered into the Takeout Agreement, and the arbitration agreement was valid on the present state of PRC law.

Issues to be determined

42 The central issue before us involves the identification of the proper law of the arbitration agreement. In this regard, it is common ground between the parties that the three-stage inquiry in *BCY* ([23] *supra*) applies to determine this question.

43 In the course of addressing this central issue, we will also touch on some of the preliminary issues dealt with by the Judge and raised by the parties. It will become apparent, however, that because of the way our analysis proceeds, not all of these call for determination in this judgment.

The *BCY* framework

44 Both parties accepted that the *BCY* framework is the appropriate framework to be applied in determining the proper law of the arbitration agreement. Thus, in coming to our decision, we proceeded on the basis of the parties' agreement to determine the proper law of the arbitration agreement as the Judge did below.

45 There are three steps, or stages, to the *BCY* framework, which mirrors the framework set out by the English Court of Appeal in *Sulamérica Cia Nacional de Seguros SA and others v. Enesa Engelharia SA and others* [2013] 1 WLR 102 ("*Sulamérica*"). Such a framework accords with the established common law rules for ascertaining the proper law of any contract: see *Sulamérica* at [9].

46 At the first stage of the test, the court examines whether the parties had expressly chosen the proper law of the arbitration agreement. If they have, the inquiry ends there. This is uncontroversial and is nothing more than giving effect to the parties' agreement that that law should govern the arbitration agreement.

47 At the second stage of the test, in the absence of an express choice, the court examines if the parties had made an *implied* choice of the proper law to govern their arbitration agreement. We note that both parties accepted that the starting point in determining the implied choice ought to be the law of the substantive contract where the arbitration agreement was integrated into and

formed part of the substantive contract. This is also in line with two other High Court decisions. In *Dyna-Jet Pte Ltd v. Wilson Taylor Asia Pacific Pte Ltd* [2017] 3 SLR 267 (“*Dyna-Jet*”), Vinodh Coomaraswamy J noted, with regard to an arbitration agreement found in a contract governed by English law, that that meant that the arbitration agreement, too, was governed by English law. Citing *Sulamérica*, Coomaraswamy J observed that “there [was] no reason … to move beyond the starting assumption that the parties intended their arbitration agreement to be governed by the proper law of the broader contract in which it is found”: *Dyna-Jet* at [31]. Similarly, in *BMO v. BMP* [2017] SGHC 127 (“*BMO*”), Belinda Ang Saw Ean J aligned herself with *BCY* ([23] *supra*) and considered that *BCY* provided “useful guidance for courts tasked with determining the law governing arbitration agreements”: at [39]. Although the appeal against the *BMO* decision was allowed, our grounds did not question the correctness of *BCY*: see *Marty Ltd v. Hualon Corp (Malaysia) Sdn Bhd (receiver and manager appointed)* [2018] 2 SLR 1207.

48 If neither an express choice nor an implied choice of the proper law of the arbitration agreement can be discerned, the third stage of the *BCY* framework provides that the system of law with which the arbitration agreement has its closest and most real connection will be the proper law: see *BCY* at [40], citing *Sulamérica* ([45] *supra*) at [9] and [25]. We accept that this last step does involve the judicial imputation of a choice of law for the arbitration agreement, because the court only arrives at this stage of the analysis if it has found that the parties have entirely failed to select a proper law themselves, whether expressly or impliedly: GD ([22] *supra*) at [56]. We agree with the Judge below that this judicial imputation is justified, however, because it rests on the underlying premise that the parties would have, if they had addressed their minds to it, selected the law which has the closest and most real

connection to the arbitration agreement. The third stage permits the court to impute to the parties "only that law which can plausibly be imputed to the parties": GD at [56].

Significance of the proper law of the arbitration agreement

49 Before applying the *BCY* framework to the facts of this case, we make some brief observations as to the significance of the proper law of the arbitration agreement so as to forestall any confusion that might arise, particularly at the stage of setting aside an arbitral award though no such concern was raised in this appeal.

50 A concern that might arise at the stage of setting-aside proceedings is the prospect of the seat court having to apply some law other than its own in determining the application to set aside the arbitral award. This possibility would arise if, for example, the proper law of the arbitration agreement is determined under the *BCY* framework to be a law other than the law of the seat. In that instance, must the seat court apply the proper law, or should it apply its own law, *ie*, the law of the seat?

51 In our view, the law that the seat court will apply in any setting-aside application will ultimately depend on the grounds of challenge raised by the applicant. This is entirely consistent with the relevant statutory provisions, in particular s 24 of the IAA and Art 34(2) of the UNCITRAL Model Law on International Commercial Arbitration ("Model Law"), which together set out the grounds upon which an arbitral award might be set aside. Section 24 of the IAA reads:

> **Court may set aside award**
>
> 24. Notwithstanding Article 34(1) of the Model Law, the High Court

may, in addition to the grounds set out in Article 34(2) of the Model Law, set aside the award of the arbitral tribunal if —

(a) the making of the award was induced or affected by fraud or corruption; or

(b) a breach of the rules of natural justice occurred in connection with the making of the award by which the rights of any party have been prejudiced.

52 Article 34(2) of the Model Law reads:

(2) An arbitral award may be set aside by the court specified in Article 6 only if:

(a) the party making the application furnishes proof that:

(i) a party to the arbitration agreement referred to in Article 7 was under some incapacity; or the said agreement is not valid under the law to which the parties have subjected it or, failing any indication thereon, under the law of this State; or

(ii) the party making the application was not given proper notice of the appointment of an arbitrator or of the arbitral proceedings or was otherwise unable to present his case; or

(iii) the award deals with a dispute not contemplated by or not falling within the terms of the submission to arbitration, or contains decisions on matters beyond the scope of the submission to arbitration, provided that, if the decisions on matters submitted to arbitration can be separated from those not so submitted, only that part of the award which contains decisions on matters not submitted to arbitration may be set aside; or

(iv) the composition of the arbitral tribunal or the arbitral procedure was not in accordance with the agreement of the parties, unless such agreement was in conflict with a provision of this Law from which the parties cannot derogate, or, failing such agreement, was not in accordance with this Law; or

(b) the court finds that:

(i) the subject-matter of the dispute is not capable of settlement by arbitration under the law of this State; or

(ii) the award is in conflict with the public policy of this State.

53 It is evident from the above statutory provisions that there are some grounds of challenge for which the seat court is mandated to apply its own law, most obviously, where the challenge is made on the grounds of arbitrability and of alleged conflict with the public policy of the seat: see Art 34(2)(b) of the Model Law.

54 On the other hand, there are grounds of challenge where the seat court in hearing the setting-aside application is mandated to apply some law *other* than its own, most obviously, when the "said agreement is not valid under the law to which the parties have subjected it": see Art 34(2)(a)(i). In such a scenario, the proper law of the arbitration agreement, as determined under the *BCY* framework, will have to be applied by the seat court to decide whether the arbitral tribunal has *jurisdiction* over the dispute under the terms of the arbitration agreement. However, Art 34(2)(a)(i) provides that the seat court

will apply its own law in the event that there is no indication as to the law to which the parties had subjected the arbitration agreement.

55 For present purposes, it is not necessary for this court to express a definitive view as regards the law that is to apply to determine *each* of the grounds of challenge under s 24 of the IAA or Art 34(2) of the Model Law as they were not before us. It suffices to say that in general, the seat court will apply the law of the seat and where that law directs it to some other system of law, usually the proper law of the arbitration agreement, then it will apply that law. However, as we have illustrated above, in general, the proper law of the arbitration agreement will be most relevant to questions as to formation, validity, effect and discharge of the arbitration agreement: David Joseph, *Jurisdiction and Arbitration Agreements and Their Enforcement* (Sweet & Maxwell, 3rd Ed, 2015) ("*David Joseph*") at para 6.53. In the final analysis, the particular system of law that the seat court will apply is that which the relevant arbitration law in the seat directs it to.

Issue 1: Did the parties make an express choice of proper law?

56 As regards the first step of the *BCY* test, the Judge was right to find that the parties had *not* made an express choice of law for the arbitration agreement in Art 14.2 of the Takeout Agreement. The mere fact that Art 14.2 follows Art 14.1 does not mean that the governing law specified in Art 14.1 to govern the Takeout Agreement should be taken as the *express* governing law of the arbitration agreement in Art 14.2. This would be consistent with the treatment of such provisions in cases such as *BCY* ([23] *supra*) and *Sulamérica* ([45] *supra*).

57 We reproduce Art 14 of the Takeout Agreement here for convenience:

ARTICLE 14: DISPUTES

14. 1 This Agreement shall be governed by the laws of the People's Republic of China.

14. 2 With respect to any and all disputes arising out of or relating to this Agreement, the [p]arties shall initially attempt in good faith to resolve all disputes amicably between themselves. If such negotiations fail, it is agreed by both parties that such disputes shall be finally submitted to the Singapore International Arbitration Centre (SIAC) for arbitration in Shanghai, which will be conducted in accordance with its Arbitration Rules. The arbitration award shall be final and binding on both [p]arties.

58 Article 14 of the Takeout Agreement bears strong parallels to the dispute resolution clause in *BCY* itself. Like Art 14, the *BCY* clause was also divided into two sub-clauses, the first expressly providing for the governing law of the main contract, and the second separately setting out the parties' arbitration agreement (see [14] and [16] of *BCY*):

9. 13 Governing Law and Dispute Resolution

9. 13. 1 This Agreement and any non-contractual obligations arising out of or in connection with it are governed by and shall be construed in accordance with the Laws of the State of New York of the United States of America.

9. 13. 2 All disputes (including a dispute, controversy or claim regarding the existence, validity or termination of this Agreement—a 'Dispute') arising out of or in connection with this Agreement shall be finally settled under the Rules of Arbitration of the International

> Chamber of Commerce by one arbitrator appointed in accordance with the said Rules, such arbitration to take place in Singapore. The seat of the arbitration shall be Singapore.

59 The High Court in *BCY* considered that the arbitration agreement did not contain an express choice of governing law. Instead, the dispute had to be decided on the application of the second step of the *BCY* test: at [41]. This was despite cl 9. 13. 1, which specified that the governing law of the agreement was New York law. By parity of reasoning, merely specifying in Art 14. 1 that the Takeout Agreement "shall be governed by the laws of the [PRC]" is, in our view, insufficient to constitute an express choice of the proper law of the arbitration agreement in Art 14. 2.

60 Similarly, the selection of Brazilian law as the governing law of the substantive contract, an insurance policy, in *Sulamérica* ([45] *supra*) was insufficient to constitute an express choice of law governing the arbitration agreement. It is true that *Sulamérica* is less analogous to our case because the governing law clause and the dispute resolution clause were separate clauses. And it is also true that the parties in *Sulamérica* accepted that no provision had been made in the arbitration agreement itself as to the proper law of that agreement: see [10]. But Moore-Bick LJ also appears to have independently concluded that the express choice of Brazilian law in the policy was *not* an express choice of the proper law of the arbitration agreement, observing instead that it was only "a strong pointer towards an implied choice of the law of Brazil as the proper law of [the arbitration agreement]": *Sulamérica* at [27].

61 In our judgment, the approaches of the courts in *BCY* and *Sulamérica* reveal that an express choice of the proper law of the main contract does not, in

and of itself, also constitute the proper law of the arbitration agreement. Instead, because it is possible for parties to expressly provide for a proper law of the arbitration agreement (*BCY* at [59]), and because it is only a "natural inference"—and not a legal conclusion in and of itself—that in the absence of such specific provision the law governing the substantive contract is also presumed to govern the arbitration agreement (*Sulamérica* at [11]), the express choice of the proper law of the main contract is only a "strong indicator of the governing law of the arbitration agreement unless there are indications to the contrary": *BCY* at [65].

Issue 2: Did the parties make an implied choice of proper law?

62 As we have observed above at [44]-[47], the parties accepted that the starting point at this stage of the *BCY* framework is that PRC law, as the governing law of the Takeout Agreement, is also the governing law of the arbitration agreement in Art 14. 2. This starting point can, however, be displaced. The choice of a seat that is different from the place of the law of the governing contract is not by itself sufficient to displace the starting point: *BCY* at [65].

63 The question therefore is whether there is anything to displace the implied choice of PRC law in this case. Such an inquiry only becomes relevant *if* the law of the seat is materially different from the law governing the arbitration agreement which, at this point in the analysis, is PRC law. In this connection, the phrase "arbitration in Shanghai" would have a significant impact on this inquiry.

The meaning of the phrase "arbitration in Shanghai"

64 Here, we respectfully part ways with the Judge. In our view, the Judge adopted a somewhat strained interpretation of Art 14. 2 to arrive at his finding at

[104] of the GD ([22] *supra*) that two geographical locations were identified in Art 14. 2 when there was in truth only a reference to one, *ie*, Shanghai. Rule 18. 1 of the SIAC Rules was instrumental to the Judge's decision, and it provides that in the absence of the parties' agreement, the default seat of the arbitration shall be Singapore, unless the tribunal determines otherwise:

> The parties may agree on the seat of arbitration. Failing such an agreement, the seat of arbitration shall be Singapore, unless the Tribunal determines, having regard to all the circumstances of the case, that another seat is more appropriate.

The critical point, however, is that the default choice of Singapore as the seat only operates *in the absence of agreement by the parties*. In order to invoke the default choice of Singapore under r 18. 1, the Judge first had to consign the reference to Shanghai as a reference to the venue and not the seat. We consider that the Judge was wrong to do so.

65 In our judgment, the natural meaning of the phrase "arbitration in Shanghai" is that Shanghai is the seat of the arbitration. Counsel for the respondents, Mr William Ong, quite candidly and fairly accepted this. We think that he was right to do so. This court, as early as 2002, in *PT Garuda Indonesia v. Birgen Air* [2002] 1 SLR(R) 401 ("*Birgen Air*") expounded on the distinction between the seat of the arbitration, and the venue(s) where arbitration proceedings and hearings may be held. The *seat* of an arbitration is *essential* to arbitration law. Its significance lies in the fact that for legal reasons the arbitration will be regarded as situated in the State or territory of the seat, and the choice of seat also identifies the State or territory whose laws will govern the arbitral process, *ie*, the curial law of the arbitration: *Birgen Air* at

[24]. The seat will also be considered to be the jurisdiction in which the arbitral award is "made" for the purposes of the New York Convention. The *venue(s)* where an arbitration might be held, on the other hand, have far less significance. The venue is simply the physical place where the arbitral tribunal will have to hold its hearings and meetings, if the parties so provide for it. It is not common for parties to do so, and it is certainly not *essential* that parties specify a venue; the choice of venue is likely to be motivated by mundane considerations of logistical and practical convenience and cost. For the same reason, venues of the arbitration, unlike a seat, can change in the life of any arbitral process. Given the stark contrast in the legal significance of the seat as compared to that of the venue, we think therefore that where parties specify only one geographical location in an arbitration agreement, and particularly where, as here, the parties express a choice for "arbitration in [that location]", that should most naturally be construed as a reference to the parties' choice of seat.

66 We are fortified in this approach by a line of authorities which have construed similar geographical references in substantially the same way. In *Naviera Amazonica Peruana SA v. Compania Internacional de Seguros del Peru* [1988] 1 Lloyd's Rep 116 ("*Naviera*"), a decision of the English Court of Appeal, Kerr LJ at 119 essentially adopted the phrase "arbitration in London" as a colloquial way of referring to London as the seat of the arbitration, when he noted that the question was "whether the 'seat' ... of any arbitration ... was agreed to be London or Lima, or—to put it colloquially—whether this contract provided for arbitration in London or Lima". Indeed, this was how Clarke J read that sentence in the subsequent English High Court decision of *ABB Lummus Global Ltd v. Keppel Fels Ltd* [1999] 2 Lloyd's Rep 24 ("*ABB Lummus*") at 31, where he observed that the expression "arbitration

in London” or “arbitration in New York” had been treated by Kerr LJ in *Naviera* “as ordinary or colloquial language describing the seat of the arbitration”. In line with these authorities, the use of the expression “arbitration in Shanghai” in our case ought similarly to be construed as a reference to the seat.

67 More recently, the English High Court in *Shagang South-Asia (Hong Kong) Trading Co Ltd v. Daewoo Logistics* [2015] 1 Lloyd’s Rep 504 (“*Shagang*”) had the occasion to consider an arbitration clause that provided: “Arbitration: Arbitration to be held in Hong Kong. English Law to be applied”. Hamblen J considered a line of authorities, including *Naviera* and *ABB Lummus*, and took the view that the use of the phrase “to be held in Hong Kong” ordinarily carried with it an implied choice of Hong Kong as the seat of the arbitration, and of the application of Hong Kong law as the curial law. Clear words or significant contrary indicia would be necessary to establish that some other seat or curial law had been agreed, and the provision that English law was to be applied was insufficient to amount to such contrary indicia: at [38] and [39]. On our part, we can discern no meaningful difference between the phrases “arbitration to be held in”, and “arbitration in”. Thus *Shagang*, too, supports the reading we have given to Art 14. 2.

68 In addition, the approach we take also finds support in the academic commentaries. *David Joseph* ([55] *supra*) at para 6. 40 notes that “certain expressions such as ‘arbitration in London’ or ‘arbitration in New York’ will without more be taken as colloquial expressions for a choice of seat”. Notably as well, Gary B Born, *International Commercial Arbitration* (Kluwer Law International, 2nd Ed, 2014) states the following (at pp 2074-2075):

> … [P]arties sometimes refer merely to a geographic location, without

> specifying for what purpose (*e. g.*, as the arbitral seat, location for hearings, location of an arbitral institution, or something else.) ***In general, courts and arbitral institutions interpret such references as specifying the arbitral seat.*** *For example, an arbitration clause which read 'Arbitration: Hamburg' with no explanation, has been held to constitute an agreement on the place of arbitration.* [emphasis added in italics and bold italics]

The situation at hand is precisely that described in the extract above. Article 14.2 provides for "arbitration in Shanghai" without specifying the purpose of the reference to Shanghai. The general approach therefore is to interpret the reference as specifying Shanghai as the seat.

69 In summary, we think that the phrase "arbitration in Shanghai" in Art 14.2 of the Takeout Agreement is most naturally construed as a reference to the seat of the arbitration. This, however, is not the end of the analysis. We are prepared to accept, as Hamblen J did in *Shagang*, that the natural reading can be displaced by contrary indicia. We turn then to examine whether such contrary indicia exist on our facts.

Whether contrary indicia point to Shanghai being anything other than the seat

70 Having quite fairly accepted that "arbitration in Shanghai" would ordinarily and naturally be construed as a reference to the seat being in Shanghai, Mr Ong nevertheless urged us to find that there were contrary indicia that displaced the natural reading of this phrase. Mr Ong's argument that Shanghai was *not* the seat was twofold. He argued that the background contextual material, including the earlier drafts of the Takeout Agreement, and the e-mail correspondence between the parties, would show that the parties intended for their arbitration to be seated in a neutral forum which, in this case, could *not* be the PRC, and

must instead be Singapore. He further argued that the potentially invalidating effects of PRC law on the arbitration agreement, on the state of PRC law as at the time the parties entered into the Takeout Agreement, militated against a finding that the parties had chosen Shanghai as the seat. This would have created the absurd result that the parties had expressed a manifest intention to arbitrate while simultaneously defeating it by their choice of seat. We will address these arguments in turn.

The admissibility of evidence of the parties' pre-contractual negotiations

71 The background contextual material upon which the respondents rely is essentially evidence of the parties' pre-contractual negotiations. This evidence was put forward by one Mr Kim, who negotiated the Takeout Agreement on behalf of the respondents. Mr Kim filed an affidavit in the court below setting out his recollection of the negotiations, and exhibiting the e-mail correspondence between the parties in the negotiation. This e-mail correspondence also enclosed various earlier drafts of the Takeout Agreement; these drafts contained the parties' markups and comments.

72 The thrust of Mr Kim's evidence is as follows: (a) the Takeout Agreement was one of a set of four agreements relating to a common facility; (b) the four agreements were related and were finalised at about the same time; (c) the respondents were clear throughout the negotiations that they would not agree to "local" arbitration in the PRC, and desired "international" arbitration conducted by a trustworthy, neutral third party such as Singapore; (d) the drafts of the Takeout Agreement and the other three agreements reflect the appellant proposing arbitration in China, with the respondents counter-proposing arbitration in Korea; and (e) the other three agreements were finally executed without reference to Shanghai as a location, and only mentioned the SIAC.

73 Mr Kim elaborated that the changes made to the arbitration clauses in the

four agreements across the various drafts reveal that the "intentions of all parties were to have a neutral third party in the arbitration clauses". Mr Kim also explained that the reason why the reference to Shanghai was left in the Takeout Agreement, but not in the other agreements, was that he had read a Korean translation of the draft dated 15 March 2011 which read "the CIETAC Shanghai Arbitration Commission *located in* Shanghai" [emphasis added]. He therefore understood "for arbitration in Shanghai" to "simply mean the geographical location of the branch office of SIAC". He also emphasised that he personally did not realise the legal significance of an arbitral seat and what that entailed in respect of the court having supervisory jurisdiction over the arbitration. He reiterated that at the time of the negotiations "[a]ll parties wanted an independent or neutral forum like Singapore to conduct any arbitration, as opposed to say China or Korea".

74 The appellant did not put forward any witnesses of its own to attest to the parties' pre-contractual negotiations. As we have already noted above at [24], the Judge refused to admit this evidence, holding that the entire agreement clause in Art 16. 3 of the Takeout Agreement operated to exclude such evidence.

75 Before us, the respondents contended that the Judge was wrong to have disregarded this evidence. They submitted that there was no prohibition against the admissibility of such evidence whatsoever, because the parol evidence rule does not apply at all for cases arising out of an arbitration. They cited the High Court decision in *BQP* ([39] *supra*) as authority for this proposition. They further asserted that the Judge wrongly interpreted the entire agreement clause in Art 16. 3 of the Takeout Agreement; the correct interpretation would have revealed that that clause allowed evidence to be admitted to aid in the interpretation of the Takeout Agreement, but not to contradict, vary, add to, or

subtract from it.

76 We consider that the respondents' reliance on *BQP* was misplaced. The parol evidence rule and its exceptions find statutory expression in ss 94 to 99 of the Evidence Act (Cap 97, 1997 Rev Ed) (the "Evidence Act"). These sections are contained within Pt Ⅱ of the Evidence Act. Section 2(1) of the Evidence Act mandates that Pt Ⅱ applies to all judicial proceedings in the courts, but it does not apply to proceedings before an arbitrator:

> **2.** —(1) Parts Ⅰ, Ⅱ and Ⅲ shall apply to all judicial proceedings in or before any court, but not to affidavits presented to any court or officer nor to proceedings before an arbitrator.

77 *BQP* was a case where the High Court did make reference to the parties' pre-contractual negotiations for the purposes of interpreting a clause in the agreement. But in that case, neither party objected to the admissibility of the evidence. Even more crucially, the evidence had already been admitted before the tribunal: *BQP* at [42], [43], [45] and [98]. Thus, by the time the High Court heard the jurisdictional challenge, the evidence had already formed part of the record of the proceedings before the tribunal. The High Court itself did not have to consider the question of admissibility of the evidence.

78 In our case, however, Mr Kim's evidence was only proffered in the jurisdictional challenge in the High Court. It was not evidence placed before the tribunal. This, in our view, makes all the difference. The hearing of the jurisdictional challenge in the High Court simply did not fall within the province of "proceedings before an arbitrator", for which s 2(1) of the Evidence Act provides that the exclusionary rule does not apply. The High Court, unlike an arbitrator, was bound by s 2(1) read with ss 94 to 99 of the Evidence Act to

apply the parol evidence rule and its exceptions. Further, the High Court heard the jurisdictional challenge *de novo*: see *BCY* ([23] *supra*) at [36] and *BXY and others v. BXX and others* [2019] 4 SLR 413 at [18]. Thus, no deference was due to the arbitral tribunal that would have required some attenuation of the rules of evidence so as to align the High Court's review proceedings with the first instance proceedings before the tribunal.

79 The point we have just made also disposes of the respondents' arguments that the parties had effectively contracted out of the exclusionary rule, by incorporating the SIAC Rules and agreeing that the tribunal would be guided by the International Bar Association Rules on the Taking of Evidence in International Arbitration 2010. While that argument might have some force if it were made in relation to the admissibility of evidence before the tribunal, the High Court was bound, as are we, to give effect to the parol evidence rule and its exceptions in the Evidence Act.

80 The respondents are therefore wrong to contend that *BQP* is authority for the proposition that the parol evidence rule does not apply at all in cases that arise out of an arbitration. *BQP* is, if anything, only authority for the far more limited proposition that the High Court can consider evidence of pre-contractual negotiations that have already been admitted by the arbitral tribunal.

81 The question that follows is whether the High Court, applying the law relating to the admissibility of evidence of pre-contractual negotiations as it presently stands, should have admitted Mr Kim's evidence. Our law does not mandate a *blanket* prohibition against the admissibility of pre-contractual negotiations, as our decision in *Zurich Insurance (Singapore) Pte Ltd v. B-Gold Interior Design & Construction Pte Ltd* [2008] 3 SLR(R) 1029 ("*Zurich Insurance*") makes clear at [132(d)]. But this does *not* mean that such evidence is freely to be admitted as a general rule either. Instead, the issue

as to whether evidence of pre-contractual negotiations should generally be freely admissible remains open: see *Sembcorp Marine Ltd v. PPL Holdings Pte Ltd and another and another appeal* [2013] 4 SLR 193 ("*Sembcorp Marine*") at [75] and *Xia Zhengyan v. Geng Changqing* [2015] 3 SLR 732 ("*Xia Zhengyan*") at [62]. For the time being, we have cautioned in *Sembcorp Marine* at [75] that any attempt to rely on such evidence should be made with full consciousness of the concerns we expressed and the pleading requirements we prescribed in that judgment, which requirements accord with the limits set down in *Zurich Insurance* at [132(d)] that extrinsic evidence will only be admitted if it is "relevant, reasonably available to all the contracting parties, and relates to a clear or obvious context".

82 We consider that this is not the appropriate occasion to grapple with the complex and difficult question whether evidence of pre-contractual negotiations should generally be freely admissible. The parties did not make arguments to that effect and the respondents, in particular, were content in oral argument before us to proceed on the basis that the criteria set out in *Zurich Insurance* had to be, and were, satisfied.

83 In our judgment, Mr Kim's evidence was neither reasonably available to all the contracting parties nor did it relate to a clear and obvious context. In *Xia Zhengyan* at [65], we cautioned that draft agreements would rarely establish the clear and obvious context necessary for the evidence of pre-contractual negotiations to be admitted:

> ... In most circumstances, the reliance on draft agreements, without more, cannot amount to a clear and obvious context in so far as the court is very much left in the dark with regard to the actual bargaining process undertaken by the contracting parties in the course of

negotiations. The addition, removal, or variation of any contractual term is, more often than not, the result of bargains and exchanges struck between the parties. It is a dynamic process and the surrounding context is likely to be as important as, if not more so than, the actual words found in the draft agreements. Furthermore, the court is not likely to be acquainted with such evidence as these bargains and exchanges are often oral in nature. Therefore, any reliance on these draft agreements alone, without more, may give rise to the risk of construing these documents *out* of context. [emphasis in original]

84 The situation we are faced with here fits the description set out in *Xia Zhengyan*: a "clear and obvious context" is absent. The respondents seek to admit earlier drafts of the Takeout Agreement and the e-mail correspondence enclosing those drafts, but, as Mr Kim himself attests, some of the negotiations took place in person, so the discussions at those meetings that led to the draft agreements being amended is not before the court. Indeed, our perusal of the e-mail correspondence enclosing the drafts shows that it was generally brief and succinct, which suggests that the bulk of the negotiations did not take place in the written correspondence. The drafts and the e-mail correspondence therefore do not give us the full picture of the parties' positions, concessions, bargains and compromises in the course of the negotiations.

85 In addition, we find it difficult to see how admitting Mr Kim's affidavit evidence attesting to his recollection of the negotiations would assist the respondents. The purpose of admitting this evidence is to show that Shanghai was *not* intended by the parties to be the seat, and the evidence purportedly establishes this by showing that the parties wanted to have a neutral forum in

which to arbitrate their dispute. But Mr Kim's own affidavit evidence undermines that argument entirely, because he quite candidly admits that "[he] did not understand the concept of the seat of the arbitration" at the time he was negotiating the Takeout Agreement on behalf of the respondents. Mr Ong appreciated the weakness of that admission to his case, and emphasised that although Mr Kim did not understand the *legal* significance of the seat, it was nevertheless his evidence that it was the parties' common understanding and agreement that they required a neutral forum like Singapore, which was, in substance and effect, "not much different" from the concept of an independent arbitral seat.

86 We find this submission untenable. Quite apart from this being only Mr Kim's subjective appreciation of the negotiations and of the significance of the reference to "Shanghai", the desire for neutrality could be, and was, fulfilled when the parties selected what they perceived to be a neutral arbitral institution, the SIAC, and made express provision for it in Art 14. 2. The desire for neutrality did not have to manifest itself *only* in the choice of a neutral seat. Further, if Mr Kim was perceptive enough to understand the *substance* of the choice of seat—amongst other things, that it would engage the supervisory jurisdiction of that territory's courts and result in the award being made in that territory for the purposes of enforcement under the New York Convention—we find it difficult to accept that the significance of the words "arbitration in Shanghai" in indicating the seat of the arbitration was lost on him. With the knowledge he is suggested to have possessed, we find it striking that he failed to ask that it be specified that Shanghai was merely the *venue* of the arbitration, or that he could have justifiably considered that adequate provision had been made for Singapore to be the seat by the simple reference to the SIAC alone, when the SIAC is only an arbitral institution, and not a legal jurisdiction of

itself. In addition, nothing in the evidence shows that the parties intended Shanghai to be only the *physical venue* of the arbitration and not its *legal seat*.

87 Mr Kim's evidence to the effect that the words "in Shanghai" were inadvertently left in Art 14. 2, when they were excised from the equivalent clauses in the other three agreements, is similarly unpersuasive. It is only Mr Kim's subjective view that the words "in Shanghai" were inadvertently left in. And if it truly were a mistake, then, as we pointed out at the hearing, the respondents should have applied for rectification of the Takeout Agreement, which they have not done.

88 In short, Mr Kim's evidence of the pre-contractual negotiations do not satisfy the *Zurich Insurance* criteria for the admissibility of extrinsic evidence. It is therefore unnecessary for us to go further to consider whether the Judge was correct in finding that the entire agreement clause would have operated to exclude Mr Kim's evidence in any event.

The effects of PRC law on the arbitration agreement

89 The other indicium which Mr Ong argued indicated that Shanghai was not the seat was the invalidating effect PRC law would have had on the arbitration agreement, based on the state of PRC law as existed at the time the parties entered into the Takeout Agreement. It was said that because the parties could not have chosen to invalidate their arbitration agreement at the same time as they expressed a manifest intention to arbitrate, Shanghai therefore *cannot* be the seat. If it was, there would be nothing to displace PRC law as the proper law of the arbitration agreement, which would lead in turn to the absurd result of the arbitration agreement being invalidated. Mr Ong therefore urged us to consider the PRC law position as part of the contextual interpretation of Art 14. 2 and the Takeout Agreement more generally.

90 We disagree that the state of PRC law can be taken into account in the way that Mr Ong suggests. For the respondents to advance this argument they would have to show that the parties were, at the very least, *aware* that the choice of proper law of the arbitration agreement could have an impact upon the validity of the arbitration agreement. But there is nothing in the evidence to show that the parties were sensitive to the interplay between PRC law and choosing the SIAC as the administering institution, much less the invalidating effect of this particular combination of choices. Instead, the evidence suggests that this consideration did not operate in their minds at all. It therefore cannot form part of the context in construing Art 14. 2.

The relevance of Shanghai not being a law district

91 Our analysis above addresses the two main planks of Mr Ong's arguments before us. We turn then to deal briefly with the Judge's reasoning that "arbitration in Shanghai" is more naturally read as a reference to Shanghai as the venue, given that Shanghai is not itself a law district, whereas Singapore is a law district: GD ([22] *supra*) at [110]. Mr Ong adopted this point in his written case.

92 We think this argument does not assist Mr Ong. This was not an argument raised or addressed by either party in their written submissions below, nor was it relied upon by the tribunal. More importantly, it seems to us that commercial parties often do only specify either the city or country in their arbitration agreements. The authorities we have canvassed above at [66]-[67] reflect this practice. Similarly, the earlier or even current model clauses ("Model Clauses") of some arbitral institutions and associations suggest it is sufficient for parties to refer to the "City and/*or* Country", for example, the London Court of International Arbitration Recommended Clauses: "The seat, or legal place, of arbitration shall be [City and/or Country]."

93 We recognise that it is probably best practice to specify both the city *and* the country, as most Model Clauses now do, including the present edition of the SIAC Model Clause. Certainly doing so will help to avoid arguments being raised about where precisely the seat is. But the omission to do so will not render a clear reference to a seat, as here, a reference to a venue instead.

Summary on the seat of the arbitration

94 The sum result of the above analysis is that Shanghai is the seat. The natural reading of the phrase "arbitration in Shanghai" is that Shanghai is the seat of the arbitration, and there are no contrary indicia to point away from this natural reading. This in turn means that the law of the seat and the parties' implied choice of proper law of the arbitration agreement are one and the same: PRC law. It follows that PRC law is the proper law of the arbitration agreement. Hence the question whether the implied choice of PRC law as the proper law should be displaced by the law of the seat in order not to nullify the parties' intention to arbitrate simply does not arise. There is also no need to go into the third stage of the *BCY* framework.

95 In addition, it is apparent from the analysis above that it becomes unnecessary to deal with some of the points considered by the Judge—specifically the validation principle and the effective interpretation principle. These issues would only have arisen for consideration if there was some *other* law that could compete with PRC law to be the proper law of the arbitration agreement. But there is no such other law. Moreover, it is also unnecessary for us to express a view on the doctrine of separability and whether it applies even where the validity of the main or substantive contract is not impugned. Here, on the *BCY* analysis, all the factors point to PRC law as the proper law of the arbitration agreement.

Issue 3: The court's orders in the appeal

96 The analysis on the *BCY* framework shows that Shanghai, and not Singapore, is the seat. We therefore allowed the appeal when parties were before us on 15 October 2019, but only to the extent that Singapore was not the seat. We expressly indicated in our oral grounds given at that time that we did not take any concluded view as to whether the tribunal did or did not have jurisdiction.

97 The limited scope of our decision might seem somewhat surprising given that the appeal arose out of a jurisdictional challenge mounted under s 10 of the IAA. On one view, it might be contended that a jurisdictional challenge ought naturally to culminate in a decision on the tribunal either having or not having jurisdiction. That view, however, would be incorrect. In our judgment, it was only proper and logical that we express no view as to jurisdiction once we had determined that Singapore was not the seat. If Singapore was not the seat, any decision of the Singapore courts on jurisdiction would not be binding upon the tribunal anyway. The Singapore courts would simply have no supervisory jurisdiction over the arbitration.

98 We add that the making of this declaration was by no means inconsistent with the structure of s 10 of the IAA. Section 10 of the IAA does not mandate that the court make a positive finding as to jurisdiction either way: ss 10(6) and 10(7) only set out the powers of the court to make certain consequential orders if it does find that the tribunal has or does not have jurisdiction. Further, it was appropriate to make this declaration despite it not having been specifically sought by the appellant because the issue of the seat was placed before the Singapore courts by the very nature of the s 10 IAA application itself. It was necessary first to determine the seat in order to determine whether the law of the seat might be available to displace the law of the main contract, which law, it

was said, might invalidate the arbitration agreement. Thus, the declaration that Singapore is not the seat was a necessary part of, and a sufficient ruling in, the jurisdictional inquiry triggered by the s 10 IAA application.

99 We further observe that it was particularly appropriate in *this* case that the question of jurisdiction, which we consider ought to be determined under PRC law as the proper law of the arbitration agreement, be given to the PRC courts to decide. This was because the parties were not agreed as to what PRC law truly provides, and whether PRC law will truly have an invalidating effect on the arbitration agreement. The Judge perceived the PRC law position to be "fraught with difficulty and rapidly evolving": GD ([22] *supra*) at [116]. And the parties' positions in the appeal were similarly not any clearer than below. This was therefore a question best left to the relevant PRC court having supervisory jurisdiction over the arbitration to decide.

100 We should add, however, that this does not mean that the jurisdictional challenge was not properly brought in the High Court. It might seem surprising that the appellant, having taken the position that Shanghai was the seat, did not pursue its jurisdictional challenge before the PRC courts as the courts of the alleged seat, instead of coming to the Singapore High Court. But we think that the appellant was entirely justified in mounting its s 10 IAA challenge here.

101 It is significant to bear in mind that the appellant's application was filed in the Singapore High Court because the majority of the tribunal had decided that Singapore was the seat. It was therefore entirely correct for the appellant to seek relief from the seat court, *ie*, the Singapore High Court, as determined by the majority of the tribunal. Besides, the parties *disagreed* about the location of the seat and whether there was even a valid arbitration agreement to begin with. That being the case, the Singapore High Court had as good a claim as the Shanghai courts to hear the jurisdictional challenge. In our view, it was

unnecessary or even unworkable that the court hearing the jurisdictional challenge be the court of the seat in a situation such as the present case where the location of the seat was *precisely* the subject of the jurisdictional challenge. To require that the court hearing the jurisdictional challenge be the court of the seat would create an unsolvable contradiction: the court which should hear the challenge ought to be the court of the seat chosen by the parties, but the court hearing the challenge would have to decide what was the seat and, by extension, whether it was the seat court.

102 It is now for the parties to decide what further actions they wish to take. The majority of the tribunal had determined that it had jurisdiction, but that determination was made on the erroneous premise that Singapore was the seat and Singapore law as the proper law would have kept the arbitration agreement alive. That conclusion might no longer stand now that Shanghai is determined to be the seat, and PRC law is the proper law of the arbitration agreement. It might be that the appellant is content to have the arbitration administered by the SIAC, but under the supervision of the PRC courts, if that can be done at all under PRC law. Equally, the appellant might still adhere to its original position that the arbitration agreement is invalid and the dispute must be litigated in the PRC courts. That is for the appellant to decide, and for the respondents to make the necessary responses as they so desire.

Conclusion

103 For the reasons given above, we determined that Shanghai is the seat of the arbitration, and not Singapore. We therefore allowed the appeal to that limited extent, without expressing any concluded view as to whether the tribunal did or did not have jurisdiction.

104 The essential point we make is that the parties' manifest intention to

arbitrate is not to be given effect at all costs. The parties did not only choose to arbitrate—they chose to arbitrate in a certain way, in a certain place, under the administration of a certain arbitral institution. Those all have to be given effect to by a process of construction which critically gives the words of the arbitration agreement their natural meaning, unless there are sufficient contrary indicia to displace that reading. If the result of this process of construction is that the arbitration agreement is unworkable, then the parties must live with the consequences of their decision.

Reported by Tan Jia Qi, Rachel and Victor Yao Lida.

捷安特轻合金科技(昆山)有限公司
v.
雅柯斯(远东)私人有限公司

——有关承认与执行外国判决的普通法规则以及新加坡法院承认与执行符合相关规定的中国法院判决

高等法庭——2012 诉讼第 105 号

法官翁安德烈

2013 年 7 月 23 日、25 日、26 日、31 日;2013 年 8 月 6 日、7 日;2014 年 1 月 28 日

【简要案情】

2010 年 12 月 16 日,捷安特轻合金科技(昆山)有限公司(以下称“原告”)在中华人民共和国江苏省苏州市中级人民法院(以下称“中国法院”)取得判雅柯斯(远东)私人有限公司(以下称“被告”)败诉的判决(以下称“中国判决”)。原告之后寻求在新加坡对被告执行中国判决,索讨各笔款项。双方于 2003 年签订合同,原告向被告购买两台发电机组,并支付 19 万美元。由于所交付的发电机组货不对板,原告因此于 2005 年 7 月 25 日在中国法院对被告提起民事诉讼(以下称“2005 年诉讼程序”)。被告就申索提交抗辩书,也派代理人出席法庭审讯。后来,2005 年诉讼程序于 2007 年 9 月 10 日中止,以便双方进行和解谈判。庭外谈判失败,原告于 2008 年 5 月 9 日在中国法院就同一申索重新展开诉讼程序(以下称“2008 年诉讼程序”)。被告未在该诉讼中应诉,因此被判败诉(即中国判决)。中国判决内容包括:

(1) 撤销合同;(2) 原告将发电机组返还给被告;(3) 被告退还原告19万美元货款;(4) 被告赔偿原告交货时将发电机组从码头搬运到原告工厂的7088元人民币运输费。虽然原告愿意随时让被告领取发电机组,但是被告并没有这样做。被告亦没有给付中国判决所判定的款项。因此,原告于2012年2月10日在新加坡展开本诉讼,索讨包括中国判决判定的19万美元和7088元人民币,已由原告支付的被告应支付的中国法院费用,以及利息和诉讼费。

【裁判要旨】

裁定,准予申索:

(1) 一方是否自愿接受外国法院管辖的问题,应根据新加坡国际私法规则来解决。然而,就国际司法管辖权而言,法官决定一方是否愿受某法院管辖时,也会考虑作出外国判决的法院的国内法,以了解各方在外国诉讼程序中所采取的措施的意义:见[25]和[26]。

(2) 就国际管辖权而言,被告在2005年诉讼程序中应诉时便已接受了中国法院的管辖:见[27]。

(3) 中国法院对2008年诉讼程序行使管辖权的依据并非是被告已根据中国国内法接受中国法院的管辖。尽管如此,中国法院根据其法律对2008年诉讼程序妥当地行使管辖权,因此被告的接受已没有必要:见[31]—[36]。

(4) 被告在2005年诉讼程序中提交抗辩书就已明确同意了接受中国法院管辖,而且可能由此认定后续诉讼程序(即2008年诉讼程序)也有该同意:见[42]和[43]。

(5) 因此,可归因于先前诉讼程序已同意接受法院管辖,换言之,当后续诉讼程序关乎同一标的物或与原诉讼程序相关时,即可说已初步接受法院管辖。至于后续诉讼程序是否关乎同一标的物或与原诉讼程序是否相关,则是一个视情况而定的程度问题:见[49]。

(6) 法官在作出决定时会考虑对双方是否公平,也希望避开在外国和诉讼地法律下因程序规则所造成的技术障碍:见[49]。

(7) 本案中,法官须就被告已初步接受2008年诉讼程序的法院管辖作出裁定,推定被告已同意接受法院管辖对被告并无不公平,但如果允许被告利用失败的庭外谈判来逃避其应承担的过错责任,则将对原告不公平:见[50]和[51]。

(8)鉴于上述推定同意或初步接受法院管辖,依据新加坡国际私法,被告在2008年诉讼程序中确实已接受了中国法院的管辖,因此,就承认和执行判决而言,中国判决是由具有国际管辖权的法庭作出的判决:见[52]。

(9) 在外国判决有权得到承认的情况下,执行该外国判决应采取的普通法诉讼行为,是将外国判决中的判定款项当作债务提起诉讼:见[62]。

(10)外国判决所依据的法律将决定外国判决中义务的性质:见[66]。

(11) 在中国判决下,原告返还发电机组给被告的义务仅意味着原告必须在其场所提供发电机组让被告领取:见[68]和[69]。

(12) 原告已经做了中国判决所规定的所有事项,在新加坡执行该判决中,被告须给付中国判决所判定的欠款,这一义务构成债务的根据:见[70]和[71]。

(13)尽管中国判决包含其他与确定数额金钱无关的义务,原告依然可以提出申索:见[74]—[76]。

【专家点评】*

一、案情

原告(一家在中国注册成立的公司)与被告(一家在新加坡注册成立的公司)签订合同,购买由一家英国公司制造的两台新发电机组。原告收到这两台发电机组后发现,它们既不是新的,也不是英国制造的,而且无法使用。原告于2005年在中国江苏省苏州市中级人民法院(以下称“中国法院”)对被告提起诉讼。双方尝试庭外和解,诉讼程序因而中止。和解失败后,原告

* 本评注撰写人:张瑞岑(Adeline Chong),新加坡管理大学法学院副教授。

于2008年在中国法院重新对被告提起同一诉讼程序。诉讼文件在被告的新加坡注册办事处送达被告,但被告没有参与2008年诉讼程序。中国法院最终判被告败诉,并判定:(1)撤销双方之间的合同;(2)原告将两台发电机组返还给被告;(3)被告退还原告购货款;(4)被告赔偿原告违约所造成的损失。被告没有对此判决提出上诉。

尽管原告愿意随时让被告取回发电机组,但被告并没有这样做,也没有支付判定款项。原告于是在新加坡提起诉讼,要求执行中国判决,而是否承认与执行中国判决则是根据新加坡的普通法规则来判断的。①根据这些规则,针对个人的外国判决如符合以下标准,有权获得承认与执行:(1)判决是有关债务或确定数额金钱的,且不涉及应付税款、罚款或其他罚金;(2)判决是终局性的;(3)外国法院对被告有国际管辖权;(4)不能针对承认与执行提出抗辩理由。捷安特轻合金一案的判决执行程序得以成功有赖于上述第一项和第三项标准。

二、中国法院对被告是否有国际司法管辖权

根据新加坡法律,外国法院是否有国际司法管辖权是依据新加坡的法律冲突规则进行评估的。新加坡法律还规定,如果被告在诉讼展开时身在或居住在外国法院的司法管辖区内,或被告愿意接受外国法院管辖,外国法院就有国际司法管辖权。

没有任何事实情况显示被告在关键时候身在或居住在中国。不过,被告曾在2005年诉讼程序中就案件的是非曲直提交了抗辩书,这显然相当于被告在这起诉讼程序中接受了中国法院的管辖。但是,2005年诉讼程序被中止,所以系争点在于,被告在2005年诉讼程序中接受了管辖是否就意味着被告在2008年诉讼程序中,即使没有参与诉讼程序,也同样接受了管辖。

接受管辖是指一方当事人“在诉讼程序中采取了措施,必须涉及放弃对

---

① 承认和执行外国判决的其他机制是法定的,即 the Reciprocal Enforcement of Commonwealth Judgments Act (Cap 264, Rev Ed 1985; repealed by Act No. 24 of 2019 with effect from a date to be determined by the government); the Reciprocal Enforcement of Foreign Judgments Act (Cap 265, Rev Ed 2001); and Part 3 of the Choice of Court Agreements Act 2016 (Cap 39A)。

外国法院管辖提出异议”。[①] 2005 年和 2008 年的诉讼程序是独立的诉讼程序,有着不同的案件编号。不过,翁法官指出,这两起诉讼程序都涉及相同的申索和相同的当事人。[②]法官参考了英国的案例,[③]这些案例承认了推定接受管辖或初步接受管辖的概念,即一方当事人就特定申索同意接受外国法院的管辖,此时就可认定其涉及同一标的物或与原申索有关的进一步申索也同意接受外国法院的管辖。

法院在评估是否可以认定“同意”时应关注是否对双方公平。[④] 法官认为,由于“技术性”问题,2005 年和 2008 年的诉讼程序是独立的诉讼程序。[⑤] 正如法官所指出的,如果先前的诉讼程序是被中止而不是被撤销,便能清楚得出被告接受中国法院的管辖。[⑥] 进一步说,认定被告同意并非不公平;反之,如果让被告利用庭外谈判失败而使中国判决不能执行,则对原告不公平。[⑦] 因此,法官裁定被告在 2008 年诉讼程序中接受了中国法院的管辖,从而赋予了中国法院国际管辖权。

三、中国的判决是否因为不是纯粹的金钱判决而被禁止执行

普通法以义务原则为承认与执行外国判决的基础。[⑧]外国判决只要符合某些特定规定,被告就有义务服从外国判决。这一义务是根据当地法律产生的,因此原告必须以外国判决作为申索依据,向当地法院提起初始诉讼。因此,翁法官认为,称其为执行外国判决是“不当的”,因为根据普通法规则,在新加坡执行的任何判决都是新加坡法院作出的判决。[⑨] 法官提到,执

---

① *WSG Nimbus Pte Ltd v. Board of Control for Cricket in Sri Lanka* [2002] 1 SLR(R) 1088 at [54].

② [2014] 2 SLR 545 at [42].

③ Namely, *Murthy v. Sivajothi* [1999] 1 WLR 467; *Lawrence Robert Whyte v. Marsha Whyte* [2005] EWCA Civ 858; *Joint Stock Company "Aeroflot-Russian Airlines" v. Boris Abramovich Berezovsky* [2012] EWHC 3017 (Ch).

④ [2014] 2 SLR 545 at [49].

⑤ Id, at [50].

⑥ Ibid.

⑦ Id, at [51].

⑧ *Godard v. Grey* (1870) LR 6 QB 139, 149-150; *Schibsby v. Westenholz* (1870) LR 6 QB 155, 159; *Adams v Cape Industries plc* [1990] Ch 433, 513; *Owens Bank Ltd v. Bracco* [1992] 2 AC 443, 484.

⑨ [2014] 2 SLR 545 at [60].

行外国判决的正当性历史根源是简约诉讼(action *in assumpsit*),而这种诉讼是为了追讨简单合同下确定数额的金钱,所以原告要求执行非金钱的外国判决必然遭到阻止。①

这一案件的问题是,中国判决包含了金钱和非金钱的判令。关于这一点,被告辩称没有义务支付金钱款项,因为发电机组仍在原告手中,这使得双方有必要确定在中国判决下须承担的义务的性质。法官在审理时认为,应适用中国法来确定这一问题。② 中国判决并没有详细说明必须在何处将发电机组返还给被告。然而,中国判决裁定被告须赔偿原告将发电机组运送到其场所安装的费用及由此产生的相关损失。综上所述,翁法官对中国判决的解释是,原告的义务仅是在其场所提供发电机组让被告取回,迫使原告先垫付返还发电机组的费用,然后再向中国法院提出进一步申索是不公平的。③既然原告已履行了其在判决中的义务,发电机组没在被告手上与被告是否有义务支付应付金钱款项是无关的。④

另一个问题是,原告的申索是否因为中国判决包含了非金钱义务就理应败诉。关于这一点,翁法官指出,即使外国法院没有根据案件的是非曲直判给原告一笔固定数额的金钱作为补偿,原告也可提出简约诉讼要求判令被告支付诉讼费。⑤因此,“如果外国法院的判令包括支付一笔确定数额金钱(除了诉讼费外)的判令,那么该支付确定数额金钱的判令应该能够作为债务诉讼的根据”。⑥ 法官的结论是,中国判决的金钱部分能够作为在新加坡法院提起债务诉讼的根据。

四、讨论

捷安特轻合金一案说明了普通法规则在承认与执行外国判决方面的运

① [2014] 2 SLR 545 at [62]-[63].
② Id, at [66].
③ Id, at [69].
④ Id, at [71].
⑤ Id, at [74].
⑥ Id, at [75].

作,特别是规定外国法院必须对被告有国际管辖权,以及外国判决必须是针对固定数额的金钱。前者是大多数法律体系,无论是普通法系还是大陆(民法)法系的共同标准。事实上,关于承认与执行外国法院的判决,中国也规定外国法院须有国际管辖权。①虽然各国对于赋予外国法院国际管辖权的标准可能有些许不同,但一般都赞同接受外国法院管辖是国际管辖权的根据。② 捷安特轻合金一案具有重要意义,不仅划定了接受管辖概念的范围,也让法院接受了"推定接受管辖"的概念。此外,法院强调必须考虑是否对双方都公平,这应该可以缓解对任何可能的不合理归责的担忧。

法院对于承认和执行的外国法院判决必须是有关金钱标的物的立场反映了传统普通法的立场。话虽如此,一些普通法国家现已接受非金钱的外国判决原则上是可执行的。③新加坡的《外国判决相互执行法》④最近也作出了修订以反映这一现代立场。⑤

然而,捷安特轻合金一案的意义并不限于此。中国和新加坡之间没有关于外国判决的双边条约。在这种情况下,中国关于承认和执行外国法院判决的法律规定必须证明中国法院和被诉求执行判决的法院之间有事实互惠关系。⑥ 这意味着必须证明后者之前曾执行中国法院的判决。这不同于新加坡关于承认和执行外国法院判决的普通法规则,新加坡没有要求证明互惠关系。捷安特轻合金一案中,江苏省苏州市中级人民法院的判决在新加坡高等法庭获得执行。江苏省南京市中级人民法院后来在"高尔集团股

① Yujun Guo, "China" in A Chong (ed) *Recognition and Enforcement of Foreign Judgments in Asia* (ABLI, 2017) at [18]-[19].

② See, eg, Convention of 2 July 2019 on the Recognition and Enforcement of Foreign Judgments in Civil or Commercial Matters, Art 5(1)(e) and (f).

③ *Pro Swing Inc v. Elta Golf Inc* [2006] 2 SCR 612 (Supreme Court of Canada); *Miller v. Gianne* [2007] CILR 18 (Grand Court, Cayman Islands); and *Brunei and Bandone v. Fidelis* [2008] JRC 152 (Royal Court, Jersey).

④ Cap 265A, Rev Ed 2001.

⑤ See, in particular, REFJA s 4(3A).

⑥ Yujun Guo, *supra* n 17, at [11].

份有限公司对江苏省纺织工业(集团)进出口有限公司”①一案中援引捷安特轻合金一案,作为中国和新加坡法院之间存有互惠关系的证据,南京市中级人民法院因此基于互惠原则执行了新加坡高等法庭的判决,这标志着中国法院首次承认与执行新加坡的判决。此后,中国与新加坡两国首席大法官于2018年8月31日签署了《关于承认与执行商事案件金钱判决的指导备忘录》,②进一步确认中国与新加坡法院之间建立互惠关系。2019年8月2日,第二份新加坡判决也在浙江省温州市中级人民法院获得了承认。③

五、总结

捷安特轻合金一案的裁决意义重大,尤其是在确立中国和新加坡法院之间的互惠关系方面。由于两国没有签订有关承认和执行外国法院判决的双边条约,确立中国和新加坡法院之间的互惠关系是重要的,这为外国判决在中国法院的执行消除了一大阻碍。鉴于“一带一路”倡议下各方面持续迅速发展,消除承认和执行新加坡判决所面对的这一障碍因而变得更为重要。新加坡最高法院(包括新加坡国际商事法庭)以及在深圳和西安设立了两个中国国际商事法庭的中国最高人民法院,凭借着在国际商业纠纷方面的专业知识,有望在审理涉“一带一路”纠纷案件方面占据优势。捷安特轻合金一案为中国和新加坡法院之间的互惠关系奠定了基础,自此诉讼当事人无论选择在新加坡还是在中国提起诉讼,都有理由相信所获得的判决在另一个国家同样可以得到执行。④

---

① (2016) Su 01 Xie Wai Ren No. 3.

② Memorandum of Guidance between the Supreme People' s Court of the People' s Republic of China and the Supreme Court of Singapore on Recognition and Enforcement of Money Judgments in Commercial Cases <https: //www. sicc. gov. sg/docs/default - source/guide - to - the - sicc/spc - mog - english - version—signed. pdf> (accessed 29 June 2020).

③ *Oceanside Development Group Ltd v. Chen Tongkao & Chen Xiudan* (2017) Zhe 03 Xie Wai Ren No. 7.

④ 当然,前提是判决须符合该国法院的法律下有关承认与执行的(其他)规定。

Giant Light Metal Technology (Kunshan) Co Ltd

v.

Aksa Far East Pte Ltd

—Common Law Rules on the Recognition and Enforcement of Foreign Judgments, and that a Singapore Court Will Recognise and Enforce Judgments of a Chinese Court If the Relevant Requirements are Satisfied

High Court — Suit No 105 of 2012

Andrew Ang J

23, 25, 26, 31 July; 6, 7 August 2013; 28 January 2014

Facts

On 16 December 2010, Giant Light Metal Technology (Kunshan) Co Ltd ("the Plaintiff") obtained judgment against Aksa Far East Pte Ltd ("the Defendant") in the Suzhou Intermediate Court, Jiangsu Province, in the People's Republic of China ("the PRC Court") for breach of contract ("the PRC Judgment"). The Plaintiff then sought to enforce against the Defendant in Singapore the PRC Judgment for the payment of various sums of moneys. In 2003, the parties had entered into a contract for the Plaintiff to purchase from the Defendant two generators sets ("the Contract"), for which the Plaintiff paid US $190, 000. The generator sets delivered were not what the Plaintiff bargained for, and it accordingly instituted civil proceedings against the

Defendant in the PRC Court on 25 July 2005 (“the 2005 Proceedings”). The Defendant filed a defence to this claim and also sent a representative to attend the court hearings. Subsequently, the 2005 Proceedings were discontinued on 10 September 2007 so that the parties could negotiate a settlement. The out-of-court negotiations failed, and on 9 May 2008 the Plaintiff re-commenced proceedings for the same claim against the Defendant in the PRC Court (“the 2008 Proceedings”). The Defendant did not enter an appearance in the later proceedings and judgment was entered against the Defendant as a result (*viz*, the PRC Judgment). The PRC Judgment ordered, *inter alia*, that: (a) the Contract be rescinded; (b) the Plaintiff return the generator sets to the Defendant; (c) the Defendant refund the price of US $ 190, 000 to the Plaintiff; and (d) the Defendant compensate the Plaintiff RMB7, 088 for transport costs paid for moving the generator sets from the dock to the Plaintiff's factory during delivery. The Defendant did not collect the generator sets although the Plaintiff was ready and willing for the Defendant to do so. Neither did the Defendant pay the judgment sums ordered under the PRC Judgment. As a result, the Plaintiff on 10 February 2012 commenced the present action in Singapore, claiming, *inter alia*, the sums of US $ 190, 000 and RMB 7, 088 as ordered under the PRC Judgment, and the Defendant's share of the PRC Court fees which had been paid by the Plaintiff, interest and costs.

Holding

Held, allowing the claim:

(1) Whether a party had voluntarily submitted to the foreign court's jurisdiction was a question for Singapore private international law rules. However, the court in deciding whether there was submission for the purposes of international jurisdiction will also take into consideration the domestic law of

the court from which the foreign judgment originated in order to appreciate the significance of the steps taken by the parties in the foreign proceedings: at [25] and [26].

(2) The Defendant by entering a defence in the 2005 Proceedings had submitted to the jurisdiction of the PRC Court for the purposes of international jurisdiction: at [27].

(3) The basis upon which the PRC Court took jurisdiction over the 2008 Proceedings was not submission by the Defendant to the jurisdiction of the PRC Court under PRC domestic law. Nonetheless, the PRC Court had properly taken jurisdiction over the 2008 Proceedings under its own laws such that submission was unnecessary: at [31] to [36].

(4) The Defendant by filing its defence to the 2005 Proceedings had unequivocally consented to the jurisdiction of the PRC Court, and it was possible to impute that consent to the subsequent proceedings (*viz*, the 2008 Proceedings): at [42] and [43].

(5) Consent to the jurisdiction of the court in earlier proceedings could be imputed or, in other words, inchoate submission could be said to arise where the subsequent proceedings concerned the same subject matter or were related to the original proceedings. Whether subsequent proceedings concerned the same subject matter or were related to the original proceedings was a matter of degree based on the circumstances: at [49].

(6) The courts in making such a decision would be informed by concerns of fairness to both parties, and also a desire to disregard technical impediments created by procedural rules under both foreign and forum law: at [49].

(7) The present case was one that warranted a finding of inchoate submission by the Defendant to the 2008 Proceedings. There was no unfairness to the Defendant in imputing such consent, but there would be unfairness to the Plaintiff were the Defendant allowed to take advantage of abortive out-of-court

negotiations to escape liability for its wrongdoing: at [50] and [51].

(8) By reason of such imputed consent or inchoate submission, the Defendant had submitted to the jurisdiction of the PRC Court in the 2008 Proceedings under Singapore private international law and, accordingly, the PRC Judgment was a judgment of a court that had international jurisdiction for the purposes of recognition and enforcement: at [52].

(9) The common law action to enforce a foreign judgment where that judgment was entitled to recognition was to commence proceedings claiming the judgment sum under the foreign judgment as a debt: at [62].

(10) The law from which the foreign judgment originated would determine the nature of the obligations owed under the foreign judgment: at [66].

(11) Under the PRC Judgment, the obligation for the Plaintiff to return the generator sets to the Defendant meant only that the Plaintiff was to make the generator sets available at its premises for collection by the Defendant: at [68] and [69].

(12) The Plaintiff had done all that was required of it under the PRC Judgment, and the Defendant's obligation to pay the Plaintiff the judgments sums owed under the PRC Judgment could found the claim in debt for the purposes of enforcement in Singapore: at [70] and [71].

(13) The Plaintiff's claim was not precluded because the PRC Judgment comprised other obligations which were not for a definite sum of money: at [74] to [76].

Commentary *

Facts

The plaintiff (a PRC incorporated company) entered into a contract with

* Author: Adeline Chong, Associate Professor, School of Law, Singapore Management University.

the defendant (a Singapore incorporated company) for the purchase of two new generator sets which were to be manufactured by a company in England. Upon receipt of the generator sets, the plaintiff discovered that they were neither new nor manufactured in England, and were not useable. The plaintiff commenced proceedings against the defendant in the PRC in 2005 before the Suzhou Intermediate People's Court, Jiangsu Province ("PRC court"). These proceedings were abandoned when the parties attempted to reach an out-of-court settlement. After negotiations failed, the plaintiff re-commenced the same proceedings against the defendant in the PRC court in 2008. The defendant was served at its Singapore registered office address but did not take part in the 2008 proceedings. The PRC court ultimately handed down a judgment against the defendant ordering that: (i) the contract between the parties be rescinded; (ii) the plaintiff to return the two generator sets to the defendant; (iii) the defendant to refund the purchase price to the plaintiff; and (iv) the defendant to compensate the plaintiff for losses caused by the breach of contract. The defendant did not appeal this judgment.

Although the plaintiff was ready and willing for the defendant to collect the generator sets, the latter did not do so, nor did it pay the judgment sums. The plaintiff thereupon commenced proceedings in Singapore seeking the enforcement of the PRC judgment. The recognition and enforcement of the PRC judgment fell for consideration under Singapore's common law rules.[①] Under these rules, a foreign judgment *in personam* is entitled to recognition and enforcement if: (i) the judgment is for a debt, or definite sum of money, not

---

① The other regimes dealing with the recognition and enforcement of foreign judgments are statutory, i. e. the Reciprocal Enforcement of Commonwealth Judgments Act (Cap 264, Rev Ed 1985; repealed by Act No. 24 of 2019 with effect from a date to be determined by the government); the Reciprocal Enforcement of Foreign Judgments Act (Cap 265, Rev Ed 2001); and Part 3 of the Choice of Court Agreements Act 2016 (Cap 39A).

being a sum payable in respect of taxes, a fine or other penalty; (ii) the judgment is final and conclusive; (iii) the foreign court had international jurisdiction over the defendant; and (iv) no defences can be raised against recognition and enforcement. The success of the enforcement proceedings in *Giant Light Metal* turned on the first and third of these criteria.

Whether the PRC court had international jurisdiction over the defendant

Under Singapore law, whether the foreign court had international jurisdiction is assessed in accordance with Singapore conflict of law rules. This in turn provides that the foreign court had international jurisdiction if the defendant was either present or resident within the jurisdiction at the time proceedings were commenced or the defendant submitted to the jurisdiction of the foreign court.

Nothing on the facts indicated that the defendant was present or resident in the PRC at the material time. However, the defendant had filed a defence on the merits in relation to the 2005 proceedings. This clearly amounted to submission by the defendant to the PRC court's jurisdiction with respect to that set of proceedings. However, the 2005 proceedings were discontinued. The issue was whether the defendant's submission to the 2005 proceedings meant that the defendant had likewise submitted to the 2008 proceedings even though it did not take part in the latter proceedings.

Submission requires that a party "had taken a step in the proceedings which necessarily involved waiving their objection to the jurisdiction" of the foreign court.① The 2005 and 2008 proceedings were separate proceedings with different case numbers. However, Ang J observed that both proceedings involved the same claims and the same parties.② His Honour referred to English

---

① *WSG Nimbus Pte Ltd v. Board of Control for Cricket in Sri Lanka* [2002] 1 SLR(R) 1088 at [54].

② [2014] 2 SLR 545 at [42].

cases[①] where the concept of imputed submission or inchoate submission had been accepted, ie where a party's consent to the jurisdiction of a foreign court in relation to certain claims may be imputed to further claims either concerning the same subject matter or related to the original claim.

In assessing whether consent may be imputed, the court is guided by concerns of fairness to both parties. [②] His Honour held that the 2005 and 2008 proceedings were separate proceedings because of a "technicality". [③] As his Honour pointed out, if the earlier proceedings were stayed rather than withdrawn, it would have been clear that the defendant had accepted the jurisdiction of the PRC court. [④] Further, it was not unfair to impute consent to the defendant; conversely, it would be unfair to the plaintiff if the defendant was allowed to exploit the failed out-of-court negotiations to render the PRC judgment unenforceable. [⑤] Thus, his Honour held that the defendant had submitted to the jurisdiction of the PRC court in respect of the 2008 proceedings and this in turn conferred international jurisdiction to the PRC court.

Whether enforcement of the PRC judgment was prohibited as it was not a pure money judgment

The doctrine of obligations underlies the recognition and enforcement of foreign judgments at common law. [⑥] A foreign judgment, provided certain requirements are fulfilled, gives rise to an obligation on the part of the

---

① Namely, *Murthy v. Sivajothi* [1999] 1 WLR 467; *Lawrence Robert Whyte v. Marsha Whyte* [2005] EWCA Civ 858; *Joint Stock Company "Aeroflot-Russian Airlines" v. Boris Abramovich Berezovsky* [2012] EWHC 3017 (Ch).

② [2014] 2 SLR 545 at [49].

③ *Id*, at [50].

④ *Ibid*.

⑤ *Id*, at [51].

⑥ *Godard v. Grey* (1870) LR 6 QB 139, 149-150; *Schibsby v. Westenholz* (1870) LR 6 QB 155, 159; *Adams v. Cape Industries plc* [1990] Ch 433, 513; *Owens Bank Ltd v. Bracco* [1992] 2 AC 443, 484.

defendant to obey the foreign judgment. This obligation arises under local law, thus the plaintiff must bring original proceedings before the local court, with the foreign judgment forming the basis of its claim. Thus, Ang J recognised that it was a "misnomer" to refer to the enforcement of foreign judgments as any judgment enforced in Singapore under the common law rules is one which is given by the Singapore courts. ① His Honour referred to the historical origins of the proper action for the enforcement of a foreign judgment being an action in *assumpsit* which, being an action for recovery on a simple contract for a definite sum of money, necessarily prevented plaintiffs from pursuing the enforcement of non-money foreign judgments. ②

The problem in this particular case was that the PRC judgment comprised both money and non-money orders. On this point, the defendant argued that it was not obliged to pay the money sums because the generator sets were still with the plaintiff. This argument entailed ascertaining the nature of obligations owed by the parties under the PRC judgment. His Honour proceeded on the basis that PRC law would apply to determine this issue. ③ The PRC judgment did not detail where the generator sets were to be returned to the defendant. However, it had ordered the defendant to compensate the plaintiff for losses reflecting the costs incurred by the plaintiff in transporting the generator sets to its facility for installation. Taken together, Ang J interpreted the judgment to mean that the plaintiff was only obliged to make the sets available on its premises for collection by the defendant as it would not be fair to oblige the plaintiff to be out of pocket until it made a further claim before the PRC court for the costs of returning the generator sets. ④ Since the plaintiff had

① [2014] 2 SLR 545 at [60].
② *Id*, at [62]-[63].
③ *Id*, at [66].
④ *Id*, at [69].

complied with its part of the judgment, the fact that the defendant was not in possession of the sets was irrelevant to the question of whether the defendant was obliged to pay the money sums due. ①

The next issue was whether the plaintiff 's claim ought to fail because the PRC judgment included a non-money obligation. On this point, Ang J noted that an action in *assumpsit* for costs awarded against a defendant could be brought even where the foreign court did not award a fixed sum of money as a remedy on the merits of the case. ② Thus, "where a foreign court makes an order for payment of a definite sum of money (other than for costs) amongst other orders, the order for payment of a definite sum of money should be capable of founding an action in debt". ③ His Honour concluded that the monetary parts of the PRC judgment was capable of founding an action in debt before the Singapore court.

Discussion

Giant Light Metal illustrates the operation of the common law rules on the recognition and enforcement of foreign judgments, in particular, the requirement that the foreign court had international jurisdiction over the defendant and that foreign judgment must be for a fixed sum of money. The former requirement is a common denominator in most legal systems, whether of common law or civil law origin. Indeed, this requirement that the foreign court had international jurisdiction is also found under the PRC's rules on the recognition and enforcement of foreign judgments. ④ While the criteria on what would confer international jurisdiction on the foreign court may differ somewhat from country to country, submission to the foreign court's jurisdiction is

① *Id*, at [71].

② *Id*, at [74].

③ *Id*, at [75].

④ Yujun Guo, "China" in A Chong (ed) *Recognition and Enforcement of Foreign Judgments in Asia* (ABLI, 2017) at [18]-[19].

generally accepted to be one of the grounds of international jurisdiction. ① The importance of *Giant Light Metal* is in drawing out the scope of the concept of submission and the court's acceptance of the concept of "imputed submission". In addition, the court's emphasis that fairness to both parties must be considered ought to ease concerns about any potentially unwarranted imputation.

The court's position on the requirement of a money sum reflects the traditional common law position. That said, some common law countries now accept that non-money foreign judgments are in principle enforceable. ② Singapore's the Reciprocal Enforcement of Foreign Judgments Act③ was recently amended to reflect the modern position. ④

The significance of *Giant Light Metal*, however, extends beyond these points. There is no bilateral treaty between the PRC and Singapore on foreign judgments. Given this, PRC law on foreign judgments requires that *de facto* reciprocity be shown between the court in the PRC and the court whose judgment it is asked to enforce. ⑤ This means showing that the latter court had previously enforced a judgment of the court in the PRC. This is unlike the Singapore common law rules on foreign judgments which do not require reciprocity to be shown. In *Giant Light Metal*, a judgment of the Suzhou Intermediate People's Court, Jiangsu Province, was enforced by the Singapore High Court. *Giant Light Metal* was subsequently cited by the Nanjing Intermediate People's Court, Jiangsu Province in *Kolmar Group AG v. Jiangsu*

① See, eg, Convention of 2 July 2019 on the Recognition and Enforcement of Foreign Judgments in Civil or Commercial Matters, Art 5(1)(e) and (f).

② *Pro Swing Inc v. Elta Golf Inc* [2006] 2 SCR 612 (Supreme Court of Canada); *Miller v. Gianne* [2007] CILR 18 (Grand Court, Cayman Islands); and *Brunei and Bandone v. Fidelis* [2008] JRC 152 (Royal Court, Jersey).

③ Cap 265A, Rev Ed 2001.

④ See, in particular, Reciprocal Enforcement of Foreign Judgments Act s 4(3A).

⑤ Yujun Guo, *supra* n 17, at [11].

Textile Industry (Group) Import & Export Co Ltd[1] as evidence of reciprocity between the PRC and Singapore courts. The Nanjing Intermediate People's Court thereupon enforced a judgment of the Singapore High Court on the basis of the principle of reciprocity. This marked the first occasion on which a court in the PRC had recognised and enforced a Singapore judgment. Since then, the establishment of reciprocal relations between the PRC and Singapore courts has further been confirmed by the signing of a Memorandum of Guidance on the Recognition and Enforcement of Money Judgments in Commercial Cases by the Chief Justices of the two courts on 31 August 2018.[2] A second Singapore judgment has also been recognised by the Wenzhou Intermediate People's Court, Zhejiang Province, on 2 August 2019.[3]

Conclusion

Giant Light Metal is a significant decision on a number of counts, not least for its role in establishing reciprocity between the PRC and Singapore courts. Given the absence of a bilateral treaty on foreign judgments between the two countries, the establishment of reciprocity between the PRC and Singapore courts is important as it does away with a large hurdle against foreign judgments being enforced in the PRC courts. The removal of this hurdle in relation to Singapore judgments is all the more important given that progress on the Belt and Road Initiative ("BRI") is continuing apace. One can anticipate that both the Supreme Court of Singapore, which includes the Singapore International Commercial Court, and the Supreme People's Court of China, which has established two Chinese International Commercial Courts located at Shenzhen

---

① (2016) Su 01 Xie Wai Ren No. 3.

② Memorandum of Guidance between the Supreme People's Court of the People's Republic of China and the Supreme Court of Singapore on Recognition and Enforcement of Money Judgments in Commercial Cases <https://www.sicc.gov.sg/docs/default-source/guide-to-the-sicc/spc-mog-english-version—signed.pdf> (accessed 29 June 2020).

③ *Oceanside Development Group Ltd v. Chen Tongkao & Chen Xiudan* (2017) Zhe 03 Xie Wai Ren No. 7.

and Xi’an, would be well placed to hear disputes regarding the BRI given their expertise in international commercial disputes. Ever since *Giant Light Metal* first laid the foundation for reciprocity between the PRC and Singapore courts, litigants can be confident that regardless of whether they choose to litigate in Singapore or the PRC, the resulting judgment would be equally enforceable in the other country. ①

Grounds of Decision

Giant Light Metal Technology (Kunshan) Co Ltd

v.

Aksa Far East Pte Ltd

[2014] 2 SLR 545

28 January 2014

Andrew Ang J:

Introduction

1 This was an action concerning the recognition and enforcement at common law of a foreign judgment obtained from the Suzhou Intermediate Court, Jiangsu Province, in the People’s Republic of China (“the PRC Court”). In particular, the case raised novel issues as to when a foreign court is said to have international jurisdiction and how a foreign judgment is enforced by the Singapore courts under Singapore private international law.

2 On 16 December 2010, Giant Light Metal Technology (Kunshan) Co Ltd

① Provided, of course, the judgment fulfils the (other) requirements for recognition and enforcement under the law of the court addressed.

("the Plaintiff") successfully obtained judgment against Aksa Far East Pte Ltd ("the Defendant") in the PRC Court for breach of contract ("the PRC Judgment"). The Plaintiff then sought to enforce against the Defendant in Singapore the PRC Judgment for the payment of various sums of moneys.

Background facts

3 The Plaintiff is a company incorporated in the People's Republic of China ("the PRC") and is engaged in designing and producing aluminium and alloy materials for the purposes of industrial and commercial use.

4 The Defendant is a company incorporated in Singapore and is in the business of general wholesale trade, including general import and export of goods.

5 On or around 18 December 2003, the parties entered into a contract for the Plaintiff to purchase from the Defendant two new generator sets with new engines, which were to be manufactured by the Cummins Engine Company Inc in England, United Kingdom ("the Contract"). The total purchase price of the generator sets was US $ 200, 000 of which the Plaintiff paid US $ 190, 000.

6 A further party to the Contract was Shanghai Yates Genset Co Ltd ("Shanghai Yates"), a company incorporated in the PRC which acted as guarantor for the Defendant in the purchase of the generator sets. Shanghai Yates was a sub-distributor of the Defendant in the PRC at the relevant time.

7 After receiving the generator sets from the Defendant, the Plaintiff was not satisfied with them: they were not new generator sets nor manufactured in England and were not capable of use. The Plaintiff thereafter instituted a civil claim against the Defendant and Shanghai Yates for breach of the Contract in the PRC Court on 25 July 2005 ("the 2005 Proceedings"). The Defendant responded by filing a "Statement of Defence" and also sent its representative, Mr You Tian Fen ("Mr You"), to attend court hearings. Subsequently, the

2005 Proceedings were discontinued on 10 September 2007 "to enable parties to attempt to resolve the matter".

8 In the event, the out-of-court negotiations failed. On 9 May 2008, the Plaintiff re-commenced proceedings for the same claim against the Defendant and Shanghai Yates in the PRC Court ("the 2008 Proceedings"). The relevant court documents were served on the Defendant in Singapore at the Defendant's registered office address via diplomatic channels on 6 November 2008. The Defendant did not dispute that it was properly served. The Defendant, however, chose to ignore the 2008 Proceedings and did not enter an appearance, taking no part in the proceedings.

9 Shanghai Yates on its part filed two defences to the Plaintiff's claim in the 2008 Proceedings and attended hearings in the PRC Court on 17 April 2009 and 20 October 2010. The PRC Court heard submissions by representatives of the Plaintiff and Shanghai Yates and, upon further consideration, awarded judgment in favour of the Plaintiff in the PRC Judgment. The section of the PRC Judgment which sets out the orders made is reproduced as follows:

> In summary, as the subject delivered by [the Defendant] was not consistent with the contract, [the Defendant] was in material breach. The claim of [the Plaintiff] for rescission of the contract, refund of price and return of goods, and compensation for damages were consistent with the law. In respect of the loss of US $ 145, 383. 28 claimed by [the Plaintiff], loss of freight of RMB 7, 088 was admitted by the court, and the remaining amount of loss lacked basis and was not upheld by the court. In accordance with Sections 97, 126, 130, 135, 136 and 148 of PRC Contract Law, Section 28 of Rules of Supreme Court on Evidence in Civil Proceedings, and Section 136 of PRC Civil Procedure

Law, it is judged as follows:

1. [The Contract] between [the Plaintiff] and [the Defendant] be rescinded;

2. [The Plaintiff] to return two AC-1130 Cummins diesel generator sets to [the Defendant];

3. [The Defendant] to refund the price of US $ 190, 000 to [the Plaintiff];

4. [The Defendant] to compensate [the Plaintiff] for the loss of RMB 7088;

Paragraphs 2, 3 and 4 above shall be performed within one month after this judgment comes into effect.

5. Other claims of [the Plaintiff] be rejected.

If any party fails to make payment within the period specified by the court, it shall pay double interest on the outstanding amount in the period of delay in accordance with Section 229 of PRC Civil Procedure Law.

The court cost for this case shall be RMB 25, 560 for which [the Plaintiff] shall pay RMB 11, 034 and [the Defendant] shall pay RMB 14, 626.

If any party feels aggrieved by this Judgment, [the Plaintiff] or [Shanghai Yates] may, within 15 days from the date of service of this judgment thereon, and [the Defendant] may, within 30 days from the date of service of this judgment thereon, file a petition for appeal with this court, with such number of copies corresponding to the number of the opposite parties, to appeal to the Jiangsu Higher Court …

10 The PRC Judgment was served on the Defendant at its registered office in Singapore on 25 March 2011 through diplomatic channels, and the deadline within which the Defendant could have brought an appeal to the Jiangsu Higher Court expired on 25 April 2011.

11 The generator sets were thereafter not collected by the Defendant. Neither did it pay the judgment sums ordered to be paid to the Plaintiff. This was despite a letter of demand sent by the Plaintiff to the Defendant on 22 July 2011. It appeared that the Defendant was not interested in collecting the generator sets despite the Plaintiff being ready and willing for the Defendant to do so. A director of the Defendant, Ms Yong Yit Yeng Mavis, even went so far as to say in cross-examination that she was not interested in taking the generator sets back and would rather dispose of the generator sets in the PRC.

12 As a result of the Defendant's non-compliance with the PRC Judgment, the Plaintiff, on 10 February 2012, commenced the present action in Singapore, claiming, *inter alia*:

(a)the sums of US $ 190,000 and RMB 7,088 as ordered in the PRC Judgment ("the PRC Judgment Sums");

(b)the Defendant's PRC court fees ordered under the PRC Judgment of RMB 14,626 which had been paid by the Plaintiff ("the PRC Court Fees");

(c)interest on the PRC Judgment Sums and the PRC Court Fees; and

(d)costs.

The issues

13 Counsel for the parties submitted that the present case concerned the common law rules on recognition and enforcement of a foreign judgment, and brought to the court's attention the paucity of Singapore case law in this area. In particular, the parties highlighted to the court the lack of precedent in relation to the issues which

arose directly for decision before me. As a result, parties relied (as a starting point) on the principles as stated in *Dicey, Morris and Collins on The Conflict of Laws* (Lord Lawrence Collins gen ed) (Sweet & Maxwell, 15th Ed, 2012) ("*Dicey, Morris and Collins*") at vol 1, paras 14R-020 and 14R-054:

> **Rule 42**—(1) Subject to the Exceptions hereinafter mentioned and to Rule 62 (international conventions), a foreign judgment in personam given by the court of a foreign country with jurisdiction to give that judgment in accordance with the principles set out in Rules 43 [and Rules 44 to 46 which relate to when such jurisdiction does not exist], and which is not impeachable under any of [Rules 49 to 54 which relate to when the foreign judgment is impeachable], may be **enforced** by a claim or counterclaim for the amount due under it if the judgment is
>
> (a) for a debt, or definite sum of money (not being a sum payable in respect of taxes or other charges of a like nature or in respect of a fine or other penalty); and
>
> (b) final and conclusive,
>
> but not otherwise.
>
> Provided that a foreign judgment may be final and conclusive, though it is subject to an appeal, and though an appeal against it is actually pending in the foreign country where it was given.
>
> (2) A foreign judgment given by the court of a foreign country with jurisdiction to give that judgment in accordance with the principles set out in Rules 43 [and Rules 44 to 46 which relate to when jurisdiction does not exist], which is not impeachable under any of [Rules 49 to 54 which relate to when the foreign judgment is impeachable] and which is final and conclusive on the merits, is entitled to **recognition**

at common law and may be relied on in proceedings in England.

(3) No proceedings may be brought by a person on a cause of action in respect of a judgment which has been given in his favour in proceedings between the same parties or their privies in a court in another part of the United Kingdom or in a court in an overseas country unless that judgment is not enforceable according to clause (1), or not entitled to recognition according to clause (2), of this Rule.

This Rule must be read subject to Rule 59.

…

Rule 43—Subject to Rules 44 to 46 [which relate to when jurisdiction does not exist], a court of a foreign country outside the United Kingdom has jurisdiction to give a judgment *in personam* capable of **enforcement or recognition** as against the person against whom it was given in the following cases:

First Case—If the person against whom the judgment was given was, at the time the proceedings were instituted, present in the foreign country.

Second Case—If the person against whom the judgment was given was claimant, or counterclaimed, in the proceedings in the foreign court.

Third Case—If the person against whom the judgment was given, submitted to the jurisdiction of that court by voluntarily appearing in the proceedings.

Fourth Case—If the person against whom the judgment was given, had before the commencement of the proceedings agreed, in respect of the subject matter of the proceedings, to submit to the jurisdiction of that court or of the courts of that country.

[emphasis in original in italics; emphasis added in underline and bold underline]

14 Indeed, there does not appear to have been an occasion when a Singapore court was required to deal with the same scope of issues relating to the recognition and enforcement of a foreign judgment under the common law as in the present case. However, the common law rules in the other major common law jurisdictions on these issues are well established. Therefore, I accepted that the principles as stated in *Dicey, Morris and Collins* served as an appropriate starting point for analysis of the issues that arose. I also noted that Prof Yeo Tiong Min in *Halsbury's Laws of Singapore* vol 6(2) (LexisNexis, 2009) ("*Yeo*") also referred to case law from England (and other common law jurisdictions) and used the English position as the basis for his analysis of this area of Singapore private international law (see generally paras 75. 155-75. 240).

15 In order to make clear the framework for analysis of the issues in the present case, it is apposite that I draw attention to an important distinction between the recognition of a judgment and its enforcement, as summarised by Prof Adrian Briggs ("Prof Briggs"), in Adrian Briggs, *The Conflict of Laws* (OUP, 2nd Ed, 2008) at pp 119-120:

> An important distinction must be drawn at the outset between the recognition of a judgment and its enforcement; and between these and the other effects which can be derived from a foreign judgment. Recognition of a judgment means treating the claim which was adjudicated as having been determined once and for all. It does not

matter whether it was determined in favour of the claimant or the defendant, though judgments in personam are only ever recognized as effective against particular parties, and the material question will be whether that person is bound. …

…

Not every judgment entitled to recognition may be enforced in England, but to be enforced, a foreign judgment must first be recognized. If it is to be enforced at the behest of the successful claimant, the judgment must meet further conditions; but if enforcement is ordered, the judgment may be executed as if it had been given by an English court, either because it is ordered that the judgment be registered pursuant to statute which provides for this effect or (if enforced under the common law) because an English court gives its own judgment which itself becomes the order which may be enforced.

[emphasis in original in italics; emphasis added in bold italics]

16 This distinction was not made clear in the present case since the Plaintiff sought only the enforcement of the PRC Judgment and did not expressly indicate that the PRC Judgment should be recognised. However, I found that it must follow, as a matter of logic and principle, that the PRC Judgment be recognised before it can be enforced. In the words of Prof Briggs, quoted by Lord Rodger of Earlsferry in *Clarke v. Fennoscandia Ltd* [2007] UKHL 56 at [21], “the logic of the law is that recognition is the necessary primary concern”.

17 What determines whether a foreign judgment is capable of recognition and enforcement according to the common law rules of private international law is broadly stated in *Dicey, Morris & Collins* ([13] *supra*), para 14R-020 (“Rule

42") (see [13] above). However, a short summary of these requirements can be found in *The Conflict of Laws* (at pp 136 and 149) which I reproduce as follows:

> A judgment will be *recognized* at common law if it is *the final and conclusive judgment of a court* which, as a matter of English private international law, had '*international jurisdiction*', and as long as there is *no defence* to its recognition. ...
>
> ...
>
> As a matter of theory, *a foreign judgment which satisfies the criteria for its recognition creates an obligation which the judgment creditor may sue to enforce in an action*, founded on the foreign judgment, at common law. *The action is brought as one for debt; it follows that only final judgments for fixed sums of money can be enforced by such proceedings*. ...
>
> [emphasis added]

18 Parties made their submissions based on these general requirements, and were agreed on what were the issues necessary for me to decide the case. Importantly, the Defendant did not raise any objection that the PRC Judgment was not final and conclusive on its merits, allege any impropriety on the part of the Plaintiff in the PRC Court when obtaining judgment in their favour, nor raise any other defences to recognition and enforcement of the PRC Judgment.

19 Accordingly, the issues in determining whether the PRC Judgment should be recognised and enforced under the common law rules of Singapore private international law were as follows:

(a) Whether the PRC Court had international jurisdiction over the

Defendant for the purposes of recognition and enforcement of the PRC Judgment ("Issue 1").

(b) Whether the Plaintiff's claim satisfied the requirement that only foreign judgments for a definite sum of money are enforceable ("Issue 2").

Analysis of Issue 1

Preliminary considerations

20 It is widely accepted that in deciding the issue of international jurisdiction, the common law is generally not concerned with how the foreign court had assumed jurisdiction over the party under its own laws (see *Buchanan v. Rucker* (1808) 9 East 192 at 194; 103 ER 546 at 547). Instead, as stated by Prof Yeo in *Yeo* ([14] *supra* at para 75. 170):

> The principal question is whether the foreign court had jurisdiction over the party sought to be bound, in the private international law sense according to the law of the forum, such that the court of the forum will recognise an obligation on the party to obey the foreign judgment.

Therefore, whether the PRC Court had international jurisdiction over the Defendant was to be determined by Singapore private international law.

21 In general, *Dicey, Morris & Collins* at para 14R-054 ("Rule 43") (see [13] above) sets out four situations where a foreign court can be said to have international jurisdiction over a party such that a judgment *in personam* issued by that court may be recognised and enforced in the Singapore courts. Counsel for the Plaintiff, Ms Rebecca Chew ("Ms Chew") relied on two of these situations: (a) the Defendant had *voluntarily submitted* to the PRC Court at the

relevant time (the first situation in Rule 43); and (b) the Defendant was *present* in the PRC at the material time (the third situation in Rule 43). Ms Chew then made two further submissions in the alternative. The first was that Shanghai Yates was the Defendant's privy for the purposes of submission to the PRC Court or presence in the PRC and, secondly, that the "real and substantial connection" approach adopted by the Canadian Supreme Court in *Beals v. Saldanha* [2003] 3 SCR 416 should be applied in Singapore, the PRC having a real and substantial connection to the dispute between the parties.

22 Ms Chew also submitted, rightly, that if I were to find for the Plaintiff on just one of the above mentioned grounds that would be sufficient to establish that the PRC Court had international jurisdiction over the Defendant. Counsel for the Defendant, Mr Francis Goh ("Mr Goh"), agreed with this submission and accordingly resisted each ground.

Voluntary submission to the PRC Court

23 The case for finding that a foreign court has international jurisdiction over the defendant based on voluntary submission, as explained in *Dicey, Morris & Collins* ([13] *supra* at para 14-069), "rests on the simple and universally admitted principle that a litigant who has voluntarily submitted himself to the jurisdiction of a court by appearing before it cannot afterwards dispute its jurisdiction". The question then is: what constitutes voluntary submission to the foreign court for the purpose of international jurisdiction?

24 In *WSG Nimbus Pte Ltd v. Board of Control for Cricket in Sri Lanka* [2002] 1 SLR(R) 1088 at [54], Lee Seiu Kin JC held that what must be considered is whether the party "had taken a step in the proceedings which necessarily involved waiving their objection to the jurisdiction". The learned authors in Jonathan Hill and Adeline Chong, *International Commercial Disputes: Commercial Conflict of Laws in English Courts* (Hart Publishing,

2010) (“*Hill & Chong*”), further elaborate on what constitutes taking “a step in the proceedings” (at para 12. 2. 5):

> *A defendant is to be regarded as having submitted to the jurisdiction of the original court if he voluntarily appears in the proceedings to defend the claim on the merits*, if he counterclaims in those proceedings or if he agrees to submit to the jurisdiction of the court (for example, in a contractual jurisdiction clause). Contesting the jurisdiction and the merits of the case in the alternative also amounts to submission. In a situation where the original court rejects the defendant's challenge of its jurisdiction and the defendant proceeds to fight the case on the merits (without reserving the position on jurisdiction), the defendant must be regarded as having submitted. [emphasis added in italics]

25 Consistent with the general principle that whether a foreign court has international jurisdiction depends on the private international law rules of the forum and not the law of the foreign court, whether a party has voluntarily submitted to the foreign court is a question for Singapore private international law rules. This was stated unequivocally in the recent United Kingdom Supreme Court decision of *Rubin v. Eurofinance SA* [2013] 1 AC 236, where Lord Collins of Mapesbury observed (at [161]) thus:

> The characterisation of whether there has been a submission for the purposes of the enforcement of foreign judgments in England depends on English law. The court will not simply consider whether the steps taken abroad would have amounted to a submission in English

proceedings. The international context requires a broader approach. Nor does it follow from the fact that the foreign court would have regarded steps taken in the foreign proceedings as a submission that the English court will so regard them. Conversely, it does not necessarily follow that because the foreign court would not regard the steps as a submission that they will not be so regarded by the English court as a submission for the purposes of the enforcement of a judgment of the foreign court. The question whether there has been a submission is to be inferred from all the facts.

26 Importantly, Lord Collins qualifies the oft-cited proposition found in *Adams v. Cape Industries plc* [1990] Ch 433 ("*Adams v. Cape*") (*per* Scott J at 461) that the fact that the foreign court considers there to have been a submission is a necessary, but not a sufficient, condition for the foreign court to have international jurisdiction. Instead, Lord Collins preferred the more nuanced approach taken in deciding whether there was submission for the purposes of international jurisdiction, and further reinforced this view by citing with approval the view of Thomas J in *Akai Pty Ltd v. People's Insurance Co Ltd* [1998] 1 Lloyd's Rep 90 at 97:

> The Court must consider the matter objectively; it must have regard to the general framework of its own procedural rules, but also to the domestic law of the Court where the steps were taken. This is because the significance of those steps can only be understood by reference to that law. If a step taken by a person in a foreign jurisdiction, such as making a counterclaim, might well be regarded by English law as amounting to a submission to the jurisdiction, but would not be

regarded by that foreign Court as a submission to its jurisdiction, an English Court will take into account the position under foreign law. …

27 This was also the approach Ms Chew suggested I take in deciding the matter, and I agreed. On that basis, Ms Chew submitted to the court that it was clear that the Defendant by entering a defence had submitted to the jurisdiction of the PRC Court in the 2005 Proceedings. It was apparent to me that no other conclusion could be drawn, and Mr Goh rightly accepted this to be the case as well. As mentioned above, however, the 2005 Proceedings were discontinued in 2007 for the purposes of out-of-court negotiations, and later re-commenced as a fresh set of proceedings (*viz*, the 2008 Proceedings). The Defendant then ignored the 2008 Proceedings without even appearing in the PRC Court to raise a jurisdictional objection. Ms Chew submitted that the Defendant had nevertheless submitted to the PRC Court in relation to the 2008 Proceedings.

28 The submissions by both parties necessitated a careful analysis of a number of issues:

(a) first, what was the basis for the PRC Court's jurisdiction over the proceedings brought by the Plaintiff;

(b) secondly, whether the 2005 Proceedings and the 2008 Proceedings can be seen as one unit of litigation or a contiguous whole; and

(c) thirdly, whether consent to the jurisdiction of the PRC Court in the 2005 Proceedings should be imputed to the Defendant in the 2008 Proceedings.

I will deal with each of these issues in turn.

The basis for the PRC Court's jurisdiction over the proceedings brought by the Plaintiff

29 This was obviously a question relating to PRC civil procedure and

jurisdiction rules, and required the aid of PRC legal experts. A joint expert report for this purpose was filed by Mr Tang Linfeng ("Mr Tang"), the expert witness on behalf of the Plaintiff, and Mr Hua Yin ("Mr Hua"), the expert witness on behalf of the Defendant. Both PRC legal experts were also cross-examined in court via the "hot-tubbing" procedure.

30 Significantly, Mr Tang and Mr Hua (especially after cross-examination) did not give vastly different legal opinions. Both experts agreed that the 2005 Proceedings and the 2008 Proceedings were technically different proceedings with different case numbers. Mr Tang, however, sought to downplay the significance of this.

31 Mr Tang opined that given the submission by the Defendant to the jurisdiction of the PRC Court in the 2005 Proceedings, its subsequent failure to object to the jurisdiction of the same court in respect of the same claim after having been served with the relevant court documents amounted to an acceptance of the PRC Court's jurisdiction. Unsurprisingly, Mr Hua did not agree. Mr Hua took the position that under Art 243 of the Civil Procedure Law of the People's Republic of China (2007) ("CPL 2007") ("Art 243"), there were two conditions which had to be fulfilled before a party is deemed to have accepted the jurisdiction of a PRC Court, *viz*, that (a) the party does not raise an objection to the court's jurisdiction; and (b) a defence is filed with the court. Article 243 states that:

> If in a civil action in respect of a case involving foreign element, the defendant raises no objection to the jurisdiction of a people's court and responds to the action by making his defence, he shall be deemed to have accepted that this people's court has jurisdiction over the case.

32 Mr Hua gave further evidence that it was incumbent on a defendant to raise his objection to the adjudicating court in the PRC if it took issue with the jurisdiction of that court, but reiterated that no defence was filed in the 2008 Proceedings by the Defendant. On a plain reading of Art 243, it appeared to me that Mr Hua's evidence on this matter was more persuasive on the issue of whether the Defendant had accepted the jurisdiction of the PRC Court. That was, however, not the end of the matter.

33 Mr Tang gave further evidence that the PRC Court in both the 2005 Proceedings and the 2008 Proceedings would have taken jurisdiction over the matter under Art 241 of the CPL 2007 ("Art 241") and would not have had to refer to Art 243 at all. Article 241 states that:

> In the case of an action concerning a contract dispute or other disputes over property rights and interests, brought against a defendant who has no domicile within the territory of the People's Republic of China, if the contract is signed or performed within the territory of the People's Republic of China, or if the object of the action is located within the territory of the People's Republic of China, or if the defendant has distrainable property within the territory of the People's Republic of China, or if the defendant has its representative office within the territory of the People's Republic of China, the people's court of the place where the contract is signed or performed, or where the object of the action is, or where the defendant's distrainable property is located, or where the torts are done, or where the defendant's representative office is located, shall have jurisdiction.

34 It was agreed by both parties that the contract had been signed in the PRC, delivered on a cost, insurance and freight basis in Shanghai, and installed at the Plaintiff's premises in Suzhou. Further, it was not disputed that the PRC Court would have jurisdiction over the 2005 Proceedings and the 2008 Proceedings because one of the requirements of Art 241 was satisfied. It was also confirmed by both experts that where the PRC Court had jurisdiction under Art 241, Art 243 would not be applicable. This was because a "case involving foreign element" in Art 243, was taken to mean a case which did not meet any of the requirements under Art 241.

35 The experts also gave evidence that the PRC Court would investigate on its own motion whether they had jurisdiction over any particular matter. This was supported by the fact that the PRC Court issued a "Notice of Case Acceptance" dated 12 May 2008, which indicated that they would be accepting the case as they had "conducted [their] examination and found [that the case] had met the acceptance conditions stipulated in the 'Civil Procedure Law of the People's Republic of China'", notwithstanding that the Defendant had clearly not filed a defence in the 2008 Proceedings.

36 Therefore, I accepted the evidence by Mr Tang that Art 243 was not actually applicable to either the 2005 Proceedings or the 2008 Proceedings. Whether the Defendant had voluntarily accepted the PRC Court's jurisdiction under PRC law was not relevant to the PRC Court's determination that it had jurisdiction over the proceedings brought by the Plaintiff. It was also clear that the experts were agreed that the PRC Court had properly taken jurisdiction over the 2008 Proceedings under its own laws.

Whether the 2005 *Proceedings and the* 2008 *Proceedings can be seen as one unit of litigation or a contiguous whole*

37 Ms Chew submitted that taking an objective assessment of all the facts,

including how the PRC Court took jurisdiction over the 2005 Proceedings and the 2008 Proceedings, the Defendant's failure to appear in the 2008 Proceedings must be viewed in conjunction with its voluntary submission to the 2005 Proceedings. Ms Chew took the position that although the 2005 Proceedings and 2008 Proceedings were technically two separate proceedings, for the purposes of submission to jurisdiction they had to be viewed as a contiguous whole. This would mean that the submission by the Defendant to the PRC Court in the 2005 Proceedings would constitute submission in the 2008 Proceedings as well. The heart of this argument was that the 2005 Proceedings and the 2008 Proceedings were separate proceedings only as the result of a mere technicality; the Defendant had conducted itself in such a way that it had clearly consented to the jurisdiction of the PRC Court, and allowing the Defendant to deny its payment obligations under the PRC Judgment would go against any reasonable conception of fairness.

38 Mr Goh, on the other hand, maintained that the 2005 Proceedings and the 2008 Proceedings were separate proceedings that could not be viewed as "one unit of litigation" or treated as a contiguous whole. If I agreed with Mr Goh on this point, then Ms Chew's submission would not get off the ground.

39 In support of his objection, Mr Goh relied on the seminal English case on international jurisdiction of *Adams v. Cape* ([24] *supra*). *Adams v. Cape* involved a situation where Cape and Capasco, both English companies, presided over a group of subsidiaries engaged in the mining of asbestos in South Africa and the marketing of the mined asbestos. The mined asbestos was sold for use in a factory in Texas where its employees later suffered personal injury from exposure to asbestos dust. In 1974, 462 workers commenced proceedings against a number of companies, including Cape and Capasco, in Tyler, Texas ("the Tyler 1 Action"). Cape and Capasco protested the jurisdiction of the

Tyler court. Those proceedings were eventually settled after the parties entered into a consent order where the workers were paid a sum of money by the defendants. Subsequently, another 206 workers instituted legal proceedings in the same court against the same defendants ("the Tyler 2 Action"). This time, Cape and Capasco chose to ignore the proceedings; they had by then removed their assets from the jurisdiction. The plaintiffs in the Tyler 2 Action, as a result, obtained default judgment against Cape and Capasco and sought its enforcement in England.

40 Before the English court, the plaintiffs sought to argue that the Tyler 1 Action and the Tyler 2 Action involved the same defendants and the same subject matter, and should be viewed as "one unit of litigation", despite there being different plaintiffs in both actions. The purpose of this was so that the submission to the Tyler court by Cape and Capasco in the Tyler 1 Action could constitute submission to the Tyler court in the Tyler 2 Action. Scott J rejected this argument, and held (at 462-463) that:

> ... the "one unit of litigation" theory, when used to translate a submission to the jurisdiction in Tyler 1 into a submission to the jurisdiction in Tyler 2, ignores the essential basis of English law concerning submissions to the jurisdiction. *Where steps taken in proceedings are being examined in the context of an alleged submission to the jurisdiction, what is being sought is evidence of consent on the part of the defendant to the exercise by the court of jurisdiction over him. Until the settlement negotiations in September* 1977 *the jurisdiction objection which Cape and Capasco had taken was being maintained. I have already expressed the view that the pre-settlement procedural steps taken by Cape and Capasco in Tyler* 1

could not, in the context of the federal procedure applicable in the Tyler court, be regarded as a waiver of the jurisdiction objection. But even if that is wrong, those steps could not possibly be regarded as evidencing Cape's and Capasco's consent to jurisdiction being exercised over them in future actions not yet started. Nor could Cape's participation in the application to Tyler 1 *for a consent order, under which the existing actions against Cape were to be dismissed "with prejudice," be regarded as evidencing that consent. Any other conclusion would, in my view, be grossly unfair to Cape and would divorce a submission to the jurisdiction from the bedrock of consent that ought to underlie it*. Accordingly, in my judgment, there was no submission to the jurisdiction by Cape or Capasco in the Tyler 2 actions. [emphasis added]

41 The reasoning of the judge is of particular import. First, Scott J focused on the lack of consent to the jurisdiction of the Tyler court by Cape and Capasco even in the Tyler 1 Action. Cape and Capasco had consistently objected to the jurisdiction of the Tyler court. It was only for the purposes of recording a consent order that Cape and Capasco entered an appearance in the Tyler 1 Action. Secondly, by extension, this meant that Cape and Capasco could not be taken to consent to the jurisdiction of the Tyler court in relation to any future proceedings which were not yet started regardless of the similarity of such proceedings with the Tyler 1 Action. Thirdly, the judge found that it would be "grossly unfair" to Cape and Capasco if consent to the jurisdiction of the Tyler court in the Tyler 2 Action was imputed to them merely because they were parties to a consent order in the Tyler 1 Action while maintaining their objection to the jurisdiction of the Tyler court at all times. Therefore, Scott J dismissed

the "one unit of litigation" argument essentially because he found that Cape and Capasco had never properly consented to the jurisdiction of the Tyler court even in the earlier proceedings.

42 Such was not the case before me. The subsequent proceedings did not just involve the same claims and the same defendants; even the plaintiffs were identical. Leaving aside the indistinguishability between the 2005 Proceedings and the 2008 Proceedings, the Defendant by filing its defence had unequivocally consented to the jurisdiction of the PRC Court in the 2005 Proceedings. Therefore, if the Defendant's acceptance of the jurisdiction of the PRC Court in the 2005 Proceedings was indeed imputed to it in relation to the 2008 Proceedings, it would not "divorce a submission to the jurisdiction from the bedrock of consent that ought to underlie it" as would have been the case in *Adams v. Cape*.

43 Therefore, I could not agree with Mr Goh on this issue. There was an earlier consent by the Defendant to the jurisdiction of the PRC Court such that it was *possible* for such consent to be imputed to the Defendant in respect of the later proceedings (*ie*, that the two sets of the proceedings could be seen as one unit of litigation or a contiguous whole). Whether such consent should be imputed, however, is a separate issue, and it is to this issue which I now turn.

Whether consent to the jurisdiction of the PRC Court in the 2005 *Proceedings should be imputed to the Defendant in the* 2008 *Proceedings*

44 Submitting in favour of an affirmative answer to the question, Ms Chew cited the English Court of Appeal decision in *Murthy v. Sivajothi* [1999] 1 WLR 467 ("*Murthy*"). In *Murthy*, the plaintiffs who were resident in Florida were induced by the first defendant to transfer large sums of money to him purportedly for the purpose of establishing a trust fund for the plaintiffs'

children. The plaintiffs also agreed to convey two properties to the first defendant for use as collateral on a loan to finance the first defendant's alleged business venture. The first defendant then mortgaged the properties to a third party who later brought proceedings in Florida for foreclosure against the plaintiffs, the first defendant and the first defendant's company. The parties to the proceedings then entered into a stipulation for settlement agreement, which was a document drawn up to settle or stay the foreclosure proceedings. The plaintiffs subsequently advanced in the same proceedings, claims to set aside the stipulation for settlement agreement, and cross-claims against the first defendant for having fraudulently deprived the plaintiffs of their properties and moneys. The plaintiffs obtained judgment in default against the first defendant in respect of those cross-claims, and then sought to enforce the judgment in England. The first defendant argued in England that when he submitted to the jurisdiction of the Florida court, it was only in relation to the mortgagee's foreclosure action and not to the cross-claims made by the plaintiffs against him.

45 Disagreeing with the first defendant, Evans LJ (at 476E) held that:

> ... when a person submits to the jurisdiction of a foreign court in respect of a claim made against him by the plaintiff or claimant in those proceedings, then he can also be taken to have submitted to its jurisdiction in respect of, first, claims concerning the same subject matter and, secondly, related claims in the sense described above. This is provided, of course, that such claims may properly be brought against him under the rules of procedure in the foreign court, either by the original claimant or by others who are parties to the proceedings there at the time when he makes the submission.

The other judges agreed with the approach adopted by Evans LJ and concluded that the submission in the foreclosure action could extend to the cross-claims advanced by the plaintiffs against the defendant, since those claims were "related claims". This was so even though the initial claim was by a mortgagee for foreclosure while the cross-claims were based on fraud with respect to both the moneys transferred to the defendant and the two mortgaged properties. Evans LJ further held (at 477D) that:

> … Whether a particular claim should be regarded as related in this sense must always be a question of fact and degree. It may not be enough that its joinder is permitted by the rules of procedure in the foreign court, and, as stated above, I am willing to accept [the defendant's] submission that the English court's rules should not be unfair to the defendant. But I do not see that it can possibly be unfair to the defendant to hold that claims which resulted in the judgment, which the plaintiffs now seek to enforce against him, were related to the claims made against him by [the mortgagee] and in respect of which he accepted the jurisdiction of the Florida court.

46 Ms Chew also sought to rely on two later cases that applied *Murthy*, *viz*, the English Court of Appeal case of *Lawrence Robert Whyte v. Marsha Whyte* [2005] EWCA Civ 858 ("*Whyte*") and the English High Court case of *Joint Stock Company "Aeroflot-Russian Airlines" v. Boris Abramovich Berezovsky* [2012] EWHC 3017 (Ch) ("*Aeroflot*"). In *Whyte*, the wife submitted to the jurisdiction of the Texas Court in relation to divorce proceedings which resulted in a custody order providing that her daughter should reside in Texas. In breach

of this order, the wife abducted her daughter to Russia. The girl was subsequently recovered by the husband. In Texas, the husband had the option of taking up an application based on the custody order for costs and expenses of recovering his daughter, but chose instead to institute an originating petition under Chapter 42 of the Texas Family Code seeking costs of recovery of the daughter, damages for pain and suffering, and punitive damages. He obtained default judgment against the wife and subsequently sought to enforce the judgment in England. The wife argued that she did not submit to the proceedings brought under the Chapter 42 originating petition, and so the requirement of international jurisdiction was not satisfied. Buxton LJ held (at [8]) that an action relating to the breach of the custody order was actually part of the original subject matter, and that it would be "quite impossible to say that the mother did not submit to [the Texas court which applied the Texas Family Code] when she submitted to the divorce decree that it enforces". Thorpe LJ added further (at [12]), that:

> … *The objection to jurisdiction seems to me to depend on the purely technical point that the father elected to seek the redress to which he was clearly entitled by originating petition under chapter* 42 *rather than by an application in the divorce proceedings*. Had he obtained an order for the reimbursement of his costs and expenses under clause 20 of the consent order the mother would clearly have no ground on which to contest jurisdiction. He might have limited his order under chapter 42 to the reimbursement of the same costs and expenses. *That only illustrates how unrealistic it would be to find a submission to the jurisdiction in the first instance but not in the second*. [emphasis added]

47 In *Aeroflot*, Justice Floyd held that based on the principle in *Murthy*, it was "realistically arguable" that a judgment obtained in Russia against the defendant to uplift or index the amount of damages awarded under an earlier Russian judgment to account for inflation could be a related claim. Therefore, the defendant in submitting to the jurisdiction of the Russian court for the earlier claim could be taken to have submitted to the later indexation proceedings.

48 Underlying all three of these cases is the principle that the courts are willing to recognise, for the purposes of international jurisdiction, that a party's consent to the jurisdiction of a foreign court in relation to certain claims may be imputed to further claims in some circumstances. Prof Briggs in a case commentary on *Murthy* ([44] *supra*) in Adrian Briggs, "B: Private International Law" (1998) 69 BYIL 332 at 352, suggested that "the effect of a submission in *Murthy* was that it amounted to an inchoate submission to other claims, reasonably closely related to that one commenced by the writ". Such "inchoate submission"—as seen in *Whyte* and *Aeroflot* —is also possible in relation to claims which are brought pursuant to subsequent and separate proceedings in respect of the same parties, rather than just to claims which are part of the same proceedings.

49 The question then is when consent will be imputed or "inchoate submission" be said to arise. *Murthy* provided two factual reference points for consent to be so imputed: where the subsequent claim concerns the same subject matter; and where the subsequent claim is related to the original claim. Which subsequent claims will fall under these categories is then a matter of degree based on the circumstances. The courts in making this assessment seemed to be informed by concerns of fairness to both the plaintiff and the defendant, and also a desire to disregard technical impediments created by procedural rules

under both foreign and forum law. With respect, I agree with such an approach.

50 In my view, the present case was one that warranted a finding of inchoate submission by the Defendant to the 2008 Proceedings. The Defendant had consented to the jurisdiction of the PRC Court in the 2005 Proceedings. There was then a break in the proceedings due to the Plaintiff's attempt to resolve the matter out-of-court. Mr Tan Chian Huat, a director of the Defendant at the material time, gave evidence that he was relieved at this development; he was thankful that the case was withdrawn because he believed that the Plaintiff would have succeeded in its claim in the PRC Court. When the proceedings were restarted in 2008 by the same plaintiff against the same defendant for the same claim in the same court, the later proceedings were separate from the 2005 Proceedings only because of a technicality. The Defendant then sought to exploit this procedural technicality by ignoring the 2008 Proceedings based on legal advice that any judgment awarded in such circumstances would not be enforceable in Singapore. To bring home the point, if the 2005 Proceedings were *stayed* rather than *withdrawn*, there would have been no dispute at all that the Defendant had accepted the jurisdiction of the PRC Court.

51 I found that although the facts of the present case were different from *Murthy*, *Whyte* ([46] *supra*), and *Aeroflot* ([46] *supra*)—the subsequent proceedings were exactly the same as the earlier proceedings, and the earlier proceedings did not finally dispose of the parties' rights—this was one instance where consent to the jurisdiction of the PRC Court by the Defendant should properly be imputed. To my mind, there was no unfairness to the Defendant in imputing such consent. *Per contra*, there would be unfairness to the Plaintiff were the Defendant allowed to take advantage of abortive out-of-court negotiations to escape liability for its wrongdoing.

52 Therefore, I found that the Defendant had voluntarily submitted to the jurisdiction of the PRC Court in the 2008 Proceedings and, accordingly, the PRC Judgment was a judgment of a court that had international jurisdiction for the purposes of recognition and enforcement.

***Conclusion on Issue* 1**

53 Since international jurisdiction may be established on alternative grounds and having found that the Defendant had voluntarily submitted to the jurisdiction of the PRC Court for the purposes of recognition and enforcement of the PRC Judgment, I did not consider further the other grounds for international jurisdiction raised by the Plaintiff.

54 At this juncture, the Plaintiff had satisfied all the necessary requirements for the PRC Judgment to be *recognised* in Singapore. The only question then was whether this PRC Judgment should be *enforced* in Singapore. This question is the subject of the analysis of Issue 2 below.

Analysis of Issue 2

55 Mr Goh submitted that the "law is clear that an enforceable foreign judgment must be a pure money judgment". He pointed out that the PRC Judgment was for the rescission of the Contract and consisted in the main of two obligations: the return of the generator sets by the Plaintiff and the refund of the purchase price by the Defendant. He maintained that the two obligations flowed from the rescission of the Contract and "[could not] be separated", with the result that the PRC Judgment was not a judgment for a definite sum of money and was unenforceable in Singapore.

56 In support of his submission, Mr Goh relied on the Court of Appeal's decision in *Poh Soon Kiat v. Desert Palace Inc* [2010] 1 SLR 1129 ("*Poh Soon Kiat*"). That case concerned the recovery of a foreign gambling debt

owed by the defendant to the plaintiff. Summary judgment was sought by the plaintiff in Singapore based on a foreign judgment obtained in the Superior Court of the State of California for the County of Santa Clara which set aside a fraudulent transfer of the defendant's interest in a particular property while ordering that the property be sold and the proceeds applied to satisfy judgment debts arising from an earlier judgment of the same Californian court for the gambling debts owed. The Court of Appeal allowed the defendant's appeal on a number of grounds, in particular that the Californian judgment sought to be enforced in Singapore was not for a definite sum of money but was for the setting aside of a fraudulent transfer of property instead.

57 Ms Chew did not seek to challenge the requirement that only foreign judgments for a definite sum of money are enforceable as applied in *Poh Soon Kiat* and, understandably so, as this court is bound by that decision in any case. Instead, Ms Chew disagreed with the Defendant's characterisation of the PRC Judgment. She submitted that the judgment merely entailed two separate obligations which the parties had to satisfy and that the Defendant was still liable to pay the Plaintiff the PRC Judgment Sums even though the Defendant was not in possession of the generator sets. Importantly, Ms Chew clarified that the real issue was whether "the Defendant [was] somehow absolved from performance of its obligation to make payment under the PRC Judgment". In that regard, Ms Chew submitted that that could not be the case and that there was "nothing preventing this Court from ordering that the Defendant [perform its obligation to make payment under the PRC Judgment]," the Defendant's obligation to pay the Judgment Sums not being contingent on the Defendant having received the generator sets. Ms Chew maintained that the enforcement action (by way of a debt claim) did not fall foul of the requirement that only judgments for a definite sum of money are enforceable.

58 The submissions by both parties raised the following issues for consideration:

(a) The conceptual basis for the enforcement of foreign judgments in Singapore.

(b) Whether the Defendant's obligation to pay the Plaintiff the PRC Judgment Sums could be enforced, given that the generator sets were still in the Plaintiff's possession.

(c) Whether the Plaintiff's claim was precluded because the PRC Judgment comprised other obligations which were not for a definite sum of money.

The conceptual basis for enforcement of foreign judgments in Singapore

59 A foreign judgment has no direct operation in Singapore and cannot be enforced immediately without more in the Singapore courts by way of execution. This accords with the common law. As explained in *Dicey, Morris & Collins* ([13] *supra*) at para 14-002, "[t]his follows from the circumstance that the operation of legal systems is, in general, territorially circumscribed". The process by which a foreign judgment is recognised and enforced was explained by Prof Briggs in Adrian Briggs, "Recognition of foreign judgments: a matter of obligation" (2013) 129 LQR 87 ("*Briggs*") at 88 – 89 (albeit in the context of recognition and enforcement of foreign judgments in England):

> … A successful litigant with a foreign judgment in his favour cannot enforce that judgment in England. No measures of execution may be taken on the strength of it. *The claimant must instead bring original proceedings before the English court, in order to obtain, speedily or eventually, an original English judgment, which alone is the judgment which can be enforced*. The nature of these English

proceedings will depend on the nature of the anterior foreign judgment. If the foreign judgment took the form of a final order to pay a sum of money, the claimant may sue to recover that sum as a debt due and owing: the issue of a claim form followed by an application for summary judgment will in many cases produce an enforceable English judgment in short order. If the foreign judgment is otherwise, no debt action will lie, with the result that the claimant must fall back and sue on the underlying cause of action. However, if the foreign judgment was entitled to recognition, the usual course of proceedings from issue of process to English judgment will be to use the foreign judgment as a short-cut, allowing and requiring the issue of substance to be treated as *res judicata*; after which the English court will be able to give judgment. Its order may not be in precisely the same terms as that made by the foreign court, but in most cases, the English order will be close to the one the foreign court made. Either course results in a judgment of the English court and it is this which is enforceable in England. [emphasis added]

60 The present proceedings were instituted on this very basis; the PRC Judgment *per se* did not afford the Plaintiff any direct rights against the Defendant in Singapore. In that sense, it is indeed a misnomer—as suggested by Prof Briggs in *Briggs* at 87—that the common law is said to allow for the enforcement of foreign judgments. Any judgment enforced in Singapore (under the common law) is ultimately one given by the Singapore courts. The foreign judgment merely “prepare[s] the ground for the making of a local order” (see *Briggs* at 89).

61 Whether a particular foreign judgment is given legal effect in Singapore is

then based upon the rules for recognition and enforcement under the common law as established earlier. Importantly, as long as the requirements for recognition and enforcement are met, the validity of the foreign judgment will not be scrutinised. The court will not re-examine the merits of the underlying claim in the foreign judgment (see the English case of *Godard v. Gray* (1870) LR 6 QB 139 and the Straits Settlement Court of Appeal decision in *Ralli v. Anguilla* [1915-23] XV SSLR 33; Lawnet neutral citation [1917] SSLR 2). This is commonly attributed to the theory that where a judgment is issued by a court of competent jurisdiction over the parties, that judgment creates an obligation on the parties to abide by it which the courts of other countries ought to recognise and enforce (see generally: *Dicey, Morris & Collins* at paras 14-007 and 14-008; *The Conflict of Laws* ([15] *supra*) at p 136; and *Hill & Chong* ([24] *supra*) at para 12. 1. 2). Therefore, the Singapore courts in recognising and enforcing a foreign judgment are holding the parties to their obligation to abide by the foreign judgment, and nothing more.

62 Specific to the common law action to enforce a foreign judgment, where that judgment is entitled to recognition, "[t]he action will be commenced by the issue of process in the usual way, claiming the judgment sum as a debt" (Adrian Briggs and Peter Rees QC, *Civil Jurisdiction and Judgments* (Informa London, 5th Ed, 2009) ("*Briggs &Rees*") at para 7. 70). This position in law has its roots in the division between law and equity prior to the enactment of the Supreme Court of Judicature Act 1873 (c 66) (UK). A foreign judgment was generally thought to be enforceable only in a Court of Law—as opposed to a Court of Chancery (but see R W White, "*Enforcement of Foreign Judgments in Equity*" (1980–1982) 9 Sydney L Rev 630 ("*White*"))—necessitating that the action be by way of a claim in *assumpsit* (*ie*, an action for recovery on a simple contract for definite sums of money).

63 The nature of the enforcement action at common law is put down as a reason for the requirement that only foreign judgments for a fixed sum of money may be enforced. Since the proper action for the enforcement of a foreign judgment was an action in *assumpsit*, it follows that an action for the enforcement of non-money foreign judgments cannot be countenanced (see generally: *Dicey, Morris & Collins* at para 14-022; *Briggs & Rees* at para 7.71; *The Conflict of Laws* at pp 149-150; White; S Pitel, "*Enforcement of Foreign Non-Monetary Judgments in Canada (and Beyond)*" (2007) 3 JPIL 241; R F Oppong, "*Enforcing Foreign Non-Money Judgments: an Examination of Some Recent Developments in Canada and Beyond*" (2006) 39 UBC L Rev 257; K Pham, "*Enforcement of Non-Monetary Foreign Judgments in Australia*" (2008) 30 Sydney L Rev 663; and V Black, "*Enforcement of Foreign Non-Money Judgments: Pro Swing v. Elta*" (2005) 42 Can Bus LJ 81). This reason has been the subject of criticism that the form of the remedy should not affect substantive rights and that, as described in *The Conflict of Laws* by Prof Briggs (at p149), "[t]he tail may be wagging the dog". Nevertheless, this requirement constituted the basis for one of the grounds of the Court of Appeal's decision in *Poh Soon Kiat* ([56] *supra*), and it was neither the occasion nor the place of this court to examine its propriety.

64 Be that as it may, the parties did not dispute that the PRC Judgment Sums were fixed and ascertained sums of money. The question was whether the PRC Judgment could constitute the basis of such a debt claim.

The nature of the obligations owed by the parties under the PRC Judgment

65 Parties (and in particular the Defendant) did not dispute that the orders made in the PRC Judgment gave rise to an obligation on the part of the Defendant to pay the Plaintiff certain ascertained sums of moneys. The point of contention here was whether the obligation of the Defendant to pay the Plaintiff

the PRC Judgment Sums could be enforced given that the generator sets were still in the Plaintiff's possession.

66 As a preliminary point, this issue raised the question as to which law should govern how the obligations owed by parties under a foreign judgment should be characterised for the purposes of enforcement. This was addressed by the Court of Appeal in *Poh Soon Kiat* which found (at [19]) that whether the Californian judgment was a "fresh foreign money judgment" was a matter to be determined according to Californian law. I respectfully agree. The court cited three authorities: *Carl Zeiss Stiftung v. Rayner & Keeler Ltd* [1967] 1 AC 853 at 927; *Colt Industries Inc v. Sarlie (No 2)* [1966] 1 WLR 1287 at 1293; and *Beatty v. Beatty* [1924] 1 KB 807 (CA) at 816. I note that the three authorities cited stood for the proposition that the foreign law (and not the *lex fori*) determines whether a foreign judgment is final and conclusive for the purposes of recognition and enforcement, and did not directly concern the determination of the nature of the obligations owed under the foreign judgment. However, this issue was not raised before me by the parties whom—given the extensive expert evidence led on the matter—I took to accept that PRC law would apply in determining the issue. I therefore proceeded on that basis.

67 In that regard, the parties sought to lead evidence from the PRC legal experts on the interpretation of the PRC Judgment and what the order for the Plaintiff to return the generator sets to the Defendant entailed. Both the experts were agreed that under PRC law principles of fairness and good faith informed the resolution of this issue. Mr Tang interpreted that to mean that the party who was in breach of the contract would have to bear the expenses of returning the generator sets. The orders made in the PRC Judgment were then scrutinised with that premise in mind.

68 The PRC Judgment ordered that the Defendant was to compensate the Plaintiff for the loss of RMB7, 088 in addition to the reimbursement of the purchase price of US $ 190, 000. This RMB7, 088 was for the costs incurred by the Plaintiff, after it had taken delivery, in transporting the generator sets from the dock to the Plaintiff's facility for installation. That the Plaintiff was compensated for this was not surprising given that the PRC Court found the Defendant liable for breach of the Contract. The PRC Judgment was, however, silent as to where the generators sets were to be returned to the Defendant. To my mind, the order for the Plaintiff to return the generator sets to the Defendant meant only that the Plaintiff was to make the generator sets available at its premises for collection by the Defendant. Were it otherwise, so that the Plaintiff was obliged to deliver the same to a location of the Defendant's choice, the PRC Court would have made further provision for the Plaintiff to be compensated for such expenses to be incurred. Only then would it be consistent with the PRC Court's order that the Defendant was to compensate the Plaintiff's transportation costs of RMB7, 088. Mr Tang agreed with that analysis.

69 Mr Hua, however, disagreed. He was of the view that the PRC Court would not consider such matters until any subsequent claims for expenses incurred in fulfilling its obligations were in fact made by the Plaintiff. Mr Hua opined further that this would be the case even if, for example, the Plaintiff had an obligation to deliver the generator sets from the PRC to Singapore. I found that this was not consistent with the general principle of fairness and good faith which *both* experts agreed must inform the Plaintiff's obligation to return the generator sets. It would not be fair if the Plaintiff's obligation under the PRC Judgment entailed that it be put out of pocket until such time that it made a further claim before the PRC Court, notwithstanding that it was the innocent party.

70 As mentioned earlier (see above at [11]), the Plaintiff was at all times ready and willing for the Defendant to collect the generator sets from them. The Defendant, however, had no such intention to do so. I found that the Plaintiff's obligation being simply to allow collection of the generator sets by the Defendant, it had done all that was required of it under the PRC Judgment. Indeed, that was all that could reasonably be expected of it.

71 To that end, the experts' view that "the obligations set out in the PRC Judgment are to be performed simultaneously" was really beside the point. Whether the Defendant was in possession of the generator sets or not in this case had no bearing on its obligations to pay the Plaintiff the PRC Judgment Sums since it did not make any arrangement to collect the generator sets. It did not lie in the Defendant's mouth to say that it did not have to perform its obligation to pay the Plaintiff the PRC Judgment Sums because it did not collect the generator sets.

Whether the Plaintiff's claim was precluded because the PRC Judgment comprised other obligations which were not for a definite sum of money

72 Since the Defendant owed an obligation to the Plaintiff for the payment of the PRC Judgment Sums, the question was whether this could be enforced here notwithstanding that the PRC Judgment also included the Plaintiff's obligation to return the generator sets to the Defendant, the latter not being an order for payment of a fixed sum of money.

73 Ms Chew's submission in this regard was that a "judgment is enforceable so long as it orders the payment of 'a definite sum of money'", and it was beside the point that the PRC Judgment made further orders which were otherwise. The order for the Defendant to pay the Plaintiff the PRC Judgment Sums constituted a debt obligation which could found an action for enforcement in Singapore. Mr Goh submitted, on the other hand, that as long as the PRC

Judgment contained obligations besides payment of a debt, the Plaintiff would be precluded from bringing a claim under the PRC Judgment.

74 I could not agree with Mr Goh. It is established that an action in *assumpsit* or debt may be brought against a defendant for costs awarded against him in a foreign judgment so long as the order for costs was final and for a definite and ascertained sum of money (see *Dicey, Morris and Collins* ([13] *supra*) at para 14-022). Importantly, such an action could be maintained even where the costs order arose from a judgment where the substantive merits did not result in orders for definite sums of moneys. This was the case in *Russell v. Smyth* (1842) 9 M & W 810, where an order for costs awarded in a foreign divorce suit was held to be enforceable (at 817):

> … The question arises in Scotland, and *the decree of the Court of Session creates a duty in the party to pay a debt*, and does not give rise to the question of jurisdiction. It is plain that this is not a decree of an ecclesiastical Court, *but of a Court of competent jurisdiction awarding costs*, and not having the power by its own process of enforcing the payment of them in this country. *An action of assumpsit, or debt, therefore, lies for the recovery of them.* … [emphasis added]

75 Consistent with the conceptual basis for the enforcement of foreign judgments explained earlier, the order for the defendant to pay costs of the divorce proceedings in *Russell v. Smyth* constituted an obligation to pay a debt which could establish an action in *assumpit* or debt in England. *A fortiori*, where a foreign court makes an order for payment of a definite sum of money (other than for costs) amongst other orders, the order for payment of a definite

sum of money should be capable of founding an action in debt.

76 It followed that in the present case, the PRC Judgment ordering that the Defendant pay the Plaintiff the PRC Judgment Sums was capable of founding the Plaintiff's debt claim in Singapore.

77 As an aside, I should add that Ms Chew also sought to rely on the doctrine that objectionable parts of a foreign judgment could be severed from the rest of the judgment such that the unobjectionable parts of the judgment may be enforced. In support of her submission, Ms Chew cited *Yeo* ([14] *supra*) at para 75. 168:

> A foreign judgment that is objectionable in part may be severed and the unobjectionable parts enforced, if the unobjectionable part could be clearly identified and separated from the objectionable part. …

78 At first blush, Prof Yeo would seem to suggest that Ms Chew's submission had some merit. However, this warranted further consideration. The basis behind Prof Yeo's statement was the case of *Raulin v. Fischer* [1911] 2 KB 93 which was also relied upon by Ms Chew. As pointed out by Mr Goh, the component of the judgment that was deemed objectionable in *Raulin v. Fischer* was a penal payment based on a criminal sanction. Since a foreign penal law was unenforceable under private international law (see the English cases of *Huntington v. Attrill* [1893] AC 150 and *United States of America v. Inkley* [1989] QB 255), the English court severed that part of the judgment and enforced only the non-penal component of the foreign judgment. Ms Chew also relied upon the English Court of Appeal decision in *Lewis v. Eliades* [2004] 1 WLR 692 ("*Lewis v. Eliades*"). In *Lewis v. Eliades*, the claimant obtained a judgment in the United States court which he sought to enforce in England. The

judgment was for damages for breach of fiduciary duty and fraud, and damages based on statute. For the statutory damages, the claimant was entitled to treble damages, which were not enforceable in the English courts by reason of s 5 of the Protection of Trading Interests Act 1980 (c 11) (UK). Accordingly, the English court severed the statutory damages from the rest of the judgment and enforced that part of the judgment awarding damages for breach of fiduciary duty and fraud. The orders made in the PRC Judgment, however, were of a different nature entirely and did not involve the enforcement of foreign penal, revenue or other public laws. In that regard, I did not think it was appropriate to extend the concept of severance to the present case.

***Conclusion on Issue* 2**

79 In the light of my conclusion that the PRC Judgment ordering the return of the generator sets did not require the Plaintiff to transport the same to a location of the Defendant's choice (it being the Defendant's obligation to collect the same), I held that the Defendant's obligation to pay the PRC Judgment Sums was enforceable in Singapore. To be clear, in arriving at this conclusion, I did not have to consider nor place any reliance on the validity or otherwise of the underlying claim in contract sued upon in the PRC Judgment.

Overall conclusion

80 For the foregoing reasons, I found for the Plaintiff, and made the following orders:

(a) The Defendant shall pay the Plaintiff the PRC Judgment Sums as ordered in the PRC Judgment.

(b) The Defendant shall reimburse the Plaintiff the PRC Court Fees ordered under the PRC Judgment.

(c) The Defendant shall pay interest on:

(i) the PRC Judgment Sums; and

(ii) the PRC Court Fees at the rate of 6.56% per annum for the period from 26 April 2011 to 7 August 2013, amounting to US$28,513.53 and RMB3,258.65 respectively.

(d) The Defendant shall pay interest on:

(i) the PRC Judgment Sums; and

(ii) the PRC Court Fees at the rate of 5.33% per annum from 8 August 2013 until date of full payment.

(e) The Defendant shall pay the Plaintiff costs to be taxed unless agreed.

Reported by Joel Quek.

Quoine Pte Ltd
v.
B2C2 Ltd

——计算机交易系统生成的合同如何适用传统合同法原则

上诉庭——2019 民事上诉第 81 号

大法官梅达顺、上诉庭法官潘文龙、上诉庭法官朱迪柏拉卡斯、国际法官 Robert Shenton French 及国际法官 Jonathan Hugh Mance

2019 年 10 月 14 日;2020 年 2 月 24 日

【简要案情】

上诉方(以下称"Quoine")是加密货币交易平台(以下称"平台")的运营商。该公司也是该平台的做市商,通过下买卖交易单以创造流动性。Quoine 通过其"Quoter 程序"进行做市交易。

答辩方(以下称"B2C2")在事发时是该平台的交易商,利用公司董事(以下称"Boonen 先生")设计的算法交易软件(以下称"交易软件")进行交易。该交易软件能在极少人为干预的情况下运行,且提供确定性交易,只要输入相同信息,就会产生相同结果。输入交易软件的信息是平台上最佳 20 张订单,并生成平台上买卖订单的报价。计算程序也编入了以每 10 个比特币(以下称"BTC")兑换 1 个以太坊(以下称"ETH")的自动保险"底价",如果软件无法从平台获得输入信息,底价就会生效。

2017 年,Quoine 因对平台的关键操作系统疏于作出必要修改,导致 Quoter 程序无法生成新的订单,交易软件的底价于是生效。最终,B2C2 的卖出订单与另两方交易商(以下称“对手方”)的买入订单配对成功,B2C2 及对手方之间最后以每 9.99999 个 BTC 或每 10 个 BTC 兑换 1 个 ETH 的价格完成了 13 笔买卖交易(以下称“争议买卖”)。当时的市场价格约每 0.04 个 BTC 兑换 1 个 ETH,成交价大约是当时市价的 250 倍。

争议买卖由平台自动结算,从对手方的账户扣除的 BTC 进入了 B2C2 的账户,从 B2C2 的账户扣除的 ETH 则进入了对手方的账户。当 Quoine 于隔日得知该争议买卖时,便以交易是以极为异常的价格完成为由,单方面取消了这笔买卖,并逆转了早前结算的交易。

B2C2 随后起诉 Quoine,称 Quoine 单方面取消买卖及逆转结算交易属违约行为或违反信托行为。听审的国际法官(以下称“法官”)驳回了 Quoine 所有的抗辩理由,并准许了 B2C2 的两项索偿。Quoine 之后就法官的裁决提出上诉。

【裁判要旨】

裁定,驳回关于违约行为申索的上诉,但准许关于违反信托行为的申索的上诉(国际法官 Jonathan Hugh Mance 持异议):

(1)争议买卖的合同(以下称“买卖合同”)是 B2C2 与其对手方之间直接订立的。这种合同关系与有关平台使用的协议条款(以下称“协议”)中的约定最为相符。协议清楚列明 Quoine 仅提供服务给平台使用者,而平台使用者会在平台上与其他使用者兑换加密货币,进行买卖:见[50]及[51]。

(2)协议中没有允许 Quoine 取消争议买卖的明示或默示条款。虽然 Quoine 想要依据一项据称允许公司取消以异常价格完成交易的条款,但在该条款被视为纳入协议之前,必须就纳入该条款一事给予平台使用者充分通知,而 Quoine 没有这么做:见[66]。

(3)对于 Quoine 提议的能让自己在某些情况下逆转平台买卖交易的默示条款(以下称“提议的默示条款”),法院不允许引入该提议的默示条款。所提议的默示条款与协议中的一项明示条款是相互矛盾的。该明示条款规定订单一旦成交,交易方就会获得平台通知,且是不可逆转的:见[71]。

(4)可以逐步调整关于单方错误原则的现有法律,以顺应算法交易的情况:见[79]。

(5)在探讨单方错误应如何适用于计算机买卖交易系统生成的合同这一问题之前,我们应先考虑另一个更根本的问题:这类合同是如何订立的。一个具有确定性的计算程序受限于程序员所设的参数,因此程序员的知情状况才是相关的,程序员的知情状况也应视作当事人的知情状况。法院审理的相关内容是,程序员在编写计算程序时,是否实际或推定知道交易方仅在出现错误时,才会接受有关的要价以及程序员是否有利用该错误。要评定程序员或运行算法的人所知情的状况,相关的时间段应从开始编写程序开始计算,直到合同订立为止:见[93],[98],[99]和[103]。

(6)本院驳回 Quoine 在普通法及衡平法上关于单方错误的抗辩理由。对手方误以为自己以没有明显偏离市价的价格用 BTC 买入 ETH,这本身不是买卖合同条款的错误,而是下买入订单时的前提出现错误,或是错误地假设平台一定会正常运作。即便我们假设有操作错误,Boonen 先生并不实际或推定知道对手方的错误想法:见[114],[115]和[126]。

(7)本院驳回 Quoine 在普通法上关于共同错误的抗辩理由。B2C2 及对手方参与争议买卖时,不可能同时在共同错误假设的情况下误以为他们是以 ETH 当时大约的市价进行交易。这是因为只有在特意预先设定的底价(每 10 个 BTC 兑换 1 个 ETH)生效后,B2C2 才会在平台上以每 9.99999 个 BTC 或每 10 个 BTC 兑换 1 个 ETH 的价格下卖出订单:见[129]。

(8)即使假设 Quoine 正确提出不当得利作为抗辩理由,该抗辩理由也不能成立。Quoine 提出的不当因素所依据的论点与本院分析单方错误时驳回的论点是一样的。另外,鉴于结论是买卖合同并未失效,B2C2 是从有效合同中获得利益的,不能说其不当得利:见[132],[134]和[135]。

(9)本院准许 Quoine 就信托问题提出上诉,原因是 B2C2 账户里的 BTC 不存在明示信托。本案中,设立信托的意图存在不确定性。Quoine

的资产与其客户的剥离这一事实本身不足以使本院认定存在信托关系:见[144]及[145]。

(10)尽管如此,鉴于本院裁定买卖合同是有效且可执行的,B2C2 按合同有权从 Quoine 获得争议买卖的所得:见[149]。

国际法官 Jonathan Hugh Mance(持异议):

(11)在适用关于单方错误的法律时,我们应考虑一般在适用该法律时的核心因素,即周遭情况或市场状况是否高度不寻常,来合理解释为何出现如此异常的价格,或者唯一可能的结论是发生了根本错误导致出现了对方不可能合理设想或合理预期的交易。法律必须适应算法程序及人工智能下的新世界,所产生的结果于理于义应是人们所预期的。真诚且理性的交易方一旦察觉发生了根本错误,就应获得救济:见[192][193][194][198]。

(12)任何理性的交易方立即就能确定交易是主要计算机系统故障造成的,而 B2C2 也确定了这一点。这类错误可以在不损害 B2C2 或任何相关第三方利益的情况下被纠正。支持逆转交易的考虑因素超过了导致该故障的任何错误或过失,关于交易基于单方错误而无效的申索应获得支持:见[194]及[195]。

(13)达成交易的不合情理不可能也不应该在这种新情况下起作用。这种新情况更倾向于实际知悉,而不是推定知悉。“不合情理”的交易是指交易商明知并且第一时间就知道交易利益是因严重错误产生的,仍选择保留利益,这一做法在任何情况下都是不合情理的:见[204]及[205]。

意见(大法官梅达顺、上诉庭法官潘文龙、上诉庭法官朱迪柏拉卡斯、国际法官 Robert Shenton French):鉴于本案中建立信托的意图存在不确定性,本院无须就加密货币是否属于能够以信托方式持有的财产一事作出最终结论。尽管如此,加密货币应被纳入与财产相关的一般概念的看法还是有许多可取之处的:见[144]。

【专家点评】*

加密货币交易所能否在双方当事人对系统错误没有争议的情况下取消通过交易算法进行的交易,通过上诉庭裁决这一问题,尚属首例。B2C2 通过自己的交易算法(交易软件),利用交易平台(Quoine)定价算法(Quoter程序)的错误,以当时市价 250 倍的价格进行对自己有利的交易。这项对交易商 B2C2 有利的裁决解决了争议,让 B2C2 获得 3092.517116 个比特币(以当前汇率计算,价值约 3870 万新元)的暴利,而交易所也因此没有追索权。法院首先审查双方合同中规定的救济措施,再研究合同错误的可能救济措施,才作出裁决。

法院裁定,双方的平台协议没有赋予交易所以错误为由逆转这些交易的合同权利,主要原因有二。虽然"异常价格条款"[上述要旨(2)中所指的"AVC"]表面上授权交易所可在系统计算虚拟货币买卖价格出现错误时取消交易,但交易所对这类错误的定义过于狭窄,如系统故障和妨碍交易发生的故障(见[69])。这一裁定是及时的,对狭义的系统错误除外条款之危险性作出了警示。法院必然会通过适用疑义条款解释(*contra proferentem*,即解释不得有利于起草人)规则来解释这些除外条款,因为它们试图免除平台服务提供商的基本责任。因此,系统错误条款应该清楚地描述电子平台上由外部和内部环境以及由平台各方、代理方、承包商和第三方造成的各种错误。

法院也裁定,尽管有"单方面变更条款"和"无须通知条款",但平台并未给予用户充分的通知去说明平台协议纳入了载于另一份文件的"异常价格条款"。这一裁决不利于"以提述方式纳入"和"继续使用视为接受"条款在网络上和电子商务合同中被广泛使用(和滥用)。法院强调,对于通知的规定不会因这类条款而被取代,这似乎由较久远的案例{例如,*Ri Jong Son v. Development Bank of Singapore* [1998] 1 SLR(R) 824}所创设的规则转向以 *Berkson v. Gogo LLC*, 97 F. Supp. 3d 359 (E. D. N. Y., 2015) 案为代表产

* 本评注撰写人:曾俊华(Daniel Seng),新加坡国立大学法学系副教授。

生的更现代、更“有利于消费者”的做法。这当然是一个值得欢迎的发展。法院尽管未对此进行讨论,但也否定了交易所要求的隐含条款,因为平台协议几乎就像一份标准的格式合同,而且是由交易所起草的。

谈到本案的主要系争点,法官们对于交易所平台是否可以利用单方错误原则使有关的争议交易无效,意见不一。但他们都认为,有关的“错误”不是普通法上的单方错误(见[114],[182]—[183]),因为“错误”并不涉及交易的条款。这是一个令人意外的结论,需要加以说明。

首先,应该注意的是,这个“错误”是由于交易所的 Quoter 程序配置不当而导致的加密货币定价错误。这种配置错误反过来又影响到交易所各种加密货币的买卖价格,特别是因为 Quoine 也是做市商(积极在其交易所下买卖交易单)(见[10]—[11])。换句话说,不仅是 Quoine 和 B2C2 之间的交易,在 Quoine 交易所进行的所有交易都受到配置错误的影响。

尽管构成整个加密货币交易基础的错误属于根本错误,但法院认为这是对订立或将要订立合同的情况的错误假设,而不是对合同条款的错误假设(见[82],[85]—[88],[115]),从而为其结论提供了依据,并援引 *Smith v. Hughes* (1871) LR 6 QB 597 (以下简称“*Smith*”) 和 *Statoil Asa v. Louis Dreyfus Energy Services LP* (“Harriette N”) [2008] 2 Lloyd's Rep 685 (以下简称“*Statoil*”) 支持其论点。然而,*Smith* 案和 *Statoil* 案都不是真正的“定价”错误案例——*Smith* 案是关于燕麦“陈旧”是不是合同条款,因为卖方向买方提供了燕麦的样本,而 *Statoil* 案被 Aikens 法官描述为一份折中合同,其中卸货日期(用来计算滞期费)不是合同条款(见[91])。事实上,*Statoil* 案中引用了 *Chwee Kin Keong and others v. Digilandmall.com Pte Ltd* [2005] 1 SLR 502(以下简称“*Chwee Kin Keong*”)案。这是新加坡上诉庭本身的判决,其主张是,如果双方对合同最基本的条款——价格不能达成一致,而买方知道发生了错误,但却进行“抢购”,则卖方有权单方面将合同作废(见[95])。一个没有被法庭引用但更为切题的“定价”错误案例是 *Deputy Commissioner of Taxation* (*NSW*) *v. Chamberlain*, 93 A. L. R. 729 (1990)。

该案中,澳大利亚联邦法院得出的结论是,一方意识到另一方因打字错误而对实际应纳税责任产生误解,从而导致了有效的单方错误,却以超乎寻常的速度“接受”了错误评估的纳税责任,依据衡平法和解,应予作废(接下来将对此进行进一步讨论)。

法院支持前述观点,将该交易定为“错误地理解下买入订单的前提”(见[114]),并将追加保证金通知和相应的 B2C2 的买入指令类比为由交易所传播的虚假信息,而对手方既不知道也没有参与其中。有人会问,是否有更好的例子说明因各种情况引起的价格错误,或导致的价格错误,从而导致合同条款的错误。毕竟,有关的加密货币由于其相互间的价格关系,具有交易代币的作用。更根本的是,定价错误破坏了算法交易的基础,算法交易下交易方利用程序进行高速交易,以求利用买卖价格的差异套利。这样的错误确实曾在证券交易所发生过:当定价错误由计算错误造成或产生时,这些交易所有取消这类交易的规则或机制[①]。这些规则被认为是建立与支持对市场和交易所的信任和信心所必需的机制,一旦出现错误,交易所的买卖双方都会严格遵守。因此,最理想的做法是由法律构建一个更宏大,与交易所的错误救济措施相一致的框架。

其次,在试图将单方错误应用于计算机交易系统所订立的合同时,多数法官也许并不确定具有“确定性”机制的算法如何反映程序设计员在相关交易合同订立前的实际或推定知悉的状况。因此,法庭似乎不愿将意识到定价错误或按之行事的或然不当行为归咎于 B2C2 的交易软件开发人员(例如,见[129])。但即使这类算法“不具确定性”(在人工智能系统发展的现阶段,可以有把握地说,没有任何机器学习系统是完全“不具确定性”的),代理制度的法律对信使和其他代表委托人行事的行政代理人一向都有健全的管理制度(见例子,*Bowstead and Reynolds on Agency*,2018 年版,第 1-047 段和以下各段)。在这个方面,《电子交易法》(第 88 章,2011 年修订

① See e. g. , Nasdaq R. 11890; NYSE R. 128; SGX-ST, Rule 11. 1. 2. 这也是判决书的[47]中援引了宣誓书的一个论点,尽管宣誓书的相关部分被认为不可接纳为证据而被删除。

版)第15条也给予了一定的支持。此外,尽管存在基于商业秘密的反对意见,交易软件可能不仅需要双方的软件专家,而且需要双方的加密货币专家进行更加深入且客观的审查,看起来专家们要审查的具体问题的范围有点狭隘。正如国际法官 Mance 所指出的,把编写软件程序以伺机利用所谓的“底价”进行交易和在 Quoine 交易所出现流动性不足时进行交易的意图归于开发人员并不为过(引述主审法官的意见,例如,见[158],[190]—[191]),尤其是因为众所周知,加密货币的价格波动很大,而且不清楚 B2C2 或交易软件是否也为交易的目的参考外来加密货币交易价格(B2C2 似乎可在一定程度上接触到这些价格——见审判判决[90]—[91])而受益。毕竟,这就是算法交易的操作目标(参见第[119]条)。

最后,即使认为很难将此案的评量标准纳入普通法的单方错误框架,多数法官大可以利用在 *Chwee Kin Keong* 案中提出的公平的解决办法逆转交易并取回 B2C2 的意外收益。但法院认为 B2C2 对这一错误既不实际知悉,也没有推定知悉(见[114]—[115]),因此没有这么做。对此,国际法官 Mance 持不同意见,他倾向于按衡平法解决问题和采用“诚实与理性的交易方”的测试标准{类似于法官在 *O. T. Africa Line Ltd v. Vickers PLC* [1996] 1 Lloyd's Rep. 700 案中提出的意见;见上述要旨(1)},允许交易所废止这一交易。有人会问,如果交易软件的使用特点是能够投机性地进行加密货币交易,那么多数法官是否会作出不同的裁决,如国际法官 Mance 似乎暗示的那样,它也可以归因于 B2C2,即通过自动化实现不择手段或不合情理的营利。程序员或软件用户是否意料到自动化的结果,这一更大的议题比软件的确定性或不确定性更适合作为系争点。但是,如果 B2C2 没有做出任何不择手段的行为,但却让人怀疑有效的交易是否存在(见[125]),那么最好是将这个问题设定为,对于 Quoter 程序的(错误)操作,是否能从所有受影响方的共同错误中找到救济办法。这一论点在法庭上获得的关注极少。

尽管本评注已很长,但必须指出,法院不将 Quoine 持有的加密资产定为财产是正确的,因为在交易和平台协议中并没有明确的信托模式,再加上账户管理的配置是基于账户(而不是基于加密钱包),*Ruscoe and Moore v. Cryptopia Ltd* [2020] NZHC 728 案的特点就是如此。毫无疑问,法院裁决交易所持有的加密资产是作为账户持有人的应计债务,而不是代他们持有的财产是正确的。

Quoine Pte Ltd

v.

B2C2 Ltd

—The Applicability of Traditional Contract Law Principles to Contracts Made by Computerised Trading Systems

Court of Appeal — Civil Appeal No 81 of 2019

Sundaresh Menon CJ, Andrew Phang Boon Leong JA, Judith Prakash JA, Robert French IJ and Jonathan Mance IJ

14 October 2019; 24 February 2020

Facts

The appellant ("Quoine") was the operator of a cryptocurrency exchange platform ("the Platform"). Quoine also functioned as a market-maker on the Platform by placing buy and sell orders to create liquidity. Quoine conducted its market-making trades through its "Quoter Program".

The respondent ("B2C2") was a trader on the Platform at the material time. B2C2 traded using algorithmic trading software ("the Trading Software") designed by its director ("Mr Boonen"). The Trading Software was designed to function with minimal human intervention, and was deterministic in the sense of always producing the same output given the same input. The inputs to the Trading Software, which would be used to generate quotes for sale and purchase orders on the Platform, were to be the best 20 orders from the

Platform. Built into the algorithm was a fail-safe "deep price" of 10 Bitcoin ("BTC") to 1 Ethereum ("ETH"), which would be invoked should input data from the Platform be unavailable.

In 2017, Quoine's oversight in making certain necessary changes to the Platform's critical operating systems led to the Quoter Program's failure to generate new orders. This led to the deep price in the Trading Software taking effect. B2C2's sell orders were eventually matched with the buy orders of two other traders ("the Counterparties"). Eventually, 13 trades ("the Disputed Trades") were concluded between B2C2 and the Counterparties at a rate of either 9. 99999 BTC or 10 BTC for 1 ETH. These rates were approximately 250 times the then going rate in the market of around 0. 04 BTC for 1 ETH.

The Disputed Trades were automatically settled by the Platform, with BTC debited from the Counterparties' accounts and credited into B2C2's account, and ETH debited from B2C2's account and credited into the Counterparties' accounts. When Quoine became aware of the Disputed Trades the next day, it unilaterally cancelled the Disputed Trades and reversed the settlement transactions on the basis that these trades were concluded at highly abnormal rates.

B2C2 commenced proceedings against Quoine alleging that its unilateral cancellation of the Disputed Trades and reversal of the settlement transactions were in breach of contract or breach of trust. The International Judge who heard the matter ("the Judge") rejected all of Quoine's defences and allowed both of B2C2's claims. Quoine appealed against the whole of the Judge's decision.

Holding

Held, dismissing the appeal with respect to the breach of contract claim and allowing the appeal with respect to the breach of trust claim

(Jonathan Mance IJ dissenting):

(1) The contracts underlying the Disputed Trades ("the Trading Contracts") were formed directly between B2C2 and the Counterparties. This characterisation best accorded with the terms of the agreement governing the use of the Platform ("the Agreement"), which made clear that Quoine was merely providing a service to the Platform's users, who would transact with one another in the exchange of cryptocurrencies on the Platform: at [50] and [51].

(2) There were no express or implied terms in the Agreement that allowed Quoine to cancel the Disputed Trades. Although Quoine had sought to rely on a clause that purportedly allowed it to cancel transactions that had taken place at an aberrant value, sufficient notice of the incorporation of this clause had to be given to users of the Platform before the clause could be regarded as having been incorporated, and this had not been done: at [66].

(3) It was not permissible to imply the terms proposed by Quoine which would allow it to reverse trades on the Platform under certain circumstances ("the Proposed Implied Terms"). The Proposed Implied Terms were incompatible with an express term of the Agreement, which provided that once an order was filled, the trader was notified via the Platform and such an action was irreversible: at [71].

(4) The existing law on the doctrine of unilateral mistake could be meaningfully adapted through incremental adjustments to suit the context of algorithmic trading: at [79].

(5) The question of how unilateral mistake should apply to contracts made by computerised trading systems should be answered by first considering the more fundamental issue of *how* such contracts were formed. Because a deterministic algorithm was bound by the parameters set by the programmer, it

was the programmer's state of knowledge that was relevant and to be attributed to the parties. The relevant inquiry was whether, when programming the algorithm, the programmer was doing so with actual or constructive knowledge of the fact that the relevant offer would only ever be accepted by a party operating under a mistake and whether the programmer was acting to take advantage of such a mistake. The relevant time frame within which the knowledge of a programmer or the person running the algorithm should be assessed was from the point of programming up to the point that the relevant contract was formed: at [93], [98], [99] and [103].

(6) Quoine's defences of unilateral mistake at common law and in equity were rejected. The Counterparties' mistaken belief that they were buying ETH for BTC at prices that did not deviate significantly from the market price was not a mistake as to a *term* of the Trading Contracts. Rather, this was a mistake as to the premise on which the buy orders were placed, or a mistaken assumption that the Platform would not fail. Even assuming there was an operative mistake, Mr Boonen did not have actual or constructive knowledge of the Counterparties' mistaken belief: at [114], [115] and [126].

(7) Quoine's defence of common mistake at common law was rejected. B2C2 and the Counterparties could not have entered into the Disputed Trades under a shared mistaken assumption that they were transacting at or around the going market rate for ETH, given that B2C2 had placed its sell orders for ETH at prices of 9. 99999 BTC and 10 BTC to 1 ETH on the Platform *because* the *intentionally* pre-programmed deep price of 10 BTC to 1 ETH took effect: at [129].

(8) Quoine's defence of unjust enrichment, even assuming this was properly raised as a defence, could not succeed. The unjust factors that Quoine raised were premised on the same points that had been rejected in relation to the

analysis on unilateral mistake. Further, given the conclusion that the Trading Contracts were not vitiated, B2C2's enrichment would have been pursuant to valid contracts and could not be said to be unjust: at [132], [134] and [135].

(9) Quoine's appeal on the trust question was allowed because no express trust arose over the BTC in B2C2's account. There was no certainty of intention to create a trust; the mere fact that Quoine's assets were segregated from its customers' could not in and of itself lead to the conclusion that there was a trust: at [144] and [145].

(10) B2C2 nonetheless remained contractually entitled to the proceeds of the Disputed Trades from Quoine, given the decision that the Trading Contracts were valid and enforceable: at [149].

***Per* Jonathan Mance IJ (dissenting):**

(11) The law of unilateral mistake should not be applied in a manner that left out of consideration elements which were normally central to its application, namely, whether there was anything drastically unusual about the surrounding circumstances or the state of the market to explain on a rational basis why such abnormal prices could occur, or whether the only possible conclusion was that some fundamental error had taken place, giving rise to transactions that the other party could never rationally have contemplated or intended. The law had to be adapted to the new world of algorithmic programmes and artificial intelligence, in a way which gave rise to the results that reason and justice would lead one to expect. Relief should be available if it would at once have been perceived by an honest and reasonable trader that some fundamental error had occurred: at [192] to [194] and [198].

(12) Any reasonable trader would at once have identified, as B2C2 did identify, a fundamental computer system breakdown as the cause of the

transactions, and such error could be rectified without any suggested detriment to B2C2 or any relevant third party. The considerations in favour of reversal of the transactions outweighed in the balance any errors or faults which had led to that breakdown. The claim that the transactions were voidable for unilateral mistake should have succeeded: at [194] and [195].

(13) Unconscionability in bringing about the transactions could not and should not have a role in relation to this novel situation, which was closer to one of actual knowledge than of constructive notice. To the extent that unconscionability might be relevant, it was in any event clearly unconscionable for a trader to retain the benefit of transactions which he would and did at once recognise as due to some major error as soon as he came to learn of them: at [204] and [205].

Observation (*per* Menon CJ, Phang JA, Prakash JA and French IJ): Given that there was no certainty of intention to create a trust, it was not necessary to come to a final position on whether cryptocurrency was a species of property that was capable of being held on trust. However, there might be much to commend the view that cryptocurrencies should be capable of assimilation into the general concepts of property: at [144].

Commentary *

This is believed to be the first case in the world decided by an appellate court on the issue of whether a cryptocurrency exchange is able to cancel transactions made by trading algorithms, in circumstances which the parties did not dispute were caused by system errors. By resolving the issue in favour of the trader B2C2, who by way of its own trading algorithm (the Trading Software)

* Author: Daniel Seng, Associate Professor, Faculty of Law, National University of Singapore.

opportunistically leveraged off the error in the exchange platform's (Quoine) pricing algorithm (the Quoter Program) to make a trade at 250 times the going market rate to its advantage, B2C2 was allowed to reap a windfall of 3,092.517116 Bitcoins (worth approximately S$38.7m by the current exchange rate), and the exchange was left with no recourse. The Court reached its decision by first examining the parties' contractual remedies, before looking at possible remedies in mistake in contract.

The Court found that the parties' platform agreement afforded the exchange no contractual rights to reverse these trades for errors for two main reasons. While the "Aberrant Value Clause" ("AVC", referred to in headnote (2) above) would ostensibly empower the exchange to cancel transactions for errors in the buy or sell price of virtual currencies calculated by the system, the exchange had too narrowly defined such errors as system failures and malfunctions which prevented trades from taking place (at [69]). This holding is timely and warns as to the dangers of crafting narrow exclusionary clauses for systems errors. Courts will necessarily read down such exclusions, by applying the *contra proferentem* rule, because they seek to absolve platform service providers of their fundamental responsibilities. Therefore, systems error clauses should clearly describe the broad range of errors in electronic platforms, caused by external and internal circumstances, and by parties to the platform, agents, contractors and third parties.

The Court also held that insufficient notice was given to users of the platform of the incorporation of the AVC, which was in a separate document, into the platform agreement, notwithstanding the "Unilateral Variation Clauses" and the "Without Notice Clause". This is a ruling that militates against the widespread use (and abuse) of "incorporation by reference" and "continued use as acceptance" clauses in online and e-commerce contracts. The Court emphasized that the requirement of notice is not displaced by such clauses, which seems to move the compass away from the older cases (see e. g., *Ri Jong Son v. Development Bank of Singapore* [1998] 1 SLR(R) 824) towards the more modern, "pro-consumer" approach typified by that set out in *Berkson v. Gogo LLC*, 97 F. Supp. 3d 359 (E. D. N. Y., 2015). This is a development that is certainly to be welcomed. And though it was not discussed as such, the Court also took a dim view of the implied terms sought by the exchange, because the platform agreement operated almost like a standard form contract and was authored by the exchange.

Turning to the main issue on this segue, the majority and the minority *disagree* on the issue of whether the exchange platform could avail itself of the doctrine of unilateral mistake to vitiate the disputed trade in question. However, *both* the majority and minority actually *agree* that the "mistake" in question is *not* one of unilateral mistake *at common law* (see [114], [182]-[183]) as the "mistake" was one that did not go to a *term* of the transaction. This is a surprising conclusion that requires explication.

Firstly, it should be noted that the "mistake" is a cryptocurrency pricing error caused by the exchange's misconfiguration of its Quoter Program. This misconfiguration in turn affected the buying and selling prices of various cryptocurrencies *on the exchange*, particularly since Quoine was also a "market-maker" (it was actively placing buy and sell orders on its own exchange) (see [10]-[11]). In other words, *all* trades taking place on the Quoine exchange were affected by the misconfiguration, and not just the trade between Quoine and B2C2.

Notwithstanding the fundamental nature of the mistake that underpins the entire cryptocurrency exchange, the Court justified its conclusion by characterizing this as a mistaken assumption about the *circumstances* under which the contract was or would be concluded, rather than as to its *terms* (see [82], [85]-[88], [115]), citing in support *Smith v. Hughes* (1871) LR 6 QB 597 ("*Smith*") and *Statoil ASA v. Louis Dreyfus Energy Services LP* (The "Harriette N") [2008] 2 Lloyd's Rep 685 ("*Statoil*"). But neither *Smith* nor *Statoil* were really "pricing" mistake cases: *Smith* was about whether the oats were "old" was a term of the contract, given that the seller supplied a sample of the oats to the buyer, and *Statoil* was characterized by Aikens J as a contract of compromise in which the discharge date (which was used to calculate the demurrage) was not a term of the contract (see [91]). In fact, *Statoil* cited *Chwee Kin Keong and others v. Digilandmall.com Pte Ltd* [2005] 1 SLR 502 ("*Chwee Kin Keong*"), a decision of the Singapore CA itself, for the proposition that where parties were not agreed as to the most fundamental term of the contract, *the price*, and where the buyer knew that the mistake had been made but went ahead and "snapped up the offer", there was a unilateral mistake by the seller which entitled the seller to vitiate the contract (see [95]). A more pertinent case about a "pricing" mistake, not cited to the Court, would be *Deputy Commissioner of Taxation (NSW) v. Chamberlain*, 93 A. L. R. 729 (1990). In that case, the Federal Court of Australia came to the conclusion that a party who was aware of the misapprehension as to the actual assessed tax liability that arose from a typing error had induced an operative unilateral mistake by *acting with extraordinary expedition* to "accept" that wrongly assessed tax liability, and that the settlement was to be vitiated *in equity* (a further discussion of that follows).

The Court supported this observation by characterizing the transaction as one "mistake[n] as to the premise on which the buy orders were placed" (see [114]), and analogized the margin calls and the corresponding B2C2 buy orders as transactions being elicited by falsehoods propagated by the exchange, in which the counterparties were neither aware of nor involved in. It may be asked if there is a better example for a mistake that originates from various circumstances which goes to, or causes an error in, the price, and thus a term of the contract. After all, the cryptocurrencies in question have utility as exchange tokens because of their prices *inter se*. Even more fundamentally, pricing mistakes undermine the very basis for algorithmic trading—where programs execute trades at high speeds seeking to arbitrage off differences in buying and selling *prices*. Such mistakes have indeed happened with stock exchanges: when pricing errors are caused by or arise from computing errors, these exchanges have rules or mechanisms to cancel these trades. ① These rules are seen as necessary to engender trust in and bolster confidence in the markets and exchanges, and are scrupulously observed by both buyers and sellers on trading exchanges whenever errors arise. Thus it will be ideal for the law to advance a larger proposition that is consonant with the exchange industry's remedy for mistake.

Or perhaps the majority, in seeking to apply unilateral mistake to contracts made by computerized trading systems, were unsure as to how algorithms as "deterministic" mechanisms reflect the programmer's state of actual or constructive knowledge up until the point when the relevant trading contract was formed. For this reason, the Court seems unwilling to impute any such awareness of the pricing mistake or possible malfeasance for acting on it to B2C2's developer of the Trading Software (see e. g., [129]). But even if

① See e. g., Nasdaq R. 11890; NYSE R. 128; SGX-ST, Rule 11. 1. 2. This was a point also made at [47] of the trial judgment, quoting from affidavits, although the relevant sections of the affidavit were struck out as inadmissible.

such algorithms were "non-deterministic" (and at the current stage of the development of AI systems, it can safely be said that no machine learning system is completely "non-deterministic"), agency law has always had a robust treatment of nuntius and other ministerial agents acting on behalf of their principals. (See e. g., *Bowstead and Reynolds on Agency*, 2018 ed, para. 1-047 et seq.) Some support for this can also be found in s 15 of the Electronic Transactions Act (Cap. 88, 2011 Rev. Ed.). Furthermore, the Trading Software could have been subjected to deeper objective scrutiny by not just software experts but also cryptocurrency experts on both sides notwithstanding the trade-secret objections, as it would appear that specific issues to be reviewed by the experts were framed somewhat narrowly. As Mance IJ observed, it is not beyond such an exercise to attribute to the developer the intent to program the Software to *trade opportunistically* with reference to the so-called "deep prices" and to trade when *there is illiquidity on the Quoine exchange* (see e. g., [158], [190]-[191], quoting from the trial judge). This is especially the case when it is well-known that cryptocurrency prices are highly volatile, and it is unclear if B2C2 or the Trading Software also benefited from referring to *exogenous cryptocurrency trading prices* for trading purposes (which B2C2 appears to have some access to—see trial judgment, [90]-[91]). After all, that is the very operative objective of algorithmic trading (cf. [119]).

Finally, even if it is considered difficult to fit the rubrics of this case within the framework of unilateral mistake at common law, the majority could have availed itself of the equitable solution advanced in *Chwee Kin Keong* to reverse the transaction and relieve B2C2 of its unexpected gains. But it desisted, holding that B2C2 had neither actual nor constructive knowledge of such a mistake (see [114]-[115]). Upon this point Mance IJ dissented, preferring to resolve the issue in equity and adopting the test of "an honest and reasonable trader" (similar to that which his Honour took in *O. T. Africa Line Ltd. v. Vickers Plc*, [1996] 1 Lloyd's Rep. 700; see headnote (1) above) to allow the exchange to avoid the transaction. It may be asked if the majority would have decided differently if the use of Trading Software is characterized as enabling the conduct of opportunistic cryptocurrency trades, such that it can also be ascribed to B2C2 the possibility of any sharp practice or unconscionable conduct enabled through automation, as Mance IJ appeared to suggest. The determinism or non-determinism of the software is not as pertinent as the larger question of whether the programmer or software user intended the result of automation. But if B2C2 did not engage in any sharp practice yet it evinced doubts as to whether there was a valid transaction made (see [125]), it may be better to frame the issue as one of whether a remedy can be found in the common mistake of all affected parties as to the (mis-)operation of the Quoter Program, an argument that received only minimal attention before the courts.

At the risk of adding to an already long note, it should be observed that the Court was right to not characterize the holding of cryptoassets by Quoine as property. In the absence of an express trust model in the trading and platform agreements, coupled with the account-based (rather than crypto-wallet-based) setup of the management of the accounts—characteristics of which were found in the case of *Ruscoe and Moore v. Cryptopia Ltd* [2020] NZHC 728—there is no doubt the Court is correct in holding that the cryptoassets held by the exchange were held as debt accruing to the account holders rather than as property on their behalf.

Grounds of Decision

Quoine Pte Ltd

v.

B2C2 Ltd

[2020] 2 SLR 20

24 February 2020 Judgment reserved.

Sundaresh Menon CJ (delivering the judgment of the majority):

Introduction

1 The world of cryptocurrency trading is not for the faint-hearted. It can involve computer-generated, high frequency transactions in digital quasi-currencies (otherwise known and referred to in this judgment as "cryptocurrencies") which manifest on computer screens or printouts but are not otherwise in a physical form. The transactions which have led to this appeal were conducted by way of algorithms created by the appellant, Quoine Pte Ltd ("Quoine"), and by the respondent, B2C2 Ltd ("B2C2"). Quoine operated a cryptocurrency exchange platform known as QUOINExchange ("the Platform"), and B2C2 traded on the Platform at the material time. Both Quoine and B2C2 were also market-makers on the Platform, which meant that they created liquidity on the Platform by actively placing orders to buy and sell cryptocurrencies, and in so doing, helped to minimise volatility in the market on the Platform. As is typical of algorithmic trading, the buy and sell contracts on the Platform were concluded without any direct human involvement, save that involved in the creation of the algorithmic processes leading to their formation. Algorithmic trading has been described as follows (see Alain

Chaboud *et al*, "Rise of the Machines: Algorithmic Trading in the Foreign Exchange Market", *International Finance Discussion Papers*, 29 September 2009 <http://www.federalreserve.gov/pubs/ifdp/2009/980/ifdp980.pdf> at p 1):

> In algorithmic trading ... [traders'] computers directly interface with trading platforms, placing orders without immediate human intervention. The computers observe market data and possibly other information at very high frequency, and, based on a built-in algorithm, send back trading instructions, often within milliseconds. ...

Sometimes things can go wrong, as they did in the present case.

2 It transpired that Quoine's failure to make certain necessary changes to several critical operating systems on the Platform set off a chain of events that eventually led to the transactions which are at the heart of this appeal. On 19 April 2017, a total of 13 trades ("the Disputed Trades") were concluded between B2C2 and two other users of the Platform, namely, Pulsar Trading Capital and Mr Yu Tomita ("Pulsar" and "Mr Tomita" respectively, and "the Counterparties" collectively), where B2C2 sold one type of cryptocurrency, Ethereum ("ETH"), for another type, Bitcoin ("BTC"), at a rate of either 9.99999 BTC or 10 BTC for 1 ETH. The rates at which the Disputed Trades were concluded were approximately 250 times the then going rate in the market of around 0.04 BTC for 1 ETH. The Disputed Trades were automatically settled by the Platform, and 3092.517116 BTC was debited from the Counterparties' accounts and credited into B2C2's account, while 309.2518 ETH was debited from B2C2's account and credited into the Counterparties'

accounts. As the Counterparties' accounts did not have a sufficient BTC balance to meet the amount that was debited, this resulted in a negative BTC balance in the Counterparties' accounts. When Quoine became aware of the Disputed Trades the next day, it considered the rates at which the trades were concluded to be highly abnormal and unilaterally proceeded to cancel the trades. The debit and credit transactions involving B2C2's account and the Counterparties' accounts were also reversed.

3 B2C2 subsequently commenced proceedings against Quoine on the basis that its unilateral cancellation of the Disputed Trades and reversal of the settlement transactions were in breach of contract and/or breach of trust. The International Judge who heard the matter ("the Judge") rejected all of Quoine's defences and allowed B2C2's claims for both breach of contract and breach of trust. The Judge did not address the issue of damages given that the trial was bifurcated (see *B2C2 Ltd v. Quoine Pte Ltd* [2019] 4 SLR 17 ("Judgment") at [134]).

4 A central plank of Quoine's defence both at trial and on appeal was the contention that the contracts underlying the Disputed Trades ("the Trading Contracts") were void or voidable for unilateral mistake. This requires us to consider how the doctrine of unilateral mistake should operate where the contracts in question were entered into by way of the parties' respective algorithms, as transpired here.

5 So far as the asserted breach of trust is concerned, this raises the complex question of whether the relevant cryptocurrency, BTC, may even be regarded as a species of property capable of attracting trust obligations.

6 Both these questions were the subject of extensive analysis by Prof Goh Yihan ("Prof Goh"), whom we appointed as *amicus curiae*. We are deeply grateful to Prof Goh for the extensive research he conducted and the excellent

assistance he afforded us on both issues. However, the latter question was not explored in detail in the court below, where the parties appeared to have proceeded on the common ground that BTC *was* a species of property that *was* capable of being the subject of a trust. Despite Prof Goh's able assistance, for reasons which we develop later, we think that the question as to whether BTC can be the subject of a trust should not be dealt with here but should be kept open for another day, in a case in which this issue is properly before the court.

7 In our judgment, for the reasons that follow, the Judge was correct to find that there were no terms in the various contractual documents, whether express or implied, which entitled Quoine unilaterally to cancel the Disputed Trades. We also agree with the Judge that there was no operative mistake on the part of the Counterparties that could be relied upon to vitiate the Trading Contracts. Additionally, given that the BTC was credited into B2C2's account pursuant to valid contracts, B2C2 could not be said to have been unjustly enriched. We therefore dismiss Quoine's appeal with respect to the breach of contract claim. However, we are satisfied that no trust could have arisen over the BTC in B2C2's account, even assuming that the BTC could be the subject of a trust. Therefore, we allow Quoine's appeal with respect to the breach of trust claim and reverse the decision of the Judge in that regard.

The factual background

8 The detailed facts are set out in the Judgment at [14]–[26] and [69]–[105]. It suffices for us to reproduce the salient facts which are relevant to understanding the arguments made in this appeal.

Quoine and the Quoter Program

9 We begin with a brief introduction of Quoine and the program it used for its

trades as a market-maker. Quoine is a Singapore-incorporated company which operated the Platform at all material times. The Platform allows users to trade cryptocurrencies, like BTC and ETH, for other cryptocurrencies or for fiat currencies. It uses an electronic ledger as an order book for all the orders that are placed by users wishing to buy and sell cryptocurrencies. Real time information on the available buy and sell orders are also displayed on the right panel of what was referred to as the "Trading Dashboard" located on the Platform's website.

10 As mentioned, apart from being the operator of the Platform, Quoine also functions as a market-maker on the Platform. In actively placing buy and sell orders, Quoine adds depth to the order book and ensures that there is a continuous two-sided market on the Platform, thus creating liquidity on the Platform and helping to minimise volatility in the market (see Judgment at [18]). A market-maker also profits from what is known as the "bid-ask" spread, which is the difference between the price at which the market-maker is willing to *buy* or *bid for* a particular currency and the price at which it is willing to *sell* or *ask for* that currency. In the material period, Quoine was the principal market-maker on the Platform. Mr Mario Antonio Gomez Lozada ("Mr Lozada"), Quoine's Chief Technical Officer, estimated that Quoine was responsible for around 98% of the market-making trades on the Platform (Judgment at [73]).

11 Quoine's market-making trades on the Platform are conducted through its "Quoter Program". The Quoter Program retrieves external market prices from other cryptocurrency exchanges and uses this data to determine the orders that Quoine will place on the Platform for market-making purposes. Importantly, the Quoter Program is proprietary to Quoine and the information generated by it is not available to other users of the Platform (Judgment at [18] and [72]).

The Counterparties and margin trading

12 We touch on some basic aspects of trading on the Platform as described in Quoine's Trading Rules dated 17 March 2017. There are two types of trading offered on the Platform which are relevant to the present dispute. The first is spot trading, where trades are settled instantly with payment for a trade being effected as soon as the trade is completed. The second is margin trading, which is a variant where trades are entered into using borrowed funds (including borrowed cryptocurrencies). Margin traders may obtain loans directly from Quoine, or from other users of the Platform willing to offer them. For margin traders with loans from Quoine, the assets in their accounts serve as the collateral for the loans, which has a bearing on how the Platform's operating system functions. The Platform is designed to close out a margin trader's open positions when it detects that the margin trader may not be able to repay its loans. In the event that the collateral in the margin trader's account falls below a pre-determined percentage of the loan, a margin call is triggered against the margin trader and the Platform automatically force-closes its margin positions by placing market orders on the Platform to close out its open positions. This is known as a "margin sell-out position".

13 The Platform continually monitors a margin trader's "live profit and loss" in respect of each open position ("live P & L") for the purposes of determining how much collateral the margin trader has available in its account. The live P & L is calculated by multiplying the quantity of borrowed cryptocurrency by the difference between its open price and its theoretical close price. The theoretical close price is calculated by simulating the closing of the margin trader's position against the current price ladder on the Platform's order book. The price ladder refers to the available buy and sell orders with bid and ask prices that are presently on the Platform's order book. Therefore,

abnormally priced orders placed on the order book and/or an abnormally thin order book can affect the calculation of the margin trader's live P & L, and cause the Platform to detect that the margin trader is in a margin sell-out position and take steps to force-close the margin trader's positions. In such circumstances, the Platform's operating system will automatically execute the force-closures as market orders to buy or sell the relevant currency at the *best available price on the Platform*. Further, the margin trader is not contacted in advance of the force-closures being executed; nor will it know the precise prices at which the force-closures will be executed (Judgment at [17]).

14 At and around the time of the Disputed Trades, the Counterparties were trading in the ETH/BTC market using ETH borrowed from Quoine (Judgment at [25]).

B2C2 and the Trading Software

15 Next, we introduce B2C2 and its trading software. B2C2 is incorporated in England and Wales and amongst its business interests is that of being a market-maker. As with other exchange platforms on which B2C2 conducts market-making, its entire trading process on the Platform is automated using its algorithmic trading software ("the Trading Software") which was designed to function with minimal human intervention (Judgment at [13]). The Trading Software was designed almost exclusively by Mr Maxime Boonen ("Mr Boonen"), a director of B2C2 and its key witness at the trial. It should be noted that the Trading Software's algorithm is *deterministic* (Judgment at [82]), which, as defined by both the Judge and Prof Goh, is one which will always produce precisely the same output given the same input. To put it another way, the Trading Software will do just what it was programmed to do and does not have the capacity to develop its own responses to varying conditions. Hence, faced with any given set of conditions, it will always

respond to that in the same way. The fact that the Trading Software's algorithm is deterministic is significant to our analysis below in relation to Quoine's defence of unilateral mistake.

16 As explained in the report of Quoine's expert witness, Mr Vikram Kapoor, the Trading Software's algorithm for placing buy and sell orders on the Platform comprises different "layers" at which different algorithmic trading "strategies" are applied. The first layer contains 12 different algorithmic trading strategies that are programmed to work in sequence, and such a series of trading strategies is known as a "strategy chain". The "PureQuote" strategy, which the Judge discussed at [83]-[84] of the Judgment, is the first strategy in the strategy chain of the First Layer. For the relevant sell (or buy) order B2C2 wishes to place on the Platform, the PureQuote strategy first constructs an order book that is internal to the Trading Software based on the 20 best sell (or buy) orders already placed on the Platform's order book. This information is *received from the Platform*. In constructing the internal order book, the PureQuote strategy will also disregard any sell (or buy) order that has been placed for less than a certain quantity of the cryptocurrency. The PureQuote strategy then processes the information on the internal order book and produces an "output" price. In other words, based on the parameters that have been pre-programmed into the PureQuote strategy, the PureQuote strategy determines the optimal output price given the information it has received from the Platform. This output price that is produced by the PureQuote strategy, however, is not the price that the Trading Software will ultimately quote for the sell (or buy) order it eventually places on the Platform. The output price from the PureQuote strategy merely serves as an input variable for the next trading strategy in the strategy chain, which in turn produces another output price. This process continues through all the trading strategies in the strategy chain, until all the strategy chains in the layers of the

Trading Software's algorithm that are running at the material time have been applied. At the end of this process, the final output price produced is that which the Trading Software quotes for the sell (or buy) order it places on the Platform.

17 Where the Platform is functioning properly with a healthy order book, the PureQuote strategy can construct the Trading Software's internal order book by drawing on the 20 best orders from the Platform's order book. However, it was anticipated that there might be situations where the Platform's order book would be either empty or populated by a large number of low volume orders which the PureQuote strategy would disregard, such that the PureQuote strategy would have no or insufficient input from the Platform's order book. This was explained by Mr Boonen as follows:

> ... [The output prices from the PureQuote strategy form] the basis of what orders we could later on send into the market, but the prices themselves are, so to speak, the best prices that we would compute on the basis of the order book proposed to us, but then other strategies can worsen those prices for a variety of reasons. So they form a sort of building block ...*there must at all time[s] exist such a building block, otherwise the rest of the strategy stack fails.* That's why we use *that method of adding* ***virtual prices*** *that are not necessarily present in the market*, because in a *completely empty order book*, for instance, the strategy cannot run, as ... it doesn't have an anchor from which it could create its output. [emphasis added in italics and bold italics]

18 As alluded to in that extract from Mr Boonen's evidence, when the

PureQuote strategy has no or insufficient input from the Platform's order book, it would not be able to "run" and so to produce an output price. Such a situation would be undesirable, given that the Trading Software was designed to function continuously with minimal human intervention. Mr Boonen therefore programmed the PureQuote strategy to always add a "virtual price" for the sell (or buy) orders of the Trading Software's internal order book. The "virtual price" is also known as a "deep price". The price is "virtual" in the sense that it is not obtained from the Platform, but is inserted into the Trading Software's internal order book so that the PureQuote strategy always has a price input to work with so as to produce an output price, even if there happened to be no or insufficient input from the Platform's order book. In this way, the Trading Software's algorithm would continue functioning and placing orders on the Platform. After some changes, Mr Boonen settled on programming a deep price of 10 BTC to 1 ETH for the sell orders for ETH. This was done before the events with which we are concerned.

The terms of use of the Platform

19 We turn to the terms and conditions of the agreement governing the use of the Platform ("the Agreement"), which were set out on Quoine's website. The Agreement recited that it was "effective upon the date of electronic acceptance" and that it was "entered into by and between [Quoine] and the user of [Quoine's Platform]". We highlight some of the relevant provisions of the Agreement.

20 Under the heading "General Terms", the Agreement stated:

> …
>
> This Agreement sets forth the terms and conditions governing the access and use of the Platform. *This Agreement may be changed at*

> *any time by the Company. It is the responsibility of the User to keep himself/herself updated with the current version of the Agreement.* Users and Members waive any claim regarding this issue. This Agreement may only be amended with the express consent of the Company. ...
>
> ...
>
> [emphasis added]

The same text, which purported to allow Quoine unilaterally to vary the Agreement, also appeared under the heading "Membership And Users Of The Platform".

21 Similarly, under the heading "Representations and Warranties", the Agreement provided as follows in sub-para (h) (which we will refer to as "the Without Notice Clause"):

> *You agree that the Company reserves the right to change any of the terms, rights, obligations, privileges or institute new charges for access to or continued use of services at any time, with or without providing notice of such change.* You are responsible for reviewing the information and terms of usage as may be posted from time to time. Continued use of the services or non-termination of your membership after changes are posted or emailed constitutes your acceptance or deemed acceptance of the terms as modified. [emphasis added]

We will refer to the clauses excerpted at [20]-[21], which purported to allow Quoine unilaterally to vary the terms of the Agreement without giving notice to the users of the Platform, collectively as "the Unilateral Variation Clauses".

22 Under the heading "Trading & Order Execution", the Agreement provided that:

> Only registered users or Members are allowed to buy, sell and use the services provided by the Platform. The exchange functions of [t]he Platform will fill in orders at the best possible available market price. Note that as markets move continuously, the prices displayed on user interfaces, on our web app or on mobile apps are in no way guaranteed. The Platform, however, has been designed to allow members to fill at best possible prices and in a timely manner. Nevertheless the Company will not be liable under any circumstances for the consequences of any delay in order filling or failure to deliver or perform.
>
> *Furthermore, once an order is filled, you are notified via the Platform and such an action is irreversible.*
>
> ...
>
> [emphasis added]

B2C2 relied specifically on the italicised portion, which we will refer to as "the Irreversible Action Clause", to argue that Quoine breached the Agreement by unilaterally cancelling the Disputed Trades.

23 As part of Quoine's defence, it asserted that in addition to the Agreement, the services it provided to the users of the Platform were governed by all other terms and conditions posted on Quoine's website, including those contained within the "'Risks in Virtual Currency Transactions' statement ... which was posted on [Quoine's] website on 22 March 2017" ("the Risk Disclosure Statement").

24 The Risk Disclosure Statement began with an explanatory paragraph:

> There are many risks associated with virtual currency transactions. Please read the following to gain a sufficient understanding of the features, mechanisms, and risks in virtual currency transactions. Please execute your transaction with understanding such features, mechanisms and risks without objection and based on your own judgment and responsibility.

25 A class of risks designated "System Risks" was set out as follows in the Risk Disclosure Statement:

> **8. System Risks**
>
> …
>
> Please be aware that in the event that a customer loses any opportunity (e. g., the Company is unable to receive a customer's order and the customer therefore loses the opportunity to place the order, losing profits that he or she ordinarily would have earned) due to emergency system maintenance or a system failure, the Company will not be able to execute a process to fix the error because it will be unable to identify the order details that the customer intended to place (the original order). *The system may produce an aberrant value for the buy or sell price of the virtual currency calculated by the system. Please be aware that if the Company finds that a transaction took effect based on an aberrant value, the Company may cancel the transaction.* Your understanding is appreciated.
>
> [emphasis added]

26 Quoine contended at trial, and on appeal, that when the Risk Disclosure Statement was posted on Quoine's website in March 2017, it introduced a new term into the Agreement (referring to the italicised text in the preceding paragraph) which permitted Quoine to cancel a transaction if it had taken place at an "aberrant value". We will refer to this as "the Aberrant Value Clause".

The events leading to the Disputed Trades

27 Against that background, we outline the events that led to the Disputed Trades. On 13 April 2017, Quoine changed some login passwords for several critical operating systems on the Platform but, due to an oversight, certain necessary changes to the Quoter Program were not implemented (Judgment at [71]). The effect of this was that the Quoter Program could not access external market data from other cryptocurrency exchanges, which prevented it from generating new ETH/BTC orders on the Platform for market-making purposes (Judgment at [72]). Given that Quoine was the primary market-maker on the Platform at the material time, the fact that it stopped placing new orders resulted in the Platform's order book gradually thinning out.

28 It was not until 19 April 2017 that the pre-existing ETH/BTC orders depleted to the point that Mr Lozada described the Platform's order book as "abnormally thin". This affected the Counterparties' live P & L and caused the Platform to conclude that they were in margin sell-out positions (see [12]-[13] above). This, in turn, triggered margin calls against them and the Platform automatically force-closed their positions by placing market orders to buy ETH at the *best available price on the Platform*, in order to repay the Counterparties' ETH loans. When the margin call was triggered against Pulsar, the market orders to buy ETH were first matched with the lowest priced sell orders available on the Platform's order book at that time. Working its way through

the sell orders, Pulsar, through the Platform's algorithm, bought ETH at prices that were increasingly higher in order to fulfil the margin call (see Judgment at [78]-[79]). It became apparent that the loss of liquidity on the Platform also caused the trading systems of other users of the Platform to place sell orders at increasingly higher prices.

29 As for B2C2, the Platform's thinning order book resulted in the PureQuote strategy of the Trading Software having no or insufficient input from the Platform's order book (see [16]-[17] above). This caused the deep price of 10 BTC to 1 ETH for the sell orders for ETH, which had been programmed into the PureQuote strategy, to take effect in the Trading Software's algorithm such that the Trading Software eventually placed sell orders to sell ETH at prices of 9.99999 BTC and 10 BTC to 1 ETH on the Platform (see [18] above). When B2C2's orders became the lowest priced sell orders available on the Platform's order book, they matched with Pulsar's market orders to buy ETH. The force-closure of Mr Tomita's positions was slightly different, but it was not suggested that anything turned on this (Judgment at [80]). Eventually, a total of 13 trades were concluded between B2C2 and the Counterparties, these being the Disputed Trades which were concluded at approximately 250 times what had been the prevailing market rate of around 0.04 BTC for 1 ETH. The relevant amount of BTC was accordingly debited from the Counterparties' accounts and credited into B2C2's account, while the corresponding amount of ETH was debited from B2C2's account and credited into the Counterparties' accounts (see [2] above).

30 Mr Lozada, upon becoming aware of the Disputed Trades, and with the strenuous encouragement of Pulsar, decided that these should be cancelled and the resulting debit and credit transactions reversed. The Disputed Trades were thus cancelled on 20 April 2017 by Quoine with the corresponding debit and

credit transactions reversed.

The decision below

31 At the trial, B2C2 argued that Quoine's unilateral cancellation of the Disputed Trades and reversal of the settlement transactions were in breach of contract and/or breach of trust. In response, Quoine raised the following defences to defend its unilateral cancellation of the Disputed Trades: (a) it was contractually entitled to cancel the trades by reason of two terms it sought to imply into the Agreement; (b) it was contractually entitled to cancel the trades by reason of the Aberrant Value Clause in the Risk Disclosure Statement; (c) the Trading Contracts were void on the basis of unilateral mistake at common law, or, in the alternative, voidable on the basis of unilateral mistake in equity; (d) the Trading Contracts were void on the basis of common mistake at common law; and (e) B2C2 would otherwise be unjustly enriched at the expense of the Counterparties. As mentioned, the Judge rejected all of Quoine's defences and allowed B2C2's claims for both breach of contract and breach of trust. We briefly set out the Judge's findings in relation to B2C2's claims and Quoine's defences.

The contractual relationship

32 We first set out the Judge's findings in relation to the contractual relationship between B2C2, Quoine and the Counterparties. This in particular shaped the Judge's analysis of Quoine's defence of unilateral mistake. B2C2 argued that Quoine was a common counterparty to all the trades made between the users of the Platform. On this basis, it was said that the concluded trades took the form of back-to-back contracts between the buyer and Quoine at one end, and the seller and Quoine at the other. Quoine, on the other hand, contended that the trades were concluded directly between the buyer and the

seller, and that it only provided the Platform on which the trades would be conducted. The Judge agreed with Quoine and held that the contract in respect of each concluded trade was made directly between the buyer and the seller (see Judgment at [131]), though each of the parties was also contractually bound with Quoine under the Agreement which governed the terms of use of the Platform.

B2C2's breach of contract and breach of trust claim

33 With respect to B2C2's breach of contract claim, the Judge held that Quoine's unilateral cancellation of the Disputed Trades was a breach of the Agreement, and in particular of the Irreversible Action Clause (see [22] above; Judgment at [136]-[137]).

34 As for B2C2's breach of trust claim, the Judge found that Quoine held the BTC in B2C2's account, which had been credited following the Disputed Trades, on trust for B2C2, and so Quoine was in breach of trust when it reversed the relevant credit transaction (see Judgment at [146]). The Judge found that Quoine held the BTC on trust for B2C2 on the basis that the "three certainties" had been fulfilled, namely, certainty of subject matter, certainty of objects and certainty of intention to create a trust. First, the Judge held that there was certainty of subject matter because cryptocurrency should be treated as property that was capable of being held on trust, on the basis that it satisfied the definition of a property right in *National Provincial Bank v. Ainsworth* [1965] 1 AC 1175 ("*Ainsworth*") at 1248, in that it was definable, identifiable by third parties, capable in its nature of assumption by third parties, and had some degree of permanence or stability. In any case, the Judge noted, Quoine did not dispute this (Judgment at [142]). Second, the Judge found that there was certainty of objects, given that the beneficiaries were identifiable from the individual accounts of the users of the Platform (Judgment at [143]). Third,

the Judge found that there was certainty of intention, based on the fact that the users' assets were managed separately from Quoine's own assets, thereby indicating that Quoine intended to hold the assets of an individual user on trust for that user (Judgment at [145]).

Quoine's defences

35 Turning then to Quoine's defences, Quoine first sought to contend that two terms ought to be implied into the Agreement (collectively, "the Proposed Implied Terms"), namely:

(a) Quoine may reverse any trades which had been executed at any abnormal rate or price as a result of any technical and/or system failure and/or error affecting the Platform.

(b) Quoine may reverse any trades resulting from orders placed in breach of the terms of the Agreement, including any trade resulting from any orders which amounted to market manipulation and/or abuse and, therefore, entailed an "unauthorised use" of the Platform.

36 The Judge found that the Proposed Implied Terms, which would allow Quoine to reverse trades on the Platform under certain circumstances, contradicted the Irreversible Action Clause which was an express term of the Agreement (Judgment at [152]). The Judge also found that in any event, the Proposed Implied Terms were not necessary to give business efficacy to the Agreement. It was instead the Irreversible Action Clause, the express term, that brought certainty to the Platform and led to a clear apportionment of risk (Judgment at [153]-[154]).

37 Second, Quoine argued that the Aberrant Value Clause in the Risk Disclosure Statement (see [25]-[26] above) allowed it unilaterally to cancel the Disputed Trades. The Judge, however, disagreed that this had been incorporated into the Agreement.

38 Third, Quoine argued that it was entitled to cancel the Disputed Trades because the Trading Contracts were void on the basis of unilateral mistake at common law. Quoine submitted that the Counterparties had entered into the Trading Contracts under two mistaken beliefs: (a) that it was necessary to close out their positions in response to the margin calls which the Platform made on them ("the First Mistaken Belief"); and (b) that they were buying ETH for BTC under contracts at prices which accurately represented or did not deviate significantly from the true market value and/or price of ETH relative to BTC on 19 April 2017 ("the Second Mistaken Belief"). Quoine argued in the alternative that the Trading Contracts were voidable on the basis of unilateral mistake in equity. Quoine submitted that by deliberately including the deep prices in the Trading Software, B2C2's conduct was unconscionable and amounted to sharp practice.

39 In considering the issue of unilateral mistake, the Judge held that where it was necessary to assess the state of mind of a party in situations where acts of *deterministic* computer programs were in issue, regard should be had to the state of mind of the programmer of the relevant program at the time it was written—which in the present case would be that of Mr Boonen (Judgment at [211]). The Judge rejected Quoine's contention that the court should instead approach the matter on the basis of considering what the contracting parties were likely to have known and intended if, hypothetically, they had met on the "floor of the exchange" for the purpose of entering into the Disputed Trades on 19 April 2017 (Judgment at [200]). The Judge found this approach wholly artificial given that the contracting parties had chosen to use deterministic algorithms as the means of entering into the Trading Contracts (see Judgment at [204]).

40 The Judge held that the Trading Contracts were not void on the basis of

unilateral mistake at *common law*. With regard to the First Mistaken Belief, the Judge found that Mr Tseung Wai Kit ("Mr Tseung"), a co-founder of Pulsar, did genuinely hold such a mistaken belief. But the Judge was of the view that this was not a mistaken belief as to a term of the Trading Contracts (see Judgment at [220] and [222]). As regards the Second Mistaken Belief, not only did the Judge find that Mr Tseung did in fact hold such a mistaken belief, the Judge also held that it was a mistake as to a term of the Trading Contracts (Judgment at [227]-[228]).

41 In considering whether Mr Boonen had actual knowledge of the First Mistaken Belief and the Second Mistaken Belief, contrary to Quoine's assertions, the Judge did not think that there was any malicious motive on Mr Boonen's part in designing the Trading Software and including the deep prices in the manner that he did. Mr Boonen had settled on programming a deep price of 10 BTC to 1 ETH for the sell orders for ETH (see [18] above) after reducing it twice, first from an initial price of "a very high number" of BTC to 1 ETH to 50 BTC to 1 ETH, and then to 10 BTC to 1 ETH, and the Judge accepted that these reductions were done for a variety of legitimate reasons (see Judgment at [96]-[97]). The Judge also accepted that although Mr Boonen knew, at the time he designed the Trading Software, that it would place sell orders at the deep price if the Platform's order book became empty, Mr Boonen did not ever consider that there was a real possibility of the deep price orders being executed (see Judgment at [123]). The Judge found that Mr Boonen's design of the Trading Software and choice of the deep price were chiefly directed to ensuring that the Trading Software remained operational rather than exploiting the existence of illiquidity on the Platform or a thinning order book (see Judgment at [121]). The Judge concluded that while Mr Boonen's programming was opportunistic in the sense that B2C2 should be best placed to

make a profit if the unlikely became a reality, it was in no respect sinister (Judgment at [125]).

42 The Judge also accepted Mr Boonen's evidence that he was unaware of the glitches causing illiquidity on the Platform until after the events of 19 April 2017. While Mr Boonen had also made changes to the Trading Software's code on 13 April 2017, the Judge accepted that he had done so independent of and without knowledge of Quoine's failure, on the same day, to take certain necessary steps to secure the continued proper functioning of the Quoter Program (see Judgment at [100]-[102]). There was also no evidence to show that Mr Boonen had turned his mind to the relationship between the margin traders and those who had loaned them money, much less programmed the Trading Software to exploit this relationship by causing its deep prices to consummate force-closures of the positions of margin traders (see Judgment at [124] and [223]). The Judge found that Mr Boonen also did not turn his mind to the circumstances that might lead to trades being executed at the deep prices (Judgment at [230]). Therefore, the Judge concluded that Mr Boonen did not have actual knowledge of the First Mistaken Belief and the Second Mistaken Belief. He accordingly found that there was no basis for Quoine to rely on unilateral mistake at common law to void the Trading Contracts.

43 The Judge also held that the Trading Contracts were not voidable on the basis of unilateral mistake in *equity*, because he found Mr Boonen had no constructive knowledge of either the First Mistaken Belief or the Second Mistaken Belief (see Judgment at [233]). The Judge further held that there was no impropriety on B2C2's part, and its conduct, even if opportunistic, was not sinister (Judgment at [236]).

44 Fourth, Quoine argued that it was entitled to cancel the Disputed Trades because the Trading Contracts were void on the basis of common mistake at

common law. Quoine contended that at the time the Disputed Trades were concluded, both the Counterparties and B2C2 wrongly assumed that (a) the Platform was working correctly and (b) the trades were therefore being transacted under normal market conditions, meaning at prices which accurately reflected or did not deviate significantly from the true market value and/or price of ETH relative to BTC on 19 April 2017. The Judge held that this defence failed because even if Quoine held a mistaken belief as to the prices at which the Disputed Trades were to be concluded, Mr Boonen (and thus B2C2) did not (see Judgment at [237]-[239]).

45 Fifth, Quoine argued that it was necessary to cancel the Disputed Trades in order to prevent B2C2 from being unjustly enriched at the expense of the Counterparties. The Judge acknowledged that as a matter of legal formality, a cause of action in unjust enrichment would only accrue if B2C2 succeeded in its suit, and it would technically accrue to the Counterparties and not to Quoine. However, since B2C2 had not applied for this defence to be struck out, the Judge decided to treat it as a potential defence (Judgment at [242]-[244]). He found that the fact that the Trading Contracts were valid and enforceable operated as a bar to any action in unjust enrichment (Judgment at [247], [249] and [252]).

46 As for the relief sought by B2C2, the Judge declined to allow B2C2's prayer for specific performance, on the basis that the price of BTC at the time of the Judge's decision was significantly higher than that when the Disputed Trades were concluded, and this would therefore cause substantial hardship to Quoine (Judgment at [256]).

The issues on appeal

47 The issues that arise in this appeal and that we will address in this

Judgment are the following:

(a) What were the contractual arrangements between B2C2, Quoine and the Counterparties?

(b) Was Quoine contractually entitled to cancel the Disputed Trades by reason of any express or implied terms of its contract with B2C2?

(c) In relation to Quoine's defence of unilateral mistake, did the Judge err in finding that Mr Boonen did not have actual or constructive knowledge of a relevant mistaken belief on the part of the Counterparties in relation to the Disputed Trades?

(d) Were the Trading Contracts void on the basis of common mistake at common law?

(e) Was Quoine entitled to cancel the Disputed Trades on the basis that B2C2 would otherwise be unjustly enriched at the expense of the Counterparties?

(f) Did Quoine hold B2C2's cryptocurrency assets on trust?

Our decision

The contractual relationships

48 We begin with the question of how the contractual relationships between B2C2, Quoine and the Counterparties should be characterised. As the Judge noted, the resolution of this question is relevant to the subsequent analysis on unilateral mistake, in so far as it is first necessary to identify which contract was affected by any asserted mistake and who the mistaken party was (Judgment at [129]).

49 B2C2 contended that the correct way to understand the contractual relationships was to see the Trading Contracts as part of a "spider's web" of contracts, with Quoine as the central counterparty to both sides of each

trade. In this way, the Platform would enable trading to be conducted on an anonymous basis as between the ultimate buyers and sellers. B2C2 argued on this basis that there could be no operative mistake as to the terms of the trading contracts made *between Quoine and B2C2* in relation to the Disputed Trades. Any alleged unilateral mistake would be that of the Counterparties, and so Quoine's defence of unilateral mistake would fail at the threshold. Quoine, on the other hand, argued that the Agreement made it plain that Quoine merely provided a service to the users of the Platform, and that the trading contracts were made directly between the buyers and the sellers.

50 We affirm the Judge's analysis of the contractual arrangements between the various parties, in which he accepted Quoine's characterisation of the contractual relationships. In essence, he held that the Trading Contracts were formed directly between B2C2 and the Counterparties (Judgment at [131]). The Trading Contracts constituted one of three categories of contracts the Judge identified, as follows (see Judgment at [126]):

(a) The first category was the "Platform contracts", which governed the use of the services provided by the Platform, the parties to which were Quoine and the individual users of the Platform, and the terms of which were found in the Agreement.

(b) The second category was the "Margin contracts", which concerned the arrangements based on which the margin traders would have their transactions financed. In the present case, the parties to these were Quoine and the Counterparties.

(c) The third category was the "Trading contracts", which were the contracts that came into existence when trades were concluded and governed the relationship between the parties to those trades. For the avoidance of doubt, we refer to this category of contracts as "trading contracts". As for the specific trading contracts that underlay the Disputed Trades, we refer to these as Trading Contracts, as noted at [4] above. The Judge held that B2C2 and the Counterparties were the parties to the Trading Contracts in question in this case.

51 In our judgment, this characterisation of the trading contracts best accords with the terms of the Agreement, which made clear that Quoine was merely providing a *service* to the users of the Platform which would transact with one another in the exchange of cryptocurrencies on the Platform.

52 First, the "General Terms" of the Agreement stated as follows:

> Quoine is a platform that provides services that allow the exchange of virtual currencies such as [BTC] for fiat currencies. ...
>
> ...
>
> This Agreement sets forth the terms and conditions governing the access and use of the Platform. ...
>
> ...

The same was repeated under the heading "Membership And Users Of The Platform".

53 Second, under the heading "Fees, Funding & Withdrawals", it was stated that "[a]s compensation for [t]he Platform services ... [Quoine] charges a fee on each transaction initiated by [the users of the Platform]". This lent support to the contention that Quoine was merely providing a service to the users of the Platform for which it charged a fee.

54 Third, under the heading "Trading & Order Execution", it was stated that:

> Only registered users or Members are allowed to buy, sell and use the

> services provided by the Platform. The exchange functions of [t]he Platform will fill in orders at the best possible available market price. ...
>
> ...

This suggested that Quoine's primary function was to operate the Platform which would fill orders placed by its users at the best *available* market price.

55 We therefore agree with the Judge that Quoine was only providing the services available on the Platform and that it was the parties to the trading contracts that were responsible for whether and on what terms they would place or fill orders. This, however, is not to say that there was no contractual relationship between Quoine and the users of the Platform. First, as we have noted at [50(a)] above, Quoine as the provider of the Platform's services entered into Platform contracts with the users of the Platform. Second, as noted at [50(b)] above, Quoine could be and was party to Margin contracts. Third, given that Quoine also acted as a market-maker on the Platform, there would have been situations where Quoine was the counterparty to a concluded trade, in which case it would have been party to a trading contract with a user of the Platform. However, the trades that we are concerned with in the present case, specifically the Disputed Trades, did not involve that situation.

56 In addition, we do not accept B2C2's other arguments as to why the contractual relationships ought to be seen as a "spider's web" of contracts. B2C2 contended that Quoine must have interposed itself as a "middle-man" in any trade and was obliged to underwrite the risk of a counterparty not being able to fund a trade, given that trading on the Platform was conducted anonymously and the users of the Platform would not have visibility of the creditworthiness of potential counterparties. We do not accept this because the terms of the

Agreement seem to us to say the very opposite:

> **Trading & Order Execution**
>
> …
>
> [Quoine] and its affiliates *assume no responsibility for any loss or damage incurred by members or users as a result of their use of [t]he Platform* …
>
> …
>
> **Representations and Warranties**
>
> As a Member or User, you agree to the following:
>
> > …
> >
> > **d.** You agree that use of the service is *at your own risk* and you are solely responsible for interactions … with any other Member or User of the service. [Quoine] … *assume[s] no responsibility whatsoever for harm that may come to you as a result of your interactions with any other Member or User of the service* …
>
> …
>
> [emphasis added]

57 It is evident from these terms that Quoine had expressly sought to disclaim any liability for losses that users of the Platform might suffer arising from their use of the Platform. This would include the credit risk of a counterparty.

58 We also do not accept B2C2's argument that the trading contracts could not have been formed directly between the buyers and sellers on the Platform because all trading was done anonymously. Even if the traders were unaware of who their potential counterparties might be before the conclusion of the trades,

once a trade was completed, the identity of the parties to the trade became ascertainable by way of a unique user identification number (Judgment at Annex 3). Further, there is no difficulty in the fact that the traders would not know who their counterparties were until after the trades were concluded, given that they were agreeing in effect to enter into contracts with such other users of the Platform as accepted their bids or asks as the case might be. We will discuss this in greater detail when we examine the formation of contracts by algorithmic trading (at [94]-[96] below).

Express and implied terms of the Agreement

59 Quoine argued that there were terms in the Agreement, both express and implied, which allowed it to cancel the Disputed Trades. We do not accept these contentions for the following reasons.

The Aberrant Value Clause

60 Quoine argued on appeal (as it did at trial) that the Aberrant Value Clause in the Risk Disclosure Statement (see [25]-[26] above) entitled it to cancel the Disputed Trades. It also contended that the Unilateral Variation Clauses (see [20]-[21] above) allowed it unilaterally to vary the terms of the Agreement when it uploaded the Risk Disclosure Statement on its website *without* giving notice to the users of the Platform. On the other hand, B2C2 maintained that neither the Risk Disclosure Statement nor the Aberrant Value Clause had been incorporated into the Agreement. B2C2 further submitted that even if the Aberrant Value Clause had been incorporated into the Agreement, it did not assist Quoine because it would only have permitted Quoine to cancel transactions in which the prices of the trades had been incorrectly calculated by Quoine's system due to a "system failure" or "malfunction". "System failure" and "malfunction" were defined terms in the Risk Disclosure Statement, and required there to be a situation where customers could "no longer ... place

orders over the Internet”, or the orders “arrive[d] late or [could not] be placed” (see also [68] below). The Disputed Trades were not such transactions.

61 The Judge found that the Unilateral Variation Clauses, properly construed, did not allow Quoine to change the terms of the Agreement without its drawing this to the attention of the users of the Platform in some way. Quoine thus had to provide notice to the users in order to effect a change to the terms of the Agreement. The Judge also found that merely uploading the Risk Disclosure Statement on Quoine's website without any indication that it was intended to have legal effect did not constitute such notice that changes had been made to the Agreement. This was because the Risk Disclosure Statement purported only to be a summary of risks with no indication that it was intended to have legal effect (see Judgment at [174]-[176]).

62 We affirm the Judge's analysis on this point. Although it was not necessary for Quoine to obtain the consent of a user of the Platform before changing the terms of the Agreement, we are satisfied that a user had to have reasonable means of knowing that there had been a modification to the terms and what that modification was before any such change could have legal effect. Armed with such knowledge, the user could then decide whether or not it would continue to use the Platform. In this case, all Quoine did was to upload the Risk Disclosure Statement onto its website without more. This could not on any basis have sufficed to constitute the requisite notice.

63 Further, in determining whether notice of changes to the Agreement had to be given, we also have regard to the Unilateral Variation Clauses, which include the Without Notice Clause (see [21] above). We reproduce the Without Notice Clause here:

> You agree that [Quoine] reserves the right to change any of the terms, rights, obligations, privileges or institute new charges *for access to or continued use of services at any time, with or without providing notice of such change*. You are responsible for reviewing the information and terms of usage as may be posted from time to time. *Continued use of the services or non-termination of your membership after changes are posted or emailed constitutes your acceptance or deemed acceptance of the terms as modified.* [emphasis added]

64 We note that the Without Notice Clause *expressly* stated that Quoine was permitted to effect changes to any of the terms, rights, obligations, privileges or to institute new charges for access to or continued use of services "without providing notice of such change". However, the changes contemplated by this clause were restricted only to changes pertaining to "access to or continued use" of Quoine's services. We assume, without finding, that incorporating the Aberrant Value Clause into the Agreement would be such a change. Even so, we think that it was *implicit* within the Without Notice Clause that a user of the Platform ought to be given the opportunity to consider the change in question, so that it could decide whether to continue using Quoine's services. We say this for three reasons.

65 First, the Without Notice Clause stated that changes to the terms would be "posted or emailed", which suggested that Quoine would take positive steps to bring the changes to the attention of the users of the Platform. Second, the clause stated that continued use of Quoine's services after such changes had been posted or e-mailed would amount to an affirmation or deemed acceptance of the terms as modified. This part of the clause would not make sense if the

users did not have an *awareness* of those modified terms to begin with. Third, the "General Terms" of the Agreement provided that the users of the Platform were responsible for reviewing the changes to the Agreement:

> … This Agreement may be changed at any time by [Quoine]. *It is the responsibility of the User to keep himself/herself updated with the current version of the Agreement.* Users and Members waive any claim regarding this issue. …[emphasis added]

This contemplated that users would have the *opportunity* to review the changes in the first place, which in turn necessitated them being given notice of these changes.

66 For these reasons, we do not think that the requirement of notice was displaced by the Without Notice Clause. Sufficient notice of the incorporation of the Aberrant Value Clause as a term of the Agreement had to be given to users of the Platform before it could be regarded as having been incorporated into the Agreement. We acknowledge that pursuant to the "General Terms" of the Agreement, the onus was on the users of the Platform to keep themselves updated with the latest version of the Agreement. However, there must at least have been some indication on Quoine's website to inform users about amendments to the Agreement. We therefore agree with the Judge that simply uploading the Risk Disclosure Statement onto Quoine's website without alerting users to the fact that a new term had been introduced was insufficient to constitute the requisite notice (see Judgment at [176]).

67 Moreover, as the Judge pointed out, the Risk Disclosure Statement appeared to be nothing more than a summary of the various risks that users would expect to face when using the Platform (see [24] above), and there

would have been no reason for a user reading it to think that amendments to the terms of the Agreement were embedded within it. We also find no reason to disturb the Judge's finding that there was nothing on Quoine's website, the Agreement, or the Risk Disclosure Statement to alert the user to the need to read these documents together.

68 In any case, even if the Aberrant Value Clause had been incorporated into the Agreement, we do not think that it had the effect that Quoine suggested it did of entitling it to cancel the Disputed Trades. The relevant portion of the Risk Disclosure Statement which contained the Aberrant Value Clause (the italicised text below) stated:

> There is the risk that a system failure may occur due to changes to the external environment, etc., and this may disrupt a customer's ability to execute transactions. A 'system failure' is when [Quoine] finds that a malfunction (not including obstructed network lines or problems with a customer's computer, etc.) has clearly arisen in the system required to provide [Quoine's] services, and customers are no longer able to place orders over the Internet ([Quoine's] website, mobile site, or applications) or customers' orders arrive late or cannot be placed.
>
> Please be aware that in the event that a customer loses any opportunity (e.g., [Quoine] is unable to receive a customer's order and the customer therefore loses the opportunity to place the order, losing profits that he or she ordinarily would have earned) due to emergency system maintenance or a system failure, [Quoine] will not be able to execute a process to fix the error because it will be unable to identify the order details that the customer intended to place (the original

> order). *The system may produce an aberrant value for the buy or sell price of the virtual currency calculated by the system. Please be aware that if [Quoine] finds that a transaction took effect based on an aberrant value, [Quoine] may cancel the transaction.* Your understanding is appreciated.
>
> [emphasis added]

69 In our judgment, having regard to these portions of the Risk Disclosure Statement, the Aberrant Value Clause was meant to apply in situations where there was a discrepancy between the value input by a user of the Platform and the value generated or calculated by the system "due to emergency system maintenance or a system failure". In short, this would be the case where the value generated by the Platform was not the value intended by the user. We come to this conclusion because of the words "[Quoine] will not be able to execute a process to fix the error because it will be unable to identify the order details that the customer *intended to place*" [emphasis added]. It would be unsurprising in such circumstances that Quoine could cancel the transaction; this was simply never an intended transaction. In the present case, however, the only alleged "malfunction" in the Platform's system was the Quoter Program not being able to access external price data and therefore not being able to generate new orders, which led to a gradual thinning out of the Platform's order book. Apart from that, the market orders placed by the Platform on the Counterparties' behalf were executed exactly as intended, which was to purchase ETH at the best available price on the Platform at the material time. The prices of B2C2's sell orders for ETH, at prices of 9.99999 BTC and 10 BTC to 1 ETH, which orders were matched with the Counterparties' market orders, were similarly not "aberrant" in the sense that they were exactly what

B2C2 intended them to be; they were simply the result of the pre-programmed deep price of 10 BTC to 1 ETH in the PureQuote strategy taking effect (see [29] above). The Disputed Trades were concluded based on prices *correctly* quoted by the Trading Software for B2C2, and market orders that were *correctly* placed by the Platform for the Counterparties.

70 Aside from this, if we were to accept Quoine's position, it would seem to lead to the conclusion that the Aberrant Value Clause enabled Quoine to undertake some sort of "reasonableness" check on transactions entered into by others and then to cancel whatever transactions *it* thought was beyond the bounds of reason. We do not think this can possibly be correct.

The Proposed Implied Terms

71 We turn then to Quoine's contention that it was entitled to cancel the Disputed Trades on the basis of the Proposed Implied Terms (see [35] above). We agree with the Judge that the terms sought to be implied are incompatible with the Irreversible Action Clause (see [22] above). The Proposed Implied Terms would allow Quoine to reverse trades on the Platform which (a) had been executed at abnormal prices as a result of any error affecting the Platform, or (b) resulted from orders placed in breach of the terms of the Agreement. The Irreversible Action Clause, however, provided that "once an order is filled, [the user is] notified via the Platform and such an action is irreversible".

72 In *Sembcorp Marine Ltd v. PPL Holdings Pte Ltd and another and another appeal* [2013] 4 SLR 193 at [94]–[95], we held that a term may only be implied into a contract where the parties did not contemplate the issue at all and so left a gap in their contractual arrangements. If the question is whether the Agreement made provision for whether and when a concluded trade could be reversed, the answer to this was that the Irreversible Action Clause made it clear

that once an order had been filled and the parties to the trade had been notified by the Platform, such an action was *irreversible*. In this regard, the Proposed Implied Terms are inherently incompatible with the Irreversible Action Clause given that they purport to allow Quoine to reverse trades which had been executed and had become irreversible.

73 Quoine sought to meet this by contending that the Irreversible Action Clause only applied to the users of the Platform and not to Quoine itself as the owner and operator of the Platform. We disagree. It is clear from the plain words of the Irreversible Action Clause and the adjacent terms that it was meant to apply to all orders that had been filled, regardless of whether it was a user of the Platform or Quoine itself that was seeking to reverse the trades. The Irreversible Action Clause (the italicised text below) was found under the heading “Trading & Order Execution”, which provided as follows:

> Only registered users or Members are allowed to buy, sell and use the services provided by the Platform. The exchange functions of [t]he Platform will fill in orders at the best possible available market price. Note that as markets move continuously, the prices displayed on user interfaces, on our web app or on mobile apps are in no way guaranteed. The Platform, however, has been designed to allow members to fill at best possible prices and in a timely manner. Nevertheless [Quoine] will not be liable under any circumstances for the consequences of any delay in order filling or failure to deliver or perform.
>
> *Furthermore, once an order is filled, you are notified via the Platform and such an action is irreversible.*
>
> [Quoine] and its affiliates assume no responsibility for any loss or

damage incurred by members or users as a result of their use of [t]he Platform …

[emphasis added]

74 As the Judge noted at [151] of the Judgment, the Agreement governed the contractual relationship between Quoine and all the users of the Platform. Therefore, the terms of the Agreement would presumptively be equally applicable to Quoine. This view is supported by the sentence immediately preceding the Irreversible Action Clause, which sought to limit *Quoine's* liability for the consequences of any delay in the filling of an order or any failure to deliver or perform. Similarly, the sentence that immediately followed the Irreversible Action Clause limited *Quoine's* liability for any loss incurred by a user as a result of its use of the Platform. These sentences would have been unnecessary if the provisions under the heading "Trading & Order Execution" did not apply to Quoine. Furthermore, the Irreversible Action Clause itself provided that once an order had been filled, and the users of the Platform had been notified through the Platform, "such an action", which in this context could only mean the filling of the order, was irreversible. As the Judge noted at [152] of the Judgment, the word "irreversible" was plainly not qualified in any way and drew no distinction between the users of the Platform and Quoine as the operator of the Platform.

75 Subsequent to the hearing of this appeal, Quoine drew our attention to an article which commented on several aspects of the Judgment: see Kelvin Low & Eliza Mik, "Unpicking a Fin(e)tech Mess: Can Old Doctrines Cope in the 21st Century?", *Oxford Business Law Blog*, 8 November 2019 <https://www.law.ox.ac.uk/business-law-blog/blog/2019/11/unpicking-finetech-mess-can-old-doctrines-cope-21st-century> (accessed 14 November 2019) ("*Low &*

Mik"). The authors argued that if Quoine itself was not a counterparty to the Disputed Trades, then it must have been acting as agent for B2C2 and the Counterparties, and the users of the Platform in general, for the purposes of matching trades. On that basis, the authors contended that the Irreversible Action Clause should be construed to mean that only the *instructions* given by the users to Quoine as agent were irreversible, and not the trades themselves. We respectfully disagree.

76 First, it appears that the authors' underlying premise was that the relationship between Quoine and the users of the Platform was binary—either Quoine was the central counterparty to all trades on the Platform, or it acted as agent for the users. However, we have held that the trading contracts were formed directly between the parties to the respective trades (see [50(c)] above) and this did not require a finding that Quoine acted as agent for the parties. We consider the function of the Platform to be somewhat similar to that of an Internet messaging application, which allows users of the application to communicate with one another. If a contract is formed between two users on this messaging application, it would be artificial to suggest that the owner or operator of the Platform acted as an agent for these users. There was no suggestion that trading instructions were first passed to Quoine as a third party before they were uploaded on the Platform. Second, and more fundamentally, we consider the authors' interpretation of the Irreversible Action Clause to be contrary to the plain words of the clause. The irreversibility applies to the action of filling an order, as we have held at [74] above.

77 For these reasons, we do not think that it is permissible to imply the terms that Quoine was contending for.

Unilateral mistake

78 We turn to the central feature of Quoine's defence, and one which the

Judge acknowledged was "the most troubling and difficult in this case" (Judgment at [183]). Quoine relied on both unilateral mistake at common law and in equity to argue that the Trading Contracts should be vitiated, and therefore that its cancellation of the Disputed Trades was warranted. There is a threshold question whether Quoine, which was not a party to the Trading Contracts, could invoke the doctrine by way of defence to the claim that it breached *its* contract with B2C2 (meaning, the Irreversible Action Clause in the Agreement). In other words, the question is whether Quoine would necessarily be excused of its breach even if the Trading Contracts were vitiated. We assume, without deciding, that the defence of unilateral mistake was available to Quoine in the indirect way argued. The parties did not dispute this specific point. As noted at [45] above and [132] below, a broadly similar approach was taken by the Judge and by us in the context of the claim in unjust enrichment. Leaving this to the side, the complexity arose because the defence of unilateral mistake was being raised for the first time, as far as we are aware, in the context of algorithmic trading and the formation of contracts by such means. B2C2 and the Counterparties had entered into the Trading Contracts by means of B2C2's and Quoine's deterministic algorithms. B2C2 and the Counterparties therefore did not know until *after* the Trading Contracts had been entered into, whether an offer would be made or accepted, or the terms on which a contract would be concluded. How then could the doctrine of unilateral mistake apply in this situation, where the contracting parties did not know the specific terms on which the Trading Contracts would be entered into? It is therefore necessary to consider the principles behind the doctrine before considering its application to this novel situation.

79 We state at the outset that we approach this issue of unilateral mistake on the footing that as a court applying the common law, our task is to apply the

existing law on the doctrine subject to incremental adjustments being made in order to suit the particular context. Algorithmic trading is an area of dynamic change, and it might be more appropriate for legislative intervention in due course, if it were thought that a more fundamental redesign of the applicable legal framework is called for. That is certainly not our view at this time and we consider that the existing body of law can be meaningfully adapted to deal with the situation at hand.

Doctrine of unilateral mistake at common law and in equity

80 We begin by setting out the requirements for unilateral mistake at common law and in equity, and in so doing, we highlight their differences in requirements and consequences. This was the subject of our decision in *Chwee Kin Keong and others v. Digilandmall.com Pte Ltd* [2005] 1 SLR(R) 502 ("*Digilandmall.com*"). In essence, one party must have transacted while operating under a mistake as to a *fundamental term* of the contract (see *Digilandmall.com* at [34] and [80]). As we note below, there is a question as to whether this also applies in the context of the doctrine in equity. But beyond this:

(a) For unilateral mistake at common law, the non-mistaken party must have had *actual* knowledge of the mistaken party's mistake, and if this is established, the contract will be rendered *void*.

(b) For unilateral mistake in equity, the non-mistaken party must have had at least *constructive* knowledge of the mistaken party's mistake and must have engaged in some *unconscionable* conduct in relation to that mistake, and if this is established, the contract will be *voidable*.

81 We begin with the rationale underlying the doctrine of unilateral mistake at common law. As we alluded to in *Digilandmall.com*, the reason for the doctrine is that "a party who is aware of the error made by the other party cannot claim

that there is *consensus ad idem*" (at [31]). It follows that the doctrine is best understood by having regard to the principles governing offer and acceptance. A contract cannot be formed unless the contracting parties agree as to the *terms* of the contract. Unilateral mistake at common law voids a contract because the contracting parties have not in fact reached an agreement when one party is mistaken as to the terms put forward by the other party, and that other party knows this to be the case. In such circumstances, there is no correspondence between offer and acceptance. To explain this, it is helpful to set out what has been explained in *The Law of Contract in Singapore* (Andrew Phang Boon Leong gen ed) (Academy Publishing, 2012) at para 10.144:

> ... By [the theory of 'promisee objectivity'], there is no contract where the non-mistaken party knows ... that the mistaken party does not intend to contract on the intended terms. There is no departure from an 'objective' view of agreement because the law, in looking at the non-mistaken party's knowledge of the mistaken party's intention is not asking what the mistaken party intended. Instead, it is looking at what the non-mistaken party had reason to believe for the purpose of interpreting the communication made by the mistaken party to the non-mistaken party. ...

In short, where the non-mistaken party knows that the mistaken party made a mistake in communicating a term, the non-mistaken party cannot treat the mistaken party as having agreed to the term. Absent such knowledge, however, the position is otherwise because it would give rise to intolerable uncertainty in contractual arrangements if a party could be permitted to assert its own subjective view that it had operated under a mistake, even though there appeared objectively to be a concluded contract and the non-mistaken party was fairly operating on that basis.

82 Significantly, for the relevant mistake to void the contract, it must be about a *term* of the contract, and cannot merely be a mistaken assumption about the circumstances under which the contract was or would be concluded. A contract can be concluded as long as the contracting parties agree as to its terms, regardless of their beliefs and assumptions about the contract. This proposition was alluded to in the decision of *Smith v. Hughes* (1871) LR 6 QB 597 ("*Smith v. Hughes*").

83 In *Smith v. Hughes*, the plaintiff farmer sued the defendant racehorse trainer for breach of a contract for the sale of oats. The plaintiff had given the defendant's manager a sample of the *new* oats that he intended to sell and the defendant agreed to purchase those oats of which he received a sample. The defendant subsequently refused to complete the contract on the ground that the contract had been for the sale and purchase of *old* oats. At the trial, it was disputed whether the plaintiff and the defendant's manager discussed the subject of the oats being old oats. At the end of the trial, the judge put two questions to the jury: (a) whether the word "old" had been used with reference to the oats in the conversation between the plaintiff and the defendant's manager; and (b) whether the plaintiff had believed that the defendant believed that he was contracting for old oats. The judge directed the jury to find for the defendant if either question was answered in the affirmative. The jury found for the defendant but did not give specific answers to the two questions.

84 On appeal, the court held that the judge's direction in respect of the first question was correct. However, it found that the judge's direction in respect of the second question was either wrong or likely to be misunderstood by the jury, and a new trial was therefore necessary. In the words of Hannen J, for the jury

to find for the defendant pursuant to the second direction, "the jury should find not merely that the plaintiff believed the defendant to believe that he was buying old oats, but that he believed the defendant to believe that he, the plaintiff, was *contracting* to sell old oats" [emphasis added] (*Smith v. Hughes* at 611).

85 The decisions of Cockburn CJ and Blackburn J too illustrate the point that the relevant mistake to void a contract, on the basis of unilateral mistake, had to be about a *term* of the contract, and not merely about the circumstances under which the contract was or would be concluded.

86 Blackburn J put it in these terms at 606-607:

> ... on the sale of a specific article, unless there be a warranty making it part of the bargain that it possesses some particular quality, the purchaser must take the article he has bought though it does not possess that quality. ... *even if the vendor was aware that the purchaser thought that the article possessed that quality*, and would not have entered into the contract unless he had so thought, still the purchaser is bound, unless the vendor was guilty of some fraud or deceit upon him, and that a mere abstinence from disabusing the purchaser of that impression is not fraud or deceit ... [emphasis added]

87 Cockburn CJ identified "the fallacy of confounding what was merely a *motive* operating on the buyer to induce him to buy with one of the essential *conditions* of the contract" [emphasis added] (at 606). If a contracting party made a mistake about the circumstances under which the contract was or would be concluded, *caveat emptor* would apply, and the contract would not be vitiated so long as the parties did reach an agreement on the *terms* of the contract. In

emphasising this point, Cockburn CJ also observed that “the passive acquiescence of the seller in the self-deception of the buyer [in thinking that the oats were old oats]” would not entitle the buyer to avoid the contract (*Smith v. Hughes* ([82] *supra*) at 602–603).

88 The requirement that the relevant mistake to void a contract on the basis of unilateral mistake must concern a *term* of the contract was also applied more recently in the decision of the English High Court in *Statoil ASA v. Louis Dreyfus Energy Services LP (The "Harriette N")* [2008] 2 Lloyd's Rep 685 ("*Statoil*"). In *Statoil*, the relevant question was whether a contract of compromise between the parties was binding on the claimant when its employee had made an error in calculating the amount of demurrage due from the defendant, because the claimant's employee thought that the vessel in question had completed discharging her cargo on 13 October 2006 when in fact she only completed discharging on 24 October 2006. Prior to concluding the contract of compromise, the defendant's employee realised that the claimant's employee made this error but opted to say nothing about it. Aikens J held that it was *not a term* of the contract that the compromise was reached on the premise that the discharge had been completed on 13 October 2006 (at [91]). He accordingly held that there was no operative unilateral mistake as to a term of the contract, which therefore remained binding. Citing *Smith v. Hughes* in coming to his decision, Aikens J framed the relevant proposition of law as follows (*Statoil* at [88]):

> … if one party has made a mistake about a fact on which he bases his decision to enter into the contract, but *that fact does not form a term of the contract* itself, then, *even if the other party knows that the first is mistaken as to this fact*, the contract will be binding. …[emphasis added]

89 We turn next to the rationale behind the doctrine of unilateral mistake in equity. We held in *Digilandmall.com* ([80] *supra*) that we have an equitable jurisdiction with regard to unilateral mistake and that this jurisdiction exists to assist us in achieving the ends of justice in appropriate cases (see *Digilandmall.com* at [74] and [77]). To invoke this jurisdiction, it must be shown that the non-mistaken party had constructive knowledge of the mistaken party's mistake and further, that it was *unconscionable for the non-mistaken party to insist on the performance of the contract* because it had engaged in some unconscionable conduct or sharp practice in relation to that mistake (see *Digilandmall.com* at [80] and [83]).

90 There is a question as to whether unilateral mistake in equity can extend beyond a mistake as to a term of the contract, and related to this, whether a mistaken assumption about the circumstances under which the contract was or would be concluded can itself be an operative mistake. The English authorities seem to suggest, on balance, that there is no equitable jurisdiction to vitiate a contract for unilateral mistake and if there were, they appear to doubt whether it extends beyond a mistake as to a term of the contract: see *Chitty on Contracts* (H G Beale gen ed) (Sweet & Maxwell, 33rd Ed, 2018) ("*Chitty*") at para 3-027; Edwin Peel, *The Law of Contract* (Sweet & Maxwell, 14th Ed, 2015) at para 8-058; Jack Beatson, Andrew Burrows & John Cartwright, *Anson's Law of Contract* (Oxford University Press, 29th Ed, 2010) at p 278; see also *Clarion Ltd and others v. National Provident Institution* [2000] WLR 1888 at 1905C–1905H; *Great Peace Shipping Ltd v. Tsavliris Salvage (International) Ltd* [2003] QB 679; *Huyton SA v. Distribuidora Internacional de Productos Agricolas SA de CV* [2003] 2 Lloyd's Rep 780; *Statoil*. The High Court of Australia in *Taylor v. Johnson* (1983) 151 CLR 422 treated relief for unilateral

mistake as to a fundamental term as equitable in character; see also N C Seddon & R A Bigwood, *Cheshire and Fifoot Law of Contract* (LexisNexis Butterworths, 11th Australian Ed, 2017) at para 12.44 in which it is said that an equitable principle of mistake has probably displaced any possible common law doctrine of mistake.

91 As for the position in Singapore, although there is a recognised equitable jurisdiction for dealing with unilateral mistake, the question as to whether this extends beyond a mistake as to a term of the contract remains open. In *Digilandmall.com*, the mistake in question was undoubtedly one as to a fundamental term of the contract, namely, the price, and there was no detailed discussion about whether any other type of mistake could be relied upon to invoke the defence (see *Digilandmall.com* at [34] and [80]). It is true that in *Digilandmall.com*, the court did go on to observe that "[o]ne suggested way" to differentiate between unilateral mistake at common law and in equity would be to hold that the former was "limited to mistakes with regard to the subject matter of the contract", while the latter "[could] have regard to a wider and perhaps open-ended category of 'fundamental' mistake" (at [75]). This, however, was not explored or developed in detail.

92 The issue of whether unilateral mistake in equity can extend beyond a mistake as to a term of the contract was not fully argued before us. In addition, we are satisfied that it is not necessary for us to determine this question in this case. Even on the Judge's view of the relevant belief (the Second Mistaken Belief) being treated as a mistake for the purposes of the equitable jurisdiction, there are the further requirements of constructive knowledge of the mistake and unconscionability and those simply did not exist in this case.

93 If the doctrine of unilateral mistake is to be understood in terms of the principles governing offer and acceptance, or in other words, the formation of

the contract, then, as Prof Goh suggested, the question of how the doctrine should apply to contracts made by computerised trading systems should be answered by first considering the more fundamental issue of *how* such contracts are formed. We therefore turn to consider this.

94 The decision of the English High Court in *R (on the application of Software Solutions Partners Ltd) v. Her Majesty's Commissioners for Customs and Excise* [2007] EWHC 971 (Admin) ("*Software Solutions Partners*") is of some assistance. There, the court considered an automated electronic process of contracting involving the software of the applicant, Software Solutions Partners Ltd ("SSP"). Insurance brokers who used SSP's software could enter into insurance contracts on behalf of their customers with insurers who were using the same software. A broker would input the details for the required insurance product into the software, which would calculate quotes available from those insurers based on pre-determined qualification criteria as agreed between the insurers and SSP, and also electronically determine whether the risk was acceptable to the insurers without referring it back to them. Once the customer accepted the price and terms of an insurance cover, the software would process the customer's data automatically and generate the relevant policy contract and the relevant insurer would be bound by it. All the information necessary for contract formation was pre-programmed in the software according to parameters laid down by the insurer. The court concluded in these circumstances that the insurer using the software had, expressly or impliedly, invited the insurance broker to use the software as the medium for contract formation and undertook to be bound by the automatically generated policy contract even if the insurer was temporarily unaware of it (see *Software Solutions Partners* at [65] and [67]). Put another way, the insurer made a binding offer to provide insurance and the broker, on the customer's behalf, could accept it and that would be

effective when received by SSP's information system (see *Software Solutions Partners* at [19]).

95 The court in *Software Solutions Partners* analogised that case to *Thornton v. Shoe Lane Parking Ltd* [1971] 2 QB 163 where Lord Denning MR discussed the situation of a customer putting money into an automatic machine and being issued with a ticket. There, Lord Denning MR held that the offer was made when the proprietor of the machine held it out as being ready to receive money and the customer accepted the offer by inserting money into the machine (at 169).

96 What is clear in our case is that the Trading Contracts had been entered into pursuant to the parties' respective deterministic algorithms. As was the case in *Software Solutions Partners* for the insurers using SSP's software, the contracting parties and Quoine did not know beforehand that the Trading Contracts would be entered into; and they were also unaware of the specific terms on which the contracts would be concluded. These factors did not prevent the formation of the policy contracts in *Software Solutions Partners*, and, in our judgment, did not here prevent the formation of a contract at the point of time when an offer made by one algorithm was accepted by the other.

97 This was also the view of the Judge and it drove him, in our judgment, inevitably, to adopt a certain analytical model when considering the issue of unilateral mistake. Specifically, he refused to consider the matter by reference to what the position would have been and what the contracting parties were likely to have known, intended and agreed had they had face-to-face negotiations at a hypothetical meeting on the "floor of the exchange" to enter into the Trading Contracts, at the time these were entered into, because this was simply not how they had agreed to form their contracts. Instead, they had decided to form contracts using the relevant deterministic algorithms (see

Judgment at [200] and [204]). We agree with this characterisation of the parties' method of contracting and we think it would be wholly artificial to recast the relevant matrix of fact, which was one where the contracting parties did not in fact know beforehand that they were going to enter into the Trading Contracts or their terms, and were content to abide by what the relevant algorithms did at least as long as this was within the ambit of their programmed parameters. We also agree with the Judge that it follows from this that in cases where contracts are made by way of *deterministic* algorithms, any analysis concerning knowledge of a mistake or unconscionably taking advantage of one must be done by reference to the state of mind of the programmers of the algorithms at the time of the programming (see Judgment at [211]).

98 As we have noted at [15] above, a deterministic computer program or algorithm is bound by the parameters set by the programmer, and can (and generally will) only do what the programmer has programmed it to do. Given a particular input, it will produce a particular output; on each occasion, the output should and will be the same if the former does not change. Therefore, when it comes to assessing the state of knowledge that is to be attributed to the parties at the time of a contract made by way of deterministic algorithms, the relevant inquiry cannot be directed at the parties themselves, who had no knowledge of or direct personal involvement in the formation of the contract. Rather, working backwards from the output that emanated from the programs, we are driven to assess the relevant state of knowledge by examining that of *the programmers*. This approach is consistent with that which was advocated by Prof Goh.

99 Apart from determining whose knowledge is relevant, it is also important to consider the relevant *time* for assessing that person's knowledge. In our judgment, the relevant time frame within which we should assess the knowledge

of a programmer or the person running the algorithm would be from the point of programming up to the point that the relevant contract is formed. As Prof Goh noted, the point of programming is when the programmer's knowledge is the most concretised. The question can first be framed in this way: if the algorithm was programmed to produce a particular output, *why* was this done? But the inquiry cannot end there and must extend past that point of time because there may be situations where a programmer or the person running the algorithm who did not contemplate the relevant mistake at the point of programming came to learn of it subsequently *before* the contract had been formed, and yet allowed the algorithm to continue running, intending thereby to take advantage of the mistake. In such a case, it would be wrong to ignore the subsequent acquisition of knowledge. This is why it is appropriate to have regard to the state of knowledge up to the time of the contract.

100 Prof Goh cited Nik Yeo & Joseph Farmer, "Mapping the Landscape: Cryptocurrency Disputes under English Law (Part 2)" (2019) 5 JIBFL 290 at 291. This was a commentary on the Judge's decision in which the authors note as follows:

> An issue to which the case gives rise is an apparent timing mismatch: the traders' mistakes must necessarily have arisen, or at least have been continuing, at the point of the original trades, whereas the last human input into the programming must by practical necessity have occurred *before* those trades. *How then could the state of mind of the programmer when originally programming B2C2's 'deep price' methodology ever include knowledge of the relevant mistake?* ... the law might need to recognise that so long as the knowledge or intention of the original programmer was that there ought not to be the sort of

> mistake which subsequently arose, then it does not matter for the rules of unilateral mistake if the particular instantiation of that mistake post-dates the last act of a human being, so long as the programmer's state of mind could be said still to be extant at the time the mistake is made (in other words, that the code has not changed by then in a way which would be inconsistent with that state of mind). [emphasis added]

101 We also note that *Low & Mik* ([75] *supra*) made some similar points in commenting on the Judge's decision as follows:

> ... Being unaware of the conclusion of a contract, a contracting party utilising automated contracting is *ipso facto* incapable of having any actual knowledge of any mistake on the part of its counterparty at the time of contracting, however egregious the mistake. But this would have the effect of immunising any contracting party employing algorithmic contracting from the doctrine of unilateral mistake entirely, which cannot be correct. ...
>
> ... it is unrealistic to attempt to attribute knowledge of a future mistake to a past programmer a la Nostradamus. ...

102 We have two observations on these extracts. The first relates to the level of knowledge of the mistake while the second relates to the time when the knowledge is assessed. Turning to the first point, it is true that it may be artificial, even unrealistic, to conduct the analysis on the basis of an expectation that the non-mistaken party must have knowledge of the specific and precise details of the mistake that has arisen. Programmers are not expected to be

prophets and mistakes can take a wide range of forms. But the law on unilateral mistake is concerned:

(a) with a type or class of mistake, that is one concerning the fundamental terms of the contract (at least at common law); and

(b) with the mental state of the non-mistaken party—whether it knew (or ought to have known) of the (type of) mistake and was acting to take advantage of it.

103 In our judgment, keeping the focus on these considerations enables us to address the authors' concern that the state of mind of the programmer when originally programming the algorithm could never have included knowledge of the particular manifestation of the relevant mistake. That is not and should not be the inquiry and we do not think it was the inquiry that the Judge pursued. Rather, the relevant inquiry might be framed thus: when programming the algorithm, was the programmer doing so with actual or constructive knowledge of the fact that the relevant offer would only ever be accepted by a party operating under a mistake and was the programmer acting to take advantage of such a mistake? In our judgment, this was the essential methodology applied by the Judge at [229]-[230] of the Judgment, which we set out at [124] below.

104 The second point which pertains to timing is resolved by the approach that we have set out at [99] above. If at the point of programming, the programmer contemplated or ought to have contemplated that a mistake might arise on the part of a counterparty to a future contract and designed the algorithm to exploit such a mistake, then it does not matter for the purposes of establishing the requisite knowledge that the relevant mistake had occurred *after* the algorithm had been programmed. Further, as we have noted, the framework we have developed also enables the court to examine and consider the knowledge

actually acquired after the point of programming and the actual conduct of the parties up to the time of the contract. However, we emphasise that this is directed at *actual* conduct. This is to be contrasted with the approach that Quoine urged upon us, which we have rejected (see [97] above), which was to analyse the matter by reference to a "hypothetical meeting on the trading floor that notionally took place just before the contract was concluded in the light of the information available at that time". On that approach, the question posed is whether the parties *would have agreed* to the contract with knowledge of the mistake. With respect, this is, as we have mentioned, a wholly artificial analysis that has no relation to the reality of the situation, which is that the trades were conducted by way of algorithmic trading and not by way of an imagined meeting on some trading floor. The consequence of this is that the parties had *committed* to transact with each other in a certain way which entailed that they would not even know whether a contract would be formed, and if it were, on what terms that would be, *and* they chose in these circumstances not to bargain for a right to review, confirm or invalidate any ensuing contract that might emerge out of the arrangements that they had committed to. This simply did not accommodate the court artificially (or "equitably") interposing another last look at the proposed terms immediately prior to the algorithms concluding the contract and, for that matter, still less *after*. Having committed to transact in this way, and in the absence of any basis upon which equity's intervention could be justified up to the time the relevant offer was accepted and the contract formed, we cannot see a principled basis for such intervention premised on a review of the reasonableness of the ensuing contract *after* it had been formed without any mistake as to its terms.

105 We turn to the *type* of knowledge required on the part of the non-mistaken party of the mistaken party's mistake, which, as stated at [80] above, differs

depending on whether a party is seeking to invoke the doctrine of unilateral mistake at common law or in equity. The former requires proof that the non-mistaken party had *actual* knowledge of the mistake at the time of the contract, while the latter requires *constructive* knowledge (coupled with an element of unconscionability). The distinguishing line between actual knowledge and constructive knowledge can be difficult to draw, if not in theory then in practice. This is not least because both forms of knowledge require the court to adopt an objective inquiry (see *Digilandmall.com* ([80] *supra*) at [44]; *Wellmix Organics (International) Pte Ltd v. Lau Yu Man* [2006] 2 SLR(R) 117 at [66]).

106 The test for establishing actual knowledge is set out in *Digilandmall.com* at [41]-[42] as follows:

> 41 As is so often alluded to in the cases, in the absence of an express admission or incontrovertible evidence, the fact of knowledge would invariably have to be inferred from all the surrounding circumstances, *including the* ***experiences and idiosyncrasies*** *of the person and what* ***a reasonable person*** *would have known in a similar situation. If a court, upon weighing all the circumstances, thinks that the non-mistaken party is* ***probably aware*** *of the error made by the mistaken party, it is entitled to find, as a fact, that the former party has actual knowledge of the error.* Following from that holding, the court should declare the contract so formed as void on the ground of unilateral mistake.
>
> 42 In order to enable the court to come to the conclusion that the non-mistaken party had actual knowledge of the mistake, *the court would go through a process of reasoning where it* ***may consider what***

> ***a reasonable person, placed in the similar situation****, would have known.* In this connection, we would refer to what is called 'Nelsonian knowledge', namely, wilful blindness or shutting one's eyes to the obvious. Clearly, if the court finds that the non-mistaken party is guilty of wilful blindness, it will be in line with logic and reason to hold that that party had actual knowledge.
>
> [emphasis added in italics and bold italics]

107 Actual knowledge is concerned with the *subjective* knowledge of the non-mistaken party. In other words, for actual knowledge to be made out, it must be shown that the non-mistaken party actually knew of the relevant fact. However, the means by which the *subjective* knowledge of the non-mistaken party is ascertained may include considerations of the matter from an objective perspective. This was consistent with the approach that Prof Goh urged upon us at para 137 of his submissions on the mistake issue:

> What is the criterion to be applied in so far as the ascertainment of the presence of knowledge ... is concerned? **The answer would appear, by the very nature of the doctrine itself, to hinge upon the subjective knowledge of the party concerned.** However, it is submitted that such ' subjective knowledge' must be **objectively ascertained**, and, indeed, the case of *Hartog v. Colin & Shields* [[1939] 3 All ER 566] supports this proposition. In that case, the reference to verbal and written negotiations prior to the sale concerned as well as expert evidence as to the prevalent trade practice ... tilted the decision in favour of the defendant sellers who, Singleton J decided, had obviously made a mistake which was equally clear to the

plaintiff buyer, having regard to the *objective facts* just mentioned. As Singleton J observed:

> '[T]here was an accident. The offer [by the defendant sellers] was wrongly expressed, and the defendants *by their evidence, and by their correspondence*, have satisfied me that the plaintiff could *not reasonably* have supposed that that offer contained the [defendants'] *real* intention.'

[emphasis in original in italics; emphasis added in bold; footnotes omitted]

108 In contrast to actual knowledge, constructive knowledge involves *imputing* knowledge to the non-mistaken party. The inquiry is not directed at whether the non-mistaken party *actually* knew of the mistaken party's mistake, but whether a reasonable person in the position of the non-mistaken party would have known of the mistake. If the answer to that is yes, then the non-mistaken party is *deemed* to have constructive knowledge of the mistake, notwithstanding that it could not be proved that it did indeed have that knowledge. Here the inquiry that is adopted by the court is necessarily an objective one.

109 The final requirement to establish unilateral mistake in equity is that the non-mistaken party must also be found to have engaged in some *unconscionable* conduct in relation to the relevant mistake. In *Digilandmall.com*, this was also referred to as "sharp practice" and "impropriety" (see *Digilandmall.com* at [77] and [80]). Much more recently, in *BOM v. BOK and another appeal* [2019] 1 SLR 349 ("*BOM*"), we elaborated on what constitutes "unconscionable conduct" although this was not in the context of unilateral mistake in equity. In *BOM*, we were required to consider the circumstances in which a deed of trust might be set aside on the basis of unconscionability, and in that context held

that "the narrow doctrine of unconscionability" [emphasis in original omitted] applies in Singapore (at [142]):

> ... To invoke the doctrine, the plaintiff has to show that he was suffering from an infirmity that the other party exploited in procuring the transaction. Upon the satisfaction of this requirement, the burden is on the defendant to demonstrate that the transaction was fair, just and reasonable. In this regard, while the successful invocation of the doctrine does not require a transaction at an undervalue or the lack of independent advice to the plaintiff, these are factors that the court will invariably consider in assessing whether the transaction was improvident.

In relation to the requirement for the plaintiff to be suffering from an infirmity, this refers to the plaintiff being poor and ignorant or suffering from other forms of infirmities of sufficient gravity, whether physical, mental and/or emotional in nature, as to have acutely affected his ability to "conserve his own interests" (*BOM* at [141]). Admittedly there is a potential tension between requiring, on the one hand, that unconscionability be shown, this necessarily being a subjective inquiry premised on what the non-mistaken party actually knew—see *Digilandmall.com* at [78]—and, on the other, that the non-mistaken party have at least constructive knowledge of the mistake, this being, as we have already noted, an objective inquiry.

110 Aside from this, a narrow conception of unconscionability limits excessive subjectivity in determining what amounts to unconscionable conduct, and instead promotes certainty and predictability for contracting parties (see *BOM* at [176]). Given the circumstances of this case, and for reasons we will shortly

develop, we consider that we would not on any footing have been able to find that there was unconscionable conduct on the part of B2C2 or Mr Boonen, and thus it is not necessary for present purposes either to resolve the tension we have alluded to or to decide the question as to whether the same narrow conception of unconscionability should apply in the context of unilateral mistake in equity. We therefore leave this open for the present.

111 Further, it is also relevant when considering unilateral mistake in equity to have regard to the degree of carelessness or negligence on the part of the mistaken party to determine where the equities fall, even if a mistaken party's carelessness would not in and of itself disentitle it from relief (*Digiland-mall.com* ([80] *supra*) at [79]).

Application to the facts of this case

112 On appeal, Quoine focused on the Second Mistaken Belief as the operative mistake held by the Counterparties, which was that they believed they were buying ETH for BTC under contracts at prices which accurately represented or did not deviate significantly from the true market value and/or price of ETH relative to BTC on 19 April 2017 (see [38] above). Quoine argued that Mr Boonen had actual or at least constructive knowledge of the Second Mistaken Belief, because his main objective in programming the Trading Software to place sell orders for ETH at the deep price of 10 BTC to 1 ETH when the Platform's order book became empty or abnormally thin was to unconscionably profit from potential errors of the other market participants. Against this, B2C2 submitted that there was no mistake as to the prices quoted and accepted for the Disputed Trades, and that Mr Boonen had not engaged in any unconscionable conduct when programming the Trading Software.

113 To recapitulate, B2C2 had through its algorithm placed sell orders for ETH on the Platform at prices of 9.99999 BTC and 10 BTC to 1 ETH. On the

other side of the transactions, orders had been placed on behalf of the Counterparties to buy ETH at the best available price on the Platform. These orders had been placed by the Platform's operating system, which had done just as it had been programmed to do in the light of the conditions presented on the Platform. These were the two sides of the trades that were matched and resulted in the Trading Contracts.

114 It is helpful to pause here and examine the position a little more closely. Because the Trading Contracts had been entered into pursuant to deterministic algorithmic programs that had acted exactly as they had been programmed to act, it is not clear what mistake can be said to have affected the formation of the contracts. The mistake, if anything, was in the way the Platform had operated as a result of Quoine's failure to make certain necessary changes to several critical operating systems, which led to a series of steps that force-closed the Counterparties' positions and triggered buy orders for ETH being placed on their behalf. This might conceivably be seen as a mistake as to the premise on which the buy orders were placed, but it can in no way be said to be a mistake as to the terms on which the contracts could or would be formed. If a party A is told a falsehood by B which causes A to accept C's offer to transact at a price A would not otherwise have transacted at, in circumstances where C was neither aware of nor involved in B's falsehood, we are unable to see how that falsehood can be said to be a mistake that vitiates the contract. Here, the problems with the Quoter Program and the subsequent force-closure of the Counterparties' positions are akin to a "falsehood" told by Quoine to the Counterparties. This cannot be a mistake that vitiates the Trading Contracts between B2C2 and the Counterparties.

115 Accordingly, although we find no reason to disagree with the Judge's finding that the Counterparties held the Second Mistaken Belief that they were

buying ETH for BTC at prices which did not deviate significantly from the market price on 19 April 2017 (see Judgment at [228]), we respectfully disagree that this mistake was as to a *term* of the Trading Contracts. The Second Mistaken Belief was characterised as a mistake as to the prices at which the Trading Contracts were entered into. In our judgment, this was incorrect. The prices that the Disputed Trades were concluded at were arrived at by operation of the parties' respective algorithms, and it was common ground that these had operated as they were meant to. In fact, the precise mistake in this case was a mistaken *assumption* on the part of the Counterparties as to how the Platform would operate. In other words, their real belief was that the Platform would not fail; and as the Judge found, the premise for the Second Mistaken Belief was that the Platform would either always operate as intended or, alternatively, there would be adequate error identification and protection systems to prevent trading from continuing if the Platform operations deviated from this assumed state of affairs (Judgment at [227]). However, we do not see how this can assist Quoine because the Second Mistaken Belief was not a mistake as to the terms of the Trading Contracts, but instead was a mistaken assumption as to the circumstances under which the Trading Contracts would be concluded. This is not an operative mistake at least in the context of unilateral mistake at common law. In this regard, the position of the Counterparties (with their mistaken assumption) is analogous to the position of the claimant in *Statoil* ([88] *supra*), where the court found that there was no operative unilateral mistake as to a contract term and the contract of compromise in question thus remained binding (see [88] above). In fact, the claimant in *Statoil* would, on the face of things, seem to have been in a better position than the Counterparties in the present case, because the defendant in *Statoil* was actually aware that the claimant had entered into the contract on a mistaken assumption;

in contrast, as we discuss below, Mr Boonen did not have actual or constructive knowledge of the Second Mistaken Belief (see [126] below).

116 In a sense, this might be sufficient to dispose of the case on unilateral mistake (at least at common law). However, since we have left open the issue identified at [92] above, we proceed on the assumption that there was an operative mistake, and examine whether the non-mistaken party, B2C2, had the requisite knowledge of this mistake.

117 In relation to B2C2, the Judge made the following findings:

(a) There was plainly no mistake on B2C2's part in designing its algorithm to place the sell orders on the Platform at the deep price.

(b) There was no sinister motive behind Mr Boonen programming the Trading Software with the deep prices. Specifically, at the time the Trading Software was designed, the deep prices had *not* been programmed with either the awareness or the intention to take advantage of a mistaken bid by a counterparty or to enter into a contract on that basis.

118 Quoine did not (and plainly could not) challenge the first finding and although it mounted a challenge of sorts against the second finding, we consider that this challenge was bound to fail. The Judge gave detailed reasons for his findings and there is neither reason nor basis for us to overturn those findings. In this regard, we are cognisant of our position as an appellate court. We did not have the benefit of hearing the parties' evidence at trial or grappling with the minutiae of that evidence as the Judge did, and thus appropriate caution demands that we should be slow to overturn primary findings of fact made by the Judge. In any event, we accept the Judge's findings for the following reasons.

119 First, there were no grounds for concluding that Mr Boonen had ever turned his mind to the relationship between the margin traders and those who

loaned them money (Judgment at [124] and [223]). It is difficult to see how Quoine could even begin to mount a challenge against this finding. It was not suggested that the deep prices were programmed with margin trades in mind. If Mr Boonen did not programme the deep prices with awareness or consideration of the terms on which margin trading was done, he could not have programmed the Trading Software with the *knowledge* that in situations of illiquidity on the Platform when the order book was abnormally thin, margin calls would be triggered and market orders would be placed to purchase ETH at the best available price, thereby creating an opportunity for exploitation.

120 Second, the Judge accepted that the programming of the deep prices was in part to ensure that the PureQuote strategy would always have price inputs so that the Trading Software would function continuously (see [18] above), and in part to ensure that in the unlikely event that a trade were to occur at a deep price, it would adequately protect B2C2 against any adverse consequences of such a trade (see Judgment at [83] and [85]). The Judge acknowledged that Mr Boonen's strategy might not have been wholly defensive, but nevertheless held that the overriding reason for programming the deep prices was to protect B2C2 in the event of the unexpected happening (see Judgment at [119] and [230]).

121 Third, the Judge accepted that when Mr Boonen designed the Trading Software, he knew of the *possibility* that the Platform's order book might become empty and that in that event the deep prices would be inserted into the Trading Software's internal order book. However, the Judge also stated that Mr Boonen had never considered that there was a *real* possibility of orders placed on the Platform at the deep prices being filled. Mr Boonen in fact considered that this was unlikely and the Judge found that he did not turn his mind in any detail to the circumstances in which this might happen (Judgment at [121] and

[123]).

122 The first finding at [117(a)] above is fatal to any argument resting on common mistake since it is plain that B2C2 was never acting under a mistake (see [129] below).

123 The second finding at [117(b)] above, in our judgment, is fatal to any argument resting on unilateral mistake. This is because it excludes any notion of the Trading Contracts having been concluded in circumstances where B2C2 either actually knew or must be taken to have known that these had been or must have been the result of a mistake having been made by either of the Counterparties. This follows from the analysis of the law that we have set out above. Further, as we have observed at [42] above, the Judge also accepted that Mr Boonen had no knowledge of the glitches causing the illiquidity on the Platform until after the Disputed Trades had been transacted.

124 Following from our analysis of the law at [103] above, the relevant inquiry in this case could be framed thus: when programming the Trading Software with the deep prices, was the programmer doing so with actual or constructive knowledge of the fact that sell orders at those prices would only ever be accepted by a party operating under a mistake and was the programmer acting to take advantage of that mistake? In our judgment, this was the essential methodology applied by the Judge at [229]-[230] of the Judgment and which led him to conclude that Mr Boonen neither had such knowledge nor programmed the Trading Software to take advantage of any such mistake:

> 229 It is next necessary to determine whether Mr Boonen had actual knowledge of the mistaken belief at the time he inserted the deep prices ... Can it be said that Mr Boonen knew that 'it was never contemplated by [any trader] that any trades would be transacted on

the Platform at prices which deviated so substantially from the actual market prices'? This amounts to a belief held by Mr Boonen at that date *that the price was so abnormal that no trader would trade at that price otherwise by way of a mistake*.

230 … I have concluded on the basis of those findings of fact that Mr Boonen did not insert the deep prices with that belief. He foresaw that a number of factors might arise which would cause the deep prices to be inserted and the overriding reasons for them being inserted was to protect B2C2 in the event of the unexpected happening. He did not exclude the possibility of trades at those prices being executed. Whilst he was aware that one possible cause was that it could be the result, wholly or in part, of some error or omission on the part of someone, including himself, he did not turn his mind in any detail to the circumstances that might lead to such trades being executed. He knew that the Platform was an automated system and that therefore no opportunity would arise for any particular trade to be reviewed by the parties in advance. In the circumstances of this case, in order for him to have actual knowledge that other traders believed that in no circumstances would a trade be transacted on the Platform at prices which deviated so substantially from the actual market prices, I consider that it would be necessary for it to be demonstrated that he held that belief himself, which he did not …

[emphasis added]

125 We have also observed above at [99] that the programmer's knowledge, or indeed the knowledge of anyone running the algorithm, is relevant *past* the point of programming, and up till the Disputed Trades occurred. Examining the

state of B2C2's knowledge at this later point in time, however, we consider that Quoine could not establish or adduce any evidence to show that B2C2 and/or Mr Boonen had become aware of the problems with the Quoter Program or the fact that the Platform's order book had gradually thinned out in the period *after* the Trading Software had been programmed and *prior* to the Disputed Trades (which was when the Trading Contracts were entered into). Quoine did seek to rely on the e-mail that was sent by Mr Boonen on 20 April 2017, the morning *after* the Disputed Trades had occurred but in our view, this does not help its case at all. That e-mail simply stated in the subject line "Major Quoine database breakdown, please call us urgently". Quoine argued that Mr Boonen's reaction showed that he knew that there must have been some mistake. However, this, at its highest, showed Mr Boonen's state of mind *after* he became aware of the Disputed Trades, which is not part of the relevant time frame. Further, the e-mail, if anything, supports the Judge's finding that Mr Boonen did not programme the Trading Software with the deep prices with any sinister intent, because his reaction was simply inconsistent with that of a man who had anticipated the possibility of such a mistake occurring and designed his algorithm to exploit it.

126 Taking the evidence above together, it is apparent to us that Mr Boonen did not have actual or constructive knowledge of the Second Mistaken Belief. Mr Boonen would have had to foresee a perfect storm of events that began with the problems with the Quoter Program and ended with the Disputed Trades being concluded at the deep price for him to have had, or be taken to have had, the Second Mistaken Belief. Despite Quoine's considerable efforts to mount a case suggesting even a hint of this, there was simply no evidence to suggest that Mr Boonen had ever contemplated anything of the sort. We therefore reject Quoine's case on this aspect of the appeal.

127 We add for completeness that the second finding of the Judge described at [117(b)] above, that there was no sinister motive behind programming the Trading Software with the deep prices, also excludes any notion of the Trading Contracts having been entered into in circumstances where B2C2 had acted unconscionably. We find no reason to disagree with the Judge's finding that although Mr Boonen's inclusion of the deep prices was an opportunistic business decision, it was not motivated by sinister intent (Judgment at [236]).

128 For all these reasons, we are satisfied that Quoine's defences of unilateral mistake at common law and in equity fail.

Common mistake

129 Quoine also argued that the Trading Contracts were void for common mistake, since B2C2 and the Counterparties had entered into the Disputed Trades under a shared mistaken assumption that they were transacting at or around the going market rate for ETH. However, B2C2 could not have been labouring under such an assumption, given that it had placed its sell orders for ETH at prices of 9.99999 BTC and 10 BTC to 1 ETH on the Platform *because* the *intentionally* pre-programmed deep price of 10 BTC to 1 ETH in the PureQuote strategy took effect (see [117(a)] above). Therefore, Quoine's defence of common mistake at common law fails.

Unjust enrichment

130 We turn to Quoine's argument that it was entitled to cancel the Disputed Trades on the basis that B2C2 would otherwise be unjustly enriched at the expense of the Counterparties and/or Quoine. Quoine's and B2C2's arguments on unjust enrichment hinged on whether we accepted that the Trading Contracts were vitiated for mistake. If the Trading Contracts remained valid and enforceable, that would seem to bar any action in unjust enrichment.

131 In his discussion of the unjust enrichment point below, the Judge applied

our decision in *Singapore Swimming Club v. Koh Sin Chong Freddie* [2016] 3 SLR 845 at [90], which sets out the three requirements for an action in unjust enrichment to succeed: (a) a benefit has been received or an enrichment has accrued to the defendant; (b) the benefit or enrichment is at the claimant's expense; and (c) the defendant's enrichment is unjust.

132 As a preliminary point, we agree with the Judge's conclusion that if the Disputed Trades were not cancelled, B2C2 would stand to receive a substantial benefit in terms of the considerable value of BTC that had been credited into its account. However, as the Judge noted, this benefit would have been at the expense of the *Counterparties*, which would have had to make up the shortfall between the BTC actually in their accounts and the amount that had been debited from their accounts pursuant to the Disputed Trades. Therefore, the cause of action in unjust enrichment should if at all vest in the Counterparties, and not Quoine. However, B2C2 did not attempt to strike out this aspect of Quoine's defence, and the Judge therefore proceeded with the trial on the basis that it was properly raised as a defence. We therefore proceed on the same basis.

133 As to the first element, there is no doubt that B2C2 was enriched or derived a benefit from having the proceeds of the Disputed Trades credited into its account. Assuming that the Counterparties are able to bring a claim against Quoine for the losses they might suffer as a result of the Disputed Trades if the Trading Contracts remain valid and enforceable, it might then be said that B2C2's enrichment was at least indirectly at the expense of Quoine. On this basis, the first two requirements of unjust enrichment would be made out. We turn then to the last requirement, which is that there must be an unjust factor.

134 The unjust factors that were pleaded by Quoine were first, that the benefit was conferred upon B2C2 pursuant to a mistake, and second, that there was a

lack of consent in the formation of the Trading Contracts by which B2C2 was enriched. In truth, these were the same points raised in relation to the case on unilateral mistake, which we have rejected.

135 Further, given our conclusion that the Trading Contracts are not vitiated, B2C2's enrichment would have been pursuant to valid contracts and it is difficult to see how this could be said to be unjust. As stated in *Goff & Jones: The Law of Unjust Enrichment* (Charles Mitchell, Paul Mitchell & Stephen Watterson eds) (Sweet & Maxwell, 9th Ed, 2016) at para 9-94 (see Judgment at [249]):

> Where a benefit is mistakenly conferred by one party on another *under a contract*, a claim in unjust enrichment will commonly fail *even if the mistake would otherwise support such a claim*. ... the contract will bar the claim, to the extent *that it entitles the defendant to receive the relevant benefit*. For the claim to succeed, the claimant will need to show that the contract is invalid, being either non-existent, void or voidable. ...[emphasis added]

136 Therefore, we are satisfied that Quoine's defence of unjust enrichment cannot succeed.

The trust question

137 Finally, we turn to B2C2's contention that Quoine was holding the BTC which was credited into B2C2's account pursuant to the Disputed Trades on trust and that Quoine breached that trust when it reversed that credit transaction. This raises the threshold issue of whether cryptocurrency, specifically BTC, is a species of property that is capable of being held on trust.

138 This point was not disputed by the parties when they were before the Judge and was only raised belatedly by Quoine on appeal. Nevertheless, the Judge briefly considered the question, and concluded that cryptocurrency satisfied all the requirements in the classic definition of a property right set out in the decision of the UK House of Lords in *Ainsworth* ([34] *supra*) at 1248. However, he left open the question of what the precise nature of the property right was, having been satisfied that cryptocurrency could be treated as property in a generic sense.

139 There have been some other cases in the Commonwealth that have implicitly accepted that cryptocurrency may be regarded as property, although we are not aware of any court that has attempted to identify the precise nature of the property right if any. In *Elena Vorotyntseva v. Money*-4 *Limited and others* [2018] EWHC 2596 (Ch), the English High Court issued a proprietary injunction preventing the removal of specific ETH and BTC holdings. In coming to his decision, Birss J observed that there had been no suggestion that cryptocurrencies could not be a form of property.

140 In *Copytrack Pte Ltd v. Wall* [2018] BCSC 1709, the Supreme Court of British Columbia ordered that some C $400, 000 worth of ETH be traced, which suggests that ETH was recognised as a species of property susceptible to tracing. The action was brought by Copytrack Pte Ltd ("Copytrack"), a company engaged in the business of digital content management and automated copyright enforcement. Copytrack created its own cryptocurrency, Copytrack tokens, and mistakenly transferred a more valuable cryptocurrency, ETH, to the defendant investor instead of Copytrack tokens. The ETH was then transferred by the defendant to third parties. Copytrack sought to trace and recover the ETH. The court characterised the issue of whether the property law doctrines of conversion and wrongful detention could apply to cryptocurrencies

as a "critical issue" and the "real issue on this application". While the court did not go so far as to rule on whether cryptocurrencies could, in fact, be subject to specific property law claims, the court held that it would be unreasonable and unjust in the circumstances to deny Copytrack a remedy, and so allowed Copytrack to trace and recover the wrongfully transferred ETH.

141 Academic commentators broadly agree that BTC may be regarded as a property right, although they disagree as to the precise nature of this right. In Jean Bacon *et al*, "Blockchain Demystified: A Technical and Legal Introduction to Distributed and Centralised Ledgers" (2018) 25(1) Rich J L & Tech 1, the authors suggest (at para 182) that holders of digital tokens such as BTC should be regarded as having a property interest at common law, because they hold a bundle of rights that include the right to control the token. This interest is identifiable through entries on the blockchain, can be transferred by entries of the blockchain, and has a high degree of permanence and stability.

142 To similar effect is Kelvin F K Low and Ernie G S Teo, "Bitcoins and other cryptocurrencies as property?" (2017) 9(2) *Law, Innovation and Technology* 235 (available at https://ink.library.smu.edu.sg/sol_research/2806), where the authors argue that the property right relating to BTC is the right to have one's public BTC address appear as the last entry in the blockchain in relation to a particular BTC. Such a right provides exclusive control to the holder in the form of universal exigibility and can be seen as involving a true property transfer when one transfers BTC from one's public BTC address to another's BTC address.

143 Most recently, the UK Jurisdiction Taskforce ("UKJT") chaired by Sir Geoffrey Vos released its "Legal Statement on Cryptoassets and Smart Contracts" (November 2019), where it considered the question of whether English law would treat a particular cryptoasset as property. The UKJT defined

cryptoassets as generally having the following characteristics (at para 31): (a) intangibility; (b) cryptographic authentication; (c) use of a distributed transaction ledger; (d) decentralisation; and (e) rule by consensus. The UKJT stated (at para 85) that cryptoassets have all the indicia of property, and that their novel or distinctive features as aforementioned do not disqualify them from being property. The UKJT also stated that cryptoassets are not disqualified from being property simply because they might not be classifiable either as things in possession or as things in action. The UKJT therefore concluded that cryptoassets could be treated, in principle, as property.

144 There may be much to commend the view that cryptocurrencies should be capable of assimilation into the general concepts of property. There are, however, difficult questions as to the type of property that is involved. It is not necessary for us to come to a final position on this question in the present case. This is because even if BTC were to be regarded as a species of property which is capable of being the subject of a trust, we are satisfied that B2C2's breach of trust claim would fail because, contrary to what the Judge found, we consider that there was no certainty of intention to create a trust. In this regard, we agree with the observations made by French CJ in the High Court of Australia decision of *Korda v. Australian Executor Trustees (SA) Ltd* (2015) 255 CLR 62 ("*Korda*"). French CJ stated that the process of ascertaining whether the necessary intention to create a trust should be imputed is "one of construction of the relevant text or oral dealings in their context" (*Korda* at [11]). He clarified that an intention is not to be imputed and a trust inferred "simply because a court thinks it is an appropriate means of protecting or creating an interest".

145 The Judge held that the "decisive factor", which led him to find that a trust had arisen over the BTC that had been credited into B2C2's account, was

that B2C2's assets were held separately as assets of an individual user of the Platform rather than as part of Quoine's trading assets. He regarded this as a "clear indication" that Quoine claimed no title to the user's assets and acknowledged that it was holding them to the order of the user who could demand withdrawal at any time (see Judgment at [145]). In our respectful view, the mere fact that Quoine's assets were segregated from its customer's cannot in and of itself lead to the conclusion that there was a trust. In *Vintage Bullion DMCC (in its own capacity and as representative of the customers of MF Global Singapore Pte Ltd (in creditors' voluntary liquidation)) v. Chay Fook Yuen (in his capacity as joint and several liquidator of MF Global Singapore Pte Ltd (in creditors' voluntary liquidation)) and others and other appeals* [2016] 4 SLR 1248, we stated as follows at [61]:

> Counsel for Vintage ... submitted at the hearing before us that the Company had in effect by its conduct made a declaration of trust over the sum representing the Unrealised Profits by computing the gains and losses in relation to the Unrealised Profits daily, and thereafter setting aside and segregating the funds. In our view, however, the concepts of segregation and trust need to be clearly distinguished. *The mere segregation of money into separate bank accounts does not equate to the creation of a trust and is not sufficient to establish a proprietary interest in those funds in anyone other than the account holder* ... Put simply, *segregation is a necessary but not a sufficient condition* to give rise to an express trust over the Sums in favour of the Customers. What is further required is to establish that the Company had *the requisite certainty of intention for the funds to be held on trust* ...[emphasis in original omitted; emphasis added in italics]

146 In any event, the manner in which BTC was *actually* stored by Quoine in the cold storage wallet suggests that there was, *in fact*, *no* segregation, which militates against the inference that it was being held on trust. The manner in which BTC was set aside for users of the Platform was explained by Mr Lozada as follows at the trial:

> Q. … even though the asset in the wallet is not specifically identifiable to each customer, Quoine has an internal book which identifies the amount of assets that are held to the credit of each customer; correct?
>
> A. Yeah, ***the database has each customer account has the balance***. *It's like*—***think of it as a bank***. You have your US dollar and how much US dollar you hold in your account. That is in … Quoine's database.
>
> Q. Let's assume there were only 100 ETH in a cold storage wallet of Quoine, and you have 100 customers with a credit of 1 ETH each. Then, in a sense, you would be able to identify that 1 ETH belongs to each customer in the cold storage wallet; correct?
>
> A. We don't normally do that. We base our accounting on what we have in the database. As I said before, ***what's in the cold storage doesn't necessarily have to match what the customer balance has***. As I explained, if we sell a [BTC] to a customer and the database gets updated, we will have to go and procure it. ***The database will say they own*** 1 ***[BTC] or*** 1 ***ETH. The wallet may have a different amount***.
>
> [emphasis added in bold italics]

147 Given that the amount that was reflected in the account balance of a user of the Platform as it appeared on Quoine's database did not necessarily match the amount in the cold storage wallet, it could not be said that Quoine was holding the amount stated in the user's account balance on trust. From Mr Lozada's explanation, it appears that the only amount which a user was concerned with was what was reflected on Quoine's database. The actual amount in the cold storage wallet did not matter because, if there were insufficient assets to meet the account balance reflected in the database, Quoine would simply purchase the required amount from other sources to make up the shortfall. We find this arrangement to be more akin to deposits being made with a bank (as Mr Lozada suggested at the trial). The account balance that was stated in Quoine's database was the amount Quoine owed a user, and it was up to Quoine to take steps to ensure that it could repay that debt as and when the user called on it.

148 Further, cl 9 of the Risk Disclosure Statement seem to us to contradict the suggestion that there was an intention to create a trust. Clause 9 provided that:

> …
>
> … [Quoine] does not, however, take client fund safety measures such as depositing [the assets deposited by customers] in an account with a trust bank, etc. regarding these assets, so if [Quoine] goes bankrupt, [Quoine] will not be able to return customer assets, and customers may suffer losses.

Assets held on trust would generally not be subject to the trustee's insolvency creditors.

149 For these reasons, we are satisfied that no express trust arose over the BTC in B2C2's account. We therefore allow Quoine's appeal in this regard. That said, given our decision above that the Trading Contracts are valid and enforceable, B2C2 is nevertheless contractually entitled to the proceeds of the Disputed Trades from Quoine.

Conclusion

150 In the circumstances, we dismiss Quoine's appeal on the breach of contract claim, and allow its appeal on the breach of trust claim. Unless the parties are able to come to an agreement on costs, they are to furnish written submissions limited to six pages each, within three weeks of the date of this judgment, as to the appropriate costs orders.

151 Finally, we would like to record our deep gratitude to Prof Goh for his submissions, which were characteristically thorough, meticulously researched and extremely clear and greatly assisted us in coming to our decision.

Jonathan Mance IJ (dissenting):

Introduction

152 Do conventional legal principles work, or may they need to adapt, when traders hand their affairs to computers operating by algorithm? These questions are raised by this appeal. The computers in issue were "deterministic", meaning that they operated according to pre-determined algorithmic programs, set by humans. This is therefore a case about the legal rules applicable when machines contract in mechanistic fashion by reference to their data input, and by mistake the data input is interrupted and so the outcome becomes fundamentally distorted. The contracts here, made in the middle of the night, were for the supply of BTC by or through Quoine in exchange for the supply of

ETH by B2C2-I adopt throughout the abbreviations used by the majority ("the Majority") in their judgment ("the Majority Judgment"). In the event, the BTC were undervalued or the ETH over-valued by some 250 times, compared to any "normal" price. This occurred because Quoine's computer had, by accident, been cut off from outside world information. But it takes two to contract, and the programming of B2C2's computer to bid or offer at "deep" prices played an important role which will require further examination.

153 B2C2 maintains that, whatever went wrong, a contract so made must stand. For reasons which will appear, I consider that it is correct to approach the case on the basis that it would have been obvious to any human that a wholly untoward breakdown or error had occurred. Since the contracts were made around midnight on 19 April 2017, no human was around to make this observation, but at 6：15am next morning B2C2 did make it, by sending to Quoine the simple message: "Major Quoine database breakdown" and asking Quoine to call B2C2 urgently. The question is whether the contracts were and are, nonetheless, binding.

The facts

154 The facts have been set out in the Majority Judgment. In brief outline:

(a) The Platform operated by Quoine in Singapore provided (i) a facility for trading virtual currencies against each other, together with (ii) a real-time price chart of completed trades for each currency pair executed on the Platform and several other major cryptocurrency exchanges. The real-time prices so displayed were "calculated, consolidated and published" to the trading dashboard through a software program used by the Platform known as the "Quoter Program": Judgment at [14] and Mr Lozada's affidavit at [9(f)].

(b) Quoine also acted as a market maker on the Platform, using the external price information obtained by its Quoter Program to generate buy and sell orders, thereby generating liquidity and depth, minimising volatility and ensuring a continuous two-sided market on the Platform: Judgment at [18] and [72].

(c) Quoine extended credit to certain margin traders on the Platform, which monitored such trades and was programmed, in the event of any margin shortfall, to close them out automatically, selling at the best available price the assets in the relevant trader's account serving as collateral: Judgment at [16]–[17].

155 The Platform and the Quoter Program were therefore designed and expected to operate integrally. However, on 13 April 2017 the login passwords for several critical systems on the Platform were changed for security reasons, and, by oversight, the corresponding necessary changes to the Quoter Program were not implemented. As a result, the Quoter Program ceased to be able to access data from external exchanges and stopped creating new ETH/BTC orders on the Platform. This did not generate an exception message, because the notification flag for such messages had itself been disabled (see the Judgment at [71]–[72]).

156 The volume of trades shown on the Platform gradually diminished, as outstanding orders were filled, with the effect that in the middle of the night of 19 April 2017 the Platform concluded that two margin traders, Pulsar and Mr Tomita, who had borrowed ETH from Quoine in order to speculate in BTC, were in a "margin sell-out position". The Platform therefore triggered calls to force-sell their BTC assets in exchange for ETH at the best available market price. Adding to the chapter of misfortunes, though not centrally relevant to the issues before this court, the Platform, by design oversight, lacked a facility to check that there were sufficient assets available as security to cover any

perceived margin shortfall, and so purportedly sold considerably more BTC than the margin traders had—3000 BTC were sold in the case of Pulsar, which in fact only had some 13.5 BTC: Judgment at [73]-[74].

157 B2C2 is a trader on the Platform. Its software program operated primarily by examining to the first 20 price levels on both the bid and the offer side, and calculating by a series of steps appropriate order levels. But, against the possibility that the available price levels might be too few or too low in value, the program included "deep prices" on the bid and ask side to prevent the program "erroring out". As at 19 April 2017 these deep prices were 10 BTC/ETH on the ask side and 0.00001 BTC/ETH on the bid side. On the bid side (B2C2 buying ETH in return for BTC) an artificial limit would in practice prevent quotes reaching the Platform, on the ground that the bid quantity was too small. On the ask side (B2C2 buying BTC), the only limit was by reference to a threshold based on a notional exchange rate, regardless of the actual sale value.

158 Bid and ask orders at deep prices were, it appears, regularly sent out into the market on the Platform by B2C2's program, but under normal conditions they were ignored, as they would be entirely out of line with available market prices. In evidence which the Judge accepted (Judgment at [113]), Mr Boonen, the proprietor of B2C2, explained that the purpose of the deep prices was "to cover the risk to B2C2 of uncertain liquidity and market conditions" (Judgment at [112]), so catering for very remote market circumstances. Mr Boonen also stated:

> Now, this check or this feature that we're talking about, that price of 10, it's not the sort of day-to-day measure, right. It is a circuit breaker. It is when something very unusual happens. It's when the

> unfathomable actually crystallises. I think it's important to add that clarification.

The Judge accepted that Mr Boonen was not thereby referring to the possibility of errors of which the programme might take advantage. He was "affronted at the suggestion" that he had designed the software with this in mind (Judgment at [117]). On the contrary, the Judgment recites that:

> 118 ... [H]is primary concern when writing the program was to protect the integrity of the B2C2 trading system so as to minimise the risk of any unwarranted exposure.
>
> ...
>
> 121 ... [H]e would have appreciated that the deep prices would only be likely to be executed when there was illiquidity in the order book for that was one of the reasons underlying the addition of the deep prices in the software in the first place. His reasoning was however directed to ensuring the B2C2 system remained operational in such circumstances rather than exploiting the existence of illiquidity.
>
> 122 ... He might have appreciated that one contributing factor to illiquidity could be due to an oversight or error on the part of someone but there are no grounds for concluding that he considered that these would be the only circumstances that would lead to illiquidity. ...

159 What in the event happened was that, in the absence of any other market liquidity, the force-close orders put out by Quoine's Platform, following Pulsar's and Mr Tomita's perceived defaults, were matched with seven of B2C2's deep price bids for BTC at or around 10 BTC/ETH. This "was at a

rate approximately 250 times the rate of about 0. 04 BTC for 1 ETH which had been the previous going rate" (Judgment at [4]). Next morning, when human eyes spotted what had happened overnight, Quoine purported to reverse the trades. The present case is about whether it had valid grounds to do so.

Issues

160 The trial and the appeal have raised a large number of issues, on most of which I am in full agreement with the Majority. In particular, and for the reasons given at [48]-[58] of the Majority Judgment, I agree that the force-out sales which the Platform brought about were between Pulsar and Mr Tomita ("the Counterparties" on whose behalf Quoine was acting) and B2C2. I also consider, if there was any basis for their reversal, that Quoine was acting on behalf of Pulsar and Mr Tomita and was entitled to act on their behalf in taking advantage of it. A security holder is bound to have regard to the interests of a margin trader in executing against margin, and here that clearly required the reversal of the trades, if legally possible.

161 Further, for the reasons given at [60]-[67] of the Majority Judgment, I agree that the contracts brought about by the computers did not incorporate the Aberrant Value Clause, on which Quoine relied. I prefer to reserve my position in relation to the construction and ambit of that clause had it been incorporated, addressed at [68]-[70] of the Majority Judgment, it being unnecessary to determine this. I also agree, for the reasons provided at [71]-[77] of the Majority Judgment, that it is not possible to identify any relevant implied term, unless (I would add) it were one simply mirroring the principles, as I analyse them below, governing mistake; those principles in my view reflect precisely what honourable and reasonable traders would also regard as axiomatic in the present context, whatever the other contractual terms. Finally, I agree with the

Majority's reasons at [129] – [149] for concluding that there was here no common mistake of the nature there identified, and no unjust enrichment or trust.

Unilateral mistake—*Digilandmall.com*

162 The central issue, in my opinion, addressed at [78] – [128] of the Majority Judgment, is whether the doctrine of unilateral mistake applies in these circumstances to enable the reversal of the trades. The law regarding unilateral mistake has been considered in Singapore in *Digilandmall.com* ([80] *supra*). The actual decision in *Digilandmall.com* was based on findings of actual knowledge in relation to each appellant: see *Digilandmall.com* at [88] *et seq*. The court's discussion of the potential role of equity in the context of unilateral mistake was therefore *obiter*, though it is of great assistance in the analysis and merits close attention. The court was clear that, outside the sphere of common law mistake, there was room for equity to operate. The contrary simple approach (that unilateral mistake only exists at common law) would not, it thought, always lead to a just result.

163 There are two particular respects in which equity may supplement the common law relating to unilateral mistake. One is to give the court jurisdiction in cases of fundamental mistake of a nature not covered by the common law. The other is to give it jurisdiction in cases where the non-mistaken person lacks whatever is the requisite mental state for common law relief. The court in *Digilandmall.com* alluded to both these aspects. It focused in the main on the latter aspect, and, as the Majority Judgment notes at [91], did not explore the former aspect in detail. But it came down in favour of a "flexible" doctrine of mistake in equity (further explored at [166] below), in terms which could countenance a wider and perhaps open-ended category of "fundamental"

mistake. The court in *Digilandmall.com* stated at [75] that one possible approach to equity's role would be:

> ... to hold that the former [*ie*, common law mistake] is limited to mistake with regard to the subject matter of the contract (like that in *Bell v. Lever Bros*), while the latter [*ie*, mistake in equity] can have regard to a wider and perhaps open-ended category of 'fundamental' mistake: see *William Sindall Plc v. Cambridgeshire County Council* [1994] 1 WLR 1016, *per* Hoffmann LJ at 1042.

It went on at [76] to note that another possibility would be:

> ... to take a clear simplistic approach, namely, where there is actual knowledge, the contract would be void at common law. But where there is no actual knowledge, the contract ought to be performed. There would then be no room for equity to operate. But we believe that simplicity may not always lead to a just result, especially where innocent third parties are involved.

164 The court concluded therefore that there is a role for equity. However, it did not endorse the precise distinction suggested at [75] of that case. That is because it saw common law mistake as extending beyond mistake with regard to the "subject matter" of the contract. Denning LJ had, in its view, erred in *Solle v. Butcher* [1950] 1 KB 671 at 692 in suggesting (in relation to both common and unilateral mistake) that, following *Bell v. Lever Bros* [1932] AC 161, "only mistake relating to identity or subject matter would come within the common law doctrine of common mistake", whereas any other "common

mistake, even on a most fundamental matter", such as a mistake "about the terms of an offer, or the identity of the person by whom it was made", would not render a contract void at law. So thought the court in *Digilandmall.com* at [58], and I respectfully agree.

165 The limitation suggested by Denning MR would restrict common law mistake radically (although he would have counterbalanced this with a correspondingly wider role for equity). However, the English authorities, considered in the Majority Judgment at [83]-[90], indicate that, contrary to what Denning LJ thought in *Solle v. Butcher*, mistake under English common law extends to all situations involving a sufficiently fundamental mistake as to the subject matter or a term, though no further. That being the scope of common law mistake under the English law, it is, as the Majority Judgment indicates at [90], unresolved to what, if any, extent there is, under English law, a further equitable jurisdiction to relieve against other situations of fundamental mistake. In contrast with English common law, the High Court of Australia has, I note, endorsed the limited role given to common law mistake by Denning LJ, but again counterbalanced this with a recognition of equitable relief in other cases: *Taylor v. Johnson* ([90] *supra*) at [9]-[11]. I note in this connection that the High Court spoke of the nature of mistake "in relation to a fundamental term" as capable of leading to the grant of equitable relief where one party was aware that the other was "entering [into] the contract under some serious mistake or misapprehension about either the content or subject matter of that term" (*Taylor v. Johnson* at [14]). Further, it granted such equitable relief on the facts when all that could be said was that the non-mistaken party (Mr Taylor) "believed that [Mrs Johnson] was under some serious mistake or misapprehension about either the terms (the price) or the subject matter (its value) of the relevant transaction" (at [15]).

166 The court in *Digilandmall.com* went on to consider and disagree with Canadian authority which also suggested a composite analysis, whereby mistake in equity would subsume the common law. It went on at [55] to hold that there was a role for both common law and equitable mistake, along lines indicated in *Associated Japanese Bank (International) Ltd v. Crédit du Nord SA* [1989] 1 WLR 255, where Steyn J (as he then was) said this:

> No one could fairly suggest that in this difficult area of the law there is only one correct approach or solution. But a narrow doctrine of common law mistake (as enunciated in *Bell v. Lever Brothers* [1932] AC 161), supplemented by the more flexible doctrine of mistake in equity (as developed in *Solle v. Butcher* [1950] 1 KB 671 and later cases) seems to me to be an entirely sensible and satisfactory state of the law …

Subject to the qualification, which the court in *Digilandmall.com* had already made at [58], that common law mistake should not be understood as narrowly as Denning LJ had suggested in *Solle v. Butcher*, Singapore law therefore recognises both the common law and equity as having relevant roles in cases of unilateral mistake. The recognition of a clear role of equity comes with the advantage that Steyn J pointed out, which the court in *Digilandmall.com* echoed at [77], namely, that "[a] great attribute … of equity, is its flexibility to achieve the ends of justice".

167 The court specifically identified in this connection the ability of equity to address situations of constructive notice. By this, it made clear that it was referring to situations falling short of actual knowledge: see *eg*, *Digilandmall.com* ([80] *supra*) at [76], [77], [83] and [88]. Of such situations, the

court said (at [77]):

> … Constructive notice is a concept of equity and whether constructive notice should lead the court to intervene must necessarily depend on the presence of other factors which could invoke the conscience of the court, such as ' sharp practice ' or ' unconscionable conduct '. Negligence *per se*, on the other hand, should not be sufficient to invoke equity. Parties to a contract do not owe a duty of care to each other.

One important consideration that may, of course, arise is that the exercise of any equitable jurisdiction can and will always take care to protect legitimate third party interests. Here, however, it was not suggested that any such interests which arose in the very short period before the mistake came to light precluded the avoidance by Quoine of the transactions. (Paragraph 256 of the Judge's first instance judgment mentions—but only as a reason for not ordering specific performance against Quoine—that, "[b]efore the trades were reversed", B2C2's software generated sales of slightly under one-third of the BTC "on nine different exchanges". Since any such sales were not relied on as a bar to avoidance, no consideration was, it seems, given to their terms or prices, though these may of course become material to damages.)

168 The court in *Digilandmall.com* developed its reference to unconscionability in the following *dicta* (at [78]):

> However, ' unconscionability' cannot be imputed based on what a reasonable person would have known. It must be based on matters the non-mistaken party knows: see *Can-Dive Services v. Pacific Coast*

> *Energy Corp* (2000) 74 BCLR (3d) 30 ('*Can-Dive*') per Southin JA at [142]. One cannot act unconscionably if one does not know of facts which could render an act so. Thus, we do not think we can accept the views of Shaw J, the lower court judge in *Can-Dive*, that constructive knowledge alone would suffice to invoke equity's conscience. However, as we have indicated earlier, Canadian jurisprudence has moved in that direction.

169 The judgment in *Digilandmall.com*, therefore, indicates that unilateral mistake in equity can exist where there is a combination of factors: (a) constructive notice of a mistake which would, if actual knowledge existed, render the contract void; and (b)(i) behaviour by the non-mistaken party which is unconscionable (b)(ii) based on knowledge by the non-mistaken party of the facts involved in the unconscionability. It is also consistent with the further proposition, which I would endorse, that the flexible equitable doctrine is capable of covering situations of unilateral mistake, where the mistake, although not strictly as to subject matter or a term, is sufficiently "fundamental" to justify equitable intervention-subject again, if the analysis in *Digilandmall.com* is followed through, to the presence of factors (b)(i) and (b)(ii).

170 The analysis in *Digilandmall.com* does, however, give rise to two points, which I mention although their resolution is not in my opinion necessary for the determination of this appeal. First, if unconscionable behaviour based on knowledge by the non-mistaken party is understood as behaviour conducing to the mistaken party remaining mistaken, then it is difficult to see how there could ever be constructive notice. As the court in *Digilandmall.com* recognised at [76], [77], [83] and [88], constructive notice comes into consideration where there is no actual knowledge of the mistake. Second, the primary basis

for equitable relief on the ground of unilateral mistake is the mistake of which the non-mistaken party has constructive notice. Where unconscionability operates, it is as an additional element (see *Digilandmall.com* at [77], [80] and [83])—in effect a control mechanism. Authorities such as, most recently, *BOM* ([109] *supra*) deal with the situation, materially different therefore from the present, where unconscionability is all that is relied on to justify the setting aside in equity of an otherwise valid transaction. The limited view of unconscionability taken in *BOM* (linking it closely with what was called "class 1 undue influence") must be seen in that context. Where the primary basis for relief is a mistake of which the non-mistaken party has constructive notice, no reason appears why unconscionability should not operate on a flexible basis to meet the equity of the particular case.

171 Consistently with the first point, unconscionable behaviour conducing to the mistaken party remaining mistaken is a typical—though not essential—hallmark of unilateral mistake at common law based on *actual* knowledge of a mistake as to a term which the non-mistaken party "snaps up". Thus, in common law cases such as *Tamplin v. James* (1880) 15 Ch D 215, quoted in *Hartog v. Colin & Shields* [1939] 3 All ER 566, courts spoke in terms of a party "snapping up the offer", which, as also in *Digilandmall.com*, the non-mistaken party actually realised to be mistaken. (The position is different in Australia, where, for reasons explained at [164] above, the role of equity is much greater and embraces situations of "snapping up" with actual knowledge, like that in *Taylor v. Johnson* ([90] *supra*) itself, which would under English and Singapore law fall within common law mistake.) But "snapping up" or unconscionable behaviour conducing to the mistake is not an essential feature of unilateral mistake at common law, because this can occur where there is simply knowing and silent "standing by".

172 There can be marginal situations where a non-mistaken party suspects a mistake by the other party and "proceeds on a course of wilful ignorance designed to inhibit his own actual knowledge of the other's mistake" (in the words of McLachlin CJBC, as she then was, in *First City Capital Ltd v. British Colombia Building Corp* (1989) 43 BLR 29 ("*First City Capital*") at [30]). But, just as shutting a blind eye may be equated with actual knowledge or recklessness with intention, such situations are best equated with actual knowledge, rather than treated as cases of constructive notice. That is in my opinion correctly stated by the court in *Digilandmall.com* ([80] *supra*) at [42], where it referred to "what is called 'Nelsonian knowledge', namely, wilful blindness or shutting one's eyes to the obvious", and went on to state:

> … Clearly, if the court finds that the non-mistaken party is guilty of wilful knowledge, it will be in line with logic and reason to find that that party had actual knowledge.

However such situations may be analysed, it is clear that the court in *Digilandmall.com* understood the concept of constructive notice to extend to a different, broader range of situations.

173 It follows that if constructive notice is to have the relevant role in relation to unilateral mistake in Singapore law, which the court in *Digilandmall.com* in my view correctly assigned to it, unconscionability cannot relate to behaviour with knowledge of the mistake conducing to the mistaken party remaining mistaken. Equity's conscience must be capable of being affected by behaviour in seeking to retain the benefit of the mistake, once it is discovered. Taking words which were used by the court in *Digilandmall.com* itself at [80], the court is then:

> ... entitled to intervene and grant relief when it is unconscionable for the non-mistaken party to insist that the contract be performed. ...

174 Two passages from prior Canadian authority cited by the court in *Digilandmall.com* at [49] and [51] need to be read with caution and in context, in so far as they may at first reading appear to link unconscionability and " snapping up " to equitable relief in circumstances of constructive notice. The two passages come from the first instance decision in *First City Capital Ltd* at [34] and the British Colombia Court of Appeal decision in 256593 *BC Ltd v.* 456795 *BC Ltd* (1999) 171 DLR (4th) 470 ("256593 *BC Ltd*") at [25]. In the first passage, McLachlin CJBC said that, on a hypothesis of no actual knowledge:

> ... [T]his is most certainly a case where [the defendant] ought to have known that [the owner] had no right to sell the building to it. Nevertheless, [the defendant], in its negotiations with [the owner], pursued a course designed to inhibit discovery of the mistake, moving with uncharacteristic haste to snap at [the owner's] mistaken offer.

On its facts, *First City Capital* falls fairly clearly into the category of Nelsonian knowledge: see in particular at [18] – [20] of *First City Capital*, where McLachlin CJBC concluded that BCBC "at very least suspected" a mistake and checked with a superior the authority of the junior with whom it was dealing "without, significantly, asking ... about the substance of the transaction, a course which might have disclosed the error".

175 The second passage is attributed in *Digilandmall.com* to Donald JA, giving the judgment of the Court of Appeal in 256593 *BC Ltd*. But it was actually a quotation by Donald JA, from (once again) the judgment of McLachlin CJBC in *First City Capital*, about which Donald JA went on to make this reservation (at [26]-[28]):

> [26] Counsel for Ace submits there is no evidence of snapping up the offer in the present case. Assuming that to be so, I do not think that conduct so characterized is necessary for rescission on mistake. I respectfully agree with the reasoning of Shaw J. in *Can-Dive* ... where he said at 69-70 that:
>
> > While I agree with what Madam Justice McLachlin said so far as it goes, I do not believe she intended to imply that there must be a conscious taking advantage by one party of the other in all cases. The element of constructive knowledge based upon what a reasonable person 'ought to know' is premised upon that person not being conscious of the error. Thus, while the idea of 'snapping up' may well apply in cases where one side is aware of the other side's error, I do not think it can be applied literally in the constructive knowledge cases. Rather, in my opinion, constructive knowledge alone will suffice to invoke equity's conscience. [...]
>
> [27] Baker J. in *Craig Estate v. Higgins* (1993), 86 B. C. L. R. (2d) 64, put in summary form at 72 a statement of the law with which I respectfully agree:
>
> > The court may grant relief from a contract entered into on

the basis of unilateral mistake where the plaintiff has established, and has met the high burden imposed upon it of doing so, that a mistake has been made and that it would be unjust or inequitable for the court to allow the other party to uphold the bargain. One of the grounds on which a court may find that it would be unfair or inequitable is if the party seeking to enforce it had actual knowledge or constructive knowledge that a mistake had been made prior to acceptance of the offer.

[28] All the elements for rescission on unilateral mistake are present here: (1) a mistake; (2) on a material term; (3) known actually or constructively by the non-mistaken party; and (4) an unconscionable result if the settlement agreement is enforced. It is my opinion that the mistake gives Ace a huge windfall that it had never bargained for and leaves Earl's with an outstanding debt while simultaneously transferring Earl's interest in the very asset underlying that debt. [Donald JA's emphasis in 256593 *BC Ltd*]

176 Other passages in McLachlin CJBC's judgment in *First City Capital* in my opinion actually support the analysis adopted in British Colombia by the Court of Appeal as well as by Shaw J and Baker J. Thus, referring to *McMaster University v. Wilchar Construction Ltd* [1971] 3 OR 801, 22 DLR (3d) 9 (HC) at p 18, McLachlin CJBC said ([26]-[27]):

[26] In *McMaster*, the Court held that the offeror was to be relieved from a contract involving a mistake known to the offeree because ' it would be unconscionable, unfair and unjust *to permit the plaintiff to*

maintain the contract' (p. 22). This test was applied by Gould, J. of this Court in *Beverly Motel (1972) Ltd. v. Klyne Properties Ltd.* (1981), 30 B.C.L.R. 282 ... :

> Provided there is mistake as to the promise or as to some material term of the contract, if the court finds that there has been honest, even though inadvertent, mistake, it will afford relief *in any case where it considers that it would be unfair, unjust or unconscionable not to correct it* ...

[27] ... Fraud in this wider sense refers to transactions falling short of deceit *but where the Court is of the opinion that it is unconscientious for a person to avail himself of the advantage obtained* ...

[emphasis added]

177 At [78] of *Digilandmall.com* ([80] *supra*), quoted at [167] above, the court cited Southin JA who said at [142] of *Can-Dive Services v. Pacific Coast Energy Corp* (2000) 74 BCLR (3d) 30 that "questions of unconscionability are not matters to be determined on what someone ought to have known, but what he did know". The context was a claim to rectify a subcontract to give a right to claim extra remuneration for working in difficult soil conditions, in circumstances where it was thought (as it turned out mistakenly) that such a right anyway followed from the back-to-back terms of the head contract. The claim failed on the basis that "[t]he critical 'fact'—the true meaning of the head contract—was unknown to both parties to the subcontract until the learned trial judge handed down his judgment": *Can-Dive* at [143]. Both parties had "agreed to be bound by the head contract, whatever it meant", and the claim amounted to an attempt to rectify the bargain, rather than the subcontract

(*Can-Dive* at [141] and [144]). But what is of current interest is that Southin JA, with whose judgment Ryan JA agreed, gave at [141], as an example of a situation where equitable relief against mistake could be given, a scenario where a mistake occurred in the course of "mechanical" transcription and was only subsequently discovered. She said:

> In the case at bar, if, when the subcontract had been typed up, the typist had omitted to put in the weather clause upon which the parties had struck a bargain, it would, in my opinion, be equitable fraud for the head contractor to say, in effect: 'Well, too bad, see the words of the contract.' But that is not what happened here. ...

178 The court at [78] of *Digilandmall.com* also expressed some disagreement with the views of Shaw J at first instance in *Can-Dive*, while going on to recognise that Canadian jurisprudence "has moved in that direction"—quite possibly a reference to the British Colombia Court of Appeal's reasoning in 256593 *BC Ltd* ([174] *supra*). But the problem is not just one of preference, it goes to the heart of any significant doctrine of constructive notice as a basis for equitable relief. It is not however critical, as I see it, to resolve the problem in this case, which is concerned with a different issue: how, if at all, a doctrine based on a need for either actual or constructive notice can operate in circumstances where neither party was or could have been aware of the mistake as and when it occurred. As will appear, I consider that this conundrum can be resolved in this case by considering what B2C2's actual state of mind would have been, given knowledge of the circumstances of the transactions as and when they occurred. To that extent, the case parallels situations of actual knowledge, rather than constructive notice.

Conceptual basis of unilateral mistake

179 Before considering further how the law of unilateral mistake may apply in the present case, I should say something about its conceptual basis. The court at [31] of *Digilandmall.com*, in a phrase quoted in the Majority Judgment at [81], suggested that it is "self-evident" that "a party who is aware of the error made by the other party cannot claim that there is *consensus ad idem*". There is a long-standing academic debate about the foundational principle underpinning the law of contract at common law. Is contract based on objective evaluation of the parties' communications against the background of all the circumstances which were or are to be taken to have been within their knowledge? Or is it based on subjective consensus, modified in almost every case by the consideration that each party will be effectively precluded from relying on any interpretation different from that which they objectively agreed between them (an approach similar to that which I understand the French Civil Code to adopt: see *eg*, *Dallah Real Estate and Tourism Holding Company v. The Ministry of Religious Affairs, Government of Pakistan* [2011] 1 AC 763 at [19])? If the former, then unilateral mistake operates as a limited exception to the objective approach, which is how it is explained in *Chitty* at para 3-022; see also *Treitel on The Law of Contract* (Sweet & Maxwell, 14th Ed, 2015) at paras 1-002, 2-002 and 8-047; and John Cartwright, *Misrepresentation, Mistake and Non-Disclosure* (Sweet & Maxwell, 3rd Ed, 2012) at para 13-02. If the latter, then unilateral mistake is one limited situation where estoppel cannot and does not operate, because there is no reliance.

180 In *Taylor v. Johnson* ([90] *supra*), the High Court of Australia concluded at [9] that "[w]hile the sounds of conflict have not been completely stilled, the clear trend in decided cases and academic writings has been to leave the objective theory in command of the field". I agree with this, and it

corresponds with the terms in which other common law courts have described the principles governing contract: see *eg*, *Reardon Smith Line Ltd v. Yngvar Hansen-Tangen* [1976] 1 WLR 989 at 997; *Investors Compensation Scheme Ltd v. West Bromwich Building Society* [1998] 1 WLR 896 at 912; *Charter Reinsurance Co Ltd v. Fagan* [1997] AC 313 at 384; and *Wood v. Capita Insurance Services Ltd* [2017] AC 1173 at [10] ("The court's task is to ascertain the objective meaning of the language which the parties have chosen to express their agreement"). On that basis, unilateral mistake is an exception, recognised by the law to further the ends of justice, of a similar character to the principles underlying the law of misrepresentation, undue influence or mistake. The court in *Digilandmall.com* effectively recognised this at [31] when it said:

> ... The law should not go to the aid of a party who knows that the objective appearance does not correspond with reality. It would go against the grain of justice if the law were to deem the mistaken party bound by such a contract.

This analysis also has the further consequential advantage of explaining why and how the law can establish, as the court recognised that it should in *Digilandmall.com*, different rules for common law mistake in circumstances where a fundamental mistake as to a term is involved (the contract is void), and for equitable mistake (the contract is potentially voidable). The logic of the theory of subjective consensus is that there is no contract at all in any case of unilateral mistake, whether common law or equitable. The High Court of Australia pointed this out in *Taylor v. Johnson* at [8].

181 The value of a differentiated analysis of unilateral mistake, operating both

at common law and in equity, is that it enables the court to address in a circumstance-specific way situations where, for one reason or another, parties objectively reach agreement on a contract which, as one party knows or ought to know, differs in some fundamental respect from what the other party thinks it is or means. The mistake may, I add, come to the former party's knowledge quite independently of and outside the contractual discussions. Take for example, a contract made for oats or even for new oats, where the seller, unknown to the buyer, is told by a third party with no authority to act for the buyer (or discovers by reading without permission a piece of paper on the buyer's desk while the buyer is out of the room), that the buyer believes it to be a term of the contract that the oats will be old. The offer and acceptance and the contract made all objectively permit or call for the delivery of new oats, but the seller's knowledge of the buyer's actual misapprehension prevents the seller from insisting on performance. The underlying rationale is not a lack of correspondence between offer and acceptance, but a principle of justice.

The application or adaption of the above principles

182 I turn to the application, or adaption, of the above principles in the present circumstances. For the reasons given by the Majority at [114], I agree that the present case cannot readily be analysed as involving an actual mistake as to a term of the transactions as executed. That is because of the very fact that the transactions were effected by computers operating mechanistically according to algorithms, leading inexorably, although blindly, to such transactions. The case does not therefore fit within the principles governing unilateral mistake at common law, and it would not be right to extend these to cover such a situation, since the operation of the algorithms might also have led (though it did not do so here) to relevant third party interests arising before any human

discovery of the mistake. What can however be stated with confidence is that the mistake and its outcome in the form of the transactions was in human terms just as fundamental as the sort of mistake at issue in *Digilandmall.com* ([80] *supra*). The reaction of any human trader viewing the transactions as executed would have been that they were fundamentally misconceived—the result of some fundamental mistake leading to terms for the sale of BTC to which no seller of BTC would, in prevailing market conditions, agree.

183 In these circumstances, the enquiry therefore moves to the more flexible area of unilateral mistake in equity. For that purpose, the Judge's findings, in particular at [227] were and are, to my mind, clear. There was a fundamental mistake, in that Quoine's system operated (and led to the sale of BTC on terms) in a way that was not conceived as possible and would never have been accepted by Quoine or the Counterparties in the prevailing circumstances. Further, although B2C2 had no knowledge of the mistake as and when it occurred, the position is that, as soon as it inspected the computer printouts next morning, it knew at once that there had been such a mistake, and e-mailed its message to Quoine: "Major Quoine database breakdown", to which I referred at the outset of this judgment and to which I shall return at [203]. The question is whether, where two parties well know that there has been a fundamental mistake as soon as a computerised transaction comes to their attention, where no detriment has occurred and no relevant third party interests intervened, and where the mistake could readily be rectified, the law will enforce the contract regardless. For the reasons I will give, in my opinion, the law should and can in such circumstances hold that the contract is voidable, as Quoine claims.

184 Certainty in contract is of course important, but it is not everything: see, *eg*, *Golden Strait Corporation v. Nippon Yusen Kubishka Kaisha (The "Golden*

Victory") [2007] 2 AC 353; *Bunge SA v. Nidera BV* [2015] 3 All ER 1082. Like all great judges, Lord Mansfield could see the force of both considerations. In *Vallejo v. Wheeler* (1774) 1 Cowp 143 at 153 he said that:

> In all mercantile transactions the great object should be certainty: and therefore, it is of more consequence that a rule should be certain, than whether the rule is established one way or the other. Because speculators in trade then know which ground to go upon.

But in another famous decision, *Alderson v. Temple* (1768) 4 Burr 2235 at 2239, he showed a different concern:

> ... [T]he most desirable object in all judicial determinations, especially in mercantile ones, (which ought to be determined upon natural justice, and not upon the niceties of the law,) is, to do substantial justice. ...

There are cases where justice outweighs in the balance the interests of legal certainty. The court in *Digilandmall.com* recognised this in the present context, endorsing at [81] a statement of Assoc Prof Yeo Tiong Min that "[t]he fear that the use of 'elastic' equitable principles will lead to uncertainty and encourage litigation is arguably exaggerated" and adding it "is not more difficult to determine what is 'equitable' than what is 'reasonable' at common law".

185 The critical problem which Quoine faces in this case is that, in conventional cases of unilateral mistake, the relevant knowledge or constructive knowledge either exists or not, as a matter of fact, as and when the contract is made. The focus of the enquiry is then on the actual state of mind and conduct

of human beings involved in the making of the contract. That approach is by definition impossible in the different context of a contract made between computers programmed by humans. But the right approach is less obvious. The Judge dealt with the issue as follows (at [200]–[211]):

> 200 Quoine submits that the Court should consider what the parties are likely to have known and intended if, hypothetically, they had met on the 'floor of the exchange' for the purpose of reaching an agreement on the trades on 19 April 2017. On this basis, as I understand it, it is contended that mistakes can be identified by comparing theoretically what would have happened in face-to-face negotiations with what actually happened at the computer interface.
>
> …
>
> 202 B2C2 contends that there must be a mistake as to a term of the contract and that the party placing the order, albeit by a computer, must be the person mistaken. It was not sufficient if there was a mistake as to facts surrounding that term. In this respect therefore B2C2's position was that the assessment of a relevant mistake was no different in the case of computer transactions than in face-to-face transactions.
>
> 203 Further, relying on *Chwee* [*ie*, *Digilandmall.com*], B2C2 contends that the only relevant knowledge is knowledge at the time of contracting and suggests that it is wrong to assess knowledge or constructive knowledge at the time the deep price mechanism was programmed.
>
> 204 So far as concerns the nature of the mistake, I cannot accept Quoine's hypothetical meeting contention. The question is not what

would have happened if the computer element was absent. The parties have chosen to use computers as the means of entering the Trading contracts. They have entered Platform contracts with Quoine so as to be able to enter Trading contracts and, in the case of margin traders, they have entered the Margin trading contracts to regulate their position vis-à-vis the lender, in this case Quoine. All parties were therefore aware that there was to be no human element in the trades and it is wholly artificial to work on the basis of what might have happened if a human element was involved. Equally whilst B2C2's position identifies what the nature of the mistake must be, it does not assist in determining how and when to identify it.

205 In the circumstances of this case, I have concluded that the relevant mistake must be a mistake by the person on whose behalf the computer placed the order in question as to the terms on which the computer was programmed to form a Trading contract in relation to that order. This mistake will have to be in existence at the date of the contract in question but may have been formed at an earlier date. The existence of a relevant mistake will be a question of fact in each case.

206 Turning to knowledge of the mistake, the law in relation to the way in which ascertainment of knowledge in cases where computers have replaced human actions is to be determined will, no doubt, develop as legal disputes arise as a result of such actions. This will particularly be the case where the computer in question is creating artificial intelligence and could therefore be said to have a mind of its own.

…

210 Where it is relevant to determine what the intention or knowledge was underlying the mode of operation of a particular machine, it is logical to have regard to the knowledge or intention of the operator or controller of the machine. In the case of the kitchen blender, this will be the person who put the ingredients in and caused it to work. His or her knowledge or intention will be contemporaneous with the operation of the machine. But in the case of robots or trading software in computers this will not be the case. The knowledge or intention cannot be that of the person who turns it on, it must be that of the person who was responsible for causing it to work in the way it did, in other words, the programmer. Necessarily this will have been done at a date earlier than the date on which the computer or robot carried out the acts in question. To this extent I reject B2C2's contention that that the only relevant knowledge is knowledge at the time of contracting. I agree with Quoine that regard should be had to the knowledge and intention of the programmer of the program in issue when that program (or the relevant part of it) was written.

211 Accordingly, in my judgment, in circumstances where it is necessary to assess the state of mind of a person in a case where acts of deterministic computer programs are in issue, regard should be had to the state of mind of the programmer of the software of that program at the time the relevant part of the program was written. In the present case that person is Mr Boonen.

186 The Judge then gave effect to this approach, by examining first the state of mind of Pulsar and Mr Tomita operating as margin traders on the market and

then that of Mr Boonen when he programmed the B2C2 computer and set it into operation to trade on the market. As to the former, the Judge focused on the state of mind of the margin traders, and, on the basis of the evidence given by Mr Tseung of Pulsar, accepted that both Pulsar and Mr Tomata held a mistaken belief which was fundamental to the trades. The Judge explained this conclusion as follows (at [227]-[228]):

> 227 Mr Tseung, however, gives evidence that because the trades were carried out at the highly abnormal price, they were clearly invalid and that Pulsar did not consider them to be valid. He went on to state '[i]t was never contemplated by Pulsar that any trades may be transacted on the Platform at prices which deviated so substantially from the actual market prices'. Although he gave no reasons for holding this belief, he was not cross-examined on this statement and I therefore accept that this was a genuinely held belief. Indeed, having heard all the evidence, I can well understand that a trader on the Platform who was not a market maker might well have formed such a belief even having read the Agreement and the Risk Disclosure Statement. It is a belief which is founded on the premise that the Platform would either always operate as intended or, alternatively, if for some reason it did not, there would be adequate error identification and protection systems in place to prevent trading continuing in such circumstances.
>
> 228 I therefore accept that the Counterparties held this mistaken belief and that it is a belief which is fundamental to the Trading contracts.

187 The evidence was, in substance, that Pulsar never contemplated that trading could occur at such deviant prices other than as a result of some egregious error. The Judge said he could well understand that a trader on the Platform who was not a market maker might well have formed such a belief. The reservation "who was not a market maker" deserves a word. 98% of the relevant market making on the Platform was done by Quoine, as the Majority Judgment recites at [10], and there is every reason to think that it would and did view the relevant trades in exactly the same way as Mr Tseung of Pulsar, and sought to set them aside on that basis. The Judge's reservation presumably arises because B2C2 did some market making, and at the same time also issued its "deep" bids and offers which it contemplated might be accepted for some reason other than a mistake (though the suggested unfathomable market event had never in fact arisen). The reservation therefore takes one back to the core of the issue—whether B2C2's accepted intention to cater for wholly unfathomable events (which in fact never occurred) is the answer to the claim of unilateral mistake.

188 A collateral observation which it is convenient to interpose at this point is that it is, to my mind, odd that attention at trial should have been so focused on the margin traders, and not on Quoine. It was Quoine whose computer was programmed to instruct the trades. Moreover, most of the BTC sold did not exist as assets of Pulsar, and there must at least be a question whether Quoine could have had ostensible authority to bind Pulsar by a sale of non-existent assets which Quoine can have had no actual authority to sell on Pulsar's behalf. These points were not explored before us, and I need say no more about them, save to repeat that, if attention had been focused on Quoine's state of mind, rather than that of the margin traders, I feel confident that the Judge would have made the same finding with regard to Quoine that he made with

regard to the margin traders.

189 Having found a fundamental mistake on the side of the suppliers of BTC, the Judge turned to consider the other side of the issue, whether the mistake was sufficiently known to B2C2 as the supplier in exchange of ETH. As to this, he said (at [229]-[231]):

> 229 It is next necessary to determine whether Mr Boonen had actual knowledge of the mistaken belief at the time he inserted the deep prices and I thus return to the findings of fact in [118]-[125] above. Can it be said that Mr Boonen knew that 'it was never contemplated by [any trader] that any trades would be transacted on the Platform at prices which deviated so substantially from the actual market prices'? This amounts to a belief held by Mr Boonen at that date that the price was so abnormal that no trader would trade at that price otherwise by way of a mistake.
>
> 230 This is the aspect of this case that I have found to be most troubling but I have concluded on the basis of those findings of fact that Mr Boonen did not insert the deep prices with that belief. He foresaw that a number of factors might arise which would cause the deep prices to be inserted and the overriding reasons for them being inserted was to protect B2C2 in the event of the unexpected happening. He did not exclude the possibility of trades at those prices being executed. Whilst he was aware that one possible cause was that it could be the result, wholly or in part, of some error or omission on the part of someone, including himself, he did not turn his mind in any detail to the circumstances that might lead to such trades being executed. He knew that the Platform was an automated system and

that therefore no opportunity would arise for any particular trade to be reviewed by the parties in advance. In the circumstances of this case, in order for him to have actual knowledge that other traders believed that in no circumstances would a trade be transacted on the Platform at prices which deviated so substantially from the actual market prices, I consider that it would be necessary for it to be demonstrated that he held that belief himself, which he did not: see [123] above.

231 Accordingly, whilst I accept that the Counterparties held the second mistaken belief relied upon by Quoine, I do not accept that Mr Boonen had actual knowledge of that belief. The defence of unilateral mistake at common law therefore fails.

190 The paragraph numbered [123], to which the Judge referred at the end of [230] read as follows:

I therefore accept that when Mr Boonen configured the code he knew of the possibility that the order book might become empty and that in that event the deep prices would be placed on the order book but I do not accept that he ever considered that there was a real possibility of the deep price orders being executed. He considered that this was unlikely and I do not believe that he turned his mind in any detail to the circumstances in which this might happen. That was not the motivation for designing the software as he did. He did not consider that the deep prices were irrational. Indeed he gave cogent reasons for the selection of the prices which were directed to protecting the integrity of his system but at a level which he felt would not be so high as to cause a circuit break on the Platform: see [86] above. This

> last factor is inconsistent with any assertion that Mr Boonen understood that trades would only be matched by the Platform at prices at or near the previously existing prevailing market price: see [230] below.

The Judge went on at [124]:

> The evidence does not support the conclusion that when designing the code Mr Boonen perceived that no trader would ever agree to buy ETH at such a price unless he had made a mistake and included the deep prices with this in mind. …

191 In relation to Mr Boonen the Judge therefore thought that the relevant enquiry was whether he knew or believed when he programmed B2C2's computer, prior to and in June 2016, that *no trade would ever take place at the deep prices* which he had programmed his computer to output to the Platform at apparently random times *other than as a result of some fundamental error*. Since the Judge had held that Mr Boonen had a rational motive for inserting the deep prices (which Mr Boonen had explained as being to cover very unusual or unfathomable market conditions: see the Judgment at [113], quoted at [158] above), he could not be said to know or believe when programming his computer or at any time in advance of the actual transactions that, if a transaction took place at the deep prices, it *must involve a mistake and nothing else*.

192 On such an approach, before any relief could be granted, it would have to be shown (a) that Mr Boonen knew by prophetic foresight that the particular transactions would occur at the deep prices over the night of 13 April 2017 due

to some fundamental error (which is obviously impossible); or (b) that each and every transaction which might ever occur at the deep prices he offered would be the result of some mistake, *ie*, that any transaction at his deep prices could *only* arise from some fundamental mistake. The latter approach, which the Judge adopted, therefore looks at the position in the abstract and in advance, without any regard for the actual transactions or the market circumstances surrounding them. This is a different approach to that which applies when considering mistake in the context of a transaction completed by human intervention, when the first question is the actual state of mind of each party in the light of the surrounding circumstances. If one of them by mistake refers to a price per "pound", rather than per "piece", the other, if aware of the state of the market, will know in that light when a wholly mistaken word has been used. The Judge's approach involves omitting a usually important element in any appraisal of such a situation, namely, (here) whether there was anything drastically unusual about the surrounding circumstances or the state of the market to explain on a rational basis why such abnormal prices could occur, or whether the only possible conclusion was that some fundamental error had taken place, giving rise to transactions which the other party could never rationally have contemplated or intended.

193 The key question is, therefore, whether the law of unilateral mistake falls to be applied in a manner which leaves out of consideration circumstances which are normally central to its application, simply because the parties entrusted their dealings to computers which can have no such consciousness. In my opinion, it does not and should not. The law must be adapted to the new world of algorithmic programmes and artificial intelligence, in a way which gives rise to the results that reason and justice would lead one to expect. The introduction of computers no doubt carries risks, but I do not consider that these include the

risk of being bound by an algorithmic contract, which anyone learning of would at once see could only be the result of some fundamental error in the normal operation of the computers involved. Computers are outworkers, not overlords to whose operations parties can be taken to have submitted unconditionally in circumstances as out of ordinary as the present. I do not think that the obvious malfunctioning of a computer-based system should be given the dominance that B2C2's case implies.

194 In my opinion, it is necessary to revisit the Judge's refusal to take as the relevant test what Mr Boonen or anyone in his position could or would have known or believed, if he or they had known of the circumstances which have actually occurred. That is a test which relates what actually occurred to natural human reactions, given knowledge of what occurred. It matters not whether one assumes such knowledge at the time of the transactions, or prophetically in advance. The answer is the same. If it would at once have been perceived that some fundamental error had occurred, relief should be available. There is no difficulty here about identifying the circumstances to which, given such knowledge, the objective test would and should be applied.

195 For the reasons indicated at [182] and [183] above, any relief should be equitable, rather than at common law. The fact that computers were involved makes this appropriate. B2C2's computer might have on-sold the BTC by algorithm at a normal price to a *bona fide* purchaser for value. Equity could then refuse to set aside the transaction whereby B2C2 acquired the BTC. The fact that Quoine was at fault should not however point decisively away from relief. There was here certainly a series of avoidable errors, which some might suggest should preclude relief. But the question is whether the errors were so egregious as to justify imposing (on whichever of Pulsar and Mr Tomita or Quoine might end up holding the parcel) a loss of perhaps millions of dollars,

and benefitting B2C2 to the tune of perhaps millions of dollars by way of what some would call an uncovenanted windfall. In circumstances where B2C2 would and did know at once that some fundamental error had occurred, which error could be rectified without any detriment being suggested to B2C2 or any third party, I have no doubt about the answer. Unilateral mistake commonly involves fault, even if the fault only consists in failure by the mistaken party to appreciate what impression they have, objectively, given to the other party. Where the error is known, the fact that it is or may be attributable to fault cannot axiomatically outweigh the considerations of fair dealing that lead to relief both at common law or, *a fortiori* as here, in equity. The High Court of Australia cited in this connection, with apparent approval, at [13] of *Taylor v. Johnson* ([90] *supra*), the position in the United States that:

> [I]t matters not that the mistake is, or may be, due to negligence or want of care on the part of the party who is mistaken when the other party has not materially changed his position and third party rights are not in question (*De Paola v. City of New York* (1977) 394 NYS (2d) 525, at pp 527–528).

But it is unnecessary to go that far. There is on any view a balance. In the present case, where any reasonable trader would at once have identified, as B2C2 did identify, a fundamental computer system breakdown as the cause of the transactions, the considerations weighing in favour of reversal of the transactions outweigh in the balance any errors or faults which led to that breakdown.

196 It should also be remembered that fundamental errors of the present nature can and do occur in computerised exchanges without any fault. Suppose in the

present case that a mouse had eaten, or a third party using a mechanical digger had cut, a cable linking the Platform to the Quoter Program. Or suppose someone had hacked into Quoine's computer and disconnected the link. The same question, whether relief could be granted, would arise, without there being necessarily any background of fault. The law must be capable of addressing such a situation in a manner which corresponds with what I would regard as the clear justice of the case, as well as with the natural expectations of reasonable traders.

197 It was suggested that all such problems, including the present, could have been dealt with by appropriately framed conditions of business. No doubt that is so. But the same could said in many of the situations in which the common law has developed principles of relief, to achieve just results. The law governing mistake is itself a classic example, as is the law of misrepresentation, duress, undue influence, *etc*. The question is not whether the parties might have regulated such situations generally, or the present situation in particular, by specific agreement, but whether in the circumstances they should be taken to have accepted the risk of their occurrence so as to preclude application of such common law principles, adapted as necessary to the age of algorithms.

198 There is nothing surprising about the law applying a test which asks what an honest and reasonable trader would have understood, given knowledge of the particular circumstances. The law of contract itself is, as I have indicated at [179]-[181], based generally not on what the parties actually thought or knew was the effect of particular words or conduct, but upon what they must reasonably be taken to have understood or known in all the relevant circumstances.

199 A similar objective approach is also found in tort and criminal law. Take the tort of knowing or dishonest assistance. This is committed where a breach of

fiduciary duty has been committed by A, and B is said to have assisted it dishonestly. But dishonesty is judged objectively in the light of the circumstances known to the alleged assister. In other words, there are two stages: the first is to ascertain what the alleged assister knew; but, once that is ascertained, the honesty or dishonesty of their conduct falls to be judged by an objective standard of honesty to be expected and applied in the light of such knowledge: see *Barlow Clowes International Ltd and others v. Eurotrust International Ltd and others* [2006] 1 WLR 1476; see also two recent judgments of the Court of Appeal of England and Wales applying this test: *Group Seven Ltd v. Notable Services LLP* [2019] EWCA Civ 614 and *Simetra Global Assets Ltd v. Ikon Finance Ltd* [2019] EWCA Civ 1413. This objective approach also applies in the criminal law: see *Ivey v. Genting Casinos (UK) Ltd* [2018] AC 391, indicating that the decision in *R v. Ghosh* [1982] QB 1053 should no longer be followed in so far as it stated that a defendant must be conscious subjectively that his conduct was dishonest.

200 There is nothing surprising, impermissible or unworkable therefore about a test which asks what any reasonable trader would have thought, given knowledge of the particular circumstances. That is the proper approach, in my opinion, in the present situation. Whether the unknown activities of two computers in the middle of the night should bind the parties should be judged by asking whether any reasonable trader, on the relevant exchange, knowing what was happening (or what had happened) could or would have thought, in the otherwise prevailing circumstances, that this was anything other than the consequence of a gross and unintended "major database breakdown" or error with equivalent effect. Since this is how B2C2 actually categorised it, the answer is doubly obvious. Of course, this test involves a hypothetical, as the Judge said at [204]. But it does not work on the basis of speculation as to what

"might" have happened if a human element had been involved. On the contrary, it provides relief in equity in the present case because any reasonable person, knowing of the relevant market circumstances, would have known that there was a fundamental mistake. It is the Judge's approach which seems to me, to use his word, "artificial" in assessing whether the contract can stand, not by reference to the circumstances and time when it was made, but on the basis that Mr Boonen would have to be shown to be aware *in advance* that the only circumstances in which a contract could come into existence at his deep prices would be if some fundamental mistake occurred. That prevents any assessment of the validity of computer-made contracts as and when made, and potentially enables traders to make what an honourable and reasonable trader would, I believe, identify as an unjustified windfall—and would expect to forego because it was such.

201 In the present case, there can only be one answer to the question of what any reasonable trader with knowledge of the market circumstances would have thought. There was not and never has been any suggestion that Mr Boonen's very unusual or unfathomable market developments occurred. The only explanation of the transactions, whether hypothesised in advance, observed concurrently or considered early next morning, was and is major error—as B2C2 at once saw.

202 Mr Boonen was very well informed about actual world and market circumstances. The Judge recorded (at [102]):

> ... He explained that B2C2 was connected to 15 exchanges at the time, on some of which up to ten pairs were traded. The market for BTC/ETH on the Platform was relatively small ...

As to Mr Boonen's state of mind when next morning he observed the overnight trades, the Judge recorded (at [114]):

> ... Mr Boonen gave evidence that he was surprised when he first saw that the orders had been filled and that he considered the possibility that there was an error on the Platform or an error in the B2C2 system. Having checked that there were no apparent errors in either system he thought 'Wow, there must have been something incredible happened [*sic*] in the market overnight'.

Mr Boone's reaction that something incredible must have happened in the market overnight cannot have lasted more than a second, since his connection to 15 world exchanges would have informed him that no such thing had happened.

203 Curiously, but very relevantly on this appeal, the Judge also omitted from the Judgment reference to one key document which above all others gives a key to Mr Boonen's actual state of mind, on learning of the transactions next morning. He sent the e-mail at 6 : 15am to Quoine's support team requesting that it call B2C2 urgently as he had detected a "Major Quoine database breakdown". That is what the Judge said he could well understand might be the reaction of an ordinary trader on the Platform, and it was evidently what Mr Boonen thought. The present case is one, in my judgment, where any reasonable trader would expect the general law to afford relief, as it does in more conventional cases of mistake.

Unconscionability

204 In so far as it is suggested that unconscionability is a prerequisite to

equitable relief, I would repeat what is indicated at [178] above. First, the present situation is one where the primary vitiating factor relied on is mistake, and, second, it is not one where relief is being sought on the basis of constructive notice. The question in the present case is not whether B2C2 had constructive notice, because constructive notice depends, like actual knowledge, on human involvement during the relevant transaction. The present case is one where the law needs to fashion an appropriate principle to cater for a situation where it is clear that there would have been actual knowledge of mistake had the actual transactions been foreseen in advance or had there been human involvement at the time (and where it is also the fact that there was such knowledge as soon as they were discovered). Unconscionability in bringing about the transactions cannot and should not have a role in relation to this novel situation, which is, as I have indicated at [178], closer to one of actual knowledge than of constructive notice. I add that is unnecessary on the facts to consider in this case whether equitable relief would extend to the (probably unlikely) situation in which all that could be affirmed was that the party in B2C2's position, knowing of the transaction against the relevant market background, *should* have realised that it had only come about as a result of some fundamental error. In this case, it can unhesitatingly be affirmed that B2C2 would actually have realised this, and did do so as soon as it knew of the transaction.

205 To the extent that unconscionability may be relevant, it is in my view clearly unconscionable in the present context of unilateral mistake for a trader to retain the benefit of transactions which he would—and did—at once recognise as due to some major error as soon as he came to learn of them. This parallels the analysis taken, in my view appropriately, by the Court of Appeal of British Colombia took in 256593 *BC Ltd* ([174] *supra*) at [26] - [28], and is

consistent with other statements of principle: see [172]-[175] above. I may also be forgiven for quoting here from a judgment of my own in the area of unjust enrichment—*McDonald v. Coys of Kensington* [2004] EWCA Civ 47. In that case, a purchaser insisted on holding onto a valuable registration number plate or mark (with the initials TAC 1) for which he had not contracted and which had remained on the vehicle as transferred to him by a mistake on the part of the vendor. The issue was whether the purchaser had been unjustly enriched. His defence was that he had done nothing wrong and had simply acquired the number plate as part of the car which was now his. Giving the sole reasoned judgment of the Court of Appeal of England and Wales and holding that he had been unjustly enriched, I said this at [37]:

> Looking at the matter generally, I have no doubt that justice requires that a person, who (as a result of some mistake which it becomes evident has been made in the execution of an agreed bargain) has a benefit or the right to a benefit for which he knows that he has not bargained or paid, should reimburse the value of that benefit to the other party if it is readily returnable without substantial difficulty or detriment and he chooses to retain it (or give it away to a third party) rather than to re-transfer it on request. Even if realisable benefit alone is not generally sufficient, the law should recognise, as a distinct category of enrichment, cases where a benefit is readily returnable. A person who receives another's chattel must either return it or pay damages, commonly measured by reference to its value. The mark is not a chattel, and it was not suggested before us that its return could at any stage (even before the gift to the partner) have been enforced, or that its non-return could sound in damages. (There were

allegations below of implied duties to co-operate in the return of the mark, but the judge did not accept them, and there is no appeal in that respect.) However, Mr McDonald's insistence on keeping the mark and the absence of any obvious means of compelling its re-transfer are reasons for analysing this case in terms of unjust enrichment. Mr McDonald knew that he had not bargained or paid for the mark. The mark or its benefit was in practice easily returnable. If Mr McDonald chose to keep it, then I see every reason for treating him as benefited.

206 In my opinion, a parallel analysis applies here. Equity will look at all aspects of a transaction. If it is immediately obvious that a mistaken transfer has occurred, a failure to do the honourable thing and return the benefit can be as unconscionable as the conduct of someone who plays some positive part in bringing the transaction about.

Conclusion

207 In these circumstances, and on the basis that the test in law is that which I have suggested it should be, the claim that the transactions were voidable for unilateral mistake should have succeeded. I would have allowed this appeal accordingly.

Reported by Andre Soh, Chua Xyn Yee and Iris Ng.